Iserson's Getting Into A Residency

Iserson's Getting Into A Residency

A GUIDE FOR MEDICAL STUDENTS

Seventh Edition

Kenneth V. Iserson
M.D., MBA, FACEP, FAAEM

Galen Press, LTD. • Tucson, Arizona

First Published 1988
Second Edition 1990
Third Edition 1993
Fourth Edition 1996
Fifth Edition 2000
Sixth Edition 2003
Seventh Edition 2006

GALEN PRESS, LTD.
P.O. Box 64400
Tucson, AZ 85728-4400
Phone (520) 577-8363   Fax (520) 529-6459
Orders (U.S. & Canada) 1-800-442-5369

www.galenpress.com

Bulk purchase terms are available. Please contact our special sales department.

ISBN-10: 1-883620-09-0

ISBN-13: 978-1-883620-09-7

KENNETH V. ISERSON, M.D., MBA, FACEP, FAAEM
Professor of Emergency Medicine
University of Arizona College of Medicine
1501 N. Campbell Avenue
Tucson, AZ 85724

FREIDA is a registered trademark of the American Medical Association.
Windows is a registered trademark of Microsoft, Inc.

Library of Congress Cataloging-in-Publication Data
Iserson, Kenneth V.
  Iserson's getting into a residency : a guide for medical students / Kenneth
V. Iserson. – 7th ed.
    p. ; cm.
  Rev. ed. of: Getting into a residency / Kenneth V. Iserson. 6th ed. 2003.
  Includes bibliographical references and index.
  ISBN-10: 1-883620-09-0 (pbk.)
    1. Residents (Medicine)–Selection and appointment–United States. 2. Medical
education–United States. I. Title: Getting into a residency. II. Iserson, Kenneth V.
Getting into a residency. III. Title.
    [DNLM: 1. Internship and Residency–United States. 2. Education, Medical,
Graduate–United States. W 20 I78i 2006]
RA972 .I74 2006
610'.71"550973–dc21   06-

Printed in the United States of America.
10 9 8 7 6 5 4 3 2 1

Contents

List of Figures ix
Acknowledgments xiii
A Personal Note xv
Preface to the First Edition xvii

1 Overview 1
   The Problem 1
   The Process 4

2 The Specialties 7
   The Choices 7
   Medicine's Future 13

3 Specialty Descriptions 27

4 Choosing A Specialty 113
   Your Personal Aptitudes—Assess Them Honestly 113

5 Important Factors When Choosing A Specialty 133
   Monetary Rewards 134
   Length of Training 138
   Work Hours/Lifestyle 139
   The Potential Future 140
   Difficulty of Getting a Residency Position 143

6 Starting The Process 145
   Choosing an Adviser/Mentor 145
   Testing Your Specialty Choice 150

7 Grades, Tests, & Clinical Clerkships 159
   Putting Your Effort Where It Counts 159
   Honor Grades 159
   Licensing Examinations 165
   Summer Work 207
   Research 208
   Arranging Your Senior Schedule 212
   Awards 219

8 Putting Off A Decision 223
   The Fine Art of Procrastination 224
   Taking Time Off 225
   Win-Win Decisions 225
   Advantages & Disadvantages of a Transitional Year 227
   Quick Decisions & Forty Years of Sadness 229
   Switching Careers 231
   Dangers of Indecision 232

9 Gathering Information 233

10 Finding Programs That Meet Your Needs 247
   The First Cut 247
   What Do You Want in a Program? 248
   Factors to Consider 254
   Narrowing the Choices 287

11 Playing The Odds: How Many Program Applications? 295
   How Competitive Is the Specialty You Want? 295
   How Competitive Are You? 296
   What Do You Have to Lose? 297

12 Buffing Your File: The Paperwork 299
   Your Name 301
   The Application 302
   The Résumé 317
   The Personal Statement 327
   Reference Letters 329
   A Picture? 344
   The Transcript 345
   Timing—It's Your Future at Stake 347

13 Special Situations 351
   Women 352
   Marriage, Pregnancy, & Children 357
   Couples Matching 362
   Part-Time (Shared-Schedule) Positions 363
   Gay, Lesbian, Bisexual, & Transgender Applicants 366
   Psychiatric Illness 367
   Underrepresented Minorities 368
   Physically Impaired Applicants 373
   Osteopathic Physicians 375
   Older Applicants 382
   Military/Public Health Service 384

14 International Medical Graduates 389
   ECFMG Certification 394
   Tips for All IMGs 399
   Non-U.S./Non-Canadian Citizens (FNIMGs) 400
   U.S. International Medical Graduates (USIMGs) 402
   Canadian Citizens 405

15 Preparing For The Interview 407
   The Mock Interview 407
   Timing 409
   Wait-Listed? 412
   Travel Arrangements 412

Updating Information about the Programs 419
Communicating with the Programs 419

16 **Looking The Part: Interview Attire** 421
Men 422
Women 424
Packing 426
Tax Tip 429

Feedback Form 430

17 **The Visit** 431
Timeliness 431
Attitude 433
Uniqueness 434
Knowledge 435
Talk to Residents for the Real Story 436
Basic Rules 437
Materials for the Interview 440
Behavior at Lunch 444

18 **The Perfect Applicant** 447

19 **The Interview** 453
Know Your Questions 453
The List—To Ask Faculty 455
The List—To Ask Residents 466
Confirm Questionable Points 474
Things Not to Ask 474
Things Not to Do 477
Stressful Interviews 479
Control the Interview—Gently 482
Reasons Why Interviews Fail 482
Sell Yourself 487

20 **The Questions—The Answers** 489
Presenting Yourself 490
Types of Questions 492
Interview Techniques 493
Questions & Answers 494
Illegal Questions 528

21 **Post-Visit Follow-Up** 531
Thank-You Letter 531
Telephone Follow-Up 533
Specific Information 534
Analyze Your Visit 534
Ranking the Programs for Success 535

22 The NRMP & Other Matches 539
  The NRMP Match 540
  NRMP Match Rules—General 549
  Student Candidates 558
  Physician Candidates 564
  Military Appointments 564
  Don't Believe Anything You Are Promised 564
  What to Do If You Don't Match 565
  Matching in Advance (PGY-2 & Above) 568
  Not Using a Match 570
  Osteopathic Matching Program 575

23 You've Matched—Now What? 581
  Telephone Follow-Up to Program 581
  Letter Follow-Up 581
  Post-Purchase Dissonance 582
  Contracting with the Program 583
  Debt Management 583
  Your New Home 584
  Moving 585
  Conclusion 586
  A New Beginning 586

Glossary 587
Annotated Bibliography 592
Medical Organizations' Contact Information & Websites 605
Index 611

List of Figures

Fig. 1.1   Getting a Residency—The Component Parts 5-6

Fig. 2.1   Essentials of Specialty Selection 9

2.2   The Process of Choosing a Specialty 10

2.3   Factors Important to Students When Selecting a
Residency Program 11

2.4   States with the Most Physicians per Capita 13

2.5   Reasons Why Students Choose Primary Care/
Non-Primary Care Specialties 16

2.6   Percentage of Specialty Physicians in Practices with
Managed Care Contracts 19

2.7   American Board of Medical Specialties (M.D.)-Approved
Specialty Boards, Certifications, and Special
Qualification Categories 20-22

2.8   Approved Specialty Boards, Certification, and Special
Qualification Categories (D.O.) 23-25

2.9   M.D. and D.O. Physicians in Practice by Specialty 26

Fig. 3.1   Length of Postgraduate Training for M.D. Physicians 108

3.2   Length of Postgraduate Training for Osteopathic
(D.O.) Physicians 109

3.3   Is This Specialty for You? 110-11

Fig. 4.1   Number of PGY-1 and First-Year Specialty Positions
Offered, 2005–2006 115

4.2   Personal Trait Analysis 117-18

4.3   Personal Trait Analysis—An Example 119

4.4   Personal Trait Synthesis—An Example 120

4.5   Personal Trait Synthesis 121

4.6   Characteristics Strongly Associated with the Practice
of Some Major Specialties 122-25

4.7   Selecting a Specialty for You—An Example 126-28

4.8   Selecting a Specialty for You 128-30

4.9   Correlation of Personal Traits and Specialty
Characteristics 131

4.10   Correlation of Personal Traits and Specialty
Characteristics—An Example 132

Fig. 5.1   Median Physician Annual Income 135
     5.2   Average Weekly Work Hours and Workloads of
            Different Specialists 140
     5.3   Change in Number and Percentage of M.D. Physician
            Specialists, 2005, 2010, and 2020 142

Fig. 6.1   Maslow's Hierarchy of Needs 157

Fig. 7.1   Questions about Clerkship Expectations 164
     7.2   USMLE Eligibility Requirements and Contacts 170
     7.3   Recent USMLE Pass Rates 175
     7.4   USMLE Step 1 Content 178
     7.5   USMLE Step 2CK Content 179
     7.6   USMLE Step 2CS Contents 181
     7.7   USMLE Step 3 Content 184
     7.8   COMLEX-USA Examination Blueprint 195
     7.9   Examination Pathways for U.S. Licensure 196
     7.10   Graduate Education Requirements for Licensure 197

Fig. 8.1   Win-Lose Decision-Making Model 226
     8.2   Win-Win Decision-Making Model 227

Fig. 9.1   Questions to Ask about Requirements for Specialty
            Certification 236

Fig. 10.1   "Must/Want" Analysis—The Instructions and
            The Form 250-52
     10.2   "Must/Want" Analysis—An Example 253-54
     10.3   Percent of Residency Programs, Residents, and
            Fellowships by Geographic Region 261
     10.4   Health Benefits Provided to Housestaff and Dependents 278
     10.5   Non-Health Benefits for First-Year Housestaff 280
     10.6   Programs in Representative Specialties with On-Site
            Childcare 283
     10.7   "Must/Want" Analysis—Example #1 288-89
     10.8   "Must/Want" Analysis—Example #2 290-91
     10.9   "Must/Want" Analysis—Example #3 292-93

Fig. 11.1   Applicants and 1st-Year Positions, 1952–2005 296
     11.2   Average Number of Applications Submitted to
            Programs in Various Specialties 298

Fig. 12.1   Requirements for Applications to Different Programs—
            Example 303
     12.2   Résumé Disaster Areas 319

12.3   Action Words for Your Résumé 320
12.4   A Résumé Checklist 321
12.5   Sample Résumé—The Disaster 322
12.6   A Sample Résumé—Style #1 323
12.7   A Sample Résumé—Style #2 324
12.8   Two Other Acceptable Résumé Formats 325
12.9   Format for Personal Statement 328
12.10 Alternative Style for a Personal Statement 330
12.11 Frequency of Appearance of Information in
       Dean's Letters 331
12.12 AAMC's Template for Medical Student Performance
       Evaluation 332-35
12.13 Disparaging Comments about Applicants 338
12.14 Elements of a Reference Letter 342
12.15 A Completed-Application Postcard 349

Fig. 13.1   Women's Representation in Selected Specialties 353
13.2   Gender of Medical School Faculty, by Rank 354
13.3   Women M.D. Faculty in Various Specialties 355
13.4   Relative Incidence of Sexual Harassment 356
13.5   Pregnancies and Complications 361
13.6   Shared-Schedule/Part-Time Positions Offered
       by Specialties 365
13.7   Minority Representation on Medical School
       Faculties in Various Clinical Specialties 369
13.8   Osteopathic Internships 376
13.9   Osteopathic Graduates in ACGME-Approved Programs 380

Fig. 14.1   IMGs Practicing Medicine in Various Specialties 391
14.2   Types of Applicants (Percentages) Filling PGY-1 and
       Advanced Positions in Specialties through NRMP Match .. 394
14.3   Requirements to Practice Medicine, Do Post-Graduate
       Training, or Be a Clinical Research Fellow in the
       United States (Patient Contact) 395

Fig. 15.1   Air Travel Made Easier 416-17

Fig. 16.1   Packing a Suitcase 428

Fig. 17.1   Elements in the Communication Process 434
17.2   Interview Notes 442
17.3   "Must/Want" Analysis As an Interview Checklist—
       An Example 443-44

Fig. 18.1   Relative Importance of Academic Criteria When
            Selecting Residents in Various Specialties 449
     18.2   Importance of Information to Residency When
            Selecting Interviewees and Ranking Applicants 450
     18.3   Items in Applicant's History That Worry
            Residency Directors 451

Fig. 19.1   Typical Interview from the Interviewer's Viewpoint 454
     19.2   Guidelines for Effective Listening 483
     19.3   Factors Influencing an Interviewer's Behavior 485
     19.4   Warning Signs for Interviewers 486
     19.5   Personality Traits Interviewers Seek 487
     19.6   Interviewer's Rating Form 488

Fig. 20.1   Illegal Questions—Sex Discrimination 528
     20.2   Other Questions—Legal and Illegal Forms 529

Fig. 21.1   Follow-up Letter Format 532
     21.2   How Applicants Evaluate Residency Programs 536

Fig. 22.1   PGY-1 Training Accepted by Various M.D. Specialties 544
     22.2   Medical Specialties, Programs, and Entry-Level
            Positions Offered 545-48
     22.3   Average Number of Programs on Applicants' ROLs 553
     22.4   NRMP Rank-Order List Decision Tree 554
     22.5   Important Dates in the NRMP Application Process 557
     22.6   NRMP Couples Match Results, 1987–2005 560
     22.7   Example of a Couple's Worksheet 561
     22.8   Example of a Couple's Rank-Order List 562
     22.9   Selected Specialties' Programs and Positions Available
            through Other (Non-NRMP-PGY-1) Matches 569-70
     22.10 Osteopathic Specialties' Programs and Number
            of Positions 578-79
     22.11 Osteopathic Intern/Resident Registration
            Program Schedule 580

Acknowledgments

Those having torches will pass them on to others.

– Plato, The Republic

Of the making of books, there is no end.

– Ecclesiastes, 12

THIS BOOK WOULD NOT EXIST but for the significant help I received from others. First and foremost is the fantastic assistance and support from my wife, Mary Lou Iserson, C.P.A. Acting as both a skilled and persistent editor, and the resident computer whiz, she midwifed every edition.

I greatly appreciate the help of the many students and physicians who took time to add to the book's content by using the *Feedback Form*, letters, and e-mail to send me comments (some of which are quoted in this edition).

As always, I owe a debt of gratitude to my friends at the University of Arizona Health Sciences Library, who find sources of information in inscrutable ways. I am especially grateful to Nga T. Nguyen, B.A., B.S., Senior Library Specialist, and Ms. Hannah Fisher, R.N., M.L.S., AHIP, who helped to update important details, such as organization addresses and bibliographic references. Also thanks to an ingenious and always reliable researcher, Robert Fisher, M.L.S, Tucson, AZ.

Special thanks also goes to Donald Witzke, Ph.D., now at the University of Kentucky Medical Center, Lexington, who has strongly supported this book's concept and has acted as a superb content reviewer for many editions.

A variety of people at the organizations mentioned in this book helped supply valuable updated information for this edition. These include Douglas Perry, Executive Director, San Francisco Matching Program; James W. Tysinger, Ph.D., Department of Family and Community Medicine, University of Texas Health Sciences Center at San Antonio; Walter "Waldo" Wentz, Assistant Director, National Residency Matching Program; George V. Richard, Ph.D., Director, and Jeanette Calli, Program Manager, Careers in Medicine Program, Association of American Medical Colleges; Don M. Majors, SFC, USAREC; Jill Birdwhistell Pierce, Ph.D., Sr. Marketing Director, American Medical Women's Association; Joyce L. Obradovic, Director, Division of Postdoctoral Training, American Osteopathic Association; Wendy Klein, M.D., FACP, Sr. Deputy Director, and Janett Forte, MSW, LCSW, Coordinator, the Virginia Commonwealth University Center of Excellence in Women's Health.

A number of individuals associated with, and departments within, the American Medical Association, also provided invaluable assistance. These included David W. Emmons, Ph.D., Director, Center for Health Policy Research; Derek R. Smart, Data Release Manager; Alk Widge, Chair, Medical Student Section; Sylvia Etzel, Online Manager, *FREIDA*; J.D. Kinney, Director, Department of Marketing & Strategic Analysis; and Harry Bauer, AMA Alliance.

Aside from our Library's reference staff, those from the University of Arizona College of Medicine who assisted in updating this book include Chris Leadem, Ph.D., Sr. Associate Dean, Admissions & Student Affairs; Pat Oltman, Coordinator, Office of Student Affairs; and James M. Woolfenden, M.D., Professor of Nuclear Medicine.

Not only I, but also the medical students at the University of Arizona, express our gratitude to the Arizona Medical Association, to its Executive Director, Chic Older, and to the Mallory Trust, who believe that this book is so essential to medical students' careers that they supply each student with a copy.

My special appreciation goes to George H. Zimny, Ph.D., for graciously allowing a markedly abbreviated version of his Medical Specialty Preference Inventory to be included in this text.

I would be remiss if I did not also thank the people at Galen Press: Mary Lou Sherk and Jennifer Gilbert, who have been wonderful in supporting this project and helping make it the success it has been. Part of that success is due to Lynn Bishop, who produced the cover design, and to Anne Olson-Scribner, who gave the book its wonderful interior design.

Finally, I wish to thank Dr. Louis Olsen, M.D., of Baltimore, Maryland. One of the few ideal physicians I know, this Family Physician suffered the strain of acting as my mentor throughout medical school—-for which I will be ever grateful. It is to him that I owe much of what I am as a clinician and teacher.

A Personal Note

To cure sometimes, to relieve often, to comfort always.
— Anonymous, 15th C. or earlier

WHEN THIS BOOK'S FIRST EDITION went to press, there were few methods available to help medical students select specialties or residency programs. They gathered information by sending postcards to ask for written program materials, submitted paper applications, took the "National Boards" without a clinical component, and waited for their Dean to distribute their Match results. At that time, Osteopathic students had no matching program.

That was only twenty years ago! Today, the Web has overtaken the residency application process. Students can gather a wealth of information from *FREIDA*, specialty webpages, and other online resources using a home computer. USMLE and COMLEX are computerized and include a clinical component. You can even access your Match results in complete privacy! Each year, the system continues to evolve at a faster pace.

Because a casual reader (including a reviewer of the last edition!) might conclude that not much has been changed in this latest edition, I wanted to point out some of the substantial modifications as well as the particular challenges that acquiring this information has posed over the last year. Information for the seventh edition was scrounged from all valid sources. In some cases, this information is changing so fast that no two sources agreed. The difficulties were compounded by the lack of cooperation by some national medical organizations.

Despite the increasing sophistication of institutional websites, information about graduate medical education has become more difficult to access each year. Rather than becoming more transparent, major medical educational organizations are restricting access to much of their previously available data. The Association of American Medical Colleges and the American Osteopathic Association either refuse to release information or make it so obscure that it is meaningless. While the American Medical Association's website is a marvelous resource, it is so user-unfriendly that, without very specific search parameters, much of the information remains hidden in the bowels of their enormous computer system. A lot of work went into determining how to access the best sources on their website. I assume that the AMA will correct this in the future.

The National Residency Matching Program, on the other hand, continues to be open with their data. The San Francisco Matching program has also generously shared their information for this book.

So, what's new? All the "nitty-gritty" information, the URLs, e-mail addresses, phone and fax numbers, costs of tests, courses, materials, etc., have been checked for accuracy. In most instances, current URLs have replaced street addresses, signifying the importance that an online presence now has for most institutions. (If the URLs don't work, shorten them to see if the primary address leads you to the site.) Of course, specialty details have been updated and new specialties have been added.

All figures that contain current information (approximately 100 of them!) have been updated, new figures have been added, and others with data that is no longer relevant or verifiable have been deleted. Those figures that remain and that are based on older research signify that we could not find updated material in the medical literature but that the topic remains of interest.

The description of the Electronic Residency Application Service (ERAS) reflects program changes, the addition of new specialties, and the inclusion of Osteopathic programs. There is also an updated description of the USMLE, in particular the new Step 2 Clinical Skills requirement, and an extensively revised description of COMLEX. Sections on the NRMP Main Match, the NRMP Fellowship Match, the San Francisco Match, and the Osteopathic Intern/Resident Registration Program reflect those institutions' changes, including the specialties with which they now work (2006).

There are also significant additions to the Questions and Answers chapters, both those questions that you should have in mind when talking to faculty or residents and those questions that they could ask you.

Licensure requirements have also changed, and, while that is not your primary concern at the moment, it is important to consider your training program in light of the requirements for the state in which you want to practice. This is especially true for international medical graduates and D.O.s. In addition, the numerous rule changes pertinent to IMGs are reflected in the book.

Finally, the *Annotated Bibliography* has been checked to see that the material is still available, and new references have been added. A list of URLs that are used in the book has been compiled as well.

Overall, this is the most up-to-date, complete, and accurate resource that I could provide. My hope is that, as with prior generations of residency applicants, this helps you to decide what your goal is and how to best achieve it.

Kenneth V. Iserson, M.D., 2006

Preface To The First Edition

Knowing how to get a job is as important as knowing how to do a job.

– Robert Half

OVER THE YEARS, MANY STUDENTS have come to me seeking career advice. In some cases, the advice was about my own specialty. But often it concerned the mechanics of finding a personal niche in medicine and assuring that the individual was able to get a training position in his or her area of interest. Sadly, most of these medical students had not spent enough time investigating all the choices available. Many believed that since they had chosen medicine as a career, and since they had achieved the long-sought-after goal of entering medical school, the significant choices were behind them. Nothing could be further from the truth.

Medicine is a diverse and complicated profession. The physician practicing Pathology is in a different world from the Family Practitioner or Physiatrist. The Radiologist's practice has little in common with that of the Anesthesiologist. Unfortunately, these differences are not as obvious as they might be in many medical school settings.

While students know, or will know, something about the practices of the Internist, Family Physician, General Surgeon, Pediatrician, Obstetrician, and Psychiatrist from their required third-year rotations, even here their knowledge may be skewed toward picturing the individuals only in the hospital setting. Rarely does this setting constitute the majority of the clinician's practice. This is insufficient knowledge upon which to base a career. In addition, most medical students are unaware of their many training options. (Many haven't even heard the term "Physiatrist" before. This is a specialist in Physical and Rehabilitation Medicine.)

The first part of this book briefly describes the specialty choices available to you. It also provides you with a method of analyzing your own interests to compare them with those of physicians practicing in various medical fields.

Even if you do make a career decision, how do you use your medical school experience to optimize your chances of getting into the specialty and program that you finally decide upon? The basic medical school wisdom is that an industrious student will get his or her just rewards. Not necessarily! There is so much to do and so little time in which to accomplish it. You need to know how to maximize your efforts. The second part of the book encompasses this.

And then, how do you know where to interview, how to get an interview, and how to interview? Although students in other professions are given basic information on how to get their first job, this information is not generally passed on to medical students. You need this knowledge as you prepare to get your first job in medicine. You will find it in the third part of the book.

Finally, how to best utilize the Matching systems? What pitfalls must you avoid? What opportunities can you take advantage of? The last part of the book deals with these questions.

This text, in concert with your mentor and Dean of Students, is designed to guide you through the process of selecting a specialty field, helping you to maximize your efforts toward getting into your chosen specialty and program, selecting programs that meet your personal needs, getting interviews at these programs, doing well at the interviews and ultimately matching with these programs.

This book is intended to serve as a guide for the student who wants to be a winner—who is actively participating in taking those steps necessary to get into the residency he or she wants. Different parts of the book will be relevant to different students with diverse goals in mind. To make this book work for you, you should read it all, charting the course to your goal. This can be done by *checking* or *flagging* those items relevant to *your* goal and what you must do to achieve it. After you have charted your course, you can then use this as a plan for action. As you complete each activity, check it off. Write in the book, highlight what is relevant, and make it work for you.

If you are reading this book, it means that you are willing to put forth a little effort in preparing for your upcoming major career step. Just owning the book will not be sufficient. You must read it and apply the information diligently. Success can be yours if you expend the energy.

If any part of this book particularly helps you, or you find errors or omissions, please let me know. You can be assured that any insights you share will be considered for the future editions of this book.

Best of luck in your exciting life in medicine!

K.V. Iserson, M.D.
December, 1987

1

Overview

Luck is a crossroad where preparation and opportunity meet.

– Anonymous

The Problem

IF YOUR RICH RELATIVE JUST DONATED $3 million to endow a desperately needed chair of advanced biohypergraphics at the institution you would like to attend, you may not have much of a problem securing a residency slot there. Unfortunately, most of us are not in this position. Residencies are getting rather picky about their selections, since it costs about $157,820 per year (2006 dollars) to educate a resident. And, with the rapidly decreasing number of quality residency positions, even the rich-relative ploy may not guarantee you entrance.

In recent years, 7% or more of the U.S. medical students attempting to find a residency position through the National Residents Matching Program (NRMP) did not match. Not exactly the kind of odds you would choose! And the odds are even worse in some of the specialties that do not go through the NRMP.

Getting a residency in the specialty you desire, at the institution you crave, is a COMPETITION. It has RULES, which you may not know unless you have been out in the working world as a professional before entering medical school. These rules correspond in many ways to those used to get executive positions in business. They even more closely approximate the rules you will follow to get a job after residency—assuming that you, like more than half of your colleagues, join a group practice of some type.

In many ways, resident-selection rules are arcane—having been derived from the ancient art of choosing an apprentice. One thing is certain: just as in the days of our ancestors, choice apprenticeship positions are few and far between.

A physician from the Philippines related a horrifying story of his experiences not many years ago. As now, the Philippines had very good quality medical schools. They taught from American texts and used the same curriculum. But they produced more medical graduates than there were spaces available for residency training. Since physicians were required to have advanced training to get a medical license, many medical school graduates ended up doing odd jobs (this individual drove a taxicab) until they could get residency positions in the United States. That situation is now being duplicated in many other countries.

These events happened when we had a severe shortage of doctors in this country, and physicians graduating from U.S. medical schools could get into almost any specialty that they desired. The only real question was where.

Today's graduating medical students are part of an increasing pool of physicians. While there were 142 physicians per 100,000 population in 1960 (one physician per 703 persons), in 2003, there were 298 per 100,000 (one physician per 336 persons). This represents more than a 200% growth in the number of physicians, while the population increased by only 60%.

According to the AAMC's Center for Workforce Studies, by 2020, the U.S. physician workforce will increase by about 30,000, from 972,000 in 2005 to 1,002,000. Existing M.D. and D.O. schools will add between 1,100 and 1,800 graduates per year, and new schools will add between 250 and 950 new graduates annually.

Nevertheless, in late 2004, the Council on Graduate Medical Educations reported that by 2020, even if medical schools would increase the number of graduates by 3,000 per year, the United States probably will have fewer physicians than necessary. In part, this stems from younger physicians working fewer hours than their forebears, an increase in the elderly who will need more healthcare, and persistent geographic physician maldistribution. The federal government estimates that, depending on changes in healthcare use, staffing patterns, and insurance availability, the U.S. will need between 28% and 40% more physicians in 2020 than in 2000.

In today's medical marketplace, primary care providers are in short supply, while specialists and subspecialists abound. Severe geographic and specialty disparities exist, with relatively few physicians in rural areas and in primary care practices. Therefore, the federal government is targeting many non-primary care training programs for destruction. Positions in most of these specialties, already difficult to obtain, will become extremely competitive.

In 2005–2006, there were approximately 100,000 residency and fellowship positions approved by the Accreditation Council for Graduate Medical Education (ACGME). This was essentially the same number as in 1993–94. In 2004, nine subspecialties had no training programs. While the number of U.S. residents and fellows has increased 95% since 1970, their percentage in relation to the total physician population has decreased from 15.3% in 1970 to 11.5% in 2005.

In 2005, international medical graduates (IMGs) (27%) and Osteopathic physicians (D.O.s) (6%) comprised a steadily increasing percentage of all residents, while the percentage of Canadians (<1%) remained constant and U.S. medical graduates (67%) decreased. There were about 21,500 PGY-1 positions available to students, which is about the same number as existed in 1994. The number of residency and fellowship *programs*, however, increased from 7,435 in 1994 to more than 8,250 in 2005.

Applicants already overwhelm the most sought-after residency programs and institutions. But don't despair. This book will show you how to get the residency that you long for. Basically, success comes from applying the **three golden rules**:

1. Be Assertive! No one can look out for your interests better than you. Determine what you want and need, then go after it. This means that you should get a mentor/adviser, research opportunities, special externships or rotations, or additional career counseling and information. Remember— the course of *your entire professional life* depends on whether you get a good residency in your chosen field!

2. Time It Right! Nothing is worse than doing all the right things— but at the wrong time. This includes getting started. As you will learn from this book, if you are just beginning the process as a senior medical student, you are probably already behind the eight ball. If you are a third-year student, you have more time to get your act together—but you had better work fast. The essence of timing is to *start early*, *apply early*, and *interview late*. While "the early bird gets the worm" is a trite expression, it is worth heeding—at least until you schedule your interviews (see Chapter 15).

3. Go for the Gold! Most medical students I know tend to "put down" both themselves and the training they received from their medical school. "It's only a state school" or "I wasn't AOA," they moan. This negative attitude makes them aim much lower than they should, both in the specialty they seek and in the institutional slots they pursue. My father was a professional salesman. His advice for success was, *"Sell yourself—no one will do it for you."* While you compete for your goal, keep these words close to your heart. Remember, it's your life and your career!

The Process

Performing well in medical school is hard enough, but then to obtain a residency position, you must learn the arcane language, processes, and alternatives associated with the licensing tests, gathering residency program information, submitting applications, and the matching programs. Even those U.S. students going into mainline specialties such as Internal Medicine or Family Medicine must learn the lingo to succeed. Those entering Neurology, Ophthalmology, Neurological Surgery, Otolaryngology, or Urology must contend with more complex systems. The system is extremely complicated for Osteopathic medical students and for international medical graduates (IMGs), who first must decide which of the multiple pathways they should follow.

Figure 1.1 is an overview of the routes and procedures for residency application. Note that some elements pertain only to Osteopaths; others pertain only to IMGs. Each of these steps is discussed in greater detail later in this book.

FIGURE 1.1

Getting a Residency—The Component Parts

EXAMS

M.D. Students/Graduates	**D.O. Students/Graduates**
USMLE	COMLEX (D.O.s only)

M.D. Students/Graduates

USMLE

- Most M.D. students must pass Steps 1, 2CK, and 2CS to get a residency position.
- M.D.s must pass all three Steps to obtain a medical license.

D.O. Students/Graduates

COMLEX (D.O.s only)

- Most D.O. residencies require passing Levels 1, 2PE, and 2CE.
- Completion of Levels 1, 2, and 3 required for licensure.

USMLE

- D.O.s may also use this exam for licensure in most states.

▼

RESIDENCY PROGRAM INFORMATION

M.D. Students/Graduates

FREIDA

AMA Graduate Medical Education Directory (the "Green Book")

D.O. Students/Graduates

AOA-net (*Opportunities*)

Individual programs' websites and printed materials.
Specialty society websites and online residency catalogs.

▼

APPLICATION SUBMISSION

M.D. Students/Graduates

Electronic Residency Application Service (ERAS)

- Used by most M.D. residency programs.

Centralized Application Service (CAS)

- Used by M.D. "Advanced" programs in San Francisco Matching Program.

D.O. Students/Graduates

Electronic Residency Application Service (ERAS)

- Used by most D.O. internships (students only).

Individual Program Applications

- Used by some M.D. and D.O. training programs, and many subspecialty fellowships (often, Universal Application).

Figure 1.1 (continued)

MATCHING PROGRAMS

M.D. Students/Graduates

National Resident Matching
Program (NRMP)

NRMP Specialty/Fellowship
Matching Programs

San Francisco Matching Program

Urology Match

D.O. Students/Graduates

AOA Intern/Resident
Registration

Military Match

No Matching Program
• Used by "off-cycle" applicants, D.O. residencies,
and many fellowship programs.

▼

INTERNATIONAL MEDICAL GRADUATES

ECFMG Certificate Required

USMLE
• IMGs must pass Steps 1, 2CK,
and 2CS for ECFMG
certification.

VISA
• Required for non-U.S. citizens/
permanent residents.

Fifth Pathway

• An alternative to ECFMG
certification for U.S. citizen
IMGs from selected schools.

2

The Specialties

If you don't know where you are going,
you won't know when you get there.

– Anonymous

The Choices

IN GOING THROUGH THE PROCESS of tentatively selecting a specialty—
because a tentative selection is all you should make if you are reading this
during your preclinical or early clinical years—*make sure to choose for
yourself*. Don't select a specialty based on:

- **What your parents want you to do.** "You're going to be a Surgeon,
  just like your old man," your father has said since you were in
  preschool.
- **What your spouse wants you to do.** "Make sure that you go into
  something where you will be home nights and weekends."
- **The specialty that your lab partner selected.** Did you forget that
  while your partner was dissecting those tiny little nerves in Anatomy
  you had trouble finding the biceps muscle?
- **Mental images from the books and television shows** that first
  attracted you to medicine. Do you really think Emergency Physicians
  see only crises interspersed with sexual escapades, as *ER* depicts?

"Knowing" the Specialty You Will Enter

Many students enter medical school "knowing" the specialty they will follow as their career. Most of them are wrong. Studies suggest that more than
one-third of medical students make a specialty selection before medical
school (although it often subsequently changes), about the same number
decide during their third-year clerkships, and fewer decide either during
their basic science years or after their basic clerkships.

Overall, only 20% of students who "know" what field they want to practice upon entering medical school actually pursue that field for residency training. More than one-third of those entering medical school who are interested in Obstetrics/Gynecology, Psychiatry, Family Medicine, or Emergency Medicine ultimately pursue those fields. In general, older students are more likely to commit to a career path early in medical school. But the likelihood is that you will change your mind as you experience new and exciting adventures on your journey through medical school.

Even in my student days (many years ago), we knew that our specialty choices would probably not last out the first year. My anatomy partner, for example, foolishly blurted out during our first day of medical school that he would be a Pediatric Surgeon. Okay, so he was good at dissection, but no one believed that he would really follow through with that goal. Of course, he was the exception. We now send mail to him at the Section of Pediatric Surgery.

A Medical Career?

An uncomfortable question needs to be raised early in your considerations about selecting a career path in medicine. That is, do you really want to be a physician? Of course you have already spent a great deal of time pursuing this goal. But is it still what you want? You now know a lot more about medicine and, hopefully, about yourself than when you started this trek toward a medical career. Perhaps now is the time to reflect upon whether this choice is still right for you.

An American Medical Association survey yielded disturbing results— *39% of practicing physicians probably or definitely would not go to medical school,* if they had known as much about a career in medicine when entering as they know now. If you also feel that way, now would be an appropriate time to consider jumping ship. Yes, this could deal a large blow to your self-esteem. And you might feel that you have failed the relatives and friends who have been cheering you on. But the bottom line is to do a personal assessment to determine whether your goals and desires will still be met by a medical career.

Medicine's Opportunities

Before you do anything too hastily, however, consider that medicine has more options for its practitioners than any other profession (Figures 2.7, 2.8, and 2.9). Many of those who say that they are not happy in medicine may only be dissatisfied with their specialty. If you choose your specialty wisely, you stand the best chance of being fulfilled by your medical career (Figure 2.1).

FIGURE 2.1

Essentials of Specialty Selection

1. Keep an open mind about your career direction in medicine. Most students enter medical school with a limited view of the range of exciting career opportunities in medicine, even (or especially) if their parents are physicians.

2. Be open to the many new possibilities and experiences that medical school offers.

3. Know that even the largest medical centers and extensive medical school curricula do not expose students to the entire scope of available medical careers.

4. Aggressively seek new, interesting career opportunities—wherever you find them.

5. Remember what excites you about a medical career.

Choose a specialty that fits your own needs, wants, and interests. Medical students considering which specialty to enter say that they give consideration to: the time they will have for their family and personal life (81%); their professional autonomy within the specialty (53%); potential income (29%); risk of malpractice (29%); and risk of contracting AIDS (10%). In assessing your own needs, you may need to consider the presence of a family in your future. You may also realize that given the increase in managed care organizations, professional autonomy is an illusion for many physicians. The debt you owe, however, is real and current.

Don't let your financial burden unduly influence your decision. Don't choose a specialty just for the big bucks. Unfortunately, that is how some of your classmates may decide upon their future direction. But 40 or more years of misery in a specialty that does not interest you is not worth it. The happiest physicians are those who enjoy their work. Between 60% and 75% of medical students change their specialty choice during medical school; 20% of residents in training switch to unrelated areas; and 16% of physicians in practice change their specialty identification. Try to figure out which area of medicine you will enjoy for your entire professional life. It will be worth the time you spend doing it.

Specialty Choice

The process of choosing a specialty is complex and involves multiple steps (Figure 2.2). Initially, you must assess your own strengths and weaknesses,

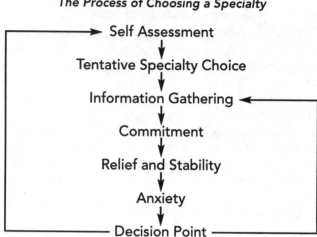

FIGURE 2.2

The Process of Choosing a Specialty

Adapted from: *New Physician.* July-August 1986, p. 19.

and likes and dislikes. The process has been described as "trying on possible selves" (i.e., projecting oneself into hypothetical career and personal roles). Medical students must make specialty choices that fit with their own personalities, so that they are compatible with other practitioners in the specialty and are able to master the specialty's content and skills. As students go through medical school, they make these choices in three ways:

1. They confirm that a pre-existing specialty choice meets their needs.
2. They select a specialty that includes many of the areas they find interesting.
3. They eliminate specialties as they discover things about themselves and the specialties that are not compatible.

The biggest decision for most students in their specialty selection is whether to enter a surgical or a non-surgical specialty. After looking over the available specialties, make a tentative choice. Then gather enough information, both by reading and through experience, to confirm that you have made the correct selection. With this commitment, you will experience some relief and stability. But making this decision can also lead to anxiety. Such anxiety is a normal part of making a major decision and is termed "post-purchase dissonance." If your anxiety is more severe than this (more than the feeling that you get after you have signed the papers on a new car or an expensive computer system), your career decision should be investigated further—and perhaps changed.

Figure 2.3 lists the significance of factors that students consider when choosing a residency program. Their importance may vary by specialty.

Once you make a career decision, expect to hear negative comments about your chosen specialty as you rotate through clinical clerkships. This behavior is typical of medical practitioners. Physicians, as well as other professionals, often believe that the "holy grail" is whatever professional area they chose, and that everyone else does less important work, works less hard, makes too much money for what they do, or is incompetent. Whether this is a way to bolster their self-esteem or reinforce their career choice, or results from their interactions with other practitioners and their

---

FIGURE 2.3

Factors Important to Students When Selecting a Residency Program

Very Important
- Quality of training program
- House officer satisfaction
- General impression at the interview
- Diversity of training experience
- Geographic location
- Resident staff quality/makeup
- Faculty/staff quality
- Personal fit with program/ personalities

Important
- Conference/didactic teaching
- High level of responsibility for patients
- Opportunities for post-residency training
- High patient volume
- Program's prestige
- Family considerations
- Proportion of IMGs in program

Not Very Important
- Department's and faculty's prestige
- Program director's qualities
- Extent of staff supervision
- Program's flexibility
- Lifestyle factors
- Manageable caseload
- Size of resident staff
- Call schedules
- Elective availability
- Physical plant
- Opportunity to conduct research
- Salary/benefits
- Cost of living

Not Important
- Management opportunities
- Affiliation with VA hospital
- Availability of support services
- Opportunity to treat AIDS patients
- Absence of AIDS from patient population
- Training in one hospital

Adapted from: Richard GV, Borges NJ: *First-year Residents' Reflections on Choice of Residency Program.* Rootstown, OH: Northeastern Ohio Universities College of Medicine, 2004 and Riley JD, Hannis M, Rice KG: Are international medical graduates a factor in residency program selection? A survey of fourth-year medical students. *Acad Med.* 1996;71(4):381-6.

patients is uncertain. However, just as professional baseball pitchers cannot allow themselves to be affected by catcalls from the stands, medical students allow these comments to influence their career decisions only at their own peril.

Jobs—The Ultimate Goal

Completing medical school and residency seems pointless if you cannot ultimately get a position in your specialty. You need to take a realistic look at the specialties. Some fields are already crowded; others, according to the best estimates, soon will be. Over the past decade, some graduates, especially in Anesthesiology, Plastic Surgery, and Pathology, have had trouble finding jobs, although in the current health care market, the situation seems to change annually. In response, many residency programs have reduced the number of training positions.

Those programs that have lost the most positions include Family Medicine, Internal Medicine, Pathology, and Pediatrics. Twice as many residency directors in university-based programs anticipate losing positions as do those in university-affiliated and community-based programs. This will dramatically increase the competition for university-based positions. However, positions have recently been added at many residencies in Anesthesiology, Emergency Medicine, and Radiation Oncology.

Residency directors foresee an increase in job opportunities for residency graduates in Anesthesiology (due to decreasing numbers of graduates to fill the positions opened by retiring anesthesiologists), Family Medicine, Internal Medicine, and Pediatrics. They believe fewer jobs will be available for new Ophthalmologists, Orthopedic Surgeons, Radiologists, and Pathologists.

Despite these predictions, any specialty that you find that you really like, whether or not it is populated by a horde of other physicians, will most likely suit you the best.

So where do all these physicians practice? The U.S. regions with the most physicians per capita are New England (CT, ME, MA, NH, RI, VT) with one physician for every 241 people and the Middle Atlantic (PA, NJ, NY) with one physician for every 267 people. The regions with the fewest physicians per capita are: the East South Central (KY, AL, MS, TN) and the Mountain (AZ, CO, ID, MT, NV, NM, UT, WY) with one physician per 403 people, and the West South Central (AR, LA, OK, TX) with only one physician per 429 people.

The states with the highest physician-to-population ratios are listed in Figure 2.4.

FIGURE 2.4
States with the Most Physicians per Capita
(Ratio of persons per each physician)

1. District of Columbia	122	6. Connecticut	252
2. Massachusetts	210	7. Rhode Island	263
3. Maryland	222	8. Hawaii	289
4. New York	236	9. New Jersey	297
5. Vermont	240	10. Pennsylvania	305

Adapted from American Medical Association: *Physician Characteristics and Distribution in the U.S.*, 2005 ed. Chicago, IL: American Medical Association, 2005, p. 331, Table 5.19.

Medicine's Future

I hope you will have a long career in medicine, during which you will see many changes, not only in the science and art of medicine, but also in health care delivery systems. Your choice of specialty will, in part, determine how well you weather these changes. At present, three important factors appear to be influencing the course of health care delivery: the role of primary care versus specialist physicians, the role of managed care delivery systems, and the number of physicians in each specialty compared to those that are needed to provide adequate care for the population. While these factors are clearly interrelated, I will attempt to provide you with a brief overview of the individual elements.

Primary Care

Before looking at individual specialties, you should know what is meant by the term "primary care"—a hot topic among health planners, politicians, and medical school deans.

Primary care is ideally the point at which patients enter the health treatment system. Primary care practitioners, now also referred to as "Generalists," should be able to diagnose and treat 80% or more of the patients that present themselves, oversee the activities of any specialists involved in their patient's care, and provide continuity of care. Whether many practitioners actually do all these is questionable. It is especially difficult to provide continuity of care, since patients frequently switch their managed care plans (HMOs, PPOs, IPAs, etc.).

What specialties are considered "primary care"? Certainly, the term encompasses General Internal Medicine, Family Medicine, and General

Pediatrics. Does it also include Obstetrics and Gynecology, Emergency Medicine, Psychiatry, Internal Medicine subspecialties, Dermatology, and Neurology? All have been proposed as being "primary care." In some cases their practitioners do exactly what the definition implies—sometimes better than those in the three generalist specialties. Most Physician Assistants and Nurse Practitioners also fall into this category. But why all this fuss?

The answer is, for money and survival. Over the past several decades, the federal government's regulatory and funding arms have attempted to limit the number of non-primary care residency and fellowship (except Geriatrics) positions. A key measure of medical school performance (especially state-financed schools) is what percentage of their graduates practice medicine in rural or underserved urban environments? The thought is that primary care physicians are more likely to practice in these underserved locales. Therefore, multiple groups continue to advocate for more primary care residency positions, although it has become clear that there may be enough primary care practitioners—they just are not adequately distributed.

About 86% of all primary care physicians practice in metropolitan areas and about 76% of those who still do patient care are office based. General Practitioners (85%) and Family Practitioners (82%) most commonly have office-based practices; only 71% of Internists are office-based.

You may have noticed that many senior faculty extol the virtues of primary care. Perhaps this is because national groups and legislators have recently been reviewing medical schools based on the percentage of their graduates that go into primary care specialties. With more than one-third of U.S. medical schools having an explicit mission to produce primary care physicians, the folks who control the purse strings are carefully reviewing whether they are meeting this goal. A primary care designation has, therefore, been politically important for survival. Medical schools have been successful in promoting primary care specialties: The number of graduates planning a career in Family Medicine, General Internal Medicine, or General Pediatrics grew from 14.6% of 1992's graduating class to about 25% in 2005.

While primary care residencies were once much more popular, 50% or more of the graduating classes at about one-third of U.S. medical schools enter a primary care residency. In 2005, for the tenth straight year, more than 50% of the graduating students took residencies in Family Medicine, Internal Medicine, or Pediatrics—although many are expected to enter subspecialties, especially those entering Internal Medicine. For the first time in many years, the number of Osteopathic medical school graduates entering M.D.-affiliated primary care residencies declined. Among M.D.-granting schools, the percentage of their graduates entering primary care varies widely. Even at many Osteopathic medical schools, which once had a much more solid primary care orientation, most of their graduates veer away from primary care.

Over the past three decades, the number of physicians in primary care specialties more than doubled, only slightly lagging behind the total number of U.S. physicians. Among them, General Internists comprise 37% of all primary care physicians; Family Practitioners, 26%; Obstetrician/Gynecologists, 13%; General Pediatricians, 19%; and General Practitioners, 4%. (General Practitioners are usually physicians who practice general medicine and do not hold Board certification; nearly two-thirds are at least 55 years old.) The subspecialists in these fields also increased, with the largest increase occurring in Pediatric subspecialties.

States with the highest ratio of primary care physicians to all physicians are Illinois (36%); New Jersey (35%); and Michigan, Texas, California, and Ohio (34% each). More than 37% of all IMGs practice in primary care, as do 33% of U.S. medical graduates and 27% of Canadian medical graduates practicing in the United States.

Nearly three-fourths (73%) of all U.S. physicians are Board certified, which is similar to the percentage (71.6%) of those practicing primary care. The highest percentage of those with primary care Board certification is in Family Medicine (80%), while Board certification among Pediatricians is 77%; Obstetrician/Gynecologists, 76%; and General Internists, 68%. About 91% of primary care subspecialists have their Boards.

Based on current residency trends, the AMA believes that the future non-specialist primary care workforce will include mostly women, IMGs, and D.O.s. Why do students choose to enter primary care, especially Family Medicine? The biggest factor is being a woman: Women comprise more than half (53%) of primary care residents. The second most important factor is being an IMG: About 50% of Family Medicine residents now are IMGs (as opposed to 22% in 1999).

Studies of U.S. medical students suggest that they are strongly influenced by many factors, perhaps the most important of which is whether they entered medical school thinking that they would be a Family Physician. They are more likely to enter Family Medicine if they have a rural background; have low income expectations and little debt; are Hispanic, married, or older; and are not concerned about control of their work hours. (Other factors are listed in Figure 2.5.) One study also suggested that students who were less Machiavellian tended to go into primary care. (Heh! Heh! Heh! Were you saying you wanted to subspecialize?)

FIGURE 2.5

Reasons Why Students Choose Primary Care/ Non-Primary Care Specialties

Factors important when selecting a primary care specialty:

1. Good match with personal interests.
2. Long-term relationship with patients.
3. Broad practice area.
4. Caring for ambulatory patients.
5. Preventive interventions.
6. Diverse patient populations.
7. Enhanced patient interactions.
8. Breadth of clinical activities and content.
9. Influence of role models and mentors.

Factors important when selecting a non-primary care specialty:

1. Good match with personal interests.
2. Lifestyle and quality of life.
3. Higher income.
4. Narrow practice area.
5. Seeing immediate results of interventions.
6. Doing procedures and having technical skills.
7. Caring for critical patients.
8. Intellectual challenge.
9. Pace of practice.
10. Specific setting: ED, OR, ICU.

Adapted from: Garibaldi RA, Popkave C, Bylsma W: Career plans for trainees in internal medicine residency programs. *Acad Med* 2005;80(5):507-12; and Burack JH, Irby DM, Carline JD, et al.: A study of medical students' specialty-choice pathways: trying on possible selves. *Acad Med.* 1997;72(6):534-41.

One warning, however. A recent survey showed that 40% of America's primary care physicians would choose another career if they could start over. According to the researchers, the most dissatisfied primary care physicians had originally entered medicine for the intellectual challenge and stimulation. They are often unhappy due to boredom and infrequent therapeutic success. Those who entered medicine primarily to "help people" were still satisfied with the choice they had made. They derive most of their satisfaction from social interactions with their patients.

No one really knows how many primary care practitioners we need. Some studies now suggest that the United States has adequate generalist physicians to meet current needs. As an AAMC spokesman said, "In recent years, there has been no insufficiency in primary care doctors. We were giving people the wrong message." The real problem seems to be an over-abundance of specialists. Plans were afoot to retrain specialists into primary care (a fruitless endeavor that has now been abandoned). Specialists, rather than primary care physicians, provide most of the care for one in five Americans, with most of these patients being elderly.

As alternative practitioners (Physician Assistants and Nurse Practitioners) assume many duties formerly performed by primary care physicians, the era of the primary care practitioner may have passed. Yet bureaucrats with little grasp of the big picture will probably determine the balance of training positions. As with their response to the "physician shortage" only a few years ago, they are certain to overreact.

At present, residency graduates intending to practice primary care are doing very well; they report that they get more than 50 recruitment offers during their residency (IMGs get fewer). Their salary expectations are also rising, although whether they will get what they hope for remains to be seen.

The Managed Care Environment

Health care delivery is changing and managed care organizations spearheaded that change. "Managed care" includes a wide variety of structures, from large group practices relying on salaried physicians and their own hospitals to every other imaginable permutation of physicians, insurance companies, and hospitals. What they have in common is that rather than emphasizing quality medical care or the physician-patient relationship (some may still have these), they emphasize cost-effectiveness. With the runaway cost of medical care and the increasing availability of high technology, high-cost diagnostic and treatment modalities, such a change was inevitable.

A wag once commented that if we treated medicine like agriculture and paid every unneeded licensed physician $100,000 to not practice medicine, we could balance the federal budget. Indeed, the more practicing physicians we have, the more medical tests and procedures are ordered and the more costs increase. Specialists do far more tests and procedures than primary care practitioners; hospitalized patients get the most tests and the most procedures. Managed care organizations, therefore, profit by keeping as many patients as possible away from specialists and hospitals. They have been very successful at doing this in many parts of the country. You can see the effects of this in the many hospitals that have closed or been forced to merge, the specialists who wish to retrain into primary care, the new specialty graduates who cannot get jobs in locales they desire, and the specialty societies that plan to close residency and fellowship programs.

Among the key skills needed to be a successful practitioner within the managed care environment are the ability to diagnose and treat a wide variety of common illnesses, the ability to recognize when you are beyond your depth clinically, an ability and willingness to see many patients quickly, an ability to work with many other physicians and non-physician health care providers, an understanding of how to effectively use information systems (computers), and a willingness to tolerate the unwieldy clinical and financial maze of managed care organizations.

These are skills that, for the most part, can and should be learned during medical school and residency. An optimal place to learn such skills is to work within a managed care framework, gaining experience either by dealing with such organizations from the outside or, better yet, by spending some time working in managed care groups. Unfortunately, only 20% of teaching hospitals use such facilities for residency training, and the amount of education in managed care settings varies by specialty.

As can be seen in Figure 2.6, it is now common for physicians to participate in managed care. Soon the full impact of managed care will be felt throughout the country. Making money (for owners and insurance companies) and saving money (by employers and government) are strong incentives. It would be wise for you to consider the impact of managed care systems on medical practice in the United States as you make your career decisions.

While managed care is the current buzzword in health care delivery, the caveat when charting your future career is to always plan for the next system—and perhaps for the system after that. For example, the emerging buzz phrase is "quality-based reimbursement." (Of course, the problems are how "quality" is defined and who does the defining.)

The "Right" Number of Physicians

Medicine and medical care delivery systems are changing so fast that no one can predict exactly how many physicians we will need or what will be the optimal balance of specialties over the course of your career—or even for the next ten years. An educated guess of how many physicians will be in the various specialties can be found in Figure 5.3. Whether these numbers represent too many or too few physicians is, at present, unclear. Some pessimistic studies suggest that about 40% of all medical specialists could be unnecessary by the end of this decade.

FIGURE 2.6
Percentage of Specialty Physicians in Practices with Managed Care Contracts

Specialty	Any Managed Care Contract	Private	Medicare	Medicaid
Obstetrics/Gynecol	98%	96%	71%	68%
Otolaryngology	98	98	72	73
Cardiology	96	94	85	65
Pediatrics	96	92	20	78
Radiology	96	92	74	72
Anesthesiology	95	92	76	76
General Surgery	93	95	75	71
Family Medicine	91	88	58	61
ALL PHYSICIANS	**91**	**87**	**62**	**62**
Gen Internal Med	90	86	67	58
Dermatology	90	85	57	34
Pathology	86	82	64	59
Emergency Med	82	72	66	66
Psychiatry	74	67	41	37

Adapted from: American Medical Association. *Physician Socioeconomic Statistics 2000–2002.* Chicago, IL: AMA, 2001. Available information suggests that the data in this figure continues to represent the current situation in 2006.

Economic necessity is pushing the health care system to encourage more non-physicians (Nurse Practitioners, Nurse-Anesthetists, Nurse- and lay-midwives, Physician Assistants, Optometrists, Clinical Psychologists, and others) to practice medicine. In some cases, they are decreasing the need for specialist physicians (Anesthesiologists, Ophthalmologists) while in other cases, such as in the primary care specialties, their numbers have not reduced the need for practitioners.

When considering what specialty to enter, you will hear conflicting opinions about the future need for physicians in various specialties. As the truism goes, "There are liars, damn liars, and statisticians." Worse yet are those who interpret those statistics, often incompletely or incorrectly, to make their points. Take all these prognostications with a grain of salt.

Your best course of action is to use all the factors you trust to be valid, including estimations of the potential job markets. Next, assess which specialty best fits your needs, your interests, and your personality. Then pursue your specialty choice with all of your determination.

The future will come, no matter what you do. Therefore, your best strategy is to prepare yourself to *enjoy* your medical career.

FIGURE 2.7

American Board of Medical Specialties (M.D.)-Approved Specialty Boards, Certifications, and Special Qualification Categories

American Board	Certification	Subspecialty
Allergy & Immunology	Allergy & Immunology	Clinical & Lab Immunology
Anesthesiology	Anesthesiology	Critical Care Medicine Pain Medicine
Colon & Rectal Surgery	Colon & Rectal Surgery	
Dermatology	Dermatology	Dermatopathology Clinical & Lab Derm Immunology Pediatric Dermatology
Emergency Medicine	Emergency Medicine	Medical Toxicology Pediatric Emergency Medicine Sports Medicine Undersea & Hyperbaric Medicine
Family Medicine	Family Medicine	Adolescent Medicine Geriatric Medicine Sports Medicine
Internal Medicine	Internal Medicine	Adolescent Medicine Cardiovascular Disease Clin Cardiac Electrophysiology Clin & Lab Immunology Critical Care Medicine Endocrinology, Diabetes & Metab Gastroenterology Geriatric Medicine Hematology Infectious Diseases Interventional Cardiology Medical Oncology Nephrology Pulmonary Disease Rheumatology Sleep Medicine Sports Medicine Transplant Hepatology
Medical Genetics	Clin Biochemical Genetics Clin Cytogenetics Clin Genetics (M.D. only) Clin Molecular Genetics Medical Genetics (Ph.D. only)	Molecular Genetic Pathology
Neurological Surgery	Neurological Surgery	
Nuclear Medicine	Nuclear Medicine	

continued

FIGURE 2.7 (continued)

American Board	Certification	Subspecialty
Obstetrics & Gynecology	Obstetrics & Gynecology	Critical Care Medicine Gynecologic Oncology Maternal & Fetal Medicine Reproductive Endocrinology/ Infertility
Ophthalmology	Ophthalmology	
Orthopedic Surgery	Orthopedic Surgery	Orthopedic Sports Medicine Surgery of the Hand
Otolaryngology	Otolaryngology	Neurotology Pediatric Otolaryngology Plastic Surgery within the Head & Neck
Pathology	Anatomic & Clinical Path Anatomic Pathology Clinical Pathology	Blood Bank/Transfusion Med Chemical Pathology Cytopathology Dermatopathology Forensic Pathology Hematology Medical Microbiology Molecular Genetic Pathology Neuropathology Pediatric Pathology
Pediatrics	Pediatrics	Adolescent Medicine Clinical & Lab Immunology Developmental-Behavioral Peds Medical Toxicology Neonatal-Perinatal Medicine Neurodevelopmental Disabilities Pediatric Cardiology Pediatric Critical Care Medicine Pediatric Emergency Medicine Pediatric Endocrinology Pediatric Gastroenterology Pediatric Hematology-Oncology Pediatric Infectious Diseases Pediatric Nephrology Pediatric Pulmonology Pediatric Rheumatology Pediatric Transplant Hepatology Sleep Medicine Sports Medicine

continued

FIGURE 2.7 (continued)

American Board	Certification	Subspecialty
Physical Medicine & Rehabilitation	Physical Medicine & Rehabilitation	Pain Medicine Pediatric Rehabilitation Medicine Spinal Cord Injury Medicine
Plastic Surgery	Plastic Surgery	Plastic Surgery within the Head & Neck Surgery of the Hand
Preventive Medicine	Aerospace Medicine Occupational Medicine Public Health & General Preventive Medicine	Medical Toxicology Undersea & Hyperbaric Medicine
Psychiatry & Neurology	Neurology Neurology with Special Qualifications in Child Neurology Psychiatry	Addiction Psychiatry Child & Adolescent Psychiatry Clinical Neurophysiology Forensic Psychiatry Geriatric Psychiatry Neurodevelopmental Disabilities Pain Medicine Psychosomatic Medicine Sleep Medicine Vascular Neurology
Radiology	Diagnostic Radiology Radiation Oncology Radiological Physics	Neuroradiology Nuclear Radiology Pediatric Radiology Vascular/Interventional Radiology
Surgery	Surgery Vascular Surgery	Pediatric Surgery Surgery of the Hand Surgical Critical Care
Thoracic Surgery	Thoracic Surgery	
Urology	Urology	

Information from: American Board of Medical Specialties, 2005.

FIGURE 2.8
**Approved Specialty Boards, Certification, and
Special Qualification Categories (D.O.)#**

American Osteopathic Board	General Certification	Certification of Special Qualifications[†]	Certification of Added Qualifications[††]
Anesthesiology	Anesthesiology		Addiction Medicine Critical Care Medicine Pain Management
Dermatology	Dermatology		Dermatopathology MOHS-Micrographic Surg
Emergency Medicine	Emergency Medicine		Emergency Med Svcs Medical Toxicology[*] Sports Medicine
Family Physicians	Family Practice (& Osteopathic Manipulative Treatment)		Geriatric Medicine Sports Medicine
Internal Medicine	Internal Medicine	Allergy/Immunology Cardiology Endocrinology Gastroenterology Hematology Infectious Dis Nephrology Oncology Pulmonary Dis Rheumatology	Addiction Medicine Critical Care Medicine Clin Cardiac Electrophysiology Geriatric Medicine Interventional Cardiology Sports Medicine

Neurology & Psychiatry	Neurology
	Psychiatry
		Child/Adolescent
		   Neurology
		Child & Adolescent
		   Psychiatry
			Addiction Medicine
			Neurophysiology
			Sports Medicine

Neuromusculo- skeletal Medicine	Neuromusculoskeletal Med & Osteopathic Manipulative Med		Sports Medicine
Nuclear Medicine	Nuclear Medicine		Nuclear Imaging & Therapy
Obstetrics & Gynecology	Obstetrics & Gynecology	Gynecologic Oncology Maternal/Fetal Med Reproductive Endocrinology	

(continued)

FIGURE 2.8 (continued)

American Osteopathic Board	General Certification	Certification of Special Qualifications[†]	Certification of Added Qualifications[††]
Ophthalmology & Otolaryngology	Facial Plastic Surg Ophthalmology Otolaryngology Otolaryngology/ Facial Plastic Surg		Otolaryngologic Allergy
Orthopedic Surgery	Orthopedic Surgery		Hand Surgery
Pathology	Anatomic Pathology Anatomic Pathology & Lab Medicine Laboratory Medicine	Forensic Pathology	Dermatopathology
Pediatrics	Pediatrics	Adolescent/Young Adult Medicine Neonatology Ped Allergy/Immunol Ped Endocrinology	Sports Medicine
Physical Medicine & Rehabilitation	Physical Med & Rehabilitation		Sports Medicine

Preventive Medicine	Preventive Med/
	    Aerospace Med
	Preventive Med/
	    Occupational-
	    Environmental Med
	Preventive Med/
	    Public Health
			Occupational Medicine
			Sports Medicine

Proctology	Proctology		
Radiology	Diagnostic Radiology Radiation Oncology		Angiography & Interventional Radiology Body Imaging Diagnostic Ultrasound Neuroradiology Nuclear Radiology Pediatric Radiology

(continued)

FIGURE 2.8 (continued)

American Osteopathic Board	General Certification	Certification of Special Qualifications[†]	Certification of Added Qualifications[††]
Surgery	Gen Vascular Surg	Gen Vascular Surg	Surgical Critical Care
	Neurological Surg		
	Plastic & Recon-		
	structive Surg		
	Surgery (General)		
	Thoracic Cardio-		
	vascular Surg		
	Urological Surg		

[#]Osteopathic training programs do not exist in most approved specialties and subspecialties.
[*]Also available to diplomates of other AOA Boards.
[†]Requires General Certification—Equivalent to "Subspecialty."
[††]Requires General Certification or Certification of Special Qualifications—Equivalent to "Subspecialty."
Adapted from: DO-Online (www.do-online.osteotech.org/), December 2005.

FIGURE 2.9
M.D. and D.O. Physicians in Practice by Specialty

Specialty	M.D. Physicians*	D.O. Physicians**	% of All Practicing Physicians***
Allergy & Immunology	4,101	43	0.5
Anesthesiology	37,754	875	5.0
Cardiovascular Disease	21,981	451	2.9
Colon & Rectal Surgery	1,197	2	0.2
Dermatology	9,988	339	1.3
Emergency Medicine	25,552	2,088	3.5
Family Medicine	76,503	18,765	12.2
Gastroenterology	11,329	227	1.5
General Practice	13,546	42	1.7
General Surgery	37,288	752	4.9
Internal Medicine, General	106,499	3,278	14.1
Internal Medicine, Other	36,546	474	4.7
Medical Genetics	433	0	<0.1
Neurological Surgery	5,008	71	0.7
Neurology	13,006	264	1.7
Nuclear Medicine	1,455	10	0.2
Obstetrics & Gynecology	41,038	1,526	5.5
Ophthalmology	18,584	298	2.4
Orthopedic Surgery	23,211	1,039	3.1
Osteo. Manipulative Med/OMT	N/A	373	<0.1
Otolaryngology	9,704	129	1.3
Pathology-Anat/Clin	18,826	136	2.4
Pediatrics, General	53,628	1,663	7.1
Pediatric Subspecialties	14,277	106	1.8
Plastic Surgery	6,506	313	0.9
Physical Med & Rehabilitation	7,042	287	0.9
Psychiatry	46,453	536	6.0
Pulmonary Diseases	9,438	203	1.2
Radiology (All)	35,757	804	4.7
Thoracic Surgery	5,056	77	0.7
Urology	10,431	182	1.4
Other Specialties	19,623	650	2.6
Others in Practice	53,780	4,897	7.5
Total	738,994	40,910	—

* Adapted from: Association of American Medical Colleges. *AAMC Data Book.* Washington, D.C.: AAMC, 2005, Table J5 and American Medical Association: *Physician Characteristics and Distribution in the U.S.* Chicago, IL: American Medical Association, 2005, Table 1.9.
** Adapted from: American Osteopathic Association. Fact Sheet 2005 and Find a D.O., http://www.osteopathic.org/directory.cfm, Accessed December 2005.
***Does not add up to 100% due to rounding.
N/A = Information not available.

3

Specialty Descriptions

*The specialist learns more and more about less and less until, finally, he knows
everything about nothing; while the generalist learns less and less about
more and more until, finally, he knows nothing about everything.*

– Donsen's Law

FIRST, LOOK AT THE WIDE RANGE of medical specialties that are available.
You may be surprised at the diversity within the house of medicine. There
are probably many specialties listed here that you have never heard of;
there definitely are many that you will have no contact with during medical school. You may have encountered others only peripherally. But they
all are options for you. Most of these specialties provide certification—
either primarily, such as Pediatrics and Surgery, or as a subspecialty, such as
Forensic Pathology and Hematology. Some, such as Trauma Surgery and
Hospitalists, are gradually being accepted as distinct subspecialties by the
medical community, but do not yet have subspecialty examinations or
certifications.

Nearly three-fourths (73%) of all U.S. physicians hold specialty or subspecialty board certification. Overall, the majority of physicians who do get
board certified have done better in medical school and residency than their
counterparts who don't. Most physicians must now pass an initial exam to
become certified, with future periodic recertifications to assess their clinical performance.

Read these descriptions to open your mind to the scope of career
choices you have. There is no point in leaping ahead until you know what
lies before you.

The ease of acquiring a residency position in each specialty varies. This
can be expressed by assigning each specialty a relative difficulty factor, just
as in competitive diving. While it is impossible to give exact numbers, it is
possible to approximate this difficulty. Beside each specialty's name in the

descriptions below, the difficulty factor is indicated by using a one (*) to five (*****) asterisk scale. *In specialties with one asterisk, you should have the least difficulty getting a residency position (or into the field, if there is no residency); and in those with five asterisks, the most difficulty.* Remember, though, that even the easiest specialties to enter have some very competitive programs, and even the most difficult to enter have some less competitive programs. So, only use the asterisk system as a *general guide, not as an absolute truth.*

Some specialties are entered through the completion of Fellowship training, which is obtained after first finishing a prerequisite residency. These specialties are designated by "(F)." The terminology PGY-1, PGY-2, etc. (or, occasionally, OGME-1, OGME-2, etc. for Osteopaths) equates to the specified "postgraduate year."

Some specialties have programs that accept new residents other than in July. The number of programs offering these slots is listed. The specific programs, as well as those that offer part-time (shared-schedule) positions, can be found by selecting "optional criteria" in *FREIDA.*

The figures in Chapter 22 contain additional information that may guide you when making a decision. This includes the prerequisites for training in the various specialties, the total number of programs in each specialty, and the approximate number of entry-level positions open each year. Figure 2.9 lists the total number of physicians currently practicing in each specialty. A visual description of the length of specialty training for both M.D. and Osteopathic (D.O.) physicians can be found in Figures 3.1 and 3.2, which follow the verbal descriptions of the specialties. Figure 3.3 ranks most specialties and subspecialties by how well they meet current practitioners' expectations of what they were seeking when they entered the specialty. Figure 13.6 lists the number of programs in each specialty that have part-time/shared-schedule positions available.

After you have looked through this chapter, use an evaluation tool such as the Pathway Evaluation Program (http://medweb.usc.edu/pathways/intro.htm) or the AAMC's Careers in Medicine (http://services.aamc.org/careersinmedicine/), as well as the Personal Trait Analysis in Chapter 4, to compare your likes and dislikes in medical practice to those of practitioners in the major specialties.

For clarification, "ACGME" stands for Accreditation Council for Graduate Medical Education, the body that approves M.D. residencies. "AOA" in "AOA-Approved Programs" stands for American Osteopathic Association, the body that approves D.O. residencies. "NRMP" stands for National Residency Matching Program, used by most medical students to obtain a residency position. It is described in detail in Chapter 22. (For M.D.s, "AOA" also stands for a prestigious medical school honorary society.)

Legend for Specialty Descriptions

*	Entry into a training program is **Very Easy**
**	Entry into a training program is **Easy**
***	Entry into a training program is **Difficult**
****	Entry into a training program is **Very Difficult**
*****	Entry into a training program is **Extremely Difficult**

(F) Fellowship training following completion of an initial residency.

The Osteopathic listings are for funded programs and positions only.

In the boxes listing the positions for each specialty, the terms mean:

"ACGME-Approved Programs"—Programs approved for M.D.s

"AOA-Approved Programs"—Programs approved for D.O.s

"1st-Yr. Spots"—PGY-1 (Intern) Positions

"Advanced Spots Avail. to M.D. Students"—Positions (PGY-2 or above) with which M.D. students can match

"Funded Entry-Level D.O. Spots"—The number of funded beginning positions available in AOA-approved programs

"All Entry-Level M.D. Spots"—All beginning positions in ACGME-approved specialty training programs

"Alt./Comp. Med Curriculum"—Programs offering some training in Alternative/Complementary Medicine

"Programs with Childcare"—Programs with on-site childcare available.

"N/A"—no data available

Information in the tables reflects the available data for that specialty. Some specialties have only limited data available and thus the whole table is not shown.

Aerospace Medicine***

Specialty Overview: Aerospace Medicine is a specialty within Preventive Medicine. Practitioners are responsible for the medical care and safety of individuals involved in military and civilian aviation and space travel. This includes crew members and ground personnel. The Federal Aviation Administration, NASA, the military, and the aerospace industry employ most flight surgeons and aviation medical examiners. They are usually engaged in clinical medicine, research and development, or administration. Medical certification of pilots for flight duty often constitutes a large part of their clinical practice, and most physicians in this field are pilots themselves.

Training: Two years of training are required after internship. One of these years must be spent obtaining an advanced degree in a relevant area, usually a master's degree in Public Health. The second residency year devotes more time to clinical Aerospace Medicine. A fourth year of training, teaching, practice, and/or research is required to take the Board examination. There are two military Aerospace Medicine programs (Brooks Air Force Base, Texas, and Pensacola Naval Air Station, Florida) and two civilian programs (Wright State University, Ohio, and University of Texas at Galveston-NASA).

Match: To be eligible for the military programs, an individual must already be in the military and practicing as a Flight Surgeon.

AEROSPACE MEDICINE			
ACGME-Approved Programs	4	All Entry-Level M.D. Spots	45
AOA-Approved Programs	0	All Entry-Level D.O. Spots	0
Adv. Spots Avail. to M.D. Students	0		

For more information, contact:

- Aerospace Medical Association, (703) 739-2240; www.asma.org.
- American College of Preventive Medicine, (202) 466-2044; www.acpm.org/residency.htm.
- American Osteopathic College of Occupational and Preventive Medicine, (800) 558-8686; www.aocopm.org.

Allergy and Immunology (F)*

Specialty Overview: Allergy and Immunology is a subspecialty of both Internal Medicine and Pediatrics devoted to the diagnosis and treatment of allergic, asthmatic, and immunologic diseases. There is a great deal of art, as well as science, in the practice of the Allergist–Immunologist. The patients seen most frequently have asthma and chronic or seasonal allergies. Practitioners get most of their patients through referrals. There is usually very little emergency or night call. Practice opportunities are more restricted than in the past, due to an increasing number of physicians, both in this field and in other fields, who do allergy testing and treatment. Allergist–Immunologists are mainly office-based and are concentrated in metropolitan areas. Research opportunities in this field are growing dramatically because of the increasing recognition of the role of immunologic factors in diseases. Allergist–Immunologists average 41 hours per week doing patient care.

Training: Training is two years after completing either a Pediatric or an Internal Medicine residency. It includes experiences in both pediatric and adult diseases. It is expected that trainees will participate in research. A special qualification in Clinical & Laboratory Immunology requires an extra year of training that prepares trainees to act as consultants in the application and interpretation of diagnostic immunology tests.

Match: Applicants should contact programs directly.

ALLERGY AND IMMUNOLOGY

ACGME-Approved Programs	72	AOA-Approved Programs	0
1st-Yr. Spots for M.D. Students	0	Funded Entry-Level D.O. Spots	0
Adv. Spots Avail. to M.D. Students	0	% IMG Residents	17
All Entry-Level M.D. Spots	150	Avg. Res. Work Hours/Week	40
% Women Residents	48	Programs with Childcare	28
Avg. Ratio of Full-Time Physician		Programs Offering a "Primary	
Faculty to Fellows	2.4	Care Track"	3
% Training in Hospital Outpatient		Programs Offering Multiple	
Clinics	56	Start Dates	9
% Training in Non-Hospital		Programs Allowing Moonlighting	37
Community Ambulatory Clinics	6	Alt./Comp. Med Curriculum	19

CLINICAL AND LABORATORY IMMUNOLOGY

ACGME-Approved Programs	1	AOA-Approved Programs	0
1st-Yr. Spots for M.D. Students	0	Funded Entry-Level D.O. Spots	0
Adv. Spots Avail. to M.D. Students	0	% IMG Residents	N/A
All Entry-Level M.D. Spots	2	Avg. Res. Work Hours/Week	38
% Women Residents	71	% Training in Non-Hospital	
Avg. Ratio of Full-Time Physician		Community Ambulatory Clinics	0
Faculty to Residents/Fellows	6.1		
% Training in Hospital Outpatient			
Clinics	17		

For more information, contact:

- American Academy of Allergy, Asthma, & Immunology, (414) 272-6071; www.aaaai.org.
- American Association of Immunologists, (301) 634-7178; www.aai.org.
- American College of Allergy, Asthma, & Immunology, www.acaai.org.
- American Osteopathic College of Allergy and Immunology, 7025 E. McDowell Rd., Ste. 1B; Scottsdale, AZ 85257; (480) 585-1580.

Anesthesiology***

Specialty Overview: Anesthesiologists give general and regional anesthesia during surgical, obstetric, diagnostic, and therapeutic procedures; function as Critical Care physicians; and give anesthetic blocks in conjunction with pain clinics. They often specialize in Pediatric, Neurosurgical, Obstetric, Cardiothoracic, or Ambulatory Anesthesia, although Critical Care (see Critical Care) and Pain Medicine (see Pain Medicine) are the only formal subspecialties. Anesthesiology remains primarily a hospital-based specialty with frequent night call for most practitioners, although the rapid expansion of outpatient surgery has changed this a little. Research continues to push the practice of Anesthesiology into an ever more elegant and scientific realm. The growing use of less-expensive Nurse–Anesthetists and a declining number of surgeries has decreased the need for Anesthesiologists, although the number of Anesthesiologists has increased about one-third in the past decade. Over the past decades, Anesthesiology's popularity as a specialty selection has varied tremendously. At present, it is again very popular.

Training: Training consists of a "base" year, essentially a Transitional, Preliminary, or Categorical internship in a clinical specialty, followed by three years of training in Clinical Anesthesiology and Critical Care. Residency programs in Anesthesiology start at either the first (PGY-1) or the second (PGY-2) postgraduate year. The training is essentially the same for Osteopathic physicians. Training in the subspecialties of Anesthesia Critical Care Medicine (49 positions), Anesthesia Pain Medicine (197 positions) or Pediatric Anesthesiology (137 positions) takes a minimum of one year after completing an Anesthesiology residency.

Match: In recent years, about 96% of the available PGY-1 positions filled through the NRMP Match. Of the PGY-2 positions available through the NRMP Match, about 95% filled in the Match. Some PGY-4 positions are available in specialty areas (Pediatric, Neurosurgical, etc.) and can be applied for separately from normal Anesthesiology programs.

Other Useful Information: Anesthesiology residencies tend to look both for good performance in preclinical Physiology and Pharmacology courses and for how well students have done in their Internal Medicine and Anesthesiology clerkships. Those going into the field are detail-oriented, dislike long-term patient relationships, and can remain calm in the face of clinical schedules over which they often have little control. Since working with a team is vital, great importance is given to the applicant's interview.

ANESTHESIOLOGY

ACGME-Approved Programs	132	AOA-Approved Programs	11
1st-Yr. Spots for M.D. Students	654	Funded Entry-Level D.O. Spots	21
Adv. Spots Avail. to M.D. Students	617	% IMG Residents	27
All Entry-Level M.D. Spots	1,271	Avg. Res. Work Hours/Week	61
% Women Residents	26	Programs with Childcare	9
Avg. Ratio of Full-Time Physician Faculty to Residents/Fellows	1.3	Programs Offering a "Primary Care Track"	1
% Training in Hospital Outpatient Clinics	11	Programs Offering Multiple Start Dates	44
% Training in Non-Hospital Community Ambulatory Clinics	2	Programs Allowing Moonlighting	60
		Alt./Comp. Med Curriculum	52

For more information, contact:

- American Academy of Pain Medicine, (847) 375-4731; www.painmed.org.
- American Osteopathic College of Anesthesiologists, 17201 E. Highway 40, Independence, MO 64055-6427; (816) 373-4700.
- American Society of Anesthesiologists, (847) 825-5586; www.asahq.org.

Cardiology (F)*****

Specialty Overview: Cardiologists (the specialty is officially known as "Cardiovascular Disease") primarily deal with adult patients who have diseases of the heart and circulatory system. They are involved in both the diagnosis and the medical treatment of these diseases. The core of the specialty is the medical history and physical diagnosis augmented by the latest medical technology and medications. Cardiologists are divided by the nature of their practices into invasive and non-invasive specialists. Invasive Cardiologists perform angiography (catheters in arteries) to visualize and treat obstructions of vessels, primarily the coronary arteries. This is an evolving, expanding, and quite lucrative area of the specialty. Cardiologists are generally office-based, but spend about one-third of their professional time in hospitals. This frequently includes long hours and significant night call.

Between 1990 and 2003, the number of Cardiologists has increased more than 40%, and the numbers keep increasing. This has resulted in a great deal of competition among Cardiologists. However, since Cardiology has been targeted as a specialty with too many practitioners, especially in

the highly paid area of invasive Cardiology, the number of available positions will decrease in the future. Cardiologists average 58 hours per week
doing patient care.

Training: Training is currently a three-year fellowship following completion of an Internal Medicine or a Pediatric residency. One year (or in a
few four-year programs, two years) is devoted to research. Specialty certification in Cardiology is time-limited, and requires periodic recertification.
An additional year of training is necessary for certification in Cardiac Electrophysiology or Interventional Cardiology. Post-fellowship training is also
available in Nuclear Cardiology. For Osteopathic physicians, training follows internship and two years of Internal Medicine residency.

Match: About 97% of ACGME-approved programs and positions in
adult Cardiology and 94% in Pediatric Cardiology are available through the
NRMP Medical Specialties Match. Match results are announced in June,
one year before the applicant starts specialty training. In recent years,
about 62% of applicants to Adult and Pediatric Cardiology programs found
positions through the Match. About 99% of available Adult Cardiology
positions filled in the Match, as did 84% of those in Pediatric Cardiology.

CARDIOLOGY (INTERNAL MEDICINE)

ACGME-Approved Programs	170	AOA-Approved Programs	15
1st-Yr. Spots for M.D. Students	0	Funded Entry-Level D.O. Spots	65
Adv. Spots Avail. to M.D. Students	0	% IMG Residents	37
All Entry-Level M.D. Spots	778	Avg. Res. Work Hours/Week	52
% Women Residents	19	% Training in Non-Hospital	
Avg. Ratio of Full-Time Physician		Community Ambulatory Clinics	3
Faculty to Fellows	1.6		
% Training in Hospital Outpatient			
Clinics	16		

PEDIATRIC CARDIOLOGY*

ACGME-Approved Programs	48	AOA-Approved Programs	0
1st-Yr. Spots for M.D. Students	0	Funded Entry-Level D.O. Spots	0
Adv. Spots Avail. to M.D. Students	0	% IMG Residents	34
All Entry-Level M.D. Spots	100	Avg. Res. Work Hours/Week	53
% Women Residents	34	% Training in Non-Hospital	
Avg. Ratio of Full-Time Physician		Community Ambulatory Clinics	2
Faculty to Fellows	2.8		
% Training in Hospital Outpatient			
Clinics	18		

For more information, contact:
- American College of Cardiology, (800) 253-4636, ext. 694 or (301) 897-5400; www.acc.org.
- American College of Osteopathic Internists, (301) 656-8877; www.acoi.org.
- American Academy of Pediatrics, (847) 434-4000; www.aap.org.

Child and Adolescent Psychiatry (F)*

Specialty Overview: Child and Adolescent Psychiatrists diagnose and treat mental, emotional, and behavioral disorders in children, adolescents, and their families. Child Psychiatrists work with Pediatricians, courts, schools, and social service agencies. They often have both inpatient and outpatient practices, and frequently work as part of a multidisciplinary team. Child Psychiatrists average 42 hours per week doing patient care. Although still a relatively small specialty, the number of Child Psychiatrists increased by 55% between 1990 and 2003. Their services remain in high demand.

Training: Fellowships for both M.D.s and D.O.s consist of two years of Child and Adolescent Psychiatry in addition to at least two years (following internship) of General Psychiatry. Child and Adolescent Psychiatry training can start any time after the internship year, but generally begins after the PGY-2 year in Psychiatry. There are also nine programs with five years of training combining Pediatrics, Psychiatry, and Child and Adolescent Psychiatry. These programs consist of two years of Pediatrics, one-and-a-half years of adult Psychiatry, and one-and-a-half years of Child and Adolescent Psychiatry, making trainees eligible for Board certification in all three specialties. For information about this training, see the list at www.aacap.org/training/tbtpd.htm and contact the individual programs. These programs are more difficult to match with than programs in either Pediatrics or Psychiatry.

Match: About 72% of ACGME-approved programs and positions in Child and Adolescent Psychiatry are available through the NRMP Medical Specialties Match. Match results are announced the January before the applicant starts specialty training. In recent years, about 81% of applicants found positions through the Match. About 86% of available positions fill in the Match. There are 22 positions combining Pediatrics, Psychiatry, and Child and Adolescent Psychiatry available to medical students through the NRMP PGY-1 Match.

CHILD AND ADOLESCENT PSYCHIATRY

ACGME-Approved Programs	115	AOA-Approved Programs	1
1st-Yr. Spots for M.D. Students	0	Funded Entry-Level D.O. Spots	1
Adv. Spots Avail. to M.D. Students	0	% IMG Residents	47
All Entry-Level M.D. Spots	438	Avg. Res. Work Hours/Week	42
% Women Residents	60	% Training in Non-Hospital	
Avg. Ratio of Full-Time Physician		Community Ambulatory Clinics	11
Faculty to Fellows	1.8		
% Training in Hospital Outpatient			
Clinics	35		

For more information, contact:
- American Academy of Child & Adolescent Psychiatry, (202) 966-7399; www.aacap.org.
- American College of Osteopathic Neurologists and Psychiatrists, 28595 Orchard Lake Rd., Ste. 200, Farmington Hills, MI 48334; (248) 553-0010, ext. 295.

Child Neurology (F)*

Specialty Overview: Child Neurologists diagnose and manage neurological disorders of the infant, child, and adolescent. They treat diseases of the brain, spinal cord, and neuromuscular system. Many such problems are congenital or developmental in nature. Practitioners, most often based at academic medical centers, usually see patients in consultation for primary care physicians. Child Neurologists average 40 hours per week doing patient care.

Training: Before entering a Child Neurology program, applicants must have completed either: (1) at least two years of an approved Pediatric residency, (2) a PGY-1 year acceptable for Neurology training (broad-based clinical experience, primarily in Internal Medicine) and a year of Pediatrics, or (3) a year of Pediatrics and a year of basic neuroscience training. Training in Child Neurology is an additional three years: one year in clinical adult Neurology and one year in clinical Child Neurology. The third year is devoted to studying Electrodiagnostic Neurology, Neuropathology, Neuroradiology, Neuro-Ophthalmology, Child & Adolescent Psychiatry, and the basic neurosciences. Trainees are eligible to take the American Board of Pediatrics examination after their second year of Child Neurology training.

Match: All Child Neurology programs are in the the Child Neurology Matching Program (CNMP), sponsored by the The Child Neurology Society (CNS) and the Professors of Child Neurology (PCN); www.sfmatch .org. The Match is for PGY-3 positions and occurs in January, before the

NRMP Match. Applicants must register with both the NRMP and the CNMP, even if they will be entering an "integrated" program that arranges the first two years of training. Open positions are often available and can be accessed through the CNMP website.

CHILD NEUROLOGY			
ACGME-Approved Programs	72	AOA-Approved Programs	0
1st-Yr. Spots for M.D. Students	0	Funded Entry-Level D.O. Spots	0
Adv. Spots Avail. to M.D. Students	0	% IMG Residents	42
All Entry-Level M.D. Spots	101	Avg. Res. Work Hours/Week	58
% Women Residents	49	% Training in Non-Hospital	
Avg. Ratio of Full-Time Physician		Community Ambulatory Clinics	1
Faculty to Fellows	7.3		
% Training in Hospital Outpatient			
Clinics	30		

For more information, contact:
- American Academy of Neurology, (651) 695-1940; www.aan.com.
- American College of Osteopathic Neurologists and Psychiatrists, 28595 Orchard Lake Rd., Ste. 200, Farmington Hills, MI 48334; (248) 553-0010, ext. 295.
- The Child Neurology Society, (651) 486-9447; www.childneurologysociety.org.

Colon and Rectal Surgery (F)*****

Specialty Overview: Colon and Rectal Surgeons diagnose and treat disorders of the intestinal tract, rectum, anal canal, and perianal areas that are amenable to surgical treatment. They are involved not only in operative treatment but also in diagnostic procedures, including colonoscopy. Other physicians refer most patients. Most practitioners in this specialty are located in medium to large cities. Colon and Rectal Surgeons average 54 hours per week doing patient care. A small specialty, the field grew by 42% between 1990 and 2005.

Training: The training consists of a complete residency in General Surgery followed by a one-year fellowship in Colon and Rectal Surgery. While there are no Osteopathic training programs in this specialty, the more limited specialty of Proctology, consisting of two years of training after internship, is available.

Match: Nearly all positions are listed in the NRMP Fellowships Match. Results of the Match for positions beginning in July are released in December of the prior year. In recent years, 78% of applicants matched and 99% of available positions filled in the Match.

COLON AND RECTAL SURGERY

ACGME-Approved Programs	39	AOA-Approved Programs	0
1st-Yr. Spots for M.D. Students	0	Funded Entry-Level D.O. Spots	0
Adv. Spots Avail. to M.D. Students	0	% IMG Residents	13
All Entry-Level M.D. Spots	72	Avg. Res. Work Hours/Week	53
% Women Residents	26	Programs with Childcare	15
Avg. Ratio of Full-Time Physician Faculty to Fellows	5.2	Programs Offering a "Primary Care Track"	1
% Training in Hospital Outpatient Clinics	18	Programs Offering Multiple Start Dates	1
% Training in Non-Hospital Community Ambulatory Clinics	19	Programs Allowing Moonlighting	8
		Alt./Comp. Med Curriculum	1

PROCTOLOGY (OSTEOPATHIC ONLY)

AOA-Approved Programs	1	All Entry-Level D.O. Spots	2

For more information, contact:

- American Osteopathic College of Proctology, 9948 State Route 682, Athens, OH 45701; (740) 594-7979.
- American Society of Colon & Rectal Surgeons, (847) 290-9184.

Complementary and Alternative Medicine*

Specialty Overview: Complementary and Alternative Medicine (CAM), also known as Integrative or Holistic Medicine, uses medical therapies not generally considered part of conventional Western medicine. This most often includes herbs and dietary supplements, mind-body therapies, massage and chiropractic therapy, homeopathy, and acupuncture. It may also include music therapy, hypnotherapy, nutrition, reflexology, yoga, aromatherapy and therapeutic touch. Practitioners can use these methods alone, but often combine them with standard therapies. About 40% of Americans may use CAM in each year, and there is increasing pressure on insurance companies to pay for this therapy.

While complementary and conventional therapies are often used simultaneously to reduce side effects and to increase well-being, alternative therapies are employed in place of conventional medicine to cure disease. Many physicians who are CAM practitioners have not completed extensive training in these areas. As insurance companies begin paying for more CAM procedures, this will change.

Training: Most Family Medicine programs and about half of all Internal Medicine Programs offer some training in CAM. However, most of this training consists only of a single rotation, an elective, or a short survey course. Some programs in other specialties offer similar experiences. Relatively few residencies offer fully integrated CAM training within the residency. While some fellowships exist, both in general CAM and in specialized areas, most are within Family Medicine and Internal Medicine departments.

Match: Students can match into residencies with CAM training. Use the American Medical Association's *GMED Companion: An Insider's Guide to Selecting a Residency Program* (published annually) to search for programs listed as offering an "Alternative/Complementary Medicine Curriculum." Once such programs are identified, go to their website or contact them (contact information is on *FREIDA*) to ascertain whether the amount of CAM training they offer meets your needs. Fellowships must be contacted individually.

Other Useful Information: This area is being driven by public demand. With its own research funding Institute at NIH and the likelihood of widespread insurance payments for such therapy, this specialty will certainly grow over the coming decade.

COMPLEMENTARY AND ALTERNATIVE MEDICINE			
ACGME-Approved Programs	0	AOA-Approved Programs	0
1st-Yr. Spots for M.D. Students	N/A	Funded Entry-Level D.O. Spots	N/A
Adv. Spots Avail. to M.D. Students	0	% IMG Residents	N/A
All Entry-Level M.D. Spots	N/A	Avg. Res. Work Hours/Week	N/A
% Women Residents	N/A		

For more information, contact:

- AMSA website on CAM: http://www.amsa.org/programs/gpit/compmed.cfm.
- Columbia University-Rosenthal Center for Alternative/Complementary Medicine College of Physicians and Surgeons, (212) 305-4755; http://cpmcnet.columbia.edu/dept/rosenthal/.
- National Center for Complementary and Alternative Medicine, National Institutes of Health; http://altmed.od.nih.gov.

Critical Care (F)***

Specialty Overview: Critical Care physicians work in hospital intensive care units managing the overall care of critically ill medical and surgical patients. The practice requires both a broad knowledge of the medical and surgical conditions that cause patients to be in the intensive care unit and a specialized knowledge of the respiratory, fluid, and cardiovascular management needed to maintain these patients. Many Critical Care physicians alternate their duties in the critical care unit with practice in their primary specialty. The majority of Critical Care physicians in adult units are Internists, most commonly specialists in Pulmonary Diseases. Night call or night duty in the intensive care unit is common. Most individuals in this specialty are located in large cities. Critical Care physicians average 66 hours (Anesthesia), 64 hours (Surgeons), 51 hours (Pediatricians), or 48 hours (Internists) per week doing patient care.

Training: At present, positions leading to certificates of special competence are offered in Critical Care from the American Boards of Internal Medicine (1 to 3 years after residency), Anesthesiology (1 year), and Surgery (1 year). Pediatrics offers Critical Care as a subspecialty (3 years after residency). Other Boards may offer a similar certification in the future. Internal Medicine offers two routes to certification: either a one-year fellowship following completion of subspecialty training, or a two-year fellowship following residency. A common program design is to incorporate Critical Care into a three-year Pulmonary Diseases fellowship leading to dual subspecialty certification (see Pulmonary Diseases).

Match: Virtually all adult Critical Care programs combined with Pulmonary Disease training (Internal Medicine), those in Pediatric Critical Care, and those in Surgical Critical Care are in the NRMP Fellowship Match. For other Critical Care training, contact the individual programs, which are listed in *FREIDA*.

ADULT CRITICAL CARE (ANESTHESIOLOGY)			
ACGME-Approved Programs	49	AOA-Approved Programs	0
1st-Yr. Spots for M.D. Students	0	Funded Entry-Level D.O. Spots	0
Adv. Spots Avail. to M.D. Students	0	% IMG Residents	66
All Entry-Level M.D. Spots	48	Avg. Res. Work Hours/Week	58
% Women Residents	11	% Training in Non-Hospital	
Avg. Ratio of Full-Time Physician		Community Ambulatory Clinics	<1
Faculty to Fellows	9.9		
% Training in Hospital Outpatient			
Clinics	<1		

ADULT CRITICAL CARE (INTERNAL MEDICINE)

ACGME-Approved Programs	32	AOA-Approved Programs	3
1st-Yr. Spots for M.D. Students	0	Funded Entry-Level D.O. Spots	5
Adv. Spots Avail. to M.D. Students	0	% IMG Residents	60
All Entry-Level M.D. Spots	91	Avg. Res. Work Hours/Week	57
% Women Residents	27	% Training in Non-Hospital	
Avg. Ratio of Full-Time Physician		Community Ambulatory Clinics	2
Faculty to Fellows	3.1		
% Training in Hospital Outpatient			
Clinics	2		

ADULT PULMONARY DISEASE/CRITICAL CARE (INTERNAL MEDICINE)

ACGME-Approved Programs	122	AOA-Approved Programs	4
1st-Yr. Spots for M.D. Students	0	Funded Entry-Level D.O. Spots	10
Adv. Spots Avail. to M.D. Students	0	% IMG Residents	41
All Entry-Level M.D. Spots	400	Avg. Res. Work Hours/Week	52
% Women Residents	25	% Training in Non-Hospital	
Avg. Ratio of Full-Time Physician		Community Ambulatory Clinics	1
Faculty to Fellows	1.8		
% Training in Hospital Outpatient			
Clinics	19		

ADULT CRITICAL CARE (SURGERY)

ACGME-Approved Programs	85	AOA-Approved Programs	1
1st-Yr. Spots for M.D. Students	0	Funded Entry-Level D.O. Spots	1
Adv. Spots Avail. to M.D. Students	0	% IMG Residents	19
All Entry-Level M.D. Spots	170	Avg. Res. Work Hours/Week	51
% Women Residents	16	% Training in Non-Hospital	
Avg. Ratio of Full-Time Physician		Community Ambulatory Clinics	<1
Faculty to Fellows	6.6		
% Training in Hospital Outpatient			
Clinics	4.3		

PEDIATRIC CRITICAL CARE*

ACGME-Approved Programs	59	AOA-Approved Programs	0
1st-Yr. Spots for M.D. Students	0	Funded Entry-Level D.O. Spots	0
Adv. Spots Avail. to M.D. Students	0	% IMG Residents	33
All Entry-Level M.D. Spots	119	Avg. Res. Work Hours/Week	58
% Women Residents	45	% Training in Non-Hospital	
Avg. Ratio of Full-Time Physician		Community Ambulatory Clinics	0
Faculty to Fellows	3.6		
% Training in Hospital Outpatient			
Clinics	5		

For more information, contact:
- American College of Osteopathic Internists, (301) 656-8877; www.acoi.org.
- Society of Critical Care Medicine, (847) 827-6869; www.sccm.org.

Dermatology*****

Specialty Overview: Dermatologists deal with patients who have both acute and chronic disorders of the skin. They diagnose skin lesions and use both chemotherapeutic agents and surgery to effect cures. Dermatologists get referrals from other physicians and see patients who refer themselves. There is little night call and very rarely an inpatient service associated with a Dermatology practice. With the increase in managed care, many patients who once would have been referred to Dermatologists are now being treated by primary care practitioners, decreasing the need for Dermatologists. Dermatologists average 40 hours per week doing patient care.

Following Dermatology training, fellowships are available in Procedural Dermatology, Mohs Micrographic Surgery, and Dermatopathology. Mohs Micrographic Surgery treats skin cancers, with the physician acting as surgeon, pathologist, and reconstructive surgeon. Dermatopathology is a subspecialty of both Pathology and Dermatology. Emphasis is placed on the diagnosis of skin disorders using appropriate microscopic techniques including light and electron microscopy, immunopathology, histochemistry, and aspects of cutaneous mycology, bacteriology, and entomology. Dermatopathologists average 52 hours per week doing patient care.

Training: Dermatology residencies are three years following initial training. There are 11 PGY-1 positions in four-year programs. Dermatopathology training consists of a one-year fellowship. It is designed for either a research or a clinical practice. At least six months of the training must be in either clinical Dermatology for those trained in Pathology, or Anatomic Pathology for those trained in Dermatology.

Match: Nearly all positions that begin at the PGY-2 level are available to medical students through the NRMP Advanced Match. Most applicants must arrange their own internship. Several programs require the prior completion of a residency in another specialty. Entrance to the specialty is very competitive. In recent years, 100% of the positions offered through the NRMP Match filled.

DERMATOLOGY

ACGME-Approved Programs	111	AOA-Approved Programs	18
1st-Yr. Spots for M.D. Students	28	Funded Entry-Level D.O. Spots	21
Adv. Spots Avail. to M.D. Students	288	% IMG Residents	4
All Entry-Level M.D. Spots	404	Avg. Res. Work Hours/Week	43
% Women Residents	58	Programs with Childcare	36
Avg. Ratio of Full-Time Physician		Programs Offering a "Primary	
Faculty to Residents	1.0	Care Track"	4
% Training in Hospital Outpatient		Programs Offering Multiple	
Clinics	75	Start Dates	7
% Training in Non-Hospital		Programs Allowing Moonlighting	48
Community Ambulatory Clinics	9	Alt./Comp. Med Curriculum	14

DERMATOPATHOLOGY (F)

ACGME-Approved Programs	47	AOA-Approved Programs	0
1st-Yr. Spots for M.D. Students	0	Funded Entry-Level D.O. Spots	0
Adv. Spots Avail. to M.D. Students	0	% IMG Residents	36
All Entry-Level M.D. Spots	85	Avg. Res. Work Hours/Week	41
% Women Residents	50	% Training in Non-Hospital	
Avg. Ratio of Full-Time Physician		Community Ambulatory Clinics	5
Faculty to Fellows	10.6		
% Training in Hospital Outpatient			
Clinics	45		

For more information, contact:

- American Academy of Dermatology, (847) 330-0230; www.aad.org.
- American Osteopathic College of Dermatology, (800) 449-2623; www.aocd.org.
- American Society for Dermatologic Surgery, (847) 956-0900; www.asds-net.org/.
- American Society of Dermatology, (916) 446-5054; www.asd.org/.

Emergency Medicine****

Specialty Overview: Emergency Physicians are mainly hospital-based and deal with the entire spectrum of acute illness and injury in all age groups. Hands-on physical diagnosis and the use of both medical and surgical therapeutic modalities are an integral part of the specialty. Emergency Physicians are trained to stabilize patients with acute injuries and deal with life-threatening conditions. Hours are long, but schedules are fixed in advance. There is rarely a call schedule outside of assigned working hours in this specialty. Most practitioners in the specialty work in medium to large cities. Many new Emergency Medicine opportunities are available at academic centers and in research. All sources agree that there will still be a shortage of Emergency Physicians in the year 2025, since the number of emergency department visits continues to climb dramatically as people have less access to primary care physicians. Less than 1% of Emergency Physicians leave the field each year. Emergency Physicians average 39 hours per week doing patient care. Between 1990 and 2003, there was an 87% increase in the number of Emergency Physicians.

Training: Training is three to four years in length. Programs also exist combining Emergency Medicine with either Internal Medicine or Pediatrics. These programs are five years long and lead to dual certification. Osteopathic physicians have the option of combining Emergency Medicine with training in Family Medicine.

Fellowships following residency leading to subspecialty certification are offered in Medical Toxicology (20 programs), Pediatric Emergency Medicine—through both Emergency Medicine (21 programs) and Pediatrics (44 programs)—and Sports Medicine (3 programs). Some Critical Care programs accept Emergency Medicine residency graduates. Fellowships are also available in Research, Hyperbaric Medicine, Medical Education, Medical Information Services, International Medicine, and Emergency Medical Service Administration.

Match: Most programs begin in the first year and are available through the NRMP PGY-1 Match. Those that begin at the PGY-2 level require at least one year of prior training in a Transitional internship or an Internal Medicine, Surgery, or Family Medicine residency, and are available through the NRMP Advanced Match. Students can also enter the five-year combined programs in Emergency Medicine–Internal Medicine and Emergency Medicine–Pediatrics.

Nearly all fellowship positions in Pediatric Emergency Medicine are available through the NRMP Fellowship Match. In recent years, of those positions available through the Fellowship Match, 100% filled and 61% of applicants obtained positions. Match day is in December, the year before the fellowship begins.

Other Useful Information: Emergency Medicine has become extremely competitive. Programs look for high United States Medical Licensing Examination (USMLE) scores, research experience, election to AOA (honorary), and outstanding performance on Emergency Medicine clerkships. In recent years, about 98% of the available PGY-1 positions filled through the NRMP Match. Of the PGY-2 positions available through the NRMP Match, about 97% filled in the Match.

EMERGENCY MEDICINE

ACGME-Approved Programs	133	AOA-Approved Programs	36
1st-Yr. Spots for M.D. Students	1,188	Funded Entry-Level D.O. Spots	172
Adv. Spots Avail. to M.D. Students	144	% IMG Residents	4
All Entry-Level M.D. Spots	1,477	Avg. Res. Work Hours/Week	54
% Women Residents	32	Programs with Childcare	47
Avg. Ratio of Full-Time Physician		Programs Offering a "Primary	
Faculty to Residents/Fellows	0.7	Care Track"	5
% Training in Hospital Outpatient		Programs Offering Multiple	
Clinics	10	Start Dates	9
% Training in Non-Hospital		Programs Allowing Moonlighting	70
Community Ambulatory Clinics	1		
Alt./Comp. Med Curriculum	33		

EMERGENCY MEDICINE–PEDIATRICS (COMBINED RESIDENCY)**

ACGME-Approved Programs	3	AOA-Approved Programs	1
1st-Yr. Spots for M.D. Students	4	Funded Entry-Level D.O. Spots	0
Adv. Spots Avail. to M.D. Students	0	% IMG Residents	6
All Entry-Level M.D. Spots	4	Avg. Res. Work Hours/Week	70
% Women Residents	49	% Training in Non-Hospital	
Avg. Ratio of Full-Time Physician		Community Ambulatory Clinics	2
Faculty to Residents	13.2		
% Training in Hospital Outpatient			
Clinics	11		

EMERGENCY MEDICINE–INTERNAL MEDICINE (COMBINED RESIDENCY)*****

ACGME-Approved Programs	10	AOA-Approved Programs	13
1st-Yr. Spots for M.D. Students	21	Funded Entry-Level D.O. Spots	22
Adv. Spots Avail. to M.D. Students	0	% IMG Residents	4
All Entry-Level M.D. Spots	21	Avg. Res. Work Hours/Week	52
% Women Residents	24	Programs with Childcare	4
Avg. Ratio of Full-Time Physician		% Training in Non-Hospital	
Faculty to Residents	9.1	Community Ambulatory Clinics	2
% Training in Hospital Outpatient			
Clinics	21		

PEDIATRIC EMERGENCY MEDICINE (F)****

ACGME-Approved Programs	44	AOA-Approved Programs	0
1st-Yr. Spots for M.D. Students	0	Funded Entry-Level D.O. Spots	0
Adv. Spots Avail. to M.D. Students	0	% IMG Residents	12
All Entry-Level M.D. Spots	84	Avg. Res. Work Hours/Week	28
% Women Residents	51	% Training in Non-Hospital	
Avg. Ratio of Full-Time Physician		Community Ambulatory Clinics	3
Faculty to Fellows	3.4		
% Training in Hospital Outpatient			
Clinics	22		

EMERGENCY MEDICINE–FAMILY PRACTICE (OSTEOPATHS ONLY)		
AOA-Approved Programs	5	1st-Yr. Funded Spots for D.O. Students 19

For more information, contact:

- American Academy of Emergency Medicine, (800) 884-2236; www.aaem.org/.
- American Academy of Emergency Medicine Resident and Student Association, www.aaemrsa.org/.
- American College of Emergency Physicians, (800) 798-1822; www.acep.org.
- American College of Osteopathic Emergency Physicians, (800) 521-3709; www.acoep.org.
- Emergency Medicine Residents Association, (800) 798-1822; www.emra.org.
- Society for Academic Emergency Medicine, (517) 485-5484; www.saem.org.

Endocrinology, Diabetes, and Metabolism (F)*

Specialty Overview: Endocrinologists treat patients with diseases of the endocrine (glandular) system and with a wide variety of hormonal abnormalities. The most common endocrine diseases include diabetes mellitus, high lipid (blood fats or cholesterol) levels, and thyroid disorders. Patients are often referred to Endocrinologists for failure to grow, early or late puberty, excess hair growth, high calcium levels, osteoporosis, pituitary tumors, or reproductive problems. Endocrinologists also consult in the rapidly growing area of Nutrition & Metabolism. This includes helping with postoperative and chronic-disease patients needing extra nutritional support. Many Endocrinologists also participate in clinical or basic-science research. Endocrinologists average 45 hours per week (Internists) and 35 hours per week (Pediatricians) doing patient care.

Training: Training is two years following an Internal Medicine residency or three years following a Pediatric residency. For Osteopathic physicians, training follows internship and two years of Internal Medicine residency.

Match: Applicants should contact individual training programs, since this specialty has no match. Programs are listed in *FREIDA*.

ENDOCRINOLOGY, DIABETES, AND METABOLISM (INTERNAL MEDICINE)

ACGME-Approved Programs	119	AOA-Approved Programs	1
1st-Yr. Spots for M.D. Students	0	Funded Entry-Level D.O. Spots	1
Adv. Spots Avail. to M.D. Students	0	% IMG Residents	42
All Entry-Level M.D. Spots	256	Avg. Res. Work Hours/Week	43
% Women Residents	57	% Training in Non-Hospital	
Avg. Ratio of Full-Time Physician		Community Ambulatory Clinics	5
Faculty to Fellows	2.8		
% Training in Hospital Outpatient			
Clinics	48		

PEDIATRIC ENDOCRINOLOGY

ACGME-Approved Programs	66	AOA-Approved Programs	0
1st-Yr. Spots for M.D. Students	0	Funded Entry-Level D.O. Spots.	0
Adv. Spots Avail. to M.D. Students	0	% IMG Residents	36
All Entry-Level M.D. Spots	85	Avg. Res. Work Hours/Week	38
% Women Residents	63	% Training in Non-Hospital	
Avg. Ratio of Full-Time Physician		Community Ambulatory Clinics	2
Faculty to Fellows	2.3		
% Training in Hospital Outpatient			
Clinics	53		

For more information, contact:

- American College of Osteopathic Internists, (301) 656-8877; www.acoi.org.
- Endocrine Society, (301) 941-0200; www.endo-society.org.
- American Academy of Pediatrics, (847) 434-4000; www.aap.org.

Family Medicine*

Specialty Overview: Family Physicians treat entire families, as did the General Practitioners of the past. They spend more than 90% of their time in direct patient care. The spectrum of their practice varies with the extent of their training, their interests, the area of the country, the number of other medical practitioners in the area, and the rules of their local hospitals. Family Physicians practice mostly in an outpatient setting. They provide primary care to a diverse population, unlimited by the patient's age, sex, organ system affected, or disease. They usually have a significant number of pediatric and geriatric patients. Delivering babies, although always a part of the training, is not always a part of the practice. Due to the rising cost of professional liability insurance, the irregular hours involved, and other factors, many Family Physicians severely limit this aspect of their practices. Dealing with the behavioral aspects of medicine, including family life-cycle events (birth, stress, grief), and delivering other psychological services are a large part of Family Medicine.

Most Family Physicians enter group practices, and most participate in some type of managed health care delivery system (HMO, PPO, IPA). Many have assumed the often-uncomfortable role of "gatekeeper" or "case manager" within these systems and end up allocating services to patients. The average Family Physician works 46 hours per week, with two-thirds of the time spent on office visits and the balance spent on hospital rounds, on other patient visits, and doing surgical/manipulative procedures.

There is a shortage of Family Physicians aggravated by an increased demand in managed care systems and rural areas. Part of the reason for this shortage is that the specialty suffers from a lack of recognition, both publicly and professionally, which discourages new physicians from entering this field. And, while many Family Physicians work longer hours than their colleagues and often must know how to treat a broader range of medical problems, their remuneration is one of the lowest in medicine. Physicians in this field get satisfaction from providing continuity of care to patients, within the context of their entire family, throughout the various stages of life.

Training: Training is three years in length. Residencies combining Family Medicine and Internal Medicine last four years; those combining Family Medicine and Psychiatry are five years long. Osteopathic residencies are generally two years in length following internship and one program exists combining Family Practice with Osteopathic Manipulative Medicine. Family Medicine faculty rely heavily on applicant interviews and performance on clinical rotations to select residents. About 10% of Family Physicians specialize. Family Medicine residency graduates (M.D.s) can take one-year Geriatric Medicine (71 positions) or Sports Medicine (111 positions) fellowships. They are approved for Adolescent Medicine subspecialty and may have such programs in the future.

Osteopaths can take a two-year Geriatrics fellowship after their first year of Family Practice residency or a two-year Osteopathic Manipulative Medicine fellowship after completing their residency.

Match: In recent years, about 79% of the available PGY-1 positions filled through the NRMP Match.

FAMILY MEDICINE

ACGME-Approved Programs	469	AOA-Approved Programs	144
1st-Yr. Spots for M.D. Students	3,442	Funded Entry-Level D.O. Spots	423
Adv. Spots Avail. to M.D. Students	0	% IMG Residents	34
All Entry-Level M.D. Spots	3,442	Avg. Res. Work Hours/Week	62
% Women Residents	51	Programs with Childcare	145
Avg. Ratio of Full-Time Physician		Programs Offering a "Primary	
Faculty to Residents	0.7	Care Track"	158
% Training in Hospital Outpatient		Programs Offering Multiple	
Clinics	20	Start Dates	145
% Training in Non-Hospital		Programs Allowing Moonlighting	290
Community Ambulatory Clinics	14		
Alt./Comp. Med Curriculum	276		

FAMILY MEDICINE–INTERNAL MEDICINE (COMBINED RESIDENCY)**

ACGME-Approved Programs	3	AOA-Approved Programs	0
1st-Yr. Spots for M.D. Students	6	Funded Entry-Level D.O. Spots	0
Adv. Spots Avail. to M.D. Students	0	% IMG Residents	5
All Entry-Level M.D. Spots	6	Avg. Res. Work Hours/Week	53
% Women Residents	55	Programs Offering a "Primary	
Avg. Ratio of Full-Time Physician		Care Track"	1
Faculty to Residents	4.2	% Training in Non-Hospital	
% Training in Hospital Outpatient		Community Ambulatory Clinics	13
Clinics	27		

FAMILY MEDICINE–PSYCHIATRY (COMBINED RESIDENCY)**

ACGME-Approved Programs	10	AOA-Approved Programs	0
1st-Yr. Spots for M.D. Students	21	Funded Entry-Level D.O. Spots	0
Adv. Spots Avail. to M.D. Students	0	% IMG Residents	13
All Entry-Level M.D. Spots	21	Avg. Res. Work Hours/Week	64
% Women Residents	33	Programs with Childcare	4
Avg. Ratio of Full-Time Physician		Programs Offering a "Primary	
Faculty to Residents/Fellows	6.7	Care Track"	1
% Training in Hospital Outpatient		Programs Offering Multiple	
Clinics	16	Start Dates	1
% Training in Non-Hospital			
Community Ambulatory Clinics	8		

FAMILY PRACTICE WITH OMM, OMT, OR NEUROMUSCULAR MEDICINE (D.O.s ONLY)

AOA-Approved Programs	7	Funded Entry-Level D.O. Spots	3

For more information, contact:

- American Academy of Family Physicians, (913) 906-6000; www.aafp.org.
- American College of Osteopathic Family Physicians, (800) 323-0794; www.acofp.org.

Gastroenterology (F)***

Specialty Overview: Gastroenterologists are Internists and Pediatricians who specifically deal with diseases of the esophagus, stomach, small and large intestines, liver, pancreas, and gallbladder. A large number of their patients have ulcer disease or chronic diseases of the liver, intestinal tract, or pancreas. Recent advances in endoscopy (esophagogastroduodenoscopy, colonoscopy, and endoscopic retrograde cholangiopancreatography) have increased the number of procedures that Gastroenterologists perform. Gastroenterologists are predominantly office-based. They take some night call and many have active inpatient services. The field of Gastroenterology grew more than 50% in the past 15 years. It is still growing rapidly and has been targeted as an over-populated specialty. The specialty's leaders are considering a 50% decrease in available training positions. Gastroenterologists average 52 hours per week (Internists) and 50 hours per week (Pediatricians) doing patient care.

Training: As a subspecialty of Internal Medicine, training consists of a two-year fellowship following completion of an Internal Medicine residency. Pediatric Gastroenterology fellowships last three years after a Pediatric residency. For Osteopathic physicians, training follows internship and two years of Internal Medicine residency.

Match: Adult and Pediatric Gastroenterology programs do not have a match. The programs are listed in *FREIDA*. Contact the programs directly. Because many programs have fall deadlines for receiving applications, it is best to contact them at least two years before your expected start date.

GASTROENTEROLOGY (INTERNAL MEDICINE)			
ACGME-Approved Programs	156	AOA-Approved Programs	7
1st-Yr. Spots for M.D. Students	0	Funded Entry-Level D.O. Spots	6
Adv. Spots Avail. to M.D. Students	0	% IMG Residents	30
All Entry-Level M.D. Spots	421	Avg. Res. Work Hours/Week	50
% Women Residents	24	% Training in Non-Hospital	
Avg. Ratio of Full-Time Physician		Community Ambulatory Clinics	3
Faculty to Fellows	1.5		
% Training in Hospital Outpatient			
Clinics	25		

PEDIATRIC GASTROENTEROLOGY*

ACGME-Approved Programs	51	AOA-Approved Programs		0
1st-Yr. Spots for M.D. Students	0	Funded Entry-Level D.O. Spots		0
Adv. Spots Avail. to M.D. Students	0	% IMG Residents		42
All Entry-Level M.D. Spots	69	Avg. Res. Work Hours/Week		41
% Women Residents	40	% Training in Non-Hospital		
Avg. Ratio of Full-Time Physician		Community Ambulatory Clinics		7
Faculty to Fellows	1.9			
% Training in Hospital Outpatient				
Clinics	28			

For more information, contact:

- American College of Gastroenterology, (703) 820-7400; www.acg.gi.org.
- American College of Osteopathic Internists, (301) 656-8877; www.acoi.org.
- American Gastroenterological Association, (301) 654-2055; www.gastro.org.
- American Academy of Pediatrics, (847) 434-4000; www.aap.org.

Geriatric Medicine (F)*

Specialty Overview: Geriatric Medicine is a primary-care subspecialty that deals with the complex medical and psychosocial problems of older adults. About 20,000 Geriatric clinicians are currently needed and the demand for physicians with special skills in Geriatric Medicine is rapidly increasing. By 2030, 20% of all Americans will be older than 65 and the United States will need more than 36,000 Geriatricians. People aged 85 and older, the "old old," are the fastest growing segment of the population, with expected growth from 4 million people today to 19 million by 2050. Currently, there are just over 9,000 certified Geriatricians, and this number is expected to decline dramatically in the next few years as practicing Geriatricians retire.

While one-third of all patients seen by Internists are over 65 years old, nearly half of Geriatricians' patients are over 75 years old. Geriatricians average 48 hours per week doing patient care.

Opportunities exist in academic medicine and research, corporate (HMO) medicine, community medicine, long-term care, and private practice. At present, most graduates of Geriatric Medicine and Geriatric Psychiatry fellowships hold academic faculty appointments, although relatively few do research or publish. Geriatricians must be able to work within a multispecialty team of both medical and non-medical personnel.

Training: Most Geriatricians begin from a base of training in Family Medicine, Internal Medicine, or Psychiatry. Some of the programs operate jointly, with both the Internal Medicine and Family Medicine programs participating. Psychiatry has its own programs. All fellowships are one year long. Osteopathic fellowships are available for those completing one or two years of any other residency.

Match: There is no matching program for any Geriatric fellowship, so contact the programs directly. *FREIDA* has a list of programs.

GERIATRIC MEDICINE (FAMILY MEDICINE)*

ACGME-Approved Programs	31	AOA-Approved Programs	5
1st-Yr. Spots for M.D. Students	0	Funded Entry-Level D.O. Spots	9
Adv. Spots Avail. to M.D. Students	0	% IMG Residents	54
All Entry-Level M.D. Spots	71	Avg. Res. Work Hours/Week	N/A
% Women Residents	49	% Training in Non-Hospital	
Avg. Ratio of Full-Time Physician		Community Ambulatory Clinics	0
Faculty to Fellows	3.5		
% Training in Hospital Outpatient			
Clinics	29		

GERIATRIC MEDICINE (INTERNAL MEDICINE)*

ACGME-Approved Programs	100	AOA-Approved Programs	1
1st-Yr. Spots for M.D. Students	0	Funded Entry-Level D.O. Spots	1
Adv. Spots Avail. to M.D. Students	0	% IMG Residents	58
All Entry-Level M.D. Spots	471	Avg. Res. Work Hours/Week	43
% Women Residents	45	% Training in Non-Hospital	
Avg. Ratio of Full-Time Physician		Community Ambulatory Clinics	17
Faculty to Fellows	3.1		
% Training in Hospital Outpatient			
Clinics	34		

GERIATRIC PSYCHIATRY*

ACGME-Approved Programs	60	AOA-Approved Programs	0
1st-Yr. Spots for M.D. Students	0	Funded Entry-Level D.O. Spots	0
Adv. Spots Avail. to M.D. Students	0	% IMG Residents	71
All Entry-Level M.D. Spots	162	Avg. Res. Work Hours/Week	38
% Women Residents	39	% Training in Non-Hospital	
Avg. Ratio of Full-Time Physician		Community Ambulatory Clinics	13
Faculty to Fellows	5.1		
% Training in Hospital Outpatient			
Clinics	36		

For more information, contact:
- American Academy of Family Physicians, (913) 906-6000; www.aafp.org.
- American College of Osteopathic Internists, (301) 656-8877; www.acoi.org.
- American Geriatrics Society, (212) 308-1414; www.americangeriatrics.org.
- American Association for Geriatric Psychiatry, (301) 654-7850; www.aagpgpa.org.

Hand Surgery (F)***

Specialty Overview: Hand surgeons primarily treat diseases of and injuries to the hand and forearm. Nearly all have training in either Orthopedic Surgery or Plastic Surgery. Advances in the specialty have come with development of new microsurgical techniques. Some Hand Surgeons do reimplantation surgery after traumatic amputations. This surgery normally requires a specialized center. One benefit to Hand Surgery is that it is usually done sitting down. Much of the surgery is now done on outpatients. Hand Surgeons average 59 hours per week doing patient care.

Training: Fellowship training in Hand Surgery lasts one year after a residency in Orthopedic Surgery, Plastic Surgery, or General Surgery.

Match: Most Hand Surgery positions (the majority through Orthopedic Surgery) fill through the Specialty Match run by the NRMP Combined Musculoskeletal Matching Program. In recent years, nearly all applicants found a position.

HAND SURGERY (ORTHOPEDIC SURGERY)

ACGME-Approved Programs	51	AOA-Approved Programs	0
1st-Yr. Spots for M.D. Students	0	Funded Entry-Level D.O. Spots	0
Adv. Spots Avail. to M.D. Students	0	% IMG Residents	12
All Entry-Level M.D. Spots	115	Avg. Res. Work Hours/Week	52
% Women Residents	22	% Training in Non-Hospital	
Avg. Ratio of Full-Time Physician		Community Ambulatory Clinics	17
Faculty to Fellows	3.5		
% Training in Hospital Outpatient			
Clinics	40		

HAND SURGERY (PLASTIC SURGERY)

ACGME-Approved Programs	14	AOA-Approved Programs	0
1st-Yr. Spots for M.D. Students	0	Funded Entry-Level D.O. Spots	0
Adv. Spots Avail. to M.D. Students	0	% IMG Residents	5
All Entry-Level M.D. Spots	20	Avg. Res. Work Hours/Week	57
% Women Residents	20	% Training in Non-Hospital	
Avg. Ratio of Full-Time Physician Faculty to Fellows	5.1	Community Ambulatory Clinics	16
% Training in Hospital Outpatient Clinics	23		

HAND SURGERY (GENERAL SURGERY)

ACGME-Approved Programs	2	AOA-Approved Programs	0
1st-Yr. Spots for M.D. Students	0	Funded Entry-Level D.O. Spots	0
Adv. Spots Avail. to M.D. Students	0	% IMG Residents	8
All Entry-Level M.D. Spots	10	Avg. Res. Work Hours/Week	1.5
% Women Residents	33	% Training in Non-Hospital	
Avg. Ratio of Full-Time Physician Faculty to Fellows	1.5	Community Ambulatory Clinics	38
% Training in Hospital Outpatient Clinics	25		

For more information, contact:

- American Academy of Orthopaedic Surgeons, (800) 346-2267; www.aaos.org.
- The American Orthopaedic Association, (847) 318-7330; www.aoassn.org/.
- American Osteopathic Academy of Orthopedics, (800) 741-2626; www.aoao.org.
- American Association for Hand Surgery, (312) 236-3307; www.handsurgery.org.
- American Society for Surgery of the Hand, (847) 384-8300; www.hand-surg.org.

Hematology–Oncology (F)**

Specialty Overview: Although separate specialties, Hematology (the diagnosis and treatment of diseases of the blood) and Oncology (the diagnosis and treatment of patients with cancer) are often combined in both training and practice. This specialty's patients, once seen as victims of hopeless diseases, frequently can now be offered significant life-extending treatments.

The specialty is predominantly office-based, but practitioners often have a large primary or consultative inpatient service. Night call and emergencies can be frequent. Most specialists in this field work in medium to large cities. Hematologists and Oncologists are drawn from the specialties of Pediatrics and Internal Medicine. Hematologist–Oncologists average 47 hours per week (Internists) and 39 hours per week (Pediatricians) doing patient care. Hematologist–Pathologists average 57 hours per week doing patient care. Oncologist–Internists average 45 hours per week doing patient care. More than 11,000 physicians currently practice Hematology, Oncology, or both.

Training: Training in either Hematology or Oncology is usually a two-year fellowship, but many programs combine the two specialties into three-year fellowships. Training follows completion of an Internal Medicine or a Pediatric residency, or three years of a Pathology residency for a one-year fellowship in Hematology. For Osteopathic physicians, training follows internship and two years of Internal Medicine residency.

Match: Lists of programs can be found in *FREIDA* and, since there is no match in the adult specialties, applicants should contact programs directly. The NRMP runs the Pediatric Hematology/Oncology Fellowship Match, with 90% of programs participating. About 80% of participants match. Match day is in May, a year before the program starts.

HEMATOLOGY (INTERNAL MEDICINE)

ACGME-Approved Programs	13	AOA-Approved Programs	0
1st-Yr. Spots for M.D. Students	0	Funded Entry-Level D.O. Spots	0
Adv. Spots Avail. to M.D. Students	0	% IMG Residents	52
All Entry-Level M.D. Spots	37	Avg. Res. Work Hours/Week	50
% Women Residents	54	% Training in Non-Hospital	
Avg. Ratio of Full-Time Physician		Community Ambulatory Clinics	3
Faculty to Fellows	2.5		
% Training in Hospital Outpatient			
Clinics	45		

HEMATOLOGY (PATHOLOGY)

ACGME-Approved Programs	77	AOA-Approved Programs	0
1st-Yr. Spots for M.D. Students	0	Funded Entry-Level D.O. Spots	0
Adv. Spots Avail. to M.D. Students	0	% IMG Residents	63
All Entry-Level M.D. Spots	130	Avg. Res. Work Hours/Week	42
% Women Residents	52	% Training in Non-Hospital	
Avg. Ratio of Full-Time Physician		Community Ambulatory Clinics	<1
Faculty to Fellows	7.0		
% Training in Hospital Outpatient			
Clinics	3		

ONCOLOGY (INTERNAL MEDICINE)

ACGME-Approved Programs	20	AOA-Approved Programs	1
1st-Yr. Spots for M.D. Students	0	Funded Entry-Level D.O. Spots	1
Adv. Spots Avail. to M.D. Students	0	% IMG Residents	44
All Entry-Level M.D. Spots	76	Avg. Res. Work Hours/Week	50
% Women Residents	28	% Training in Non-Hospital	
Avg. Ratio of Full-Time Physician		Community Ambulatory Clinics	9
Faculty to Fellows	2.7		
% Training in Hospital Outpatient			
Clinics	49		

HEMATOLOGY–ONCOLOGY (INTERNAL MEDICINE)

ACGME-Approved Programs	123	AOA-Approved Programs	1
1st-Yr. Spots for M.D. Students	0	Funded Entry-Level D.O. Spots	2
Adv. Spots Avail. to M.D. Students	0	% IMG Residents	48
All Entry-Level M.D. Spots	428	Avg. Res. Work Hours/Week	49
% Women Residents	41	% Training in Non-Hospital	
Avg. Ratio of Full-Time Physician		Community Ambulatory Clinics	2
Faculty to Fellows	2.3		
% Training in Hospital Outpatient			
Clinics	32		

PEDIATRIC HEMATOLOGY–ONCOLOGY***

ACGME-Approved Programs	60	AOA-Approved Programs	0
1st-Yr. Spots for M.D. Students	0	Funded Entry-Level D.O. Spots	0
Adv. Spots Avail. to M.D. Students	0	% IMG Residents	29
All Entry-Level M.D. Spots	123	Avg. Res. Work Hours/Week	50
% Women Residents	59	% Training in Non-Hospital	
Avg. Ratio of Full-Time Physician		Community Ambulatory Clinics	<1
Faculty to Fellows	3.2		
% Training in Hospital Outpatient			
Clinics	32		

For more information, contact:

- American College of Osteopathic Internists, (301) 656-8877; www.acoi.org.
- American Society of Clinical Oncology, (703) 299-0150; www.asco.org.
- American Society of Hematology, (202) 776-0544; www.hematology.org.

Hospitalist*

Specialty Overview: Hospitalists care for inpatients. Under current definitions, physicians are hospitalists if they spend 25% or more of their time caring for patients admitted or transferred to the hospital by their primary doctors. Their practice has been described as "caring for horizontal patients"; when patients are discharged, office-based physicians take over their care. This specialty's growth has been encouraged by managed care organizations that want their office-based physicians to primarily see outpatients while streamlining the treatment given to inpatients, i.e., reduce lengths of stay and reduce costs. Having Hospitalists see all inpatients saves the time required for the other physicians to do rounds. In some cases, Hospitalists also compensate for the reduction in resident physicians some hospitals have experienced by doing the work the residents used to do.

However, some managed care organizations require the use of their Hospitalist, rather than allowing the primary physician to provide patient care. This has raised serious, and organized, opposition to their presence.

Although the original description of Hospitalists raised the question of whether these physicians would suffer "burnout" more than others, recent studies demonstrate that their burnout rate is no greater than physicians in Emergency Medicine or Critical Care. Hospitalists must balance the demands of patients, families, primary physicians, hospitals, and insurers. They seem to be doing this well, and more hospitals and medical groups are employing them. Standard residency training, however, does not seem to adequately prepare them for this role.

Of the current 12,000 Hospitalists, 90% are Internists, about 5% are Pediatricians, and 5% are Family Physicians. It is estimated that there will be about 30,000 Hospitalists by 2010. About 7% of Internal Medicine residents plan to make this their area of practice. At some academic centers, Hospitalists do most of the inpatient teaching to residents and students. A benefit of being a Hospitalist is having set hours to work. The pay is 20% higher than what General Internists receive.

It is unlikely that Hospitalist will become an official specialty in the near future, since that may mean managed care groups and hospitals will require such certification for all primary care physicians to care for hospitalized patients—a situation no one wants.

Training: Currently, training generally consists of completing an Internal Medicine or Family Medicine residency. About 105 residency programs have special tracks to train Hospitalists. These programs, most of which are in Internal Medicine and Family Medicine, as well as the 62 Hospitalist

Fellowships, can be located by checking the "Optional Criteria" button when searching *FREIDA*. These fellowships are one or two years long. Most of these programs include special training dealing with end-of-life care, interactions with other specialists (especially surgeons), managed care, quality improvement and patient safety, teamwork, hospital systems and infrastructure, care available outside the hospital, and business and communication skills.

For more information, contact:
- Society of Hospital Medicine, (800) 843-3360;
www.hospitalmedicine.org/.

Infectious Disease (F)*

Specialty Overview: Infectious Disease specialists diagnose and treat contagious diseases. At the onset of the antibiotic era, the specialty was thought to be on the edge of extinction; it is now making a comeback. This is due to the great diversity of drug-resistant bacteria, the AIDS epidemic, the fear of bioterrorism, and the threat of a worldwide flu pandemic.

Infectious Disease specialists act as consultants to other physicians. Many are also involved in research and most work in major medical centers. With the increased importance of nosocomial infections, many Infectious Disease specialists work part-time as hospital infection control officers. Physicians in this subspecialty generally receive lower salaries than those specialists who are more procedure-oriented. Many Infectious Disease specialists also practice General Internal Medicine. Infectious Disease Internists average 43 hours per week doing patient care. There are currently about 6,000 Infectious Disease specialists.

Training: Training consists of either a two-year fellowship following completion of an Internal Medicine residency or a three-year fellowship after a Pediatric residency. For Osteopathic physicians, training follows internship and two years of an Internal Medicine residency.

Match: Applicants match with Infectious Disease fellowships by using the NRMP Medical Specialties Matching Program. About 83% of programs participate in the Match. Of the positions offered through the NRMP, 87% are filled. Match day is in May, a year before the program begins. Pediatric Infectious Diseases programs can be found in *FREIDA* and should be directly contacted.

INFECTIOUS DISEASE (INTERNAL MEDICINE)

ACGME-Approved Programs	139	AOA-Approved Programs	2
1st-Yr. Spots for M.D. Students	0	Funded Entry-Level D.O. Spots	4
Adv. Spots Avail. to M.D. Students	0	% IMG Residents	47
All Entry-Level M.D. Spots	332	Avg. Res. Work Hours/Week	50
% Women Residents	50	% Training in Non-Hospital	
Avg. Ratio of Full-Time Physician		Community Ambulatory Clinics	4
Faculty to Fellows	2.8		
% Training in Hospital Outpatient			
Clinics	18		

PEDIATRIC INFECTIOUS DISEASES

ACGME-Approved Programs	62	AOA-Approved Programs	0
1st-Yr. Spots for M.D. Students	0	Funded Entry-Level D.O. Spots	0
Adv. Spots Avail. to M.D. Students	0	% IMG Residents	40
All Entry-Level M.D. Spots	74	Avg. Res. Work Hours/Week	40
% Women Residents	56	% Training in Non-Hospital	
Avg. Ratio of Full-Time Physician		Community Ambulatory Clinics	<1
Faculty to Fellows	3.0		
% Training in Hospital Outpatient			
Clinics	15		

For more information, contact:

- American College of Osteopathic Internists, (301) 656-8877; www.acoi.org.
- Infectious Diseases Society of America, (703) 299-0200; www.idsociety.org.

Internal Medicine**

Specialty Overview: Internists (specialists in Internal Medicine, not to be confused with "interns") are divided into General Internists and subspecialists in Internal Medicine (see the subspecialties listed under "Internal Medicine" in Figure 2.8). The General Internist provides longitudinal care to adult patients with both acute and chronic diseases. In rural areas, the General Internist often acts as a consultant to other practitioners on complex medical cases. In suburban and urban areas, however, other primary care practitioners usually consult with Internal Medicine subspecialists; surgical specialists consult with both General and subspecialty Internists. Urban General Internists provide primary health care and treat non-surgical diseases such as diabetes, hypertension, and congestive heart failure on both an inpatient and an outpatient basis. They are also very active in managed care plans such as HMOs.

Students attracted to General Internal Medicine seek an intellectual challenge, have an interest in primary care, and often had a positive experience during their third-year Internal Medicine rotation. General Internal Medicine, however, has been less popular among students and housestaff in recent years. This trend may be due to several factors, including: the Internist's income being lower than that of either the average physician or the Internal Medicine subspecialist, General Internal Medicine's relatively low prestige, the perception that caring for chronically ill patients is burdensome, and the increasing hassles of practice. Many students avoid Internal Medicine because they perceive that the housestaff and attendings they work with are overworked, unhappy, and under-rewarded. Studies show that General Internists are less satisfied with their jobs than are either Family Physicians or Internal Medicine subspecialists. However, the growth of managed care plans and societal pressure to have more primary care physicians have led to increased job opportunities for General Internists. Approximately 25% of Internal Medicine Residents plan to be General Internists because they prefer to care for ambulatory patients, believe it offers them an opportunity to have long-term relationships with patients, and does not involve caring for critical patients.

Internal Medicine is often described as "less procedural and more cerebral" than other specialties. While this may be true for General Internists, it is not true of the procedure-oriented subspecialists in Gastroenterology, Critical Care, Pulmonary Disease, and Cardiology. The average Internist (General and subspecialty) has a 59-hour work week, with 47% of the time spent in office visits, 18% on hospital rounds, 27% on other patient care activities, and 3% doing surgical/manipulative procedures. In some areas of the country, the amount of hospital time is decreasing as Hospitalists assume inpatient tasks. Internists average 49 hours per week doing patient care.

Training: Training in Internal Medicine is three years in length. Programs that combine Internal Medicine with Family Medicine (see Family Medicine–Internal Medicine), Pediatrics (see below), Preventive Medicine, or Nuclear Medicine are four years long. Programs combining Internal Medicine with Emergency Medicine (see Emergency Medicine–Internal Medicine), Neurology, Physical Medicine & Rehabilitation, or Psychiatry are each five years long. These combined programs qualify graduates for board examinations in both specialties. If an Osteopathic graduate enters an Internal Medicine "specialty-track" internship, the Internal Medicine training time is shortened by one year.

One of the advantages of Internal Medicine training is the number of options available following residency. More than two-thirds of Internal Medicine residency graduates go on to subspecialize. However, individuals completing Internal Medicine residencies in markets with high managed care penetration are less likely to subspecialize than are Internal Medicine residents training in areas with less managed care impact. Many physicians do not finalize their decision to practice as either General Internists or subspecialists until well into their residency. Following residency, fellowships are available in: Cardiovascular Disease; Clinical Cardiac Electrophysiology; Critical Care Medicine; Endocrinology, Diabetes & Metabolism; Gastroenterology; Geriatric Medicine; Hematology; Infectious Diseases; Interventional Cardiology; Oncology; Nephrology; Pulmonary Disease; Rheumatology; and Sports Medicine.

FREIDA lists some positions as "Internal Medicine" and some as "Medicine–Primary." The difference between the two types of programs is that there is more, but often only slightly more, time spent in an ambulatory clinic and a continuity clinic in the latter type. Graduates of both programs take the same Board examination. Some programs, labeled "Primary Care Internal Medicine," emphasize outpatient clinic training, although they seldom have more clinic hours than inpatient training. These come closer than the usual residency programs to mimicking the actual practice of a General Internist, although all Internal Medicine programs have increased the amount of time spent in ambulatory settings over the past few years.

Match: Virtually all ACGME-approved positions in Internal Medicine are listed in the NRMP PGY-1 Match. In recent years, about 97% of the available PGY-1 Categorical (three-year) positions filled through the NRMP Match, with 45% of the positions taken by foreign graduates. About 1,600 Internal Medicine positions are listed as "Preliminary" and are for only one year of training (before beginning training in other specialties). U.S. graduates filled 77% of these positions.

Other Useful Information: Internal Medicine led the way in the reform of postgraduate education. Internal Medicine training programs have more experience with the requirement that limits the number of hours residents work to 80 hours per week, averaged over four weeks. Residents at all levels of training have, on average, at least one day per week free of hospital duties. They also must spend at least 25% of their three-year training in ambulatory settings. Not all programs, though, comply with these requirements.

INTERNAL MEDICINE

ACGME-Approved Programs	389	AOA-Approved Programs	66
1st-Yr. Spots for M.D. Students(C)	6,630	Funded Entry-Level D.O. Spots	204
1st-Yr. Spots for M.D. Students(P)	1,987	% IMG Residents	49
Adv. Spots Avail. to M.D. Students	0	Avg. Res. Work Hours/Week	65
All Entry-Level M.D. Spots	8,347	Programs with Childcare	150
% Women Residents	41	Programs Offering a "Primary	
Avg. Ratio of Full-Time Physician		Care Track"	114
Faculty to Residents	1.1	Programs Offering Multiple	
% Training in Hospital Outpatient		Start Dates	70
Clinics	22	Programs Allowing Moonlighting	239
% Training in Non-Hospital		Atl./Comp. Med Curriculum	196
Community Ambulatory Clinics	9		

INTERNAL MEDICINE–NEUROLOGY (COMBINED RESIDENCY)*

ACGME-Approved Programs	7	AOA-Approved Programs	0
1st-Yr. Spots for M.D. Students	12	Funded Entry-Level D.O. Spots	0
Adv. Spots Avail. to M.D. Students	0	% IMG Residents	39
All Entry-Level M.D. Spots	12	Avg. Res. Work Hours/Week	52
% Women Residents	27	Programs with Childcare	6
Avg. Ratio of Full-Time Physician		Programs Offering a "Primary	
Faculty to Residents	58.8	Care Track"	1
% Training in Hospital Outpatient		Programs Offering Multiple	
Clinics	22	Start Dates	3
% Training in Non-Hospital			
Community Ambulatory Clinics	5		

INTERNAL MEDICINE–PHYSICAL MEDICINE & REHABILITATION (COMBINED RESIDENCY)*

ACGME-Approved Programs	2	AOA-Approved Programs	0
1st-Yr. Spots for M.D. Students	2	Funded Entry-Level D.O. Spots	0
Adv. Spots Avail. to M.D. Students	0	% IMG Residents	83
All Entry-Level M.D. Spots	2	Avg. Res. Work Hours/Week	53
% Women Residents	0	Programs with Childcare	1
Avg. Ratio of Full-Time Physician		Programs Offering a "Primary	
Faculty to Residents	38	Care Track"	1
% Training in Hospital Outpatient		% Training in Non-Hospital	
Clinics	42	Community Ambulatory Clinics	10

INTERNAL MEDICINE–PREVENTIVE MEDICINE (COMBINED RESIDENCY)*

ACGME-Approved Programs	7	AOA-Approved Programs	0
1st-Yr. Spots for M.D. Students	7	Funded Entry-Level D.O. Spots	0
Adv. Spots Avail. to M.D. Students	0	% IMG Residents	65
All Entry-Level M.D. Spots	7	Avg. Res. Work Hours/Week	N/A
% Women Residents	36	Programs with Childcare	4
Avg. Ratio of Full-Time Physician		Programs Offering a "Primary	
Faculty to Residents	47	Care Track"	0
% Training in Hospital Outpatient		% Training in Non-Hospital	
Clinics	N/A	Community Ambulatory Clinics	N/A

INTERNAL MEDICINE, PRIMARY

ACGME-Approved Programs	65	AOA-Approved Programs	0
1st-Yr. Spots for M.D. Students	290	Funded Entry-Level D.O. Spots	0
Adv. Spots Avail. to M.D. Students	0	All Entry-Level M.D. Spots	290

INTERNAL MEDICINE–PSYCHIATRY (COMBINED RESIDENCY)*

ACGME-Approved Programs	19	AOA-Approved Programs	0
1st-Yr. Spots for M.D. Students	39	Funded Entry-Level D.O. Spots	0
Adv. Spots Avail. to M.D. Students	0	% IMG Residents	32
All Entry-Level M.D. Spots	39	Avg. Res. Work Hours/Week	61
% Women Residents	36	Programs with Childcare	10
Avg. Ratio of Full-Time Physician		Programs Offering a "Primary	
Faculty to Residents	24	Care Track"	2
% Training in Hospital Outpatient		Programs Offering Multiple	
Clinics	23	Start Dates	4
% Training in Non-Hospital			
Community Ambulatory Clinics	2		

For more information, contact:

- American College of Osteopathic Internists, (301) 656-8877; www.acoi.org.
- American College of Physicians-American Society of Internal Medicine, (800) 523-1546; www.acponline.org.
- Society of General Internal Medicine, (800) 822-3060; www.sgim.org.

Internal Medicine–Pediatrics**

Specialty Overview: Combined Internal Medicine–Pediatrics training programs are designed for the individual who wishes to have a primary care practice for families without offering obstetric and surgical services. About 80% of graduates from these programs see both adults and children in their practice, and about 20% work in rural or underserved areas.

Graduates of these combined training programs report that they feel as comfortable as other Pediatricians handling infant, child, and adolescent cases, but less comfortable than Family Physicians treating adolescent health problems. Although they are more comfortable than Family Physicians dealing with complex Internal Medicine patients, they report being less comfortable than other Internists treating intensive care and geriatric patients. Internist–Pediatricians average 51 hours per week doing patient care.

Completion of combined programs makes the individual eligible to take the specialty Board examination in both Pediatrics and Internal Medicine. The combined programs are not reviewed by the certifying bodies (Residency Review Committees) as a whole program. Rather, the Internal Medicine and Pediatrics programs are each reviewed and approved separately. The number of combined programs is growing. A listing can be found both on *FREIDA* and in the "Green Book's" Appendices.

Training: Training is four years in length, with a minimum of 20 months of Internal Medicine. The programs are, for the most part, integrated. Trainees take blocks of Internal Medicine and then blocks of Pediatrics. This often leads to spending nearly two years at the intern level of training. More than 90% of Internal Medicine–Pediatrics residents complete the program, and about 20% go on to subspecialize. Most graduates feel that they needed to spend more time in the ambulatory setting and less in intensive care.

Match: In recent years, about 87% of the available PGY-1 positions filled through the NRMP Match.

INTERNAL MEDICINE–PEDIATRICS

ACGME-Approved Programs	101	AOA-Approved Programs	2
1st-Yr. Spots for M.D. Students	465	Funded Entry-Level D.O. Spots	4
Adv. Spots Avail. to M.D. Students	0	% IMG Residents	20
All Entry-Level M.D. Spots	465	Avg. Res. Work Hours/Week	65
% Women Residents	51	Programs with Childcare	42
Avg. Ratio of Full-Time Physician		Programs Offering a "Primary	
Faculty to Residents	13.1	Care Track"	10
% Training in Hospital Outpatient		Programs Offering Multiple	
Clinics	29	Start Dates	19
% Training in Non-Hospital		Programs Allowing Moonlighting	77
Community Ambulatory Clinics	10	Alt./Comp. Med Curriculum	58

For more information, contact:

- American College of Physicians-American Society of Internal Medicine, (800) 523-1546; www.acponline.org.
- American Academy of Pediatrics, (847) 434-4000; www.aap.org.

Medical Genetics*

Specialty Overview: Medical Genetics is the newest medical specialty. Currently, more than 1,000 physicians have been certified in M.D. Clinical Genetics. Most come from the specialties of Pediatrics, Obstetrics and Gynecology, or Internal Medicine. The rapid changes occurring in clinical genetics with the deciphering of the human genome and the application of that knowledge suggest that there may be a much greater need in the future for Medical Geneticists for both diagnosis and treatment.

Training: Two years of training in another medical specialty is required before admission. Training in Medical Genetics lasts two or more additional years. Some programs offer all four years of training. Eleven programs combine training in Medical Genetics with Pediatrics in a five-year program.

Match: Nearly all Medical Genetics programs are listed in *FREIDA*. Programs must be contacted directly; only two participate in the NRMP Matching Program.

MEDICAL GENETICS

ACGME-Approved Programs	48	AOA-Approved Programs	0
1st-Yr. Spots for M.D. Students	2	Funded Entry-Level D.O. Spots	0
Adv. Spots Avail. to M.D. Students	0	% IMG Residents	45
All Entry-Level M.D. Spots	96	Avg. Res. Work Hours/Week	39
% Women Residents	53	Programs with Childcare	14
Avg. Ratio of Full-Time Physician Faculty to Fellows	5.8	Programs Offering a "Primary Care Track"	2
% Training in Hospital Outpatient Clinics	59	Programs Offering Multiple Start Dates	22
% Training in Non-Hospital Community Ambulatory Clinics	9	Programs Allowing Moonlighting	21
		Alt./Comp. Med Curriculum	6

For more information, contact:

- ·American Board of Medical Genetics, (301) 634-7315; www.abmg.org/ or www.faseb.org.

Medical Management/Administration*

Specialty Overview: Medical managers have existed almost as long as the profession. (As soon as there were two physicians, one was assuredly the administrator.) Recently, Medical Management has come into its own with the increasing complexity of Byzantine government rules, the maze of managed care organizations, and the constantly changing patient and payer demands. Also called "Medical Administration," these specialists compete with non-physicians who also try to manage health care systems.

Since managing physicians is somewhat like herding cats, it is often a thankless job. Yet many physicians try it at various stages of their careers—especially in the decade before retirement. Many such positions are available in hospitals, group practices, clinics, insurance companies, and corporations.

Closely linked to Medical Management is "Managed Care Medicine." Those taking courses in this area also intend to manage other physicians, but often with the more defined goal of working within managed care. According to the *New England Journal of Medicine* [1999;341(25):1945-8], the inherent conflicts in the medical director's role are "satisfying the desires of patients and physicians, on the one hand, and the financial profit or survival of the organization, on the other, and between the unlimited demands of individual patients and the limited resources of society."

Training: Courses are available through the American College of Physician Executives, the American College of Managed Care Medicine, and various MBA and MPH programs.

For more information, contact:
- American College of Managed Care Medicine, (804) 527-1906; www.acmcm.org.
- American College of Physician Executives, (800) 562-8088; www.acpe.org.
- American Medical Directors Association, (800) 876-2632; www.amda.com.

Medical Toxicology (F)*

Specialty Overview: Medical Toxicologists diagnose, treat, and consult on a wide variety of intentional, accidental, and industrial poisonings. Toxicology is a subspecialty of Emergency Medicine, Pediatrics, and Preventive Medicine, although no Pediatrics-based programs exist.

Training: Training programs are usually two years following the primary residency. A current list is on *FREIDA*.

Match: Fellowships, usually within Emergency Medicine or Preventive Medicine departments, are obtained by contacting each program directly.

MEDICAL TOXICOLOGY			
ACGME-Approved Programs	20	AOA-Approved Programs	0
1st-Yr. Spots for M.D. Students	0	Funded Entry-Level D.O. Spots	0
Adv. Spots Avail. to M.D. Students	0	% IMG Residents	5
All Entry-Level M.D. Spots	34	Avg. Res. Work Hours/Week	N/A
% Women Residents	50		
Avg. Ratio of Full-Time Physician Faculty to Fellows	1.5		

For more information, contact:

- American Academy of Pediatrics, (847) 434-4000; www.aap.org.
- American College of Emergency Physicians, (800) 798-1822; www.acep.org.
- American College of Occupational and Environmental Medicine, (847) 818-1800; www.acoem.org.
- Society for Academic Emergency Medicine, (517) 485-5484; www.saem.org.
- Society of Toxicology, (703) 438-3115; www.toxicology.org.

Neonatal–Perinatal Medicine (F)**

Specialty Overview: Neonatologists treat the problems associated with premature births. Their practice centers on the neonatal intensive care unit. They are Pediatricians who do critical care on those neonates who do not yet have the capacity to live without medical assistance. As with other critical care specialists, they must be able to skillfully perform procedures—but they must work on *very* small babies. The size of the infants they work with has progressively decreased. Neonatologists work closely with a specialized team of nurses, social workers, and respiratory therapists. They also work closely with families to sort out both medical and ethical issues of care. Neonatologists average 53 hours per week doing patient care.

Training: Fellowships are two years in length following a residency in Pediatrics.

Match: Contact individual training programs, since this specialty has no match.

NEONATAL–PERINATAL MEDICINE

ACGME-Approved Programs	97	AOA-Approved Programs	0
1st-Yr. Spots for M.D. Students	0	Funded Entry-Level D.O. Spots	0
Adv. Spots Avail. to M.D. Students	0	% IMG Residents	40
All Entry-Level M.D. Spots	209	Avg. Res. Work Hours/Week	52
% Women Residents	54	% Training in Non-Hospital	
Avg. Ratio of Full-Time Physician		Community Ambulatory Clinics	<1
Faculty to Fellows	3.1		
% Training in Hospital Outpatient			
Clinics	7		

For more information, contact:

- American Academy of Pediatrics, (847) 434-4000; www.aap.org.
- American College of Osteopathic Pediatricians, (312) 202-8188; www.acopeds.org/.

Nephrology (F)*

Specialty Overview: Nephrologists diagnose and (non-surgically) treat diseases of the kidney and the urinary system. Most of their patients have chronic diseases requiring long-term care. Managing dialysis and the treatment of dialysis and renal transplant patients are large parts of most Nephrologists' practices. The specialty is predominantly office-based. However, practitioners may have large primary or consultative inpatient services. Night call can be frequent. Nephrologists average 55 hours (Internists) or 42 hours (Pediatricians) per week doing patient care.

Training: Training is generally a two-year fellowship following the completion of an Internal Medicine residency or three years after a Pediatric residency. For Osteopathic physicians, training follows internship and two years of an Internal Medicine residency.

Match: Applicants should contact programs directly.

NEPHROLOGY (INTERNAL MEDICINE)

ACGME-Approved Programs	130	AOA-Approved Programs	6
1st-Yr. Spots for M.D. Students	0	Funded Entry-Level D.O. Spots	11
Adv. Spots Avail. to M.D. Students	0	% IMG Residents	42
All Entry-Level M.D. Spots	306	Avg. Res. Work Hours/Week	52
% Women Residents	33	% Training in Non-Hospital	
Avg. Ratio of Full-Time Physician		Community Ambulatory Clinics	7
Faculty to Fellows	1.8		
% Training in Hospital Outpatient			
Clinics	22		

PEDIATRIC NEPHROLOGY

ACGME-Approved Programs	37	AOA-Approved Programs	0
1st-Yr. Spots for M.D. Students	0	Funded Entry-Level D.O. Spots	0
Adv. Spots Avail. to M.D. Students	0	% IMG Residents	36
All Entry-Level M.D. Spots	39	Avg. Res. Work Hours/Week	43
% Women Residents	60	% Training in Non-Hospital	
Avg. Ratio of Full-Time Physician		Community Ambulatory Clinics	1
Faculty to Fellows	2.4		
% Training in Hospital Outpatient			
Clinics	31		

For more information, contact:

- American College of Osteopathic Internists, (301) 656-8877; www.acoi.org.
- American Society of Nephrology, (202) 659-0599; www.asn-online.org.
- Renal Physicians Association, 4701 Randolph Rd., Ste. 102, Rockville, MD 20852; www.renalmd.org.

Neurological Surgery*****

Specialty Overview: Neurosurgeons provide operative and non-operative management of lesions of the brain, spinal cord, peripheral nerves, and their supporting structures (skull, spine, meninges, CNS blood supply). Many are also involved in pain management. This requires much manual dexterity and a willingness to accept both dramatic successes and long-term failures in patient care. New developments in autologous and fetal tissue transplantation and in stereotactic surgery for epilepsy, Parkinson's Disease, and tumors may increase the need for Neurosurgeons during the next decade. Patients range in age from neonates to the elderly. Night call and emergency surgery are frequent parts of Neurosurgical practice. Neurosurgeons average 62 hours per week doing patient care.

Training: Residency training lasts five years following one year of General Surgery. Trainees must spend a minimum of 36 months in clinical Neurosurgery and three months in clinical Neurology. The balance of time can be spent studying relevant basic sciences, such as Neuropathology and Neuroradiology, or related fields, such as Pediatric Neurosurgery and Spinal Surgery. The specific areas covered during these extra months are the key differences among this specialty's training programs.

Match: All civilian Neurosurgery residency programs are in the Neurological Surgery Matching Program (NSMP), sponsored by the Society of

Neurological Surgeons, www.sfmatch.org. About 37 ACGME-approved programs participate in the NRMP Match, but these are probably all "pre-matched" in the NSMP. The San Francisco Matching Program suggests that applications be submitted to the Centralized Application Service by late August. Rank-order lists are due in December and results are distributed in late January. Students in the Neurological Surgery Match should also sign up with the NRMP PGY-1 Match for an internship position. (Although some programs have associated internships, applicants need to be in the NRMP PGY-1 Match to get a position.) Participants in the Neurological Surgery Match get their results before they must submit their NRMP Rank-Order Lists. In recent years, only 61% of applicants matched.

NEUROLOGICAL SURGERY

ACGME-Approved Programs	95	AOA-Approved Programs	9
1st-Yr. Spots for M.D. Students	19	Funded Entry-Level D.O. Spots	16
Adv. Spots Avail. to M.D. Students	131	% IMG Residents	9
All Entry-Level M.D. Spots	150	Avg. Res. Work Hours/Week	75
% Women Residents	13	Programs with Childcare	35
Avg. Ratio of Full-Time Physician		Programs Offering a "Primary	
Faculty to Residents	1.2	Care Track"	1
% Training in Hospital Outpatient		Programs Offering Multiple	
Clinics	16	Start Dates	7
% Training in Non-Hospital		Programs Allowing Moonlighting	15
Community Ambulatory Clinics	1	Alt./Comp. Med Curriculum	10

For more information, contact:
- American Association of Neurological Surgeons, www.aans.org.
- American College of Osteopathic Surgeons, (800) 888-1312; www.facos.org.

Neurology**

Specialty Overview: Neurologists diagnose and treat patients with diseases of the brain, spinal cord, peripheral nerves, and neuromuscular system. Much of the practice deals with the diagnosis and, more and more often, the treatment of patients seen in consultation. Many of these patients have headaches, strokes, or seizure disorders. Neurologists follow not only these patients but also those with chronic neuromuscular diseases. It is anticipated that the need for Neurologists will increase as the population ages. The specialty is predominantly office-based. Neurologists may, however, have large primary or consultative inpatient services. Night call can be frequent, especially in solo or small group practices. Neurologists average 48 hours per week doing patient care.

Training: Training is three years after a general PGY-1 year, most often in Internal Medicine, Pediatrics, Family Medicine, or a Transitional program. Some Neurology programs have their own PGY-1 year, and so are four years long. Combined programs, which take five years to complete, exist in Internal Medicine–Neurology (see Internal Medicine), Neurology–Nuclear Medicine, and Neurology–Physical Medicine & Rehabilitation. Three programs that are seven years long combine Neurology, Diagnostic Radiology, and Neuroradiology. Ten programs combine Neurology and Psychiatry. Post-residency fellowships exist in Pain Medicine (2 programs; 1 year), Child Neurology (72 programs, see "Child Neurology"), Neurodevelopmental Disabilities (8 programs; 4 years), Clinical Neurophysiology (90 programs; 3 years), and Vascular Neurology (22 programs; 1 year). Basic Neurology training programs are similar for Osteopathic physicians.

Match: ACGME-approved programs generally match through the Neurology Matching Program, sponsored by the Association of University Professors of Neurology, www.sfmatch.org. Most positions are filled a year ahead of time (matching for the year after internship). However, positions not previously filled are offered for the same year to those who have finished at least an internship. This Match requires that rank-order lists be submitted in December and releases results in late January. ACGME-approved programs that offer a first-year position integrated into the Neurology residency, in most cases, also use the regular NRMP PGY-1 Match. Positions in programs combining Neurology with another specialty, such as Psychiatry or Internal Medicine, generally must be obtained through the NRMP Match or negotiated directly with the program. In recent years, 76% of applicants matched.

	NEUROLOGY		
ACGME-Approved Programs	128	AOA-Approved Programs	6
1st-Yr. Spots for M.D. Students	43	Funded Entry-Level D.O. Spots	10
Adv. Spots Avail. to M.D. Students	481	% IMG Residents	38
All Entry-Level M.D. Spots	524	Avg. Res. Work Hours/Week	61
% Women Residents	38	Programs with Childcare	49
Avg. Ratio of Full-Time Physician		Programs Offering a "Primary	
Faculty to Residents	2.1	Care Track"	5
% Training in Hospital Outpatient		Programs Offering Multiple	
Clinics	24	Start Dates	17
% Training in Non-Hospital		Programs Allowing Moonlighting	43
Community Ambulatory Clinics	2	Alt./Comp. Med Curriculum	23

For more information, contact:
- American Academy of Neurology, (651) 695-1940; www.aan.com.
- American Association of Electrodiagnostic Medicine, (507) 288-0100; www.aaem.net.
- American College of Osteopathic Neurologists and Psychiatrists, 28595 Orchard Lake Rd., Ste. 200, Farmington Hills, MI 48334, (248) 553-0010, ext. 295.
- American Neurological Association, (952) 545-6284; www.aneuroa.org.

Nuclear Medicine*

Specialty Overview: Specialists in Nuclear Medicine use radioactive materials both to diagnose and to treat diseases by imaging the body's physiologic functions. The field combines medical practice with certain aspects of the physical sciences, including physics, mathematics, statistics, computer science, chemistry, and radiation biology. Specialists in Nuclear Medicine, unlike those in Radiation Oncology, use radioactive materials that are "unsealed" (i.e., free in the bloodstream) for their diagnostic studies and treatments. At some institutions, they also perform radioimmunoassay tests. Practitioners in the specialty have no primary patient-care responsibility and little night call. Many individuals who are currently practicing Nuclear Medicine have not been formally trained or certified in the specialty. However, anyone entering the field is expected to have been fully trained. The future of the specialty may be either very dynamic or rather static, depending upon how rapidly some currently innovative techniques, especially those related to PET scanning, become available to the specialty. Nuclear Medicine physicians average 52 hours per week doing patient care. The number of physicians in the field has only increased 10% in the past 15 years.

Training: Training consists of two years of Nuclear Medicine following, interspersed with, or, in a few cases, preceding two years of initial training in another clinical specialty, most commonly Radiology, Internal Medicine, or Pathology. Other fields of clinical training have also been rather freely accepted. Osteopathic programs also accept two years of initial training in Family Medicine. Radiology residents doing a year of training in Nuclear Radiology occupy some of the positions that exist for training in Nuclear Medicine. Note, however, that Nuclear Medicine is a specialty distinct from Nuclear Radiology.

Match: Nearly all positions are obtained by negotiating with individual programs. Except for the few programs in the NRMP Advanced Match, contact the programs directly.

NUCLEAR MEDICINE

ACGME-Approved Programs	61	AOA-Approved Programs	0
1st-Yr. Spots for M.D. Students	0	Funded Entry-Level D.O. Spots	0
Adv. Spots Avail. to M.D. Students	0	% IMG Residents	46
All Entry-Level M.D. Spots	72	Avg. Res. Work Hours/Week	46
% Women Residents	27	Programs with Childcare	22
Avg. Ratio of Full-Time Physician Faculty to Residents/Fellows	2.3	Programs Offering a "Primary Care Track"	2
% Training in Hospital Outpatient Clinics	38	Programs Offering Multiple Start Dates	17
% Training in Non-Hospital Community Ambulatory Clinics	<1	Programs Allowing Moonlighting	21
		Alt./Comp. Med Curriculum	5

For more information, contact:

- American College of Nuclear Medicine, (717) 898-5008; www.acnucmed.org.
- American College of Nuclear Physicians, (703) 326-1190, ext. 1216; www.acnponline.org.
- American Osteopathic Board of Nuclear Medicine, 1000 E. 53rd St., Chicago, IL 60615.

Obstetrics and Gynecology***

Specialty Overview: Obstetrician–Gynecologists manage pregnancies and treat disorders of the female reproductive tract. Obstetricians deal with pregnancy in women. Gynecologists deal with medical and surgical diseases of the female reproductive tract and with infertility. While some specialists in this field work primarily in one area or the other, most work in both Obstetrics and Gynecology. This is the only surgical specialty that is considered "Primary Care."

Obstetric practice has been greatly affected by the rising cost of medical liability insurance and the increasing propensity to sue physicians. Because of this, Obstetricians are, in increasing numbers, eliminating deliveries from their practices or reducing the provision of care to patients who have or are likely to have high-risk pregnancies. As the population ages and there is a greater awareness of women's health care needs, there will be a need for more Gynecologists.

The specialty combines both surgical and non-surgical approaches to disease, and is increasingly using endoscopic surgical techniques (minimally invasive surgery). The average Obstetrician–Gynecologist, in a 49-hour work week, spends about 50% of the time seeing patients in the office and 33% in surgery or in the delivery room.

The field of Obstetrics and Gynecology is primarily office-based, but frequently has a sizable inpatient load. A busy Obstetrics practice consists of considerable emergency and night call. An increasing number of women are entering this field. In general, the smaller the program and the fewer patients they see, the less competitive it is. This field has experienced the greatest percentage increase in female residents over recent years; about 58% of residents in 1996 and 75% in 2005 were women.

Training: The basic training program in Obstetrics and Gynecology consists of four years of training following medical school. If Osteopathic graduates enter an Obstetrics/Gynecology "specialty-track" internship, their Obstetrics and Gynecology training time is shortened by one year. The malpractice climate has had an adverse effect on some training programs, leading to Obstetrics residents not being given an opportunity to exercise a level of responsibility appropriate to their level of training. Following residency, physicians can take subspecialty fellowships in Reproductive Endocrinology (more commonly known as Infertility) or Gynecologic Oncology, which requires extra surgical training. The two newest subspecialties are Maternal–Fetal Medicine, in which physicians treat the developing child *in utero,* and Urogynecology/Reconstructive Pelvic Surgery.

Match: In recent years, about 95% of the available PGY-1 positions filled through the NRMP Match, with about one-fifth going to foreign graduates. Most positions in Gynecologic Oncology, Maternal–Fetal Medicine, Reproductive Endocrinology, and Female Pelvic Medicine & Reproductive Surgery go through the NRMP Obstetric/Gynecology Specialty Match, with rank lists due in early October and matching in early November, the year before the July start date

OBSTETRICS AND GYNECOLOGY

ACGME-Approved Programs	254	AOA-Approved Programs	31
1st-Yr. Spots for M.D. Students	1,238	Funded Entry-Level D.O. Spots	68
Adv. Spots Avail. to M.D. Students	0	% IMG Residents	21
All Entry-Level M.D. Spots	1,238	Avg. Res. Work Hours/Week	74
% Women Residents	73	Programs with Childcare	91
Avg. Ratio of Full-Time Physician		Programs Offering a "Primary	
Faculty to Residents	0.9	Care Track"	65
% Training in Hospital Outpatient		Programs Offering Multiple	
Clinics	31	Start Dates	19
% Training in Non-Hospital		Programs Allowing Moonlighting	59
Community Ambulatory Clinics	8	Alt./Comp. Med Curriculum	100

For more information, contact:

- American College of Obstetricians & Gynecologists, www.acog.org.
- American College of Osteopathic Obstetricians & Gynecologists, (800) 875-6360; www.acoog.com.
- American Society for Reproductive Medicine, (205) 978-5000; www.asrm.org.

Occupational Medicine*

Specialty Overview: Occupational Medicine is one of the specialties of Preventive Medicine. It focuses on the effects of the work environment on health and ways to protect workers. Occupational physicians work in industry, teaching hospitals, government, or occupational health clinics. As the positions in industry decrease, private practice within occupational health clinics has become a burgeoning area for those in Occupational Medicine. In these clinics, they often treat work-related injuries and evaluate patients with work-related disabilities. Specialists rarely take night call or have inpatient responsibilities.

Training: Training consists of two or three years following internship. Part of the time is used to get a graduate degree in an appropriate area, usually a Master of Public Health. A fourth year of training, teaching, practice, and/or research is required to take the Board examination. Osteopathic physicians can specialize in Preventive Medicine–Occupational Medicine–Environmental Medicine.

Match: Contact individual programs directly.

OCCUPATIONAL MEDICINE			
ACGME-Approved Programs	33	AOA-Approved Programs	0
1st-Yr. Spots for M.D. Students	0	Funded Entry-Level D.O. Spots	0
Adv. Spots Avail. to M.D. Students	0	% IMG Residents	N/A
All Entry-Level M.D. Spots	108	Programs with Childcare	9
Programs Offering a "Primary Care Track"	4	Programs Allowing Moonlighting	20
		Alt./Comp. Med Curriculum	9
Programs Offering Multiple Start Dates	12		

For more information, contact:

- American College of Occupational and Environmental Medicine, (847) 818-1800; www.acoem.org.
- American College of Preventive Medicine, (202) 466-2044; www.acpm.org.

• American Osteopathic College of Occupational and Preventive Medicine, (800) 558-8686; www.aocopm.org.

Ophthalmology*****

Specialty Overview: Ophthalmologists prevent, diagnose, and treat the diseases and abnormalities of the eye and periocular structures. A combination of office-based medical practice and surgical treatment of diseases makes this a popular specialty. Ophthalmologists treat patients of all ages, often using high-technology equipment in both diagnosis and therapy. Patients are usually seen as outpatients. Many Ophthalmologists take some night call, but they rarely have to go into the hospital after-hours. Inpatient services represent a small proportion of the care they deliver. With Optometrists performing many of the functions once reserved for Ophthalmologists, the field is rapidly becoming over-staffed. Ophthalmologists average 43 hours per week doing patient care.

Training: The training consists of three years following an internship. Residency programs place great emphasis on high class-standing and research experience. They try to officially limit each student to one "audition elective," but this has had varying success. Over the past decade, entering Ophthalmology has become slightly less difficult, although it retains its reputation as a "difficult-to-enter" specialty.

Match: Matching is through the Ophthalmology Matching Program sponsored by the Association of University Professors of Ophthalmology, and run by the San Francisco Matching Programs, **www.sfmatch.org.** They also run the Centralized Application Service (CAS) for all civilian Ophthalmology applicants. Rank order lists for PGY-2 positions are submitted in December and matching occurs in January for positions beginning 18 months later. Individuals usually arrange their own internships through the NRMP PGY-1 Match. The Ophthalmology Matching Program also runs a Vacancy Information System, available through their website. In recent years, 77% of applicants matched.

Fellowship positions, except for Ophthalmic Plastic & Reconstructive Surgery (Oculoplastics), are offered through the Ophthalmology Fellowship Matching Program run by the San Francisco Matching Program. Information can be obtained on their website. In recent years, the following percentage of applicants matched to these specialties: Cornea/External Disease, 72%; Glaucoma, 78%; Neuro-Ophthalmology, 60%; Pediatric Ophthalmology, 54%; and Retina, 74%. The Fellowship Match is held in May, one year before the July starting date. Oculoplastic fellowships are matched through the NRMP Specialty Matching Program; fewer than half the applicants find a position.

OPHTHALMOLOGY

ACGME-Approved Programs	117	AOA-Approved Programs	9
1st-Yr. Spots for M.D. Students	0	Funded Entry-Level D.O. Spots	12
Adv. Spots Avail. to M.D. Students	460	% IMG Residents	7
All Entry-Level M.D. Spots	460	Avg. Res. Work Hours/Week	51
% Women Residents	34	Programs with Childcare	36
Avg. Ratio of Full-Time Physician		Programs Offering a "Primary	
Faculty to Residents	1.3	Care Track"	11
% Training in Hospital Outpatient		Programs Offering Multiple	
Clinics	84	Start Dates	4
% Training in Non-Hospital		Programs Allowing Moonlighting	27
Community Ambulatory Clinics	5	Alt./Comp. Med Curriculum	23

For more information, contact:

- American Academy of Ophthalmology, (415) 561-8500; www.aao.org.
- American Osteopathic Colleges of Ophthalmology, Otorhinolaryngology-Head & Neck Surgery, (800) 455-9404; www.aocoohns.org.

Orthopedic Surgery*****

Specialty Overview: Orthopedic Surgeons treat diseases and injuries of the spine and the extremities. Using surgery, medications, and physical therapy, their goal is to preserve maximal function of the musculoskeletal system. Much Orthopedic Surgery that was once performed on an inpatient basis is now done as ambulatory surgery. Individuals who go into this specialty like to work with their hands. Many have hobbies such as woodworking that emphasize this, and the majority are sports-oriented. Many Orthopedic Surgeons take night and emergency call during their entire career.

Orthopedic Surgeons average 61 hours per week doing patient care. Among subspecialists, Adult Reconstructive Orthopedic Surgeons average 48 hours per week doing patient care; Orthopedic Spinal Surgeons, 53 hours; Orthopedic Sports Medicine physicians, 55 hours; and Pediatric Orthopedic Surgeons, 56 hours.

Training: Training consists of one year in a broad medical specialty followed by four years of Orthopedics. Orthopedic Surgery is one of the most competitive specialties. Programs look for high USMLE scores, research experience, election to AOA (honorary), and successful "audition clerk-ships." Both subspecialty training and certification are available in Hand Surgery (see Hand Surgery). One-year fellowship positions also exist in Musculoskeletal Oncology (12 programs), Adult Reconstructive Orthopedics (14 programs), Foot and Ankle Orthopedics (5 programs), Orthopedic Sports Medicine (see Sports Medicine), Pediatric Orthopedics (23 programs), Orthopedic Trauma (6 programs), and Orthopedic Surgery of the Spine (12 programs).

Match: In recent years, virtually all of the available PGY-1 positions filled through the NRMP Match. Orthopedic fellowship positions are arranged individually with most training programs. The exception is Orthopedic Hand Surgery, which uses the NRMP's Combined Musculo-skeletal Match. This match is held in May, a year before the July starting date.

ORTHOPEDIC SURGERY

ACGME-Approved Programs	152	AOA-Approved Programs	30
1st-Yr. Spots for M.D. Students	610	Funded Entry-Level D.O. Spots	70
Adv. Spots Avail. to M.D. Students	51	% IMG Residents	2
All Entry-Level M.D. Spots	661	Avg. Res. Work Hours/Week	71
% Women Residents	9	Programs with Childcare	53
Avg. Ratio of Full-Time Physician		Programs Offering a "Primary	
Faculty to Residents	0.7	Care Track"	4
% Training in Hospital Outpatient		Programs Offering Multiple	
Clinics	32	Start Dates	5
% Training in Non-Hospital		Programs Allowing Moonlighting	32
Community Ambulatory Clinics	5	Alt./Comp. Med Curriculum	30

ADULT RECONSTRUCTIVE ORTHOPEDICS (F)

ACGME-Approved Programs	14	AOA-Approved Programs	0
1st-Yr. Spots for M.D. Students	0	Funded Entry-Level D.O. Spots	0
Adv. Spots Avail. to M.D. Students	0	% IMG Residents	37
All Entry-Level M.D. Spots	27	Avg. Res. Work Hours/Week	53
% Women Residents	0	% Training in Non-Hospital	
Avg. Ratio of Full-Time Physician		Community Ambulatory Clinics	14
Faculty to Fellows	2.2		
% Training in Hospital Outpatient			
Clinics	27		

MUSCULOSKELETAL ONCOLOGY (F)

ACGME-Approved Programs	9	AOA-Approved Programs	0
1st-Yr. Spots for M.D. Students	0	Funded Entry-Level D.O. Spots	0
Adv. Spots Avail. to M.D. Students	0	% IMG Residents	33
All Entry-Level M.D. Spots	12	Avg. Res. Work Hours/Week	47
% Women Residents	33	% Training in Non-Hospital	
Avg. Ratio of Full-Time Physician		Community Ambulatory Clinics	13
Faculty to Fellows	3.5		
% Training in Hospital Outpatient			
Clinics	47		

ORTHOPEDIC SURGERY OF THE SPINE (F)

ACGME-Approved Programs	12	AOA-Approved Programs	0
1st-Yr. Spots for M.D. Students	0	Funded Entry-Level D.O. Spots	0
Adv. Spots Avail. to M.D. Students	0	% IMG Residents	23
All Entry-Level M.D. Spots	27	Avg. Res. Work Hours/Week	49
% Women Residents	0	Programs Offering Multiple	
Avg. Ratio of Full-Time Physician		Start Dates	2
Faculty to Fellows	2.9	% Training in Non-Hospital	
% Training in Hospital Outpatient		Community Ambulatory Clinics	1
Clinics	31		

PEDIATRIC ORTHOPEDICS (F)

ACGME-Approved Programs	23	AOA-Approved Programs	0
1st-Yr. Spots for M.D. Students	0	Funded Entry-Level D.O. Spots	0
Adv. Spots Avail. to M.D. Students	0	% IMG Residents	19
All Entry-Level M.D. Spots	36	Avg. Res. Work Hours/Week	42
% Women Residents	19	Programs Offering Multiple	
Avg. Ratio of Full-Time Physician		Start Dates	4
Faculty to Fellows	5.1	% Training in Non-Hospital	
% Training in Hospital Outpatient		Community Ambulatory Clinics	12
Clinics	42		

For more information, contact:

- American Academy of Orthopaedic Surgeons, (800) 346-2267; www.aaos.org.
- American Osteopathic Academy of Orthopedics, (800) 741-2626; www.aoao.org.

Otolaryngology****

Specialty Overview: Otolaryngologists, or Head and Neck Surgeons, specialize in the evaluation and treatment of medical and surgical problems of the head and neck region, including disorders of the ears, upper respiratory tract, and upper GI tract. The specialty is frequently referred to as ENT (Ear, Nose, & Throat). Practitioners have a substantial office practice with varying amounts of surgery, which is mostly performed in an ambulatory setting. Most practitioners have few inpatients. Since managed care organizations have targeted some of this specialty's common procedures, such as tympanotomies, for decreased use, the field may become over-staffed. Otolaryngologists average 52 hours per week doing patient care.

Training: Training consists of one or two years of General Surgery followed by three or four years of ENT training. Two-year fellowships and certification are available in Neurotology (11 programs) and Pediatric Otolaryngology (5 programs). Additional fellowships are available in Facial Plastic & Reconstructive Surgery (37 programs), and in Head & Neck Cancer Surgery. About 25% of all residency graduates take additional fellowship training.

Most Osteopathic Physicians train in the combined specialty of Otolaryngology/Facial Plastic Surgery. One approved program exists for D.O.s in Otolaryngic Allergy. Osteopathic residents who take a "specialty-track" internship in the specialty can shorten their training by one year.

Match: About one-third of ENT programs will go through the 2006 NRMP Match, and most will participate after that. Some subspecialty fellowships use the San Francisco Matching Program, www.sfmatch.org. Internship positions are obtained through the NRMP PGY-1 Match. In recent years, 78% of applicants matched.

OTOLARYNGOLOGY

ACGME-Approved Programs	102	AOA-Approved Programs	0
1st-Yr. Spots for M.D. Students	22	Funded Entry-Level D.O. Spots	0
Adv. Spots Avail. to M.D. Students	247	% IMG Residents	2
All Entry-Level M.D. Spots	269	Avg. Res. Work Hours/Week	65
% Women Residents	21	Programs with Childcare	39
Avg. Ratio of Full-Time Physician		Programs Offering a "Primary	
Faculty to Residents	1.1	Care Track"	8
% Training in Hospital Outpatient		Programs Offering Multiple	
Clinics	42	Start Dates	1
% Training in Non-Hospital		Programs Allowing Moonlighting	23
Community Ambulatory Clinics	5	Alt./Comp. Med Curriculum	20

OTOLARYNGOLOGY/FACIAL PLASTIC SURGERY (D.O.s ONLY)

AOA-Approved Programs	18	Funded Entry-Level D.O. Spots	16

For more information, contact:
- American Academy of Otolaryngology-Head and Neck Surgery, (703) 836-4444; www.entnet.org.
- American Osteopathic Colleges of Ophthalmology, Otorhino-laryngology-Head & Neck Surgery, (800) 455-9404; www.aocoohns.org.

Pain Medicine (F)*

Specialty Overview: Pain Medicine, previously called "Pain Management," is concerned with the study of pain, the prevention of pain, and the evaluation, treatment, and rehabilitation of persons in pain. A Pain Medicine physician serves as a consultant to other physicians but is often the principal treating physician and may provide care at various levels. A relatively new subspecialty of Anesthesiology, Neurology, Physical Medicine & Rehabilitation, and Psychiatry, Pain Medicine has expanded rapidly with the recognition that chronic pain control has often been poorly managed in the past. Specialists work in hospitals and independent pain control clinics, and use a variety of pain management techniques. Pain Medicine physicians average 55 hours per week doing patient care.

Training: Pain Medicine fellowships are one year following the completion of a core residency in one of the sponsoring specialties. The breakdown is: Anesthesiology (97 programs; 197 positions); Physical Medicine and Rehabilitation (8 programs; 17 positions); Neurology (2 programs; 2 positions); and Psychiatry (1 program; 1 position).

Match: Contact programs directly. They are listed in *FREIDA*.

PAIN MEDICINE			
ACGME-Approved Programs	108	AOA-Approved Programs	1
1st-Yr. Spots for M.D. Students	0	Funded Entry-Level D.O. Spots	1
Adv. Spots Avail. to M.D. Students	0	% IMG Residents	49
All Entry-Level M.D. Spots	217	Avg. Res. Work Hours/Week	46
% Women Residents	17	Programs Offering Multiple	
Avg. Ratio of Full-Time Physician		Start Dates	41
Faculty to Fellows	2.6	% Training in Non-Hospital	
% Training in Hospital Outpatient		Community Ambulatory Clinics	8
Clinics	71		

For more information, contact:
- American Academy of Pain Medicine, (847) 375-4731; www.painmed.org.

• American College of Osteopathic Pain Management & Sclerotherapy, Inc., (800) 471-6114; www.acopms.com.

Pathology**

Specialty Overview: Pathologists are laboratory-based physicians who are often said to be the "doctor's doctor." They act as consultants for other physicians, helping them to determine the nature of disease in tissue, body fluids, or the entire organism. They apply the methods of the basic sciences to the detection of disease, but generally have little or no direct contact with (live) patients; they interact with other physicians. Pathologists' lives are generally low-key and there is little or no in-hospital night call.

The field is divided into the areas of *Anatomic Pathology*, i.e., autopsies, Cytopathology, Surgical Pathology (gross and microscopic pathology); and *Clinical Pathology*, i.e., Hematology, Microbiology, Clinical Chemistry, and Blood Banking/Transfusion Medicine. Most Pathologists, especially the Anatomic Pathologists, are hospital-based. Many Pathologists also function as researchers and teachers in university medical centers or medical schools—frequently while also maintaining an active Pathology practice. In the past, the income has been very generous, especially for Clinical Pathology. However, changes in reimbursement have decreased Pathologists' income. Many recent Pathology residency graduates have had difficulty finding desirable positions. Pathologists average 44 hours per week doing clinical work. Among subspecialists, Blood Banking/Transfusion Pathologists average 40 hours per week, Cytopathologists average 44 hours per week, and Forensic Pathologists average 47 hours per week doing clinical work.

Training: A residency can be taken separately in either Clinical Pathology or Anatomic Pathology (three years), or the two can be combined (four years). A "credentialing year" is required prior to taking the Board examination. This is usually taken before beginning a Pathology residency. It can consist of a clinical year, clinical experience, or clinically related research. Subspecialty training following the initial residency is available in Neuropathology (36 programs), which requires two years; and in Forensic Pathology (39 programs), Dermatopathology (see Dermatology), Blood Banking/Transfusion Medicine (48 programs), Chemical Pathology (3 programs), Pediatric Pathology (28 programs), Hematology (see Hematology), Selective Pathology (22 programs), Cytopathology (85 programs), or Medical Microbiology (12 programs), each requiring one year.

Match: Many Pathology programs pressure students to accept a position outside of the NRMP Match (when they come for the interview), even though both the student and the program are obligated by contracts to participate in the Match. In recent years, about 90% of the available PGY-1 positions filled through the NRMP Match; nearly half were filled by foreign graduates. For subspecialty positions, contact the programs directly.

PATHOLOGY, ANATOMIC AND CLINICAL			
ACGME-Approved Programs	151	AOA-Approved Programs	0
1st-Yr. Spots for M.D. Students	633	Funded Entry-Level D.O. Spots	0
Adv. Spots Avail. to M.D. Students	0	% IMG Residents	49
All Entry-Level M.D. Spots	633	Avg. Res. Work Hours/Week	49
% Women Residents	50	Programs with Childcare	66
Avg. Ratio of Full-Time Physician		Programs Offering a "Primary	
Faculty to Residents	1.7	Care Track"	4
% Training in Hospital Outpatient		Programs Offering Multiple	
Clinics	1	Start Dates	34
% Training in Non-Hospital		Programs Allowing Moonlighting	65
Community Ambulatory Clinics	<1	Alt./Comp. Med Curriculum	6

For more information, contact:
- American Osteopathic College of Pathologists, (954) 432-9640; www.iedit.com/profiles/Health-Medical/Am .Osteopathiccollegeofpathologists.
- American Society of Clinical Pathologists, (312) 738-1336; www.ascp.org.
- College of American Pathologists, (800) 323-4040; www.cap.org.

Pediatric Surgery (F)*****

Specialty Overview: Pediatric Surgeons diagnose and treat surgical diseases in children. Depending upon their training, they deal with abdominal, urologic, and thoracic problems, as well as multiple trauma. Because a high volume of patients is needed to support such a specialized practice, most Pediatric Surgeons live in moderate- or large-size cities, and are associated with major medical centers. Since this is a subspecialty of General Surgery, applicants must first complete a General Surgery residency. Pediatric Surgeons average 73 hours per week doing patient care.

Training: Training in Pediatric Surgery is two years in length.

Match: Nearly all programs use the NRMP Pediatric Surgery Fellowship Match. In recent years, 100% of the available positions filled, but only

62% of applicants matched. Rank-order lists are due in April; results are available in May, 14 months before the July starting date.

Other Useful Information: Fellowship directors look for individuals who work well with others, do well in interviews, and who have been favorably recommended (during phone calls) by practicing Pediatric Surgeons known to the directors.

PEDIATRIC SURGERY

ACGME-Approved Programs	31	AOA-Approved Programs	0
1st-Yr. Spots for M.D. Students	0	Funded Entry-Level D.O. Spots	0
Adv. Spots Avail. to M.D. Students	0	% IMG Residents	2
All Entry-Level M.D. Spots	31	Avg. Res. Work Hours/Week	76
% Women Residents	22	% Training in Non-Hospital	
Avg. Ratio of Full-Time Physician		Community Ambulatory Clinics	1
Faculty to Fellows	3.8		
% Training in Hospital Outpatient			
Clinics	17		

For more information, contact:

• American Pediatric Surgical Association, (847) 480-9576; www.eapsa.org.

Pediatrics***

Specialty Overview: Pediatricians take care of pediatric patients. While that may sound circular, it is the only way to describe many Pediatric practices. Pediatricians may at one time have dealt primarily with children, but they have now expanded the scope of their practice to include adolescents and young adults. Twenty-two percent of the average Pediatrician's patients are from 12 to 21 years old. In some cases, Pediatricians continue to care for their patients into adulthood, especially those with illnesses like cystic fibrosis that used to be uniformly fatal during childhood. Pediatricians do a great deal of well-child and preventive care. More recently, they are being asked to fill the often-uncomfortable role of "gatekeeper" or "case manager" for prepaid health plans. In this position, they determine their patients' access to care.

Progressively fewer Pediatricians are opting for solo private practice, with two-thirds working in group practices. Much of the intensive exposure to ill children seen by residents and medical students during their training does not exist for the practicing Pediatrician. Office-based for the most part, Pediatricians rarely utilize surgical techniques such as suturing or fracture reduction. More women and fewer IMGs are entering this field.

The average Pediatrician, in a 44-hour work week, spends more than half of the time on office visits and the rest on non-clinical care activities, hospital rounds, and additional clinical activities. Pediatrics is one of the lowest paying medical specialties. Most Pediatricians choose this field because they love working with children. The field has grown 68% in the past 15 years, in part because the number of subspecialty fellowships have increased by 56%.

Training: Initial Pediatric residency training is three years. The *NRMP Directory* lists 87 positions as "Pediatrics–Primary." These positions are integrated into normal Pediatric programs, but offer slightly more outpatient and continuity clinic experience. Graduates of both types of programs take the same Board examination. There are also four-year residencies combining Pediatrics with Internal Medicine. Some five-year programs combine Pediatrics with Dermatology, Emergency Medicine, Psychiatry/Child Psychiatry, Medical Genetics, or Physical Medicine & Rehabilitation. (*See* listings under Internal Medicine, Emergency Medicine, and Child/Adolescent Psychiatry for additional information.) Osteopathic residents who take a "specialty-track" internship in Pediatrics can shorten their training by one year.

Following initial Pediatric residency training, more than one-third of all graduates specialize. Subspecialty training (each is two to three years long) following the initial residency is available in: Developmental–Behavioral Pediatrics (22 programs), Neonatal–Perinatal Medicine (97 programs), Pediatric Cardiology (48 programs), Pediatric Critical Care Medicine (59 programs), Pediatric Emergency Medicine (44 programs), Pediatric Endocrinology (66 programs), Pediatric Gastroenterology (51 programs), Pediatric Hematology–Oncology (60 programs), Pediatric Nephrology (37 programs), Pediatric Pulmonology (46 programs), and Sports Medicine (8 programs).

Fellowships are also possible in Adolescent Medicine (25 programs), Allergy–Immunology, Pediatric Infectious Diseases (62 programs), and Pediatric Rheumatology (25 programs). Child Neurology (72 programs; see "Child Neurology") training can be started after two years of a Pediatrics residency.

Match: In recent years, about 97% of the available PGY-1 positions filled through the NRMP Match; more than 25% of the positions were filled by foreign medical graduates. Fellowships in Pediatric Cardiology, Pediatric Critical Care Medicine, Pediatric Emergency Medicine, Pediatric Hematology–Oncology, and Pediatric Rheumatology go through the NRMP Specialties Matching Program.

PEDIATRICS			
ACGME-Approved Programs	204	AOA-Approved Programs	15
1st-Yr. Spots for M.D. Students	2,868	Funded Entry-Level D.O. Spots	42
Adv. Spots Avail. to M.D. Students	0	% IMG Residents	30
All Entry-Level M.D. Spots	2,868	Avg. Res. Work Hours/Week	69
% Women Residents	67	Programs with Childcare	86
Avg. Ratio of Full-Time Physician		Programs Offering a "Primary	
Faculty to Residents	1.8	Care Track"	60
% Training in Hospital Outpatient		Programs Offering Multiple	
Clinics	37	Start Dates	51
% Training in Non-Hospital		Programs Allowing Moonlighting	94
Community Ambulatory Clinics	11	Alt./Comp. Med Curriculum	72

For more information, contact:

- American Academy of Pediatrics, (847) 434-4000; www.aap.org.
- American College of Osteopathic Pediatricians, (312) 202-8188; www.acopeds.org.

Physical Medicine and Rehabilitation***

Specialty Overview: Physiatrists (specialists in Physical Medicine & Rehabilitation, or PM&R) deal with the diagnosis, evaluation, and treatment of patients with impairments or disabilities that involve musculoskeletal, neurologic, cardiovascular, or other body systems. Physiatrists diagnose and treat patients of all ages with: (1) musculoskeletal pain syndromes, industrial and sports injuries, degenerative arthritis, or lower back pain; (2) severe impairments amenable to rehabilitation from strokes, spinal cord and brain injuries, amputations, and multiple trauma; and (3) electrodiagnosis (i.e., EMG, nerve conduction, somatosensory evoked potentials). The Physiatrist's goal is to maximize the patient's physical, psychosocial, and job-related recovery, as well as to alleviate pain. Depending upon their practice, they may have frequent or no night call. Physiatrists average 48 hours per week doing patient care.

Training: Residency training is four years. This can be either three years following at least one year of prior training or a straight four-year program. Program details are listed on *FREIDA*. There are combined programs in Internal Medicine–PM&R (6 programs), Pediatrics–PM&R (5 programs), and Neurology–PM&R. Following residency, fellowship training is available in Pain Medicine (8 programs), Pediatric Rehabilitation Medicine (2 programs), and Spinal Cord Injury Medicine (21 programs).

Osteopathic physicians can also take training in Neuromuscular Medicine or take an extra year (+1) of Osteopathic Manipulative Medicine (OMM) after an AOA-approved residency. Many D.O.s with advanced training in these techniques have the "problem" of too many patients seeking their services. Some programs allow M.D.s to apply.

Match: In recent years, about 95% of the available PGY-1 positions filled through the NRMP Match. Of the PGY-2 positions available through the NRMP Match, about 90% filled in the Match; nearly half are filled by foreign medical graduates.

Other Useful Information: Many more PM&R positions are available than there are residency graduates to fill them.

PHYSICAL MEDICINE AND REHABILITATION

ACGME-Approved Programs	79	AOA-Approved Programs	3
1st-Yr. Spots for M.D. Students	78	Funded Entry-Level D.O. Spots	9
Adv. Spots Avail. to M.D. Students	278	% IMG Residents	45
All Entry-Level M.D. Spots	356	Avg. Res. Work Hours/Week	50
% Women Residents	36	Programs with Childcare	30
Avg. Ratio of Full-Time Physician		Programs Offering a "Primary	
Faculty to Residents	1.0	Care Track"	1
% Training in Hospital Outpatient		Programs Offering Multiple	
Clinics	24	Start Dates	19
% Training in Non-Hospital		Programs Allowing Moonlighting	40
Community Ambulatory Clinics	5	Alt./Comp. Med Curriculum	43

FAMILY MEDICINE–OMM or –OMT

AOA-Approved Programs	7	Funded Entry-Level D.O. Spots	23

NEUROMUSCULAR MEDICINE

AOA-Approved Programs	15	Funded Entry-Level D.O. Spots	43

For more information, contact:

- American Academy of Physical Medicine and Rehabilitation, (312) 464-9700; www.aapmr.org.
- American Osteopathic Board of Neuromusculoskeletal Medicine; (317) 879-1881; www.academyofosteopathy.org.
- American Osteopathic College of Physical Medicine and Rehabilitation, (847) 825-2515; www.aocpmr.org.
- Association of Academic Physiatrists, (410) 637-8300; www.physiatry.org.

Plastic Surgery (F)*****

Specialty Overview: Plastic Surgeons operatively treat disfigurements of the body, whether they are congenital, traumatically induced, or caused by aging. This area of Surgery is as much an art as a science, and an artist's vision is said to be necessary to excel in the field. Microsurgery and liposuction are two of the newer techniques being used in both reconstructive and cosmetic surgery. There is a large amount of night call to the emergency room, especially early in a practitioner's career. Much of Plastic Surgery is done on an ambulatory basis. While the field is quite lucrative at present, Plastic Surgery is expected to have many more practitioners than necessary in the near future. Plastic Surgeons average 56 hours per week doing patient care.

Training: Plastic Surgery offers two routes for training. The "integrated" route is aimed at senior medical students who match at the PGY-1 level. These programs, which use the NRMP Match and Electronic Residency Application Service (ERAS), accept medical students into five- or six-year Plastic Surgery programs. The "independent" route is for those who first complete at least three years of General Surgery or an entire Otolaryngology or Orthopedic Surgery residency. They then have at least two, and often three, years of Plastic Surgery training. The "independent" programs use the San Francisco Match and the Centralized Application Service (CAS).

Individual "independent" programs vary in their preferences regarding previous training. They all accept applicants who have completed General Surgery training, and most accept those who have completed Otolaryngology or Orthopedic residencies. Many programs will consider candidates with four years of General Surgery; some, mainly the three-year programs, accept applicants with only three years of General Surgery.

Applicants must ascertain the minimum requirements by contacting each program and obtaining the "Preliminary Evaluation of Training" form from the American Board of Plastic Surgery (www.abplsurg.org). This form must be completed prior to applying for residencies. Individuals with more training have a better chance of getting a position. Applicants should visit the website of the Association of Academic Chairmen of Plastic Surgery for more details.

Postgraduate fellowships and certification are available in Hand Surgery (14 programs). Additional training in Plastic Surgery and fellowships in Craniofacial Surgery (65 programs), Microsurgery, and Burn Surgery are also available following completion of the primary Plastic

Surgery residency. Osteopathic physicians can also train in Otolaryngology/Facial Plastic Surgery (see Otolaryngology).

Match: About 40% of entry-level positions are available to medical students through the NRMP Match. The rest are reserved for residents already in or about to complete their surgical training. These are available through the Plastic Surgery Matching Program, www.sfmatch.org.

PLASTIC SURGERY			
ACGME-Approved Programs	90	AOA-Approved Programs	2
1st-Yr. Spots for M.D. Students	81	Funded Entry-Level D.O. Spots	5
Adv. Spots Avail. to M.D. Students	1	% IMG Residents	6
All Entry-Level M.D. Spots	207	Avg. Res. Work Hours/Week	63
% Women Residents	19	Programs with Childcare	27
Avg. Ratio of Full-Time Physician		Programs Offering a "Primary	
Faculty to Residents/Fellows	1.3	Care Track"	3
% Training in Hospital Outpatient		Programs Offering Multiple	
Clinics	22	Start Dates	2
% Training in Non-Hospital		Programs Allowing Moonlighting	11
Community Ambulatory Clinics	7	Alt./Comp. Med Curriculum	4

For more information, contact:

- American Academy of Facial & Reconstructive Surgery, (800) 332-3223; www.aafprs.org.
- American College of Osteopathic Surgeons, (800) 888-1312; www.facos.org.
- American Society of Plastic & Reconstructive Surgeons, (800) 766-4955; www.plasticsurgery.org.
- Association of Academic Chairmen of Plastic Surgery, (703) 820-7400; www.aacplasticsurgery.org.

Preventive Medicine, General*

Specialty Overview: Preventive Medicine requires entry through one of its four subspecialties; General Preventive Medicine is one of these. (The others are Public Health, Aerospace Medicine, and Occupational Medicine.) Physicians in this field are committed to population-based approaches to disease prevention and health promotion. Training includes both clinical preventive medicine and education in epidemiology, biostatistics, informatics, environmental health, health promotion and disease prevention, and research. These physicians work in primary care settings, managed care organizations, public health, government agencies, industry, and academia.

In some cases, Family Medicine programs have made arrangements so that training in both specialties can take place concurrently. Two sub-specialty certifications are now available in Preventive Medicine: Medical Toxicology (4 programs) and Undersea & Hyperbaric Medicine (1 program). Preventive Medicine specialists average 30 hours per week in clinical work.

Training: At least one year of clinical training and a Master of Public Health or equivalent degree are required to complete the program and to be eligible to take the specialty examination.

Match: More programs in General Preventive Medicine participate in the NRMP Match than in the other Preventive Medicine subspecialties. Most physicians begin the two-year programs after some other clinical training. Applicants can usually make arrangements with individual programs to begin at the PGY-2 level. The intern year is obtained through the NRMP PGY-1 Match.

PREVENTIVE MEDICINE, ALL TYPES

ACGME-Approved Programs	67	AOA-Approved Programs	0
1st-Yr. Spots for M.D. Students	4	Funded Entry-Level D.O. Spots	0
Adv. Spots Avail. to M.D. Students	4	% IMG Residents	19
All Entry-Level M.D. Spots	234	Avg. Res. Work Hours/Week	38
% Women Residents	42	Programs with Childcare	24
Avg. Ratio of Full-Time Physician		Programs Offering Multiple	
Faculty to Residents/Fellows	3.3	Start Dates	29
% Training in Hospital Outpatient		Programs Allowing Moonlighting	41
Clinics	15	Alt./Comp. Med Curriculum	19
% Training in Non-Hospital			
Community Ambulatory Clinics	17		

For more information, contact:

- American College of Preventive Medicine, (202) 466-2044; www.acpm.org.
- American Osteopathic College of Occupational and Preventive Medicine, (800) 558-8686; www.aocopm.org.

Psychiatry**

Specialty Overview: Psychiatrists diagnose and treat disorders of the mind. They deal with the entire spectrum of mental illness, from mild situational problems to severe, incapacitating psychotic illnesses. Psychiatrists practice in a variety of settings, including private offices, community mental health centers, psychiatric hospitals, prisons, and substance abuse programs. The majority are office- rather than hospital-based. While there may be night call, it is easier than it might otherwise be, since many Psychiatrists use other health care workers to screen their calls for them. The wide diversity of new potent psychotropic medications has given the Psychiatrist a powerful pharmacological armamentarium. Treatment results that would have been unbelievable a few years ago can often be obtained, and many more disease-specific drugs are anticipated in the future. This may increase the ties between Psychiatry and other types of clinical practice. There are many job openings for Psychiatry residency graduates.

Only about 3% of medical students choose to specialize in Psychiatry, primarily due to their perceptions that treatments have little efficacy, that their ability to treat many patients will be limited due to healthcare "reform," and that the specialty lacks status within the profession. Those who go into Psychiatry do so because of the intellectual challenge, a desire to return to a humanities/social science background, the novel and unique problems, or because they want to treat the "whole person." Psychiatrists average 40 hours per week doing patient care.

Training: Training is three years following a clinical internship that is usually very similar in structure to a Transitional year. The residency consists not only of training in Psychiatry, but also a significant amount in Neurology. Subspecialty fellowships and certification are available in Addiction Psychiatry (14 programs), Forensic Psychiatry (42 programs), Geriatric Psychiatry (60 programs), Psychosomatic Medicine (14 programs), and Pain Medicine (1 program). Seventeen programs combine Psychiatry with Internal Medicine, ten combine Psychiatry with Family Medicine, and ten combine Neurology and Psychiatry.

Fellowships exist in Child & Adolescent Psychiatry (115 programs) for both M.D.s and D.O.s, and consist of a minimum of two years of Child & Adolescent Psychiatry in addition to at least two years (following internship) of general Psychiatry. The Child & Adolescent Psychiatry training can start any time after the internship year. There are also nine programs with five years of training that combine Pediatrics, Psychiatry, and Child Psychiatry. All Psychiatry, Child & Adolescent Psychiatry, and other subspecialty programs are listed in *FREIDA*.

Match: In recent years, about 95% of the available PGY-1 positions filled through the NRMP Match; more than one-third of the positions were filled by foreign medical graduates.

PSYCHIATRY

ACGME-Approved Programs	181	AOA-Approved Programs	4
1st-Yr. Spots for M.D. Students	1,383	Funded Entry-Level D.O. Spots	7
Adv. Spots Avail. to M.D. Students	6	% IMG Residents	42
All Entry-Level M.D. Spots	1,389	Avg. Res. Work Hours/Week	52
% Women Residents	51	Programs with Childcare	63
Avg. Ratio of Full-Time Physician Faculty to Residents	1.3	Programs Offering a "Primary Care Track"	17
% Training in Hospital Outpatient Clinics	11	Programs Offering Multiple Start Dates	61
% Training in Non-Hospital Community Ambulatory Clinics	2	Programs Allowing Moonlighting	112
		Alt./Comp. Med Curriculum	72

For more information, contact:

- American College of Osteopathic Neurologists and Psychiatrists, 28595 Orchard Lake Rd., Ste. 200, Farmington Hills, MI 48334, (248) 553-0010, ext. 295.
- American Psychiatric Association, (888) 357-7924; www.psych.org.
- American Society of Addiction Medicine, (301) 656-3920; www.asam.org.

Public Health*

Specialty Overview: Specialists in Public Health, an area of Preventive Medicine, deal with health promotion and disease prevention. They work in governmental and private health agencies, academic institutions, and health service research organizations. They deal with the health problems of entire communities and countries, as well as with those of individual patients. Their goals are to promote health and to understand the risks of disease, injury, disability, and death. They (1) assess information about the community's health, (2) develop comprehensive public health policies, and (3) assure the provision of services necessary to achieve the public health goals. This frequently involves dealing with the administrative and political sides of medicine. This specialty usually has no night call and very low (usually government) pay. The dearth of residency programs (a number have closed due to lack of funding) has made these specialists some of the most sought-after in medicine (although still among the worst paid).

Training: Training in Public Health consists of two years following a clinical internship. One of these years is spent obtaining an advanced degree, usually a Master of Public Health. A fourth year of training, teaching, practice, and/or research is required to take the Board examination.

Some programs in Family Medicine, Internal Medicine, and Pediatrics have dual training with various Preventive Medicine specialties, including Public Health.

Match: For the most part, there is no matching program in Public Health. Applications must be made to the individual programs. Students can arrange to begin a program following a clinical year, which should be obtained through the NRMP PGY-1 Match.

PUBLIC HEALTH			
ACGME-Approved Programs	17	AOA-Approved Programs	1
1st-Yr. Spots for M.D. Students	0	Funded Entry-Level D.O. Spots	3
Adv. Spots Avail. to M.D. Students	0	% IMG Residents	N/A
All Entry-Level M.D. Spots	64	Avg. Res. Work Hours/Week	N/A
% Women Residents	N/A	Programs with Childcare	3
Programs Offering Multiple		Programs Offering a "Primary	
Start Dates	7	Care Track"	2
Programs Allowing Moonlighting	8	Alt./Comp. Med Curriculum	3

For more information, contact:

- American Association of Public Health Physicians, (773) 632-4400; www.aaphp.org.
- American College of Preventive Medicine, (202) 466-2044; www.acpm.org.
- American Osteopathic College of Occupational and Preventive Medicine, (800) 558-8686; www.aocopm.org.

Pulmonary Disease (F)**

Specialty Overview: Pulmonologists diagnose and treat patients with diseases of the lungs in both the in- and out-patient setting. They deal most often with patients having lung cancer, asthma, and many types of chronic lung disease. Pulmonologists, because of their background, often act as full- or part-time Critical Care physicians. The specialty combines patient care and the performance of manipulative procedures with a strong underlying base of physiology. Procedures include: bronchoscopy, endotracheal intubation, management of mechanical ventilators, and placement of pulmonary artery catheters. Night call depends upon the type of practice. Pulmonologists average 51 hours per week (Internists) and 33 hours per week (Pediatricians) doing patient care. Pulmonary Disease–Critical Care physicians average 64 hours per week doing patient care.

Training: Training consists of a two- or three-year fellowship following completion of an Internal Medicine residency or three years following a Pediatric residency. Many adult three-year programs fulfill the requirements for certification in Critical Care as well as Pulmonary Disease (see Critical Care for details). For Osteopathic physicians, training follows internship and two years of an Internal Medicine residency.

Match: Fellowships, both for Pediatric Critical Care and Internal Medicine Pulmonary Disease (with and without Critical Care), go through the NRMP Specialties Matching Services. Virtually all Internal Medicine programs and positions and most Pediatric Critical Care positions are in the Match. Rank order lists are due and results of the Match are released in June, one year prior to the start of the program. Applicants for Pediatric Pulmonology training should contact the programs directly, since this specialty has no match.

PULMONARY DISEASE (INTERNAL MEDICINE)

ACGME-Approved Programs	30	AOA-Approved Programs	2
1st-Yr. Spots for M.D. Students	0	Funded Entry-Level D.O. Spots	3
Adv. Spots Avail. to M.D. Students	0	% IMG Residents	73
All Entry-Level M.D. Spots	117	Avg. Res. Work Hours/Week	48
% Women Residents	24	Programs Offering a "Primary	
Avg. Ratio of Full-Time Physician		Care Track"	1
Faculty to Fellows	2.2	Programs Offering Multiple	
% Training in Hospital Outpatient		Start Dates	4
Clinics	18		
% Training in Non-Hospital			
Community Ambulatory Clinics	1		

PEDIATRIC PULMONOLOGY

ACGME-Approved Programs	46	AOA-Approved Programs	0
1st-Yr. Spots for M.D. Students	0	Funded Entry-Level D.O. Spots	0
Adv. Spots Avail. to M.D. Students	0	% IMG Residents	42
All Entry-Level M.D. Spots	57	Avg. Res. Work Hours/Week	47
% Women Residents	41	Programs Offering Multiple	
Avg. Ratio of Full-Time Physician		Start Dates	19
Faculty to Fellows	2.8	% Training in Non-Hospital	
% Training in Hospital Outpatient		Community Ambulatory Clinics	1
Clinics	26		

For more information, contact:

- American College of Chest Physicians, (847) 498-1400; www.chestnet.org.
- Society of Critical Care Medicine, (847) 827-6869; www.sccm.org.

Radiation Oncology*****

Specialty Overview: Radiation Oncologists use radiation therapy in the treatment of malignancies and other diseases. A flood of new information about radiation and cancer biology has made Radiation Oncology a rapidly changing field. While there has previously been a scarcity of Radiation Oncologists, the specialty is now close to equilibrium. Radiation Oncologists have relatively little night call, and average 50 hours per week doing patient care.

Training: Training lasts four years after internship.

Match: Medical students obtain PGY-2 positions through the NRMP Match and usually must match separately with their first-year programs (internships). In recent years, about 98% of the PGY-2 positions available through the NRMP Match filled through the Match.

RADIATION ONCOLOGY

ACGME-Approved Programs	79	AOA-Approved Programs	0
1st-Yr. Spots for M.D. Students	0	Funded Entry-Level D.O. Spots	0
Adv. Spots Avail. to M.D. Students	121	% IMG Residents	8
All Entry-Level M.D. Spots	137	Avg. Res. Work Hours/Week	49
% Women Residents	29	Programs with Childcare	25
Avg. Ratio of Full-Time Physician		Programs Offering a "Primary	
Faculty to Residents	1.2	Care Track"	2
% Training in Hospital Outpatient		Programs Offering Multiple	
Clinics	84	Start Dates	5
% Training in Non-Hospital		Programs Allowing Moonlighting	22
Community Ambulatory Clinics	3	Alt./Comp. Med Curriculum	11

For more information, contact:
- American Osteopathic College of Radiology, (800) 258-AOCR; www.aocr.org.
- American Society for Therapeutic Radiology & Oncology, (800) 962-7876; www.astro.org.

Radiology, Diagnostic****

Specialty Overview: Diagnostic Radiologists use x-rays, ultrasound, magnetic fields, and other forms of energy to make diagnoses. While they still learn to read basic radiographs, Diagnostic Radiologists must now also learn how to interpret nuclear scans, PET scans, ultrasonography images, CT scans, and MR images. Additionally, they are trained to perform diagnostic and interventional procedures, such as angiography, guided biopsy and drainage procedures, and non-coronary angioplasty. This is an enormous body of knowledge to learn during a residency.

Most practitioners are hospital-based, although Radiologists are beginning to practice out of freestanding diagnostic facilities. Because of the increased demand for emergency CT and ultrasound studies, as well as for interventional procedures, Diagnostic Radiology night call has become very busy at many hospitals, although many studies are now being read via teleradiology from home or by "nighthawks," U.S.-trained radiologists based in countries such as Australia and Israel. Radiology has also joined Obstetrics/Gynecology as one of the most frequently sued specialties.

Diagnostic Radiologists average 50 hours per week doing clinical work. Among subspecialists, Neuroradiologists average 52 hours per week, Pediatric Radiologists average 53 hours per week, and Vascular and Interventional Radiologists average 54 hours per week doing clinical work. The field has only grown 5% in the past 15 years, although this may change as interventional procedures assume a greater role in medical care.

Training: Diagnostic Radiology programs are generally four years of training following internship. Some Diagnostic Radiology programs now require completion of a clinical first year before starting the residency. This first year can be in nearly any clinical area or combination of areas. Osteopathic training is four years after internship. Some ACGME-approved residencies in Diagnostic Radiology provide special competence in Nuclear Radiology after an additional formal year of training. This should not be confused with a residency in Nuclear Medicine, which is a distinct specialty with training only in that area.

Many residents gain an employment edge by taking one-year fellowships in Abdominal Radiology (12 programs), Breast Imaging/Women's Imaging (23 programs), Cardiothoracic Radiology (2 programs), Endovascular Surgical Neuroradiology (3 programs), Magnetic Resonance Imaging (14 programs), Musculoskeletal Radiology (9 programs), Neuroradiology (87 programs), Nuclear Radiology (21 programs), Pediatric Radiology (44 programs), Thoracic Radiology (12 programs), Ultrasound (1 program), or Vascular/Interventional Radiology (101 programs).

Match: The clinical year required before beginning a Diagnostic Radiology residency is obtained through the NRMP PGY-1 Match. In recent years, about 95% of the available positions filled through the NRMP Match. Some of the fellowship programs in Abdominal Radiology, Breast Imaging/Women's Imaging, Magnetic Resonance Imaging, Musculoskeletal Radiology, Pediatric Radiology, Neuroradiology, Special/Combined Programs in Radiology, Thoracic Radiology, Ultrasound, and Vascular/Interventional Radiology go through the NRMP Specialties Matching Service. Rank order lists are due in June, with results announced in July, one year prior to the start date.

RADIOLOGY, DIAGNOSTIC

ACGME-Approved Programs	191	AOA-Approved Programs	14
1st-Yr. Spots for M.D. Students	134	Funded Entry-Level D.O. Spots	25
Adv. Spots Avail. to M.D. Students	884	% IMG Residents	10
All Entry-Level M.D. Spots	1,118	Avg. Res. Work Hours/Week	51
% Women Residents	27	Programs with Childcare	55
Avg. Ratio of Full-Time Physician		Programs Offering a "Primary	
Faculty to Residents	1.3	Care Track"	2
% Training in Hospital Outpatient		Programs Offering Multiple	
Clinics	15	Start Dates	11
% Training in Non-Hospital		Programs Allowing Moonlighting	68
Community Ambulatory Clinics	1	Alt./Comp. Med Curriculum	25

PEDIATRIC RADIOLOGY

ACGME-Approved Programs	44	AOA-Approved Programs	1
1st-Yr. Spots for M.D. Students	0	Funded Entry-Level D.O. Spots	1
Adv. Spots Avail. to M.D. Students	0	% IMG Residents	62
All Entry-Level M.D. Spots	87	Avg. Res. Work Hours/Week	45
% Women Residents	68	% Training in Non-Hospital	
Avg. Ratio of Full-Time Physician		Community Ambulatory Clinics	0
Faculty to Fellows	3.9		
% Training in Hospital Outpatient			
Clinics	15		

For more information, contact:

- American College of Radiology, (800) 227-5463; www.acr.org.
- American Osteopathic College of Radiology, (800) 258-AOCR; www.aocr.org.
- American Roentgen Ray Society, (800) 438-2777; www.arrs.org.

Rheumatology (F)*

Specialty Overview: Rheumatologists diagnose and treat patients with a wide variety of diseases of the joints, soft tissues, and blood vessels. These include the various types of arthritides, both acute and chronic, which can affect individuals. The field has grown in recent years with the increased interest in the autoimmune diseases underlying many rheumatologic conditions. Rheumatology is one of the quieter subspecialties of Internal Medicine and Pediatrics. Yet Rheumatologists often care for very ill patients. There is usually little night call and small primary or consultative inpatient services for those not mixing their Rheumatology practice with General Internal Medicine or Pediatrics. Internist Rheumatologists average 49 hours per week doing patient care.

Training: Training consists of a two-year fellowship following completion of an Internal Medicine residency or three years following a Pediatrics residency. For Osteopathic physicians, training follows internship and two years of an Internal Medicine residency.

Match: About 80% of Rheumatology programs are in the NRMP Medical Specialties Matching Program. Rank order lists are due and the match occurs in June, a year before the program begins.

RHEUMATOLOGY (INTERNAL MEDICINE)

ACGME-Approved Programs	108	AOA-Approved Programs	3
1st-Yr. Spots for M.D. Students	0	Funded Entry-Level D.O. Spots	4
Adv. Spots Avail. to M.D. Students	0	% IMG Residents	38
All Entry-Level M.D. Spots	198	Avg. Res. Work Hours/Week	45
% Women Residents	52	Programs Offering a "Primary	
Avg. Ratio of Full-Time Physician		Care Track"	3
Faculty to Fellows	2.4	Programs Offering Multiple	
% Training in Hospital Outpatient		Start Dates	24
Clinics	52		
% Training in Non-Hospital			
Community Ambulatory Clinics	4		

PEDIATRIC RHEUMATOLOGY

ACGME-Approved Programs	25	AOA-Approved Programs	0
1st-Yr. Spots for M.D. Students	0	Funded Entry-Level D.O. Spots	0
Adv. Spots Avail. to M.D. Students	0	% IMG Residents	41
All Entry-Level M.D. Spots	28	Avg. Res. Work Hours/Week	47
% Women Residents	71	Programs Offering Multiple	
Avg. Ratio of Full-Time Physician		Start Dates	7
Faculty to Fellows	2.1	% Training in Non-Hospital	
% Training in Hospital Outpatient		Community Ambulatory Clinics	4
Clinics	67		

For more information, contact:
- American College of Rheumatology, (404) 633-3777; www.rheumatology.org.
- American Osteopathic College of Rheumatology, Inc., 193 Monroe Ave., Edison, NJ 08820-3755; (732) 494-6688.

Sports Medicine (F)* (Primary Care); (Orthopedic Surgery)***

Specialty Overview: Sports Medicine fellowships are available under the auspices of Emergency Medicine (3 programs), Family Medicine (68 programs), Internal Medicine (2 programs), and Pediatrics (8 programs). Family Medicine, Internal Medicine, and Pediatrics. This specialty is sometimes called (by the NRMP as well as others) "Primary Care Sports Medicine" to distinguish it from Orthopedic Surgery's Sports Medicine subspecialty. Specialists in this area diagnose and treat non-operative sports-related injuries. They also emphasize prevention and rehabilitation. Some perform epidemiological studies to determine the best preventive methods. Many practitioners incorporate Sports Medicine into their existing practices by offering fitness evaluations, acting as team physicians, or working with recreational athletes. Primary Care Sports Medicine physicians average 41 hours per week doing patient care.

Orthopedic Sports Medicine is a subspecialty of Orthopedic Surgery. These practitioners perform many of the same preventive and therapeutic measures as other Sports Medicine physicians; in addition, they treat injuries surgically when necessary. Orthopedic Sports Medicine physicians average 55 hours per week doing patient care.

Training: Primary Care Sports Medicine training (nearly all under the auspices of Family Medicine) is one year after the initial residency. Orthopedic Sports Medicine is a one-year fellowship following the completion of an Orthopedic Surgery residency. There are three combined Osteopathic Family Medicine–Sports Medicine programs with seven positions.

Match: Most Primary Care Sports Medicine programs are in the NRMP Specialties Match. In recent years, 69% of applicants matched and 94% of available positions filled. Results are available in the January before the start date.

Applicants to Orthopedic Sports Medicine fellowships should contact programs directly. A list of programs for both adult and Pediatric Rheumatology is on *FREIDA*.

ORTHOPEDIC SPORTS MEDICINE***

ACGME-Approved Programs	60	AOA-Approved Programs	0
1st-Yr. Spots for M.D. Students	0	Funded Entry-Level D.O. Spots	0
Adv. Spots Avail. to M.D. Students	0	% IMG Residents	5
All Entry-Level M.D. Spots	149	Avg. Res. Work Hours/Week	44
% Women Residents	4	Programs Offering Multiple	
Avg. Ratio of Full-Time Physician		Start Dates	8
Faculty to Fellows	3.1	% Training in Non-Hospital	
% Training in Hospital Outpatient		Community Ambulatory Clinics	27
Clinics	34		

PRIMARY CARE SPORTS MEDICINE*			
ACGME-Approved Programs	81	AOA-Approved Programs	10
1st-Yr. Spots for M.D. Students	0	Funded Entry-Level D.O. Spots	20
Adv. Spots Avail. to M.D. Students	0	% IMG Residents	5
All Entry-Level M.D. Spots	111	Avg. Res. Work Hours/Week	N/A
% Women Residents	37	Programs Offering Multiple	
Avg. Ratio of Full-Time Physician		Start Dates	3
Faculty to Fellows	4.0	% Training in Non-Hospital	
% Training in Hospital Outpatient		Community Ambulatory Clinics	48
Clinics	37		

For more information, contact:

- American College of Sports Medicine, (317) 637-9200;
  www.acsm.org.
- American Orthopaedic Society for Sports Medicine,
  www.sportsmed.org.
- American Osteopathic Academy of Sports Medicine,
  (608) 831-4400; www.aoasm.org.

Surgery, General****

Specialty Overview: General Surgeons primarily diagnose and treat diseases and injuries of the abdominal organs and of the soft tissues and vasculature of the neck and trunk. They are also usually called in to manage, often in concert with other surgical specialists, patients suffering injuries to more than one body area. In rural settings, the General Surgeon may still be "General," doing Orthopedic, Urologic, and, occasionally, Thoracic or Neurosurgical procedures. But for the most part, today's General Surgeon primarily works in the abdomen, on the breast, on the peripheral vasculature, on the skin, and, in some cases, on the neck. Increasingly, endoscopic and other minimally invasive surgical techniques are being used. Not all General Surgery residencies are prepared to thoroughly teach these valuable techniques.

During their 60-hour average work week in private practice, Surgeons spend about half their time on office visits, a third in surgery, and the rest on hospital rounds and other patient care activities. Nearly all surgical specialties are oversupplied with practitioners for the perceived need in the population. Yet there are still many areas of the country that are underserved by surgeons. The number of General Surgeons has decreased by more than 1% over the past fifteen years.

Training: Training in General Surgery is usually five years after medical school. It is four years after internship for Osteopathic physicians. "Categorical" General Surgery residency positions, designed for those interested in completing an entire General Surgery residency, have become relatively difficult to obtain. More than half of the available Surgery PGY-1 positions are "Preliminary" spots that only guarantee training for one or two years. They are designed for those wishing to enter other fields, particularly other surgical specialties.

Subspecialty fellowships and certification are available in Surgery of the Hand, Pediatric Surgery, Surgical Critical Care, and Vascular Surgery. Other fellowships are available in Trauma Surgery (26 programs), Minimally Invasive and Gastrointestinal Surgery (96 programs), and Abdominal Transplant Surgery (45 programs). Some educators now feel that the lack of continuity of care has harmed surgical training programs in markets dominated by managed care. Residents rarely see the same patients in the clinic, in the hospital, and during follow-up visits.

Match: In recent years, about 99% of the available Categorical PGY-1 positions in General Surgery filled through the NRMP Match. Of the available Preliminary General Surgery positions, about 65% filled through the NRMP Match. Most surgical fellowship programs, except Trauma (see Trauma Surgery), are available through the NRMP Specialties Match.

SURGERY, GENERAL

ACGME-Approved Programs	252	AOA-Approved Programs	37
1st-Yr. Spots for M.D. Students(C)	1,051	Funded Entry-Level D.O. Spots	72
1st-Yr. Spots for M.D. Students(P)	1,331	% IMG Residents	22
Adv. Spots Avail. to M.D. Students	0	Avg. Res. Work Hours/Week	77
All Entry-Level M.D. Spots	2,382	Programs with Childcare	104
% Women Residents	24	Programs Offering a "Primary	
Avg. Ratio of Full-Time Physician		Care Track"	9
Faculty to Residents	0.9	Programs Offering Multiple	
% Training in Hospital Outpatient		Start Dates	20
Clinics	19	Programs Allowing Moonlighting	40
% Training in Non-Hospital		Alt./Comp. Med Curriculum	43
Community Ambulatory Clinics	4		

For more information, contact:

- American College of Surgeons, (312) 202-5000; www.facs.org.
- American College of Osteopathic Surgeons, (800) 888-1312; www.facos.org.

Thoracic Surgery (F)**

Specialty Overview: Thoracic, or Cardiothoracic, Surgeons operatively treat diseases and injuries of the heart, lungs, mediastinum, esophagus, chest wall, diaphragm, and great vessels. The most common surgery that these specialists perform is coronary artery bypass grafting. The other common procedures include cardiac surgery for acquired valvular disease or congenital cardiac defects, pulmonary surgery for malignancies, and surgery for trauma to intrathoracic organs. Some also perform heart and lung transplants. Postoperative care for all these patients is usually the responsibility of the Thoracic Surgeon, although they may share the duties with Critical Care physicians and Cardiologists. As might be expected from the nature of the diseases treated, very long and erratic hours are often necessary. This results in Thoracic Surgery being one of the most time-consuming and stressful of all the specialties. Those in the field, though, generally feel that the rewards are worth the price. Thoracic Surgeons average 67 hours per week doing patient care.

Training: Thoracic Surgery is a subspecialty of General Surgery, and certification in General Surgery is required to take the Thoracic Surgery boards. Training lasts two to three years after completion of a General Surgery residency. Since the process of going through a General Surgery residency is itself grueling, this acts as a major deterrent to many individuals who might otherwise enter this field. Osteopathic programs in Thoracic–Cardiovascular Surgery are two years in length after completing three years of General Surgery and one year of internship.

Match: Thoracic Surgery applicants go through the NRMP Thoracic Surgery Match, with rank order lists due and results announced in June, one year prior to the July start date. In recent years, 96% of applicants matched and 72% of the available positions filled.

THORACIC SURGERY			
ACGME-Approved Programs	97	AOA-Approved Programs	2
1st-Yr. Spots for M.D. Students	0	Funded Entry-Level D.O. Spots	3
Adv. Spots Avail. to M.D. Students	0	% IMG Residents	25
All Entry-Level M.D. Spots	158	Avg. Res. Work Hours/Week	71
% Women Residents	11	Programs with Childcare	33
Avg. Ratio of Full-Time Physician		Programs Offering a "Primary	
Faculty to Fellows	2.7	Care Track"	1
% Training in Hospital Outpatient		Programs Offering Multiple	
Clinics	12	Start Dates	7
% Training in Non-Hospital		Programs Allowing Moonlighting	4
Community Ambulatory Clinics	1	Alt./Comp. Med Curriculum	13

For more information, contact:

- American College of Osteopathic Surgeons, (800) 888-1312; www.facos.org.
- Society of Thoracic Surgeons, (312) 202-5800; www.sts.org.

Trauma Surgery (F)**

Specialty Overview: While not yet an official subspecialty, Trauma Surgery is one of the fastest growing areas in Surgery. With the wide institution of trauma centers, there is an increasing need for Surgeons with training in the treatment of patients with multiple injuries. Trauma Surgeons are generally the operating surgeon for patients with major injuries. In addition, they oversee and coordinate the large team responsible for both these patients' initial and the postoperative care. In-hospital call is usually required on a frequent basis. As with firefighters, there is often the need to immediately go to full speed from a dead stop. Long hours are required, and family life can be difficult. Most Trauma Surgeons are in medium- to large-sized cities.

Training: Training normally consists of a one- or two-year fellowship at a major trauma center following a General Surgery residency. Many Trauma Surgery fellowships are combined with training in Critical Care or with research. At the present time, most practicing Trauma Surgeons have not completed such a fellowship. The necessity for completion of such a fellowship in the future is currently unknown. A list of fellowship programs that comply with AAST guidelines and with Critical Care requirements, as well as other available fellowships, can be found at www.aast.org/fellow.html.

Match: Fellowships are arranged on an individual basis during the third or fourth year of General Surgery training.

TRAUMA SURGERY			
ACGME-Approved Programs	0	AOA-Approved Programs	0
AAST-Approved Programs	26	Funded Entry-Level D.O. Spots	0
1st-Yr. Spots for M.D. Students	0	% IMG Residents	N/A
Adv. Spots Avail. to M.D. Students	0	Avg. Res. Work Hours/Week	N/A
All Entry-Level M.D. Spots	42	% Women Residents	N/A

For more information, contact:

- American Association for the Surgery of Trauma, http://aast.org/fellowships/AAST_Fellowships.html.

Urology****

Specialty Overview: Urologists diagnose and treat diseases of and injuries to the kidney, ureters, bladder, and urethra. In males, they also treat disorders of the prostate and genitals. Often they work in concert with Nephrologists (Internists and Pediatricians) and have both a surgical and non-surgical practice. Renal transplantation, investigations into fertility and male sexuality, and the use of non-invasive techniques (such as lithotripsy) are expanding areas within the field. Urologists have a moderate amount of night call and often have small inpatient services, since much of Urologic Surgery is now done in an ambulatory setting. Urologists average 56 hours per week doing patient care. The number of Urologists has increased 13% in the past 15 years.

Training: Urology training generally consists of two years of General Surgery followed by at least three years of Urology. The preliminary (first two) surgical years are at the same institution as the Urology training in about half of the programs. Eighteen programs offer Pediatric Urology fellowships. Osteopathic residents who take a "specialty-track" internship in Urology can shorten their training by one year.

Match: Urology has a separate Match run through The American Urological Association Residency Matching Program, www.auanet.org. There is a $75 application fee, and rank-order lists are submitted by early January. The results of the Match are released in late January, before participants must submit their NRMP Rank-Order Lists. The Urology Matching Program also has a list of current vacancies on its website. In recent years, 100% of positions filled and 67% of applicants obtained positions.

Applicants generally must participate in the NRMP PGY-1 Match to obtain their preliminary surgical positions. Most of the Urology positions listed as being available to medical students through the NRMP PGY-1 Match are for individuals who have already matched at that institution in Urology through the specialty's Match, since most programs require the "pre-Urology" training to be completed at their institution. These are usually Preliminary Surgery positions.

UROLOGY

ACGME-Approved Programs	120	AOA-Approved Programs	5
1st-Yr. Spots for M.D. Students	19	Funded Entry-Level D.O. Spots	32
Adv. Spots Avail. to M.D. Students	232	% IMG Residents	5
All Entry-Level M.D. Spots	251	Avg. Res. Work Hours/Week	65
% Women Residents	14	Programs with Childcare	42
Avg. Ratio of Full-Time Physician		Programs Offering a "Primary	
Faculty to Residents	1.0	Care Track"	3
% Training in Hospital Outpatient		Programs Offering Multiple	
Clinics	34	Start Dates	4
% Training in Non-Hospital		Programs Allowing Moonlighting	29
Community Ambulatory Clinics	5	Alt./Comp. Med Curriculum	26

For more information, contact:

- American College of Osteopathic Surgeons, (800) 888-1312; www.facos.org.
- American Urological Association, (410) 727-1100; www.auanet.org.

Vascular Surgery (F)**

Specialty Overview: As subspecialists of General Surgery, Vascular Surgeons diagnose and treat diseases of the arterial, venous, and lymphatic systems. Unless they are associated with a very large medical center, specialists in this field often have to perform General Surgery to make a living. This is partly because so many General Surgeons perform Vascular Surgery as a routine part of their practice. Vascular Surgeons average 62 hours per week doing patient care.

Training: Training for M.D.s is one or two years following completion of a General Surgery residency. There currently are seven Osteopathic programs.

Match: The NRMP conducts the Vascular Surgery Specialty Match for residents already in a General Surgery residency. Fourth-year General Surgery residents generally apply for these positions. Nearly all the available positions are in this Match. In recent years, 86% of applicants successfully matched and 79% of the available positions filled in the Match. Rank order lists are due and results of the Match are announced in May, one year prior to the start date.

VASCULAR SURGERY

ACGME-Approved Programs	94	AOA-Approved Programs	7
1st-Yr. Spots for M.D. Students	0	Funded Entry-Level D.O. Spots	11
Adv. Spots Avail. to M.D. Students	0	% IMG Residents	10
All Entry-Level M.D. Spots	117	Avg. Res. Work Hours/Week	62
% Women Residents	9	Programs Offering a "Primary	
Avg. Ratio of Full-Time Physician		Care Track"	2
Faculty to Fellows	3.0	Programs Offering Multiple	
% Training in Hospital Outpatient		Start Dates	1
Clinics	18		
% Training in Non-Hospital			
Community Ambulatory Clinics	2		

For more information, contact:

- American College of Osteopathic Surgeons, (800) 888-1312; www.facos.org.
- Society for Vascular Surgery, (800) 258-7188; http://svs.vascularweb.org.

Women's Health*

Specialty Overview: Female patients are treated by all medical specialists. This new area's goal, according to some advocates, is "to produce physicians with an expertise in clinical, teaching, and research aspects of women's health, and to produce physicians capable of leadership roles in the expanding field of women's health." Another program says it exists to help physicians "provide optimal care for all patients. We were clearly deficient in caring for a major sector of the population, necessitating the establishment of specific women's health activities." Hopefully, Women's Health programs will raise primary care physicians' awareness of those women's healthcare issues that are not directly related to Obstetrics/Gynecology. Whether the extra training will prove worthwhile remains to be seen.

Training: Training in Women's Health is available either combined with an Internal Medicine or a Family Medicine residency (3 years total), or as a two-year fellowship after the completion of residency training in Family Medicine, Internal Medicine, Neurology, Obstetrics/Gynecology, Psychiatry, or Surgery. Virtually all residencies are currently given through Internal Medicine. Various groups sponsor these fellowships, and each program's content depends on their specialty orientation.

While more than 180 primary care programs list themselves as having a "Women's Health Track" (see *FREIDA's* "Optional Criteria"), it is unclear what this actually means in most cases. The numbers in the chart below are from the federal *Directory of Residency and Fellowship Programs in Women's Health* (2004). A list of programs is intermittently available from the U.S. Department of Health & Human Services, Office on Women's Health: www.4women.gov/owh/resfel/index.htm. The ACP/ASIM online directory also lists Internal Medicine programs with Women's Health tracks. There is no subspecialty certification in Women's Health.

Match: All primary care residencies go through the NRMP Match. There is no match for Women's Health fellowships, so applicants should contact programs directly.

INTERNAL MEDICINE–WOMEN'S HEALTH

ACGME-Approved Programs	10	AOA-Approved Programs	0
1st-Yr. Spots for M.D. Students	33	Funded Entry-Level D.O. Spots	0
Adv. Spots Avail. to M.D. Students	0	All Entry-Level M.D. Spots	33

WOMEN'S HEALTH (F)

ACGME-Approved Programs	14	AOA-Approved Programs	0
1st-Yr. Spots for M.D. Students	0	Funded Entry-Level D.O. Spots	0
Adv. Spots Avail. to M.D. Students	0	All Entry-Level M.D. Spots	22

For more information, contact:

- American Medical Women's Association, (703) 838-0500; www.amwa-doc.org.
- Office on Women's Health, U.S. Dept. of Health & Human Services, (202) 690-7650; www.4women.gov/owh/resfel/index.htm.

FIGURE 3.1
Length of Postgraduate Training for M.D. Physicians*

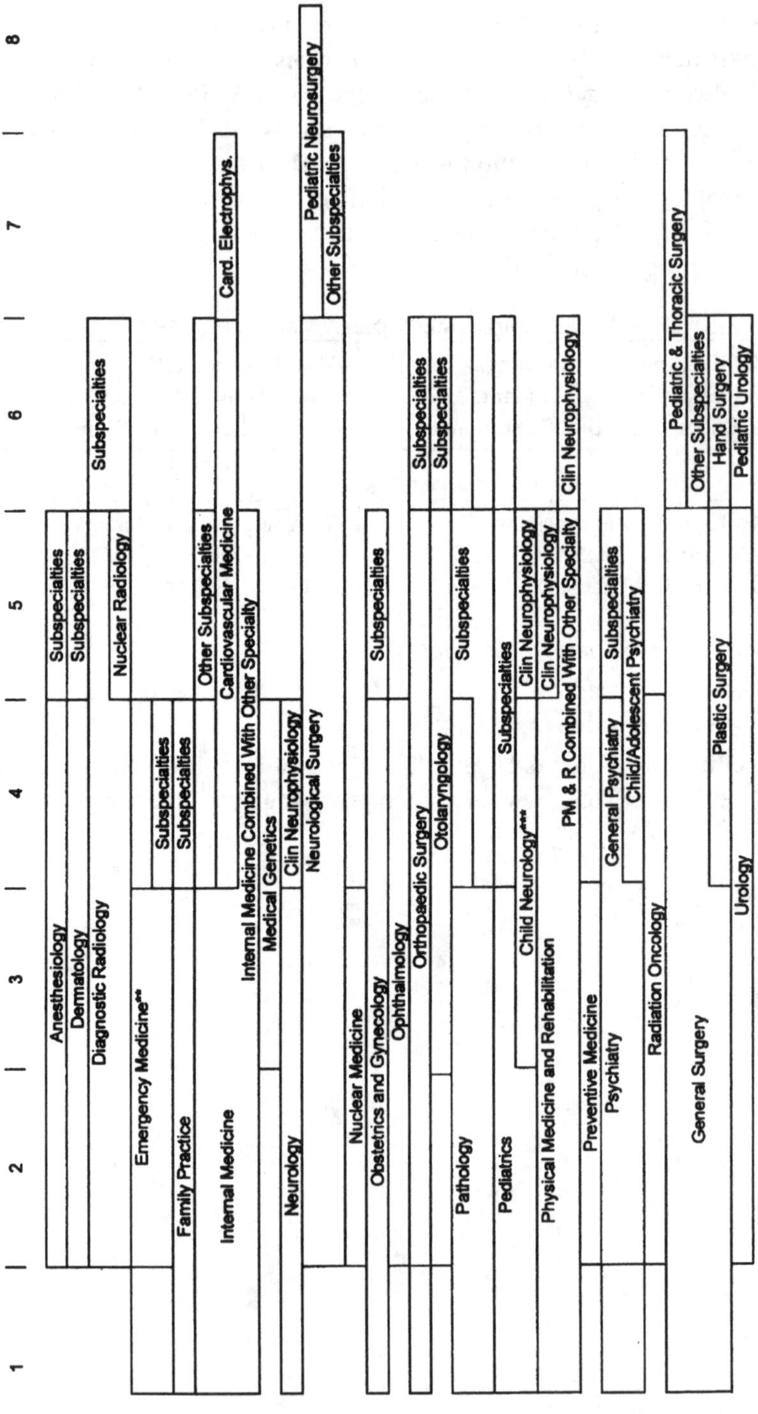

*Many programs offer a broad-based GY-1 and GY-2 years as part of their residencies.
**Emergency Medicine programs may include GY-1 through GY-3, GY-1 through GY-4, or GY-2 through GY-4.
****One broader, adult medicine year may be substituted for one year in Pediatrics.

FIGURE 3.2

Length of Postgraduate Training for Osteopathic (D.O.) Physicians

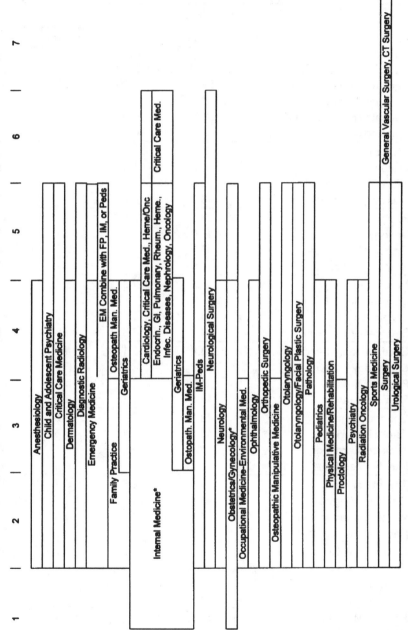

*Nearly all Internal Medicine and OB/Gyn residents take AOA-approved "specialty track" internships to shorten their training by one year.

FIGURE 3.3

Is This Specialty for You?

	% Practitioners saying that they are "Very Satisfied" with their specialty	% Practitioners saying that they are "Dissatisfied" with their their specialty	How satisfied with *current* practice position (1=unsatisfied to 5=very satisfied)	Hours per week doing patient care
Geriatric Medicine (IM)	59.6%	7.0%	3.5	49.3
Geriatric Psychiatry	*	*	4.5	47.7
Neonatal–Perinatal Medicine	58.7	13.0	3.7	52.6
Dermatology	56.1	10.8	3.7	39.6
Thoracic Surgery	53.4	17.8	3.4	66.6
Oncology (IM)	50.5	11.3	3.8	44.7
Infectious Diseases (IM)	50.0	6.3	3.6	42.7
Allergy & Immunology	48.2	10.7	4.1	41.3
Pediatrics	48.1	12.6	3.7	44.0
Urology	48.0	13.8	3.8	55.8
Orthopedic Surgery	47.1	19.3	3.7	60.5
Neurological Surgery	47.0	15.2	3.7	61.7
Nephrology (IM)	46.2	9.0	3.6	55.2
Endocrinology, Diabetes, & Metabolism	44.9	10.2	3.5	44.8
Emergency Medicine	44.4	13.3	3.8	38.7
Occupational Medicine	43.8	15.1	#	#
Cardiology	43.8	16.5	3.7	58.0
Pediatric Surgery	*	*	3.4	73.1
Plastic Surgery	43.3	23.1	3.3	55.7
General Surgery	43.0	20.4	3.5	59.9
Family Medicine	42.8	16.9	3.6	45.5
Pediatric Cardiology	*	*	3.6	43.7
Internal Medicine–Pediatrics	*	*	3.3	50.7
Rheumatology	42.6	18.0	3.7	48.6
Ophthalmology	41.4	21.0	3.5	43.4
Vascular/Interventional Rad.	*	*	3.8	53.5
Hand Surgery (Ortho)	*	*	3.8	59.1
Obstetrics & Gynecology	34.4	24.2	3.7	48.7
Child & Adolescent Psychiatry	40.6	19.8	3.5	41.8
Pathology	*	*	3.8	44.1
Child Neurology	*	*	3.7	40.4
Physical Medicine & Rehabilitation	39.1	12.6	3.7	47.9
Neurology	39.0	16.2	3.6	48.4
Radiology, Diagnostic	*	*	3.8	50.2
Otolaryngology	38.8	25.2	3.8	51.9

FIGURE 3.3 (continued)

	% Practitioners saying that they are "Very Satisfied" with their specialty	% Practitioners saying that they are "Dissatisfied" with their specialty	How satisfied with *current* practice position (1=unsatisfied to 5=very satisfied)	Hours per week doing patient care
Radiation Oncology	*	*	3.6	49.5
Gastroenterology	38.5	19.5	3.8	51.7
Pulmonology–Critical Care	*	*	3.8	63.6
Pediatric Gastroenterology	*	*	4.0	50.0
Psychiatry	38.6	38.6	3.6	40.1
Vascular Surgery	*	*	3.8	61.9
Internal Medicine	36.5	20.3	3.4	49.3
Anesthesiology	*	*	3.7	54.7
Colon & Rectal Surgery	*	*	4.0	54.0
Hematology–Oncology	*	*	3.6	46.6
Pulmonary Diseases	33.3	17.9	3.6	51.2
Preventive Medicine	*	*	4.2	29.8
Hand Surgery (Non-Ortho)	*	*	3.0	56.7
Critical Care (All)	*	*	3.4	65.8
Nuclear Medicine	*	*	3.7	51.9
Pain Medicine	*	*	3.5	54.5
Pediatric Pulmonology	*	*	3.5	33.2
Pediatric Hematology–Oncology	*	*	3.4	39.0
Gynecology	27.3	25.0	#	#
Medical Genetics	#	#	2.0	28.0

(To order specialties, numbers were not rounded, as they were in the specialty descriptions.)

*Position based on 2000 AMA survey data.

#No information available.

Adapted from: *AMA Statistics*, 2002; and Leigh JP, Kravitz RL, Schembri M, Samuels SJ, Mobley S: Physician career satisfaction across specialties. *Arch Intern Med.* 2002;162:1577-84.

4

Choosing A Specialty

"Cheshire puss," she [Alice] began . . .,
"would you please tell me which way I ought to go from here?"
"That depends on where you want to get to," said the cat.

– Lewis Carroll, *Alice's Adventures in Wonderland*

Your Personal Aptitudes—
Assess Them Honestly

THERE ARE SEVERAL METHODS you can use to assess your interests when deciding which specialty is best for you. The first one is the "try it and like it" method. Using this option, a student does a clinical rotation, likes the limited experience, and decides to make that specialty his or her life's work. This can be very misleading.

A single exposure to a specialty can be particularly stimulating because of the attending, resident team, and selection of patients—or unrealistically dismal for the same reasons. In either case, the experience may have very little to do with how well you are suited to the specialty or what the practice of the specialty is really like outside the halls of academia. Yet this is the traditional procedure medical students have used to make their career choices.

This method has, until recently, worked to the advantage of the entire medical system. Most students entered the specialties to which they were exposed during their third-year required rotations (at most schools, these are Internal Medicine, Surgery, Pediatrics, Psychiatry, Neurology, Obstetrics/Gynecology, and Family Medicine). When these were the specialties that needed the most practitioners, this process worked well. However, some of these specialties are currently, or shortly will be, oversubscribed. The available first-year positions in the various specialties (Figure 4.1), though, do not necessarily reflect the number of practitioners each specialty will need. In the case of Internal Medicine, most residents ultimately enter subspecialty practices.

Approximately 8% to 10% of the first-year slots go unfilled each year. Specialties with more "first-year positions" than "PGY-1 positions" generally require other training, such as an internship, before entering the residency. Osteopathic programs require completion of a first year of training before entry into any residency other than a "specialty-specific" program. In 2005, there were approximately 22,000 positions at the PGY-1 level in M.D. and D.O. programs (not counting newly accredited programs) and about 1,000 one-year Transitional PGY-1 positions. Many of the specialties listed in Figure 4.1 have positions beginning in the PGY-2 or subsequent years that are available to medical students through the NRMP or other matching programs.

You may also want to look at Figure 22.2 to see the total number of positions available to medical students (PGY-1 and Advanced Matches), and the total number of entry-level positions that are available to both medical students and those with additional training.

Specialty Interest Tests

The second, and more scientific, method (remember, physicians are supposed to be applied scientists) is to test yourself for your interest profile. This can be done either by taking a formal, standardized test or by self-testing.

The standardized test, the Strong Vocational Interest Inventory: Gough Medical Subspecialty Scales (a Meyers-Briggs-type preference test), is available through many Dean of Students' offices. This test compares your interests with those of current practitioners in approximately seven major specialties. It has been tested and validated on large numbers of individuals practicing in the various specialties and administered to many medical students, most of whom have found it very useful. Some schools use other Meyers-Briggs-type tests. You can access some of these (for additional fees) through the AAMC's Careers in Medicine (http://services.aamc.org/careers inmedicine/). One warning: If you take any Meyers-Briggs-type test in your first or second year of medical school, it has only a fair predictive value. The farther along you are in your training, the more valid the results will be.

A quicker but less-accurate way of assessing your interests is to test yourself by using one of three sources. The first is *How to Choose a Medical Specialty* by Anita Taylor (most medical libraries have a copy). This book contains short descriptions of all the approved specialties and many sub-

FIGURE 4.1

Number of PGY-1 and First-Year
Specialty Positions Offered, 2005–2006

	Positions Available at PGY-1 Level	All Entry-Level Positions
Specialties with Greatest Increase by 2020		
Anesthesiology	654	1,271
Cardiovascular Diseases	0	778
General Internal Medicine (C & P)*	8,347	8,347
Internal Medicine Subspecialties (other than Cardiology)	33	3,364
Other Surgical Specialties	81	1,343
Pathology	633	633
Radiology	134	1,118
Specialties with Moderate Increase by 2020		
Emergency Medicine	1,203	1,502
Family Medicine	3,442	3,442
General Surgery (C & P)*	2,382	2,382
Medical Administration/Non-patient care	0	0
Ophthalmology	0	460
Orthopedic Surgery	610	661
Other "Medical" Specialties	129	3,672
Psychiatry	1,383	1,389
Urology	19	251
Specialties with Smallest Increase by 2020		
Obstetrics/Gynecology	1,238	1,238
Otolaryngology	22	269
Pediatrics	2,868	2,868

*"C" are Categorical positions; "P" are Preliminary positions.
Categories adapted in part from: Bureau of Health Professions, Health Resources and Services Administration. *Changing Demographics: Implications for Physicians, Nurses and Other Health Workers.* Washington, DC: US Dept. of Health and Human Services. Spring 2003. Data gathered from multiple sources.

specialties with a self-assessment quiz for each one. If you do the assessment quiz for all the specialties in the book, you will be able to rank your interests. You can then compare your interests with those of practitioners in the specialty. The second, and better, way to assess your specialty interest is to take the online Pathway Evaluation Program for Medical Professionals (http://medweb.usc.edu/pathways/intro.htm). Finally, the AAMC's Careers in Medicine website (http://services.aamc.org/careersinmedicine/), although at times a bit pedantic, is an excellent, complete, and mostly free source (except for the Myers-Briggs-type testing) to help you evaluate what specialty you may want to enter.

Pathway Evaluation Program for Medical Professionals

The Pathway Evaluation Program for Medical Professionals, once an on-site short course offered by most medical schools, is now available online at http://medweb.usc.edu/pathways/intro.htm. This career-planning program provides medical students with an opportunity to determine what specialties might be the most compatible with their values and interests, helping them make informed specialty decisions. Duke University School of Medicine now administers this program in partnership with Glaxo-SmithKline.

The most interesting part of the site is the short real-time evaluation of your likes and dislikes in clinical medicine. This leads to a comparison with the results from physicians practicing in the 42 most common specialties and subspecialties. These results are based on a survey of more than 2,400 practicing physicians with a spectrum of ages and from a variety of practice settings. It also gives users a personal profile of their long-range values and interests that can be compared with practicing physicians' profiles on the site.

The profiles of physicians include their likes and dislikes about the specialty and how they rated the specific factors used on the career evaluation. These profiles, in PDF files, can be printed for later perusal. You can also review each individual factor to see how the different specialties compare with each other. Take a look at "Income satisfaction." You probably won't be too surprised to learn which specialists are most pleased with their income.

Some schools have follow-up counseling programs for career assessment. Check with your Dean of Students to see if one is available at your school.

Careers in Medicine website

The AAMC's *Careers in Medicine* (*CiM*) can be accessed after a simple registration process, at: http://services.aamc.org/careersinmedicine/. It is a four-phase course that helps medical students go through the process of choosing a specialty. *CiM* offers a structured, step-by-step way of thinking about this process. It uses a four-stage career-development model that includes: (1) self-assessment, (2) career exploration, (3) decision making, and (4) implementation. *CiM* also contains a variety of other resources, such as specialty descriptions, online career planning resources (some of which you must pay for), and a bibliography. As with the Pathway Program, some medical schools use this in conjunction with formal career counseling.

The resources above will broaden your field of vision beyond that which you have already experienced. Your whole professional life is at stake. Take the time to carefully think through your choice.

Since you already have this book, you can also quickly assess the medical specialty areas that interest you by completing the Personal Trait Analysis, Figure 4.2.

Personal Trait Analysis (Figure 4.2)

As you can see in the example (Figure 4.3) completed by a sample medical student, you should put a "+" next to each "Characteristic" that you "Like" or feel is one of your "Strengths." If you neither "Like" the "Characteristic" nor consider it one of your "Strengths," put a "0" in the appropriate place. Note that you may "Like" some of the Characteristics, but not feel that they are "Strengths." Others you may feel are personal "Strengths," but you do not particularly "Like" them. In these cases, just mark the form accordingly. The statements are purposely broad, so do not be alarmed by their general nature.

Once you have completed your Personal Trait Analysis in Figure 4.2, use the Personal Trait Synthesis form (Figure 4.5) to rearrange the "Characteristics" (as our sample student has done in Figure 4.4) under the following four categories:

High Priority—Characteristics you marked (+)"Like," (+)"Strength"

Priority—Characteristics you marked (+)"Like," (0)"Strength"

Acceptable—Characteristics you marked (0)"Like," (+)"Strength"

Reject—Characteristics you marked (0)"Like," (0)"Strength"

Next, look at Figure 4.6, which summarizes the characteristics that practitioners in some major specialties feel relate to their area. Then go to Figures 4.7 and 4.8, "Selecting a Specialty for You."

These forms are also available on the *Companion Disk for Getting Into A Residency*. This is a program that has many of the blank forms found in this book, including the forms needed for the "Personal Trait Analysis." The program will even perform all the calculations for you! Windows-based programs are available from Galen Press, Ltd. See the *Annotated Bibliography* for more information.

FIGURE 4.2
Personal Trait Analysis

Characteristic	Like	Strength
1. Deal with Many Major Diseases		
2. Treat Infectious Diseases		
3. Treat Incurable & Disabling Diseases		
4. Evaluate Neurological Functions		
5. Evaluate Reproductive Functions		
6. Deal with Complex Problems		
7. Life-Threatening Problems		
8. Treat Psychosomatic Problems		
9. Deal with Intimate Personal Problems		
10. Deal with Emotional Reactions to Illness		
11. Older Age Patients		
12. Child & Adolescent Patients		
13. Dying Patients		
14. Many Patients Daily		
15. Give Comprehensive Care		
16. Home Health Care		
17. Do Preventive Care		
18. Do Genetic Counseling		
19. Marital & Sexual Counseling		
20. Family Planning Counseling		
21. Discuss Personal Relations		
22. Patient Participation in Care		
23. See Beneficial Treatment Results		
24. Use Knowledge of Musculoskeletal System		
25. Use Knowledge of Circulat., Resp., Digest., & Excretory Systems		
26. Use Knowledge of Anatomy & Physiology		
27. Do Extensive, Precise Workups		
28. Use Lab Tests		
29. Use Proctoscopies & Arteriograms		
30. Use Complex Equipment		
31. Use Your Hands		
32. Do Repetitive Standard Procedures		
33. Do High-Risk Procedures		
34. Do Outpatient Operative Procedures		
35. Get & Use Family Information		
36. Use Socioeconomic Information		
37. Use Rehabilitation Services		
38. Use Social Services		
39. Give Psychological Services		
40. Get Referrals & Give Consultations		

FIGURE 4.3
Personal Trait Analysis—An Example

Characteristic	Like	Strength
1. Deal with Many Major Diseases	+	+
2. Treat Infectious Diseases	0	+
3. Treat Incurable & Disabling Diseases	0	0
4. Evaluate Neurological Functions	0	0
5. Evaluate Reproductive Functions	0	0
6. Deal with Complex Problems	+	+
7. Life-Threatening Problems	+	+
8. Treat Psychosomatic Problems	+	0
9. Deal with Intimate Personal Problems	0	0
10. Deal with Emotional Reactions to Illness	0	0
11. Older Age Patients	+	+
12. Child & Adolescent Patients	0	+
13. Dying Patients	0	+
14. Many Patients Daily	+	0
15. Give Comprehensive Care	+	+
16. Home Health Care	0	0
17. Do Preventive Care	0	0
18. Do Genetic Counseling	0	0
19. Marital & Sexual Counseling	0	0
20. Family Planning Counseling	0	0
21. Discuss Personal Relations	+	0
22. Patient Participation in Care	+	+
23. See Beneficial Treatment Results	+	+
24. Use Knowledge of Musculoskeletal System	+	+
25. Use Knowledge of Circulat., Resp., Digest., & Excretory Systems	+	0
26. Use Knowledge of Anatomy & Physiology	+	+
27. Do Extensive, Precise Workups	0	+
28. Use Lab Tests	+	+
29. Use Proctoscopies & Arteriograms	0	0
30. Use Complex Equipment	+	0
31. Use Your Hands	+	+
32. Do Repetitive Standard Procedures	0	0
33. Do High-Risk Procedures	0	0
34. Do Outpatient Operative Procedures	+	+
35. Get & Use Family Information	0	+
36. Use Socioeconomic Information	+	0
37. Use Rehabilitation Services	0	0
38. Use Social Services	0	+
39. Give Psychological Services	+	+
40. Get Referrals & Give Consultations	+	0

FIGURE 4.4

Personal Trait Synthesis—An Example

Our sample student has taken his results from Figure 4.3 and grouped them according to their priority for him.

Characteristic	Like	Strength
HIGH PRIORITY (4)		
1. Deal with Many Major Diseases	+	+
6. Deal with Complex Problems	+	+
7. Life-Threatening Problems	+	+
11. Older Age Patients	+	+
15. Give Comprehensive Care	+	+
22. Patient Participation in Care	+	+
23. See Beneficial Treatment Results	+	+
24. Use Knowledge of Musculoskeletal System	+	+
26. Use Knowledge of Anatomy & Physiology	+	+
28. Use Lab Tests	+	+
31. Use Your Hands	+	+
34. Do Outpatient Operative Procedures	+	+
39. Give Psychological Services	+	+
PRIORITY (3)		
8. Treat Psychosomatic Problems	+	0
14. Many Patients Daily	+	0
21. Discuss Personal Relations	+	0
25. Use Knowledge of Circul., Resp., Digest., & Excretory Systems	+	0
30. Use Complex Equipment	+	0
36. Use Socioeconomic Information	+	0
40. Get Referrals & Give Consults	+	0
ACCEPTABLE (2)		
2. Treat Infectious Diseases	0	+
12. Child & Adolescent Patients	0	+
13. Dying Patients	0	+
27. Do Extensive, Precise Workups	0	+
35. Get & Use Family Information	0	+
38. Use Social Services	0	+
REJECT (1)		
3. Treat Incurable & Disabling Diseases	0	0
4. Evaluate Neurological Functions	0	0
5. Evaluate Reproductive Functions	0	0
9. Deal with Intimate Personal Problems	0	0
10. Deal with Emotional Reactions to Illness	0	0
16. Home Health Care	0	0
17. Do Preventive Care	0	0
18. Do Genetic Counseling	0	0
19. Marital & Sexual Counseling	0	0
20. Family Planning Counseling	0	0
29. Use Proctoscopies & Arteriograms	0	0
32. Do Repetitive Standard Procedures	0	0
33. Do High-Risk Procedures	0	0
37. Use Rehabilitation Services	0	0

FIGURE 4.5
Personal Trait Synthesis

Now list your likes/strengths from Figure 4.2 according to their priority.

HIGH PRIORITY (4)

_____   _____

_____   _____

_____   _____

_____   _____

PRIORITY (3)

_____   _____

_____   _____

_____   _____

_____   _____

ACCEPTABLE (2)

_____   _____

_____   _____

_____   _____

_____   _____

REJECT (1)

_____   _____

_____   _____

_____   _____

_____   _____

FIGURE 4.6

Characteristics Strongly Associated with the Practice of Some Major Specialties

The following seven charts summarize the "Characteristics" practitioners feel relate to their specialties in Emergency Medicine, Family Medicine, Internal Medicine, Obstetrics and Gynecology, Pediatrics, Psychiatry, and Surgery. While there are *many more specialty fields than are listed here*, these charts should give you a starting point from which to look into similar, related specialty areas.

When you finish looking these over, turn to Figures 4.7 and 4.8 "Selecting a Specialty For You," to determine how your own rating of the Characteristics compares to those of specialists practicing in these fields.

Emergency Medicine

Very Common
- Life-Threatening Problems
- Many Patients Daily
- Use Your Hands

Common
- Use Lab Tests
- Child and Adolescent Patients
- Use Knowledge of Musculoskeletal System
- Use Knowledge of Circulatory, Respiratory, Digestive, & Excretory Systems
- Use Knowledge of Anatomy & Physiology
- Many Major Diseases
- Beneficial Treatment Results
- Outpatient Operative Procedures

Rare
- Deal with Emotional Reactions to Illness
- Preventive Care
- Use Proctoscopies & Arteriograms
- Incurable & Disabling Diseases
- Discuss Personal Relations
- Use Rehabilitation Services
- Family Planning Counseling
- Use Psychological Services
- Evaluate Reproductive Functions
- Home Health Care

Very Rare
- Marital & Sexual Counseling
- Genetic Counseling

Family Medicine

Very Common
- Comprehensive Care
- Use Lab Tests
- Outpatient Operative Procedures
- Child & Adolescent Patients
- Older Age Patients
- Many Patients Daily
- Intimate Personal Problems
- Use Family Information
- Treat Infectious Diseases

Common
- Many Major Diseases
- Deal with Life-Threatening Problems
- Psychosomatic Problems
- Dying Patients
- Home Health Care
- Preventive Care
- Marital & Sexual Counseling
- Family Planning Counseling
- Discuss Personal Relations
- Patient Participation in Care
- Beneficial Treatment Results
- Repetitive Standard Procedures
- Use Socioeconomic Information
- Use Rehabilitation Services
- Use Social Services

Rare
- Genetic Counseling
- Use Complex Equipment
- Do High-Risk Procedures
- Get Referrals & Give Consults

FIGURE 4.6 (continued)

Internal Medicine

Very Common
- Complex Problems
- Use Lab Tests
- Get Referrals & Give Consults

Common
- Many Major Diseases
- Treat Infectious Diseases
- Incurable and Disabling Diseases
- Life-Threatening Problems
- Psychosomatic Problems
- Intimate Personal Problems
- Older Age Population
- Dying Patients
- Comprehensive Care
- Patient Participation in Care
- Knowledge of Circulatory, Respiratory, Digestive, & Excretory Systems
- Extensive, Precise Workups
- Proctoscopies & Arteriograms
- Use Family Information

Rare
- Child & Adolescent Patients
- Genetic Counseling
- Family Planning Counseling
- Psychological Services
- Use Knowledge of Musculoskeletal System
- Evaluate Reproductive Functions

Very Rare
- Outpatient Operative Procedures

Obstetrics & Gynecology

Very Common
- Marital & Sexual Counseling
- Use Your Hands
- Family Planning Counseling
- Intimate Personal Problems
- Evaluate Reproductive Functions

Common
- Many Patients Daily
- Preventive Care
- Beneficial Treatment Results
- Use Lab Tests
- Repetitive Standard Procedures
- Get Referrals & Give Consults

Rare
- Incurable & Disabling Diseases
- Older Age Patients
- Dying Patients
- Home Health Care
- Use Knowledge of Musculoskeletal System
- Use Complex Equipment
- Do High-Risk Procedures
- Use Socioeconomic Information
- Give Psychological Services

Very Rare
- Use Rehabilitation Services
- Use Proctoscopies & Arteriograms
- Evaluate Neurological Functions

FIGURE 4.6 (continued)

Pediatrics

Very Common
- Preventive Care
- Comprehensive Care
- Many Patients Daily
- Child & Adolescent Patients
- Treat Infectious Diseases

Common
- Beneficial Treatment Results
- Use Lab Tests
- Repetitive Standard Procedures
- Use Family Information

Rare
- Incurable & Disabling Diseases
- Family Planning Counseling
- Deal with Emotional Reactions to Illness
- Use Knowledge of Musculoskeletal System

Very Rare
- Older Age Patients
- Marital & Sexual Counseling
- Use Complex Equipment
- Do High-Risk Procedures
- Dying Patients
- Evaluate Reproductive Functions
- Use Proctoscopies & Arteriograms

Psychiatry

Very Common
- Psychosomatic Problems
- Intimate Personal Problems
- Emotional Reactions to Illness
- Discuss Personal Relationships
- Patient Participation in Care

Common
- Get Referrals & Give Consults
- Give Psychological Services
- Use Social Services
- Use Socioeconomic Information
- Use Family Information
- Marital & Sexual Counseling
- Complex Problems

Rare
- Use Lab Tests
- Extensive, Precise Workups
- Genetic Counseling
- Home Health Care
- Life-Threatening Problems
- Evaluate Reproductive Functions
- Use Knowledge of Anatomy & Physiology
- Use Rehabilitation Services

Very Rare
- Use Your Hands
- Do High-Risk Procedures
- Outpatient Operative Procedures
- Many Patients Daily
- Use Complex Equipment
- Use Proctoscopies & Arteriograms
- Treat Infectious Diseases
- Use Knowledge of Musculoskeletal System
- Use Knowledge of Circulatory, Respiratory, Digestive, & Excretory Systems

FIGURE 4.6 (continued)

Surgery

Very Common
- Life-Threatening Problems
- Beneficial Treatment Results
- Get Referrals & Give Consults
- Use Your Hands
- Outpatient Operative Procedures
- Use of Knowledge of Anatomy
  & Physiology
- Use Proctoscopies & Arteriograms

Common
- Many Major Diseases
- Complex Problems
- Dying Patients
- Extensive Precise Workups
- Use Lab Tests
- Use Knowledge of Musculoskeletal
  System
- Use Knowledge of Circulatory,
  Respiratory, Digestive,
  & Excretory Systems

Rare
- Comprehensive Care
- Preventive Care
- Deal with Emotional Reactions
  to Illness
- Intimate Personal Problems
- Evaluate Neurological Functions
- Psychosomatic Problems
- Evaluate Reproductive Functions
- Use Socioeconomic Information

Very Rare
- Genetic Counseling
- Marital-Sexual Counseling
- Family Planning Counseling
- Psychological Services

Adapted from: Zimny GH. *Manual for the Medical Specialty Preference Inventory.* (revised draft) St. Louis, MO, 1977; and Zimny GH, Iserson KV, Shepherd C. A characterization of emergency medicine. *JACEP.* 1979;8(4):147-49.

FIGURE 4.7

Selecting a Specialty for You—An Example

This form summarizes the prior pages (Figure 4.6) and briefly describes those characteristics favored by current practitioners in seven common specialties. Our sample student, whose Personal Trait Synthesis can be found in Figure 4.4, would fill out the blank Figure 4.8 as seen below.

Every characteristic that the student rated as a "High Priority" [Like (+), Strength (+)] gets 4 points; each one rated as "Priority" [Like (+), Strength (0)] gets 3 points; each one rated as "Acceptable" [Like (0), Strength (+)] gets 2 points; and each one rated "Reject" [Like (0), Strength (0)] gets 1 point. That student would then fill in the numerical values for each of the characteristics [rated as Very Common (VC), Common (C), Rare (R), or Very Rare (VR)] in each of these specialties.

Once the individual numbers are filled in, a score can be calculated based upon the correlation of personal traits with the specialty characteristics.

Characteristic	IM	SUR	FM	PED	OB	PSY	EM
1. Deal with Many Major Diseases	C 4	C 4	C 4	–	–	–	C 4
2. Treat Infectious Diseases	C 2	–	VC 2	VC 2	–	VR 2	–
3. Treat Incurable & Disabling Diseases	C 1	–	–	R 1	R 1	–	R 1
4. Evaluate Neurological Functions	–	R 1	–	–	VR 1	–	–
5. Evaluate Reproductive Functions	R 1	R 1	–	VR 1	VC 1	R 1	R 1
6. Deal with Complex Problems	VC 4	C 4	–	–	–	C 4	–
7. Life-Threatening Problems	C 4	VC 4	C 4	–	–	R 4	VC 4
8. Treat Psychosomatic Problems	C 3	R 3	C 3	–	–	VC 3	–
9. Deal with Intimate Personal Problems	C 1	R 1	VC 1	–	VC 1	VC 1	–
10. Deal with Emotional Reactions to Illness	–	R 1	–	R 1	–	VC 1	R 1
11. Older Age Patients	C 4	–	VC 4	VR 4	R 4	–	–
12. Child & Adolescent Patients	R 2	–	VC 2	VC 2	–	–	C 2
13. Dying Patients	C 2	C 2	C 2	VR 2	R 2	–	–
14. Many Patients Daily	–	–	VC 3	VC 3	C 3	VR 3	VC 3

FIGURE 4.7 (continued)

Characteristic	IM	SUR	FM	PED	OB	PSY	EM
15. Give Comprehensive Care	C 4	R 4	VC 4	VC 4	–	–	C 4
16. Home Health Care	–	–	C 1	–	R 1	R 1	R 1
17. Do Preventive Care	–	R 1	C 1	VC 1	C 1	–	R 1
18. Do Genetic Counseling	R 1	VR 1	R 1	–	–	R 1	VR 1
19. Marital & Sex Counseling	–	VR 1	C 1	VR 1	VC 1	C 1	VR 1
20. Family Planning Counseling	R 1	VR 1	C 1	R 1	VC 1	–	R 1
21. Discuss Personal Relationships	–	–	C 3	–	–	VC 3	R 3
22. Patient Participation in Care	C 4	–	C 4	–	–	VC 4	–
23. See Beneficial Treatment Results	–	VC 4	C 4	C 4	C 4	–	C 4
24. Use Knowledge of Musculoskeletal System	R 4	C 4	–	R 4	R 4	VR 4	C 4
25. Use Knowledge of Circul., Resp., Digest., & Excretory Systems	C 3	C 3	–	–	–	VR 3	C 3
26. Use Knowledge of Anatomy & Physiology	–	VC 4	–	–	–	R 4	C 4
27. Do Extensive, Precise Workups	C 2	C 2	–	–	–	R 2	–
28. Use Lab Tests	VC 4	C 4	VC 4	C 4	C 4	R 4	C 4
29. Use Proctoscopies & Arteriograms	C 1	VC 1	–	VR 1	VR 1	VR 1	R 1
30. Use Complex Equipment	–	–	R 3	VR 3	R 3	VR 3	–
31. Use Your Hands	–	VC 4	–	–	VC 4	VR 4	VC 4
32. Do Repetitive Standard Procedures	–	–	C 1	C 1	C 1	–	–
33. Do High-Risk Procedures	–	–	R 1	VR 1	R 1	VR	–
34. Do Outpatient Operative Procedures	VR 4	VC 4	VC 4	–	–	VR 4	C 4

FIGURE 4.7 (continued)

Characteristic	IM	SUR	FM	PED	OB	PSY	EM
35. Get & Use Family Information	C 2	–	VC 2	C 2	–	C 2	–
36. Use Socioeconomic Information	–	R 3	C 3	–	R 3	C 3	–
37. Use Rehabilitation Services	–	–	C 1	–	VR 1	R 1	R 1
38. Use Social Services	–	–	C 2	–	–	C 2	–
39. Give Psych Services	R 4	VR 4	–	–	R 4	C 4	R 4
40. Get Referrals; Give Consultations	VC 3	VC 3	R 3	–	C 3	C 3	–

FIGURE 4.8

Selecting a Specialty for You

Your rating number, *taken from Figure 4.5,* for each "Characteristic" is inserted below the associated strength of the characteristic ("VC" = Very Common; "C" = Common; "R" = Rare; "VR" = Very Rare) for each specialty. Note that your rating number for each characteristic will be the same under each specialty. (See Figure 4.7 for the numbers to use.) Once the individual numbers are filled in, a score can be calculated based upon the correlation of personal traits with the specialty characteristics.

Characteristic	IM	SUR	FM	PED	OB	PSY	EM
1. Deal with Many Major Diseases	C	C	C	–	–	–	C
2. Treat Infectious Diseases	C	–	VC	VC	–	VR	–
3. Treat Incurable & Disabling Diseases	C	–	–	R	R	–	R
4. Evaluate Neurological Functions	–	R	–	–	VR	–	–
5. Evaluate Reproductive Functions	R	R	–	VR	VC	R	R
6. Deal with Complex Problems	VC	C	–	–	–	C	–
7. Life-Threatening Problems	C	VC	C	–	–	R	VC

FIGURE 4.8 (continued)

Characteristic	IM	SUR	FM	PED	OB	PSY	EM
8. Treat Psychosomatic Problems	C	R	C	–	–	VC	–
9. Deal with Intimate Personal Problems	C	R	VC	–	VC	VC	–
10. Deal with Emotional Reactions to Illness	–	R	–	R	–	VC	R
11. Older Age Patients	C	–	VC	VR	R	–	–
12. Child & Adolescent Patients	R	–	VC	VC	–	–	C
13. Dying Patients	C	C	C	VR	R	–	–
14. Many Patients Daily	–	–	VC	VC	C	VR	VC
15. Give Comprehensive Care	C	R	VC	VC	–	–	C
16 . Home Health Care	–	–	C	–	R	R	R
17. Do Preventive Care	–	R	C	VC	C	–	R
18. Do Genetic Counseling	R	VR	R	–	–	R	VR
19. Marital & Sex Counseling	–	VR	C	VR	VC	C	VR
20. Family Planning Counseling	R	VR	C	R	VC	–	R
21. Discuss Personal Relationships	–	–	C	–	–	VC	R
22. Patient Participation in Care	C	–	C	–	–	VC	–
23. See Beneficial Treatment Results	–	VC	C	C	C	–	C

FIGURE 4.8 (continued)

Characteristic	IM	SUR	FM	PED	OB	PSY	EM
24. Use Knowledge of Musculoskeletal System	R	C		R	R	VR	C
25. Use Knowledge of Circul., Resp., Digest., & Excretory Systems	C	C				VR	C
26. Use Knowledge of Anatomy & Physiology		VC				R	C
27. Do Extensive, Precise Workups	C	C	–	–	–	R	–
28. Use Lab Tests	VC	C	VC	C	C	R	C
29. Use Proctoscopies & Arteriograms	C	VC	–	VR	VR	VR	R
30. Use Complex Equipment	–	–	R	VR	R	VR	–
31. Use Your Hands	–	VC	–	–	VC	VR	VC
32. Do Repetitive Standard Procedures	–	–	C	C	C	–	–
33. Do High-Risk Procedures	–	–	R	VR	R	VR	–
34. Do Outpatient Operative Procedures	VR	VC	VC	–	–	VR	C
35. Get & Use Family Information	C	–	VC	C	–	C	–
36. Use Socioeconomic Information	–	R	C	–	R	C	–
37. Use Rehabilitation Services	–	–	C	–	VR	R	R
38. Use Social Services	–	–	C	–	–	C	–
39. Give Psych Services	R	VR	–	–	R	C	R
40. Get Referrals; Give Consultations	VC	VC	R	–	C	C	–

FIGURE 4.9

Correlation of Personal Traits and Specialty Characteristics

It is now time to see how your own traits, likes, and strengths match with the seven specialties analyzed. Using Figure 4.8, add the numbers associated with a particular rating for each specialty and put the result in the appropriate box in the chart below. For example, our sample student (Figure 4.7), in the Internal Medicine column, put two "4" and one "3" rating for traits listed as Very Common (VC). This equals "11." So our sample student would put the number "11" in the top left box in the chart, labeled "Very Common, IM." (See Figure 4.10 for an example.) The *Companion Disk* will do these calculations for you.

Complete the remainder of your chart in a similar manner. Then, to get the scores you will need, divide by the number specified in the box. This will give you an average score for the traits in that category.

As you can see, the higher the scores in the "Very Common" and "Common" boxes, and the lower the scores in the "Rare" and "Very Rare" boxes, the better your personal traits, strengths, and likes correlate with the practice in a particular specialty.

For an example of this form filled out by our sample student, turn to Figure 4.10.

	IM	SUR	FM	PED	OB	PSY	EM
Very Common Total:							
Divided by:	3	7	9	5	5	5	3
Score =							
Common Total:							
Divided by:	14	7	15	4	6	7	9
Score =							
Rare Total:							
Divided by:	6	8	4	4	9	8	10
Score =							
Very Rare Total:							
Divided by:	1	4	–	7	3	9	2
Score =							

FIGURE 4.10

Correlation of Personal Traits and Specialty Characteristics—An Example

	IM	SUR	FM	PED	OB	PSY	EM
Very Common Total:	11	24	26	12	8	12	11
Divided by:	3	7	9	5	5	5	3
Score =	3.67	3.43	2.89	2.40	1.60	2.40	3.67
Common Total:	37	23	35	11	16	19	33
Divided by:	14	7	15	4	6	7	9
Score =	2.64	3.29	2.33	2.75	2.67	2.71	3.67
Rare Total:	13	15	8	7	23	18	15
Divided by:	6	8	4	4	9	8	10
Score =	2.17	1.88	2.00	1.75	2.56	2.25	1.50
Very Rare Total:	4	7	–	13	3	25	2
Divided by:	1	4	–	7	3	9	2
Score =	4.00	1.75	–	1.86	1.00	2.78	1.00

This example demonstrates a pattern, which should point our sample student toward a specialty choice. Surgery and Emergency Medicine have characteristics closest to the student's likes and strengths. These two specialties also seem to rarely deal with many of the aspects of medicine the student feels are neither personal "Likes" nor "Strengths."

In general, you should look for the highest scores in the "Very Common" and "Common" characteristic areas, and the lowest scores in the "Rare" and "Very Rare" areas. A specialty that shows a reversal of this trend will be a poor match for you. The presence of very similar numbers in all four categories indicates that you may be able to generate little enthusiasm for the specialty.

However, there is one major caveat to using this scoring sheet: the subspecialty areas are not really considered in this schema. For example, while Internists very rarely do outpatient operative procedures, the subspecialty of Cardiology, especially those Cardiologists who do heart catheterizations, considers this a "Very Common" aspect of their practice. So, use these charts to get an estimate of areas that you would like to explore further. *Do not use them rigidly or without thinking beyond the results.*

5

Important Factors When Choosing A Specialty

The more alternatives, the more difficult the choice.

– Abbé D'Allainval, *L'embarras des richesses*, 1726

MANY FACTORS COME INTO PLAY when you are trying to choose a specialty. The elements you find important may not be the same ones that your classmates value. Yet it might be instructive to look at what recent graduates felt were important factors in their choice of specialty.

The most important factors that students believe influenced their specialty choice relate to how they will interact with patients. *Interest in helping people, the opportunity to make a difference in people's lives, and the type of patient problems encountered* in the specialty were the major influences for most students. This suggests that most students' altruistic reasons for entering medicine still influence them after the four-year grind of medical school. Very reasonably, most students say other persuasive factors are whether their own *personality fits with the specialty* and whether they *possess the required skills or abilities.*

Medical students seem to make bad specialty choices—either being attracted to or rejecting specialties—based on the nature of the people with whom they work, especially in their third-year rotations. There are, however, personalities inherent in different specialties—especially at each institution. Associating with specialists both at the academic center and in the community (for example, at the regional society meeting) may help you decide whether your personality fits that specialty.

Other common factors considered when making a specialty choice are the *intellectual content* of the specialty and whether the specialty has *challenging diagnostic problems.* Basically, students prefer not to be bored by the career path they take. Significantly, these are the same factors cited by physicians in practice who still enjoy their specialty 20 and 30 years after completing residency.

Unlike previous generations of medical students, recent graduates have wisely relied much less on a particular physician or a specific medical school course when choosing their specialty. However, they do still rely a bit too heavily on their experience during subspecialty clerkships. Brief and isolated experiences such as these can be misleading—both positively and negatively—so beware.

Other factors also influence career choices, but few people readily acknowledge being swayed by them. These include income, length of training, work hours, availability of jobs in the future, and the difficulty of getting a residency position.

Monetary Rewards

One aspect of selecting a specialty, which is rarely, if ever, spoken about except in a humorous fashion, is the financial remuneration you can expect. While it may be both noble and consistent with the values that brought you into the field of medicine to try to ignore financial considerations completely, it is unrealistic. No physician is likely to be poor, but most medical students accrue enormous debts to finance their education.

Specialty Income

Medical students generally believe that their educational investment will pay off handsomely. More than one-third of graduating medical students expect to be earning more than $200,000 annually within ten years of completing their postgraduate training.

Procedure-oriented specialties are the most lucrative for physicians. And the difference between incomes for physicians in these specialties and those of their non-procedurally oriented colleagues can be truly amazing. This is because, at present, the insurance payment schemes reward *doing* (procedures) at a much higher level than *thinking* (cognition). While Pediatricians have a median annual income of about $150,000, Cardio-thoracic Surgeons earn nearly four times as much (Figure 5.1).

According to recent estimates, new Internists will earn only one-fourth to one-half of the starting salary received by physicians who are trained in more procedurally or technically oriented areas. For decades, some policy makers have predicted future changes in this system as mechanisms for physician payment are rearranged at the federal, state, and private levels through "health-care reform." So far, it hasn't happened. Across the United States, the highest physician incomes are in the East South Central (AL, KY, MS, TN) and West-South-Central states (AR, LA, OK, TX), while the lowest are in the Mountain (AZ, CO, ID, MT, NM, NV, UT, WY) and the Pacific states

FIGURE 5.1
Median Physician Annual Income*

Specialty	Income
Cardiothoracic Surgery	$ 560,000
Neurosurgery	440,000
Orthopedic Surgery	360,000
Vascular Surgery	360,000
Diagnostic Radiology	350,000
Cardiology	320,000
Plastic Surgery	310,000
Anesthesiology	300,000
Colon & Rectal Surgery	290,000
Gastroenterology	290,000
Urology	290,000
Hematology/Oncology	270,000
Otolaryngology	270,000
General Surgery	260,000
Ophthalmology	260,000
Obstetrician/Gynecology	250,000
Pathology	250,000
All Physicians	**$ 230,000**
Dermatology	$ 230,000
Nephrology	230,000
Emergency Medicine	210,000
Neurology	200,000
Occupational Medicine	190,000
Psychiatry	180,000
Endocrinology	170,000
Rheumatology	170,000
General Internal Med	160,000
Family Medicine	150,000
Pediatrics	150,000

*Reports of specialty salaries vary widely. Use these numbers only as an approximation.
Adapted from multiple sources (2005, 2006).

(AK, CA, HI, OR, WA). Real physician income (adjusted for inflation) has remained relatively unchanged for the past decade.

If the past is any indicator, though, the disparity in salary between doers and thinkers will persist. For example, a major income realignment was to occur in the early 1990s with the implementation of the Resource Based Relative Value Scale (RBRVS). It never materialized. Despite predictions from the government, the American Medical Association, and other reputable sources that primary-care practitioners would benefit, they didn't. In fact, it has been shown that primary care physicians have a substantially lower return on their investment in professional education than do medical or surgical subspecialists, attorneys, dentists, and individuals in business. Based on the costs of a medical education, the "hours-adjusted net present value" of the money invested in education is $11.65 for attorneys, $11.29 for procedure-based physicians, $9.66 for dentists, $8.98 for businessmen, and $6.48 for primary care physicians. After their mid-20s, lawyers, businessmen, and dentists also work fewer hours than do physicians. Yet, no matter which specialty a physician chooses to enter, he or she is in no danger of going on the dole.

The changing health care environment, however, should eventually decrease the need for, and the income of, many specialists. This is because managed care organizations generally make money by keeping their patients away from medical specialists. So far, they have been only partially successful at doing this.

Other changes may also affect physicians' income in certain specialties. Recent rules concerning physician reimbursement have severely reduced the income of Clinical Pathologists. The government unilaterally disallowed payment for a large portion of their practice. This, as is usually the case, was followed by a similar move by all other insurers. The government is now seriously looking at making similar changes in reimbursement for other hospital-based specialists, such as Anesthesiologists, Radiologists, and Emergency Physicians. How this will affect their income is uncertain.

Then there is the malpractice insurance dilemma, cycling from a crisis level to merely being uncomfortable, which will continue to affect some specialties until broad tort reform is enacted. Obstetricians still find it difficult in some locales to deliver babies at a cost that new families can afford, while paying the ever-increasing premiums for their malpractice insurance.

In many cases, Family Practitioners have completely given up the portion of their practices that previously included Obstetrics, outpatient Orthopedics, and Surgery. Radiologists have joined the luckless group of most-frequently-sued specialties, mainly from inaccurately reading mammograms. Neurosurgeons, Plastic Surgeons, and many other specialists now face similar stiff increases in the already astronomical cost of malpractice insurance. While the highest-income specialties are still lucrative even after subtracting the cost of their malpractice premiums, the net remuneration is not quite as attractive as it would first appear.

Overall, physicians earning the highest net income live in metropolitan areas with fewer than one million people, are not in solo practice, are not linked to a managed care group, and are between 46 and 55 years old.

Debt & Specialty Choice

No one has consistently shown that most medical students make career choices based on the level of their debt. Some studies, however, suggest a trend in that direction, and one-third of graduating medical students admit that their educational debt influenced their specialty choice. Recent surveys have shown that as medical students' debt rises, their debt load influences their specialty choice. Only 18% say it influences them if they have a debt less than $50,000. However, it influences more than half of those with debts above $150,000. How it influences them is uncertain. For example, a 2003 AAMC survey of graduating medical students showed that medical students choosing Radiology (very high income) had less debt, on average, than those going into Pediatrics (relatively low income). Not measured, though, was whether the difficulty of obtaining a position in the highest-paying specialties or the longer period of residency training also influenced their specialty selection.

In 2005, medical students received more than $1.5 billion in educational loans. The 84% of 2005 medical school graduates who borrowed money to pay for their education owed an average of $115,000. This debt level has increased nearly 300% since 1985! (For perspective, the average graduating student's debt in 1971 was only $8,435, or $40,488 in 2005 dollars.) Students in private medical schools have debts nearly 50% higher than those in public schools.

This debt level will rise, given that in 2005, the mean annual tuition and fees was more than $19,000 at public medical schools and more than $36,000 at private medical schools. Many exceed $40,000 and one (University of Colorado) is in the $70,000 range for non-residents. In addition, nearly 16% of medical school graduates' spouses have debts exceeding $50,000. Also, nearly 15% of medical students take more than four years to graduate, thus increasing their debt load.

Because of the interest accruing on their loans, many medical students eventually pay back up to three dollars for every dollar they borrow. Therefore, selecting a poorly remunerated specialty without understanding the ramifications may lead to a rude awakening at the end of residency training.

During part or all of residency, physicians may either avoid paying and accruing interest on some student loans (deferment) or avoid paying on the loans but still accrue interest (forbearance or "deferment" of unsubsidized loans), depending on their overall financial situation. The requirements for implementing these options have become stricter in recent years. The rules continue to change, so check with your loan officer to find out the current regulations. Note that, unlike other government loans and most felonies, there is no "statute of limitations" on government loans to students. You owe them the money until it is repaid; even bankruptcy doesn't automatically banish these debts.

Many residents find it wise either to apply for forbearance from their lenders or to consolidate their loans and extend their payment schedule through the Federal Loan Consolidation Program. You should be aware that the federal government now publishes the names of individuals who default on student loans. There has been a move to have all residency training programs provide financial advice and administrative assistance in managing resident education indebtedness. The wise programs are beginning to do this.

An excellent, comprehensive source of information about handling medical student debt—which is conveniently staged for each level of training—is the AAMC's website, "Financing Your Medical Education" (www.aamc.org/students/financing/start.htm). Periodically updated to reflect changes in lending practices and related laws, it contains nearly all the information you will need to manage your medical school debt.

Importance of Income

A final note is in order about the importance of income at various career stages. For the entry-level physician, income is extremely important. This makes sense, since most new physicians have enormous debts, no money, and increasing financial responsibilities. At mid-career, however, income is of only medium importance—with job security being the most important factor keeping the physician in practice. At this stage of physicians' careers, job satisfaction is equally as important as income. Job satisfaction becomes of overwhelming importance for physicians in the last third of their career. Those who have high job satisfaction presumably keep working longer than those who do not, and have more fun while they are working.

Length of Training

The majority of medical students do not make specialty choices based on the length of required training. The pleasure they get out of practicing a specialty that interests them generally pays them back for the added training.

Studies show that the length of training influences some medical students' specialty choice, particularly those selecting generalist or support specialties. The amount of this influence increases as the student's debt rises, becoming particularly strong at debt levels above the mean debt level (about $110,000 in 2005). While this may be understandable, it is sad to think that after expending so much effort, an individual might make a life-long career decision on such a flimsy basis.

One point worth noting, however, is that longer training does not always equate to additional income. In the medical subspecialties, for example, Gastroenterologists, who frequently perform high-reimbursement procedures, have large incomes while Rheumatologists, who do few procedures, make scarcely more than a General Internist. This doesn't mean that those who have a calling in Rheumatology should not pursue this specialty, only that extra education does not always equal an increased income.

Work Hours/Lifestyle

Income must not be the only factor you consider. Work hours and lifestyle also become important once you complete residency. A "controllable lifestyle" has become more important to medical school graduates. Over the past 20 years, the proportion of women choosing controllable lifestyle specialties (such as Anesthesiology, Dermatology, Emergency Medicine, Ophthalmology, Otolaryngology, Pathology, Psychiatry, and Diagnostic Radiology) rose from 18% to 36%. During that same period, the proportion of men choosing controllable lifestyle specialties rose from 28% to 45%. These changes persisted even after controlling for income.

An important element of lifestyle is the hours worked. Even during residency, the hours worked by PGY-2 and higher-level residents often mimic the work hours expected in that specialty. Figure 3.3 shows the hours different specialists work in patient care, and Figure 5.2 shows patient-care hours in relation to the total time some specialists devote to professional activities. A comparison with Figure 5.1 shows that the hours worked do not correlate with income.

The hours a physician puts into his or her work will markedly influence his or her type of family life and extracurricular activities. If you expect to have any life outside of medicine, consider this carefully. Also, note that Surgeons and Obstetricians have lots of "down time" waiting for an available operating room or for a woman in labor. Much of this time may also be in the middle of the night, on weekends, and on holidays. On average, Diagnostic Radiologists work the least time each year (44 weeks), closely followed by Anesthesiologists (45 weeks/year), and Urologists, Dermatologists, and Neurologists (~46 weeks/year). Most other specialists work between 47 and 48 weeks/year.

FIGURE 5.2

Average Weekly Work Hours and Workloads of Different Specialists

Specialty	Patient Care	All Professional Activities	Patient Visits	% Time in Primary Care Activities
Cardiovascular Diseases	61	64	98	6
Anesthesiology	59	61	NA	<1
Radiology	59	58	NA	2
Gastroenterology	58	64	80	8
General Surgery	58	63	81	4
Urology	57	63	98	<1
Gen Internal Medicine	56	62	104	62
Obstetrics/Gynecology	56	61	101	24
Neurology	54	61	78	1
Orthopedic Surgery	54	60	112	4
Otolaryngology	52	58	91	3
Family Medicine	51	56	127	86
Emergency Medicine	50	56	118	30
Pediatrics	49	55	111	73
Ophthalmology	44	49	121	6
Psychiatry	44	47	NA	1
Dermatology	2	47	152	<1
Pathology	42	46	NA	<1

Adapted from: American Medical Association. *Physician Socioeconomic Statistics*, Chicago, IL: AMA, 2003.

Many specialists now join group practices to decrease their work hours and on-call time. Depending on the nature of the group, some physicians have found this quite helpful. This has resulted in a large variation in work hours not only among specialties, but also within each individual specialty. Therefore, a specialty's work hours should not be your only consideration when choosing a specialty—but they are a factor that should be taken seriously.

The Potential Future

It is difficult to predict either the need for or the supply of U.S. physicians in the future—either in total or by specialty. Physician oversupply and maldistribution has been an issue in the United States at least since an 1895 *Journal of the American Medical Association* discussion of the topic, which concluded, "our 'excess of doctors' would disappear at once" if the physician population was equitably distributed.

In the early 1990s, experts predicted an oversupply of as many as 165,000 physicians by the year 2000. Yet these predictions have not come to pass. *Anticipating future physician and specialty supply and demand is a very inexact science.*

It is now thought that there will be an increasing physician shortage that will become serious around the year 2011, with a shortage of about 200,000 physicians by 2020. The following factors support this prediction:

- The rapid aging of the population.
- A decreasing workload for residents.
- An increasing supply of women in medicine (with 20% fewer hours worked over their professional lives).
- A faster population growth rate than was expected.
- An aging physician population.
- Shorter working hours for all physicians due to the increase in alternative health plans, legislative requirements, and changing lifestyles.

Physicians may also continue to retire earlier. In recent years, physician retirement rates have increased significantly. The probability of a physician retiring between the ages of 55 and 74 has increased by 60% in the past decade. Above the age of 60, employed physicians consistently retired earlier than those in solo or group practices. According to AMA estimates, increasing retirement rates may absorb as much as one-third of the projected growth in physician supply by the year 2020.

Figure 5.3 shows estimates of the increase of physicians in the major specialties over the next 10 and next 20 years. While they are based somewhat on projected future needs, these numbers are highly speculative. For example, a decreasing birth rate may suggest a need for fewer Pediatricians, but a new health care system allowing children greater access may increase the need. Despite numerous studies, no one knows whether advances in the treatment of coronary artery disease will favor a need for more Invasive Cardiologists (those who pass catheters under x-ray guidance) rather than for more Cardiothoracic Surgeons. Changes in both the treatment of chronic renal disease and the government's and public's attitude toward chronic renal dialysis programs will profoundly affect the need for Nephrologists. Finding an organic basis for more major psychoses may reduce the need for Psychiatrists, while increasing the need for (and effectiveness of) Neurologists.

And, if history is any guide, AIDS and SARS will be only two of many epidemics requiring more Family Physicians, Internists, and Infectious Diseases specialists. The number of primary care physicians will most likely increase. Whether that will result in too many primary care physicians is uncertain.

FIGURE 5.3

Change in Number and Percentage of M.D. Physician Specialists,
2005, 2010, and 2020

Specialty	Number of Physicians			% Change 2005 to 2020
	2005	2010	2020	
TOTAL M.D.s & D.O.s	**831,447**	**891,687**	**1,038,234**	**25%**
PRIMARY CARE	**283,632**	**300,651**	**344,907**	**21**
Gen./Family Medicine	115,583	122,512	139,252	20
Gen. Internal Medicine	114,197	123,645	146,885	29
Gen. Pediatrics	53,852	54,494	58,770	9
MEDICAL SPECIALTIES	**104,145**	**113,200**	**135,331**	**30**
Medical Subspecialties	43,336	47,301	56,955	33
Cardiovascular Diseases	22,675	25,143	31,690	39
Other Med Specialties	38,133	40,756	46,687	24
SURGERY	**171,133**	**183,519**	**213,196**	**25**
General Surgery	40,605	44,473	53,641	32
Obstetrics/Gynecology	44,547	46,168	48,962	9
Otolaryngology	10,326	10,877	12,248	20
Orthopedic Surgery	24,804	26,736	31,596	28
Urology	11,455	12,448	15,122	30
Ophthalmology	20,099	21,650	25,972	30
Other Surg Specialties	19,296	21,167	25,655	33
OTHER PATIENT CARE	**221,355**	**239,224**	**280,405**	**27**
Psychiatry	46,877	49,340	54,116	15
Anesthesiology	39,547	43,188	52,493	33
Emergency Medicine	24,813	26,206	29,505	18
Radiology	33,218	36,919	45,855	38
Pathology	18,229	20,174	24,167	33
Other Specialties	58,672	63,398	74,270	27
NON-PATIENT CARE	**51,182**	**55,093**	**64,394**	**25**
U.S. POPULATION (000)	**294,100**	**307,075**	**335,444**	**14**

Adapted in part from: Bureau of Health Professions, Health Resources and Services Administration. *Changing Demographics: Implications for Physicians, Nurses and Other Health Workers.* Washington, DC: US Dept. of Health and Human Services. Spring 2003, p. 70 "Status Quo Scenario."

Basically, medicine does not remain static. Rather, it is an ocean of care with many storms and currents. The storms are the major new medical discoveries, new diseases, and changes in the population's demographics. The currents are the changes in attitudes, by both the medical community and the public concerning the popularity of various medical practices. (Yes, unfortunately, medicine is guided by more than pure science.) Your ship will sail this ocean. Care, foresight, and a willingness to occasionally alter course slightly will keep you afloat.

Difficulty of Getting a Residency Position

The difficulty you have in getting an individual residency position will vary with the amount of preparation you do, including correctly matching your aptitudes and accomplishments with a program's needs. However, you can "guesstimate" how difficult it will be to match with each specialty using the tables in the National Resident Matching Program's *Results and Data Book* (see Contact Information for address).

For example, in 2005, the average specialty offering PGY-1 positions through the NRMP PGY-1 Match filled 92.1% of the available spots (additional spots were filled outside of or after the Match). Those filling higher percentages, and thus being more difficult to match in, were Dermatology (28 spots; 100%), Pediatrics–Primary (87; 100%), General Surgery (1,051; 99%), Orthopedic Surgery (610; 99%), Emergency Medicine (1,188; 98%), Internal Medicine–Primary (290; 97%), Internal Medicine (4,768; 97%), Pediatrics (2,269; 97%), Psychiatry (1,026; 96%), Anesthesiology (463; 95%), and Obstetrics/Gynecology (1,144; 95%). Of note, however, is that U.S. senior (M.D.) students filled a relatively small number of some specialties' positions, including Primary Care Internal Medicine (59%), Pediatrics (52%), Pathology (62%), Psychiatry (64%), and Internal Medicine (56%), meaning that they are still rather easy for U.S. seniors to match with.

These numbers and those in the NRMP's charts (www.nrmp.org) do not include all the positions available to you. A more accurate picture can be seen by comparing some of these numbers with those in *FREIDA* or in Figure 22.2. Several specialties, including Child Neurology, Ophthalmology, Neurology, Neurological Surgery, Plastic Surgery, Urology, and some of the Internal Medicine subspecialties, hold separate matches for some or most of their positions (see Figure 22.9). These matches occur both through the NRMP and outside of it. Many programs in Preventive Medicine (Aerospace, Occupational, Public Health, and General Preventive Medicine), Medical Genetics, Nuclear Medicine, Trauma Surgery, many

Internal Medicine specialties, and many Osteopathic residencies require direct application to the programs.

Usually, programs accepting students for an advanced-level position require applicants to match separately in a Preliminary or Transitional internship program for their first year. The students themselves must usually arrange for this training, which means going through the NRMP Match to get a first-year slot. On occasion, the specialty program will arrange the first-year position. Find out how it usually works in the specialty of your choice by writing the specialty's board or society. However, you also need to check with the individual programs, as first-year arrangements may vary from program to program, even within the same specialty. Note that the rules for some specialties change yearly.

6

Starting The Process

There are three types of people: those who make things happen,
those who watch things happen, and those who wonder what happened.

– Anonymous

Choosing an Adviser/Mentor

SELECTING A MENTOR *is one of the most important career decisions you will*
ever make. Most students, however, don't have mentors—they only have
"advisers." These faculty members, usually chosen by the Dean, often have
multiple advisees and little time for any of them. They may not even have
any interest in actually helping students advance their careers in the right
direction. *You need a mentor!*

Selecting a mentor is serious business. When you were born, you could
not choose your parents. You now, however, have a choice of mentor. And
make no mistake about it, you are choosing a surrogate parent. At best,
your mentor can simplify the whole process of selecting your specialty,
choosing a desirable residency program, and getting into that program. At
worst, a mentor can obstruct your decision-making process by putting the
roadblocks of guilt and favors in the way of a correct personal choice.

Your mentor is the individual who will help you make the most of your
medical school education. He or she will get you over the rough spots,
show you opportunities that you otherwise might miss, guide your career,
and generally think of your interests above those of other medical students.
Your mentor is your guide, your teacher, your role model. But finding one
is up to you. It will take effort, initiative, and assertiveness on your part to
locate the right individual. The choice is yours—you can either find a mentor or resign yourself to struggling through on your own.

Choose Early

You should select your mentor early to have the widest possible selection and to fully use his or her expertise. "I'm only in my second semester," you say. "I'll wait until I have had some clinical experience." Baloney! The longer you wait, the less likely it is that your mentor will be:

- your first choice
- a mentor, rather than a standard "adviser"
- able to actually help you very much

A young man showed up in my office one day. Asking if he could have a few moments to talk to me, he explained that he had just been accepted into medical school. He would be starting classes in about six months and wanted to know if I would be his adviser. (His approach was correct. Using the word "mentor" often frightens faculty members.) He explained that he was not sure what field of medicine he wanted to enter, but thought that he had an interest in Emergency Medicine. I agreed to "advise" this student. As his mentor, I was able to introduce him to early clinical experiences, guide him to research opportunities, and help him over some rough spots in his life. Even though he had an interest in my specialty, I repeatedly challenged him on this decision—especially asking him to "tell me the worst parts about the specialty." As with any specialty, if he couldn't answer that question, he didn't know enough about the field.

During his clinical years, I showed him alternative paths to enable him to get the most out of his clinical experiences, prepared him for the entire residency matching process (in General Surgery, which he finally decided upon), and used personal contacts to get him interviews that he desired. He got into his first choice of residency programs. That, in part, was because he was savvy enough about both medical school and the residency selection process to have a mentor help him get the most out of those experiences. But, in fact, getting a supportive mentor is no different in medicine than it is in any field of endeavor. The trick is, start early!

What Type of Person?

When Odysseus went on his travels, Mentor was the person he entrusted with caring for his house and son. He looked for a wise and faithful counselor. That is also what you seek.

The individual you want as your mentor has five characteristics: clinical experience, approachability, the understanding and willingness to work through your insecurities, the character to act as your personal and professional role model, and a vested interest in helping you become successful, regardless of the specialty you ultimately choose.

How do you find a mentor? This will take some effort on your part. Start by making contacts with upper-level (third- and fourth-year) students. They should be doing clinical rotations, and so can be found at the hospital in the evening and at night. Two good places to make contact are in the hospital cafeteria and in the library. Introduce yourself as a fellow medical student and tell them that you need some advice. Unless they are in a rush to get somewhere (the life of a medical student is a harried one) they will be honored by your interest. The question you need to ask is, "Who are the best clinical teachers at the school?" Ask several students for their opinions. This will get you started.

Usually Clinical

Some students select their advisers by picking faculty members who are professors or department chairs. Some students may be lucky enough, using this method, to get counselors who are both interested in them and still knowledgeable about what they will need to do as medical students to get into a residency. But the primary requirement for becoming a full professor is research. Teaching really plays very little, if any, part in their promotion. So choose a mentor from the faculty members who are still involved in teaching, rather than from those who have "retired" to their offices and laboratories. *Your mentor must be reasonably accessible.*

Why choose a clinician rather than a basic scientist? There are three reasons. First, your career will probably be in clinical medicine. You need someone who knows the clinical ropes—not just those in the lecture hall and the lab. Second, the most difficult decisions you will face as a student will revolve around your clinical rotations. In what order should you take the required rotations? What should you do in your senior year? Clinicians are the most qualified people to answer such questions. Finally, your role model should live in the same world that you plan to enter—clinical medicine.

Pick a Known Teacher

Now you have a list of clinical teachers that other students consider excellent. Why did they choose these people? Being an excellent teacher takes effort. This effort stems from an interest in helping students to learn. It is also based on a deep and abiding interest in student welfare. Doesn't this sound like the type of person you want for a mentor? Of course, given the recognition of their excellence by other students, some of these individuals may already have many students whom they are counseling. If they cannot add another student, ask if they can recommend an individual whom they feel would be an excellent adviser. These people can usually spot the gems among their faculty, so take their suggestions seriously. If one of them feels that they can add you to his or her group, go for it. You already stand out by showing initiative so early. You can now do several other things to enhance that positive image.

Be visible. This means showing up with some regularity at your adviser's doorstep. The best and most productive way to accomplish this is to spend clinical time with him or her. This could mean doing afternoon or Saturday morning ward rounds, scrubbing in on a Saturday morning operation or procedure, or tagging along during an evening clinic or an emergency department shift. Since you have chosen a great teacher, it probably will be no time at all until you are actively participating (at your level of expertise) in patient care. If you do this, be sure to wear appropriate attire. This is the time to start looking professional. And bring along a stethoscope. Here is where you will begin to learn to use it.

Develop an image in your mentor's mind of a likable, courteous, and considerate individual. It is always pleasant to have a cheerful person around. But fawning and flattery generally have a negative effect. Mentors can see through these false habits in a minute.

Be respectful of your mentor's time. Once a clinician has agreed to be your adviser/mentor, make an appointment to see that individual whenever necessary. This is the professional thing to do and your mentor will appreciate your consideration of his or her valuable time.

Be clear about what you desire from your mentor (advice) and what your mentor can expect from you (hard work and dedication). Don't push for anything else. If you demonstrate the hard work and dedication, all else will follow.

Notice that nothing has been said yet about your mentor's specialty. Having examined your options, you probably have a general idea of what you are aiming for in the future. But, at best, it will be a very rough guess at this point. Try to select a mentor who is in a field compatible with your interests. For example, if you are contemplating Thoracic Surgery, a Dermatologist should probably not be your first choice as a mentor. If you do get a mentor who is in the specialty you finally choose, so much the better. However, *your choice of the appropriate person as your mentor actually depends more upon the individual than on his or her specialty.*

Steer Clear of Those with Blinders

Selecting someone who cannot see beyond his own chosen field of specialization is a real danger. You quickly may discover this attitude from such comments as, "The only real doctors are Surgeons," or "The only satisfaction in medicine comes from delivering babies." The key here is the word "only." At this point in your career, there is no "only," merely a lot of "maybes."

Too many medical school advisers and other faculty say "That's a bad career move" as they denigrate other specialties that students are considering. This statement is often accompanied by incorrect information about the other specialty. Instead, they should be supporting their students who are searching for the best fit of a specialty with their personality, needs, and abilities.

If you find that your selection for mentor wears specialty blinders, bail out—fast. This is the right time to get another adviser—one with a broader outlook about medical practice.

Supplement Later, If Necessary

Congratulations! You have gone through the process of getting a mentor early. This should help you through many of the rough spots in the road ahead. But now, after your exposure to Pediatrics, you are certain that you are destined to be a Pediatrician. Your mentor is an Anesthesiologist. What should you do?

First, make an appointment with your mentor. Explain that you have given the question of specialty choice a great deal of thought, and have decided on Pediatrics. If you have chosen your mentor correctly, he or she will understand and support your decision. He or she may also ask you why you made that decision and if you have thought about some important points related to your specialty decision. Being able to answer those questions may serve to deepen your resolve and help assure you that you have made the correct (initial) decision.

Next, ask if your adviser knows any Pediatricians, either from within the faculty or in the community, who could assist you in gathering more specific information about the specialty. Could he or she arrange an introduction or phone ahead to say that you will be calling for an appointment? Then, visit these referrals and get all the information and special help from them that you can.

But don't forget your mentor! He or she is still the physician who has your interests most at heart. Keep in close contact, and continue to run your major decisions by him or her for an honest appraisal. Your mentor can be a close contact and source of advice for the rest of your career—don't abandon that individual now.

No Available Specialty Adviser?

While most students will have at least one local physician in their specialty of interest to act as a mentor, no medical center has specialists in every field. Therefore, some students will be faced with the problem of no one practicing that specialty (or trained in the field) at their medical school.

What do they do? First, get an adviser who is sympathetic to your plight rather than someone who wants to steer you toward his or her specialty. Talk with the Dean of Students about this to get an appropriate person.

Next, contact the geographically closest physician practicing that specialty. If you have difficulty locating such a person, contact the national specialty organization for assistance. (See the contact information under each specialty's description in Chapter 3.) You can also check the "Doctor Finder" section of the American Medical Association's website (www.ama.org). Search for "Doctor Finder," then use the "patient" option to indicate your locale and the specialty in which you are interested. This list includes both AMA members and non-members. Contact that individual and see if they are willing to both give you long distance advice (e-mail, phone, mail) and have you visit their practice when you have time (weekends, holidays).

Testing Your Specialty Choice

Once you think you know which specialty you might like, why don't you give it a try? Would you buy a car without taking it for a test drive? Of course not! Then why consider investing time, effort, and money to train in a specialty when you really don't know if you have found the correct one?

At graduation, only 20% of medical students are still interested in entering the same specialty that they wanted when they entered medical school. That is certainly understandable. More troubling is that nearly 25% of all physicians change their specialties after graduation, either during their training or shortly thereafter. In many cases, this is due to poor planning. Be smart. Test your specialty choice before you invest too much of yourself in it.

Volunteer Time

One of the best ways to learn about a specialty is to spend some of your free time on that clinical service. This is especially true if that specialty rotation is not available early in your third year of medical school. If your mentor is in this field, you should have no problem arranging this. Otherwise, he or she might help you contact a physician in that specialty with whom you can work.

No matter where you are in your training now, you are probably saying, "What free time?" The answer is that you have time to do anything that is important to you. *This is important.* Certainly you can arrange to have a half-hour or 45 minutes to participate in a portion of morning rounds before class. How about Saturday or Sunday mornings?

What information are you seeking? Look at the specialists you're with. Do they seem happy doing what they do? Would you enjoy doing what they do? Do you want to have the same type of clinical practice as they have? Will it provide enough intellectual stimulation for you? What don't you like about it? Could you put up with it for your entire career? These are just a few of the questions that you should ask yourself during your volunteer stint. Some of the questions you will ask yourself, and the clinical experiences that you will have, will differ depending upon your level of training and prior clinical experience. The farther along you are in your training, and the more in-depth your clinical experiences have been, the more subtle the questions you will be able to ask yourself about the specialty.

But this doesn't mean you should delay volunteering for clinical experiences to explore your choices. Rather, it means you should start early. The more of this type of volunteer time that you spend, the faster you will gain experience and be able to probe your specialty choice in depth. *Also, spend some of your time in a community hospital or office setting.* This will give you a broader view of how the specialty is practiced away from the academic medical center.

Pre-med

This is an excellent time to volunteer in a specialty. You have time to spare. And you can find out something even more important than what specialty you want to enter: *You can determine if you really want to become a physician.* This must be *your* choice, not your parents', teachers', or friends' choice for you. And in volunteering, you will be able to see the amount of dedication, hard work, and commitment to continued learning that the profession requires. If a medical career is really what you want, this experience will renew your motivation. If not, it may save you a lot of frustration and help you to redirect your energies.

How do you volunteer at this stage of your training? Undoubtedly, it will be more difficult to get a volunteer position in a specific specialty now than it will be after you enter medical school. You may have fewer contacts in the medical field and less knowledge upon which to base a specialty decision.

Your best bet is to first approach your family's doctor. Tell him or her of your interest in the medical profession and of your desire to experience medicine firsthand by "tagging along and helping out." Usually the clinician will be flattered that you asked, and will let you participate in at least a limited fashion. After a few months of this (stick it out, you are learning vital information on which to base lifelong decisions), it may become obvious that you have progressed beyond the level of knowledge that this practitioner can offer. If the practitioner does not spontaneously suggest it, you should inquire as to whether there is a more in-depth (read "active") medical experience available to you. If you know this physician really well, you might even address the possibility in your first meeting. In many cases, of course, working with a practitioner of this sort will be interesting and intriguing. If that is true for you, stick with it.

Okay, you don't have a family physician and neither of your parents are physicians. (Physician-parents should generally be able to help you to arrange these experiences.) What do you do now? If you are not quite gutsy enough to walk in on a physician unannounced, try to get some leads from the staff at your college's student health center. If this does not prove useful, go to a major hospital in your area and volunteer to work in a clinical area.

The hospital you choose depends upon your interests. To start, you may want to pick the hospital that gets most of the accident victims (Level I Trauma Center). Ask to work in the emergency department. There you will see both a wide variety of illnesses and injuries and some of the activities of practitioners in many different specialties. You may even make some contacts that you can use in the future. If you have the opportunity and the time, it might even be useful for you to work as an emergency department aide. These positions are often available to individuals with little or no experience. Then you will really be part of the team and be able to interact with patients in an even closer manner. You will also get paid.

Preclinical Years

If you are reading this between studying for Physiology or Pharmacology, you may question where you will find time to volunteer clinically. You can use nights, weekends, and holidays for this clinical activity, after the demands of studying (and the absolute imperative to find some time for yourself) have been satisfied.

Volunteering to work clinically during the preclinical years is an essential part of your career preparation—not only to help you choose a specialty, but also to remind you of why you struggled so hard to get into medical school. You have more clinical opportunities available than does an undergraduate student. Remember, you are a *medical student*. You will soon be a physician, and the entire profession stands ready to help you.

Basically, you will find yourself in one of two situations, depending upon the nature of your medical school. The first results from the traditional medical school structure, in which the major teaching hospital is adjacent to the school. There you will bump into "white coats" every day. And you will have little difficulty finding the time between classes to approach clinicians about working with them. The hospital and the physicians working there are oriented toward education and will, in general, be ready to accommodate you.

The second type of medical school is less consolidated than the first type. This makes it somewhat more difficult to get a meaningful clinical experience early in your training. Either the basic science and clinical campuses are geographically separated or there is no specific or adjacent teaching-oriented hospital. (These latter are the "community-based" medical schools.) A mentor, if you have one, can be invaluable in assisting you here. If you don't have a mentor, you will have to approach local hospitals and practitioners on your own. Success depends upon your persistence; keep trying if you are initially turned down.

With community-based medical schools, there are several options for locating volunteer opportunities. As when choosing a mentor, you can get leads from upper-level medical students. If your school offers Physical Diagnosis courses in the first and second years, use your instructor as a resource. He or she might actually be an individual with whom you can work in a real clinical setting. You can also approach physicians at the largest of the affiliated community teaching hospitals. They are more attuned to education than other practitioners. And even if the first physician you contact can't help you, that clinician can probably give you some excellent leads. If nothing else proves fruitful, try the county or state medical societies. Some branches have programs designed to pair students with practitioners.

The most important reason to obtain clinical experience in your preclinical years is to learn the relationship of the basic sciences to the practice of medicine. "But why will this be important to me as a physician?" asked a first-year medical student after a rather mystifying biochemistry lecture. The lecturer, a Ph.D. who proudly proclaimed whenever he had the chance that he had never been in a hospital as an adult, could not answer the student's question. He did not even understand it.

You are in medical school to become a physician. In almost every case, physicians interact with the ill and injured on a daily basis. If you wonder why the basic sciences are important, you may find the answers in the real and immediate classroom of clinical experience. The basic sciences are not just "important," but vital to understanding clinical practice and the changes that will occur in medicine during your career. Spend some time in clinical activities. It's worth it.

Clinical Years

If you are already in your clinical years, mere additional clinical exposure is not what you need. You must spend time testing your tentative specialty choices.

"But when do I have the time?" you ask. The answer is, during "slow" rotations, on weekends, and in the evenings. If you find spending time with specialists in the field you plan to enter to be too much work, rather than a joy, perhaps you have discovered the answer to whether you are really interested in that specialty. If you don't enjoy the work now, how will you feel about it in 20 years? Or during the 20 years after that?

By your fourth year, you should have made a reasonably definite and educated decision regarding a specialty choice. Some students wait until their elective time to test their specialty choices. That is too late. Unless there is an elective opportunity in the third year, you cannot afford to wait that long to make a decision. You should use the prime elective time early in your fourth year for two vital electives.

First, take a rotation that will allow you to make decisions and take responsibility for them, such as an Internal Medicine or a General Surgery subinternship. These experiences will help you to be a "star" when you take your next elective in your chosen specialty. Use this elective to "show your stuff" to the specialists who will be writing your letters of recommendation.

At many schools, students are now allowed to postpone some required clerkships, such as Psychiatry, Neurology, and Family Medicine, until their fourth year. This allows them time earlier in their training to experience other fields, such as Anesthesiology and Radiology, which have traditionally been reserved for fourth-year elective time. If it is not overdone, this may be a good chance to get a more in-depth look at an area you have strongly considered as a career.

Reading (See the *Annotated Bibliography*)

There are several sources for material dealing with every specialty and sub-specialty.

The first source (often the easiest to access) is the Internet, although finding the right URL may be difficult. The current URLs are listed under each specialty description in Chapter 3; most provide you with additional "links." The bibliography contains more URLs, and many others are listed in appropriate sections throughout this book. They are up-to-date at the time of publication but, as you know, the Web constantly changes, so if the supplied URLs don't work, use a search engine with the organization's name. If you use Google, go to the "Advanced Search" mode (www.google.com/advanced_search) and put the name in the "exact phrase" box. Rarely, some specialty organizations dissolve, change names, or merge. If you still can't find it, look at the links on related websites.

Your medical school's library is another great source of information. If you are interested in any of the more popular specialties, there should not only be factual material on the specialty, but also biographies of individuals in the field. Also, look for articles highlighting the specialty in *The New Physician*, which regularly prints reviews of major specialties. Specialty journals, especially the "throwaways," may also give you an idea of the breadth of the discipline. This is particularly true for some of the smaller specialties, which do not get significant coverage in journal articles that usually discuss only the larger specialties. The reference librarians can also help you locate online information that you haven't been able to find.

Two other excellent sources of information are the American Medical Association Medical Student Section's *Specialty Specific Information* site (go to www.ama-assn.org/go/mss and scroll down to "Tools You Can Use"— "Residency Resources") and the *Pathway Evaluation Program's "Specialty Profiles"* (http://medweb.usc.edu/pathways/intro.htm). The Association of American Medical Colleges offers a briefer review of many specialties on its *Careers in Medicine* site (www.aamc.org/students/cim/specialties.htm). Generally, these sources review the history, economics, and practice of most of the medical specialties.

For information about the smaller or newer specialties, you may have to turn to other sources. One, discussed in more detail in Chapter 9, is the *Directory of Graduate Education Programs*. In the section on "Essentials of Accredited Residencies in Graduate Medical Education," it provides a wealth of information about each officially recognized specialty and sub-specialty.

Ask your mentor or adviser for material about the specialty that you are considering. This individual may have information from a variety of sources, or may have produced some herself. Finally, you may want to borrow a standard text for the field (assuming that you are considering a lesser-known specialty that is not well-represented in the library). This should also give you a broad idea of the discipline's scope.

Talk to Many Specialists in the Field

Specialty choices are often based on a student's interaction with one physician in a given field. Often this specialist is a parent or the family's doctor. Other times it is an assigned adviser or a respected faculty member. But no matter who the role model is, basing your entire career on only one individual's experiences can lead to disaster.

It is essential that you get input from a wide variety of practitioners as you try to decide on your medical specialty. If your interest is Dermatology, this does not mean talking only with the faculty at your school. You should also visit Dermatologists in private practice, group practice settings, and health maintenance organizations in your community. If there is a county or state society meeting for the specialty, try to attend it as a student observer. Normally, these specialty societies will welcome you. You will then have a chance to talk with a variety of specialists practicing in that field, and will also hear about the problems they face in their practices and about their general attitude toward their own specialty choice.

Many physicians practicing today would not choose the same specialty if they had it to do over again. While some of this may be due to "the grass is always greener" syndrome, in large part, it is because they made career decisions without adequate information and with inappropriate expectations. Get as much information as you can directly "from the horses' mouths." The grief you save will be your own.

Match Your Choice to Your Needs

It is vital, when choosing the direction your career will take, to consider your personal desires.

Abraham Maslow, in his famous book, *Motivation and Personality* (Harper & Row, New York, 1954), sought to explain why people are driven by particular needs at particular times. He felt that all human needs are arranged in a hierarchy, from the most pressing to the least pressing (Figure 6.1). As each level of need is satisfied, it is no longer a driving force for that individual. For nearly all medical students, the basic physiological needs, such as hunger and thirst, have been satisfied. The safety needs of security and protection will be satisfied if you believe you will complete medical school, get into a residency program, and earn a living. The factors on this level, plus those on the next most important level, the esteem needs of recognition, self-esteem, and status, are very often the driving forces behind a medical student's specialty choice. (Most medical students can see that the social needs of love and belonging will be fulfilled in the future, if not now.)

What you must do, however, is look beyond these levels and try to visualize what you will need to reach the highest level—*Self-Actualization*. Basically, you must try to determine *what will be fulfilling to you for the rest*

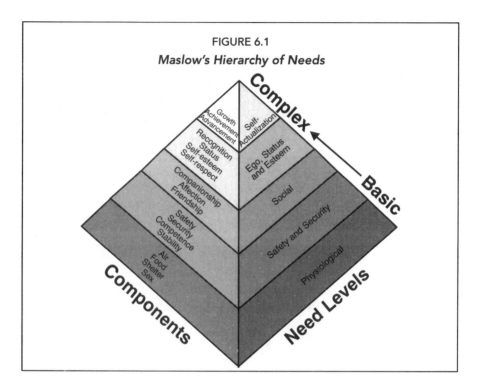

FIGURE 6.1
Maslow's Hierarchy of Needs

of your life. Will you be happy in your specialty choice at age 40? Will you be able to meet your life goals? (You are about to be a doctor so you have essentially achieved that goal.) This is something that, though easily stated, is very hard to do. Yet if you give it some serious thought—reflecting on it and talking it over with those close to you, you may very well make a much better decision than you otherwise might have made.

7

Grades, Tests, & Clinical Clerkships

Whether you think you can or think you can't, you're right.

– Henry Ford

Putting Your Effort Where It Counts

SUCCEEDING IN MEDICAL SCHOOL takes a lot of work. But since there are many areas in which to work hard and only a finite amount of time and energy available to put into them, it is important to determine where you should put your greatest effort—and how to make it pay off.

Residency programs will use your grades, test scores, and, occasionally, "audition electives" to evaluate your medical school performance. Institutions, and specific residency programs within those institutions, vary widely in how they assess the individual components of any candidate's application. How a particular program will evaluate the various criteria is almost impossible to ascertain. The best you can do is to put as much effort as possible into each of the following areas. Your personal strengths will help determine the areas in which you excel.

Honor Grades

Grades reflect your abilities over a wide range of activities. Therefore, they are one of the major factors used to differentiate you from other applicants. In the basic sciences, grades reflect your ability to gather, memorize, regurgitate, and, occasionally (especially in schools with problem-based learning), synthesize information. Grades from clinical services reflect your ability to perform basic patient care, to memorize information, and to work well with patients, staff, and physicians. This is measured by how well you regurgitate the information for exams and synthesize it on the wards. Grades from clinical rotations also reflect your social and interactive skills.

Getting "Honors" (equivalent to an "A" or a "4.0" on a four-point scale; also equivalent to "High Honors," "Outstanding," or "Superior" at some schools) sets you apart from your classmates—and, more important, other applicants. But it will be the rare individual, indeed, who will be able to get all, or even a majority of, "Honors" grades. So, it may benefit you to set your sights on particular courses and clerkships in which to make an all-out effort for "Honors," and to settle for lower (but passing) grades in the remaining classes.

If your school happens to be on a strict pass-fail system, you will have a slightly lower chance of getting into the most competitive residencies. You cannot change the grading system your school uses—at least not by yourself. So, you will have to concentrate on other demonstrable honors, awards, and letters of recommendation.

Order of Importance

Okay, so you have decided to put extra effort into certain courses to get "Honors" grades in them. How do you decide which ones? Actually, it is not that difficult.

Third-Year Required Clerkships

Your grades (not to mention your letters of recommendation) in required third-year clerkships are the most important for getting a residency. While the level of difficulty and type of experience you get in your preclinical years can vary widely among medical schools, junior-year clinical experiences are, for the most part, very similar—even though their grading varies greatly from school to school. Therefore, residency programs find them the easiest way to compare applicants. *Residency directors know that students' high honors grades in core clerkships are excellent predictors of outstanding clinical performance and consider them one of the most important factors in resident selection.* Also, unless you are going into Pathology, patient care is the job for which you will be applying. Therefore, residency programs must know whether you are competent in this area. Since you will apply to the programs very early in your fourth year, most of the clinical grades that the evaluators see when selecting candidates for interviews will be those from the third year.

If you are entering a specialty that is required in the third-year curriculum, such as Internal Medicine, General Surgery, Pediatrics, Psychiatry, Obstetrics and Gynecology, and often Neurology or Family Medicine, it will obviously be to your advantage to do well in that area. Otherwise, the two clerkships that normally carry the most weight in residency selection are Internal Medicine and Surgery. Make an extra effort to do well on these rotations.

Here is a note about your third year in general: You will probably find your junior year of medical school to be both the most exciting and the most confusing period of your professional career. As you rotate through the various specialties, you will be barraged by their differing attitudes, rules of behavior, and personalities. Even if you have a good idea about which discipline you want for a career, don't close your mind to the experiences that you encounter. You might find a field that interests you more than your original choice. But don't rely on a single experience at a single institution with a single group of physicians to make your career decision. It may be very misleading.

In what order should you take your junior clerkships? Basically, it boils down to deciding whether to take Medicine and Surgery early in the year or later, after you have been "seasoned" by completing the "lesser" clerkships. The answer depends upon two things:

1. **How much clinical experience have you obtained during your preclinical years?** If you have had significant clinical experience, it matters little when you take any particular clerkship.

2. **Do you want to go into a specialty that is offered in the third year?** If you think that you do but you are not sure, take that clerkship early to find out if you like it. On the other hand, if you are sure, take it at a time when you can be certain of doing well on the rotation. Again, if you already have a great deal of clinical experience, take it when it is convenient. If you are a clinical novice, then wait until later in your third year to "show your stuff." Going through other clinical areas first will improve your performance—and your grade.

Specialty Clerkship

Next in importance to your third-year clerkships, and often of equal or greater importance in some specialties (such as Ophthalmology and Orthopedic Surgery), is your performance in your chosen specialty's senior clerkship. Where and with whom you take this clerkship is critical. If you plan on going into Radiology, taking a Radiology clerkship at the local suburban hospital won't work, no matter what the quality of teaching or your experiences. Use that site for extra volunteer time.

For a senior specialty elective "Honors" grade that residency programs view favorably, and to obtain a beneficial recommendation letter, take this rotation *at a major teaching hospital with an attending physician who is well-known to residency directors in the field.* Since you have ample leeway in setting up your senior schedule, there is no reason why you cannot find a suitable clerkship.

Remember that the smaller specialties (e.g., Neurological Surgery, Oto-laryngology) and smaller programs in most other specialties prefer to take applicants they know. Use this to your advantage.

Preclinical

Third on the list of priorities for getting "Honors" grades are the preclinical courses. This, of course, does not include those of you who are interested in going either into Pathology or into a research-oriented career. In both of these cases, "Honors" grades in the preclinical years are very important. For a Pathology residency, preclinical "Honors" grades will often be the most important selection factor.

If you are interested in a clinically oriented career, you should pick and choose carefully where to focus your main effort during the first two years. For those entering the Surgical specialties, "Honors" in Anatomy and Pathology are very helpful. Those contemplating any of the Neurosciences (including Psychiatry) should strive for excellence in their Neuroscience course. And for almost everyone else, the key courses are Pharmacology and Physiology. This is not meant to imply that you shouldn't try to make a clean sweep by getting more "Honors" grades. But in reality, this is just not possible for most mortals. So, direct your efforts where they will count the most.

A strategy that some students find successful is to pick one major course each semester (or quarter) in which to try to achieve an "Honors" grade. Then, when you have a little extra time to study, concentrate on that course. While this strategy does not always work, many individuals have found that it gives them motivation to study just a bit harder.

Senior Electives

The grades from senior electives are the least significant to most programs when choosing residents. *This does not include electives in your chosen specialty.* Other senior grades are considered very minimally—except in extraordinary cases, such as getting all "Honors" or, at the other extreme, failing or getting "Incomplete" in a course. All experienced residency directors know that "grade inflation," that is, a higher percentage of excellent scores than is warranted, is rampant on senior electives. This is especially true for electives taken outside the main teaching hospitals. So, don't expect to correct a dismal record with a lot of "Honors" grades from fourth-year electives. Everyone will see through that ploy.

One problem for some individuals is that the grades for senior specialty electives will not be recorded in time to affect your selection for an interview. If you have done very well on a rotation in your chosen specialty, have your Dean's office send an updated transcript to the programs to which you are applying and get a letter from the elective director to give to the residency directors during your interview. Of course, if you didn't do well in some senior electives (too much time at the beach?), not having the grades on the mailed transcript will be to your advantage.

Clinical Honors = Effort + Effort + Effort

Since so much emphasis is placed on doing well during clinical rotations, understand that you do not have to be either a genius or a saint to get "Honors" grades. All it takes is a realization that you will have to expend *effort, effort, and more effort.* This includes *in-depth reading* about the patients that you have seen, are taking care of, or will see (such as those in the operating room). If you have time, also read about the other patients on the ward. If you are scheduled to do a procedure, read about it in advance. And don't just scan the *Cliff's Notes* version; get a book that will give you detailed information. If you can, also learn a few pieces of arcane trivia about the disease or procedure. These are always fun to introduce into discussions when making rounds.

Know the ropes. New rotations initially confuse all students and residents. Each service has its own culture, its own rules, its own body of basic knowledge, and its own stumbling blocks for the unwary. One way to ease your transition into a new rotation is to discover exactly what the service expects of you. (See Figure 7.1 for a list of questions to ask.) If you don't receive this information at least a week before the rotation begins, call or visit the rotation director's office to ask your questions. Often, the secretary will have a pre-printed list of information that is normally handed out the first day; get it in advance.

Round early and stay late. If you show up before the rest of your team to find out what happened on the ward overnight, you will be able to help the housestaff immeasurably. This often translates into glowing recommendations about you to the attendings. Stay late to complete any work that was left undone. If you are still there (doing something useful, not just hanging around) when the other students are gone, you will stand out as the hard worker you are.

Volunteer for extra or onerous work. Of course no one wants to put an IV into Mrs. Smith for the twentieth time or to push Mr. Jones down to radiology, but volunteer to do it with a *smile.* Not only will you make points, but you also may get priority in doing things that you want to do, such as the next thoracentesis or hernia repair.

FIGURE 7.1

Questions about Clerkship Expectations

- What are the goals and objectives for the rotation?
- What clinical responsibilities do students have?
- Where and when should I report the first day?
- At which facilities will I work?
- What is the call schedule? Is there in-house call for students?
- Is there a conference and lecture schedule?
- Do students carry pagers?
- Are there non-clinical responsibilities (such as a presentation)?
- Who is the attending? How often will I meet with him or her?
- Who will be the senior resident on the service?
- Which other students will be on the rotation?
- Is there a list of required or suggested readings?
- Are there printed descriptions of special clinical procedures?
- Are there study questions?
- Will there be written or oral exams? How many and when?
- Who evaluates students? On what basis?
- Can I see a copy of the student-performance evaluation form?
- Is housing available for out-of-town students?
- Can I interview for a residency position during the rotation?

Show enthusiasm in everything that you do on the clinical services. Be pleasant. Smile, even if it is after your bedtime (or maybe you haven't been to sleep and it's 6 A.M.). Everyone gets tired, but if you use the energy you still have to bolster everyone's spirits, you will earn big points—and will have a better time doing it than if you are sullen.

Clinical services are increasingly using problem- and case-based small-group instruction during clerkships. The hints below have helped other students perform well in these groups.

Small Group Participation

- Show up for all sessions.
- Read required material in advance.
- Listen actively (i.e., focus on the speaker).
- Participate an appropriate amount of the time.
- Ask questions that improve discussion and understanding.
- Show respect for other group members' opinions.
- Relate positively and constructively to other group members.
- Encourage other group members to participate.
- Help to keep the discussion on track.

Problem-Based Learning Hints
(Also useful for presenting cases on the wards.)
- Show up for all sessions.
- Read and research the Problem Case(s) and Learning Issues in advance.
- Prepare using MEDLINE, textbooks, journal articles, and expert faculty.
- Critically interpret information and information sources.
- Identify case issues that may lead to Learning Issues.
- Share information appropriately.
- Identify pertinent facts in the case.
- Present information in an organized manner.
- Formulate hypotheses.
- Identify the information needed to progress further with the case.
- Apply previously learned and new information to the case problems.

Finally, if there are written or oral exams at the end of the rotation—*study*. Find out early if there will be such a test (there usually is) and try to ascertain what will be on it. Then use your extra time (believe it or not there will usually be a lot of "down time" on the wards) to study. If you know what you have to study at the beginning of the rotation, the reading that you do about your patients will complement, enhance, and, often, shorten your study time.

The key to success on clinical rotations, as one student wrote in her personal statement, is to "Work like a duck: appear smooth on the surface, but paddle like crazy underneath."

Licensing Examinations

The United States Medical Licensing Examination (USMLE) is now the standard licensing examination for M.D.s who wish to practice in the United States or Canada, no matter where they were educated. Osteopathic physicians may take either their own licensing examination, the COMLEX, or the USMLE. These tests assess examinees' understanding and application of biomedical and clinical sciences and medical knowledge to the practice of clinical medicine. They are generally taken over a period of years during medical school and early clinical training.

Licensing examinations, however, are not used solely to obtain medical licenses; residency programs use them to screen applicants, many medical schools require students to pass them to advance or graduate, and some states require that physicians pass specific USMLE Steps before beginning or continuing residency training. Repeated studies in many specialties have shown that residents' performance during training and on their specialty Board examinations directly correlates to how well they do on the USMLE. Residency directors know that and select applicants accordingly.

Many schools use USMLE Steps 1 and 2 as a part of their student evaluation system: 123 (of 125 total) U.S. M.D. medical schools require students to take Step 1, 122 schools require Step 2 Clinical Knowledge (CK), and 120 require Step 2 Clinical Skills (CS). For advancement or graduation, 108 U.S. M.D. schools require a passing score on Step 1, 83 schools require passing Step 2CK, and 44 schools require passing Step 2CS. Only 17 schools do not require students to pass any USMLE Steps to advance or graduate. Some residency directors are hesitant to "rank" applicants who have not completed their school's graduation requirements.

The Federation of State Medical Boards now recommends that all medical students pass USMLE Steps 1, 2CS, and 2CK prior to entering residency programs. This means that applicants may have to prove that they passed these exams before the date that residency directors submit their rank-order lists to the NRMP (or sooner for the "early" matches). More than 60% of residency programs require applicants to submit Step 1 USMLE scores; approximately 40% require scores from Steps 1, 2CS, and 2CK. Applicants who have taken both Step 1 and the two components of Step 2 before applying to residencies may have a better chance of matching with the programs they rank highly—if they have done well on the exams. As a result of the rapid scoring possible after a computer-based exam (generally sent within six weeks) and the automatic transmission (if requested by the applicant) of scores to residency programs, more applicants are reporting their Step 2 scores.

The Educational Commission for Foreign Medical Graduates (ECFMG) also administers Steps 1, 2CK, and 2CS. These three exams fulfill the medical science examination requirement for ECFMG certification. All international medical graduates, including U.S. citizens, should apply directly to the ECFMG to take the USMLE.

United States Medical Licensing Examination (USMLE)
Overview
The USMLE (which some students paradoxically call "You Smile") has been given twice annually since 1992–94, when it replaced the old "National Board" exams. The computerized versions were introduced sequentially, with Step 1 beginning in May 1999, Step 2 in August 1999, Step 3 in November 1999, and Step 2 Clinical Skills in June 2004. The advantages of computerized exams are:

- Enhanced security (questions are drawn from a pool of content-parallel questions in a very large question bank).
- Increased flexibility for examinees in scheduling their exam time (since all Steps are now offered throughout the year).
- Shorter testing times for Steps 1 and 2.
- Wider access to the exam.
- Faster score reporting.
- The ability to add new assessment methods to the exams.

The downside to computerization is the fear engendered in those who do not feel that they are computer literate. While U.S. graduates have not reported problems, some IMGs with less computer experience have felt threatened by the computer-based format.

The computerized Step 1 is a one-day (eight-hour) examination consisting of seven 60-minute blocks of approximately 50 multiple-choice "one-best answer" questions.

As of June 2004, Step 2 is made up of two examinations: Step 2 Clinical Knowledge (CK) and Step 2 Clinical Skills (CS). Step 2CK is a one-day (nine-hour) examination consisting of eight 60-minute blocks of approximately 45 multiple-choice questions each. Step 2CS is a one-day (eight-hour) examination broken into 25-minute segments, during which students interact with 12 "standardized patients." While Step 2 was designed to be taken near the end of the final year of medical school, many U.S. medical students take it at the end of their first clinical year (year 3 in most schools).

Step 3 is a two-day (eight hours each day) exam, with a day and a half to take 480 multiple-choice questions and a half day with nine Computer-based Case Simulations (CCS). All three Steps have many tables and graphs to interpret.

While the exact questions each examinee gets will vary, everyone is tested on equivalent content. The difficulty of the questions may vary, but the results are statistically adjusted so that all examinees are treated fairly. How well an examinee does on the initial blocks of questions may determine which subsequent blocks he or she gets. Within the time period allowed for a block, examinees may answer questions in any order, go back to review responses, and change their answers. However, once the time is up, the questions and responses in that block cannot be accessed.

Examinees may take Steps 1, 2CS, and 2CK in any sequence; the components are scored and the results are reported separately. You must pass both Steps 1 and 2 before taking Step 3.

How to Apply

All applicants should obtain the *USMLE Bulletin of Information* from www.usmle.org. A separate booklet on the Step 2CS exam can also be downloaded.

Students in and graduates of accredited U.S. and Canadian M.D. and D.O schools, including foreign nationals or "Green Card" holders attending U.S. or Canadian schools, apply to the National Board of Medical Examiners (NBME) to take Steps 1, 2CK, and 2CS, and apply to their state's medical board for Step 3. Application materials are available on the NBME's website at www.nbme.org. For other questions, you can contact NBME, Department of Licensing Examination Services, 3750 Market St., Philadelphia, PA 19104; (215) 590-9700; e-mail: webmail@nbme.org.

International medical students and graduates (IMGs) should get information about the requirements to take the examination, and apply for it through the Educational Commission for Foreign Medical Graduates' (ECFMG) website (www.ecfmg.org). The ECFMG can also be reached at: 3624 Market St., Philadelphia, PA 19104-2685; (215) 386-5900. Fifth Pathway students will already have taken part of the USMLE through the ECFMG. As with other candidates, IMGs apply to the state medical board for Step 3.

Follow the instructions on the NBME or ECFMG website to apply for the USMLE. The application is usually completed online, but it can also be submitted by mail. Submit your application at least three months before you expect to take the test.

When you apply, you must select a three-month "eligibility period" during which you prefer to take the exam. Be sure that the three-month time period begins at least six weeks from the date you submit (or mail) your application, to allow time for your application to be processed. If you need to, you can ask later for a three-month extension to your eligibility period (*in writing*; the form is on the website). USMLE officials may grant the extension—*but only once, and for an additional fee.* If you do not take the test during the original or extended eligibility period, you will need to reapply with a new application and pay the full fee again.

After your application has been processed, you will receive your "Scheduling Permit," which will detail the Step for which you registered, your eligibility period, your testing region, your Scheduling Number (SN), and your Candidate Identification Number (CIN), which is a private code that you will need to take the exam. Information and instructions necessary to schedule your exam with a Prometric Center are also included. If you do not receive this material or lose it, call the NBME between 8 A.M. and 5 P.M. Eastern Time.

Eligibility (see Figure 7.2)

Steps 1, 2CK, and 2CS: Medical students should be officially enrolled in or a graduate of: (1) a U.S. or Canadian medical school accredited by the LCME or the AOA; or (2) a medical school recognized by the ECFMG (year of graduation and medical school must be listed in the *International Medical Education Directory* [IMED] of the Foundation for Advancement of International Medical Education and Research [FAIMER®]).

Step 3: Applicants must: (1) have an M.D. (or equivalent) or D.O. degree; (2) have passed USMLE Steps 1, 2CK, and 2CS (if a recent graduate) or, if an IMG, hold an ECFMG Certificate or have completed a "Fifth Pathway" program; and (3) meet any other requirements set by the Medical Board through which they are applying (see Figure 7.10). Initial applicants for a medical license who do not meet the standard eligibility criteria, but who otherwise meet all other requirements of the licensing board, may be allowed to take the examination if the licensing board makes a request to the USMLE's Secretariat.

Special Testing Arrangements

Special testing arrangements (formally called "Special accommodations"), such as a separate room or increased examination time limits for students with disabilities, can be arranged. If you have special needs due to a documented physical or learning disability that is covered under the Americans with Disabilities Act (ADA), contact the group that administers the Step (NBME, ECFMG, or state medical board) as early as possible. They will supply you with additional information and a supplementary application for special accommodations. Much of this information is also on the USMLE, NBME, ECGMG, and FSMB (www.fsmb.org) websites.

Any request for special accommodations must be submitted with supporting documentation at the time you apply to take the Step. Although you should mail these forms at the same time as your application, *send the application separately.* Special accommodations that the USMLE may provide include assistance with keyboard tasks, audio renditions of the material, extended testing time, extra breaks, large-print versions, and other adaptations. Any special accommodations used during the testing are noted on the USMLE score reports and transcripts.

Scheduling the USMLE

Test scheduling is on a "first-come, first served" basis. Therefore, contact the ProMetric scheduling representative immediately after receiving your permit to schedule your exam. (The phone number will be on the permit.) You can also schedule it online at www.prometric.com and receive

FIGURE 7.2
USMLE Eligibility Requirements and Contacts

USMLE Step	Type of Applicant	Contact to Take Examination	Contact to Send USMLE Transcript
Step 1 or Step 2 only (CK or CS)	Students officially enrolled in or graduated from medical schools in the U.S. and Canada accredited by the Liaison Committee on Medical Education (LCME) or the American Osteopathic Association.	NBME Dept. of Licensing Examination Services 3750 Market St. Philadelphia, PA 19104-3190 (215) 590-9700 e-mail: webmail@nbme.org www.nbme.org	NBME If registered through the NBME (most U.S. and Canadian medical students) and going to recipients (e.g., residency programs) other than licensing bodies (e.g., state medical boards). Results can also be sent through ERAS.
Step 1 or Step 2 only (CK or CS)	Students officially enrolled in or graduated from Foreign Medical Schools. A "foreign" medical school is one that is located outside the U.S., Canada, and Puerto Rico that, at the time of application to take the USMLE (student) or at graduation, is listed in the FAIMER *International Medical Education Directory.*	ECFMG 3624 Market St. Philadelphia, PA 19104-2685 (215) 386-5900 e-mail: info@ecfmg.org www.ecfmg.org	ECFMG If registered through the ECFMG (most international medical graduates) and going to recipients (e.g., residency programs) other than licensing bodies (e.g., state medical boards). Results can also be sent through *ERAS.*
Step 3	All medical graduates who have: (1) Passed Steps 1 and 2 (2) Met their licensing authority's requirements (varies in different locales) (3) If an IMG obtained an ECFMG Certificate or successfully completed a Fifth Pathway program.	Medical Licensing Authority (State Medical Board) – or – FSMB Dept. of Examination Services P.O. Box 619850 Dallas, TX 75261-9850 (817) 868-4041 e-mail: usmle@fsmb.org www.fsmb.org	FSMB For any transcript going to a medical licensing body (e.g., state medical board).

confirmation via e-mail, although this may be slower than speaking to the representative.

Before calling ProMetric, select several alternative dates and testing locations. (Locate ProMetric test centers near you by using their website. When scheduling your exam, you will need to have your SN. To unlock your test at the Center, you will need your CIN. (Keep these numbers confidential.) The representative will give you information about available dates at the centers near you, including, if necessary, alternative centers with open dates. Note that May, June, July, November, and December are the most popular months to take the exams in the United States and Canada. The test centers are closed on major U.S. holidays and for the first two weeks in January.

Note: To avoid problems, reconfirm your testing appointment a week prior to your scheduled testing date!

If you want to reschedule your test date within your eligibility period, you must personally speak to a ProMetric staff member about it at least five working days before your scheduled date or you will have to pay an extra fee (see below). If you do not get your first choice of test centers or dates, it is worthwhile checking back, since openings occur when other examinees change their test dates.

USMLE Cost

The fee (in 2006) to take Step 1 or Step 2CK is $445 and Step 2CS is $975. Note that the fee increases if Step 1 or Step 2CK will be taken outside the United States, U.S. territories, or Canada. If you will be doing this, call the NBME Department of Licensing Examinations at (215) 590-9700 or e-mail USMLEreg@nbme.org before submitting your application to determine the correct fee.

Unless you cancel or reschedule your Step 1 or Step 2CK appointment by noon (Eastern Time) five business days (Monday-Friday, excluding U.S. holidays) before the scheduled exam date there is an additional charge. For Step 2CS, there is an additional $150 charge (in 2006) if you cancel less than 15 days before the exam; this increases substantially ($400) if you miss your scheduled appointment without rescheduling. These fees are due when the exam is rescheduled. No rescheduling can occur after 12:00 A.M. (Eastern Time) on the day of the exam.

Since individual state licensing boards administer Step 3, the fees and rules vary. In 2005, it cost $625 in all states except Mississippi ($725), South Dakota ($775), and Vermont ($660). The number of times candidates can take Step 3 varies from once (Alaska) to no limit (in 18 states). Candidates generally have seven years to complete all USMLE Steps, although California gives candidates ten years and five states (ID, LA, MI, NY, NC) have no time limit.

The total cost for Step 3, plus a medical license, ranges from $1,465 in Alaska and $1,415 in Maryland to $625 in many states. Osteopathic physicians can become licensed most inexpensively in Pennsylvania ($565) and Oklahoma ($535).

Preparing for the USMLE

Free orientation materials for all Steps are on the USMLE website at www.usmle.org. (Click on "Orientation and Practice Materials" and then on the link to the year in which you want to take the test.) The downloadable software contains more than 100 practice test items for each Step, two videos describing Step 2CS, and five sample case simulations for Step 3. The practice test items can be taken in either a timed or an untimed mode. Be certain to remove any prior copies of these programs before downloading the new versions. This material can also be obtained on a CD-ROM from the entity (NBME, ECFMG, FSMB) through which you are registering for the exam. The NBME also sells downloadable assessment tests for $45 each (www.nbme.org).

It may be worthwhile for you to purchase a scheduling permit for a 3½-hour practice session at a ProMetric test center. Although the practice test contains the same materials as are on the USMLE website, it gives you a chance to experience it in the setting you will be in when you take the actual test. (Practice sessions are much more expensive outside the United States and Canada.) Private tutoring companies also run preparation courses.

Taking the Test

On test day, get to the test center at least 30 minutes before the exam time listed on your confirmation notice. If you are more than 30 minutes late, you will not be admitted and will have to pay a rescheduling fee if you still want to take the test. Wear very comfortable clothes. For Step 2CS, wear comfortable, professional clothes and bring a stethoscope and a white lab/clinic coat. (They may be able to supply a white coat and stethoscope if you forget them.)

On arrival, you will sign in. To take the exam, you must show them your Scheduling Permit and a photo ID with your signature (such as a driver's license, a passport, a national identity card or other form of unexpired government-issued identification, or an ECFMG-issued identification card). The name on the photo ID must *exactly match* the name on your

Scheduling Permit. Without these, you will *not be allowed to take the test*. You will need to reschedule the exam during your remaining eligibility period and pay an extra fee. They will then take a digital photo of you. (There is a reason they call this test "You Smile"!)

You are then required to place all personal items (including food, beverages, pagers, cell phones, brimmed hats, book bags, handbags, backpacks, books, notes or study materials, digital watches, watches with computer communication or memory capability, calculators, and radios) in a small locker. If you need to keep a personal item (such as food for a diabetic) with you, you will need to apply in advance for special accommodations (see above). For Step 2CS, only a coat rack and open cubbyholes are available for personal storage; do not bring anything valuable other than a white coat and a stethoscope, which you will keep with you. For all exams, there is no place for luggage storage and no waiting area for non-examinees.

For Steps 1, 2CK, and 3, a proctor will offer you a pair of earplugs and give you an erasable writing board, marker, and tissues to use for erasures. They will then escort you to a testing room and show you how to adjust the mouse and monitor. Entering your CIN will initiate a 15-minute tutorial that explains how the test works. If you wish, you can immediately exit this tutorial and begin the test. For Step 2CS, there will be an on-site orientation, after which staff members will direct you how to proceed.

One of the keys to doing well on the USMLE is time management. Each day there are at least 45 minutes of "break time" (including the lunch period) that you can take as you wish. For Steps 1, 2CK, and 3, by doing the tutorial in advance, you save 15 minutes for lunch and breaks. By limiting the number of breaks you take, you save time signing in and out (and have longer breaks). Completing sections early also gives you additional time for breaks or lunch. Those who have taken the computerized USMLE recommend that you pre-plan when and for how long you will take your breaks so that, under stress, you do not shortchange yourself on the allotted time for the test sections. Be careful not to use up all the break time early in the testing day.

For Step 2CS, the entire day is spent in the testing area. Once you check in and enter the secure testing area, you cannot leave until the exam is over. There are two breaks. The first is 30 minutes long, during which they serve a light meal and have vending machines available. Later, there is a 15-minute break.

Upon completing the test, give your Permit to the proctor, sign out of the Center, and get a Test Completion Notice.

You must complete the entire examination (although you may not have time to answer all the questions) to receive a score. If you leave the test early, you will not receive a score. If computer or technical problems develop, notify the proctors and they will make the necessary adjustments.

Scoring

Scores are usually available four weeks after the exam, although the report may take as long as six weeks to arrive. Your score report will list the three-digit scores needed to pass the Step; the two-digit minimum passing score is always 75. Unless you send a written request to the USMLE, the scores will automatically be reported to all accredited M.D. and Osteopathic schools in the United States and Canada. No scores are ever reported by phone or fax.

The pass/fail standards for all Steps are set before the exam begins. There is no set percentage of examinees that must pass or fail. This standard is statistically maintained at the same level across test administrations. Generally, examinees must correctly answer 60% to 70% of the questions on each Step or component to pass. Although the USMLE program recommends a minimum passing score for each Step, each medical licensing authority (i.e., state medical board) may establish the passing scores for their own jurisdiction. The mean three-digit scores range from 200 to 220 with a standard deviation of 20 points. In 2005, the minimum passing score for Step 1 was 182; for Step 2CK, 182; and for Step 3, 184. Changes to these scores can be found on the USMLE website. Scores are also converted to a two-digit score, since most state medical boards require a "75" to pass. This generally equates to at least one standard deviation below the mean three-digit score.

How do you interpret the scores? The percentile score that rated examinees against a standard group is no longer being reported, resulting in a more-or-less "Pass-Fail" system. This makes it more difficult for residency directors and licensing boards to determine how well examinees who passed the exam did on the USMLE (although many residency directors try to interpret the relative scores individuals get).

Unintended consequences of "Pass-Fail" USMLE scores include bland recommendation letters and an increased number of applicant interviews for each residency position, increasing the costs for applicants and programs. Figure 7.3 shows the recent performance of various groups on the computer version of the test. Although it may not be clear from the chart, the National Board of Medical Examiners (NBME) says that about 1% of graduates of U.S.- and Canadian-accredited schools do not eventually pass the USMLE, while as many as 25% of IMGs are unable to pass the exam.

FIGURE 7.3

Recent USMLE Pass Rates

Examinee	Pass Rate
STEP 1	
U.S./Canadian M.D. Students	
First-time taker	93%
Repeater	64%
D.O. Students	
First-time taker	70%
Repeater	53%
ECFMG-registered	
First-time taker	67%
Repeater	40%
STEP 2CK	
U.S./Canadian M.D. Students	
First-time taker	97%
Repeater	67%
D.O. Students	
First-time taker	80%
Repeater	23%
ECFMG-registered	
First-time taker	75%
Repeater	46%
STEP 2CS	
U.S./Canadian Students	96%
ECFMG-registered	83%
STEP 3	
U.S. M.D. Graduate	
First-time taker	96%
Repeater	69%
D.O. Graduate	
First-time take	93%
Repeater	67%
ECFMG-registered	
First-time taker	74%
Repeater	57%

Adapted from USMLE materials, October 2005.

For Step 2CS, examinees are assessed on their data-gathering and communication skills (including spoken English) by the standardized patient, and on their ability to complete an appropriate patient note by physician raters. Performance on Step 2CS is reported as pass or fail, with no numerical score. Examinees who fail will receive a performance profile, which reflects the relative strengths and weaknesses of their performance on the subcomponents of Step 2CS.

In Step 3, Computer-based Case Simulations (CCS) are scored against answers given by practicing clinicians and experts in the field. The closer you come to matching what these practitioners deem to be "ideal management," the higher your score. Potentially dangerous and unnecessary actions significantly lower the score. Scores are mailed approximately two weeks after the examination. Most state licensing boards have the results sent simultaneously to them and to the examinee. Some state boards have the scores reported to them first, and they then send results to the examinee.

Retaking the USMLE

If you fail a Step or a Component (CK/CS), you must resubmit the same application as you did the first time, and pay the fee again. However, you must wait at least 60 days before you retake the test. While there is no limit on the number of times you can take a USMLE Step or Component, you *cannot take a failed or incomplete Step or part (CS/CK) more than three times in a 12-month period.*

The USMLE recommends that state licensing boards require examinees to pass all components within a seven-year period. They also recommend that they allow candidates a maximum of six attempts to pass any Step or part (CS or CK) without demonstrating additional educational experience. Just when this seven-year "clock" begins differs among states: This can pose difficulties for M.D./Ph.D. students, who often take from seven to nine years to complete their programs. Most states will make exceptions for them.

If you *pass* a Step or a Component (CK/CS), you may not retake it unless the licensing authority requires you to do so (usually because of the seven-year rule) or you are still enrolled as a medical student six or more years after you first passed Steps 1 or 2. In either case, if you previously passed the Step but fail when you retake it, you must pass that Step to complete the USMLE requirements.

Sending your USMLE Results (Transcript)

Unless an examinee writes to request that test scores not be sent, they will automatically be sent to all accredited M.D. and Osteopathic schools in the United States and Canada. Requests that scores be sent to other agencies or institutions depend on which Step(s) you have taken and where you want to send them. Most residency applicants have their results sent electronically via the Electronic Residency Application Service (ERAS). Other requests must be made in writing to the appropriate body (Figure 7.2).

Upon receiving your written request, plus a small fee, the NBME (ECFMG for IMGs) will send copies of your USMLE transcript to residency programs. The form to use and the current cost can be obtained from the NBME, ECFMG, or your Dean of Students. This USMLE transcript includes results of all your attempts to pass USMLE Steps, as well as results from any NBME Parts or FLEX examinations (old licensing tests). It also includes notes about any examinations for which no scores were reported (incomplete examinations or indeterminate scores), any special accommodations that were provided, any incidents of irregular behavior (e.g., cheating), and any actions that credentialing or licensing authorities have taken against you. After physicians take the USMLE Step 3, the Federation of State Licensing Boards, rather than the ECFMG or NBME, sends out the transcripts.

USMLE: Irregular Testing Behavior

A USMLE examinee's "irregular behavior" is serious and, if confirmed, becomes a part of his or her USMLE record that is sent to medical licensing authorities and residency programs. The examinee may also be barred from future USMLE exams (if they haven't completed the series), meaning that they cannot be licensed in the United States if they are an M.D., or they may be required to take the test under special conditions. "Irregular behavior" includes:

- Seeking or obtaining access to examination materials prior to the exam.
- Falsifying information on the application or registration forms.
- Taking the exam without being eligible for it.
- Impersonating an examinee or hiring a proxy to take the exam.
- Copying answers from another examinee or looking at another examinee's computer screen.
- Allowing your answers to be copied.
- Making notes of any kind during the exam except on the non-removable, erasable writing surface provided for examinees.
- Failure to adhere to test center staff's instructions.
- Disruptive behavior at the test center.
- Possessing photographic, communication, or recording devices, including electronic pagers and cell phones.
- Altering or misrepresenting examination scores.
- Theft of or other unauthorized possession of examination materials.
- Any unauthorized reproduction (including memorization and distribution) of examination materials.

USMLE Step 1

Step 1 is a one-day (eight hours), 350-item multiple-choice examination that assesses examinees' understanding of and ability to apply key basic biomedical science concepts. All questions in Step 1 require "one best answer." The exam emphasizes the principles and mechanisms of health, disease, and therapeutic modalities. Integrating material across subject areas, most test items apply basic science principles to clinical situations and include interpreting illustrations or other problem-solving skills. Step 1 covers anatomy, behavioral sciences, biochemistry, microbiology, pathology, pharmacology, physiology, and interdisciplinary topics such as nutrition, genetics, and aging (Figure 7.4). The questions are not grouped by subject area (e.g., anatomy), but appear randomly.

The test is given in seven 60-minute blocks; each block has from 25 to 50 questions that cover all the subjects. The test items include pictures and tables, and require the identification of normal and pathologic gross and microscopic specimens and the integration of basic science with clinical problems. Recently, the number of factual-recall questions has decreased, while more questions that require examinees to answer based on integrating information from various subject areas have been added.

FIGURE 7.4

USMLE Step 1 Content*

1. Systems
General Principles
Normal and abnormal processes not limited
to specific organ systems   40%-50%
Organ Systems
Normal and abnormal processes that are
system specific   50%-60%

• Cardiovascular	• Endocrine
• Gastrointestinal	• Hematopoietic / Lymphoreticular
• Musculoskeletal	• Nervous / Special Senses
• Renal / Urinary	• Pulmonary / Respiratory
• Reproductive	• Skin / Connective Tissue

2. Process
Normal structures and functions   30%-50%
Abnormal processes   30%-50%
Principles of therapeutics   15%-25%
Psychosocial, cultural, occupational and
environmental considerations   10%-20%

*All percentages are subject to change.
Adapted from the *USMLE 2006 Bulletin of Information*.

Most U.S. medical students take this Step after completing their second preclinical year. The NBME's Comprehensive Basic Science Subject Examination (CBSE)—given at most U.S. medical schools—seems to predict whether students will pass the USMLE Step 1. Like the USMLE, these tests have become computerized.

USMLE Step 2

Step 2 consists of two examinations: Step 2 Clinical Knowledge (CK) that is a multiple-choice component and Step 2 Clinical Skills (CS) that is a simulated-patient encounter to assess clinical and communication skills.

Step 2 Clinical Knowledge (CK) is a one-day (nine hours), 370-item multiple-choice examination divided into eight 60-minute blocks. It assesses whether examinees have sufficient knowledge and understanding of the clinical sciences to provide safe and competent patient care under supervision. It emphasizes health promotion, disease prevention, and clinical situations commonly seen during a primary care internship (Figure 7.5). The questions are of two types: a single-best answer, as in Step 1, and "extended matching" where there is one list of up to 20 answers available for a series of questions.

FIGURE 7.5

USMLE Step 2CK Content

1. Normal Conditions and Disease Categories
Normal growth and development and general principles of care
Individual organ systems or disorders:

- Blood & Blood-forming Organs
- Cardiovascular Disorders
- Endocrine & Metabolic Disorders
- Gynecologic Disorders
- Immunologic Disorders
- Mental Disorders
- Musculoskeletal System & Connective Tissue
- Nervous System & Special Senses

- Nutritional & Digestive Disorders
- Pregnancy, Childbirth, & Puerperium Disorders
- Renal, Urinary, & Male Reproductive Systems
- Respiratory System
- Skin & Subcutaneous Tissue

2. Physician Task*

Applying principles of management	15%-25%
Establishing a diagnosis	25%-40%
Promoting preventive medicine & health maintenance	15%-20%
Understanding mechanisms of disease	20%-35%

*These percentages may change.
Adapted from the *USMLE 2006 Bulletin of Information.*

The test includes material from Internal Medicine, Obstetrics and Gynecology, Pediatrics, Preventive Medicine and Public Health, Psychiatry, and Surgery. Nearly all questions are clinical scenarios where the examinee must provide a diagnosis, a prognosis, an indication of the underlying disease mechanism, or the next step in medical care, including preventive measures. Examinees must interpret tables, laboratory data, imaging studies, photographs of gross and microscopic pathology specimens, and the results from other diagnostic studies.

Step 2 Clinical Skills (CS) was added in June 2004 to provide a minimum national standard for interpersonal and clinical skills, which a large body of literature has shown to be strongly correlated with the incidence of malpractice suits and patients' treatment compliance and satisfaction. For IMGs, Step 2CS replaces the Clinical Skills Assessment (CSA®), which was administered by the ECFMG. The Medical Council of Canada has also adopted it as part of their medical licensing exam.

This exam is a one-day (eight hours) examination, broken into 25-minute segments during which examinees interact with 12 "standardized patients." It closely parallels many elements of the Objective Structured Clinical Examination (OSCE) given at most medical schools (described on page 206). The secure test area is a series of exam rooms equipped with standard exam tables, blood pressure cuffs, otoscopes, ophthalmoscopes, non-latex gloves, sinks, and paper towels. Outside each exam room is a cubicle with a computer where the patient note can be written or typed. Bring a stethoscope and white coat; they provide you with a clipboard, blank paper, and a pen.

Examinees must pass all three components of the CS examination during a single administration: (1) an Integrated Clinical Encounter (ICE), with an assessment of data collection skills and a recorded patient note; (2) an assessment of Communication/Interpersonal Skills (CIS); and (3) an assessment of Spoken English Proficiency (SEP). The cases are the kinds of medical problems that would commonly be encountered in a clinic, doctor's office, emergency department, or hospital. (See Figure 7.6.)

Before entering an exam room and once an announcement tells you to begin, you will read an instruction sheet about the patient's case, including the chief complaint and the patient's vital signs. (You should consider these vital signs to be accurate.) If laboratory results are included, it means that the patient is returning for a follow-up appointment. Make notes of the relevant information. After entering the room, take a *focused* history based on the chief complaint and do a *focused* physical exam, if indicated. Wash your hands before and after you do the exam. Listen *empathetically* to the patient; be careful not to interrupt patients, a common mistake when

FIGURE 7.6
USMLE Step 2CS Content

Components

1. *Integrated Clinical Encounter (ICE)*

   Data gathering: Take a patient history and perform a physical examination. (The standardized patient scores this part using a checklist.)

   Documentation: Complete a Patient Note summarizing the findings of patient encounter, diagnostic impression, and initial patient work-up.

2. *Communication and Interpersonal Skills (CIS)*

   (The standardized patient scores all CIS components using a checklist and rating scales.)

   Questioning skills: includes the use of open-ended questions and transitional statements and not interrupting the patient.

   Information-sharing skills: such as avoiding jargon, responding to patient questions/concerns, and providing counseling when appropriate.

   Professional manner and rapport: such as showing concern for patient's comfort/modesty, the examinee's personal hygiene (wash hands before and after physical exam), and expressing interest in the impact of the illness on the patient.

3. *Spoken English Proficiency (SEP)*

   Clarity of spoken English communication within the context of the doctor-patient encounter, including pronunciation, word choice, and minimizing the need to repeat questions or statements.

Patient Note

The written form and computer form are essentially identical.
Remember to focus on the *patient's chief complaint*.

History: Include significant positives and negatives from the patient's history of present illness; past medical, social, and family history; and a review of system(s).

Physical Examination: Indicate only pertinent positive and negative findings related to the patient's chief complaint. If no physical exam was required or possible (e.g., you spoke on the phone with a patient or caregiver), leave this section blank.

Differential Diagnosis: In order of likelihood (with #1 being the most likely), list up to 5 potential or possible diagnoses for this patient's presentation. *In many cases, you may list fewer than 5.*

Diagnostic Workup: List immediate plans (up to 5) for further diagnostic workup. If a part of the physical exam (i.e., a pelvic exam) is indicated, list it here. *Do not include treatment, consultations, or referrals.*

Adapted from: *USMLE 2006 Bulletin of Information.*

taking a history. Do a *gentle exam.* (If you don't normally do a gentle exam, have someone teach you how; all your patients will appreciate it.) If you would normally do an exam that is not part of the test (genitourinary, pelvic, female breast, and corneal reflexes), note that on your proposed "diagnostic workup" when you write up the case. In some cases, you may be asked to perform the workup on a mannequin or a simulator.

In some instances, you may be making a phone call. Follow the instructions and, once connected, do not press any button on the phone until you are done. As with the patient encounter, you only get one chance. Once you leave the room or hang up the phone, you cannot go back. An announcement will tell you when you have five minutes left with the patient. Although no children will be simulated patients, you may need to discuss a child's case with their caregiver.

Immediately after the patient encounter, you will have ten minutes to write or type (on a computer) a patient note. If you finish the patient encounter early, you can use that extra time for your note. If you choose to write your note by hand, *write or print it legibly!* If the scorers cannot read it, it will count against you. You may use the abbreviations on the sheet posted at every station and other common medical abbreviations. However, if in doubt that your abbreviation will be understood, write it out. You can write your note in full sentences, in the short phrases more typical of physicians' notes (e.g., "Abd: non-distended, NL BS"), or a combination of both.

The test is meant to present examinees with a broad spectrum of cases from a physician's typical workday in U.S. medical practice, and is composed of interactions with 12 "standardized patients," people trained to act like patients from a broad range of age, racial, and ethnic backgrounds. Examinees have 15 minutes to examine each patient, establish a rapport, elicit pertinent information, and perform a physical examination. They then have 10 minutes to record a patient note, including pertinent history, physical findings, diagnostic impressions, and plans for possible further evaluation. If you do not use the entire 15 minutes for the patient encounter, the remaining time will be added to the time you have to record the patient note. Presentation categories include cardiovascular, constitutional, gastrointestinal, genitourinary, musculoskeletal, neurological, psychiatric, respiratory, and women's health. The cases must be taken in the order that they are presented and be completed in the time allowed. A few of these cases may, in fact, be tests of possible new cases; these will not be scored.

While the specific cases used vary from day to day, each examinee will get a combination of cases with an equal degree of difficulty. Each group of cases will reflect common and important symptoms and diagnoses. In any case, the simulated patients will respond to similar questions in the same way.

For Step 2CS, if you do not begin every case, your performance may be assessed on those cases you completed. If this assessment would result in a "pass" no matter how poorly you might have done on the skipped case(s), you will get a "pass" score. The reverse is also true: if you failed the completed cases, you will get a failing score. Otherwise, your attempt will be noted as an "incomplete examination."

Of the 17,700 students who took the exam between June 2004 and March 2005, about half were U.S. or Canadian medical students, with a 96% pass rate; IMGs, who made up the rest of the students, passed 85% of the time.

Fifth Pathway students must have taken either the prior CSA exam or Step 2CS to be eligible to take Step 3.

USMLE Step 3

Step 3 is a two-day examination (eight hours each day) with 480 multiple-choice items, which are divided into blocks of from 25 to 50 items, and approximately nine Computer-based Case Simulations (CCS). Unlike Steps 1 and Step 2CK, all multiple-choice questions in each block relate to the same clinical setting. You will have from 45 to 60 minutes to complete each multiple-choice block and a maximum of 25 minutes to complete each CCS. Step 3 is administered after graduation, usually during the PGY-1 year, and assesses whether examinees have sufficient knowledge and understanding of biomedical and clinical science to practice medicine without supervision. The knowledge base is what would be expected of a generalist physician, including non-emergency and emergency encounters with regular and new patients in various settings, such as clinics, offices, nursing homes, hospitals, emergency departments, and via telephone. It is heavily weighted toward clinically oriented knowledge and situations (Figure 7.7).

Candidates can take this exam after they have passed Steps 1, 2CK, and 2CS; have received an M.D. or D.O. degree from a school accredited by the Liaison Committee on Medical Education (LCME) or the American Osteopathic Association (AOA); and have completed their state medical board's required amount of graduate medical education (Figure 7.10). Graduates of foreign medical schools must have an ECFMG Certificate or have completed a "Fifth Pathway" program. (See Chapter 14, "International Medical Graduates.")

FIGURE 7.7

USMLE Step 3 Content*

1. Physician Tasks

Applying scientific concepts and mechanisms of disease	8%-12%
Formulating most likely diagnosis	8%-12%
Evaluating severity of patient's problems	8%-12%
Managing the patient:	45%-55%

- Health Maintenance
- Clinical Intervention
- Clinical Therapeutics
- Legal and Ethical Issues

Obtaining history and performing physical examination	8%-12%
Using laboratory and diagnostic studies	8%-12%

2. Clinical Encounters

Continued care	50%-60%
Emergency care	15%-25%
Initial care	20%-30%

*These percentages may change.
Adapted from the NBME materials, August 2005.

Registered applicants should write to their state's board for the additional information contained in *USMLE Step 3 General Instructions, Content Outline, and Sample Items.* The address and phone numbers of individual state licensing boards are listed in the *USMLE Bulletin of Information,* which can be obtained from the Federation of State Medical Boards of the United States, Inc., e-mail: alpp@fsmb.org; www.fsmb.org. Depending on state requirements, this Step can be taken during or after the PGY-1 year.

Note that the application material for Step 3 is sent to your residency program director. If you change training programs after the Match or you do not receive an application, contact your state licensing board or the Test Administration Office, Step 3, National Board of Medical Examiners, 3750 Market St., Philadelphia, PA 19104-3190. Include your full name as it appeared on Steps 1 and 2, your NBME Identification Number that is on your Step 1 and 2 results, your medical school, the year of graduation, and your current address.

Step 3: Computer-based Case Simulation (CCS). In the Computer-based Case Simulation (CCS), the examinee provides care to approximately nine simulated patients. Given the information in the clinical problem, examinees decide what treatment to give and when to initiate it. They must also monitor patients' responses to their interventions (or non-interventions). The cases must be completed in the order presented.

During the CCS, examinees type on the "order sheet" their requests for information from the history and physical, orders for laboratory studies and procedures, requests for consults, and instructions to begin medications and other therapies. These are drawn from thousands of possible entries. As the case progresses, you can advance the time clock and re-evaluate the patient, check on test results, and learn the results of any interventions. By looking at the patient's chart, you can review vital signs, progress notes, nurses' notes, and test results—all under different tabs. Time is suspended (neat idea) as you consider what steps to take next. You cannot go back in "time," but you may change orders as the situation changes and as you move the patient between the office, home, emergency department, intensive care unit, and ward.

The computer monitors each action the examinee takes, with the highest score being given for thoroughness, efficiency, avoiding risks, timeliness, and avoiding unnecessary or potentially dangerous actions.

To do well, you must become familiar with the Computer-based Case Simulation (CCS) software and understand how the simulated cases work before taking the exam. Review all the orientation materials and do all the practice cases sent with your application packet and available at the USMLE website (www.usmle.org) or at LCME- and AOA-accredited medical schools. The NBME recommends that all Step 3 applicants review the Primum® CCS tutorial and the practice cases well in advance of the testing day to have a thorough understanding of how Primum CCS works.

USMLE Sample Questions

Three types of questions (described below) make up the multiple-choice part of the exam: single item, matching sets, and case clusters. The questions concentrate on therapy and management. They are based upon pictorial and graphic presentations of data (radiographs, EKGs, pictures of patients, photomicrographs, patient charts, etc.) and patient management problems designed to simulate actual patient encounters.

One-Best-Answer Questions: Steps 1, 2CK, and 3

Single-item questions are typical multiple-choice questions in which you must select the one best answer. The question can be phrased in the positive, such as "What is the next appropriate laboratory test?" or in the negative, such as "What organism is NOT likely to cause the patient's problem?" For both types of questions, first read the case and the question carefully and eliminate the answers you know are wrong. Then, from those remaining, select the answer you think is the most correct. (This strategy does not work for extended-matching questions where there are up to 20 choices.) A typical single-item question is:

1. A 32-year-old man comes to your office with severe flank pain radiating into his right groin. The pain began suddenly about one hour before his arrival. On physical examination, you find normal bowel sounds, no abdominal wall guarding, rigidity or mass, no costovertebral angle tenderness, and no evidence of a hernia. His chest and rectal examinations are normal. The most appropriate next step is to:

(A)   do an intravenous pyelogram.
(B)   get a surgical consultation.
(C)   obtain abdominal radiographs.
(D)   obtain blood for a complete blood count and electrolytes.
(E)   test his urine for blood.

(Answer: E)

Matching Sets: Steps 2CK and 3

Matching sets questions also require one best answer, but with a twist: You are given a series of questions on a common topic with a list of between 4 and 26 possible answers. The questions are not linked, and each answer may be used more than once or not at all. An example of a matching set question is:

> The response options for the next two items are the same. You will be required to select one answer for each item in the set.

For each patient with a cough, select the most likely diagnosis.

A. Asthma   D. Pneumonia
B. Cancer   E. Pulmonary embolus
C. Congestive heart failure F. Tuberculosis

1. A 62-year-old, previously healthy man has had several days of right-sided pleuritic chest pain, a cough productive of yellow-green sputum, fever, sweats, and increased difficulty breathing. He has never used tobacco. His chest radiograph shows consolidation of a portion of the right lower lobe.

(Answer: D)

2. A 62-year-old, previously healthy man has had progressively increasing right-sided pleuritic chest pain, recent hemoptysis, increased difficulty breathing, and weight loss. He has never used tobacco and has had no fever. His chest radiograph shows mediastinal fullness on the right with obstructive atelectasis and a right-sided pleural effusion.

(Answer: B)

END OF CASE

Case Clusters

Case clusters are vignettes followed by from two to six questions. Additional information is supplied as the case develops, so it is extremely important to answer these questions in the order presented. An example of this format is:

A 5-year-old girl's parents bring her to the emergency department because of difficulty breathing. She has previously been in good health and began complaining of pain in her throat about three hours ago. She now is wheezing, sitting forward, and drooling.

1. When auscultating her lungs, you most likely hear:

(A) diminished breath sounds
(B) expiratory wheezes
(C) inspiratory wheezes
(D) rales in both bases
(E) unilateral inspiratory wheezes

(Answer: B)

2. The patient's oxygen saturation on room air is 87%. She does not want an oxygen facemask and pushes it away. Your next step should be:

(A) admit her to the intensive care unit
(B) do an arterial blood gas analysis
(C) examine her throat for a foreign body
(D) have her parent hold the oxygen near her mouth
(E) perform a thoracostomy

(Answer: D)

3. Soft-tissue radiographs of the neck demonstrate [a swollen epiglottis. *On the test, you would interpret the radiograph.*] The most likely etiologic agent is:

(A) *Bacteroides melaninogenicus*
(B) *Haemophilus influenzae*, type B
(C) *Mycoplasma pneumoniae*
(D) Parainfluenza virus, type 1
(E) *Staphylococcus aureus*

(Answer: B)

4. If you saw a similar patient who presented with a barky cough and whose chest radiograph showed "steepling" of the tracheal shadow, immediate treatment might include:

(A) endotracheal intubation
(B) immediate tracheostomy
(C) inhaled albuterol
(D) inhaled racemic epinephrine
(E) topical cocaine

(Answer: D)

END OF CASE

Comprehensive Osteopathic Medical Licensing Examination-USA (COMLEX-USA)

The National Board of Osteopathic Medical Examiners, Inc. (NBOME™), first established in 1934, administers this licensing examination for Osteopathic physicians in the United States. All 50 states accept the COMLEX-USA for licensure (in this book, referred to as "COMLEX"). It is designed to assess whether the Osteopathic physician has the requisite knowledge to practice medicine without supervision.

This examination parallels the USMLE in content and format. COMLEX consists of three computerized tests (Levels 1, 2 Cognitive Evaluation [CE], and 3) and a clinical skills test (Level 2 Performance Evaluation [PE]). Level 3 was first administered in February 1995; Level 2CE, in March 1997; and Level 1, in June 1998. Level 2PE is similar to the OSCE exams and USMLE Step 2CS, and was first given in September 2004. COMLEX Levels 1, 2, and 3 must be taken in sequence, but the two parts of Level 2—CE and PE—can be taken in any order.

The primary difference between the COMLEX and the USMLE is that COMLEX has elements of Osteopathic Principles and Practice in all Levels. Osteopathic medical students and graduates may take the COMLEX, the USMLE, or both exams.

Eligibility

For Level 1, applicants must have satisfactorily completed the first half of the second year at (or graduated from) a medical school accredited by the American Osteopathic Association's Commission on Osteopathic College Accreditation (COCA) at the time they apply for the examination. For Levels 2CE and 2PE, applicants must have passed COMLEX Level 1 and satisfactorily completed the third year in a medical school accredited by COCA. The Dean's office at each Osteopathic school submits a list of eligible students to the NBOME for Levels 1, 2CE, and 2PE.

Applicants for COMLEX Level 3 must have a D.O. degree from a medical school accredited by COCA and have passed Levels 1, 2CE, and 2PE. (D.O.s who graduated prior to January 1, 2005, do not have to pass Level 2PE if they passed COMLEX Level 2CE prior to June 30, 2005.) All candidates for Level 3 must currently be in a PGY-1 training program approved by the AOA's Post-Graduate Education and Training Review Committee (PTRC) or by the ACGME, or they must have successfully completed such an internship or program. The Director of Medical Education or the program director must submit verification that an applicant is in good standing. Applicants who have completed an internship or program must submit a notarized copy of their internship or PGY-1 certificate.

Registration/Scheduling

For COMLEX Levels 1, 2CE, and 2PE, the applicant's name must be on the list from their Dean before they can register for exam. Alternatively, if the candidate has graduated, a notarized copy of his or her medical school diploma will be accepted.

All candidates *must* use the NBOME's online registration system (at www.nbome.org) to register and pay for, schedule, cancel, withdraw from, or reschedule an examination. The applicant should follow instructions and on-screen prompts. The NBOME will mail you an 11-digit Registration Code to use to access the system. You will then chose your own password, enter additional information, and pay by credit card. After a short delay, you may then schedule your exam.

COMLEX Levels 1, 2CE, and 3 exams are available at more than 300 test centers in the United States. The exact location of the test centers and the availability of the site for the scheduled test dates are listed on the NBOME website at the Examination Scheduling page. Level 2PE is administered at NBOME's National Center for Clinical Skills Testing in Conshohocken, Pennsylvania (bordering Philadelphia).

Eligible candidates may register and schedule an examination as early as six months in advance of a scheduled test date for COMLEX Levels 1, 2CE, or 3. For Level 2PE, you may register and schedule as early as a year in advance of the exam. To obtain the best choice of dates and locations, you should schedule it at least 90 days before your desired test date. To schedule the exam, you must have your NBOME six-digit identification number. After scheduling, you will receive a confirmation number from the NBOME and an e-mail confirmation notice.

Warning: Applicants must schedule their test at least 120 hours in advance of the selected date and time. If they fail to do so, they will be denied access to the examination, and they will be charged a non-refundable fee (in addition to the regular fee) when they schedule a new test date.

For more complete instructions about how to register, see "Registration Information" in the CBT Tutorial at www.nbome.org. The NBOME website has the most current information about policies and procedures applicable to testing, as well as other items of interest to candidates.

Cancelling/Rescheduling

For COMLEX Levels 1, 2CE, and 3, applicants may cancel anytime until a full 30 days prior to the scheduled test date with no penalty. If the cancellation occurs between 30 full days and 120 hours before the exam, an additional $85 is charged when the test is rescheduled. If the cancellation occurs less than 120 hours before the exam but not on the actual test date, there is an additional $190 fee charged when the test is rescheduled. If the examinee simply doesn't appear for the exam or withdraws on the test date, the additional fee is $225.

For COMLEX Level 2PE, applicants who cancel or reschedule their exam more than 30 days before their scheduled test date are charged an additional $50 when they re-register. If applicants cancel from 30 days to 48 hours before their scheduled test date, the charge is $150. For cancellations within 48 hours, the fee is $400. *Warning:* if you don't show up for a Level 2PE exam and haven't notified the NBOME prior to the start of the exam, you will be charged $650.

In the event of severe inclement weather, candidates should contact their scheduled test center to determine whether the test will still be administered. For Level 2PE, contact the NBOME National Center for Clinical Skills Testing (610-825-6551 or power-independent emergency line, 610-825-4240). In the unlikely event that a test center is closed or is forced to close during testing, candidates will be rescheduled by the NBOME (Level 2PE) or the Thomson Prometric Help Desk (Levels 1, 2CE, 3) for the next available test date.

Special Accommodations

If a candidate has a disability as defined under the Americans with Disabilities Act (ADA) and requires special accommodations to take the test, the individual must obtain "accommodation application materials" *from the NBOME office in Chicago* (NBOME, 8765 W. Higgins Rd., Suite 200, Chicago, IL 60631-4101; (773) 714-0622; fax (773) 714-0631). ADA candidates are strongly advised to submit the required ADA accommodation application and all necessary documentation early to receive consideration for their requested accommodations. A review of an application may take up to 12 weeks in some instances. The NBOME strongly recommends that all requests for accommodation applications and the supporting documentation be sent to the NBOME by a traceable means of delivery (e.g., UPS, FedEx, Certified Mail). Keep copies of everything you send them.

Candidates will be notified in writing of their accommodation status prior to the examination. They should then register for and schedule the COMLEX exam through the NBOME's office in Chicago, rather than through the online registration system.

Retaking COMLEX

If you fail a Level or a Component (CE/PE), you may apply to retake the test on the next available date that is at least 90 full days after the date of your failed exam. You must still meet the eligibility criteria and must re-apply as if you are taking the examination for the first time. Candidates may not take Level 2PE more than three times in any 12-month period. Examinees who have passed a Level or part may not retake that exam to improve their score.

Applicants requesting special accommodations who must retake a Level or a part (2CE or 2PE) must contact the NBOME office directly and must re-apply for the appropriate accommodation. A candidate may not reschedule his or her accommodation examination without notifying the NBOME office.

Although the NBOME does not limit the number of times a candidate who fails a Level may retake it, they recommend that medical licensing authorities

> consider that the candidate [should] successfully complete Levels 1, 2CE, 2PE, and 3 within a seven-year period, beginning when the candidate passes COMLEX Level 1; and allow no more than three attempts to pass each Level without demonstration of additional educational experience acceptable to the medical licensing authority.

Since this is not a mandate, the time period within which all Levels must be completed, the allowed number of attempts to pass a Level without additional education, and the required passing scores vary among the state medical licensing authorities. Each state's licensing board website (accessed through www.fsmb.org) has more specific information.

Cost

The standard fees (2005) for COMLEX are: Level 1, $445; Level 2CE, $445; Level 2PE, $965; and Level 3, $595. Additional fees may be assessed for cancellations within 30 days of the exam or for not showing up (see above).

Taking the Test

COMLEX Level 1, Level 2CE, Level 3: You should dress comfortably, since testing may take the full day. If you need to use hearing aids or earplugs during the test, contact the NBOME prior to your test date. Bring two pieces of identification; at least one must be a government-issued picture ID such as a current driver's license or passport. Candidates are not permitted to bring any food or drink into the testing area. If you will require food or drink during the testing period, you may request an unscheduled break that will be charged against the allocated test session during which the break is taken.

Be sure to arrive early for the test; candidates who arrive at the test center more than 15 minutes after the scheduled start time will not be allowed to take the test—no exceptions! (You won't get your money back either, and will pay additional fees to re-register.)

There are three optional breaks: one 10-minute break during the morning after completion of Section 2 and another 10-minute break in the afternoon after Section 6. The actual time spent on breaks is deducted from the total time allocated to complete the exam. There is also an optional 40-minute lunch break following the morning session that does *not* count against the total exam time.

COMLEX Level 2PE: Dress professionally for Level 2PE, including a white lab coat, and bring your own stethoscope. You should arrive 30 minutes prior to the scheduled start time of the exam. Be sure to allow extra time: travel delays are common in the greater Philadelphia area. Candidates will be given a boxed lunch at the first of the two scheduled breaks; you may bring your own food (not requiring refrigeration) and beverages for use during the breaks if desired. During the 7-hour test session, candidates will not be allowed to have contact with anyone outside the test center. This includes the use of cell phones. Information regarding the testing sequence is detailed in the *(annual) Orientation Guide for COMLEX Level 2PE*, available on the NBOME website.

Scoring

Scoring for COMLEX is essentially the same as for the USMLE; the number of items answered correctly (the raw score) is converted to 3-digit and 2-digit standard scores. The passing score for all COMLEX examinations is based solely on a candidate's performance, and the percentage of examinees that pass or fail is not predetermined.

The mean standard score for each of Levels 1, 2CE, and 3, regardless of when the exams were given, is 500. A minimum standard score of 400 (75 for 2-digit scores) on Level 1 or Level 2CE is required to pass the exam. A standard score of at least 350 (75 for 2-digit) on Level 3 is required to pass the exam.

COMLEX Level 1 and Level 2CE results are available online about four weeks after the test. Score reports are mailed to both examinees and their Dean approximately 10 to12 weeks after the test. Examinees and Deans' offices may access COMLEX scores online using a secure system. (Examinees may establish a secured NBOME web account during the exam registration process.) COMLEX Level 3 score reports also may be released to the Director of Medical Education at the candidate's internship hospital. No scores will be reported by phone, fax, or e-mail.

COMLEX Level 2PE scores are reported as Pass or Fail only. To achieve a "Pass," examinees must pass both the Humanistic Domain, which is a measure of physician-patient communication, interpersonal skills, and professionalism, and the Biomedical/Biomechanical Domain, which includes history-taking, physical examination, Osteopathic principles and

Osteopathic manipulative treatment, written communication (synthesis of clinical findings in a SOAP Note format), integrated differential diagnosis, and clinical problem-solving. Examinees who "Fail" receive additional feedback to help them identify their areas of strength and weakness.

Sending Your COMLEX Results (Transcript)

To have an NBOME transcript with COMLEX scores sent to a third party, such as ERAS, a residency program, or a licensing Board, send a written request and the appropriate fee to the NBOME. Information and the form can be obtained at NBOME's website. Requests are processed within two weeks; additional fees can speed the process.

NBOME transcripts include: a complete history of all exams taken, including scores if reported; information documenting "indeterminate" results of any exams; information concerning any irregular behavior during testing; and notifications of any actions taken against the candidate by a medical licensing authority or other credentialing entity that were reported to the NBOME.

The NBOME transcript will only reflect the Pass/Fail grade for COM-LEX Level 2PE. The candidate's certified transcript is the only verification sent by the NBOME to state boards for licensure applications. The processing of a certified transcript for candidates who have passed the Level 3 exam will begin no earlier than two weeks after the original release of scores. Additional certified transcripts will be sent only upon receipt of a written request from the candidate, and the normal processing time applies.

Preparing for COMLEX

The COMLEX exams are not "computer-adaptive." That is, the questions for each exam are determined before the test is administered. Usually, the questions will be identical regardless of when and where the test is administered. (For testing hints, see "Tips for taking USMLE-type Tests," below.)

Materials for COMLEX preparation, including the NBOME *Bulletin of Information*, are available at: www.nbome.org. For questions not answered on this site, contact National Board of Osteopathic Medical Examiners (NBOME), Inc., 8765 W. Higgins Rd, Suite 200, Chicago, IL 60631-4174; (773) 714-0622.

The NBOME provides a wealth of information on their website for those traveling to the Philadelphia area to take Level 2PE. This includes maps and written directions for those coming by train, shuttle, and car. In addition, they have arranged airline discounts. For additional questions about Level 2PE, contact National Center for Clinical Skills Testing, 101 W. Elm St., Suite 150, Conshohocken, PA 19428; (610) 825-6551. Inquiries about any part of COMLEX can also be sent via e-mail to admin.@ nbome.org or testing@nbome.org.

COMLEX Content

The computer-based Levels 1, 2CE, and 3 each have 400 multiple-choice questions, grouped into 50-question blocks. You can review and change answers only on the questions in the current section: You cannot return to a prior section to change your answers. A clock on the screen assists with time management, and you will be warned about the amount of time remaining.

The majority of the test items are "one-best-answer" questions, although a few will be matching questions. Most of the one-best-answer questions are single, stand-alone items; the rest consist of a case history with two or more related one-best-answer questions. Some have "exhibits" or "lab values" that can be accessed by pressing the appropriate buttons.

The COMLEX exams are designed to assess the Osteopathic medical knowledge and clinical skills considered essential for Osteopathic generalist physicians to practice medicine without supervision. COMLEX is constructed in the context of medical problem solving, which involves clinical presentations and physician tasks. Candidates are expected to utilize the philosophy and principles of Osteopathic medicine to solve medical problems.

All Levels follow the same two-dimensional "Examination Blueprint," although the emphasis changes to reflect examinees' educational level (see Figure 7.8). The examination blueprint has two main components: "Dimension I," or Clinical Presentation, identifies high frequency and/or high-impact health issues that Osteopathic generalist physicians encounter in practice. "Dimension II," or Physician Task, specifies the major steps Osteopathic physicians generally undertake to solve medical problems. Detailed topics covered by each category are in the CBT Tutorial, available on the NBOME website.

Level 1, usually taken in June of the sophomore year, is a one-day exam comparable to USMLE Step 1. It covers the basic medical sciences of anatomy, behavioral science, biochemistry, microbiology, osteopathic principles, pathology, pharmacology, and physiology. Examinees must demonstrate that they understand the mechanisms of health, medical problems and disease processes.

Level 2CE, usually taken in August of the senior year, is a one-day exam comparable to USMLE Step 2CK. It integrates the clinical disciplines of Emergency Medicine, Family Practice, Internal Medicine, Obstetrics and Gynecology, Osteopathic Principles, Pediatrics, Psychiatry, Surgery, and other areas necessary to solve medical problems. Examinees must demon-

FIGURE 7.8

COMLEX-USA Examination Blueprint

Dimension I: Patient Presentation

Level 1, Level 2CE, Level 3

Asymptomatic/General Symptoms	8-16%
Symptoms/Disorders of Digestion & Metabolism	4-10%
Symptoms/Disorders of Sensory Alternations	28-38%
Symptoms/Disorders of Motor Alternations	6-12%
Symptoms/Disorders Related to Human Sexuality & Urination	3-8%
Symptoms/Disorders of Respiration & Circulation	8-16%
Symptoms/Disorders of Thermoregulation	2-6%
Symptoms/Disorders of the Tissues and Trauma	8-16%
Symptoms/Disorders of Human Development	3-8%

Dimension II: Physician Tasks

	Level 1	Level 2CE	Level 3
Health Promotion/Disease Prevention	1-5%	15-20%	15-20%
History & Physical	5-15%	30-40%	10-20%
Diagnostic Technologies	1-5%	10-20%	15-25%
Management	2-7%	10-20%	25-40%
Scientific Understanding of Mechanisms	70-85%	5-15%	5-10%
Health Care Delivery	1-3%	5-10%	5-10%

Adapted from the NBOME website (www.nbome.org), October 2005.

strate the clinical concepts and principles necessary to make appropriate medical diagnoses through patient history and physical examination findings.

COMLEX Level 2PE, a one-day (seven hours) exam comparable to USMLE Step 2CS, uses 12 standardized patients in simulated ambulatory medical settings with problems and symptoms that are either acute, chronic, or provide opportunities for health promotion and disease prevention. It is designed to test the following clinical skills: doctor-patient communication, interpersonal interactions, professionalism, medical history-taking, physical examination, Osteopathic principles, Osteopathic manipulative treatment, and written communication (including synthesis of clinical findings, integrated differential diagnosis and formulation of a diagnostic and treatment plan). The NBOME website has the annual Orientation Guide for Level 2PE, as well as a 28-minute video. The video has also been distributed to all Dean's offices at Osteopathic medical schools.

COMLEX Level 3, usually taken in December of the first internship/ residency year, is comparable to USMLE Step 3. It is a one-day problem- and symptom-based assessment integrating the clinical disciplines of Emergency Medicine, Family Practice, Internal Medicine, Obstetrics and Gynecology, Osteopathic Principles, Pediatrics, Psychiatry, and Surgery. Examinees must demonstrate that they can make the appropriate patient management decisions and solve medical problems at the level of an inde- pendently practicing Osteopathic generalist physician.

Irregular Testing Behavior
Examinee behaviors that are not tolerated are essentially the same as those for the USMLE (see above). The penalties are also similar.

Licensure
Passing all three parts of the USMLE or COMLEX (for D.O.s only) and completing the required amount of ACGME-approved or AOA-approved graduate medical training can be used to gain an initial medical license (Figures 7.9 and 7.10).

In most states, since the licensing bodies are the same for both M.D.s and D.O.s, physicians can use either examination for licensure. However, Arizona, California, Florida, Hawaii, Maine, Michigan, Nevada, New Mex- ico, Oklahoma, Pennsylvania, Tennessee, Vermont, Washington, and West Virginia have separate Osteopathic licensing boards. These states, as well

---

FIGURE 7.9

Examination Pathways for U.S. Licensure

U.S. Graduate Pathway

M.D. Student | D.O. Student
USMLE Step 1* | USMLE Step 1*
USMLE Step 2CK & 2CS* | USMLE Step 2CK & 2CS*
USMLE Step 3 | USMLE Step 3
  | – or –
  | COMLEX Levels 1-3

IMG Pathway

ECFMG Certification:
   USMLE Step 1*
   USMLE Step 2CK & 2CS*
  USMLE Step 3

* May be taken in any order.

FIGURE 7.10
Graduate Education Requirements for Licensure

Number of years of accredited U.S. or Canadian graduate medical education (residency) required for a medical license.

One Year

Alabama[1]	Iowa[14]	New Jersey[1]	Tennessee[1]
Arizona[1]	Kansas[1]	New Mexico[3]	Texas[1]
Arkansas	Louisiana[1,9]	New York[1]	Vermont[1]
California[1,11]	Maine[3]	North Carolina[1]	Virgin Islands
Colorado[1]	Maryland[1,4]	North Dakota[1]	Virginia[1]
Delaware[1]	Massachusetts[1]	Ohio[1]	Washington[3]
Florida[1]	Michigan[3]	Oklahoma[1]	West Virginia[1]
Georgia[1]	Minnesota[1]	Oregon[1]	Wisconsin
Hawaii[1,13]	Mississippi[1]	Pennsylvania[3]	Wyoming[1]
Idaho[1]	Missouri[1]	Puerto Rico	
Indiana[1,4]	Nebraska[1]	South Carolina[1]	

Two Years

Alaska[1]	Indiana[2]	Minnesota[2]	Rhode Island[1,7]
California[2]	Kansas[2]	Montana[1]	South Dakota[5]
Connecticut	Kentucky	New Hampshire	Utah
District of Columbia[1]	Maine[1,7]	New Mexico	Virginia[2]
Florida[2]	Maryland[2,4]	Ohio[2]	Washington
Hawaii[2]	Massachusetts[2]	Oklahoma[2]	
Illinois	Michigan	Pennsylvania[1]	

Three Years

Alabama[2]	Idaho[2]	New Jersey[2]	Tennessee[2]
Alaska[2]	Louisiana[2,10]	New York[2]	Texas[2]
Arizona[2]	Maine[2,7,8]	North Carolina[16]	Vermont[2,6]
Colorado[2]	Mississippi[2,15]	North Dakota[2,16]	West Virginia[2]
Delaware[2]	Missouri[2]	Oregon[2,17]	Wyoming[2,18]
District of Columbia[2]	Montana[2]	Pennsylvania[2,8]	
Georgia[2]	Nebraska[2]	Rhode Island[2]	
Guam[12]	Nevada	South Carolina[2,15]	

[1]Graduates of U.S. or Canadian M.D. or D.O. medical schools only.
[2]International medical graduates only.
[3]D.O.s only.
[4]Additional year of residency required if applicant failed any Step of licensing exam three or more times.
[5]Must complete a residency program.
[6]Canadian training not accepted.
[7]May accept GME completed in Canada, England, Scotland, and Ireland for credit toward a license.
[8]May accept IMG qualifications equivalent to standard licensing requirements.
[9]Only ACMGE-approved (M.D.) training accepted.
[10]May count Fifth Pathway as one year for licensure.
[11]Must include at least 4 months of General Medicine.
[12]Sufficient GME to be eligible for U.S. specialty board certification.
[13]May not accept Canadian GME.
[14]IMGs will need 2 years of GME for licensure after 2006.
[15]ABMS Board Certification required for Fifth Pathway graduates.
[16]IMGs may have 2 years of U.S. or Canadian GME waived if they have equivalent professional experience.
[17]IMGs need at least 3 years of progressive GME in no more than 2 specialties at no more than 2 hospitals.
[18]IMGs must take an oral examination.
Adapted from: State Medical Licensure Requirements & Statistics: 2005. Chicago, IL: AMA, 2005, Tables 6 and 8.

as some others, have distinct requirements for D.O. licensure. For further information about licensure, see *State Medical Licensure Requirements and Statistics*, published annually by the American Medical Association.

One important note: NBME policy states that individuals who demonstrate "irregular behavior" and/or those who "subvert the NBME assessment or certification process" (i.e., cheat) will be permanently barred from certification by the Board. In addition, reports will be sent both to the individual's medical school and to the Federation of State Medical Boards. Don't say that you weren't warned.

Suggested New Medical Licensing Requirements

Medical licensing, the resident experience, and the prospect of resident moonlighting all were shaken by the Federation of State Medical Boards' (FSMB) May 1998 "Recommendations on Licensure." This body, comprised of representatives of all state medical licensing bodies, recommended that these boards adopt the following policies:

1. All M.D. and D.O. students are required to pass Steps 1 and 2 of the USMLE (M.D. or D.O.) or Levels 1 and 2 of the COMLEX (D.O.s only) prior to entering residency training.

2. Residents must complete three years in an ACGME- or AOA-approved postgraduate training program before becoming eligible to apply for full licensure.

3. Residents must apply to their state board for a state permit to practice as a resident, with the program director reporting to the board annually on any disciplinary or other problems that could impair the resident's ability to function.

4. All residents seeking training permits will undergo a criminal background check.

Some medical boards have either accepted these recommendations or are considering adopting them. This will mean that all physicians will need at least three years of residency training to practice medicine in the United States. It will also mean that, in states that adopt these recommendations, residents will only be able to moonlight (and begin paying back their enormous debts) at their own institutions. This may conflict with the ACGME's requirements, thus leaving residents no moonlighting opportunities.

Special Purpose Examination (SPEX®)

State licensing authorities use this one-day computer-administered examination, containing 420 multiple-choice questions, to test the knowledge-base of physicians who have held a valid, unrestricted medical license in a

U.S. or Canadian jurisdiction and are seeking licensure in a new state, or relicensure in the same state, *at least five years after graduation from medical school.*

Increasingly, state medical boards require that physicians who were previously licensed in another state pass the SPEX before getting a license in their state. Medical boards also use the test before reinstating the license of physicians who have been inactive for a period of time. In recent years, the pass rate has been about 68%. This test is *not* available as a licensing mechanism for graduating medical students. As with the USMLE, Pro-Metric administers the exam.

Importance of Passing the Tests

Residency directors know that if applicants they match with do not pass the tests their schools require for graduation, they may not have enough residents in July. That is why even moderately competitive residencies may require you to submit evidence that you have passed any examinations required for you to graduate from medical school. Students at schools that require passing Step 2 to graduate may need to take this Step in August/September of their senior year to assure residency directors that they have passed the test and, presumably, will graduate on time. In addition, if you do not eventually pass the USMLE (or the COMLEX for Osteopaths), you will never practice medicine in the United States.

How Important Are the Scores in the Resident-Selection Process?

Although the tests are not designed for this purpose, many—if not most—residencies use applicants' USMLE or COMLEX scores as a *primary screening device.* Because of the unavailability of other information about candidates, the scores on licensing examinations, especially Steps 1 and 2 of the USMLE, have become outrageously important. This is not the fault of program directors. They would like nothing better than a useful transcript (not all "Pass" grades), a specific Dean's letter (not saying that everyone "will be a fine clinician"), and school honors (such as AOA election) that are given out before they make Match decisions. However, even in this, the best of all possible worlds, the licensing examination scores are often the only objective way to evaluate a large pool of candidates from multiple schools with varying amounts of background and support material.

Residency directors want their residents to be able to pass the specialty's Board examination because reviewers and residency applicants look at how many of a residency's graduates pass their Board examination. (This information is in *FREIDA.*) As one residency director said, "Our residency program is judged, in part, on how well our graduates do on their Board examinations. Doing well on the USMLE says that they are at least good test takers—and that's important." Good USMLE scores do correlate with passing specialty board examinations. In general, they also correlate with students' clinical performance in at least their PGY-1 year.

Although this practice has been officially condemned, the NBME has sent residency directors information on how to interpret the USMLE scores to screen applicants. At the most competitive programs and in the most competitive specialties, you must obtain minimum scores on these exams for them to consider you, despite any other credentials. The specific minimum scores vary directly with the specialty's and the program's competitiveness. Scores may not be considered at all in non-competitive programs, while some very competitive specialties and programs reportedly use USMLE scores greater than 210 to determine whether they grant applicants an interview (the mean score ranges from 200 to 220; 20 points is the standard deviation). This alone suggests that the scores may be very important to you and that you should take the test very seriously.

For most applicants to programs in the NRMP PGY-1 Match, and for nearly all those applying to specialties with an advanced Match, only Step 1 scores will be available, since most students do not take the August/September Step 2 administration. This magnifies the problem of placing so much emphasis on these scores; for all but the future Pathologists among you, clinical experience is the most important factor in your success as a resident. Step 1 emphasizes the basic sciences; much of the tested material is not clinically applicable. Nevertheless, Step 1 is an important part of most residency programs' selection process.

How Much Effort Should You Expend?

Since the USMLE is so important to your career, it is worthwhile to make the extra effort to do well on the Steps. Educators refer to these tests as "high-stakes evaluations," because they may determine whether you graduate from medical school, the type and quality of the residency program you enter, and whether you are ever licensed to practice medicine. Take heed.

Most medical schools use USMLE-type questions for many of their examinations, so you will already be familiar with the format. (Some courses, however, have not changed their examinations in years, so they still use the format that the USMLE has abandoned; i.e., single questions with multiple true-false options.) You have probably also learned some of the tricks about how to take these kinds of tests. A few basic tips are listed in the next section.

Each of you knows how you learn best. For some, it is by reviewing their own notes and textbooks. For others, it may be by going over any one of the available specialized review texts. Nearly all students use the special USMLE review texts, rather than their textbooks or the study materials that the NBME supplies. Many students recommend using the books from the National Medical Series for Independent Study (John Wiley & Sons) and the "Blueprints Series" (Blackwell Science). Regardless of the source, remember to focus on "high-yield" information (start with the "high-yield" section of *First Aid for the USMLE Step 1* or 2). Don't get mired in unimportant details!

For *Step 1*, begin by reviewing your notes and books from your two basic-science years. Focus on the basic science principles related to common life-threatening and debilitating conditions, to normal development, and to prevention.

For *Step 2*, be able to diagnose and initially manage common life-threatening and debilitating conditions, and review normal development across the life span (including pregnancy) and anything pertaining to prevention. Definitely study for Step 2—regardless of what your buddies say. The test has become harder in recent years. It may be more difficult to prepare for Steps 2 and 3, since these require you to integrate material from several sources. Also, it will help you stay sane if you pass Step 2 before starting residency—you will have much less time to study for the exam during your residency.

Regardless of the Step, review previously studied material (the key is to *review* material rather than trying to learn it for the first time). This builds on your strengths and minimizes your weaknesses. Take practice tests to identify your content strengths and needs. Start with the free tests on the USMLE website.

The well-publicized national review courses are primarily for those students whose academic performance has been marginal, for those who have failed the test once, or for IMGs who are not native American-English speakers. These courses can be expensive. If this list doesn't include you, use your money to have dinner with a spouse/friend once a week as a reward for studying or to have a nice vacation after the test. Take the test and assume you pass (over 90% of test takers do!) until you get your score.

Whatever the method or methods you use, it is important for you to take this test seriously and to do the best that you possibly can.

If you did not do as well as you thought you should—or could—have the first time, *you do not have the option of repeating the test.* You can retake the exam only if you fail. If you retake and pass a Step, the passing score becomes the official National Board record, although transcripts that are sent out will list all your attempts to pass the USMLE. Even if you success-fully complete several subsections of a Step on the initial attempt, the entire Step must be retaken. Steps 1 and 2 may be taken as many times as are needed to pass.

Many of the students who fail Step 1 may do so because of reading problems or learning disabilities. Most medical schools are not prepared to deal with these difficulties. If you fail Step 1 and feel that a learning dis-ability is the reason, you might want to contact either your school's educa-tion department or one of the following medical school-based programs:

- **Rosalind Franklin University of Medicine and Science.** Their Step 1 review course lasts 15 weeks between January and May (five days/wk with an occasional practice exam on weekends). Their Step 2 review course is being re-evaluated and may resume in the future. Contact Dr. Gordon Pullen, Ph.D. at (847) 578-8603; e-mail: gordon.pullen@rosalindfranklin.edu. The website is: http://66.99.255.20/cms/educational affairs/.

- **University of Missouri–Kansas City, Institute for Professional Preparation.** Their programs, held since 1981, are available to enrollees in or graduates of U.S. medical schools. They provide programs of varying length (up to 17 weeks) for those with prob-lems at any stage of the licensing exam process. Specific infor-mation and applications can be found at http://web1.umkc.edu/ipp/.

- **The Medical H.E.L.P. Program at Marshall University in West Virginia.** This five-week program is designed for those with learning disabilities and dyslexia. Call (304) 696-3170 or (800) 642-3463; e-mail: moorek@marshall.edu; or visit their website at www.marshall.edu/medicalhelp.

If an applicant fails Step 3, the licensing board may require evidence of additional training before allowing him or her to retake the exam. For licensure, most states require that all Steps be completed within a seven-year period. The time limit begins when an applicant first passes a USMLE Step.

Tips for Taking USMLE-Type Examinations

Listed below are several things you can do to maximize your scores on licensing examinations. The first, of course, is to know the material as well as you can. If you don't know the material, there are few tips that can help, especially on tests that have been written and field-tested by experts.

1. Know the material.
2. Get enough sleep the night before.
3. Follow a normal routine the day of the exam.
4. Wear comfortable clothing.
5. Arrive early enough to sign in and get your entire allotted time for the exam.
6. Check the test information to be certain that you bring all needed materials, e.g., admission card or identification with picture.
7. Be familiar with the test format so that you don't waste time taking the tutorial or floundering with the computerized test. (Do this by taking a computerized practice test and the tutorial on the CD supplied with the registration materials.)
8. Be familiar with the types of questions (single answer) that will be used.
9. Know how the test will be scored.
10. Use your time efficiently.

Mental preparation is the next key. Most people are familiar with pretest anxiety. Butterflies in the stomach, sweaty palms, rapid heartbeat and respiratory rate, and fear of failure do not necessarily mean you have lost the war of nerves. You merely have to steady yourself. It is said that Johnny Carson (during whose show you were probably conceived) had a heart rate approaching 160 just before he went out to do his monologue. And he did this for 25 years! The trick for you is to do everything as normally as possible. Get enough sleep the night before the exam and follow your normal routine the day of the test. Dress in comfortable clothes. Large testing sites are often too warm, too cold, or alternate between these extremes. Wear clothing that can be removed or loosened to cool off and bring something extra to wear in case it gets too cold. Arrive at the testing site early to avoid hassles. Do not be caught short by failing to bring your picture ID or the admission card.

Read over testing materials well in advance of the exam date. For the USMLE, if you become familiar with the testing method by taking a practice session, you can skip the tutorial and gain 15 minutes of time. COMLEX candidates can review a CD-ROM with a practice test at their school's Dean's office.

The testing materials you receive in advance will also tell you how the test will be scored and explain the types of questions used on the exam. The USMLE is scored by crediting the correct answers; there is no numeric penalty for getting a question wrong, although it will affect the subsequent questions you get for that block. (COMLEX does not alter the questions during the exam based on the examinee's responses.) If you don't know the answer, it pays to guess. Therefore, you need to know how to guess effectively.

Guessing effectively means knowing how to best answer the types of questions on the test. As medical students, most of you will be very familiar with the standard A-Type (single-answer, multiple-choice) questions used on the exams. These are essentially variations of simple true-false questions. To answer them correctly, use the following hints:

1. Even if "A" seems to be the correct answer, look over the other answers to be certain that a more correct answer does not exist. This is especially important on USMLE Steps 2 and 3.

2. If you cannot spot which answer is "true," read each alternative and mark the ones you believe are "false." If you can mark three answers (out of five) as "false," you have increased your chance of correctly answering the item from 20% to 50%.

3. Use the information you get from other parts of the test to help answer questions you otherwise would not know. A great deal of information is given in the stems (first part) of the exam's questions. Use this to your advantage.

4. Try not to change your answers. Change an answer only if you are *certain* that your initial answer was incorrect.

5. Look for long introductory clauses (foils) or the qualifying word "may" in true answers. Look for the limiting words "never" or "always" to spot false answers.

When faced with questions concerning a clinical case, first review the questions. These will often suggest the parts of the case that are most important and the key points to look for when reading the clinical description.

When taking computerized tests, two-thirds to three-fourths of examinees who go back and change their answer for a prior question go from a wrong to a right answer. This is true if they change the answer because they (1) reread and better understand the test item, (2) use clues or cues in subsequent items, or (3) are correcting a clerical error. Examinees are less likely to select a correct answer if they are replacing one wild guess with another or if they just have a "gut feeling" that the new answer is better.

Finally, use your time effectively. This is possibly the most important strategy for successful test-taking. Do not spend too much time on any one question. If you don't pace yourself and then have to randomly guess the answers to too many questions, you will fail the exam. On the USMLE, you have only about one minute per question. Remember that, during each USMLE and COMLEX timed computer module, you may answer the questions in any order, review your responses, and change your answers. Since each question counts the same, if a question is too difficult to be answered in a reasonable amount of time, make an educated guess at the answer immediately and make a note to go back to it after you have finished the rest of the items in that module. (For the USMLE, mark questions to review with the available check mark [√]. These marks will appear on the navigation bar on the left side of the screen.) After you exit the module, or when time expires, you can no longer access those test items.

Simulated Patient cases (Step 2CS and Level 2PE) and Step 3 case simulations must be answered in the order presented. After you exit the case or session, or when time expires, you no longer have access to those test items or cases and their answers.

If you run out of time in a module, but are still working on a question, you are allowed to finish that question. The time, however, is deducted from your total time allotment. Even so, it is generally worthwhile to try to answer that last question.

Note that the NBME suggests that examinees answer each question as it appears. Since you have taken examinations of this sort in medical school, you should know which path works best for you.

If You Don't Have to Take the USMLE

A number of schools do not require their students to take Steps 1 and 2 of the USMLE. Some only require that the student pass Step 2. But unless you are an Osteopathic student, there is only one route to getting a medical license in the United States—the USMLE. You must pass all three USMLE Steps. In general, you will never be as prepared to take the basic-science-oriented Step 1 as you are during medical school. Take the test; not all residency programs require that you send a copy of your scores—and you must remember your priorities. While a low score on Step 1 might put you out of the running for a residency position, you will have passed the first hurdle to practicing medicine. Take Steps 1 and 2 while you are in medical school. Taking the USMLE during your preclinical years may well result in a high score to promote your candidacy for a residency position.

"But I took Subject Exams (also called "Shelf Exams") in my preclinical courses," you say. Residency directors place little stock in these test results, with good reasons. Performance on these tests, taken from prior

Board examinations, is not directly comparable to performance on the USMLE Step 1. That is because rather than having to study for, and know, all the basic sciences at once, you take the Subject Exams immediately after you have intensively studied each subject, usually as a final examination for the course. These exams also do not contain the newer type of test questions or the inter-subject questions now found on the USMLE. This is similarly true for Subject Exams given in the clinical years. For example, students with marginal passing scores on the Subject Exams for Biochemistry, Physiology, Pathology, Pharmacology, and Microbiology still had a 25% or greater chance of failing the same section when they took their licensing examination.

Are the Examinations Fair?

Some subgroups have consistently different results when taking both the USMLE and the COMLEX. This has raised some doubts about these exams' fairness. Although neither the NBME nor COMLEX releases this information any longer, it may be instructive to look at the information they previously released.

At least in the past, both gender and race seemed to influence students' USMLE scores on Steps 1 and 2. (These findings were actually drawn from the very similar NBME Parts I and II.) White men had the highest pass rate, followed in order by Asian/Pacific Islander men, White women, Asian/Pacific Islander women, and Hispanic men. Trailing badly were, in order, Hispanic women, Black men, and Black women. Many of the differences in test results could be predicted from the MCAT scores for reading or science problems

On the COMLEX precursor, the NBEOPS exam, men consistently scored higher on Part I, and women scored higher on Part III. Men and women performed equally well on Part II. These findings remained consistent for all Osteopathic schools. Some researchers suggest that these findings result from a difference in men's and women's academic growth rates.

The debate continues as to whether the variance in scores on the USMLE and COMLEX reflects real differences in individuals' clinical competence.

Objective Structured Clinical Examination (OSCE)

Relatively new in medical schools, the Objective Structured Clinical Examination (OSCE) tests a student's clinical abilities. The OSCE uses "standardized patients"—either patients with stable physical findings (e.g., arthritis, heart murmurs) simulating disease symptoms or staff members trained to simulate such symptoms. These standardized tests evaluate how well students deal with real patients' problems, not just how well they score on tests, in class, or on the licensing examinations. Ideally, the OSCE tests whether a student can

- perform a focused history and physical examination.
- recognize pathological processes.
- interpret laboratory data.
- establish a relevant differential diagnosis.
- develop a management plan.
- clearly document clinical findings and plans.

OSCE examinations normally take about 6 hours (including breaks), with each station requiring from 5 to 40 minutes to complete. Some stations may be coupled, so that the second station relies on clinical information from the first station. Time and the number of stations are the two variations that do not seem to affect the test's validity. Students are scored at each station using a standardized checklist of tasks.

More than 94 (of 125 total) U.S. and all Canadian medical schools now use the OSCE for clinical evaluations. Many require their students to pass it before graduation. The results will also appear in Deans' letters, most probably showing the student's results in comparison to his or her classmates. Since all specialties value clinical abilities in their residents, these test results may carry enormous weight with residency directors.

OSCE-type "simulated patient" encounters became part of the USMLE Step 2 in June 2004.

Summer Work

The Beach Boys sang "you'll have fun, fun, fun 'til your daddy takes the T-Bird away." Even if you don't have any idea what a T-Bird is (a car) or who the Beach Boys are (a '60s California singing group), you certainly know about summer fun. Unfortunately, now that you are in medical school, the sun and fun will have to be put in proper perspective. Summer, especially the summer between your first and second years of school, is your only free time to explore the tentative selections you have made concerning a specialty choice. But it also will probably be the last "free" summer that you will have for many years. The question for you is, "What is most important?"

There is no question that the pull to escape from the bookwork and laboratories of your first year is great. That is only natural. But escape into the world of clinical medicine. This should be an exciting and interesting experience on several counts.

First, it will be completely different from the classroom you have labored in for the past nine-plus months. Second, it will allow you to do what you got into medical school to do—practice medicine. This might rejuvenate you for your second year of studies. Third, it will enable you to see in more detail just what aspects of medicine you enjoy and what parts you dislike. Finally, you might even make some money.

The two places to start when exploring options for summer work are your mentor and the Student Affairs office. The latter will probably have lists of those clinical (and research) fellowships that are offered to medical students. While some fellowships are available through national programs (though not necessarily to first-year students), others are generally specific to a particular institution.

What you are looking for is *clinical experience*. In some cases, this will be obvious, e.g., it is labeled as a student clinical fellowship. Other times the clinical experience may come disguised as research, as in a Pediatric project where you will have to do specific parts of a physical examination on children to collect the necessary data. The point in summer work is to try, if at all possible, to be around clinicians, learning and doing some of what they do.

The second source to use for finding a summer clinical experience is your mentor. This individual may not only be aware of opportunities at your institution of which the Dean's office is uninformed, but also may know of opportunities in the community or at other institutions. Your mentor may also invite you to work with him or her during the summer. This could be an outstanding experience. But you may not receive any money for it.

If you are in serious need of money to continue living through the next year, you may have to balance the time you spend in an unpaid clinical experience with time spent in a paying job. However, do not neglect this unique opportunity to get your feet wet and your hands dirty in the clinical sphere. It will help crystallize your idea of what you want to do when you finish medical school, as well as improve your attitude and ability to learn in your second year.

Research

Common wisdom nowadays, meaning the scuttlebutt among the rest of your class, is that it is vital to do research if you are going to get into a good residency program—especially if it is in one of the competitive specialties like Emergency Medicine, Orthopedics, Neurological Surgery, or Otolaryngology. As with all rumors, there is a kernel of truth imbedded in the lie. It isn't mandatory to do research. If you have no desire to do research at this time, if you have no knack for it, or if you have no access to research opportunities, forgo it for now. Put your energy into some of the other areas in which you do have an interest and that, therefore, will pay off more handsomely for the amount of energy that you expend.

If you do have an interest in research, it is important to make any such endeavor a meaningful experience. First of all, *try to do a project that is clinically related to the field to which you will be applying.* Too many applications list research projects dealing with such obscurities as the genetic makeup of the hummingbird. This is not the kind of research that will endear you to most clinicians. Though that type of research can be important and the students who do it probably learn many fine laboratory techniques, they are misdirecting a lot of energy if their goal is to get into a clinical residency program. So, how do you go about getting the most out of your research effort?

First, you must choose the correct preceptor. Hopefully, your mentor either will be willing to act as your research preceptor or can direct you to someone else who is suitable. Make certain the individual you choose has previously worked on student and resident research projects. Many students suffer under the tutelage of either experienced researchers who see medical students only as "gofers," or individuals without adequate research experience (the blind leading the blind).

Doable Project

Next, select the project. It can be your idea or, more likely, it will be your preceptor's idea. The key to choosing the correct project is to *select one that interests you.* You should also be able to do the project with relatively little assistance. This usually rules out the use of a linear accelerator or other complicated instruments unless you have prior experience, or the time and interest to learn how to use such equipment. It must be a project that you can do in the time that you will have available to you. If you will only be working on it at night and during weekends, it is foolish to take on a project that requires your intervention six times a day for a month. If you have a period of time, say a month or six weeks, that you want to block out to do the research, make sure that you plan to do the work in less time than that. Research *always* takes much more time and energy than is initially allotted.

Finally, make sure that your research is at least somewhat related to your specialty choice. If you are not certain yet of what that is, aim for something with broad clinical applicability—something that affects all aspects of medicine. Projects dealing with an aspect of hypertension, diabetes, wound healing, or sepsis are some examples.

Make It Count

Other than the factors listed above, there are several key parts of the project that will provide you with extra benefits. There are *two things that must be decided before any work is performed.* The first is to make sure that a *publication* will come out of the research, and that the work won't just be either relegated to the circular file or used as a footnote in a larger piece of work. While nearly half of all medical students are involved in research projects, only one-third of this group gets listed as authors on publications. The issue of *authorship* is very important. Even if you do 90% of the work, you may only get fifth billing on any publications, meaning that you will be listed after four other individuals. You would like to be listed first, or at least second, on the paper that comes out of the research. Of course, make sure that you do enough work on the project to warrant this.

You should also be aware that clinical research seems to be much easier to publish than basic science research. It also often seems to require less time to actually perform the research—particularly if you retrospectively study already available data, such as in a chart review. (Institutional Review Board approval for projects with student participation, however, may take much longer than for other projects. So start that part of the process ahead of time.) And, if you do not wish to or do not have the time to do actual research, a case report with a literature review is a reasonable alternative. All these are excellent learning experiences. Okay, so you won't get a Nobel Prize for it, but that publication will help you get the residency you want. If you broach this subject at the start of discussions about your research project, you may find that you will have a much easier time getting both a publication and appropriate authorship.

The other item to arrange ahead of time is the question of *presentation at a scientific meeting.* A scientific article may take a long time to get published, often a year or more after submission. And the words "submitted for publication" next to an article on a résumé or application are not as impressive as "published" or "presented." The quickest way to upgrade the firepower of your paper and the research behind it is to present the findings at a national scientific meeting. If the research is of decent quality, you should have no problem doing this. If it is to be presented, an abstract of your paper is normally published ahead of time in a scientific journal; you will still be able to submit the entire paper later for publication. But if you are considering this, be sure to think, early in the planning stages, about both the project's content and the deadlines for the meeting. That way you will be able to finish the project in time to meet the meeting's deadline. Plan ahead.

Sources of Funding for Student Research

Aside from programs associated with your school, several national organizations provide funding for students with identifiable research projects. These include:

- Alpha Omega Alpha (AOA) Student Research Fellowships, www.alphaomegaalpha.org/AwardsPrograms/StudentResearchPrize.htm
- American Academy of Child & Adolescent Psychiatry Minority Fellowship in Drug Abuse & Addiction, www.aacap.org/research/spurlck1.htm
- American College of Rheumatology, www.rheumatology.org/ref/awards/index.asp?aud=stu
- American Federation for Aging Research (AFAR), www.afar.org/grants.html
- American Urological Association/American Urological Association Foundation, www.afud.org/research/application/info.asp
- American Gastroenterological Association/Foundation for Digestive Health and Nutrition, www.fdhn.org/html/awards/awards.html
- American Heart Association Student Scholarships in Cardiovascular Disease & Stroke, www.americanheart.org/presenter.jhtml?identifier=9713
- American Society for Clinical Nutrition/National Clinical Nutrition Internships, www.faseb.org/ascn/intern.htm
- American Society of Hematology, www.hematology.org/education/awards
- Society for Academic Emergency Medicine/Emergency Medicine Foundation, www.saem.org/awards/grants.htm

Organizations that provide funding for students who will devote a year or more to specific research projects:

- Howard Hughes Medical Institute, www.hhmi.org/resources/students.html
- National Institutes of Health Clinical Research Training Program, www.training.nih.gov/crtp
- Stanley J. Sarnoff Fellowships, www.sarnoffendowment.org

For those with no clue about a project, but who would like some research experience over a one- to two-month period, the following may be of interest:

- American Academy of Child and Adolescent Psychiatry Minority Fellowship, www.aacap.org/research/spurlck2.htm
- American Medical Student Association (AMSA) Washington Health Policy Fellowship Program, http://www.amsa.org/whpfp/index.cfm
- American Pediatric Society/Society for Pediatric Research, www.aps-spr.org/Programs/programs.htm

- Memorial Sloan-Kettering Cancer Center Summer Student Fellowship Program, www.mskcc.org/mskcc/html/2637.cfm
- National Institutes of Health Summer Research Fellowship Program, www.training.nih.gov/student/index.asp

Arranging Your Senior Schedule

One of the major questions that medical students ask their advisers is "How do I arrange my senior schedule?" Although there is a movement away from the previous *laissez faire* attitude toward the senior year at many medical schools, most, if not all, of the senior year is still wide open for anything that the student wants to take. But, by now, you understand that you will need to arrange your schedule so that you maximize the results of your hard work and have the best chance of getting into a residency. So, your choices, or at least your timing, become somewhat more limited. How do you arrange your schedule?

Let's start with the second half of your senior year. Mid-February until June of your fourth year is when you should take the balance of your allotted vacation, any exotic international electives for which you have a yearning, and electives in areas in which you feel that you need more training. The average senior medical student takes more than seven weeks of electives outside his or her medical school, with the average school allowing students to take 24 weeks of electives.

Many senior students bolster their training in Radiology, Anesthesiology, Emergency Medicine, Pediatrics, Orthopedics, Cardiology, and Critical Care with senior electives. This is definitely not the time to take more electives in your chosen specialty. It is, instead, an opportunity to fill in some of the gaps in your training. However, when planning these exciting electives, remember that there is a cost for travel, housing, and maybe even tuition for electives away from your school. Look into it before you sign onto an away experience.

Working backward, you need to block out the next period for interviews. Remembering that you want to interview as late as possible, this means January and early February for those matching through the NRMP, and December for those in one of the early Matches. You will either have to use up some of your vacation or be on a *very* flexible rotation during this period.

Now we need to consider those *critical months at the beginning of your fourth year. First, do not take any vacation between your third and fourth years.* Immediately following the end of your third-year clerkships, start your subinternship (described below). You will need both the intense experience of this rotation and an excellent reference letter from the clinicians with whom you work for your application. Next, take a rotation in the specialty that you have chosen. If you think it will be useful to you, opt for more than one. But remember, your time is limited to those months between the end of your subinternship (often up to eight weeks long) and the beginning of your interviews.

Once these rules for arranging your senior year have been laid out, it doesn't seem so difficult, does it? If you remember that your twin goals are to use the first half of your senior year preparing to get into a residency and the second half obtaining training in your areas of clinical deficiency, you won't go wrong. And, as you can see, such rotations will give you the type of solid clinical experience that no adviser can fault.

Subinternship

As a subintern, medical students are given more responsibility and authority than they have previously experienced. This is the rotation, if done correctly, in which the student assumes all or part of the intern's role on a clinical service. This is where learning how to practice medicine actually takes place. Advisers often scorn the subinternship (a.k.a., junior internship, advanced clerkship). They say, "Why do your internship early?" Your answer is that you need to learn how to practice medicine, and that *you learn when you take responsibility.*

The most effective subinternships for senior students to take, therefore, are the ones that offer the most responsibility for patient care. These are often located at the municipal or Veteran's Administration hospitals. While these rotations are never as "cushy" as others that are available, they do provide the experiences that teach you the independence of thought and action which a good clinician, and a "standout" senior student, must learn.

Most frequently, the rotation, no matter what career specialty you have selected, will be on an Internal Medicine service. Because of these services' large patient loads, and the difficulty of doing any major damage before being stopped, students often can be given enough responsibility to become effective clinicians. In some cases, this will also be true of other services, but it is less likely. For the most part, because so much of the decision making on Surgery services is irreversible, the staff will be less likely to offer this kind of responsibility to students. But this varies from institution to institution.

Try to get information from the class ahead of you and from your Dean of Students about the nature of the various subinternships available. If possible, get a prestigious individual as an attending so he or she can write a letter about your performance. You can do this primarily by investigating who will attend at the institutions that are available to you during the appropriate time period. *But don't pick a stellar attending over a stellar experience.* The latter is much more important.

A second option available to some of you may also give you the same responsibility. This is working at a medical mission in a remote, usually foreign, area. While this is often an exciting and broadening learning experience, there are some drawbacks. This experience may not be universally available or affordable. In addition, it may teach you some thought processes and methods that are frowned upon in the United States, at a time in your training when it may be hard to distinguish these adequately. And, most important of all, many faculty may look upon it as mere senior-student flightiness.

Senior-Year Specialty Rotations

Questions constantly arise about whether, when, and how many rotations you should take in your chosen specialty field. By now you have heard at least some snatches of the debate on this subject. From the halls of academia, the pronouncement often goes something like, "Don't use your senior electives to train in the specialty for which you are applying. You will get enough of this training in your residency. Use your senior year to broaden your medical education." This is, of course, advice from academicians who are firmly ensconced in tenured posts. But is this the advice that they followed as medical students? Is it advice that they would give to their children? Probably not. Nearly 95% of medical students take electives in their first-choice specialty, and more than a third take three or more such electives.

What should you do? This depends first upon your perceived competitiveness for the specialty. As a candidate for a particular specialty, you fall into one of three categories: a star, middle-of-the-pack, or a struggler. How should students in each of these categories approach the idea of a senior-year specialty rotation? Assuming that you have done adequate preparation and now are reasonably certain that you do want to enter a particular area of medicine, your use of the senior specialty rotation should be directed toward maximizing your chance of getting the residency you want.

Advantages & Disadvantages

For the few of you who qualify as *stars*, you can use the rotation to demonstrate to residency programs that you are as good as your file says. Physicians, being generally conservative in nature, tend to prefer working with people whom they know, in lieu of those whom they have not met or have met only briefly in interviews. Some residency directors require that candidates do student rotations at their program if they wish to be considered. More than 35% of programs suggest to applicants that they are more likely to be seriously considered for selection if they take an elective at that program. If you truly are a "star" academically, personally, and clinically, show them your stuff!

If you fall into the *struggler* category, where it is obvious that your paperwork will not even get you an interview, much less the residency slot of your choice, you will need to do more than one specialty rotation. Put your greatest effort forward; you need to demonstrate to the faculty at the residency programs not only that you are capable of doing a solid job as a resident, but also that you will fit in well with their department. Demonstrate to them that you are a pleasure to have around and that you will acquit yourself well now that you have found the area of medicine for which you have been searching. Many students, after doing poorly in medical school, have used this strategy to land excellent residency positions. The key to succeeding with this strategy, however, is to work very hard—both clinically and at fitting in with the team.

Most of you are in the *middle-of-the-pack* group. While you should do at least one senior specialty elective, both to confirm your interest in the specialty and to get an additional reference letter, you run a great risk if you do more than that. There are only two types of performance for senior students doing electives in their chosen specialties. They are either "standouts" or "shutouts." There are relatively few individuals who shine both clinically and personally. If you can achieve that status, you are as good as in the residency. But even the "stars," and these are the best of the best, cannot always achieve that ranking in the minds of the specialty faculty during a rotation.

If you do not become a "standout," you are a "shutout." As Dr. Alan Langlieb wrote just after he went through the interviewing process, "One experience shared by me and other students I have met on interviews was the 'so-this-is-what-we're-getting' or the 'we-can-do-better' phenomenon. Faculty are honored that someone took the trouble and had the interest to spend from four to six weeks at their institution, but often do not know the best place to put you. They don't want to work you too hard. Anyway, you spend half your time getting accustomed to a new hospital . . . The program may see too much of the student and feel as though they could do better . . . My advice is to spend a night or weekend on call. This lets the program know of your interest and makes you stand out from other applicants, but you are not around long enough to become a part of the wallpaper."

The student who looks really good on paper, but who has not rotated through the department, will be seen as a potentially much stronger candidate than one who has rotated through and done anything less than a stellar job. Simply getting "Honors," while essential, does not necessarily mean that you were perceived as a "standout." It may only be a reflection of easy grading or it may have been based upon your clinical performance alone. The faculty may have thought that you would be impossible to work with for the duration of a training program. And there is no way to really know this. So, you take a big risk by doing a rotation at a residency where you would like to go.

But if programs require that all applicants do a rotation at their facility, you are stuck. More than one-third of students report that programs to which they applied at least suggested that they were more likely to be considered if they did a rotation with them. If you really want to go into such a program, you will need to do the rotation. These are normally rather small programs in selected specialties. In most cases, Orthopedics, Ophthalmology, and Neurological Surgery only rank students who have done an "audition clerkship" at their program. However, this requirement severely limits their applicant pool and, therefore, you may stand a better chance than you would otherwise expect. There are, of course, ways to improve your clinical performance on the specialty rotation. This takes a little preparation.

Preparation

How do you prepare for an elective rotation in the specialty that you have chosen? First, of course, you should have been preparing over the past several years by reading about the specialty, talking with many practitioners in the field, and spending volunteer time with physicians in the specialty.

But now you are getting ready to "show your stuff" to a residency faculty and you want to be a "standout." Clinically, a residency faculty is looking for an individual who

1. Knows enough of the specialty's factual material to have a solid basis for future training.
2. Is able to use these facts in an intelligent manner to deliver good patient care.
3. Delivers patient care in a manner consistent with the specialty's personality.

This almost sounds as idealistic as "motherhood and apple pie." But it is what you have to achieve.

The first requirement, *knowing the basic facts*, can be satisfied through exposure to specialists in the field, reviewing your notes from the relevant basic science courses, and reading specialty textbooks. (Make sure to read at least one cover-to-cover prior to taking the rotation. If you are pressed for time, it can be the shorter "Essentials of . . ." version.)

The second requirement, *using those facts in an intelligent manner to deliver good patient care,* is more difficult to achieve. This means having the skill to integrate the facts that you have learned and then apply them in clinical situations. It also means, in almost all cases, demonstrating a certain degree of independence by devising and carrying out diagnostic and treatment plans without guidance, though not without supervision. How, as a fourth-year student, will you possibly be able to do this? You will be able to do this as a result of the training and experience you gained while doing a subinternship.

The third attribute specialty faculties look for is whether you *deliver care in a manner consistent with that field's personality*. What does this mean? One of best examples of this is expressed in a story about a new General Surgery intern at a prestigious institution. As he was walking across the hospital's cafeteria one day, he was pointed out to the surgical chief resident by the chairman of the department with the comment, "He's just not aggressive enough to be a *real* surgeon. He'll have to go." Perhaps this quiet, studious physician was too stubborn to be kicked out (also maybe too good), but he didn't go. And, as is true in all such stories, he went on to succeed—in fact, he became a world-famous Pediatric Cardiovascular Surgeon. But the fact remains that a particular type of person tends to be drawn to each specialty, and the medical care in that field is generally given with a certain overlay of that personality.

While there are many exceptions (you probably know of some), a certain aggressiveness is expected in applicants for Surgery, most Surgical subspecialties, and Emergency Medicine. Warmth and understanding is looked for in applicants to programs in Psychiatry, Pediatrics, Family Medicine, and Physiatry. Calmness and a low-key nature are often sought in applicants for Internal Medicine, Radiology, Anesthesiology, Pathology, and Neurology residencies. It is not clear whether current practitioners' personalities guide the specialty's personality, or whether the nature of each specialty attracts and molds particular individuals. But the important point to remember is: if you stand out as a significantly different personality type than individuals already in the specialty, it will be more difficult for you to get a training position in that specialty.

Home or Away?

Many factors involved in taking a specialty rotation at home or away have already been discussed. However, there are still three points worth noting.

First: *There can be significant expenses* involved in the travel, meals, and lodging associated with taking an away rotation. While you may assume that there is housing available for rotating medical students, and some of you might even expect free meals, much of the time you would be mistaken. Find out about these costs before arranging the rotation.

Second: *The expense might be worth it.* If you rotate at the site of your first-choice residency only to find out that it really does not meet your needs, you have spent the money wisely. In such a case, the one-month rotation may save you several years of unhappiness. Remember, specialty rotations work both ways—they look you over and you look them over.

Third: *Apply for externships early!* Very popular clerkships, either at your own school or away, are often filled a year or more in advance. Even if you make your specialty choice at a late date, you may still have a good chance of obtaining a rotation in the specialty at your own school. This is not true of away rotations. If you are strongly considering doing an away elective in your chosen specialty, get information and sign up for the externship as early as possible. If you change your mind later, you can always cancel.

The Association of American Medical Colleges (AAMC) has a website with information about medical student electives (http://services.aamc.org/eec/student.cfmon-line). Unfortunately, it is not organized by specialty, but only by medical school, state/province, and geographic region. The University of Kansas School of Medicine has a wonderful website (www.kumc.edu/som/medsos/opp.html) listing many types of "Unique Electives" and summer "Fellowships" with their URLs.

The AMA's Medical Student Section also has a great site with International elective opportunities. (Go to www.ama-assn.org/go/mss and scroll down to *"Tools You Can Use"—"International Opportunities."*) Another source for finding yearlong international medical student fellowships is via the AAMC's "Resources for Medical Students" page (www.aamc.org/students/medstudents/). Many specialty societies also have lists of electives in their specialty.

Timing

When should you do your specialty rotation? If you are applying to one of the specialties that does not match early, you have some leeway. But if you will be in an early Match, you may be pressed for time. In either case, you should do a strong subinternship immediately following your junior year, usually on an Internal Medicine service. That's right—no vacation for now; you will have to wait until much later in the year.

A subinternship is usually a six- or eight-week block, so you should finish near the end of August. Then you should take a specialty rotation. If you take it at a program to which you are applying, you will probably be able to interview near the end of the rotation—especially if you notify them of your desire to do this in advance and reconfirm your intent upon arrival. If you have the time, and you feel that you will be exceptionally weak clinically for a fourth-year student in your selected specialty, you may want to first do a specialty rotation at a program that you do not rank highly. Then, if you think that doing another rotation will help your individual chances, you can do it at one of your top choices. Consider, though, that many students have found that the programs that they thought would be lowest on their rank-order list ended up at or near the top.

As you did with your third-year clinical rotations, try to arrange your schedule so you can work with an attending who is well-known by residency directors in the specialty. Ask that individual at the start of the rotation if, contingent upon your performance, he or she would be willing to write you a letter of recommendation. Attendings are normally very amenable to this. Then make sure that you supply the necessary names and addresses so that the letters can be sent. There won't be much time. These letters will have to go out *fast*.

You will have now used up all the time that you have available for rotations that will be of any help (or hindrance) in getting into a residency. You can finally spend some time broadening your medical horizons and, certainly, taking a well-deserved vacation.

Awards

Not everyone receives awards during medical school. But getting them may help you obtain a residency position, and make you feel good in the process. Who doesn't like getting an award? The acknowledgments you received as an undergraduate are passé. Not that you shouldn't list Phi Beta Kappa or other undergraduate achievement awards on your résumé, but remember that everyone else has similar achievements. That is why you were accepted into medical school. And anyway, you received those awards a long time ago. Residencies want to know what you have done recently. Awards, in part, answer that question. They are also an important factor in making you and your application stand out as being unique among the crop of applicants to the programs.

AOA

Alpha Omega Alpha (AOA) is the national M.D. medical school honorary society. (Note that this is not the American Osteopathic Association [AOA]. Residency directors know the difference.) Students are elected to AOA based primarily on their grades. In most schools, students can be elected to AOA either at the end of their third year or during their fourth year. Because it is found in most schools, AOA is the best-recognized medical school award. Students elected to the honorary are generally assured of serious consideration by residency programs. This means that many will get most of the interviews they desire. After that it will, of course, be up to them to do well in these interviews.

Some schools do not have AOA chapters. Generally, this is due to the school's philosophy that they should attempt to reduce competition among students. Other schools do not elect anyone to AOA until late in the senior year. Their assumption is that this gives those students at the bottom of the class a better chance of competing against their classmates for residency slots. It is, however, not just your classmates but, rather, all medical students who are the competition.

If your school has an AOA chapter, find out from the Dean of Students what the requirements are to be elected. If you think that you can satisfy these requirements, then go for it. Getting into AOA can somewhat ease the burden and anxiety of getting a residency position.

If you are elected to AOA after you submit your residency applications, or even after you have been interviewed, send the programs an official notification from the registrar. Most schools will ask you for the necessary addresses since they know this is very important.

But AOA is not the only award that you can get.

Just for Women

The American Medical Women's Association gives several awards to its members. These include a merit-based scholarship, an essay award, a certificate to top medical school graduates, and a research award. They also occasionally have month-long, special-project "internships." For further information, contact: AMWA, (703) 838-0500; e-mail: info@amwa-doc .org; www.amwa-doc.org (go to "Member Services").

Special Awards

Many other awards are given out both nationally and locally. However, they may have to be sought out. Your Dean of Students should have a list of the awards given at your school, and probably knows a good bit about other national prizes. The University of Kansas School of Medicine website also has a fine list of nationally available scholarships and awards (www.kumc .edu/som/medsos/opp.html).

The most obvious awards are those that you in all probability investigated as soon as you were accepted into medical school. These are *scholarships*. Since these are awards, they should be noted as such on program applications. If you were given renewals of these scholarships because of your good performance in medical school, so much the better. Note, however, that bartering service for money, such as signing up for the Health Professions Scholarship Program, doesn't count.

Another type of award given in most schools is for *excellence in particular courses or clerkships*. For example, the outstanding student in Anatomy or in Family Medicine may get an award (often with money as well as a plaque). If you have been selected for such recognition, it is a big deal! Note it prominently on your applications. If the specialty for which you are applying has an award, find out the requirements for it and see if you can be the one to receive it. Your interest in the specialty alone should go a long way toward getting you this honor.

Unfortunately, many schools do not announce award recipients until graduation. This is long past the time when it will help you to get a residency position. While speaking to your Dean of Students about awards in general, find out if this is your school's policy. If it is, can it be changed? If it can't, and you know that you have been designated for such an award, try to at least have it mentioned in your Dean's letter or in a separate letter that you can include with your applications.

One way you can get recognition and also buff up another area of your application is to receive a *research grant*. Very often either medical schools or individual departments, or both, have monies specifically set aside for medical student research. If you plan to do research anyway, it wouldn't be a bad idea to apply for some of this research money. Not only is it a significant accolade, but it will also make your foray into research much easier.

There are also awards, usually given by major drug companies, for *medical writing, biomedical illustration*, and other specialized endeavors. If you have talent in any area where such a prize is given, go after it. You will often be able to find out about these awards from your Dean of Students, notices on your class's bulletin board, or advertisements in *The New Physician*.

8

Putting Off A Decision

If you carry a lantern, you will not fear the darkness.

NOT MAKING A DECISION about a specialty choice is, as the saying goes, equivalent to deciding not to go into a specialty—at least for the present. In the past (forty or more years ago), medical students routinely put off choosing a specialty until they were well into their internship year. This is the tradition of Ben Casey and Marcus Welby (maybe you saw them in reruns) and of *Arrowsmith* (perhaps you read it in high school). This tradition stemmed from a time, now happily past, when many, if not most, physicians went into practice with little more than an internship as their postgraduate training.

Today, it is dangerous—if not insane—to go into practice so unprepared. Advanced training is now necessary to understand the increasing complexity of medical practice. Without advanced training, today's medical school graduates will usually neither qualify for malpractice insurance nor be granted hospital privileges.

Sadly, we still routinely allow physicians with only an internship to practice in both our Public Health Service (treating Native Americans and poor people) and the military. If you plan to follow these career paths, you can do so with only a PGY-1 year of training. Without advanced training, however, you will probably not progress very far within these services.

Admittedly, making a specialty choice is difficult. It is yet another step in the maturation process, and will remove you from the comfort you have felt for a number of years—ever since you received your acceptance into medical school.

Now, instead of seeing yourself as "a doctor," you must generate another image of yourself. Looking in the mirror, you now must see a Pediatrician, a Pathologist, a Family Physician, a Surgeon, or another specialist. This much narrower focus may be an uncomfortable fit if you have envisioned yourself as the omniscient healer. But it is a fit to which you are going to have to adjust. The only question is, when should you make the decision?

More medical students make their initial specialty decision during their third year of medical school (46%) than at any other time. Another 24% select a specialty during their fourth year, while 23% make a decision before beginning their clinical years of medical school.

The Fine Art of Procrastination

Despite the common wisdom, making a life-changing decision is not easy and may not completely succumb to rational analysis. A decision about which specialty to enter is just such a decision. Writing a list of pros and cons will just not hack it. Such a decision must take into account many intangible factors, such as your past experiences, willingness to take risks, and unspoken dreams.

Everyone has procrastinated about making a major decision. The question to ask is why are you procrastinating? Usually it is because you fear making a "wrong" decision, especially if that decision seems irrevocable. Any major decision involves risk—personal, financial, or both. Some decisions don't work out the way you planned. That's okay. Obviously, choosing a specialty to enter is a gigantic step. It is not, however, permanent, since up to 20% of physicians change their career direction at least once.

Several techniques may help you make a decision, especially if you have already gathered the basic information about the specialties you are considering, including spending time with both academic and community physicians practicing those specialties.

Discuss your options with close friends and family. Allow yourself to express your emotions, not just "the facts." Your career choice is emotional, so "let it all hang out."

Weigh what is most important in your own life: personal satisfaction, family, money, prestige, time off. Actually give every one a weight (like in the "Must-Want" Analysis) and see how each specialty you are considering will fulfill them.

When you are alone, *imagine yourself* in each of the specialties you are considering. Are you enjoying yourself or stressing out? Do you feel satisfied or frustrated? Maybe most important, do you want to go to work tomorrow?

The key is to not hem and haw while you are in the middle of the road about which way to go. It will only make you middle-of-the-road kill—not a pretty picture.

Taking Time Off

There are several reasons to take time off during or immediately after medical school. Residency directors are used to seeing this type of hiatus in medical training, so this should not hurt an applicant's chances of getting into a program.

If you have a choice, when should you take time off? One student suggested that if she took time off between her first and second years, she could go straight into third year without losing any clinical skills or knowledge. Some students take time off between their second and third years, others between the third and fourth years. Few take time off immediately after graduation.

Taking leave for medical, personal, and family reasons, especially to have a baby, is now fairly common. If you do that, be sure your reason for taking time off is clearly stated in your personal statement. With the increasing debt load many medical students carry, some schools allow students to take a year off to work. In the long run, this is probably not a wise financial decision, but it should not penalize residency applicants. If you put something in your personal statement, however, it is fair game to ask about during the interview. For example, if you mention your chronic illness, they may ask if it is under control or how often you have exacerbations requiring time off.

If the time off was to acquire another degree, do extended research, or have an unusual medical experience (such as doing volunteer work in a disaster area), describing what you learned and why you did it should probably be the focus of your personal statement. This may also be the focus of most of your interviews. In many cases, this type of extra experience and knowledge may make you an even *more desirable* candidate.

Others who take time off may have less-clear motivations. Often, the individuals were not sure whether they really wanted to pursue a medical career, or they had so much academic difficulty that they were asked to temporarily drop out. These types of breaks during training may seriously hurt applicants' chances of getting a desirable residency position, especially if they cannot demonstrate they have used the time to make certain that medicine is the career they want or to correct their academic deficiencies.

Win-Win Decisions

Fear of making decisions often keeps people from moving ahead with their lives and their careers. The motto for most medical students—those who have traveled the normal route to medical school—is often "Be careful! You might make the wrong decision." They believe that, at any juncture, an incorrect career choice could deprive them of those things that the "correct" decision is supposed to bring: money, love, respect, and security. They may also, by making the "wrong" decision, find that they are neither perfect nor in complete control of their lives. But, like the donkey that couldn't choose between two bales of hay, it is possible for them to waiver in their decision just long enough to starve to death.

To feel better about making a career decision, you must adjust your view of the possible outcomes. First, realize that your decision will not determine your life or death. The decision need not be permanent. It can be reassessed at a later time when you have more information. Second, instead of thinking of your career decision in terms of the "right" path (you win) versus the "wrong" path (you lose), consider that any of the paths you have reasonably investigated can offer you exciting, although not necessarily equivalent, opportunities.

By thinking of your career decision as a Win-Lose situation (Figure 8.1), you will doom yourself to forever thinking "What if I had taken the other route?" every time something in your career, or your life, is not perfect. This results in a life of misery and depression. By following a Win-Win model (Figure 8.2), you allow yourself to feel good and gain the rewards you desire from whichever path you take.

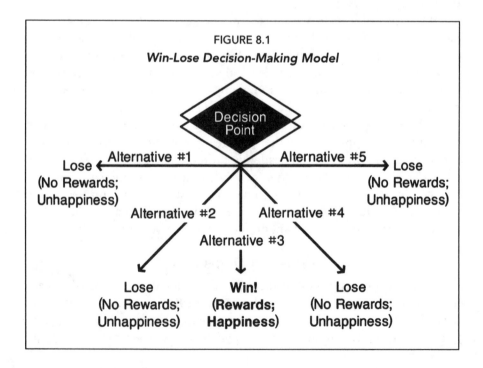

FIGURE 8.1

Win-Lose Decision-Making Model

Decision Point

Lose ← Alternative #1   Alternative #5 → Lose
(No Rewards;   (No Rewards;
Unhappiness)   Unhappiness)

Alternative #2   Alternative #4

Alternative #3

Lose   Win!   Lose
(No Rewards;   (Rewards;   (No Rewards;
Unhappiness)   Happiness)   Unhappiness)

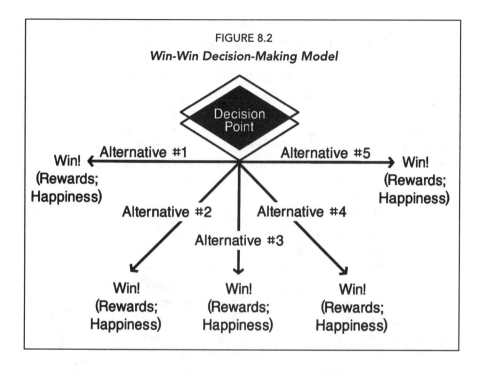

FIGURE 8.2
Win-Win Decision-Making Model

Advantages & Disadvantages of a Transitional Year

Taking a transitional internship without having obtained a commitment for PGY-2-level training has both advantages and disadvantages.

The Transitional internship is similar to the internships of old. It exposes physicians to Medicine, Surgery, Emergency Medicine, Obstetrics and Gynecology, Pediatrics, and, perhaps, Psychiatry. Very similar in many ways to a repeat of your third year of medical school, albeit with upgraded responsibility, it provides another general overview of the practice of medicine. The additional knowledge and abilities you acquire may be very useful throughout your career. This is especially true if you are thinking of using this as your first year of training prior to beginning a program that starts in the second year, such as Anesthesiology, Radiology, or Ophthalmology. But if you are merely postponing a decision about which specialty to enter, and assume you will use the Transitional year to decide, you may be in for a rude awakening.

First, look at the time schedule for the NRMP application process (Figure 22.5). You will see that going into a Transitional year allows you to put off making a decision, at best, only until the end of your senior year of medical school. Matching in the advanced Matches (PGY-2 and above) and with programs not participating in the Match usually occurs even earlier. If you plan to start specialty training the year after your internship, you will have to have made a decision before the end of your senior year. So, what price do you pay for procrastinating?

Internship is tough on both body and soul. It doesn't matter whether you are in a Transitional program or in a Categorical internship. (For an explanation of the types of internships, see Chapter 22.) You will work long hours and get little sleep. That is the nature of the beast. So, now you have moved the very grueling process of applying for a training position to what will probably be the most difficult time in your entire life—the first half of your internship. Not a pretty prospect. It is so difficult to deal with the added stress that many interns give up and take the easiest route to a decision. That is, they agree to take virtually any open position, even if it is not in the specialty they want. They promise themselves that they will look for a better position later. They rarely do.

Another problem relates directly to the Transitional year. Many specialties, including most Surgical areas, Internal Medicine, Pediatrics, and Family Medicine, will not accept a Transitional year as counting toward completion of a residency (Figure 22.1). Therefore, you may have to either avoid going into these specialties or repeat your internship—a dismal thought and nearly always an unhappy experience. No matter how much you think you won't mind repeating the intern year—you will hate it. I have seen many individuals, all of whom truly believed they would not mind going through internship again, be absolutely miserable when having to repeat the experience. Most people emerge from their internship with a wealth of new clinical knowledge and the ability to make clinical decisions and work in a clinical setting. Repeating this experience will not substantially increase these abilities. Instead, it will often cause frustration, since your supervising residents may not have the same level of skills that you do.

An alternative, if you can at least decide between Surgery and Medicine, is to take a "Preliminary" Surgery or Medicine internship. These are not broadly based, as are the Transitional programs. They are essentially the same programs as those the Categorical Medicine or Surgery interns go through. The benefit is that more possibilities exist for you following such training. Surgery and its associated areas will accept a Preliminary Surgery internship; Medicine will accept a Preliminary Medicine internship. Some Preliminary spots may be relatively easy to obtain: only 65% of those in Surgery filled in the 2005 Match, although 90% of Preliminary Internal Medicine positions filled. Specialties that accept Transitional programs will also accept either of these. So, perhaps part of a decision is better than none.

You may still decide to do a Transitional year, as did nearly 5% of 2005 graduates, either because you cannot make up your mind about a specialty or because your specialty requires a preliminary clinical year before beginning specialty training, such as in Anesthesiology, Radiology, and Ophthalmology. About 80% of residents in a Transitional year plan to follow that year with a residency. Another 12% intend to follow the year with required federal service, and a small number plan to go into research. With more confidence than common sense, 1% plan to go into practice after just this one year of training!

If you intend to do a Transitional year, a good information source, aside from *FREIDA,* is the *Transitional Year Program Directory* (also called *The Purple Book Online*), published by the Association for Hospital Medical Education (http://www.ahme.org/publications/transitional.html). See Chapter 9 for descriptions of these sources.

Quick Decisions & Forty Years of Sadness

More than half of all medical school graduates believe that deciding on a specialty before beginning their third year gives them an advantage in obtaining their choice of residency program. While this may have some validity, there are dangers in making a specialty decision too quickly. Many physicians with whom I have come in contact or have counseled over the years are disappointed, if not frankly frustrated and bored, by their specialty (see Figure 3.3). This is not as surprising as it may seem. When asked how they had made a specialty decision in the first place, many said that they were influenced by an exciting third-year rotation, a dynamic teacher in medical school, a childhood physician, or a physician-parent.

During training, some got a hint that the specialty was not for them. They may have lacked a feeling of excitement when they were about to go to the operating room. Or they became depressed taking care of patients with chronic illnesses on the wards. But they did not listen to their feelings and continued their training. By the time they finished their residencies, they felt that they had committed too much time to the specialty to change.

Others liked their training immensely. The diagnostic challenges and therapeutic dilemmas seen in the tertiary-care teaching facility stimulated them. But once they got into practice, they found that they rarely used most of their skills. Rather, they dealt with a parade of patients with the same mundane problems. And this was not what they had anticipated.

Physicians also change specialties because of the process of self-discovery that accompanies most educational endeavors. It is not uncommon for medical students (maybe not you, but certainly most of your friends) to be service-oriented, obsessive-compulsive individuals. They receive much of their stimulus to achieve from a self-sacrificing posture designed to win approval from superiors, relatives, and friends. Yet, while training in clinical medicine, some individuals find that their route to personal satisfaction is not through their chosen specialty; some find that the route does not include medical practice at all.

In the past, I have gotten calls not only from physicians in practice, but also from their spouses. Our discussions were always variations on the same theme. The physicians had been in practice from eight to ten years and were very unhappy, even though they were often in what most people consider to be very desirable specialties. The physicians repeatedly stated that life would be much better if only they could change their specialty. The caller now wanted advice about how to make that change. What could not be ascertained, however, was whether the initial specialty choice, or something much more profound, was the problem.

I am saddened when I see a 45-year-old physician who is unhappy that he or she ever entered the field of medicine. It is less sad, but still somewhat unnerving, to see the same physician reenter a training program to change specialties at such an advanced stage in his or her career. So, there definitely can be reasons to wait to make a specialty decision. Investigating your options early will help to prevent you from making a foolish or uninformed choice. But just procrastinating in making that decision will not make the final selection either easier or better.

Some residency programs may now hesitate to take physicians who have completed too much prior residency training. The federal government, through the Medicare program, reimburses hospitals for much of the cost of resident education. This support is at its maximum for the time required to meet the requirements for initial Board certification—with a maximum of five years. They calculate this time period beginning with the first year of Categorical residency (not counting a Transitional or Osteopathic internship year). Although the amount of money is relatively small, the impact makes some programs wary of accepting residents who have already done training in another specialty or in a Transitional year. An exception, of course, is when that year is required as part of the training, such as before beginning Otolaryngology, Urology, Neurology, etc. This also applies to those who have entered another field, even decades ago, and now want to retrain in another specialty.

In reality, however, the Medicare payments hospitals receive for these residents are not decreased as much as one might believe. They continue to get the substantial "indirect" reimbursement; it is only the "direct" payment that is partially decreased. While programs and hospitals may consider this as one factor, generally it will not prevent residents from changing their residency program. *This relatively minor reduction in hospital reimbursement should never cause residents to work for free, as some have suggested.*

Switching Careers

Medicine, more than any other profession, tenaciously hangs onto its practitioners. Physicians are expected to remain committed to the field until death or voluntary retirement, either through a sense of altruism, because of the benefits they gain, or simply because they believe that their focused education eliminates other forms of employment.

Each year, however, about 3% of U.S. medical school graduates go into other careers. If you find that you are interested in another career, you may want to look at the AMA publication *Leaving the Bedside: The Search for a Nonclinical Medical Career.*

Numerous physicians have successfully either combined other careers with medicine or switched completely. Most of these names are well known to you, although you may not know that they were physicians. These include:

- **Philosophers:** John Locke and Oliver Wendell Holmes, Sr.
- **Astronomers:** Nicholas Copernicus (physician to the Heilsberg Bishopric)
- **Scientists:** Luigi Galvani (Italian physiologist), Carol Linnaeus (Swedish taxonomist), and Thomas Huxley (English biologist)
- **Politicians:** Jean Marat (French Revolution), Georges Clemenceau (World War I French Premier), Sun Yat Sen (first president of the Chinese Republic), and Che Guevara (modern communist revolutionary)
- **Writers:** Arthur Conan Doyle, Tobias Smollett, A.J. Cronin, Thomas Campion, Anton Chekhov, Johann Schiller, John Keats, William Somerset Maugham, and Michael Crichton
- **Others:** Galileo, Charles Darwin, and Gertrude Stein went on to fame after dropping out during medical school. (In Ms. Stein's case, it was during her 4th-year OB/Gyn clerkship at Johns Hopkins.)

So there is life outside medicine. One of the most common alternative careers that physicians now consider is the law. The AMA estimates that there are as many as 6,000 physician-lawyers in the United States. Each year, many physicians enter law school for uncertain reasons, but drop out because they find it tedious or boring. If you consider changing from a medical career, go toward a positive goal—don't just run away.

Dangers of Indecision

Some students think that because they have been unable to make a specialty decision, they will let the luck of the Match—not at all like the luck of the Irish—decide for them. They interview in two or more specialties. And, although they may give preference in their rank-order list to one field or another, it is clear that they are not committed to a particular specialty. (This is not to say that you should not list some appropriate internships at the bottom of your rank-order list—that is just being careful. See Chapter 22.)

In such cases of indecision, the question must be raised, "Is the indecision based upon a lack of knowledge about the specialties, or about one's self?" Unfortunately, it is common for students to apply to multiple types of specialties. If you are contemplating such a move, it is time to get some serious counseling. And one of the items that needs to be discussed is *whether you really want a career in medicine.* Of course you have already spent a lot of time in school, but consider that residency will be another three to seven years. Nevertheless, if you still think you really do want to work as a physician and you intend, for some reason, to apply to multiple specialties, consider the two biggest problems involved.

The first, and most obvious, problem with applying to multiple specialties is the time and cost involved. If you plan to research the specialties, and perhaps take senior electives in them, you will use up your available time very quickly. Expenses also mount up rapidly if you are applying to multiple specialties.

The second problem is that you will have broken a basic tenet of the residency application process. You will have shown that you are not committed to a specialty. And if the reason you are applying to multiple specialties in this fashion is to stay within a defined geographic area, be assured that most of the programs will know or soon discover this. If the programs are anything more than "bottom-rung" and you are anything less than a "star," they probably will not consider you seriously. Consequently, you may very well end up in a poor, nondescript program, which probably will, either then or later, make you very unhappy. It is better to make an informed choice about a single specialty and then go after the position with maximum effort.

9

Gathering Information

Just to look costs nothing.

– Folk Saying

NOW THAT YOUR SPECIALTY DECISION IS MADE, it is time to collect information, not on the specialty in general, but on that specialty's individual training programs. You need to discover the differences among training programs, where they are located, how difficult it is to get a position at each, and what variables and options exist for completing your training.

With the limited time and money you have to invest in searching for the best programs for you, it is essential that you do some priority shopping—spending your resources in a manner to give you the highest probability of finding what you want. To do this, you must get enough information about each program that you seriously consider to allow you to complete your own "Must/Want" Analysis (Figure 10.1). If you know where to look, much of this information is readily available.

You will be sifting through a lot of information, so get organized first! One method that many students find useful is to set up a file for each program they consider. If you do this, then you can put the material in the file as you collect it. Paste a copy of your "Must/Want" Analysis on the *inside* cover of each file folder.

When you take this file with you to your interview (or "audition" elective), you can fill in your "Must/Want" Analysis as you go along, and no one else will see it. It would be a good idea to also paste in a copy of "Interview Notes" (Figure 17.2). (The *Companion Disk* contains these two vital forms for you to customize and print out.) Since most students do not have their own filing cabinet, you may find it useful to purchase a sturdy cardboard file box (sometimes called a "bankers box"). A 12″ x 15″ x 10″ box can hold about 35 files. Of course, many applicants will simply put them in a file in their computer or PDA. One warning: be sure to back up these files frequently!

Now that you have a method for organizing program information, let's consider some information sources in detail. (For more sources and how to get them, see the *Annotated Bibliography*. Also see *Contact Information* for addresses.)

Graduate Medical Education Directory

The American Medical Association (AMA) issues this substantial book annually. Usually referred to as the "Green Book," it lists all "approved" M.D.-run training programs; i.e., those accredited by the Accreditation Council for Graduate Medical Education (ACGME). Most of the information in this book has been supplanted by the AMA's *FREIDA* system (see below). However, there are a few areas that are still important to residency applicants. These are mainly Section II, which describes the requirements that each residency program must fulfill, and Appendix B: Board Certification Requirements. This information is also available on the CD-ROM titled *Graduate Medical Education Library*, issued annually by the AMA.

Section I: Information Items

This section contains only the technical information about how programs become, and stay, accredited.

Section II: Requirements for Accreditation of Programs

This section has the "Institutional Requirements" (also called "General Requirements") that residencies must fulfill to obtain accreditation, including the responsibilities of institutions, the organization and responsibilities of programs, the eligibility and selection of residents, and the relationships between programs and residents. In addition, there is a list of the minimum elements for contracts between the residency programs and the applicants.

More important, this section includes the "Program Requirements" (also called "Special Requirements") for each approved specialty and subspecialty. These requirements detail each specialty's training philosophy, programs' expected general characteristics, the required scope of training (including special exceptions, acceptable prerequisite training, and alternative routes to accomplish training, if they exist), programs' expected content, the nature of the teaching staff and facilities, and any other requirements unique to the specialty.

One caveat, however: When reading the Program Requirements, remember that you will be reading what the specialty's leaders would like their ideal residency program to encompass. Few, if any, training programs ever meet all these requirements. To be accredited, they are expected to have met most of them and, where possible, to work on meeting the others. The pertinent questions for you to ask will be: (1) Does the program meet enough requirements so that it will most likely remain accredited throughout my period of training? and (2) Are the factors that I consider important present at that program?

Section III: Accredited Graduate Medical Education Training Programs

This section constitutes the bulk of the book and was once the most familiar to applicants. It contains a list of residency programs and their basic contact information. It has been supplanted by *FREIDA*. The "Supplement" that comes out each year may prove useful, however, since it includes programs that are too new to be in *FREIDA*.

Section IV: New & Withdrawn Programs

Here you will find a list of new programs, which are also included in Section III. There is also a list of programs that have been withdrawn (listed by specialty). This may be useful to look at if you cannot find the program you are looking for (it may no longer exist).

Section V: Graduate Medical Education Teaching Institutions

This is a listing, city by city, of the "sponsoring" institutions for graduate medical education programs and the "major participating" institutions. Residents generally spend less time at participating institutions, because they often host only a few or elective rotations. This information is also in *FREIDA*.

Appendices

Several of the appendices are useful. Most important for all applicants are the requirements for certification by the recognized American Specialty (M.D.) Boards in Appendix B. Figure 9.1 lists some specific information you should obtain. Now would be a good time to look at these requirements, especially if you are not going directly from medical school into residency training, or if you are anticipating something out of the ordinary for your training experience. Better to learn the rules now than to suffer later.

One appendix lists the combined specialty training programs, such as Pediatrics–Emergency Medicine; *FREIDA* contains the specifics. Another section lists U.S. (M.D.) medical schools and their addresses. There is also a glossary of terms frequently used in Graduate Medical Education.

FIGURE 9.1

Questions to Ask about Requirements for Specialty Certification

1. Is this residency program accredited? If not, will I still be qualified to take the Boards if I take my training here?
2. Can I take the specialty Boards if I do my residency outside the United States?
3. Will I be penalized if I switch programs within this specialty, or if I switch into this specialty from another specialty?
4. What are the rules about taking sick leave, family leave, and other breaks during my training? Is there a maximum time period allowed for absences or for completing training by the Board?
5. When can I take the Board exam? Are there requirements in addition to residency training (e.g., time in practice, advanced degree) that I will need? When should I apply for the exam(s)?
6. Are there different ways to become certified in this specialty?
7. Do I need an unrestricted U.S. medical license to take the Boards?
8. How many times can I take the exam? What are the pass-fail rates?
9. What are the rules regarding recertification?

GMED Companion: An Insider's Guide to Selecting a Residency Program

The AMA's annual *GMED Companion* offers basic descriptions of graduate medical education programs, including relevant data, such as the availability of shared-schedule/part-time positions. It also contains information about ERAS and the National Resident Matching Program (NRMP), as well as a general description of residency training in the Armed Services. Some of this information, plus additional information on topics such as Hospitalist and Women's Health programs, is included on the CD-ROM titled *Graduate Medical Education Library*, issued annually by the AMA.

Of particular interest for IMGs who are attempting to obtain residency positions in the United States are sections on the requirements for ECFMG certification, the types of visas that permit graduate medical education or training, and the history and requirements of the Fifth Pathway Program.

Fellowship & Residency Electronic Interactive Database Access (FREIDA)

The AMA's *Fellowship and Residency Electronic Interactive Database Online®* (commonly called *FREIDA*) is an applicant's major source of information about training programs. Instituted at the request of the AMA's Resident

Physician Section, the system provides students with a wealth of information. Indeed, so much information is available that the unprepared can be overwhelmed. *FREIDA* now lists about 7,800 ACGME-approved residency and fellowship programs and about 200 programs for combined-specialty residencies. It also offers specialty-specific workforce information and an overview of each specialty's residency programs.

Before using this database, the prudent move would be to review the section on the "Must/Want" Analysis to determine which characteristics of residency programs are of importance to you.

FREIDA can be accessed online through the American Medical Association's website. There is NO CHARGE to use this system! To access *FREIDA* on the Web, go to either www.ama-assn.org/go/freida to get to the main page or www.ama-assn.org/vapp/freida/srch/ to begin searching.

From the main *FREIDA* page, to begin searching in the specialties, click "Choose Specialty." A list of all ACGME-approved specialties, combined specialties (such as Internal Medicine–Pediatrics), and subspecialties will appear. Select one or more specialties that interest you. Then press "Continue" at the bottom of the page (or "Clear Form" to start over). At that point, *you can get a brief overview of up to 250 programs in the specialty by selecting "Search Plus."* This is a side-by-side comparison of the programs using some basic information. This function can be used again to compare programs selected with the criteria listed below. (If the specialty you choose has more than 250 programs, *FREIDA* requires that you narrow your search, as described below, before the information can be displayed.)

You now have the option of narrowing your selection criteria. By clicking "Choose Location," you can limit your search to specific states or regions. Use "Optional Criteria" to search for programs meeting any or all of the criteria chosen from the various information items below. For example, you can search for programs that participate in the NRMP, require prior residency training, offer preliminary or shared-schedule/part-time positions, and offer start dates other than in June or July.

Each program with a complete *FREIDA* listing has more than 100 information items available in the database. *FREIDA* divides the data into several categories:

1. **Basic Information:** Program name, *FREIDA* identifier (useful for returning to this entry), e-mail, snail-mail address, and phone/fax numbers of the program director and the contact person (if different); the program's website URL (if any); program length; whether they are accepting applications for the current and following years; program start date(s), whether they participate in ERAS; whether

they are affiliated with the U.S. government; and which institutions are sponsors and participants. You can link to information about each listed institution from this location.

2. **General Information:** Some programs place extra information in a "Comments" section. Number of positions in each PGY year; primary teaching site and type of hospital (such as university, military, or community); whether prior residency training is required; availability of "preliminary" positions; if applicants must pass USMLE Step 2CS before beginning their residency; participation in, and the code number for, the NRMP or other matching programs; the number of residency interviews granted in the past year; the number of required reference letters; the deadline for applications; and the interview period.

3. **Program Faculty:** The number of physician and non-physician full-time and part-time faculty; percentage of full-time female physician faculty; and the ratio of full-time-equivalent paid faculty to residents.

4. **Work Schedule:** Average hours on duty per week, excluding beeper call; maximum consecutive hours on duty during first year, excluding beeper call; number of 24-hour off-duty periods per week during the first year; whether moonlighting is allowed within the institution; whether there is a "night float" system; and the "most taxing" schedule and the beeper or home-call schedules for each year of the program.

5. **Educational Environment:** Educational conference frequency; hospital/non-hospital ambulatory experience; formal mentoring program; educational benefits (debt management/financial counseling, teaching skills programs, Continuous Quality Improvement training, international experiences, resident/fellow retreats, off-campus electives, hospice/home-care experiences, cultural competence curricula, instruction in medical Spanish or other languages, alternative medicine curricula, MPH/MBA/Ph.D. training, research rotations); educational features (Primary Care, Women's Health, Rural, or Hospitalist tracks; residents supervise medical students); and evaluation (annual in-service exams required, completion rate for program, methods for evaluating program quality).

6. **Employment Policies and Benefits:** Availability of part-time/shared-schedule positions; on-site or subsidized childcare; stipend for professional expenses; educational leave and reimbursement; moving

allowance; housing stipend; on-call meal allowance; PDAs; placement assistance upon program completion; cross-coverage in case of illness/disability; salary and vacation/sick days policy for each year in the program; the length of and pay during maternity/paternity/family medical leave; whether written policies exist on substance abuse, mental health impairment, physical disability, and cross-coverage for illness/disability; and whether medical, dental, mental health, and disability insurance is paid, shared-cost, or not paid for the residents and their dependents.

7. **Institutional Information** (available for each clinical site in the program): Hospital size; size of the medical staff; number of annual admissions and emergency and non-emergency department outpatient visits; specialized inpatient units; and other graduate medical education programs sponsored by or affiliated with that institution.

If you like what you see in a program's description, add it to your personal folder by clicking the icon in the top right-hand portion of the screen, labeled "Add to Folder."

There is an enormous amount of information, but the necessity of molding the database to all specialties has resulted in a poor fit for some. For example, for some specialties (especially Surgery, Radiology, Anesthesiology, and Pathology), applicants want to know the number of procedures performed. This information is not available. Yet the *FREIDA* system represents a vast improvement over the "Green Book."

Two caveats: Residency directors supply their own program information and no one verifies that it is accurate. When using *FREIDA*, applicants should be careful about how they interpret the information, and should double-check it if it seems questionable. Verify all important information before and during your interview. Programs can update their information, but may not have done so recently. The date listed under "Basic Information" tells you the last time the information was updated. Also, *FREIDA* may not list very new programs and programs (e.g., Maternal–Fetal Medicine, Trauma Surgery, Alternative–Integrative Medicine) which are not ACGME-approved or for which there are not yet approved program requirements. You need to contact these programs directly for their information.

The AMA asks every graduate medical education program to provide data for its listing. However, while all ACGME-approved graduate education programs are listed, some fellowships, small residencies, and residencies with few positions have incomplete listings, showing only their name, information on how to contact them, and the number of positions offered. This suggests that you should double-check the "Green Book" to be certain that you locate all the programs in which you may be interested.

Program Codes. Each program's NRMP Code (listed in *FREIDA*, on the NRMP website, and in the *Green Book*) specifies whether the program is Categorical, Preliminary, or Advanced. *FREIDA* allows searches using these categories. For example, the program code 1015110C0 (*not* the *FREIDA* "identifier" number that includes hyphens and has no letter) means that the program is at institution #1015 (University Medical Center, Tucson, AZ), that it is in specialty #110 (Emergency Medicine), that the program is Categorical (C), and that it is the first (and usually only) track that they offer. In cases where a department offers multiple types of programs, such as a primary care, rural, or women's health-emphasis track, the last digit designates how many tracks they offer.

Other Information. *FREIDA's* main page offers additional information. On the left side of the page, you can access "Graduate Career Plans" or "Specialty Training Statistics," which provide additional information about each specialty. Another option, "Institution Search," allows you to search by the healthcare facilities used by medical education programs.

Mailing Labels. *FREIDA* allows you to print mailing labels for the programs you choose. AMA student and resident members can obtain mailing labels for free (up to 30 programs), and can get them for up to 70 more programs for $50. Non-members should e-mail *FREIDA@ama-assn.org* to find out how much it costs for these labels. (It is usually a much better deal to join the AMA for this service, plus you receive the *Journal of the American Medical Association* [*JAMA*] and other benefits.) Another option is to print the program information for each program and then cut out the address information.

FREIDA is remarkably easy to use, even for the computer illiterate. Just turn on the machine or connect to the website and follow the instructions. Have fun with it.

National Residency Matching Program (NRMP) Online Directory

The *NRMP Directory* is no longer supplied in printed form, but a list of registered residency programs is posted at the National Resident Matching Program website (http://www.nrmp.nrmp.org/). It contains up-to-date, but basic, information about the registered programs. Since programs must register each year, only those registered for the current year are listed. Although the program listing opens earlier, many programs can't get their act together to submit their information before November or December.

Both medical student and Independent Applicants (IMGs, Osteopathic students, and non-medical-school-sponsored physicians) use the same website.

The *NRMP Online Directory* can be searched for "All Programs" in one or more specialties (up to a limit of 250 programs). It can also be searched for "Advanced Programs (A)," "Categorical (C)," "Preliminary (P)," "Physician Only," or "Primary Care" (labeled "M"). Primary Care programs can only be searched for Pediatric and Internal Medicine programs. Within the *NRMP Online Directory*, click on "Details" for additional information about a program.

More detailed information about residency programs, including whether they plan to participate in the NRMP Match and their NRMP program code, can be found in FREIDA.

NRMP Program Results & Data— Listing of Filled & Unfilled Programs

This information, released on the NRMP website two days before Match Day each year, shows, by specialty, the positions offered *through the NRMP Match* and what percentage were filled in the current Match, as well as similar data from previous years. The website also shows the percentage of couples that matched. This is vital information for you to read, especially if you think that you might have difficulty getting a position, as it shows you which programs might be a bit easier to enter in the coming year. In April, the NRMP publishes this information in "hard copy" as *NRMP Results and Data—[Year] Match* book. Medical libraries and residency directors should have copies.

Transitional Year Program Directory

If you are searching for information on a Transitional PGY-1 year, this annual publication, now on the Web as *The Purple Book Online,* may be of some use to you. The Association for Hospital Medical Education makes this list available at www.ahme.org/publications/transitional.html. The most important information not found in *FREIDA* is the "Comments" section, found under "Unique Features" at the bottom of each listing.

Individual Programs

Once you have used the information from the sources described above to narrow your program choices at least a little, acquire additional information directly from the programs themselves. To get this information, send them an e-mail. You can obtain the address from *FREIDA*. Be certain that you put "Residency Information Request" on the e-mail subject line. In the body of the e-mail, ask for information on residency programs beginning in a specific year. If you want to know about student elective rotations, include that request as a separate line so that it has less chance of being overlooked. Also, include your full name, a good mailing address, and a phone number in case they need to contact you. Be sure to proofread your e-mail, including the address and subject lines, before pressing that pesky "send" button.

One caveat about e-mails: If you have a "cute" name as part of your e-mail address, for example "sexyguy@xyzmail.com" or "most-wanted-gal@xyzmail.com," change it to your name, your initials, or the anonymous moniker that large systems provide to clients. You're a professional and your e-mail address should reflect that. Also, change those too-cute messages that callers get on your cell phone, answering machine, or similar device. "Thanks for calling. I'll get back to you as soon as possible," is the type of bland alternative that you should use.

For some reason, if you cannot use e-mail, send a letter, postcard, or fax. While the rumors about programs keeping this first request letter on file are not true—they start a file when they actually receive application materials—it doesn't hurt to make these requests legible. Also, include a legible return address. Each year our program receives about ten requests without legible, or even any, return addresses. It also helps to print or type your name. Many information requests have only signatures. And true to form, fewer than half of these can be deciphered.

If you write or call early—that is, before the interviewing process is over for the prior year—be prepared to get material applicable to trainees a year ahead of you. Usually this will not be much different from the material that is finally ready for your year, but be sure to compare the information you received with more current information for those programs with which you interview. In some cases, there may be substantial changes from year to year. Also, if you request your information during the early part of the year (February to April), be prepared for some delay while new material is being prepared. It is best to get preliminary information that describes the year before you wish to enter the program, and then update the materials for the "short list" of programs to which you intend to apply.

Information from residency programs varies widely. It ranges from websites with all the bells and whistles and glossy brochures with lots of pictures and very little solid information to detailed descriptions of the program, institutions, faculty, and resident responsibilities and benefits. You will probably not be able to tell the good programs from the marginal ones based only on the material you view on the Web or receive in the mail. Essentially, that is because the information is not of uniform quality. Also, some residency programs are good at marketing; others are not. Nevertheless, the information that you receive directly from the programs may assist you in working out your own "Must/Want" Analysis (Figure 10.1) and in winnowing the programs down to a reasonable number for further consideration.

The *FREIDA* system described above supplies information that is in a more consistent format than that from the individual programs and institutions. Yet the programs' materials may supply you with more recent, as well as additional, information, so requesting it is worthwhile.

The Internet

The Internet has exploded with information in recent years. Nearly every specialty now has a website with extensive information, and increasing numbers of individual residencies also have websites. Check the specialty listings in Chapter 3 and "Important Contacts" at the end of this book for some of these Web addresses.

One good website that may be around longer than others is www.aamc.org/students/medstudents (click on "Careers in Medicine"). It contains, among other things, links to specialty organizations and some career planning tools. A website with detailed reviews of individual programs from students who have actually done rotations there is www.scutwork.com. It provides some enlightening information. The American Medical Student Association (AMSA) also has a website; however, it lists only a limited number of residency programs.

Many specialties also have online discussion groups that you may be able to join. These may provide you with valuable information. The list servers can be found most easily through the specialties' national organizations. You may be required to join their medical student/resident organization (usually very inexpensive) to participate. If you are seriously considering a specialty, join their Society; it's worth the minimal cost.

Specialty Society Publications

At least six specialties publish directories of residency programs. These are:
- Emergency Medicine (http://saem.org/rescat/contents.htm)
- Family Medicine (www.aafp.org/residencies)
- Internal Medicine (www.acponline.org/residency)
- Preventive Medicine (www.acpm.org/ataglance.htm)
- Physical Medicine & Rehabilitation
  (www.physiatry.org/education/index.html)
- Urology (www.auanet.org/students_residents/index.cfm)

Each directory contains significantly more information than can be obtained by writing to the residency programs. And, though their information is updated only sporadically, they provide an excellent picture both of the scope of residencies in the specialty and of the individual programs. Each directory is described in the *Annotated Bibliography*.

Specialty Faculty

Your mentor or specialty adviser is another source of information about programs. This individual may have enough knowledge about the programs in the specialty to assist you in your search. Usually, he or she will be familiar with programs in one or more specific geographic areas. If your mentor has been in the field for some time, he may have visited other training programs in the course of professional activities. This will provide a wider knowledge base from which to counsel you. But an adviser's input must still be considered in light of both your personal needs and the other information you collect.

Remember, no matter what your specialty adviser or mentor thinks is the best program, *you* are the one who will be going through the training. However, do not discount his inside information about, and personal contacts at, specific programs. You will not find this in any book. And your adviser's influence may get you an interview at your most desired program.

Journals

If you are looking for programs with a strong academic or research bent, you may want to scan the major specialty journals to see which programs are most heavily represented. In addition, either from these journals or from mailings your specialty adviser receives, you can discern which programs are most heavily represented at national scientific meetings. Obviously, this will be only supplemental knowledge. But it may come in handy when selecting programs and also give you an inside track (with your special information) during interviews.

If you seek a program that will be relatively easy to match with, look at the advertisements in *The New Physician*. Programs normally advertise here if they have difficulty filling their slots. Many such programs are at well-known institutions, and some are even in hard-to-match-with specialties. Similar advertisements also appear, although not in as great a quantity or with as much information, in *JAMA* and the *New England Journal of Medicine*.

A program's or an institution's national reputation is not usually of major importance unless you are shooting for an eventual high-profile research or academic position. In that case, your training institution's reputation may play a role in landing you that position. Information about some institutions and their reputations for treating certain disease processes can be found in the annual "Best of" issue of *U.S. News & World Report*. This issue normally comes out in late July. Note that this listing says nothing about the quality of their training programs.

Dean of Students

Another source of information about specific residencies is your Dean of Students. You should already have had numerous opportunities to contact him or her while you were searching out a mentor, trying to decide upon your interests and how they matched with different specialty fields, and arranging your schedule to best meet your needs. While this person may not know very much about specific programs in the specialties, he or she is usually very conversant about the difficulty or ease of getting into various fields. Often, he or she can be invaluable if you perceive that you will have difficulty getting a position in your chosen specialty. The Dean of Students often knows, or can find out, where extra positions will open up, and about Transitional programs and other first-year slots that you might be able to fill.

Some Student Affairs offices have a "contact book" which lists the contacts various faculty members have with programs around the country. So, especially if you think you are in really big trouble, go see your Dean of Students—the sooner the better.

Residency Fairs

Many medical schools and some hospitals have residency fairs where students have an opportunity to hear residency directors talk about their specialties. Students can also often talk with and question physicians involved in several specialties' training programs. Some schools combine these fairs with the distribution of NRMP Match materials. Often, residency programs from within the institution (and elsewhere) have booths with glossy materials and people to answer questions. These fairs may give you some leads, as well as some additional program and specialty information.

10

Finding Programs That Meet Your Needs

If the doors of perception were closed, everything would appear as it is–infinite.

– William Blake, *A Vision of the Last Judgement*

The First Cut

NOW THAT YOU HAVE SOME initial information about residency programs, it is time to start weeding. But like any good gardener, be cautious. Don't be so anxious to get rid of the "bad choices" that you inadvertently discard the daffodils with the dandelions. Be prudent when eliminating potential programs from your list. Only reject them after you have carefully reviewed their information. Don't eliminate programs you want to enter simply because you suspect you are not a strong enough candidate—at least wait until after they tell you they do not want to interview you.

You will probably want to consider about 30 programs seriously enough to get all their information. Out of this group, apply to about 15 programs (more if you are stretching to get into some very competitive programs) and interview at ten. These numbers will vary depending upon your personal needs and the difficulty of getting a residency slot in that specialty. Nearly 40% of medical students interview at ten or fewer programs, and nearly two-thirds interview at 15 or fewer.

There are good reasons to be liberal in your selection criteria and leery of discarding programs from consideration too soon. The main reason is that often residencies that appear superficially unacceptable actually turn out to be the ones that best fit your personal needs. Written material from programs varies with the marketing sophistication of the residency and the hospital. You do not want to miss a great opportunity just because a program doesn't know how to present itself on paper; but you also don't want to pursue only those programs with excellent marketing.

What Do You Want in a Program?

What do *you* want in a residency program? You can't get to the right place until you figure out what the "right place" looks like. Your situation is similar to that of a pilot who says to his passengers over the intercom, "I have good news, and I have bad news . . . We are making good time, but I have no clue where we are going." Take the time to figure out where you want to go.

Both your residency and your subsequent career will differ markedly from medical school. In deciding about the best residencies for you, you will consider a large number of factors that you may never have had to think about previously. Most of these factors apply to everyone. But how much weight you put on each factor will be a function of your personal needs. Although it may be somewhat onerous to find some of the information you need to make a decision, the sources listed in the previous chapter, especially *FREIDA*, make it much easier than it was in the past.

Weighing the Factors—The "Must/Want" Analysis

How do you weigh the many factors involved in deciding to which residencies you should apply (and then how do you rank them in the Match)? The simplest method is to use a "Must/Want" analysis.

As shown in Figure 10.1, you make a list of all the possible factors that could influence your decision about the type of program that you would like. (Do not complete your own "Must/Want" Analysis or fill in Figure 10.1 now; wait until after you have read all the following descriptions of the factors to consider.) Some of the items may be absolute necessities for you, such as full family health care. *If an item is an absolute, a "Must," you have decided that the factor is so important that it must be present or else you will eliminate the program from consideration regardless of the program's other qualities.*

Other items will be relatively more or less important to you. For example, you may have compelling personal reasons for living in a certain part of the country or in a certain city. In that case, you would rate "geography" higher than other factors. However, if where you live is less important than other factors, you would give "geography" a low rating, or you might even eliminate it from your list.

Assigning "Weights" to each factor rates their relative importance to you. Refer to Figure 10.2 to see how a sample student assigned "Weights" to the factors important to her. After you have read the descriptions, use Figure 10.1 as a master form from which to build your own list.

Deciding What You Want—The Most Difficult Task

Completing the "Must/Want" Analysis has consistently been each student's most arduous task in the residency selection process. It is not because the concept is difficult, but because it requires you to assess what you really are searching for in a training program. It helps you answer three questions:

1. What "Must" I have to go to a program?
2. What do I "Want" in a program?
3. How important are the various factors to me?

I require my advisees to complete their own list of important factors and assign "Weights" to each before discussing which programs they might want to consider. (Our medical students get this book free from the Arizona Medical Association Foundation.) This process often precipitates constructive discussions between students and their families, significant others, and mentors, especially about where they feel they would like to (or must) live during residency training.

Once students have puzzled through what is important to them, they find that they are much better prepared to discuss why they might want to apply to certain programs. The focus of the discussion changes from what the adviser thinks are the "best" programs to which programs best meet the needs described by a student's "Must/Want" Analysis.

I have talked with numerous students who followed much of the advice contained in this book, got the residency they wanted, and then found that it did not meet their needs or expectations. As the saying goes, "Be careful what you wish for—you might get it." In nearly every case, they neglected to complete their "Must/Want" Analysis, and found out later that their "wish" was not what they really wanted. In many cases, the program's reputation or location overwhelmed every other consideration, to the individual's subsequent regret. Avoid years of dissatisfaction: Take the time to complete your own "Must/Want" Analysis. And, once you complete it, be sure to use it!

Now, skim Figure 10.1 and read the descriptions of the various factors you may want to consider. Then I will explain in detail how to complete your own "Must/Want" Analysis using Figure 10.1 as a base.

FIGURE 10.1

"Must/Want" Analysis—The Instructions

Read the following instructions *before* filling out this form. Once you have adapted this form to reflect your needs and wants, you should make several copies. One copy of this form will be used for each residency program you consider.

1. Add any personal factors that are not already listed.

2. Select any factors that absolutely MUST be present for you to consider the program. Put the word "MUST" in the "Weight" column instead of assigning it a number value. This means the factor is so important to you that if it is not present, you will not go to that program.

3. Next, select those factors that are not at all important to you and, therefore, that you will not consider in making your decision. Put a "0" next to these in the "Weight" column. Delete these factors from your final list.

4. Finally, determine how important each of the remaining factors is to you in selecting a residency position. Put a number next to each factor in the "Weight" column, so the *total of all the "Weights" equals 100*. To do this easily, first rate factors of minimal importance with a "1," and rate those of slightly more importance "2." Continue in this fashion until the total for all assigned "Weights" equals "100." You will probably need to make multiple changes until you are happy with the result.

Congratulations! You have now completed the most difficult part of the process. Make multiple copies of your "Must/Want" Analysis Form with the "Weight" column completed. You will use one of these for each residency program you consider. (The *Companion Disk* has this form, see *Annotated Bibliography*.) Figure 10.2 shows how one hypothetical student completed this first step.

Later, as you get information about each program, you will assign a "Score" (on a 1-10 scale; 10 is "perfect") that is your estimate of how well that residency program fulfills your initial expectations in the category. Then you multiply the "Weight" by the "Score" to give the factor "Total" for that program. All factor "Totals" are added to get your "Program Evaluation Score." Examples of this are shown in Figures 10.7, 10.8, and 10.9. These "Program Evaluation Scores" will be what you use to make your Rank-Order List (ROL) for the Match. (Don't worry; I'll explain this in more detail as we get to it.)

FIGURE 10.1

"Must/Want" Analysis—The Form

PROGRAM _____

Clinical Experience	WEIGHT	X	SCORE	=	TOTAL
On-Call Schedule					
Patient Population					
Responsibility					
Setting					
Volume					
Geographic Location					
Inner City, Suburb, Rural					
Part of Country					
Specific City					
Spouse/Mate/Dependent Needs					
Reputation					
Institution's Reputation					
Program's Reputation					
Program Age and Stability					
Faculty					
Availability					
Interest					
Stability					
Curriculum					
Curriculum Structure					
Interaction with Other Specialties					
Number of Conferences					
Special Training					
Types of Conferences					
Esprit de Corps					
Research Opportunities/Training					
Knowledge					
Materials					
Time					
Local Job Prospects After Training					
Facilities					
Clinical Laboratory Support					
Computerized Records/Lab Results					
Hospitals' Ages, Atmosphere					

FIGURE 10.1 (continued)

	WEIGHT	X SCORE	= TOTAL
Library/Media			
Parking			
Resident Call Room Ambiance			
Safety/Security			
No Restrictive Covenant			
Benefits: Health			
Dental			
Drug Prescriptions			
Employee Health Services			
Health Insurance			
Health Promotion			
Hospitalization			
Optical			
Psychiatric Counseling			
Sick Leave			
Benefits: Non-Health			
Association Dues			
Childcare			
Disability Insurance			
Educational Leave: Funding Available			
Time Off			
Family Educational Benefits			
Housing (Allowance)			
Laundry/Uniforms			
Liability Insurance			
Life Insurance			
Parental Leave			
Meals			
Photocopying			
Vacation			
Organized Housestaff/Union			
Moonlighting			
Shared/Part-time Positions			

TOTAL OF ALL WEIGHTS = <u>100</u>

PROGRAM EVALUATION SCORE = _____

FIGURE 10.2
"Must/Want" Analysis—An Example

Clinical Experience	WEIGHT	X	SCORE	=	TOTAL
On-Call Schedule	5				
Patient Population	2				
Responsibility	14				
Setting	7				
Volume	10				
Geographic Location					
Part of Country	1				
Specific City	1				
Reputation					
Program Age and Stability	2				
Faculty					
Availability	5				
Interest	7				
Stability	3				
Curriculum					
Number of Conferences	1				
Special Training	6				
Types of Conferences	2				
Esprit de Corps	8				
Research Opportunities/Training					
Knowledge	5				
Materials	2				
Time	7				
Facilities					
Clinical Laboratory Support	1				
Library/Media	2				
Safety/Security	3				
No Restrictive Covenant	MUST				
Benefits: Health					
Health Insurance	MUST				
Hospitalization	MUST				
Benefits: Non-Health					
Childcare	MUST				
Disability Insurance	MUST				

FIGURE 10.2 (continued)

	WEIGHT	X	SCORE	=	TOTAL
Educational Leave: Funding Available	1				
Time Off	2				
Liability Insurance	MUST				
Vacation	1				
Moonlighting	2				

TOTAL OF ALL WEIGHTS = 100

Note that this individual, who is a single mother, feels that disability, liability, and health insurance, as well as childcare, are absolute necessities for any position she might take. She also gives rather a high priority to research and subspecialty training since she plans an academic career. However other educational benefits, local job prospects after training, and the availability of a shared-schedule position are of no interest at all, and her interest in the geographic location of the program is minimal. This allowed her to shorten her "Must/Want" Analysis form to include only the items she considered important. How this individual will score specific programs will be discussed in Figures 10.7, 10.8, and 10.9

Factors to Consider

The following is a discussion of the most common factors encountered when choosing a residency program. The importance of some factors, which may not seem obvious at first, is explained. Read the discussion carefully. Next, complete your own "Must/Want" Analysis form (Figure 10.1) by adding any factors that are applicable to your situation and deleting those factors that are not. Then assign either a "Must" rating or a "Weight" to each factor on your list.

Medical students are often given the advice about big name programs that "If you can get into that program, go for it!" Fellow students, residents, and faculty give the advice. This advice is worth just what you have paid for it: Nothing! No residency program, no matter what its reputation, is right for everyone. You are an individual. Start treating yourself like one. Look at your own needs, both for now and those you can foresee for the future. Examine your personal desires and your dreams. The program you choose, the contacts you make during training, and the type of training you receive will determine the course of your future professional and, possibly, your personal life.

A resident I knew at a very prestigious, high-powered, research-oriented institution spent most days moping through the halls. She was halfway through her second year of training and completely miserable. She confided that she had come to this program because of its great reputation, but was now completely disheartened because she was not receiving the "nuts and bolts" primary care experience she knew she would need when she went into rural practice. Rather than deciding for herself what needs she wanted filled by a residency program, she had let others make her choice for her. After some soul-searching and counseling, she switched to a program that emphasized rural primary care—where she was much happier. Choose carefully. Choose for yourself. It's your life, not your peers', friends', mentor's, or family's.

Clinical Experience

Clinical experience is the basis of any residency program. This is true whether you go into a field that acts as a primary provider, such as Family Medicine or Internal Medicine, or one that acts as a consultant, such as Radiology or Pathology. It is important to your training that the entire clinical experience, from the volume and types of patients treated to the setting of the program and the amount of responsibility that you are asked to assume, is as close to optimal as possible for your needs. *If the clinical experience isn't right for you, it is unlikely that any other factor or combination of factors can make up for it.*

On-Call Schedule

The frequency of night and weekend call varies depending upon the specialty, type of institution, specific service, and year of training. In July 2003, the ACGME's mandatory work hour regulations for all specialties went into effect in the wake of threatened federal legislation and long-standing concerns about patient safety and physician fatigue. Residents have one day off each week and are on-call no more than once every third night, averaged over four weeks (at-home call is not restricted by the every-third-night limitation, but it must be reasonable). The total hours worked cannot exceed 80/week. Some specialties may apply for an 8-hour/week increase in work hours allowed. Neurological, Orthopedic, General, and Thoracic Surgery make up the bulk of the 68 programs using an 88-hour/week limit. The guidelines for each specialty are in Section II of the "Green Book," the AMA's annual *Graduate Medical Education Directory*.

A 2004–2005 ACGME survey found that the majority of residency programs seem to be complying with the new regulations: only 3% of the responding residents worked more than 80 hours a week. The survey also found that fewer programs had received citations for non-compliance with duty-hour limits (7.3% of programs reviewed versus 12% in the 2000 report). During the 2004–2005 academic year, the ACGME received 16 resident complaints for such violations, compared with 53 complaints the previous year. The long-term benefits of limiting residents' work hours, however, remain to be studied.

Programs use a variety of approaches to deal with the decrease in available resident work hours. Some hire more residents, while others designate a person as a "night float" to handle excess new admissions for the on-call resident. Depending upon how it is structured, this may relieve much of the stress of being on-call at busy institutions—until you get tapped to be the night floater. Inner-city hospitals have been affected the most, since they rely heavily on housestaff for service needs.

Carefully investigate the call schedules at the programs that interest you. Basic work duty hours and call schedule information for each program are included in the *GMED Companion*. Be certain that you will be able to survive with the amount of rest that these schedules imply. In general, Surgery programs, particularly in the PGY-1 and Chief Resident years, have more brutal call schedules than other specialties. But this is certainly not always the case. And remember to ask about the amount of call "from home." No matter how benign this sounds, it will also deprive you of sleep. The key is to investigate the call schedule thoroughly—by asking the residents.

Patient Population

The types of patients and their prevalent problems vary greatly among institutions and in different parts of the country. Consider whether the institution offers the diversity of patients and diseases necessary for your training. Knowing only the number of patients seen tells you nothing about this important element.

Will you see a general cross section of patients that are normally encountered by practitioners in your specialty? Or will you see a population restricted to the narrow subspecialty or tertiary care interests of a particular program or institution? Will you see only middle-class neurotics at a Psychiatry program in a well-to-do suburb? Or will you see the full range of psychiatric diseases?

Will you see only tertiary referrals for complicated procedures at the world-famous mecca of surgery? Or will you get to see patients with "hot" appendices and gallbladders as well? Are virtually all the admissions scheduled and the major procedures done electively? Or is there a large population with unexpected, urgent, or traumatic disease? In large part, these answers can be ascertained from the type of institution in which a program resides.

Responsibility

As the traditional expression says, a physician "sees one, does one and then teaches one." This is how you will learn in the medical field. Yet it is not only learning to do procedures, but also deciding *whether* to do procedures (or admit patients, or pursue "work-ups") that constitute the essence of clinical maturity. Performing the procedures is relatively easy; making the hard decisions is difficult. To learn this, trainees must (with adequate backup, of course) assume responsibility for all aspects of patient care for many patients. What does this mean?

First, this means having primary clinical responsibility. Will you be the one to make the moment-by-moment decisions necessary for acute patient care? Or will every decision have to be approved in advance? Will you really be responsible for the management of a group of patients? Or will you only be the "scut puppy" for attendings and the more senior residents? Will you be doing the critical care procedures, or are these relegated to the subspecialty fellows? Will you be responsible for your patients when they enter the intensive care unit? Or will they be turned over to another specialty team? You learn by taking responsibility. In any program that you investigate, find out if you will have actual responsibility for patient care.

Second, if you choose a specialty in which procedures are a large part of the practice, make certain that you will do those procedures. Procedures are essential in all Surgical specialties, including Obstetrics and Gynecology. But procedures are also a vital part of Anesthesiology, Emergency Medicine, Radiology, Cardiology, Internal Medicine, Family Medicine, Gastroenterology, and Pathology.

Not only do you need to perform an adequate number, but you also need to do the types of procedures that you expect to be doing when you go into practice. It does you little good as an Ophthalmology resident to become an expert at drilling burr holes, or as a Family Medicine resident to refine your laminectomy skills. You certainly will not be performing these operations when you go into practice. You need to gain proficiency in at least those skills that all Board-Certified specialists in your field are expected to know. A list of these procedures can, in most cases, be obtained from the specialty Board. Concentrate on finding out whether the procedures you will need are offered in sufficient quantities so that you can hone these skills during your training.

If you are going into a Surgical specialty, you may want to know not only how many and what type of procedures you will perform as a resident, but also how soon you will get to operate. In many programs, the first-year residents, though working harder than they may have thought possible, get little or no actual operating experience. They certainly go to the operating room often, but only to watch and hold retractors. At some programs, this can last well into the second or third year. Remember, unless you are a very unusual individual, you will not only become very frustrated by this, but you will also not learn very much. For Surgeons, the question "When do I actually operate?" is vital. However, be smooth about when and where you ask this question, since it can raise the hackles of many faculty members. If you cannot ascertain this from the program's literature, find out from the residents when you make your visit. It will save you a lot of frustration in the future.

One caveat: Personnel other than resident physicians should be available to do minor procedures (scut work), such as blood draws and the placement of peripheral intravenous lines or routine catheters, once these have been mastered. While it is necessary for most clinicians to learn to do these procedures, constant repetition serves little purpose and may become an impediment to a resident's education. It is worthwhile to find out how this is handled at each institution.

Setting

The institution(s) at which a residency program is located often determine the volume of patients that you will personally see, the responsibility that you will have for these patients, and the procedures that you will perform. Hospitals in large urban areas tend to offer more patients and more responsibility to the resident physician. They are often understaffed with attendings and have an overabundance of patients. At the other end of the spectrum are those community hospital programs with an abundance of attendings and a dearth of patients.

Neither situation is ideal. What you should look for is something in-between—enough patients to satisfy your personal training needs, and enough attendings to give you adequate guidance without taking away your responsibility for most of the decisions and procedures.

Sometimes major deficiencies, such as the lack of major trauma in a Surgery program, are corrected by using "away" rotations. These are designed to supply the necessary training that the home institution lacks. These short stints are often at institutions particularly known for their expertise in the deficient areas. How well these "away" rotations work varies widely. It depends upon the residents, the "away" institution, the deficient areas, and the amount of time spent away. To evaluate this type of rotation with any accuracy, you will need to speak to the residents in the program who have already "been there and done that."

Adequate training in ambulatory, rather than inpatient, settings is becoming more desirable due to changes in the practice of medicine. It is vital in all specialties that you have significant exposure to the specific methodologies used, the problems encountered, and the patients that can be treated in an outpatient setting. The type of outpatient setting is also important. If you are planning a primary care practice, it may be helpful, for example, to have some experience working at a managed care facility. (Less than 20% of all teaching hospitals have residents spend time in health maintenance organizations.) Find out how high the acuity is in the program's outpatient clinics. This can be measured by the ratio of admissions to those seen. Emergency departments usually admit from 15% to 18% of the total patients they see. Judge from that number.

Volume

The actual volume of patients to which you will be exposed, either as the primary provider or as a consultant, is of paramount importance to the quality of your training. However, information about numbers of patients can be very misleading—and often is deliberately skewed in order to attract medical students to an institution's training programs.

The size of a particular institution, the number of patients seen at the facility or by a particular service, and the number of procedures done only indirectly give you, a prospective trainee, the information you need. You also need to know the ratio of house officers to patients. If you are going into General Surgery, and the hospitals used by a training program do a total of 4,000 resident-performed operations per year, it sounds like an adequate number. But if there are 50 General Surgery residents, each resident does only 80 cases—with probably only about 40 of these being major cases. This means that at the PGY-1 and PGY-2 levels you will rarely, if ever, hold a scalpel.

In other specialties, where ward and outpatient activities comprise most of the training, there is another danger: too few residents. *While it is important to guarantee that there will be enough patients, it is also necessary to find out if there are enough residents.* Both extremes can be harmful to your training. If the ratio of residents to patients is too high (too few patients), you may not be exposed to enough medical activity to get the training you desire. But if the ratio of residents to patients is too low (too few residents), you will be robbed of valuable reading, thinking, and discussion time. You will use this time attempting to care for an ever-multiplying patient load.

Over the past decade, the ratio of postgraduate trainees to inpatient beds has been highest at training programs in the western United States, programs at university-operated institutions, and those at state-owned institutions. Programs in the southern United States, programs with limited university affiliation, and those that are church-owned have had the lowest ratio.

Numbers can also deceive in another way. While a residency program may note that there are over 1,500 babies delivered per year at the hospital, it may not tell you that private practitioners deliver more than half of these with no resident involvement. This affects, in part, the amount of responsibility that you can assume as a resident. But it also impacts greatly on the volume of patients that you personally will encounter. Your individual patient load should be at the forefront of your mind when assessing any residency program.

Geography

Geography often plays a more important role in the selection of a residency program than it rightfully should. But, probably more than any other factor that you will consider in selecting a program, geography will be the most personal for you. The strongest factor associated with doing a residency in a particular state is having been a state resident prior to medical school. Remember, though, that geographical ignorance and prejudices should not be allowed to limit your choice of programs.

If you, like many of your cohorts, have not had time to visit most of our country, then spend some time getting an accurate picture of both the geography and the medicine in different parts of the nation from people who have actually been there. No, it's not true that everything east of the Mississippi River is concrete. Likewise, it's not true that physicians practice "cowboy medicine" between the Mississippi and the Pacific Coast. Wherever you are now, I have no doubt that you have heard horror stories about other areas of the country. Find out about these areas from faculty who have lived and worked there. Don't assume anything. You may be surprised by what you discover.

There may be a special reason to carefully consider the location of residency programs. About half of all physicians set up practice in the state where they did their residency. Those most likely to stay are those who do their residency in the same state where they went to medical school, are generalist physicians, or are women.

Note that the number of residency programs varies greatly by region (Figure 10.3). If you concentrate on a region with a small number of residency positions, your chance of matching may decrease.

FIGURE 10.3

Percent of Residency Programs, Residents, and Fellowships by Geographic Region

Regions	Programs*	Residents**	Fellowships*
Mid-Atlantic (NJ, NY, PA)	22%	24%	22%
East-North Central (IL, IN, MI, OH, WI)	17	17	16
South Atlantic (DE, DC, FL, GA, MD, NC, SC, VA, WV)	16	15	17
Pacific (AK, CA, HI, OR, WA)	11	12	11
West-South Central (AR, LA, OK, TX)	9	9	9
New England (CT, ME, MA, NH, RI, VT)	8	8	9
West-North Central (IA, KS, MN, MO, NE, ND, SD)	7	6	7
East-South Central (AL, KY, MS, TN)	5	4	5
Mountain (AZ, CO, ID, MT, NV, NM, UT, WY)	4	4	4
Territories (PR)	<1	<1	<1

*These are ACGME-accredited residency programs.
**Includes both M.D.s and D.O.s. The location of AOA-accredited programs generally correlates with these numbers.
Sums may not equal 100% due to rounding.
Adapted from Appendix II, Table 2, JAMA. 2005;294(9):1132-33; and FREIDA, accessed June 2005.

The following issues will determine how important it is for you to obtain a training position in a specific part of the country, a specific state, or a specific city.

Family Needs

Many students have family obligations which limit where they can go for training. These may include having a spouse or "significant other" in a job that he or she cannot leave or transfer, a spouse or child at a critical point in school, ill parents, or family members who need specialized medical care. In dual-profession relationships, the ability of the other partner to meet professional requirements in another locale (often for the second time) carries great weight. Dentists, lawyers, accountants, architects, and others may find obtaining a new license difficult, if not impossible, in another state. For some people, being near their extended family or religious group may also be an important consideration.

One of these constraints may make a particular geographic location a "Must" for you. Since this is so personal, little advice can be given. But be sure to talk it over with the individual involved before you assume that you need to limit your search for that person's benefit. You may be amazed at the amount of flexibility you actually have.

Personal Needs

Other needs may influence how much weight you will give to geography. Besides a desire to "see the mountains (or ocean, or trees) every day," the most common personal geographic need is compatibility with leisure-time activities. Although you probably won't have much spare time, especially during your first year of training, the desire to make the most of the free time that you do have is very reasonable. But even this may not restrict you as much as you think.

Of course, if you are a mountain climber, you need mountains (or at least some good climbing walls). And if you are a surfer, you will need surf. But if you are involved in running, swimming, hiking, or the more cerebral activities of music, art, and theater, you can find many locations that will meet your needs. By the way, if you are a skier, remember that the snow only lasts a little while—and anyway, you can always fly.

Range

Although several comments have already been made about expanding your geographic horizons when choosing programs, a word needs to be said specifically about hesitancy to leave the "nest." The "nest" is your medical school, where you know the rules, know the faculty, and generally feel at home. It would be very comfortable to stay. And, unless you are a top student from a highly respected medical school, you may feel that you are not prepared to go out into the world and work, as I have heard many students say, "with students who really know something."

My advice is: *leave if you possibly can.* You are just as capable as the medical students from other or "big name" schools. In fact, you may have much more clinical experience. And, if you stay at your medical school's hospital for residency training, you will probably be working under a handicap that will not afflict your fellow residents. That is the "Once a medical student, always a medical student" syndrome.

The faculty and staff know you as a medical student. Of course, they will know, deep down, that you are now a resident, but you may have some frustrating attitudes directed your way. You certainly will have to work harder for their respect. By the way, this factor has an exponential effect upon residents joining the faculty where they completed their residencies. They spend an inordinate amount of time making the switch, in their colleague's minds, from resident to staff physician. So, if you have aspirations of joining the faculty at a specific institution, especially your medical school, go elsewhere for residency training.

Salary

In general, resident salaries have remained stable (in constant dollars) since the late 1960s. (This means that although the total amount has increased, when it is adjusted for inflation, its purchasing power has remained unchanged.)

Although it may seem that salary should be discussed under benefits, there is an element of salary that is geography-dependent. The cost of living varies significantly across the country. In general, costs will be lower in the deep South and in the Midwest. The farther northeast or west you go, the higher the average cost of living will be. Normally this will not be a significant factor, since residents' salaries usually reflect the local cost of living. If, however, you need to repay a monster-sized school loan, this difference may be important.

Reputation

The institution's and program's reputations naturally influence applicants. Few reputations derive from excellent education. Rather, other achievements bring recognition to the institution and faculty. Nearly all residency applicants do best if they look beyond a reputation to the factors that are important to their own professional development.

Institution's Reputation

Some venerable institutions, such as Harvard, Johns Hopkins, Stanford, and the University of Chicago, have built their reputations largely on research over decades or centuries. The prestige envelops all their programs, whether deserved or not. How should this institutional reputation affect an applicant's decision about whether to go there? If the institution has a residency program that is competitive in all aspects with similar programs elsewhere, some applicants may want to consider another factor: prestige. Those physicians aspiring to careers in academia or to clinical practices in posh locales may benefit from "gold-plated" credentials. Problems arise when an applicant sacrifices an excellent education for this prestige, as sometimes happens. In general, it is best to choose programs that provide an optimal educational experience, regardless of their perceived status.

Program's Reputation

Some programs in every specialty have a reputation for excellence. Many of these provide superior education. But some programs' reputations linger long after the glow has faded. Other programs have not yet acquired a reputation for excellence, either because they are new or because information about program alterations has not permeated the specialty's intelligence network. Changes in the residency director, affiliated institutions, the patient population, and institutional funding may all affect a program. Applicants cannot simply rely on a program's reputation for past excellence; they must analyze each program as it currently exists, based on their personal needs.

Nevertheless, more than one-fourth of all applicants use a program's reputation as their primary factor in deciding among programs. Many later regret this.

Program's Age & Stability

No one wants to enter a residency program only to learn partway through training that the program will merge with another institution or close, that crucial faculty members are leaving, or that the program has lost accreditation. In these times of financial upheaval within the health care industry, no guarantees exist. Large teaching hospitals and individual residency programs are closing; faculty members leave for better personal opportunities.

Increasing numbers of teaching hospitals are now merging for economic reasons. This provides them with economies of scale, may reduce operational expenses by eliminating redundant services, and makes them more attractive for managed care contracts. These mergers, though, may disrupt resident education. Teaching faculty, especially in subspecialty areas, may be diminished, as may indigent or resident clinics and ancillary services that ease the workload. Remaining faculty may be pressured to decrease teaching and increase patient care while shifting many of their duties to physician assistants, nurse practitioners and other allied health personnel. While these changes are ongoing in many institutions, the rate may be accelerated during and just after large mergers. It would be wise to check to see whether such a merger is in the works at programs to which you are applying.

A reasonable method for testing a program's stability is to look at its history. How long has it existed? Has it ever had difficulty with accreditation? Has the program's faculty been stable? The answers to these questions cut two ways. They may indicate a stable program, but they also may point to programs and faculty that are rigid and unable to change with the times. And none of this information provides a guarantee. For example, the Mount Sinai Medical Center in Cleveland and the Manhattan Eye, Ear and Throat Hospital in New York suddenly closed their residencies in June 1999, just as 150 new residents were arriving. In 2000, St. Elizabeth Medical Center in Dayton, Ohio, closed on July 31, eliminating positions for its

32 Family Medicine residents. And, in 2001, Des Moines' Metropolitan Medical Center closed their residency program, making 28 residents jobless just a week into the new training year.

Strong Faculty

A large part of what makes any residency program unique is the faculty. Their interests, strengths, and involvement in the institution, national specialty activities, and the local community are all important factors in making any residency solid. Without a dynamic faculty, it does not matter what else is present—the residency will be weak.

Current residents can best answer your questions about the faculty. They interact (or don't) with the faculty every day, and will either highly praise them or barely give them a lukewarm endorsement. There is rarely a medium ground.

Availability

Even if the faculty is intensely interested in teaching, there might be either too few of them or too much extra work, such as administrative duties, added clinical responsibilities, student teaching, research, or writing, for them to be around when you need them. Specifically, you need to know whether teachers are readily available to you in three situations.

Clinical setting. Do program faculty just make rounds or take morning report, or are they there for you when you feel that you have gotten in over your head? Can they be relied upon to respond in the middle of the night and on weekends? Will you be left "hanging" in clinics without anyone to guide you through tough or unfamiliar territory? And do they show up promptly when you need to go to the operating room or do a procedure under emergency conditions? Sadly, the answers at many programs are not optimal. Recently, non-physician staff has supervised residents in some programs. While this is not permitted under ACGME rules, find out if it occurs at the programs in which you are interested.

Personal counseling. The second time you need faculty to be available is for personal counseling. As with any job, no residency will be without its ups and downs—moments of personal crisis and indecision. More mundane will be the day-to-day administrative problems of scheduling your days off appropriately, getting your research started, or getting a nagging administrator off your back. Eventually, there will also be the question of a job search and the process of going out into the "real world." All of this can, and should, be eased by personal interaction with your faculty. That is one of the reasons they are there. If they are not available for this, you may have nowhere to turn.

Formal teaching. Last, and perhaps least important, is the faculty's participation in formal teaching. This includes grand rounds, journal clubs, and other formal conferences. While generally regarded as the most important of a faculty member's duties, it will actually be of less importance to you than the other activities.

The point is, for faculty to be effective, they not only have to be interested, but they must also be available. Part-time faculty, those with too many other duties, and those who just don't have the concern to be available to residents are not what you are seeking. Reviewing the often-inflated faculty-to-resident ratios that many programs advertise will not help you to answer this question. Get this information during your program visits.

Interest

The key ingredient for any individual faculty member, or any faculty group, is that they have a strong interest in training residents.

This may seem to be a foregone conclusion. They are faculty members at a training institution, aren't they? But individuals choose the academic path for a variety of reasons, many of which do not include teaching. They may have a strong research interest, want to avoid night call as much as possible, or just want the easier or more distant clinical experience that teaching institutions often permit. Or, they may have had, at one time, a strong interest in teaching, but are now burned out. This is not to say that there aren't many wonderful teachers at residency programs. But the quality varies widely, and it is up to you to check it closely. Without real faculty interest, you will essentially be on your own.

Stability

Along with faculty interest and a presence, there needs to be some continuity. Look for how long faculty members have been with the program, especially the residency director. Each year, about 20% of residency directors quit their positions. If there is a high turnover, there may be significant problems. How much experience have the faculty members had in the specialty? If most of them are fresh out of residency training themselves, you will probably not get the wisdom (yes, indeed—there really is some) that comes with experience, if not age. You may be getting instruction from a group who are themselves still "wet behind the ears" in their practice of medicine. While some individuals at this level may give a program an instillation of vigor and enthusiasm, too many may lead to a less-than-satisfactory training experience.

The key, then, is to check into the interest level, availability, and stability of the faculty. They are the residency program's foundation.

Curriculum

What educational opportunities, in what setting, and with what outcomes does the residency program say it offers? Standard specialty requirements may determine some of this. Some of what they say may be exaggerated. Remember that whatever they say about the curriculum is always subject to modification based on financial changes, institutional reorganization, faculty transitions, and patient care needs.

Structure

What will you do and when? Which services will you be on, for how long, and in which training years? These elements, the most basic part of a program's curriculum, are the easiest to compare among programs. Will you do the intensive care service in the first year? Do you work in the clinic during your second and third years? If particular programs interest you because of either specific rotations or the order or length of rotations, ask about these during your interview to be certain that the program anticipates no changes in them.

Curriculum structure matters in some specialties more than in others. Child/Adolescent Psychiatry programs, for example, may mix the Psychiatry and Child Psychiatry years in different ways. Similarly, all the "hyphenated programs," such as Pediatrics–Physical Medicine and Rehabilitation, Internal Medicine–Emergency Medicine, or Psychiatry–Neurology, combine time in each specialty in different ways. If this is important to your educational needs, find out how the program has structured its curriculum.

Interaction with Other Specialties

To get the most benefit from a residency program, residents should be exposed to the knowledge that other specialists provide. During the course of your training, you will most often interact with the residents (rather than attendings) from other specialties. They are an excellent, non-threatening source of information about the diseases and procedures common to their specialty. Such interactions also provide you the opportunity to learn about the thought processes used by other specialists. In addition, other specialty training programs often have organized conferences and teaching rounds that you can attend.

In some cases, the presence of another specialty's residents or fellows may interfere with your residency training. Family Medicine seems to be the most commonly affected, since specialty residents' involvement in cases often precludes Family Medicine residents from first-assisting in surgery, delivering babies and doing Cesarean sections, or getting adequate experience in Orthopedics. Many Family Medicine programs use rotations at alternative institutions to solve this problem. Not so obvious may be the decreased experience some residents get due to the presence of subspecialty fellows. Surgery residents may not get a full thoracic surgery experience if fellows do, or first-assist on, most of the cases. Internal Medicine or Pediatric residents may lack some procedural skills if Critical Care, Hematology–Oncology, or Cardiology fellows constantly upstage them.

The presence of other specialists and subspecialists is a mixed blessing. Consider each institution's blessings in light of your own needs.

Conferences

How many conferences does the residency program offer? This number is usually a prominent part of the program's literature. Rather than the absolute number, however, look at the amount of time devoted to conferences per month. (Use conferences per month as the comparison figure, since some programs hold their conferences only once or twice a month, while others may have them daily or weekly.)

Also important are the answers to these questions: How many of these conferences will you be able to attend? Is coverage of your clinical duties provided? Which takes precedence, conferences or patient care? (Conferences do you no good unless you can attend.) Also, does the program require attendance at a minimum number of conferences? If so, do penalties exist for non-attendance? Ask residents these questions for a more balanced answer.

Not only is the quantity of conference time important, but so are the *types and quality of these conferences.* Some types of conferences are mandated by the specialty's Board. Others are at the whim of or reflect the educational savvy of the residency's faculty.

It is relatively easy to determine what conferences a program holds. More difficult to determine is how good an educational experience they provide. Conference quality varies with the organization, faculty participation, relevance, and ambiance. Relevance refers to the importance of the topics to your education, rather than to the faculty's research interests or a sponsoring drug company's latest wonder drug. Do the conferences regularly enhance your ability to perform patient care or expand your knowledge of the specialty? Are some conferences joint projects between your department and complementary specialties? These are the qualities that make conferences useful.

Ambiance refers to the amount of tension that faculty and senior residents produce, especially during morbidity and mortality conferences.

Education need not be an ego-destructive experience, although some residency programs have yet to figure that out.

Lastly, how many of these conferences are resident-run? This is less important than the conference quality, although it points to another area of resident responsibility.

Special Training

Residency programs differ in their orientation. This is true for all specialties. This orientation depends partly on the values and philosophy of the institution, partly on the residency director, and in large measure on the faculty's interests and abilities.

At present, there are recognized subspecialty areas within nearly all medical specialties (Figures 2.7 and 2.8). Some are well defined, with specialty boards in place. Others, such as Trauma Surgery, have been defined both through need and by the medical community's acceptance. If you think you have a desire for training in a subspecialty, make sure that you will be exposed to it during your residency program. If you are not certain about your long-term goals, you should make sure that you will at least have exposure to several of these areas. You might just develop an interest in one of them.

If you are certain you want to enter a specific subspecialty training program after residency, find out if that area is particularly strong at the institution(s) in which the residency is located. Will you have an easier time getting into the subspecialty program (if one exists) at that institution if you do your residency there? Find out now. It may save you time, money, and a great deal of effort in the future.

Esprit de Corps

An important factor for your well-being is the amount of esprit de corps (i.e., fellowship and camaraderie) found in the department. This aspect of a training program is hard to measure, and can only be assessed by your perception of the *gestalt* of the program. But it is important to most residents, and affects how much they enjoy their residency experience. About one out of five applicants rate this as their main consideration in deciding among programs.

The attitude that pervades any department helps to determine the ease with which residents, faculty, and staff perform their duties. If there is a feeling of calm serenity, with people genuinely liking and trusting their coworkers, then the resident's job is much easier. But if there is a feeling of strain, anxiety, and perhaps fear, a resident's entire life becomes much more difficult.

The important attitudes are the day-to-day interpersonal interactions at all levels within the department, rather than those during episodic medical crises. Do the secretaries respond to you as if you are a welcome guest, or a miserable underling? Do the residents and faculty seem to get along with each other? Is there an underlying feeling of tension and bitterness?

The problem, of course, is how to assess this nebulous quality. The trick is to open your personal sensors and record your experiences after every interaction, including phone calls, with each program. When you visit the program, try to discover their feelings. Pump the residents, and if possible the ancillary staff, for their attitudes toward the people in the department. While inexact, this is the best method for assessing the departmental attitudes that may be very important for your happiness during your training.

Research Opportunities/Training

If you plan to skip this section because you don't have any interest in research, please stop and reconsider. The availability of research opportunities and training at a residency program means that you will

1. Sharpen your ability to critically read the medical literature—as you know, there is a lot of junk out there.
2. Keep abreast of the latest knowledge—at least in the areas being researched.
3. Be exposed to enough research to see whether you actually get "turned on" by it.

Quite a few residents have entered residency programs intending to never do any research after their training, only to discover that they actually liked searching for answers to pithy questions. In fact, some of them found that research added a necessary and fulfilling dimension to their professional life. While they are still in the minority, an increasing number of new medical school graduates seem to be interested in research. More than 40% plan to include a period of research in their postgraduate training.

The presence of research activity suggests that clinical service, such as patient care, is not the only reason that the faculty and residents are at a particular institution. There is more to that department and institution than merely treating patient after patient. To have research, a spirit of learning and education must be present. This is what you are looking for in a training program. Value it highly when you find it.

Knowledge

No one learns to do research by him- or herself. You may have done some research as a medical student. However, it is unlikely that you either had the primary responsibility for the project or had to acquire the in-depth knowledge of scientific methodology, statistical analysis, writing, or any of the other elements of a successful research project. You are looking for faculty members who are experienced in doing (and publishing) research in your specialty. If you have developed an interest in one particular area, you may look for that. The important thing is to find at least one faculty member experienced in research who will be willing to work with you during your training. This individual will act as a research mentor, much like your mentor in medical school.

Of course, it is best to have a selection of experienced researchers to choose from, but this is not always possible. The things you should learn about research from any particular program are:

- How to design a research project.
- How to perform those techniques needed to complete the project.
- How to statistically analyze your research.
- How to coherently write a scientific article.
- Where and how to present and/or publish your results.

How is this information about doing research presented? Is it given as lectures, assigned readings, personal tutelage, or learned by trial and error? Usually, programs use a combination of these methods. But the most important element is exposure to a faculty experienced in all phases of research.

Materials

If you plan to do research, especially if your time will be limited, find out what materials for research are available to you. The more that are readily available, the less time and energy you will have to spend hunting down needed supplies, space, and equipment.

The first, and often the most essential, material is *money*. While it is the root of all evil, money is also the key to getting research done. Does the department or institution have funds set aside for resident research? Are there other sources that can be tapped easily? Are the amounts limited? Does their availability depend on the type of research being done?

The second material you may need is *laboratory facilities*. If you are planning on doing either bench or animal research, you need both laboratory space and equipment at your disposal. You will often be able to "squeeze into" a faculty member's lab and use "borrowed" equipment. But these first have to be available. Also find out if there are support personnel, such as veterinarians and technicians, to help you. Are there animals for research? This will vary markedly due to both state law and the amount of funding you have at your disposal. Are there individuals outside the department who are supportive enough of resident research to help with space, equipment, or expertise?

Often forgotten is the question of whether you can get *secretarial support*. Whether or not you are a "hunt-and-peck" typist, those keys can get mighty blurry when you are doing the third revision of a manuscript after making ward rounds at 8 P.M. Although not essential, secretarial support is a great asset.

Finally, how about *computers*? Are there some you can use? Are they compatible with your personal computer? Is training available if you have yet to be indoctrinated? Even if you aren't interested in any other aspect of research, inquire about computers. It is essential for the modern physician, no matter what their specialty, to be acquainted with at least basic computer operation—which means being computer literate. All large hospitals in the country, as well as most physicians' offices, use computers for business management. Most also use them for the management of clinical records and other information, such as lab results. In research, computers are essential. Knowledge of databases, spreadsheets, statistical packages, and word processors is necessary for all but the simplest research being conducted today. Be sure that you come out of your residency training computer literate.

Time Allotted

If you anticipate doing serious research during your residency training, you will need adequate time. Programs vary widely in how they supply that time. Some assign specific blocks of time in which to do research. Often this is because of, or at least consistent with, specialty Board requirements.

Other options are either doing research during an elective time period or working on research while attending to other clinical duties. The former may deprive you of necessary extra clinical experiences, which are often in subspecialty or complementary areas (such as neonatal ICU for an Obstetrics resident). The latter, unless the clinical load is very light, will deprive you of sleep. And during a residency, as you will find out, sleep is a commodity in very short supply. As early as possible, determine how research time is allocated in the programs that you investigate.

Local Job Prospects after Training

You may believe that you already know where you want to live and set up practice once you have finished training. If that is true, you might want to think about this when selecting a residency site. But first, consider whether jobs in your chosen specialty are even available in the particular geographic area that interests you. More important, with the ongoing changes in health care delivery systems, will jobs still be available by the time you complete your training? Will training in that geographic area help you get a local job when you finish? Will you still be interested in living in that area when you finish?

Remember, your attitudes change as you mature. In some instances, residents who train in a particular area have an advantage getting local jobs, since they have been able to make contacts during their residency. In other cases, it may be a better strategy to train at a respected program and then look for jobs in the geographic region that interests you. Determine this by checking with clinicians or the medical society in the communities you are considering. Do not make a residency selection based on erroneous assumptions. Always check the facts first.

Also, career counseling should not end with deciding upon a specialty or entering a residency. With the proliferation of subspecialties and the wide variety of practice options, residents should actively seek advice on career decisions, beginning as soon as they enter their residency program. This may stimulate the faculty to provide some of this information in a standardized fashion, and even if they do not, it suggests to them that you are a top-notch resident who has his or her eyes focused on having a fulfilling and meaningful career. Is such counseling available at the residency program?

Facilities

As a resident, many factors will influence your day-to-day stress and comfort levels. The nature and organization of the facilities in which you work, however, are major contributing factors. While many residency applicants discount these elements, you would be wise to consider how important they will be to your education, your lifestyle, and your sanity.

Clinical Laboratory Support

Waiting for the results of an urgent, pre-operative, or outpatient laboratory test can cost both residents and patients their most valuable resource, time. Delays can frustrate everyone involved. Questions about the speed and comprehensiveness of clinical laboratories may be very important. How extensive are the tests an institution's clinical laboratories run? Is a stat lab available? Can you only get commonly needed tests during certain hours? Will lab technicians (or nursing staff) draw blood at all hours?

The days of running your own laboratory tests came and went, and now have come again—at least to a limited extent. Performing these and similar tests are part of medicine's new age. Can you perform the common "point-of-service" tests, such as Strep screens and pregnancy tests, done in your clinic? Some laboratories have stopped clinicians from performing tests in the clinics in the name of quality control (or is it revenues?). Yet, you need this experience to be prepared for medical practice after residency.

Computerized Records/Lab Results
The world is moving toward computerization. While medicine has generally moved more slowly than many other fields, financial pressures pushed many medical practices to produce first computerized laboratory results and then computerized patient records. Both save physicians an enormous amount of time when waiting or searching for information. Most training institutions have incorporated computerization to at least a limited degree, and the more they have done so, the less time you will waste.

Hospitals' Ages & Atmosphere
The bricks and mortar (and plastic, steel, and wood) that make up the institution(s) in which you work may look chic and modern or staid and ivy-covered on the outside, but you will work on the inside. How well is the facility maintained? Is its structure so outmoded that it makes working there difficult? Do its piecemeal additions mean that you will be walking endless miles to do the simplest tasks? Or are the new "modern" conveniences unworkable? Does the place look shabby and unkempt, or does it look neat and clean, despite its age?

You are going to spend many hours here. The hospital's or clinic's appearance and structure may not be your first consideration, but it will impact your daily existence.

Library/Media
How good is the *library*? Even if you do not plan to do research, the library is essential for house officers to prepare talks and investigate unusual findings in their patients. Likewise, what facilities are there to do *computer searches*, to learn about and use the *Internet*, and to *photocopy*? These services are an essential part of medical education and are available through most medical libraries. Also, do residents have Internet access on the wards, in the clinics, in the emergency department, and from their call rooms?

Parking
Parking may not only be expensive, but it can also be a hassle—as you probably already know from your medical school experience. The amount of frustration involved in parking a vehicle can be ascertained by talking to

current residents. The cost, though, is a commonly offered benefit. Seventy-two percent of teaching hospitals pay at least part of the parking costs for PGY-1 housestaff. Additional questions to ask are: How safe is the parking area? How safe is the area between where I will park and the hospital?

Resident On-Call Room Ambiance

The on-call rooms will be your home-away-from-home. Don't expect them to resemble even the quality or size of a low-rent motel room. They should, however, be clean and quiet, have ready access to a phone, have reasonable air flow and temperature control, and be private. The rooms should be cleaned daily and have fresh bed linens, although this is not the case at some institutions. Privacy is necessary so that your sleep will not be interrupted by phone calls or pages to other residents sharing the sleeping quarters. The room should also have a lock so that both you and your personal items remain safe. Ideally, you should have easy access to a bathroom and shower.

These requirements do not describe five-star accommodations, but rather one step above tent camping. Yet, if the on-call rooms meet them, they should suffice for your nocturnal hospital stays. Ask to see the on-call rooms during your visits.

Safety/Security

Most medical students feel that they are immortal (at least until they take Pathology). Since age brings some wisdom, most residents recognize that they must not only learn but also be safe in their clinical environments. News stories about physicians being killed only suggest the level of danger faced by physicians in and around hospitals. Many institutions in traditionally high-crime areas have tight security in place at their facilities. Yet even there, injuries and deaths have occurred. Some institutions have not yet come to grips with their changing environment and lack adequate security. If you recognize that no place is absolutely safe, you can reasonably balance your security concerns with your educational needs.

Restrictive Covenants

Restrictive covenants, also called "non-compete clauses," are sections of employment contracts that prevent individuals from subsequently working within a specified geographic radius. For residents, this often meant not being allowed to work in the city where the residency was located or within a specified number of miles of the residency's main clinical site.

The AMA's Council on Ethical and Judicial Affairs has said, "It is unethical for a teaching institution to seek a non-competition guarantee in return for fulfilling its educational obligations. Physicians-in-training should not be asked to sign covenants-not-to-compete as a condition of their entry into any residency or fellowship program." According to ACGME rules, residencies must not require individuals to sign these types of covenants in order to become or remain a resident.

Unless there are extenuating circumstances, *do not apply* to programs that have restrictive covenants. Therefore, in your Must/Want Analysis, "No Restrictive Covenants" should be completed as a "Must."

Benefits

The benefits a residency program provides determine your real compensation level, and, in part, how endurable your life will be during residency. They suggest how much of your salary will have to be spent on some of life's necessities, or whether you can afford to do your residency at all.

At present, programs may offer any benefit package that allows them to compete for applicants. They must, however, provide professional liability (malpractice) coverage for the duration of a resident's training and for any lawsuits filed after they leave the program that arise from events that occurred as part of their educational program. The AMA, through its representation on the ACGME, is urging that residency programs be required to also provide health, life, and disability insurance for all residents.

When you are told about the benefits that programs offer, be aware of the fine print. Many programs offer certain benefits only if the resident contributes a share of the cost. Often this portion of the cost can be considerable. If you need a particular benefit, such as parking, dental care, or insurance, find out in advance how much you will need to pay to get it.

Note that you pay no tax (or very little) on most benefits offered by a program. Since these are expenses that you otherwise would have to pay, essentially they are additional salary. But a benefit is only worthwhile to you if you need it. Obstetric care and family education fee waivers do you no good if you are a single male. Nearly half of all institutions now offer flexible (cafeteria-style) benefit plans in which the employee selects the specific benefits that he or she wants from a menu of available options.

Salary

Salary is the bedrock of all other benefits. Unlike most individuals aspiring to a professional position, residency applicants never negotiate salary—it is fixed in advance. Generally, an institution pays the same salary to all residents in the same postgraduate year of training. Yet these salaries can vary considerably among institutions, and from one region of the country to another.

In general, PGY-1 residents receive the highest average salary ($42,625) in the northeastern United States and the lowest ($40,227) in the western U.S. Nationwide, PGY-1 average salaries also vary depending on who owns the hospital: medical school-owned hospitals pay the least ($39,056) and not-for-profit private hospitals pay the most ($41,485). Salaries increase about 5% per year during training. Housestaff salaries have remained fairly constant over the past 37 years, if adjusted for inflation. (A 2005 salary of $40,788, the national average PGY-1 salary, is barely more than the $7,212 that your older professors earned as interns in 1968.)

If there is a large variation in housestaff salaries among the institutions within a particular region, think about why a particular institution has to pay higher salaries to their housestaff. Often it is because the housestaff have reasons, such as a deficient training program, to be dissatisfied.

Salary is not an absolute number. Rather, it should be compared to the cost of living in a particular locale. An apparently high salary may not go very far in Washington, DC; San Francisco; Boston; New York City; or parts of Los Angeles. (Los Angeles, by the way, has one of the lowest average first-year housestaff salaries.) However, a much lower salary may allow a rather nice lifestyle in many smaller, southern, or midwestern cities.

Health Benefits

Health benefits vary. Since you really are getting older and you probably don't plan to sit in a chair and vegetate during your time off, you need an affordable way to stay healthy and to get necessary medical treatment. This is without even considering the needs of any dependents (e.g., spouse or children) that you have or might acquire along the way.

Health benefits you might find available through your employer at a residency program include coverage for hospitalization, dental services, drug prescriptions, employee health services, psychiatric counseling, vision services (glasses), and additional health insurance. These are often grouped under various types and styles of health insurance. The bottom-line question, though, is: What services are paid for by the employer?

You may never have had to purchase *health insurance*. In the past, your parents or your school may have paid for your health insurance. If so, you will be shocked at the cost. Health insurance is very expensive. In addition, what you get for your money varies a great deal (Figure 10.4).

The major elements to consider when looking at insurance that a residency program offers are: (1) who is covered, (2) what is covered, and (3) how much you will still have to pay. If you have dependents, it is very important to know whether they will also be covered. If you expect to need obstetric care, or if you or a member of your family needs special medical

FIGURE 10.4

*Health Benefits Provided to Housestaff and Dependents**

Benefit		Resident	Family
Group Medical Insurance	Offered/Fully Paid	38%	26%
	Offered/Cost Shared	62	70
	Not Offered/Not Paid	0	2
Dental Insurance	Offered/Fully Paid	32%	19%
	Offered/Cost Shared	51	59
	Not Offered/Not Paid	17	22
Drug Prescriptions	Offered/Fully Paid	29%	3%
	Offered/Cost Shared	68	27
	Not Offered/Not Paid	3	71
Psychiatric Treatment	Offered/Fully Paid	25%	15%
	Offered/Cost Shared	45	75
	Not Offered/Not Paid	30	10
Vision Plan	Offered/Fully Paid	15%	12%
	Offered/Cost Shared	33	33
	Not Offered/Not Paid	53	55

*Some totals may not add up to 100% due to rounding.
Adapted from: Association of American Medical Colleges. *2004 AAMC Survey of Housestaff Stipends, Benefits and Funding.* November 2004 Report. AAMC Division of Health Care Affairs.

services, be certain that these will be covered by the policy. In addition, are prescriptions, glasses, and dental care covered? If they aren't, these items can take a big bite out of your salary.

Finally, if the insurance does cover your specific health needs, what is your copayment? *A copayment is the amount that you must pay*, and may be a flat fee or calculated as a percentage of the charges for specific health services. If the copayment is large or the total amount of covered services is relatively small, you could be put at financial risk if you or your family members need extensive health services. More than half of all institutions charge residents copayments for inpatient medical care, ranging from $5 to more than $1,500. For ambulatory services, about two-thirds have copayments, ranging from $5 to $50 or more. Most programs state whether they offer, pay for, or share the cost of medical, mental health, dental, and vision insurance under "Major Medical Benefits" in *FREIDA* (if the residency director completed it).

Group medical coverage is offered to residents and their families by nearly all teaching institutions. Most hospitals have from two to eight plans, with varying benefits, to choose from. In recent years, more western hospitals (75%) have paid the full cost of residents' medical insurance than did those elsewhere in the country (<53%). Programs in the West also most commonly pay in full for a resident's family to be covered (39%); this is least frequent in the Northeast (25%). Who owns the hospital also influences whether they are likely to pay for this coverage. HIV/AIDS coverage is included in most policies.

Dental plans for housestaff are offered by about 83% of hospitals, with about 78% offering this benefit for dependents. *Prescription drug* benefits for residents are offered by more than 90% of teaching hospitals. *Psychiatric* benefits are offered to housestaff by 70% of teaching hospitals, but only 25% fully pay for it. The percentage offering this benefit has drastically decreased in recent years. *Vision plans* are offered at low or no cost at less than half of teaching hospital residency programs. Although this may appear to be a minor benefit, glasses can be expensive.

Health promotion has become a cost-effective benefit for an increasing number of non-hospital employers. At least one-third of major employers have on-site exercise facilities and classes. An additional one-third provide employee discounts for health club memberships. The increasing awareness of and interest in fitness should soon make this benefit available at many teaching hospitals. Health promotion comes in two forms: *screening* and *risk-avoidance*. Residency applicants dislike pre-employment screening, such as that for drugs or HIV. They respond positively, however, to risk-avoidance measures, such as a smoke-free workplace.

Sick leave is one benefit few people look forward to using. Since you will work around ill patients and colleagues, you will probably get sick enough to stay home at some point during your residency. What provisions does the program have for this? The other side of the coin is: What requirements are there for you to act as "back-up" for other residents who take sick leave? The general requirements are often set by the specialty's residency review committee, but the details about the amount of time and how to arrange it are set by the institutions and programs.

Non-Health Benefits

Non-health benefits are designed to make your life as an employee easier. They include some of the necessities that you will have to pay for if the teaching institution does not. So, if you need a particular benefit, having it paid for by your employer will make your salary go that much farther. Of course, if the benefit is of no use to you, do not consider it as a real part of your benefit package.

Non-health benefits that may be offered to housestaff or their dependents include: life insurance, disability insurance, parking, housing allowance, meals, vacation, educational time off, educational funding, liability insurance, childcare, laundry (uniforms), association dues, family educational benefits, and photocopying allowances. It is important to consider each institution's salary and benefit package to ensure that you will have the means to survive. You may find it useful to compare a program's benefits with those offered nationwide (Figures 10.5 and 10.6).

Life insurance is a necessity if you have dependents (especially if they are children). If anything should happen to you, this is what they will use for survival for the first several months after your death. Premiums are fully paid by most teaching institutions, and partially paid by nearly all others. Most teaching hospitals also have provisions for housestaff to purchase additional life insurance if they so desire. The amount of life insurance provided averages about $48,000, and ranges from $1,000 to $600,000 or more.

Disability insurance is an absolute necessity for you from now on. You have invested an enormous amount of time, effort, and money getting into and through medical school. Your potential earning power is sizable. However, if anything should happen to you that would prevent you from practicing medicine, or even practicing in your specialty once you have been trained, you will lose it all. Disability insurance will cover some of

FIGURE 10.5
Non-Health Benefits for First-Year Housestaff*

Benefit	Hospital Contribution	Percentage with Benefit
Parking	Offered/Fully Paid	58%
	Offered/Cost Shared	16
	Not Offered/Not Paid	27
Housing	Offered/Fully Paid	2%
	Offered/Cost Shared	10
	Not Offered /Not Paid	88
Meals when on call	Offered/Fully Paid	74%
	Offered/Cost Shared	20
	Not Offered/Not Paid	6
Meals when working	Offered/Fully Paid	25%
	Offered/Cost Shared	27
	Not Offered/Not Paid	48

*Some totals may not add up to 100% due to rounding.

Adapted from: Association of American Medical Colleges. *2004 AAMC Survey of Housestaff Stipends, Benefits and Funding.* November 2004 Report. AAMC Division of Health Care Affairs.

this loss. Current standard policies for residents pay a maximum of 60% of salary per year.

It is worthwhile to consider purchasing additional disability insurance especially since you, like nearly 80% of residents, may have substantial education-associated debts. Depending upon the type of coverage, you will be paid a set amount regularly for a defined period of time if you cannot work as a physician (or as a specialist once you have been trained). A special "HIV Indemnity Plan" is available through some insurance companies, including the AMA, that pays a lump sum if a resident becomes HIV-positive. Many disability policies will not pay unless the individual becomes incapacitated.

Most teaching hospitals pay some or all of the costs of disability insurance for housestaff. Disability policies usually may be continued (are "portable") after a resident leaves the program, if someone (usually the resident) continues to pay the premiums. Often, additional coverage can be purchased. Most programs state whether they offer, pay for, or share the cost of disability insurance under "Major Medical Benefits" in *FREIDA*.

Housing is a necessity, although you may not see much of your personal housing as an intern. Only about 12% of teaching hospitals offer to pay all or part of the cost for housing. This benefit is primarily offered in the Northeast. Most programs state whether they offer a housing stipend under "Employment Policies and Benefits" in *FREIDA*.

Meals are provided at no cost for most (74%) first-year housestaff while on call, and to many (25%) when they are working but not on call. Many other hospitals subsidize a portion of housestaff meals. Two important considerations are whether the food is edible and whether it will be available when you have time to eat, such as at 3 A.M. Most programs state whether they offer an "On-Call Meal Allowance" under "Employment Policies and Benefits" in *FREIDA*. You will need more information about this, so ask the residents when you visit the program.

Vacation and educational leave are important to rejuvenate your mind and body. First-year housestaff typically get 15 days of vacation and PGY-2s typically get 23 days. Educational leave to attend conferences in excess of vacation time is granted by most teaching hospitals. While many institutions have a general vacation policy, two-thirds let individual programs determine the amount of a resident's educational leave. Most hospitals contribute about $400 toward seminar registration and per-diem costs for PGY-1s, and $700 for PGY-2s. Most programs state the amount of vacation and sick days allotted each year under "Compensation and Leave" in *FREIDA*.

Lab coats are less critical than many other benefits, but their purchase and upkeep are often expensive. Will the hospital pay for your lab coats and also wash them?

Liability insurance (malpractice) is a "Must" for all residents. The cost is astronomical if you pay for it personally, and is even higher if you should need it and not have it. This is one expense that *must* be covered by the institution. It is not too difficult to consider as a "Must" since, for their own protection, all teaching institutions cover your malpractice insurance. There is no harm in double-checking, however.

House-officer groups have recently questioned whether hospitals are supplying residents with the appropriate type of malpractice insurance. The more inclusive type of coverage is the "occurrence" policy, which covers all alleged negligent acts occurring during the policy period. "Claims-made" policies are less comprehensive, and cover policyholders for all lawsuits filed during the period of coverage. (The alleged negligent act must also have occurred during the period of coverage.)

In essence, an occurrence policy will cover you for any malpractice allegations that happen during your residency—no matter when the lawsuit is filed. This is the type of professional liability coverage that the General Requirements for residency accreditation strongly suggest that all programs have in place. Governing bodies also strongly suggest that occurrence-type professional liability coverage be provided.

The claims-made policy only covers you while you are still at the same institution. If lawsuits are subsequently filed, you are not covered by the insurance unless separate "tail coverage" has been purchased. So far, no former resident is known to have been forced to pay damages. But it could happen.

Although the General Requirements for all residency programs mandate that applicants must be provided with the details of the professional liability coverage, programs might forget to do so—especially if the coverage is inadequate. Ask for details, including the type of insurance and the amount of coverage the hospital provides.

Childcare, a result of the increasing number of working mothers, is offered by about one-third of teaching institutions (see Figure 10.6). Approximately 49% of medical students are now women. Nearly 13% of all graduating medical students have children, and half of these have two or more.

Childcare allows parents to perform their jobs and not spend all their earnings to pay for their offspring's care. Unfortunately, most childcare services only cover normal working hours, meaning Monday through Friday,

FIGURE 10.6

Programs in Representative Specialties with On-Site Childcare

Specialty	Percent of Programs
Anesthesiology	39%
Dermatology	32
Emergency Medicine	35
Family Medicine	31
Internal Medicine	39
Neurology	41
Obstetrics/Gynecology	36
Ophthalmology	31
Orthopedic Surgery	35
Otolaryngology	38
Pathology	44
Pediatrics	42
Psychiatry	35
Radiology, Diagnostic	29
Surgery, General	41

Data derived from: American Medical Association. *GMED Companion: An Insider's Guide to Selecting a Residency Program 2005–2006.* Chicago, IL: AMA, 2005.

8:00 A.M. to 5:00 P.M. As a resident, your hours will be neither that regular nor that short. Only 15% of existing childcare facilities are open weekends and holidays, and only 5% are open overnight (6:00 P.M. to 7:00 A.M.).

Some teaching hospitals, in recognition of the need for childcare services for parents who work long and irregular hours, have on-site childcare for housestaff. Hospitals offering childcare services to their housestaff find that this not only helps attract residents, but also decreases absenteeism. Most programs state whether they offer on-site or subsidized childcare under "Employment Policies and Benefits" in *FREIDA.*

Most teaching institutions will help residents find childcare if they don't offer it. Many subsidize childcare; the average maximum subsidy is 30% of the cost. However, even if institutions offer childcare, you may not be able to use it: 78% have waiting lists for housestaff's children. The average wait to enroll an infant (0 to 1 year) is six months, for children two years old and above, the wait is two months.

Besides the convenience, having on-site childcare as a benefit can save you a lot of money. Hospitals normally charge residents between $45 and $100/week per child for this service. This is usually a marked financial, as well as emotional, reward over having to arrange comparable services outside the institution. The institutional services are reliable (your only sitter does not get sick), often have flexible hours matching yours, do not require transporting your child to another site, and usually provide care for sick children. Having childcare available for children when they are ill is a new movement. This allows parents to continue working with the assurance that their children are being cared for.

If you think you could use childcare, inquire. But, since children and the responsibility that they entail are sensitive issues, inquire discreetly.

Parental leave, once called maternity leave but now also available to fathers, is a rapidly spreading benefit since passage of the federal Family Leave Act. (*FREIDA* still lists "Maternity Leave" and "Paternity Leave" separately. In fact, each of these has subsections for birth and for adoption.) Most residency programs now provide paid maternity and paternity leave for births, although not necessarily for adoptions. The programs generally limit the amount of time that can be taken. Most programs state whether they have a parental leave policy and the amount of paid and unpaid time available under "Employment Policies and Benefits" in *FREIDA*. If they have not completed that part of their listing, you can justifiably assume they have a somewhat antiquated attitude toward employment benefits.

Note: Regardless of a residency program's stated policy on parental leave, childcare, or other family matters, the attitude of the residency director matters most. If a resident's supervisor is supportive, then the policies work; if not, they fail. All applicants, not just women, should ask current residents about this during their site visit. This is the only way to discern a particular department's attitude on family-related matters.

Family leave covers a wide range of reasons to take time off, including paternity and maternity leave. While nearly 94% of teaching hospitals have family leave policies, fewer than 60% of those institutions have had anyone take leave under their policy. (Don't any of their residents have children?) Most programs state whether they offer family leave, and some give the time limits, under "Leave Availability" in *FREIDA*.

Family educational benefits are offered by some programs, especially those associated with major universities. In some cases, the benefits include free or markedly reduced tuition for college classes. While this may not be useful to most residents, who may spend much of their free time sleeping, it may be very helpful to their spouse. Many spouses are interested in pursuing the remainder of either undergraduate or graduate training. If this benefit is used, the money saved can be substantial.

Recruitment incentives are now commonly offered in primary care specialties. While some national groups tried to halt this practice, the Justice

Department's intervention assured that it will continue. Incentives range from supplying an expense account for books and educational courses to subsidizing interview expenses. Many of these incentives are now offered only by marginal programs. In the future, better programs may also begin to adopt these tactics.

Organized housestaff/unions have become much more common. Often called Independent Housestaff Organizations (IHOs), they have helped their approximately 12,000 resident members in public hospitals address training conditions, salaries and benefits, ancillary support, and patient care with a collective voice. Joining a residency where such an organization exists (if it has been effective) may help lessen the frustrations you experience during residency. Most unionized residents are located in California, the District of Columbia, Florida, Massachusetts, New Jersey, and New York, and are represented by the Committee of Interns and Residents (CIR), an affiliate of the Service Employees International Union.

In December 1999, the National Labor Relations Board overturned a 23-year-old precedent by granting medical residents the right to organize in private institutions. They had previously said that interns and residents could not collectively bargain because they were considered students, not employees. The new ruling has been interpreted as meaning that residents should be considered both employees and students.

Moonlighting

Moonlighting means working for pay during time off while you are a resident or fellow. It is not the first thing that most medical students think of when they consider residency programs. Being allowed to work clinically at another site for pay and having opportunities available to do so, however, may make the difference between eating steak or peanut butter sandwiches—or, more important, between buying gasoline for your car so you can drive to work or having to walk.

Moonlighting also offers residents an opportunity to broaden their clinical experiences, to learn about communities in which they might want to practice, to let the communities learn about them, and to find out what clinical practice is like outside a tertiary-care mecca. Most important, it lets them experience, maybe for the first time, how it feels to be treated like a professional—and to take on a professional's responsibilities.

Most residency programs have rules about moonlighting. Some allow all moonlighting. Others don't allow any. Most restrict moonlighting either to specific amounts of time or to situations where it will not interfere with resident activities. Most moonlighting occurs in Internal Medicine and Family Medicine programs; about 30% of Internal Medicine residents and

18% of Family Medicine residents have moonlighting jobs. If you think that you might want to moonlight, find out under what conditions it is allowed.

States also may regulate moonlighting through licensure. A number of states require two or more years of postgraduate training prior to licensure—a requirement that is more common and more stringent for IMGs (Figure 7.10). This either discourages most moonlighting in these states or limits it to those in their last years of residency. The Federation of State Medical Boards has recommended that all state licensing boards require at least three years of postgraduate training for licensure.

The next question is whether moonlighting jobs are available. In some institutions, moonlighting opportunities exist within the institution itself or at satellite facilities. In other hospitals, groups of residents have acquired moonlighting jobs that are available to the entire group. In most cases, however, finding these jobs is an individual endeavor. Try to find out whether current residents have found moonlighting jobs. If so, have they been within a reasonable commuting distance?

Finally, what will moonlighting cost? How expensive is a medical license in the state? How long will it take to get? In some states, it may take six months or more after applying to get a license that allows you to moonlight. How much must you spend for malpractice insurance? If there are moonlighting opportunities within the institution, it may not cost you anything. In some cases, employers furnish insurance (claims-made rather than occurrence—see "Liability Insurance," above). If you are forced to get your own insurance, it can be very expensive. Talk to the current residents about moonlighting. The information will be more reliable, and the impression that you leave with the program will be much better than if you asked these questions of faculty members.

In an interesting twist, a substantial number of teaching hospitals now arrange moonlighting opportunities, and even subsidize malpractice insurance so that residents in some specialties can moonlight. They believe this encourages students to enter these fields, or at least these residencies. Sponsoring or arranging moonlighting opportunities is most common in Family Medicine, Internal Medicine, and Pediatrics. About 20% subsidize malpractice insurance for moonlighting.

Shared-Residency/Part-Time Positions

It may be important to you, for any number of personal or professional reasons, to do your residency on a part-time basis, even though it takes longer to complete. A shared-schedule position is one in which two residents, who usually pair up before interviewing and applying to programs, agree to each spend less than full-time in a single residency slot. In essence, they share one position. These arrangements are more fully described in Chapter 13.

Other Factors

While the discussion above has covered the most common factors to consider in choosing a training position, don't forget any other personal factors that you feel are important enough to guide this decision. One rather exhaustive list of possible factors can be found in "An Applicant's Evaluation of a Medical House Officership," by Martin Raff and Ira Schwartz (1974, *The New England Journal of Medicine*). Even though the article is old, its list is as pertinent today as it was then.

Narrowing the Choices

If you have read through the description of some of the factors to consider in selecting a residency position, and if you understand the process for assigning "Weights" to the factors in a "Must/Want" Analysis, then you are ready to complete your own "Must/Want" Analysis Form. Use Figure 10.1 as a master form to develop your own list. You will use one "Must/Want" Analysis Form for each program that you evaluate, *so make several copies of the form once you have adapted it for your needs.* They will be completed first by using the programs' written information alone, and then updated using any additional information you get while interviewing.

The Companion Disk for Getting Into A Residency, available from Galen Press, Ltd., has a master copy of the "Must/Want" Analysis that you can customize to fit your needs. It will save and print multiple copies of the form. After you enter weights and scores for the programs, it will also calculate the totals for you. (It even keeps track of your "Weights" total so you can easily tell when it reaches "100.") See the *Annotated Bibliography* for more information.

Personal "Must/Want" Analysis

To decide on the programs to which you wish to apply, complete the *Must/Want Analysis Form* (see Figure 10.1). Once you have listed the factors and assigned the "Weights" in your "Must/Want" Analysis, you should be able to go through the mass of information you have collected about the residency programs in an organized and rational manner.

How does the residency that you are assessing stack up against your ideal for that particular item? For each program you evaluate, every factor is given a "Score" ranging from "1" (farthest from your ideal) to a "10" (exactly what you are looking for). You record this result in the "Score" column of the "Must/Want" Analysis. For example, if you ideally would like to have faculty available in the hospital for consultation 24 hours/day, you would score any program in which this was true a "10" for this factor. If faculty were available only every third Thursday, you would probably feel obliged to give this factor a "Score" of "1." (The scores do not have to add up to anything! Feel free to give any applicable score to any factor.) The scoring is subjective, but then, you are the subject and what counts is how you perceive the situation.

Let's see how our hypothetical applicant (from Figure 10.2) filled out her "Must/Want" Analysis Forms for three separate programs. Remember, she has not yet gone for interviews, so some of the information is not yet available. See Figures 10.7, 10.8, and 10.9 for her evaluations of three hypothetical programs.

FIGURE 10.7

"Must/Want" Analysis—Example #1

PROGRAM #1–BACKWATER STATE HOSPITAL

Clinical Experience	WEIGHT	X	SCORE	=	TOTAL
On-Call Schedule	5		7		
Patient Population	2		7		
Responsibility	14		9		
Setting	7		8		
Volume	10		6		
Geographic Location					
Part of Country	1		4		
Specific City	1		1		
Reputation					
Program Age and Stability	2		3		
Faculty					
Availability	5		?		
Interest	7		?		
Stability	3		10		

FIGURE 10.7 (continued)

	WEIGHT	X SCORE	= TOTAL
Curriculum			
Number of Conferences	1	6	
Special Training	6	7	
Types of Conferences	2	2	
Esprit de Corps	8	3	
Research Opportunities/Training			
Knowledge	5	8	
Materials	2	?	
Time	7	9	
Facilities			
Clinical Laboratory Support	1	2	
Library/Media	2	3	
Safety/Security	3	9	
No Restrictive Covenant	MUST	Yes	
Benefits: Health			
Health Insurance	MUST	Yes	
Hospitalization	MUST	Yes	
Benefits: Non-Health			
Childcare	MUST	**NO!**	
Disability Insurance	MUST	Yes	
Educational Leave: Funding Available	1	Yes	
Time Off	2	3	
Liability Insurance	MUST	Yes	
Vacation	1	4	
Moonlighting	2	?	

TOTAL OF ALL WEIGHTS = ___100___

PROGRAM EVALUATION SCORE = Not Applicable

Program #1 is completely eliminated from this applicant's consideration because of the lack of childcare. It doesn't matter what the scores are for any of the other factors—even though it scored well in several major areas. Note that a number of factors are scored as question marks. This is because the information was not available from the written material she received or from her adviser.

FIGURE 10.8

"Must/Want" Analysis—Example #2

PROGRAM #2–MAKO GENERAL HOSPITAL

Clinical Experience	WEIGHT	X	SCORE	=	TOTAL
On-Call Schedule	5		5		25
Patient Population	2		3		6
Responsibility	14		9		126
Setting	7		8		56
Volume	10		8		80
Geographic Location					
Part of Country	1		2		2
Specific City	1		1		1
Reputation					
Program Age and Stability	2		5		10
Faculty					
Availability	5		?		?
Interest	7		?		?
Stability	3		3		9
Curriculum					
Number of Conferences	1		7		7
Special Training	6		9		54
Types of Conferences	2		3		6
Esprit de Corps	8		?		?
Research Opportunities/Training					
Knowledge	5		?		?
Materials	2		8		16
Time	7		8		56
Facilities					
Clinical Laboratory Support	1		4		4
Library/Media	2		3		6
Safety/Security	3		5		15
No Restrictive Covenant	MUST		Yes		OK
Benefits: Health					
Health Insurance	MUST		Yes		OK
Hospitalization	MUST		Yes		OK
Benefits: Non-Health					
Childcare	MUST		Yes		OK
Disability Insurance	MUST		Yes		OK
Educational Leave: Funding Available	1		?		?
Time Off	2		9		18

FIGURE 10.8 (continued)

	WEIGHT X	SCORE =	TOTAL
Liability Insurance	MUST	Yes	OK
Vacation	1	7	7
Moonlighting	2	?	?

TOTAL OF ALL WEIGHTS = 100

PROGRAM EVALUATION SCORE = 505 (+ ?)

Program #2 has scored very well against our applicant's criteria. The "Program Evaluation Score" is at least 505. However, just as in the first program, some factors could not be scored. In most cases, the same or related factors for each program will not be able to be scored without a visit to the program. These include the faculty's availability and interest, the esprit de corps of the program, and the "knowledge" of available research. Other factors may only have partial information available and may need to be further elucidated in person. The scores can then be adjusted as necessary.

If a particular factor is either a "Must" or a very important (high "Weight") element for you, it is worthwhile to call the program and obtain any needed information before you make your decision about where to interview. Failing to do this may either result in wasted interviews or cause you to overlook some programs that might meet your needs.

FIGURE 10.9

"Must/Want" Analysis—Example #3

PROGRAM #3–SAGUARO COMMUNITY HOSPITAL

Clinical Experience	WEIGHT	X SCORE	= TOTAL
On-Call Schedule	5	6	30
Patient Population	2	5	10
Responsibility	14	4	56
Setting	7	10	70
Volume	10	3	30
Geographic Location			
Part of Country	1	10	10
Specific City	1	10	10
Reputation			
Program Age and Stability	2	7	14
Faculty			
Availability	5	?	?
Interest	7	?	?
Stability	3	?	?
Curriculum			
Number of Conferences	1	4	4
Special Training	6	6	36
Types of Conferences	2	9	18
Esprit de Corps	8	?	?
Research Opportunities/Training			
Knowledge	5	?	?
Materials	2	8	16
Time	7	4	28
Facilities			
Clinical Laboratory Support	1	?	?
Library/Media	2	1	2
Safety/Security	3	5	15
No Restrictive Covenant	MUST	Yes	OK
Benefits: Health			
Health Insurance	MUST	Yes	OK
Hospitalization	MUST	Yes	OK

FIGURE 10.9 (continued)

	WEIGHT	X SCORE	= TOTAL
Benefits: Non-Health			
Childcare	MUST	Yes	OK
Disability Insurance	MUST	Yes	OK
Educational Leave: Funding Available	1	8	8
Time Off	2	?	?
Liability Insurance	MUST	Yes	OK
Vacation	1	4	4
Moonlighting	2	?	?

TOTAL OF ALL WEIGHTS = 100

PROGRAM EVALUATION SCORE = 361 (+ ?)

Since the information that was available for Programs #2 and #3 was not the same, they cannot be directly compared (yet). But the information available does give a general ranking for the programs. One piece of information had to be obtained by phone about Program #3, but that residency's secretary was happy to answer a potential applicant's questions. The call provided the facts that our applicant needed in order to make an informed decision. From this group, Program #2 is the one to which our applicant will be sure to apply. Depending upon how the other programs she rates stack up, she also might decide to apply to Program #3. Program #1, of course, has been eliminated for not fulfilling one of her required "Musts." By the time she finishes interviewing at programs, she should have enough information to eliminate the question marks on her forms.

11

Playing The Odds: How Many Program Applications?

There is no certainty without some doubt.

– Elias Levita, *Tishbi*

Forecasting is hard, particularly of the future.

– Anonymous

MEDICAL STUDENTS FREQUENTLY ASK, "To how many programs should I apply?" There is no easy answer, since *the real answer depends upon your wants and needs, including your specialty choice.* No magic number exists. No one factor will give you an answer. As with all other aspects of the competition for a residency slot, the number of programs to which you should apply must be individualized. You must consider the competitiveness of the specialty you have chosen, the geographic and academic restrictions you are placing upon a residency choice, and your own competitiveness. Then, after discussions with your mentor or your specialty adviser, apply to a generous number of programs.

How Competitive Is the Specialty You Want?

First, consider how competitive your chosen specialty is. For example, Otolaryngology, Neurological Surgery, and Orthopedics require applications to more programs to be assured of an adequate number of interviews than do Psychiatry or Pathology (see Figures 4.1, 22.2, and 22.10). For many years, students have been told (with only a little exaggeration), "If your parents did not submit your Ophthalmology application while you were in diapers, it is too late." While the situation for most competitive specialties is not that bad, a few remain difficult to enter. Some specialties fluctuate widely in their competitiveness from year to year. Ophthalmology, for example, has become markedly less competitive over the past decade. Also, one of the least competitive specialties in the 1970s, Anesthesiology, became extremely competitive in the 1980s, but once again is relatively easy to enter. Generally, the more competitive the specialty, the more programs to which you should apply. Figure 11.1 demonstrates the change in total PGY-1 applicants and positions over the past 50 years. See the specialty descriptions in Chapter 3 for information on each specialty's relative competitiveness.

How Competitive Are You?

How competitive are you—really? List the qualities that are viewed as plusses in your desired specialty. Do you have strengths or weaknesses in these areas? Be objective. If you cannot be objective on your own, have your adviser or a mentor in the field help you. It is generally inadvisable to have a spouse or close friend help on this—too much honesty from the wrong source can be very ego-destructive.

Do not compare yourself with others in your school who are applying to the same specialty. This will not result in an accurate assessment of your

FIGURE 11.1
Applicants and 1st-Year Positions, 1952–2005

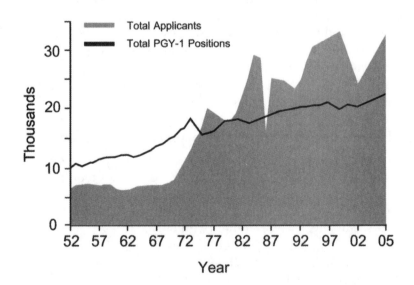

Adapted from: Association of American Medical Colleges. *AAMC Data Book.* Washington, DC: AAMC, June 2005.

competition. *The competitive pool is made up of all students from all schools who want to enter your chosen specialty.* Your best chance of success lies in assessing your competitiveness as accurately as possible. You do this by comparing the strengths that you have identified in yourself with those that you perceive the residency programs in your desired specialty want. The ideal candidate, the one who fits all the desired qualities, is the one you are competing against (see Chapter 18). But don't worry. That individual probably doesn't exist.

What Do You Have to Lose?

Professional photographers constantly tell amateurs to go ahead and take lots of pictures. "So what if you blow a few shots? You may end up with some beautiful pictures you wouldn't have gotten if you had been more conservative. Remember," they say, "the film—or the memory—is the least expensive part of system."

Just so with the application process. Applying to a few extra "pie-in-the-sky" or "reach" programs (those to which you really want to go but are afraid that they won't accept you) makes good sense for at least two reasons. First, you will never have to say to yourself, as so many physicians do in their later years when they meet up with a moron graduate from their most desired training program, "I could have gotten in if only I had applied." Second, you actually may get an interview (and then a position) at that program. It takes very little extra effort to apply to a few more programs. Since you are applying to some programs anyway, follow your dreams—they may come true. If you can dream it, you can do it!

As a general guideline, the average number of applications recent graduates submitted through ERAS to programs in various specialties is listed in Figure 11.2. Students submitted an average of 44 applications, although that number varied greatly by specialty. U.S. graduates submitted an average of 30 applications, while IMGs submitted 63 applications. Men submitted an average of 48 applications, while women submitted 39 applications.

Make up your list once and then apply to those programs. Don't continue to add to the list piecemeal. The application process is hard enough and it is very difficult to keep track of the paper shuffle under normal circumstances. Adding programs as you go along will only make the process harder on you, and on the people sending out your reference letters. One request for information to be sent to all your programs usually works well. Dribbling in those requests separately over time can spell disaster.

FIGURE 11.2

Average Number of Applications Submitted to Programs in Various Specialties

Specialty	U.S.-M.D. Applicant	Member of AOA Honor Society	IMG Applicant	Osteopathic Applicant	Ratio of Male to Female Applications*
Anesthesiology	22.1	16.7	19.1	20.2	1.14
Dermatology	44.4	52.7	17.0	14.6	0.82
Diagnostic Radiology	40.0	34.3	23.6	29.3	1.18
Emergency Medicine	24.8	18.6	17.3	18.9	1.01
Emergency Med/ Internal Med	4.5	4.3	5.0	2.7	1.36
Family Medicine	10.4	12.5	24.8	8.2	1.09
Internal Medicine	15.8	14.4	37.7	14.9	1.01
Internal Med/Pediatrics	13.2	10.6	6.9	8.1	1.07
Internal Med/Psychiatry	5.1	4.5	4.5	1.8	1.24
Obstetrics/Gynecology	21.0	18.5	23.3	20.9	0.87
Orthopedic Surgery	46.0	39.9	22.7	13.3	0.95
Pathology	16.6	13.4	18.6	14.4	0.99
Pediatrics	16.3	14.3	20.0	13.0	0.98
Pediatrics/Psychiatry/ Child Psychiatry	5.2	2.4	4.7	4.3	0.98
Physical Medicine & Rehabilitation	16.6	13.7	12.6	17.6	1.22
Plastic Surgery	26.4	31.3	14.1	7.4	0.95
Psychiatry	15.1	14.0	18.9	13.2	1.08
Radiation Oncology	29.9	29.2	13.6	30.0	1.19
Surgery, General	21.9	17.7	26.9	20.2	1.22
Transitional Year	8.2	8.5	8.3	6.0	1.11

*The ratio of the number of applications submitted by individual male applicants to those submitted by female applicants.

Adapted from: ERAS data, Association of American Medical Colleges, Washington, DC, 2005.

12

Buffing Your File: The Paperwork

A wise man recognizes the convenience of a general statement,
but he bows to the authority of a particular fact.

– Oliver Wendell Holmes, Jr.

THE KEY TO SUCCESS in preparing and gathering the information required by residency programs is the same one that got you into medical school—being compulsive. Four rules that will put you far ahead of the pack are:

1. **Be Thorough**
2. **Look Neat**
3. **Be Early**
4. **Be Organized**

Thoroughness means reading the application materials twice. Dot the i's and cross those t's. If a program requests something out of the ordinary, such as your undergraduate transcript, then make sure that you note the requirement and get them a copy. You can lose lots of points in this game if you don't read each set of rules carefully. No one is prepared to go out of his or her way to accommodate you. Some programs may not even notify you that your application is incomplete, so it's up to you to develop a system to keep track of your applications. Keep photocopies of all correspondence and detailed records of your phone calls to the programs. Be thorough.

The **lack of neatness** probably destroys more potentially successful candidates than all other factors combined. You are applying for a real job, as well as for your lifelong career. Don't send your potential employers anything unless it looks like it is the work of a professional. This means that your application and résumé should never be completed in a barely legible scrawl, in pencil, or in the middle of ward rounds. Neither should they be hacked out on the old manual typewriter in the back office, nor printed on a dot matrix printer. These documents are your representatives, your entries to the goal you seek. Make them look sharp. Make them look professional. Make them look neat.

Although there are many rumors to the contrary, programs rarely keep the correspondence you send to them requesting information and an application. They do not normally start a file on you until something more substantial, such as an application, a reference letter, or a transcript arrives. However, the postcard or short letter that you send to them requesting information must at least be legible and contain your name and address. You would be surprised how many supposedly intelligent medical students send requests that lack one of these necessary items.

Early birds catch the worm and *early applicants get the interviews*. More and more students now complete their applications at the beginning of the application "season" (August and September for programs in the NRMP PGY-1 Match). Still, many students have not even gotten application packets and information from the programs by the time they should be making their decision about which programs to apply to and completing the necessary paperwork.

No matter how good the program, nor how experienced the residency director, the question that always arises at this time of year is, "Will I get enough good candidates this year?" As a result, programs have rather liberal criteria early on for granting interviews. If you walk on water and fly through the air (without assistance, of course), you can wait and file with the rest of the applicant horde. But if you don't, get your packet completed early. Even if you can do miraculous deeds, if you apply late, optimal interview dates may not be available when you're offered one. In fact, some programs may run out of interview slots, since many have only a finite number available. Get your act together early.

Get organized. You will, undoubtedly, be flooded with material about residency programs and will be sending out lots of material to these programs (unless you apply to specialties using the Electronic Residency Application Service [ERAS®, described later in this chapter] or the Centralized Application Service [Ophthalmology, Neurological Surgery, Otolaryngology, and Neurology]). Therefore, you need to have a filing system that allows you to quickly locate, assess, and track both the material you receive and the material you send. Develop the system before you begin this process. For a system that has worked for many students, see Chapter 9.

Your Name

Everyone has a name, so what's the problem? The problem is that your name may change or have several variations. In the world of medical credentialing and verification (which you entered when you took USMLE Step 1 or COMLEX Part 1, or began the ECFMG process), variations are not tolerated. People who use first initials and middle names, change their names when married or divorced, reverse first and last names, or hyphenate their last names may encounter difficulties. The key to avoiding problems with the various bureaucrats, who must verify that you are who you say you are, is to use the same name on all your paperwork.

For example, you used T. Michael Jones on your medical school entrance materials. (You are not too keen on using Thaddeus.) Your transcript now probably reads that way—but find out from the registrar before you complete the USMLE Step 1 application. When you register for Step 1, use the same form of your name that is on your transcript. Do this for all subsequent official papers. That way, no one will confuse you with Tremont Michael Jones, Thomas Michael Jones, or even Theresa Michael Jones.

The same holds true for those who change their name when they get married or divorced. This has become more common with the increased number of women physicians. Those who get married after medical school usually have two names—their married name that they use in social situations, and their "professional name" that they use for work and for all official medical documents. That way, there is no bureaucratic confusion. Those who marry before or during medical school often begin using their married name for everything. Unfortunately, many of these marriages don't last, and so confusion may reign when the physician must use both her married and new (or old) names for the inevitable paperwork. As the number of different names increases with subsequent marriages and divorces, the confusion and resultant difficulties multiply. The best course is to have both a social name and a professional name. If possible, keep your professional name constant.

In Spanish-speaking countries (and occasionally elsewhere), a person often uses two last names—the first from their father and the second being their mother's maiden name. Therefore, a name may appear in a variety of ways on official documents—for example, Marco T. Velasco, Marco T. Velasco-Lopez, or Marco Velasco-Lopez. Others, such as those with Vietnamese names, may have their last and first names switched.

If you are in such a situation, notify all residency programs, ERAS or CAS, the ECFMG, USMLE, COMLEX, and any licensing bodies that the different names on your transcripts, Board scores, diplomas, and reference letters all belong to the same person. You do not want to be refused entrance to the USMLE because the names on your application and your ID don't match exactly. You do not want to lose out on a possible interview because of an "incomplete file" resulting from having your materials filed under more than one name. And once you go through all this hassle, you don't want problems with the matching programs because you are not listed with the residency programs under the same name you used to apply to the Match. The best course is to use only *your full name on all official documents.*

The Application

Most M.D. residency programs now use ERAS or the Centralized Application Service (CAS), which present most information in a standard format. Some M.D. residencies and fellowships, and most D.O. programs, use their own applications or the Universal Application for Residency (described on page 304). The first step is to get all the program applications you will need. Many can be downloaded from the program's website.

Application forms or the instructions specify what additional information is needed to complete the application process. Read the fine print. Make a chart of the materials required by each program. As you can see by the example in Figure 12.1, the requirements for different programs can vary widely. Nearly all will request a Dean's letter, medical school transcript, and application. Make certain that you supply at least the minimum that is required. In most instances, you should send as many excellent reference letters as you have available. Whether programs ask for one or not, always send a copy of your résumé. In general, only send a personal statement if it is specifically requested; however, if it is really good, send it anyway.

Some applicants will also need to send a copy of their ECFMG Certificate, letter of waiver from the military or Public Health Service, letters and evaluations from previous residency training, or other items. Be certain that you list all these items on your own tracking form.

Generally, the application will be the first piece of paper in your file at residency programs. The front page of the application, above all the other paperwork that you submit, must look as if the person completing it is a professional. Before you begin completing a residency program's application, it is a good idea to make copies of the form. Neatly fill out one of these copies, and then have a trusted friend review it for any spelling or grammatical errors. Such errors tend to stand out and will project a poor image of you. The reviewer, who can also evaluate your personal statement,

FIGURE 12.1

Requirements for Applications to Different Programs—Example

Hospital	Dean's Letter	Transcript	Application	Under-graduate Transcript	Personal Statement	Résumé	Ref Letters
Saw Comm	X	X	X			X	A+2
St. Mary's	X	X	U	X		X	2
Amhurt Univ	X	X	X		X		3
Smort Med Ctr	X	X	X			X	A+3
Arden St.	X		X	X	X		2
Robin Hood	X	X	X		X	X	2+P
WGMC	X	X	U		X	X	A+P
U of State	X	X	X	X	X		3

X–Required by program.
U–Requires use of the Universal Application.
A–Indicates a letter from your adviser.
#–Number of additional reference letters required.
P–At least one letter from a physician in the specialty for which you are applying.

should know you well enough to be able to suggest additional information that you were too modest to include. Then, after all your applications are ready, give these copies along with the original blank forms to a professional typist for preparation. This process will give you the best results.

Fill in all pertinent blanks on the application form with the requested information. *Never put in the words "see résumé."* Programs ask for data that they feel is necessary to make a choice among candidates, and structure their application so they can quickly screen it for this information. Of course, you will supply a résumé to the program, and there will certainly be some duplication of information. Not filling in the application with the requested information, however, can be the kiss of death. It indicates that you did not think enough of the program to do the work required to fill out their application. Instead, you left them to search around your résumé for the information they desire. Is that also how you plan to act as a resident? It is the impression that you have delivered. That is not the impression that you want the residency program to have about you as an applicant.

Finally, get your applications in early. It takes quite a bit of time to do the paperwork involved in preparing applications for submission. Since you are going to do it anyway, why not complete it early when you have a much better chance of obtaining the maximum results for your effort.

Illegal Questions

What about illegal questions? Those are the ones barred from pre-employment screening by federal and state civil rights acts. Questions dealing with race, sex, age, height, weight, national origin, military discharge status, arrest record, marital status or who lives with you, physical disability, and religion are restricted to those situations where they directly impact upon the job requirements or where the applicant raises them. Although they are not legal, many applications still contain these types of questions. How do you handle them?

First, remember that, in general, the programs are not being malicious in their use of these questions. Many times they are merely ignorant of the law. There is a fine line between questions that are illegal and those that are simply inept, curious, or friendly. Don't approach these questions in a hostile manner. Second, look over your Dean's letter, transcript, and other reference letters. How much new information are you supplying by answering these questions? Probably not much. What you are doing is putting the information down in a standard format for easy retrieval and comparison. So, the general advice is to fill in all the blanks.

The Universal Application

The Universal Application for Residency, which was an attempt to limit the amount of medical students' application paperwork, is rarely used today. Nevertheless, you may encounter it somewhere in your application process. How should you deal with it?

The ERAS and the CAS have mostly replaced the Universal Application and individual program applications. If you find that you do need this form, you may get it from the programs themselves, from your Dean of Students, or from the NRMP website (www.nrmp.org/res_match/about_res/univappl.pdf). You will usually have to use a photocopy of the original.

Some students who use the Universal Application for multiple programs photocopy one completed copy without the references and type those in individually. This looks sloppy and shows the program that they may be receiving a different reference list than other programs. As a result, they may wonder "What is this character up to?" Don't invite this kind of curiosity. Once you have completed the application using a photocopy of your original form, give it to a professional typist with clear notes about variations for individual programs. Let the typist do the labor so your application will look professional.

A note of caution is in order. Some programs specifically give applicants a choice between using the Universal Application or the program's application. If you have that choice, use the program's form. It will demonstrate more commitment, better satisfy the program's information needs, and look neater (since it will probably be an original rather than a photocopied application).

Electronic Residency Application Service (ERAS)

The Electronic Residency Application Service (ERAS), run by the Association of American Medical Colleges (AAMC), transmits residency applications, recommendation letters, Deans' letters, transcripts, USMLE scores, photographs, personal statements, ECFMG Certification, and other supporting credentials to residency programs. Starting with Obstetrics and Gynecology in the 1995–96 Match cycle, the specialties participating in ERAS 2006 include:

- Anesthesiology
- Dermatology
- Diagnostic Radiology
- Emergency Medicine
- Emergency Med/Internal Med
- Emergency Med/Pediatrics
- Family Practice
- Family Practice/Internal Med
- Family Practice/Psychiatry
- Internal Med (Preliminary & Categorical)
- Internal Med/Pediatrics
- Internal Med/Physiatry
- Internal Med/Psychiatry
- Neurology
- Neurology/Child Neurology
- Nuclear Medicine*
- Obstetrics & Gynecology
- Orthopedic Surgery
- Osteopathic Internships (D.O. students only)
- Otolaryngology
- Pathology
- Pediatrics
- Pediatrics/Dermatology
- Pediatrics/Physiatry
- Pediatrics/Psych/Child Psych
- Physical Med & Rehabilitation (Physiatry)
- Plastic Surgery (PGY-1)*
- Psychiatry
- Radiation Oncology*
- Surgery, General
- Transitional Year Programs
- Urology
- All Army & Navy PGY-1 positions

---

*Fewer than half of this specialty's programs participate in ERAS.

In principle, programs in these specialties will no longer accept paper applications, and 95% of U.S. residencies in these specialties do participate in ERAS. Most of those that do not participate are either military residencies, are located in Puerto Rico, or are in Radiation Oncology and Nuclear

Medicine. The ERAS website (www.aamc.org/students/eras/support/ proglist.pdf) lists most of the programs in participating specialties and indicates whether they participate in ERAS. *Check the ERAS website to see if the programs that interest you accept applications through ERAS.*

Osteopathic applicants can search for accredited Osteopathic programs (they are only visible to Osteopaths) by typing in a program's AOA ID or by choosing a "State/Training Type" pairing. As of 2006, Osteopathic students may also apply for Osteopathic internships through ERAS.

You cannot apply to non-participating programs using ERAS! For programs that do not use ERAS, you need to obtain paper applications. Their contact information is available online, in *FREIDA*, or in the *Green Book*. *It is the applicant's responsibility to verify with each residency program to which he or she is applying that the program is participating in ERAS.* You can check this on their website or by writing or calling the program.

Most specialties within Preventive Medicine (Aerospace Medicine, Occupational Medicine, and Public Health) require all candidates to apply directly to the programs. Neurological Surgery, Ophthalmology, and some Neurology programs use the Centralized Application Service (CAS), described on page 570. The Association of Schools of Public Health may provide applicants with a centralized application process as early as summer 2006. Many fellowships (taken after initial residency training) also require applicants to apply directly to their programs. However, for 2006, there are 18 fellowships listed on ERAS.

Components

The ERAS is comprised of four elements with which you will want to become familiar: the Dean's Office Workstation (DWS), the MyERAS website (which includes the Applicant Data Tracking System [ADTS]), the ERAS PostOffice, and the Program Director's Workstation (PDWS).

The *Dean's Office Workstation (DWS)* is software that your Dean's office uses to give you your initial code, called an "electronic token," which allows you to enter the MyERAS website. It is also where your recommendation letters, photograph, Dean's letter (also called the Medical Student Performance Evaluation [MSPE]), USMLE or COMLEX transcript, and medical school transcript are scanned before they are sent to the ERAS PostOffice. Each Dean's office (or the ECFMG for IMGs) has their own schedule for receiving and transmitting submitted materials. Their built-in delays and your tardiness may make you miss some programs' application deadlines. *It is your responsibility to know the schedule for your Dean's office, as well as the requirements and deadlines of each program to which you apply!*

The *MyERAS website* (http://services.aamc.org/eras/myeras) is your primary connection to the system. After you get the "electronic token" from your Dean's office, you can use this site to register for ERAS, receive your AAMC ID, and designate an ERAS password. (If you lose your password, go the MyERAS page and click "Forgot My Password." You should receive a copy of your password via e-mail in no more than two hours.) Once logged on, you can access virtually all the necessary parts of the system. *MyERAS* is where you complete your online residency application, create and enter your personal statement, select the residency programs to which you want to apply, and specify which materials each of those programs will receive. Until you register, however, the Dean's office cannot submit any of your materials to ERAS.

The *ERAS PostOffice* is the computer network at the AAMC to which your application materials are sent. From there, they are forwarded to the designated residency programs. Residency programs then download, collect, sort, review, and evaluate the supporting documents, and also rank the applications, using the *Program Director's Workstation (PDWS)*. Applicants have 24-hour access to the *Applicant Data Tracking System (ADTS)*, which lists each program to which you applied, when your Dean's office uploaded your documents, and when each residency program downloaded each document.

Registration

U.S. medical students/graduates: Applicants receive MyERAS electronic tokens from their school's Dean of Student's office beginning in late June. This allows them to register for and access the MyERAS website starting on July 1. Each school establishes procedures for distributing MyERAS electronic tokens and for processing ERAS applications and other materials.

Osteopathic students/graduates should be able to get this material from their Dean. Applicants can apply for Osteopathic Internship programs starting on July 1; applications for allopathic programs will not be accepted until September 1. **Canadian students** should follow the directions from their Dean of Students, since they will usually apply via the Canadian Resident Matching Service (CaRMS). **Military applicants** should contact their military counselor for any special instructions.

ERAS and International Medical Students/Graduates

To participate in ERAS, request your MyERAS electronic token from the Educational Commission for Foreign Medical Graduates' (ECFMG) website (www.ecfmg.org/eras/index.html). The $75 fee is non-refundable and must be paid prior to receiving the electronic token. This fee includes transmission of the ECFMG Status Report, which lists your passing score(s) on any tests administered through the ECFMG, to all residencies to which you apply. The ECFMG will accept ERAS applications only from individuals who have an eight-digit USMLE/ECFMG Identification Number. This number is given to individuals when they apply to take their first examination through the ECFMG.

Once you have your electronic token, you can go to MyERAS to register. After you have received your ID number through MyERAS, download the ERAS Document Submission Form (http://www.ecfmg.org/eras/index.html). Complete it and submit it with your documents to ensure direct delivery to the ECFMG's ERAS Department. Be sure to identify each of your documents with your AAMC ID or USMLE/ECFMG Identification Number and the document type (e.g., 0-123-457-6, Dean's Letter/MSPE, page 1). Write this identifying information on the *back* of your color photograph. After the ECFMG gets your Dean's letter/MSPE, color photograph, medical school transcript, and letters of recommendation, they will scan them into your file.

If your original medical school documents are not written in English, send only a high-quality copy of the translation. Be prepared to show program directors both the original-language documents and the translator's certificate at your interviews. Send good photocopies of your letters of recommendation (LORs). Keep the originals of all documents you send. Documents that the ECFMG submits to ERAS are stamped "Duplicate for ERAS use" and are shredded after they are scanned. Be sure to keep copies to use during the "scramble," in the event that you don't get a position in the Match.

The ECFMG automatically sends a "Status Report" to all residencies to which you apply. It lists your most current performance on the Clinical Skills Assessment (either "N/A" or a month/year when passed) and the date through which these results are valid. It also lists your passing score(s) on any tests administered through the ECFMG that are necessary for their certification. The USMLE transcript, which contains additional information including all the dates that you took the exam, is sent only to those programs you designate through ERAS.

Note: *All IMGs must obtain ECFMG Certification before starting a postgraduate training program.* For questions about IMG applications through ERAS that are not answered on the website, contact: eras-support@ecfmg .org. The ECFMG also sends out a free newsletter about ERAS that can be accessed or subscribed to at www.ecfmg.org/eras/erasnews.html. Technical questions about ERAS should be sent to the AAMC's website (www .aamc.org/eras).

Submitting Your Profile & Application

After you obtain your ID and password, you are ready to create your personal "**Profile.**" This contains your basic information, including contact information, social security number, NRMP Applicant Code, USMLE ID, and AOA (honorary) status. (IMGs list their visa type and ECFMG Certification status. IMGs can also apply through the ECFMG's "OASIS," see page 396.) This information can be entered piecemeal at any time during the application process. It *should be updated* with revised information, such as new phone numbers/addresses, AOA (honorary) induction, or changes in your visa status.

Once your contact information is entered, you can click on "My Application" at the MyERAS page to begin completing your "Common Application Form" (CAF). The information in your CAF is used to compile a standard résumé that is sent to program directors. This ensures that each residency program receives a résumé that contains the same information, displayed in exactly the same way, from each applicant.

Most applicants suggest that you print out the 12-page "MyERAS Application Worksheet (CAF)" and fill it in and check it for accuracy offline. This will make it much easier to complete your online CAF. Check all information carefully *before* you "certify" your CAF; once you certify it and submit it to the ERAS PostOffice for processing, it cannot be changed.

IMGs may indicate on their CAF that their medical school might not provide a Dean's letter or a transcript to the ECFMG.

Supporting Documents

The "My Documents" area of ERAS is used to create personal statements and a list of recommendation letter writers, and also to authorize the transmission of USMLE transcripts.

ERAS Personal Statement

Formatting the personal statement in ERAS can be tricky. Since the ERAS program only accepts basic computer formatting (ASCII text), any special fonts, characters, or formatting (such as italics, bold, apostrophes, quotation marks, and hard returns) will be deleted and often cause strange characters to appear in your ERAS personal statement. Many residency directors have received personal statements containing random letters and characters, truncated sentences, or one-word lines. To produce the best-looking ERAS personal statement, first create it using a word processor such as Microsoft Word or Corel Word Perfect.

After you have finished polishing your personal statement in the word processor, save it as a "plain text," "text-only," or "ASCII text format" file.

(The file name will appear with the extension ".txt".) Only after performing this step should you cut and paste the document into your ERAS application. An alternative is to type your personal statement directly into ERAS, but ERAS contains no spelling or grammar checker, so this can be risky.

If you produce more than one personal statement, give each one a unique title so you remember which one accompanies a particular application. ERAS automatically designates each statement as "PS1," PS2," etc. (If you delete one of these documents without sending it, ERAS omits that number.) You can use these numbers to track which personal statements residency programs have been downloaded via the ADTS.

Once a personal statement has been transmitted to a program, it cannot be edited. If you later find typos or need to make corrections, you should create another personal statement using a different name. This new document can then be "assigned" to any program to which you apply. The old one can be "de-assigned," although the program may already have downloaded and printed a hard copy of your original document. Using the "Program Selection Report" (from "My Reports" or "My Programs"), applicants can see a list of the programs and which personal statement has been assigned to each.

ERAS gives you the opportunity to write a very long (up to 32,000 characters, or about five pages) personal statement. Don't do this. *Limit your statement to one page.* While this may difficult to do, no one wants to read more than one page from any applicant. If a program requires specific information that is not included in your transcript, CAF, or other materials, attach it as an addendum to the personal statement you send them. IMGs may want to add specific information about their visa, Fifth Pathway, or ECFMG Certificate status. IMGs should also explain the absence of a transcript if their school will not supply one.

Since ERAS does not have a separate place for a résumé, if you wish to include one, attach this file to the end of each personal statement. Many residency directors, however, specifically request that a separate résumé not be included on ERAS, since they feel that the ERAS application contains all relevant information.

When you have finished putting a personal statement onto ERAS, print a copy for yourself using the "Print Personal Statement" button in MyERAS. If you need additional help understanding the instructions, go to www.aamc.org/students/eras/support/ by clicking the heading "My Documents."

Letters of Recommendation (LORs)

Enter the names of all the people who should get requests to write recommendation letters on your behalf in the section labeled "Letters of Recommendation." Even though the system will accept only *four* letters for each program, you do not need to limit the number of names you enter. After all, you may want to send different letters to different programs. The Dean's letter and transcript do *not* count as one of your four letters.

You need to deliver or send a request to all your letter writers. In addition, print out the ERAS form "LOR Cover Sheet/Instructions for U.S. Graduates" (or "Instructions for International Medical Graduates") and give it to them. If your school has special instructions, also include those. Be certain that you neatly fill in your identifying information in the space at the top of the standard ERAS cover letter and put the address for the Dean's office (or ECFMG) at the bottom—so the letter writer knows where to return it. These letters must be typed, so that they can easily be scanned. All letters should be addressed to "Dear Program Director." The remainder of the format is up to the writer. Letter writers must return *both* their recommendation letter and the cover sheet you sent them to either you or the Dean's office/ECFMG. These letters must *not* go directly to programs participating in ERAS.

As with all recommendation letters, if they don't quickly appear in your Dean's office or on the ADTS list as being sent, check with the letter writer to see if he or she has returned it.

IMGs applying to California programs also need to submit a copy of the "Applicant Evaluation Status Letter," issued by the Medical Board of California, www.medbd.ca.gov. This process takes several months. List "California Letter" as one of the recommendation letters. If you do not yet have the "final letter" from California, submit the temporary document they send you. When you receive the final document, send it to the ECFMG with a note attached saying that it replaces the temporary document.

IMGs should make good photocopies of their recommendation letters to send to the ECFMG. Note that the ECFMG stamps every document with "Duplicate for ERAS use" before scanning it into ERAS. This notifies the programs that the ECFMG cannot verify whether the document came from the applicant, the letter writer, or directly from the medical school.

Fifth Pathway students should send their Certificate as one of their recommendation letters.

Résumé

ERAS will not easily accommodate a personalized résumé in the system, but will generate one based on the information you provide in the CAF. If you want programs to receive your personalized résumé, you must mail it to them, take a copy with you to the interview, or send it through ERAS in place of a recommendation letter. (You can only do this if the program doesn't require that you send four letters, the maximum ERAS allows for each program.) However, sending it via ERAS is probably unnecessary unless you have a detailed history that ERAS information doesn't accurately reflect.

Photograph

While no longer required, a full-front view photograph is recommended "if you want your application to be complete." The photograph, which programs use as a visual aid, cannot be viewed by a program until you have been selected for an interview. You will probably be at a disadvantage if you fail to supply your Dean's office with a 2.5" by 3.5" (wallet size) color photo with your ID number written on the back. For more information on your photograph, see "A Picture?" on page 344.

Transcript & Dean's Letter/Medical Student Performance Evaluation (MSPE)

Your Dean's office will automatically send transcripts and the Dean's letter, which has been renamed the Medical Student Performance Evaluation (MSPE) to reflect its role as an evaluation rather than a recommendation, to ERAS for all registered residency applicants. They will be sent to all programs to which you apply, and programs can download transcripts as they are posted. Dean's letters/MSPEs for M.D. applicants will not be released by the ERAS PostOffice until November 1. Dean's letters/MSPEs for Osteopathic internships will not be held back by ERAS.

International medical students/graduates must send a copy of their transcript and Dean's letter/MSPE to the ECFMG. If these cannot be sent, either because your school does not produce them or because they are unavailable, indicate that on your CAF in the appropriate box. (At some non-U.S. schools, transcripts may be called mark sheets, time sheets, or hour sheets.) The documents must be no larger than approximately 8.5" x 14" (21 cm x 35 cm) so they will fit the scanner. Also, the ECFMG will scan only about five pages. If your transcript is longer, number the pages according to their order of importance and they will scan them in that order. Send copies made on a plain paper background. If they are on "security paper" with a background designed to make forgery difficult, the scanned image may be illegible.

Add Programs

At "Programs," you can choose between "Selected Programs" and "Applied to Programs." *Selected Programs* are those that you have reviewed, selected, and are currently assigning documents to, but that have not yet been sent your application. You can add or remove programs in the "Selected" area at any time. You can select, but not apply to, programs before you submit your CAF.

Applied to Programs are programs to which you have sent your application. Before you send materials to a program, be certain that you want to apply there—and that they participate in ERAS. Once you click on this area, an invoice appears. Your final bill reflects the number of programs to which you apply. Check it carefully, because fees paid to ERAS are not refundable!

While reviewing the lists of residency programs on ERAS, those that are "grayed out" do not participate and cannot be selected. Applicants must apply directly to those programs, as well as to those in non-participating specialties. Some programs may be listed even though they do not participate in ERAS. It is *your responsibility* to ascertain whether a program is currently an ERAS participant.

When you click on "Transmit," your application materials are immediately sent to your "Selected" programs. Once you do this, your "Selected" programs become "Applied to" programs and cannot be removed. Your Dean's office receives a list of these programs and, within their schedule, also sends their information to the programs. If you wish, you can add programs to the "Applied to" category at a later date. If you have paid for more programs than the number to which you have actually applied (see Costs, page 315), there is no additional fee to add programs later.

Osteopathic graduates can use the Program tab to search for and select Osteopathic internships by location and by type.

Assign Documents
The identical CAF, Dean's letter/MSPE, transcript, and photo will be sent to each program you apply to, but you can vary the recommendation letters and personal statements that will be sent. You can also decide whether a USMLE and/or COMLEX transcript is sent.

A maximum of four recommendation letters can be sent to any one residency program. If there is a letter writer who might help you more in one program than in another (for example, if you are applying in more than one specialty), be sure to assign their LOR to the appropriate programs. The same holds true for personal statements. You may want to individualize the statements for different programs based on their apparent interests, specialty, region of the country, etc. Some programs may also want specific information from applicants; the personal statement is where you can add it.

Once you press "Save," the LOR or personal statement assigned to a program is sent and you cannot change those specific documents. If you need to do so, you can de-assign the original document and assign a new one in its place. Remember, however, that the program may already have downloaded a copy of the original document and put it in your file. So they will have both the original and the new documents. (If you reassign documents that have not already been sent to them, they will not know.) Once a USMLE and/or COMLEX transcript is sent to a program, it cannot be de-assigned.

Applicant Data Tracking System (ADTS)

Use your ERAS ID number and password to access the ADTS through MyERAS to make sure your documents have been sent through the ERAS PostOffice. The ADTS report lists each program you applied to, when your Dean's office uploaded your documents, and when each residency program downloaded each document. Your Dean's office also has access to ADTS, although residency programs do not.

Questions

MyERAS has a detailed "Help" section that is available when you are logged in. For further information, go to the AAMC's ERAS webpage (http://www.aamc.org/students/eras/) and click on "Using MyERAS" for a breakdown of the process, or download the ERAS annual Applicant Manual under "Resources to Download". The support page also contains a path to breaking news about ERAS, which you can access by clicking on "Alerts." For technical questions you can't find answers to, e-mail the ERAS support staff at myeras@aamc.org. For faster service, include your name, AAMC ID, medical school, and return e-mail address.

International medical students/graduates can also send technical questions to the above address, but procedural problems should be sent to the ECFMG at eras-support@ecfmg.org. There is a useful FAQ page about ERAS on the ECFMG website at http://www.ecfmg.org/eras/index.html#15.

Computer Requirements

You do not need to own a computer, but you do need access to one that has 32 MB RAM and an Internet connection. The machine should have Netscape 4.77, MS Internet Explorer 5.0, AOL 5.0, or a later version of one of these browsers.

You also need a personal e-mail address to receive communications from residency directors, your Dean's office, ERAS (such as if you lose your password), and, for IMGs, the ECFMG. You will need to check your electronic mailbox, including your "bulk mail" folder, frequently. Many program directors use e-mail to ask additional questions and to offer interview slots to applicants. Individuals who use any of the free e-mail accounts must remove *all* their spam and junk mail filters.

Also, if you learn that most residency programs have downloaded your ERAS materials but you haven't heard from any of them, you may want to check to see if you received messages that your computer (or the university's computer system) rejected as "spam."

Cost

ERAS creates a "Processing Fee Invoice." Print this invoice only *after* you are ready to submit your application materials to programs, since the fee partly depends on the number of residencies applied to. *Once you pay your money, ERAS does not give refunds.*

U.S./Canadian medical students/graduates: For the 2006 cycle, the ERAS fee for medical students and graduates from U.S./Canadian schools is $60, which includes sending applications to up to 10 programs in a single specialty. Applying to between 11 and 20 programs costs $8 each, the next 10 cost $15 each, and, if you apply to more than 30 programs, each additional application costs $25. If you apply to programs in more than one specialty, you must pay an additional $60. For example, 11 Emergency Medicine programs and 3 Preliminary Internal Medicine programs will cost $128 (Emergency Medicine = $60 + $8; Internal Medicine = $60). Most students elect to have ERAS send all their USMLE or COMLEX (NBOME) transcripts to programs for a single $50 fee. For those who are arithmetically challenged, ERAS automatically computes the fees. Once the Dean's office transmits your file to the ERAS PostOffice via the Internet, all fees as detailed on the invoice must be paid within two weeks to avoid canceling your application.

International medical students/graduates: Before they can register with ERAS, IMGs must pay an extra (and separate) $75 fee for the ECFMG to act as their "designated Dean's office." After they receive your money, the ECFMG will send your ERAS "electronic token" by e-mail, scan and transmit your supporting documents, and transmit your ECFMG Status Report. To complete the application process, you must also later pay the ERAS application fees (minimum $60), the fee for your detailed USMLE score report ($50 for an ECFMG-provided transcript), and the NRMP registration fee ($65).

For billing purposes, all military programs, no matter which service or specialty, count as one specialty and require only one $60 ERAS fee for up to 10 programs. Any civilian programs also applied to would require another minimum $60 fee.

Payments can be made online using VISA credit or debit cards or a MasterCard credit card (click on "Purchase" in "My Programs" once you have your final program list). You can also send a check or money order to AAMC/ERAS, Attn. Accounting Department, 2450 N Street NW, Washington, DC 20037. Include your AAMC ID number, name, and the amount you owe.

Deadlines

Each residency program has its own deadline for receiving application information. Be certain that you know these deadlines and have your materials to ERAS before they are due. Once materials are in the ERAS Post-Office, they are normally sent to the programs within hours. Your Dean's office may take a bit longer to enter your reference letters and transcript into the system.

Transmitting & Receiving Information

Individual programs, rather than ERAS, set residency application deadlines. However, the ERAS "PostOffice" usually opens in mid-August and transmits all applications received to that time. After that, they transmit new applications daily. All Deans' letters/MSPEs that have been received are transmitted on November 1.

Get your photograph to your Dean's office as soon as possible so that it can be transmitted. Likewise, ask your letter writers to send their letters of recommendation to the Dean's office promptly. As the application season progresses, the folks responsible for submitting your information may get bogged down. The ERAS system also reportedly gets a bit slower with masses of application materials coming and going. If you have completed your online application as soon as possible, submitted your photograph, and had your recommendation letters submitted early, you should have rapid and smooth sailing. Even if there are glitches, they can be more easily fixed when both your school's ERAS staff and the folks at the AAMC have more time to work on them.

Dean's offices receive a confirmation of receipt for the application materials they send. To learn when your application was transmitted to the ERAS PostOffice and the date each residency program downloaded your file, go to the Applicant Document Tracking System (ADTS). Like the ERAS PostOffice, it begins operating at the same time each year (usually mid-August). If a program has delayed downloading your ERAS application, contact them directly to learn why.

International medical students/graduates: After completing (and proofreading) your application, make a backup copy of your materials and send them, with the ERAS Document Submission Form and your AAMC

ID or USMLE/ECFMG Identification Number handwritten on each document, to ECFMG-ERAS, P.O. Box 11746, Philadelphia, PA 19101-0746. For courier delivery, send to ECFMG-ERAS Documents, 3624 Market Street, Philadelphia, PA 19104-2685. Send only high-resolution, high-quality copies of your transcripts and Dean's letters. Keep the originals, since these materials will not be returned.

The Résumé

Your résumé, also known as a *curriculum vitae* or *c.v.*, is a word picture of yourself. Writing it will help you put your accomplishments "on paper" and identify activities needed for advancement in your specialty. Once you have your résumé, you will update and use it throughout your professional career. You should provide a copy to:

- Individuals who will write your reference letters.
- Outside programs at which you want to do electives.
- Programs where you must mail or fax your application.

Try to tailor the information you provide to the specialty for which you are applying. For example, extracurricular activities and community service may be less important to program directors in Surgery than to those in Family Medicine.

While a good résumé will not guarantee that you get into a residency, a poor résumé will certainly eliminate you from consideration. For more detailed information, see also *Résumés and Personal Statements for Health Professionals, 3rd ed.*, by James W. Tysinger, Ph.D. (Galen Press, Ltd.).

Misrepresentations

Only include true information in your résumé and personal statement. About 20% of residency applicants, and many more fellowship applicants, who list publications either falsely claimed authorship on a real paper or listed a non-existent paper. One study, for example, showed that nearly one-third of Gastroenterology fellowship applicants misrepresented their academic accomplishments. Residency directors know this. Using computer medical literature searches, programs can (and do) easily check listed publications. Such "misrepresentations" are often unintentional, and can occur when, for example, a faculty member with whom you conducted research tells you "Our study was published, and I recognized your contributions." In fact, the faculty member may have acknowledged you on the bottom of the first page and not on the author line. Consequently, it is dangerous for applicants to list any activity unless they can verify it with original documents.

Sometimes applicants misstate their manuscript's status because they do not know how to properly cite it. The Council of Residency Directors (Emergency Medicine) suggests the following guidelines:

1. **Published manuscript:** give full citation.
2. **Accepted manuscripts (in press):** list acceptance date and bring the acceptance letter to your interviews.
3. **Submitted manuscripts:** list submission date.
4. **Research experience (or manuscript in progress):** list research title/hypothesis, time period for the research, and research mentors.

Take a copy of all published works, acceptance letters, submitted articles with the submission letter, and letters from research mentors listing research dates to all your interviews. For presented papers, take a copy of the published abstract or, even better, a copy of the meeting's program.

"Headhunters" (recruiters) estimate that about one-third of résumés include lies. Many applicants think that they will be forgiven for embellishing their résumé. At least for residency applicants, forgiveness is rarely granted, and doctors' résumés are part of a paper trail that follows them wherever they go. Aside from any moral question, lying on application materials may result in not getting your desired residency position. It absolutely puts you at risk for immediate dismissal while you are a resident.

A few people each year try to enter residencies despite never having graduated from medical school; some succeed. Because of the notoriety given such cases, residency programs and state medical boards increasingly check on applicants using databanks run by the Federation of State Medical Boards, the American Medical Association, the ECFMG, and the AAMC.

Résumé Layout

Those using ERAS will have their résumé information entered in a generic style. However, you can also provide programs with your own more detailed and personalized résumé. Those not using ERAS must provide programs with a résumé.

When compiling your résumé, there are several rules to follow, and several pitfalls (Figures 12.2 and 12.5) to avoid:

1. **Emphasize your strengths.** Write the résumé so these aspects of your past are prominent.
2. **Be clear, concise, and accurate.** Unless you are extraordinary, one, or at most two, pages will suffice.

FIGURE 12.2
Résumé Disaster Areas

- Poor Organization
- Poor Grammar
- Handwritten
- Poor Photocopy
- More than Two Pages
- Lack of Name, Address, Telephone Number
- Narrative, Rather than Outline
- Misspellings of Any Kind
- Unexplained Time Periods
- Use of Onionskin Paper
- Exaggerations
- Insufficient Information

---

3. **Design your résumé to be pleasant to the eye**, clean, and uncluttered. (See "Résumé Graphics," page 326.)

4. **Use action words** (Figure 12.3) wherever possible. As Mark Twain said, the difference between the right word and the almost-right word is the difference between lightning and a lightning bug.

5. **Follow the standard layout** recommended in the checklist in Figure 12.4. Use the examples (Figures 12.6 to 12.8) when you design your own résumé. These examples are chronological résumés. This is the type preferred by most residency directors.

6. **Have it professionally typed**, or print it out only on a letter quality printer (inkjet or laser).

7. **Do not put "Résumé" or "Curriculum Vitae" at the top** of the document unless you think those reading it are idiots. Résumé formats are immediately obvious, and these words waste valuable space.

Some experts recommend that your first résumé is most easily organized using 3″ x 5″ cards (or their computer equivalent). Simply label one card for each of the topics in Figure 12.4 that applies to you. Then collect the information on each card (including names, dates, addresses, etc.) that you will need to complete the section. Put these cards in the order you want to see them on your résumé, and type the information onto your résumé.

After printing a sample copy, check it carefully for spelling errors. One medical student wrote, for example, "I am passed USMLE . . ." and "I would like to know weather . . ." As you might expect, he had a difficult time getting a position. Even if you are a native English speaker, have a literate person proofread your materials before you send them.

FIGURE 12.3

Action Words for Your Résumé

accelerated	developed	introduced	reorganized
accomplished	directed	invented	replaced
achieved	discovered	launched	represented
active member	distributed	led	researched
actively	edited	made	responsible for
adapted	effected	maintained	restored
adjusted	elected	managed	revised
administered	enlarged	modified	scheduled
advised	established	monitored	selected
analyzed	examined	motivated	served
arranged	excelled	negotiated	set up
assisted	expanded	obtained	sold
awarded	experienced in	operated	solved
built	focused	organized	streamlined
chairperson	formulated	participated in	strengthened
charted	founded	performed	studied
compiled	generated	persuaded	successfully
completed	guided	planned	supervised
conceived	headed	prepared	supplied
conducted	identified	presented	taught
constructed	implemented	produced	tested
controlled	improved	proficient at	trained
coordinated	increased	programmed	translated
counseled	influenced	promoted to	updated
created	initiated	proposed	won
delivered	installed	provided	wrote
demonstrated	instituted	published	
designed	instructed	ran	
determined	interpreted	recorded	

Only then should you decide on the graphic presentation you want. Once again, ask someone who knows you well to review it to be certain that you have portrayed yourself in the best possible manner. Figures 12.5 to 12.7 demonstrate some positive and negative examples. There is no perfect résumé style.

After further revisions, get some objective feedback, preferably from your adviser, your mentor, or the Dean of Students. If that is not possible, get someone to look at it who has experience with resident applicant résumés.

FIGURE 12.4
A Résumé Checklist

❏ Name[1]
❏ Address(es)
❏ Telephone Number(s)[2]
❏ Objective
❏ Publications
❏ Research
❏ Presentations
❏ Language/Computer Skills
❏ Honors & Awards
❏ Reference Statement
❏ Applicable Jobs
❏ Professional Memberships

❏ Extracurricular Activities[3]
❏ Personal[3]
  ❏ Birth Place & Date
  ❏ Marital Status
  ❏ Children
❏ Work Experience[4]
❏ Licenses & Certifications[5]
❏ Military[6]
❏ Education[7]
  ❏ Medical School
  ❏ Graduate School
  ❏ Undergraduate

1. If you have changed your name, be certain that there is a clear statement explaining why your name differs on your transcript, licenses, diplomas, etc. If at all possible, it is best to keep one "professional name" throughout your career, even if you plan on changing your name in a social context.

2. Include all mailing addresses, phone numbers, and e-mail addresses where you can be reached for the *next six months*.

3. Optional information. Include extracurricular activities only if they are extraordinary or applicable to medicine, such as working with the Ski Patrol or a volunteer ambulance service. Personal information can be supplied at your own discretion.

4. Include the dates that you held jobs. Other than military service, include only those jobs that you held for long periods of time, were applicable to medicine, or were full-time positions.

5. List currently held health-related licenses, such as R.N. (give states and dates), and health-related certifications, such as EMT, ACLS, ATLS, and PALS (give expiration dates).

6. The type of discharge that you received is legally privileged information. If it was anything less than honorable, don't include it.

7. Only include undergraduate and graduate school, medical school, and any other medically related course, such as an EMT or ACLS course. You have been out of high school a long time now, and no one is interested in that.

FIGURE 12.5

Sample Résumé—The Disaster

Don't you have a first name?

Isn't it obvious that this is your C.V.?

CURRICULUM VITAE

I. R. Smarte Phone/Fax/Cell phone numbers? E-mail address?

405 Campbell Ave. Washinton, DC 20043 ← Dates at this address?

Citizenship: USA ← Assumed, unless otherwise stated
Birthdate: October 27, 1967
← Who cares?

Irrelevant in all circumstances

Spouse's name: Les Smarte, I.R.S. Agent ← This will really win points!
Child: Matthew, age 4
Family:Mother: Helen S. Dingle, age 71, retired
Sister: Jean Folks, age 45, Prof. Poly Sci

Undergraduate education: Univ. Of Arizona, 1993
B.S. in Cell Biology
Honors: Phi Beta Kappa, Cum Laud Graduate. Spelling!
Extracurricular Activities: Pep Squad,
Marching Band, Biology Honorary, ← Which one?
Rescue Squad ← Which? Where? When?

Include only if your transcript is difficult to interpret

Post graduate ed: Univ. Of Cinti., ~~1987~~ 1997 Toxicology ← Spelling! Written corrections are sloppy!
Honors: Munroe Scholorship ← What is this?
Research/Publications: ``The Effect of a Sub-freezing Environment on Cellular Metabolism in Rats.'' (Thesis); Simons, G., Smarte, I.R., Sullivan, J.P. ``Cellular Inhibition of Rat Tail Growth in a Subfreezing Atmosphere.'' ← When & where were these published?

Med School-- U of MD, 2001 ← Spell out!
Honors: Sherk Scholarship, Ama stud rep ← Capitalize!
physiology, social/prventatave med, OB/GYN.
Electives: forensic sci, experimental sugr lab

Employment: 93/95 US Air Force, Staff Sgt.; ← State that job was medically related
91-93: carpenter (part-time) ← Irrelevant

Interests: Radical Student Alliance; Messianic Religious Revival ← Irrelevant Counterproductive

Why list references?

Referemces: Fr. John X. Anlen: Our Lady of Sorrow, ← Spelling! Priest
31 Ensel Street, Baltimore, MD ← Zip Code?
Michelle Rout, M.D., Radiology Resident, ← Resident
U. of AZ, 1501 N. Campbell Ave., Tucson, AZ 85724
Sally Friendly: Director, Messianic
Student Revival, 1 North St., Reuther, MD 20933 ← Friend

Counterproductive References

* Sloppy & Inconsistent Formatting *

FIGURE 12.6
A Sample Résumé—Style #1

_____ **IRENE R. SMARTE** _____

405 N. Campbell Ave.   5573 Chillum Place, Apt. D
Washington, DC 20043   Reading, PA 19601
(202) 555-9087   (610) 555-1836
e-mail: IRSmarte@medstud.net   [Use: 11/06–3/07]
[Use: 8/06–10/06 & 4/07–6/07]

OBJECTIVE   Superior training in Radiology which will give me the basis from which to practice in either the academic or the private sector for the next forty years.

EDUCATION   M.D., University of Maryland School of Medicine
Baltimore, MD
Sept. 2003–June 2007 (anticipated)
M.S., University of Cincinnati
Cincinnati, OH
Major: Toxicology
July 2001–June 2003
B.S., University of Arizona
Tucson, AZ
Major: Cellular Biology
Sept. 1995–June 1999

HONORS/ AWARDS   *Medical School:*   Sherk Scholarship (Most promising student in the sophomore class)
Class Vice-President: Junior Year
Student Representative, AMA, 2006–2007

Graduate School: Munroe Scholarship (2 years)

Undergraduate: Phi Beta Kappa
Dann-Victor Scholarship (2 years)
Cum Laude Graduate
President, Biology Honorary, 1998–1999

MILITARY EXPERIENCE   Staff Sergeant, Medical Service Corps
U.S. Air Force, 1999–2001; Honorable Discharge
Responsible for administering a 40-person Radiology department at a regional hospital.

PUBLICATIONS   Simons, G; Smarte, IR; Sullivan, JP: "Cellular Inhibition of Rat Tail Growth in a Subfreezing Atmosphere." *Journal of Arctic Biology.* 2004;3(1):12-16.

RESEARCH   "The Effect of a Subfreezing Environment on Cellular Metabolism in Rats." (M.S. Thesis) Primary Investigator: Prof. G. Simons, Ph.D.

ACTIVITIES   Member, Wheaton Rescue Squad
(Ambulance and Heavy Rescue)

PERSONAL   U. S. citizen; excellent health

REFERENCES   Furnished upon request

FIGURE 12.7
A Sample Résumé—Style #2

This is a slightly different style than the résumé in Figure 12.6. Some information has been purposely omitted. Other information has been combined. Two new sections have been added for you to use as an example.

IRENE R. SMARTE

405 N. Campbell Ave.
Washington, DC 20043
(202) 555-9087
e-mail: IRSmarte@medstud.net

OBJECTIVE
Superior training in Radiology which will give me the basis from which to practice in either the academic or the private sector over the span of my career.

EDUCATION
M.D., *University of Maryland School of Medicine*, Baltimore, Maryland
September 2003–June 2007 (anticipated)
- Sherk Scholarship (Most promising student in the sophomore class)
- Class Vice-President: Junior Year
- Student Representative, AMA, 2006–2007

M.S., *University of Cincinnati*, Cincinnati, Ohio
Major: Toxicology; July 2001–June 2003
- Munroe Scholarship (2 years)

B.S., *University of Arizona*, Tucson, Arizona
Major: Cellular Biology; September 1995–June 1999
- Phi Beta Kappa
- Dann-Victor Scholarship (2 years)
- *Cum Laude* Graduate
- President, Biology Honorary, 1998–99

MILITARY EXPERIENCE
Staff Sergeant, Medical Service Corps
U.S. Air Force, 1999–2001; Honorable Discharge
Responsible for administering a 40-person Radiology department at a regional hospital.

RESEARCH & PUBLICATIONS
Simons G, Smarte IR, Sullivan JP: "Cellular Inhibition of Rat Tail Growth in a Subfreezing Atmosphere." *Journal of Arctic Biology.* 2004;3(1):12-16.

PROFESSIONAL ORGANIZATIONS
- American Medical Student Association
- American College of Radiology, Student Member

LANGUAGES
- Spanish (fluent written and spoken)
- Russian (written only)

EXTRACURRICULAR ACTIVITIES
- Member, Wheaton Rescue Squad (Ambulance and Heavy Rescue)

REFERENCES
Furnished upon request

FIGURE 12.8
Two Other Acceptable Résumé Formats

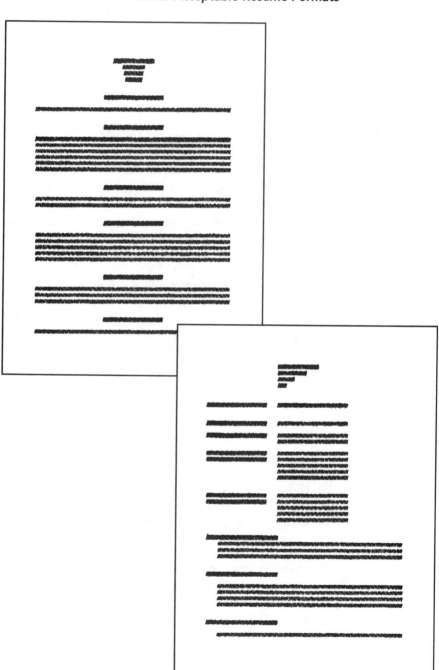

If you just can't get your act together, another option is to pay a commercial service to produce your résumé. You will, however, still have to provide the information, tell them how you want it organized, and proof it for accuracy. (Most of them proofread it for the spelling of common words.) Résumé services can be found in all large cities and around most universities. Their charges vary by location and the amount of work they need to do.

Résumé Graphics

Avoid having a résumé that looks like every other résumé in circulation! Your résumé must have a clean and distinctive appearance. Like all of your written communications, it must attract attention. Essentially, it must be more attractive than the competition. To accomplish this, you must pay attention to the paper size and appearance, margins and spacing, type size and style, and layout. The key to an effective résumé is to plan it carefully, and make sure the final product reflects the planning that went into it.

Paper

Most applicants use white bond paper. Your résumé will stand out if you use something different. Gray, ivory, or white paper with a textured or "pebble" finish will stand out among the throng of résumés. The weight of the paper is also important. Use 20- or 24-pound paper. If you plan to print your résumé on both sides of one sheet of paper, which is actually not a good idea, be sure that the paper is opaque enough so that the printing will not show through.

Paper Size

Again, most of the résumés received by residency directors are on standard 8½″ x 11″ paper. Several other sizes are available which may serve to help your résumé stand out. The most acceptable is the "Monarch" size of stationery (7¼″ x 10½″). Another possibility is using an 11″ x 17″ sheet, which will fold over into an 8½″ x 11″ folio. You can then put your name, address, e-mail address, and phone number on the outside cover.

Margins & Spacing

No matter how good your résumé is, it will look cheap, rushed, and cramped if you do not leave an ample margin. When using a standard 8½″ x 11″ sheet of paper, leave side margins of 1″ to 1½″. The space at the top of the page should be at least 1½″, and at the bottom at least 1″. If you will be using Monarch paper, leave ¾″ to 1″ margins on either side of the page. A minimum for the top and bottom margins is 1″.

Type Size & Style

Type comes in different sizes, known as "pitch," which designates the number of characters per inch. Either 11- or 12-pitch is adequate for most résumés, since it is easily readable and available in most printer fonts. If you use Monarch paper, 12-pitch type is recommended. Type also differs in height. Differing heights, known as "points," can also be used in the résumé.

Various styles of type (fonts), such as Pica, Elite, and Roman, are available. Some variety can be added to your résumé by altering these type styles appropriately. This technique is most effective when used for the captions and subheadings. Make sure that all styles are complimentary to those used for the main body of your résumé. Boldface, underlining, italics, and asterisks or bullets (circles) can also, if used sparingly, highlight important areas of your résumé. But don't get carried away and use too many font sizes and styles—they just distract the reader!

Laser Printers

Word processors and laser printers can produce amazing variations in type size and style within a document. If you have the requisite knowledge and software, you can design a magnificent résumé. If you don't though, you will need to go to a professional—including the secretaries in your adviser's or Dean's office—to get your résumé printed in this manner.

The Personal Statement

The personal statement requested by many residency programs causes more anguish among applicants than almost anything else in the application process. A great deal of time and effort is often put into these epistles—and, in general, it is mostly wasted. Although some program directors carefully read applicants' personal statements (especially those in primary care specialties), many use personal statements only to eliminate those individuals who clearly stand out as being: (1) relatively illiterate, (2) pompous or tactless, or (3) outside the mainstream of physicians in the specialty or institution.

The key to writing a good personal statement is to *be honest, but not shy* about trumpeting your virtues. Many students find this hard to do. The elements of a "safe and sane" personal statement include:

> *Section 1: Why do you want to go into the specialty?* Briefly explain what has drawn you to the specialty. If there was one particular event that stands out, describe it. Your trait analyses from Chapter 4 may help you out. Do not state that you are interested in the field primarily because of either the monetary rewards you

anticipate or the way in which it fits your lifestyle. These reasons are usually considered evidence of a shallow personality and a sloppy decision-making process.

Section 2: What do you intend to do during your career in the specialty? Be general. In a community hospital program, it is always safe to say that you are planning on a primarily clinical career with some clinical research and teaching. This question may be difficult to answer in some high-powered academic centers where there is a palpable rift between the researcher–physicians and the physician–occasional researchers. You may want to tailor this part of your personal statement to the institution to which it is being sent, as well as to your particular interests. Do not state, however, that you want to be a small-town practitioner if you are applying to a high-powered research program, or vice versa.

Section 3: Other interests. What else do you do with your life? Be brief. Discussing your family, sports, and community activities is safe. This section of your statement should be the shortest.

Additional points that may be addressed in the statement include explanations of any major problems, deficiencies, or questions that might arise after a review of your application or transcript. You might want to mention something particularly outstanding from your undergraduate career or your life outside school. *Avoid discussing politics or religion.* Neither has any place in any of your application materials. Tysinger's *Résumés and Personal Statements for Health Professionals* (see *Annotated Bibliography*) contains special instructions for addressing these issues, as well as numerous examples of personal statements.

The personal statement format (Figure 12.9) is now constrained by the limitations of ERAS (unless you apply to a specialty or program that does not participate). You still can make it interesting, and even enjoyable to read. One applicant, for example, had a five-paragraph statement, each

---

FIGURE 12.9

Format for Personal Statement

One Page

Product of Laser or Inkjet Printer

Proper Grammar, Spelling, and Composition
(Get help with this if you need it.)

paragraph beginning with a key phrase that had been said to her and that related to her specialty of choice (e.g., "Aren't you scared to take care of all those really sick people?"). There are many other interesting ways to write the personal statement. The keys are to make it

- short enough to read easily
- in readable English without spelling or grammatical errors
- based on one or more stories that illustrate your life
- interesting

As with all other materials you send to programs, review your statement for content and format before you have the final copy typed. Just as with the résumé, there is no one perfect style.

Occasionally, students ask whether they should try to make their personal statement unusual enough to stand out. Literate and witty are the best ways to make a personal statement get noticed. One applicant, for example, vividly wrote, "Activity is my oxygen." The faculty remembered her!

Generally though, you take a big risk by writing a very unusual personal statement. Remember that physicians, in general, are conservative animals. Anything odd or unusual will ordinarily be viewed negatively. "Unusual" in a personal statement is normally defined by those reading the statement as something that is cute, flippant, or crass. That is not the impression you want to create. Of course, some applicants have gotten interviews and even positions based, in part, on unusual personal statements. But it is rare. Unless your life story itself is unusual, stick with standard and boring.

Most personal statements will be in simple paragraph format and printed in the ERAS application, which allows little flexibility. Those not using ERAS may want to use an alternative format for their statements. An example of another format is shown in Figure 12.10.

Reference Letters

The reference letters that you have sent to residency programs are reflections of you in other people's eyes. They play an important part in getting you a residency position. Obtaining good reference letters, however, takes advance planning, hard work, and initiative. If you are willing to make the effort, the steps outlined below will help you to get the best possible reference letters. They will also help you make the most of the ones you do get.

FIGURE 12.10

Alternative Style for a Personal Statement

MAXWELL I. SMARTE

— Personal Statement —

hard working   I grew up in Minnesota, spending summers on my parents' farm. It was here that I learned the value of hard work.

mature   At age 18, I joined the U.S. Air Force. Rising to the rank of Staff Sergeant, this was a period of personal growth. Four years in the service as a surgical technician and OR supervisor, both stateside and in Japan, gave me a more stable view of life.

academic &
clinical skills   After completing undergraduate school in three years with a Chemistry major, I entered medical school, where I scored 212 on Step 1 of the USMLE and achieved Honors in Surgery and in Pediatrics. I spent many evenings working with one of our local Pediatric Surgeons.

career goals   The latter activity convinced me that Pediatric Surgery will provide me with what I want from a career in medicine— curing sick children, caring for those with both acute and chronic diseases, and involvement in the broadest type of General Surgery.

After residency, I would like to work at a major tertiary care teaching hospital. There I could combine practice, teaching, and research. My choice of residency reflects these long-term goals.

summary   In summary, I am a hard working, mature individual who has a clear vision of a career in Pediatric Surgery. Both my experiences and training have reinforced my dedication to this dynamic and exciting field of medicine.

Sincerely,

Maxwell I. Smarte

Dean's Letter

Each year, medical schools send about a quarter of a million Dean's letters, costing each school from $25,000 to $50,000. This averages out to more than 17 letters per student, although some students requested that more than 100 letters be sent! Each school has a standard format for these letters. Most are relatively long and detailed, averaging 3.5 single-spaced pages. The material that they contain, however, can vary greatly (Figure 12.11).

Note that ERAS now refers to the Dean's Letter as the Medical Student Performance Evaluation (MSPE). This is supposed to better reflect its role as an evaluation rather than a recommendation. So, if you are asked for "an MSPE," they just mean a Dean's Letter.

Dean's letters usually include some personal background information about the student, with reference to his or her undergraduate experience. They then detail the student's preclinical and clinical course work. Most letters include direct quotes from the student's performance evaluations.

Many schools create charts based on the Association of American Medical Colleges' guidelines (Figure 12.12) that show a student's performance on clinical clerkships compared with that of his or her classmates or

FIGURE 12.11

Frequency of Appearance of Information in Dean's Letters

Type of Information	% Never	% Sometimes	% Always
School-Related Extracurricular Activities	1	10	89
Academic Background Prior to Med School	3	9	88
Research Experience	1	13	86
Interpersonal Skills	1	19	79
Responsibility to Others*	3	30	67
Personality Descriptions	10	38	52
Personal Background Prior to Med School	6	49	45
Work Background Prior to Med School	3	55	42
Non-professional Interests (Hobbies)	10	50	40
Class Rank	66	5	29
Extent of Contact with Student	38	40	22
Statements Regarding Professional Growth	11	70	19
Statements Regarding Personal Growth**	14	74	12
Reasons for Choosing Specialty	50	38	12
Reasons for Choosing Medicine	36	54	10

*Defined as acceptance of responsibility for one's own actions, keeping agreements, and meeting obligations.

**Defined as sense of independence, purpose, and maturity.

Adapted from: Hunt DD, MacLaren CF, Scott CS, et al.: A follow-up study of the characteristics of dean's letters. *Academic Medicine*. 2001;75(7):727-33.

FIGURE 12.12

AAMC's Template for Medical Student Performance Evaluation

Template

Medical Student Performance Evaluation
for

_____
Student's Legal Name

_____
Month, Date, Year

Identifying Information

_____is a fourth-year student at_____in_____.
Student's Legal Name   Medical School   City, State

Unique Characteristics

(Provide narrative information about distinguishing characteristics exhibited and any significant challenges or hardships encountered by the student during medical school)

Academic History

Date of Expected Graduation from Medical School:

Date of Initial Matriculation in Medical School:
_____
Month, Date, Year
_____
Month, Date, Year

Please explain any extensions, leave(s) of absence, gap(s),
or break(s)in the student's educational program.
          or ❑ Not applicable

For transfer students: ❑ Not applicable
Date of Initial Matriculation in Prior Medical School:
                                                   _____
Date of Transfer from Prior Medical School: Month, Date, Year
                                                   _____
                                                   Month, Date, Year

For dual/joint/combined degree students: ❑ Not applicable
Date of Initial Matriculation in Other Degree Program:
                                                   _____
Date of Expected Graduation from Other Degree Program: Month, Date, Year
                                                   _____
Type of Other Degree Program: Month, Date, Year
                                                   _____
                                                   Degree, Major

Was this student required to repeat or otherwise   ❑ No
remediate any coursework during his/her   ❑ Yes - Please explain:
medical education?

Was this student the recipient of any adverse actions(s) ❑ No
by the medical school or its parent institution?   ❑ Yes - Please explain:

FIGURE 12.12 (continued)

Academic Progress

Preclinical/Basic Science Curriculum:
(Provide narrative information about overall, not course-specific, performance)

Core Clinical Clerkships and Elective Rotations:
(Provide a narrative evaluation about each core clinical clerkship and elective rotation taken in chronological order)

Example I
(when school policy requires that students complete all core clerkships prior to enrollment in electives)

Example II:
(when school policy permits interspersal of core clerkships and electives)

Clerkship 1:

Clerkship 2:

Clerkship 3:

Clerkship 4:

Clerkship 5:

Clerkship 6:

Elective 1:
(Provide location if an "away" elective rotation)

Elective 2:
(Provide location if an "away" elective rotation)

Clerkship 1:

Clerkship 2:

Elective 1:
(Provide location if an "away" elective rotation)

Clerkship 3:

Clerkship 4:

Elective 2:
(Provide location if an "away" elective rotation)

Clerkship 5:

Clerkship 6:

Summary

(Provide a summative assessment, in narrative format, of the student's comparative performance, relative to his/her peers, in medical school, including information about any school-specific categories used in differentiating among levels of student performance)

_____
Signature of School Official

_____
Name of School Official

_____
Title

_____
E-mail address

FIGURE 12.12 (continued)

For purposes of illustration only; school-specific course and clerkship names, grading systems, and categories of overall performance will vary by school.

Appendix A
Graphic Representations of Comparative Performance in Preclinical/Basic Science Coursework

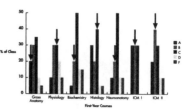

Appendix B
Graphic Representations of Comparative Performance in Core Clinical Clerkships

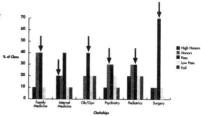

Appendix C
Graphic Representations of Comparative Performance in Professional Attributes
(Final recommendations expected by 2006)

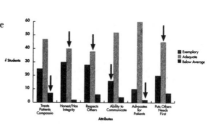

Appendix D
Graphic Representations of Overall Comparative Performance in Medical School

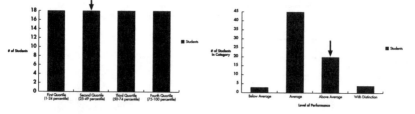

FIGURE 12.12 (continued)

Appendix E
Medical School Information Page

_____
Medical School Name

_____
City, State

Special programmatic emphases, strengths, mission/goal(s) of the medical school:

Special characteristics of the medical school's educational program:

Average length of enrollment (initial matriculation to graduation) at the medical school:

_____
Years   Months

Description of the evaluation system used at the medical school:

Medical school requirements for successful completion of USMLE Step 1, 2 (check all that apply):
USMLE Step 1:   USMLE Step 2:
❑ Required for promotion   ❑ Required for promotion
❑ Required for graduation   ❑ Required for graduation
❑ Required, but not for promotion/graduation   ❑ Required, but not for promotion/graduation
❑ Not required   ❑ Not required

Medical school requirements for successful completion of Objective/Observed Structured Clinical Evaluation (OSCE) at medical school. OSCEs are used for (check all that apply):
❑ Completion of course
❑ Completion of clerkship
❑ Completion of third year
❑ Graduation
❑ Other:_____

Utilization of the course, clerkship, or elective director's narrative comments in composition of the MSPE. The narrative comments contained in the attached MSPE can best be described as (check one):
❑ Reported exactly as written
❑ Edited for length or grammar, but not for content
❑ Edited for content or included selectively

Utilization by the medical school of the AAMC "Guidelines for Medical Schools Regarding Academic Transcripts." This medical school is:
❑ Completely in compliance with Guidelines' recommendations
❑ Partially in compliance with Guidelines' recommendations
  Exceptions:
❑ Not in compliance with Guidelines' recommendations

Description of the process by which the MSPE is composed at the medical school (including number of school personnel involved in composition of the MSPE).

Students are permitted to review the MSPE prior to its transmission:
❑ Yes
❑ No

Reprinted with permission. Association of American Medical Colleges' Dean's Letter Advisory Committee. *A Guide to the Preparation of the Medical Student Performance Evaluation.* (pamphlet). Washington, DC: AAMC, 2002, pp. 5-8.

a compilation of several recent classes. Some also include the student's results on the Objective Structured Clinical Examination (OSCE), a standardized measure of clinical performance now being used at more than 60 U.S. medical schools.

There are multiple methods used to describe a student's position within his or her class. Most (about 82%) Dean's letters include a histogram or chart that shows a student's grades in comparison with those of his or her classmates.

About 16% of the letters give the student's exact class rank. The lack of class ranking can hurt top candidates who apply for very competitive programs, since it appears that residency faculty give top-ranked individuals from "average" medical schools preference over unranked students from "top" schools. Many more letters (about 43%) give a general description of a student's position in their class.

To avoid the overblown syntax used in many recommendation letters, some schools now give a numerical breakdown of the rankings they use. For example, the top 10% of graduates (from this year or recent years) may be rated "outstanding," while the next 25% of graduates are rated "excellent." There is no question in anyone's mind where you stand (at the bottom of the class) if you get a "satisfactory" overall evaluation.

Up to half of all Dean's letters do not include information about a student's failing grades, marginal performance, leaves of absence, or even the need to repeat entire years of study. Official transcripts, however, often have this information, so the discrepancy simply reflects negatively on the letter writer and the school.

While these letters usually carry the Dean of Students' signature, 41% of schools use multiple letter writers, including subsidiary deans, administrative personnel, faculty committees, and individual faculty advisers. It is helpful to know the system at your school in case you are allowed to supply additional information. Your Dean's office will be happy to explain the system they use.

As a matter of policy, as well as common courtesy, 88% of medical schools show students their Dean's letter before they are sent out. *Your first responsibility* in regard to your Dean's letter is to *carefully review it.* Check it for mistakes. But more important, check to make sure that all good evaluations, special honors, awards, and activities have been mentioned. If there are problems or discrepancies in the letter, bring them to the Dean's attention at once. This letter will be used not only when you apply for a residency position, but also in the future when you are looking for employment after residency.

Virtually all residency programs require a Dean's letter before they invite applicants for an interview. The letters are not always a big help to residency faculty in screening applicants; however, they do serve as a gross measure of a student's achievements compared with his or her classmates. A group who reviewed Dean's letters from all U. S. medical schools felt that nearly half failed to provide either an adequate format for locating necessary information or the information itself. Nearly one-half of Pediatrics residency directors and about one-third of those in Family Practice say that they do not use the Deans' letters when making decisions about whom to interview.

The medical school deans and faculty who write the Dean's letters want all their graduates to match into the best possible residencies. They are also unreasonably threatened by a fear of tort litigation if they are too candid about a student's performance. The writer's underlying theme is the old adage, "If you can't say something nice, don't say anything at all." A letter to the *New England Journal of Medicine* once remarked that Adolf Hitler's Dean's letter might have read, "A natural leader . . . good communication skills . . . likes to find solutions to problems." The result is a bland, positive, often oblique, and incomplete picture of a graduate.

Even with all the letter's drawbacks, experienced residency directors know that if they read between the lines, the Dean's letters are an effective way of screening candidates. They look for words like "enthusiastic" (manic?), "organized" (obsessive-compulsive?), "colorful" (bizarre?), or "active social life" (flirt?). Letters that dwell on a candidate's dress and punctuality suggest that the author is hunting for something nice to say. They rarely are as explicit as are the comments heard about applicants in conversation (Figure 12.13). Finally, the Dean's letter, in combination with a transcript and a phone call, is a good method of eliminating any charlatans posing as medical students. (Yes, they really are out there.)

It is particularly disturbing when one or two schools each year cannot seem to get their Dean's letters out on time. In recent years, the schools where this has happened have been among the best in the country. Those who suffered were the medical students who did not get interview spots (most residencies only have a limited number) and therefore did not get to select from many of their top program choices.

Thus, *your second responsibility* in regard to your Dean's letter is to *keep track of when it is supposed to go out.* United States medical school Deans have agreed to a uniform date of November 1—before which no Dean's letters are to be mailed or sent via ERAS—for current medical students. (Nearly half of all graduating medical students report that programs are requesting these letters before November 1. Some Deans bypass the spirit

---

FIGURE 12.13

Disparaging Comments about Applicants
(but too witty for most faculty)

- "Works well when under constant supervision and cornered like a rat in a trap."

- "He would be out of his depth in a puddle."

- "Technically sound, but socially inept."

- "This young lady has delusions of adequacy."

- "He has the wisdom of youth and the energy of old age."

- "The nursing staff would follow him anywhere, but only out of morbid curiosity."

- "This student has reached rock bottom and shows signs of starting to dig."

- "When she opens her mouth, it is only to change whichever foot was previously in there."

- "He sets low personal standards and then consistently fails to achieve them."

---

of this requirement by announcing that they are willing to supply verbal information to program directors prior to the November 1 date.) The November date gives the Dean's offices plenty of time to write the letters. Make sure that *your* Dean's letter has been completed and is ready to be sent out by ERAS or mail on November 1. (If you have already graduated from medical school, the rules permit your old Dean's letter to be sent whenever you request it.)

Your third responsibility, if you are not using ERAS or CAS, is to supply the Dean with a correct list of program names and addresses in a timely manner. If you don't do this, it does not matter how good the letter is, or how timely the school was in getting it ready. If it cannot be sent for want of an address, you still lose.

Other Reference Letters
Whom to Ask
Most of the reference letters you will send to residency programs will come from those individuals you have personally asked to write them. It is essential for you to know whom to ask.

Residency directors know that these letters usually contain glowing references, so the more specific the authors can be—based on actually observing you or at least getting specific reports from other faculty or residents—the better the letters are viewed.

The Ideal Reference

The ideal reference letter is from an individual who is well-known to program directors in the field—a nationally recognized figure in the specialty of choice, who: (1) has worked with you clinically, (2) thinks you are a "star", and (3) came from at least one of the institutions to which you are applying. If the individual works at one of the specialty's residency programs, it is optimal if their letter says that you have been strongly encouraged to apply to his or her program. All this may be difficult to achieve in one letter. But you should think of such a reference as the "gold standard."

Other Clinical Faculty

Other good reference sources are faculty with whom you have worked clinically and who thought you did a great job. Look for those clinical rotations where you did "Honors" work to get these letters. But don't stray too far from your area of interest. Getting letters from a Psychiatry attending will not be too effective if you are applying for a Radiology position. If you have cultivated a mentor early on, whether or not he or she is in your desired specialty, it might be useful to have him or her write a letter for you. If your mentor has worked with you clinically (and if they haven't, it is *your* fault), his or her opinion will often carry a great deal of weight.

Preclinical Instructors

How about your preclinical instructors? Weak! Unless you are applying to Pathology, Public Health, or a very heavily research-oriented program these letters should only be used in addition to any required reference letters. Everyone can tell how well you did in Anatomy by your grade. The clinical programs want to know how well you treated live patients.

Researchers

"But I've done research," you say. "Can't I get a letter from my research preceptor?" Again, unless you are going into an area where this particular research will be central to your training, such a letter should be considered only as additional support. In general, medical students participating in research are used as "scut puppies." They frequently contribute very little except brute labor. Often they actually have little contact with the research director, and consequently, that individual may know very little about their clinical abilities.

Counterproductive References

Do not get letters from residents, friends, relatives, clergymen, politicians, or patients. You think I'm being funny? Not a bit. I have personally received reference letters for residency applicants from individuals in all these categories. Letters from these sources normally do not help your application. They may, in fact, be detrimental. Residency directors are interested in how well you will do in their program. They want consistent information from reputable, knowledgeable sources. That means your teachers. "If she can't get these letters, there must be something wrong with her," they say. Don't make them think that!

When to Ask

Don't be a wimp! If you want a letter from a particular individual, ask for it. But ask at the right time and in the right way. When is the right time? If you are on a clinical service with the individual, ask while you are on the service, or soon afterwards. Don't wait until six months or a year later. No matter how great a job you did, the faculty member's memory of you will fade with time. Ask if the letter can be drafted now, saying that you will give him or her the list of programs to send the letter to later.

If it is from a mentor or adviser, ask for a reference letter during a counseling session. If someone has arbitrarily selected your adviser, first think about whether he or she knows you well enough to write a letter.

If the letter you want is from a faculty member in your desired specialty, you will get it either because you have been working with the individual for some time (volunteer, fellowship, etc.) or because of your performance during a clinical rotation. If it is due to the former, just ask. If the latter, do some investigation before you start any clinical work in the department. With whom will you be working? Does this individual meet the qualifications you need for a reference? If not, is there a way of switching the schedule so you can work with someone who will be a good reference? Once you select the individual or individuals, let them know early in the rotation that you are interested in their specialty and you would like them to write you a reference letter if they think you have done an excellent job by the end of the rotation. This motivates both of you. You will know that extra scrutiny is coming your way from the faculty members, and the faculty members will pay extra attention to your performance.

How to Ask

Several years ago, I received a scrawled letter from a student who had rotated through our department some months before. Addressed to "Residency Director," it asked, "Dear Sir: Please write a letter of reference to:" and proceeded to list a number of programs. There was no return address.

Seeing no way to refuse, and personally feeling that the student had done, at best, an adequate job during his rotation, I wrote the following letter: "Mr. Student did a clinical rotation with us in July. He performed adequately." This, if you haven't guessed, is a very negative letter. I don't know if this particular student ever did match in our specialty, but his discourtesy, not to mention lack of insight and poor clinical aptitude, certainly did not help his chances of getting the residency he desired.

Don't send blind letters or coded messages. Ask for a reference letter directly. But phrase it in such a way that neither you nor the faculty member will be saddled with either a negative or a neutral (read: "negative") letter. One way of doing this is to ask if the faculty member "would feel comfortable writing me a strong letter of support?" If the answer is anything other than strongly affirmative, look elsewhere. Before he retired, one of our wisest and most experienced faculty members, Dr. Douglas Lindsey, offered to write letters for every medical student. He wrote them honestly and then showed the student the letter. It was up to the student to decide whether it was sent. This was an excellent policy of a great teacher; unfortunately, it was probably unique.

One way of circumventing the problem of a poor reference letter is to ask for a copy of the letter for your files. This gambit is somewhat tricky. If you firmly believe that the individual you have asked will write a superlative letter but will not give you a copy, go ahead—at some risk. If the individual agrees to give you a copy of the letter, then you stand a good chance of, at least marginally, upgrading the quality of the letter by discussing the content with the writer. A very few physicians make it a policy to send copies of the reference letters they write to the individuals for whom they write them. In the business world, this is standard practice and common courtesy. Too bad it isn't yet a widespread practice within the medical profession.

Once a faculty member has agreed to write a reference letter for you, hand them a nice folder containing:

1. A copy of your personal statement.
2. A copy of your current résumé.
3. Any official forms that must be included with the letter.
4. A list of elements of reference letters (see Figure 12.14).
5. A page with your name, the date you requested the letter(s), the address(es) of the recipient(s) [if you know them], and the date it is due.
6. A stamped, addressed envelope for your copy.

FIGURE 12.14

Elements of a Reference Letter

It is very useful to include the following items in reference letters for applicants to residency programs:

A. Extent of Letter Writer's Contact with Student
1. How long and intense was the contact
2. Clinical or non-clinical
3. Provide details of any specific incidents that stand out

B. Scholastic Record
1. Standing in graduating class
2. Honors/commendations in courses
3. Other honors

C. Medical Abilities
1. Interaction with patients
2. Ability to synthesize information (problem solving)
3. Diagnostic ability
4. Physical examination ability
5. Laboratory use and test interpretation
6. Technical skills
7. Use of pharmacological agents
8. Clarity of oral presentations
9. Clarity/completeness of charts
10. Knowledge of medical literature

D. Personal Characteristics
(List strongest points first.)
1. Relations with peers, faculty, ancillary staff
2. Communication skills
3. Respect for others
4. Willingness to assume responsibility
5. Ability to recognize physical limitations
6. Dependability; consistency
7. Integrity; moral and ethical qualities
8. Initiative; industriousness
9. Motivation; interest; enthusiasm
10. Maturity
11. Flexibility
12. Sense of humor

E. Overall Impression of Student
1. Rating compared with other students
2. Would you want him/her in your program

---

7. Enough stamped envelopes for the recipients. If you are using ERAS or another computerized application service, you will need to address only one envelope—to your Dean's office. If you are applying to programs that don't use computerized applications, you will need an envelope for each program.

Giving them this packet will make it easier for them to produce the letter and show them that you "have your act together."

If you do happen to get a reference letter that isn't glowing, don't panic. You have one card left to play. If the letter has not yet been sent out, don't give the author any program addresses to which he or she can send it. If you have followed the plan above, you should get a copy of the letter long before you yourself even know where you are going to apply. You will also have plenty of time to collect other, more complimentary letters. By the time you are ready to send out reference letters, you should have a file of copies of letters that have been written on your behalf. Select the best and ask these individuals to mail them to the appropriate individuals or programs. If you can pull it off, this is virtually a no-lose situation. You might also supply them with mailing labels to save them time. They will appreciate it.

A few students have been asked to sign statements that they have not seen their reference letters. This is ridiculous and unenforceable. Don't sign. However, it is common practice for students to be asked to sign a waiver of their right to request to see reference letters. If you are forced into this type of situation, you may have to sign it and hope for good letters. If possible, you do want to see those letters before they go out.

The Format

While your Dean's letter will follow the institution's format and will be professionally done on College of Medicine stationery, the same may not be true for your reference letters. It is almost unbelievable that faculty physicians send out reference letters that are not on letterhead, are printed on dot-matrix printers, or are handwritten. This is a negative reflection not only on these individuals, but also on you. If you believe that any of the individuals from whom you have requested a letter will have difficulty producing a professional-appearing document, either offer to have the letter typed for them or just ask someone else. Physicians working for the federal government and those in solo or rural practice seem to have the most difficulty producing professional reference letters. It should be noted that the best format is typewritten on letterhead stationery with a handwritten note from the writer. That gets attention.

Although most medical school faculty send out many reference letters, they have never been taught what goes in them. They might find it useful if you give them a copy of Figure 12.14, Elements of a Reference Letter, when you ask them to write your reference letter. Individuals from outside your medical center whom you are asking for a reference would almost assuredly appreciate a format to guide them in writing the letter.

Some specialties and programs now use a Standard Letter of Recommendation (SLOR). Pioneered by Emergency Medicine, SLORs are designed to improve communication about applicants. These can be more easily scanned into computers and analyzed than can normal reference letters, although many people still send both a standard letter and this form. The form includes key information, such as how likely the applicant is to match at the reference's residency program ("guaranteed," "very likely," "likely," etc.), how their grade compares with those of other students from the same year, and how the applicant measures up compared to other applicants for which the reference has written letters. Look for them to be used more frequently in the future.

A Picture?

It remains very questionable whether photographs should be a part of any employment application. Since requiring a photograph is illegal under civil rights legislation (it indicates race, gender, and age), ERAS has changed its procedures: It no longer requires a photograph, but suggests that the file will not be complete without one. The photograph is not visible to residency programs until after you have been accepted for an interview.

What kind of photograph do you include? As with everything you do in conjunction with your application, your photograph should look professional—especially because the first version they will probably see will be the black and white scanned version from ERAS. Have it professionally done. Don't sit in the drugstore photo machine that gives you five pictures for one dollar. This is your career at stake.

Go to a professional photographer and explain that you need a portrait photo. Unless you are specifically asked for a black-and-white picture, get it in color. ERAS specifies that you must submit a color photograph showing a full front view of your head and shoulders with your entire face centered in the middle of the photograph. It must have a plain white or light-colored background and be approximately 2½" x 3½" and not more than 3" x 4".

It may be less expensive to order extra copies of the photographs your school takes of students in the second or third year. But if you have noticeably altered your appearance since then, such as growing a beard or changing your hairstyle, get a new set of pictures. The benefit of using a professional photographer is that no matter what you really look like, you will appear much better in the professional's picture. Also, make sure that you look like a neat, clean professional. As you would in the interview itself, don't wear a fancy (party) hairstyle, informal clothes, or extravagant jewelry when getting the photo.

You use the color photograph once you have been granted an interview. Have a photograph ready for the program to include with your application material. Actually, it is illegal for a program to request a photograph, even after you have been interviewed in person. But you are not going to wait for them to request it—you will arrive at the interview with the photograph in hand.

Why should you do this? For a very obvious reason: You want to be remembered. Do you really think that an interviewer will remember anything specific about Jerry Glover or Mary Smythe after seeing 40 applicants? Probably not. They may even have trouble recalling applicants using the ERAS picture. But with a great color photograph to jog their memory during final selection, the good impressions that you left with the faculty will come flooding back.

Finally, before handing the picture to the residency secretary for your file, make sure that you put a gummed label on the back with your name, address, e-mail address, phone number, and the date that you are interviewing.

Oh yes, remember to say "cheese."

The Transcript

Your official medical school transcript, which will be required by nearly every program to which you apply, is a coded summary of your progress through medical school. The key word here is "coded." Symbols are used in each transcript. Familiar to most residency directors are such designations as "H" (Honors) or "A" for top grades. These symbols are widely used. Somewhat deceptively, however, some schools use "High Honors" for a top grade and "Honors" for the runners-up. Some schools, for their own reasons, use symbols that are distinctly different from those used in most transcripts. A few use "O" (Outstanding), "S" (Superior)—which indicates a less-than-Honors grade in some schools, but the top grade in others—or various numerical systems to designate a top grade. Those using numerical systems also tend to obscure the student grades with multiple columns of irrelevant data.

If you have done well in school, it is important that it be obvious to the faculty members who will review your transcript. No, the school's detailed explanation on the back of or accompanying the transcript does not help. If it needs that much explanation, the school needs to revise its method of recording grades. That, however, is something you cannot do anything about now. What you need to do is to include a separate page that summarizes your transcript with your application materials.

Your transcript summary page, *which is separate from your résumé*, should include all the following:

1. A list of all courses in which you received "Honors." Clearly specify that the grade, whatever it is called on the transcript, is in fact the top grade given out at your school.

2. A list of all courses in which you received a "B" grade, if such grades are given out at your school.

3. An explanation of any unusual grades or symbols on your transcript. This means detailing why there was an "Incomplete" listed for Biochemistry. It is very important to do this. If it was because you turned in a required project late, it is far different from what is assumed otherwise—that you failed part of the course and had to make it up.

4. A list of courses you will take in the balance of the year, but whose grades may not yet have been received or recorded by the registrar. The purpose of this is to alleviate concerns caused by misinterpretation of the transcript. Some schools use a "P" (which generally means "Pass," the average grade) to indicate that a course is "In Progress." If this appears next to the rotations taken early in your senior year (which probably will include your specialty elective), it could mean curtains for any chance to get an interview unless you explain it.

5. An explanation of any leaves of absence taken during medical school. If this needs more than a few words, state that it is further explained in your résumé or personal statement.

6. An explanation of any awards listed on your transcript. This explanation should include who gave the award and the achievement recognized.

7. Identify your class rank if your school notes this on the transcript, or if it will be to your advantage (if you are in the top half of your class) to do so.

Obviously, to intelligently write a personalized explanatory cover letter, it will be necessary for you to review a copy of your transcript. You can get this from the Registrar's office. Most individuals in these offices will be very happy to help you. Some even suggest that you come in and review your transcript periodically to ensure that they have not erred when recording your grades. Occasionally, however, some registrars may be reluctant to show you your transcript. In those cases, request help from your Dean of Students. After explaining why you want to review your record, you should have no difficulty in obtaining a copy for yourself.

Finally, you may get excellent grades in significant courses after sending in your initial transcript. It would serve you well to send, near the end of the interviewing "season," an updated transcript to the programs where you have interviewed. Make certain that the registrar has received and recorded late grades before the revised transcripts are sent out. Also, see if the Registrar's office can attach a note stating that this is an updated transcript. This will alert the programs to replace the transcript currently in their files with the new one that contains important, updated information.

A word now to those whose grades have not been stellar. An obscure transcript can often work to your advantage. You certainly do not want to call attention to it by enclosing the explanation of the transcript described above. Rather, you would like to have the transcript ignored as much as possible. It is still important, though, to explain in your résumé or personal statement any leaves of absence, failing grades, and courses-in-progress.

Finally, just as with the Dean's letter, make certain, if you are not using ERAS or CAS, that your transcript is sent out on time. Many students will be trying to send out transcripts simultaneously. This overburdens the Registrar's office. If your transcript is delayed, your work to get the right interviews might go for naught. Try to get your request in a little early. It is acceptable to forward a transcript before you have sent in, or even completed, the program's application. So, get those addresses to the Registrar's office as soon as you can. Make sure that one of the addresses is that of your mentor. When he or she receives a copy (discuss this in advance), you will know that the programs should have received their copies as well.

Timing—It's Your Future at Stake

Now that you have spent a great deal of time getting your material ready, make certain that you send it all in early. The requirements for granting interviews stiffen as the "season" progresses. When the first completed applications arrive, most programs are rather liberal about granting interviews. Later, as the vast influx of applications arrives, applicants are compared against those who have already been granted interviews. The requirements, therefore, get more demanding with each passing week. Perhaps more important, nearly half of Pediatrics residency directors and about one-fourth of those in Family Medicine and Anesthesiology use a "first-come, first-served" basis for selecting candidates to interview.

Thus, it is vital to get your materials in as soon as possible. Once you have requested that everything be sent or you have actually sent it to the programs, you can safely sit back and wait for interview requests, right? Wrong! Haven't you ever received a birthday card in the mail two months late, even though it was postmarked before your birthday? Of course you have. Not that the mail is slow or prone to frequent errors. But if your career depends upon the programs receiving all of your materials by a specific deadline, then it behooves you to be sure that they get it. And most programs do have specific deadlines.

If you use ERAS, check your application's status by using their tracking system, ADTS, accessed through the ERAS website (www.aamc.org/students/eras/start.htm). If you don't use ERAS, keep a log of everything that is supposed to be sent to each program. When you think that all of your materials should have arrived at the programs, and if you have not received any e-mail from them, call and ask. You should also do this if you are applying to non-ERAS programs.

If a program indicates that your file is incomplete, ascertain exactly what is lacking. If the missing document has been sent to multiple programs, check with more than one program. The problem may actually be that the documents are filed incorrectly or that they have not yet downloaded your materials. But it may mean that you will have to send duplicates to some programs. Remember that for programs requiring a Dean's letter, the file for graduating students will not be complete until at least the first week in November, since these letters are not released by ERAS (or sent from the Dean's office to non-ERAS programs) until November 1.

There is another method you can easily use to assure receipt of your materials for non-ERAS programs, including all Fellowships. You can enclose a self-addressed, stamped postcard with each application for the program to use to notify you when all your materials have arrived. The postcard, with a place to put a date, should say, "All necessary application materials have been received by the (name of residency program) Residency Program for (your name)." *You* should fill out the blanks before you enclose it. Attach a small note asking that the postcard be returned when all of your materials are received. Occasionally, even a detail as small as using this postcard will suggest something positive about an applicant. An example of one such postcard that our program received is shown in Figure 12.15.

In any event, once your file is complete, you should be able to e-mail the programs to find out whether you will be offered an interview. If you don't get a response in a reasonable time, call them. Calling, if you are pleasant about it, may get you an interview you might not otherwise have received.

Some students use priority mail or a courier service (FedEx, United Parcel Service overnight, etc.) to ensure that their material gets to the program (or to the ECFMG when they are acting as an IMG's Dean's office). Unless the materials are being sent from outside the United States or Canada, this is probably overkill.

The bottom line, then, is to plan ahead to get all your material to the residency programs on time—and then check to make certain it was received.

FIGURE 12.15

A Completed-Application Postcard

Date _____

Congratulations! Your application is now **complete**.

    ❏ Please call to schedule an interview.
    ❏ We will contact you to schedule an interview.
    ❏ Sorry buddy. Ever thought about law school?

Thanks for all your help.

Program _____

Telephone _____

Contact _____

13

Special Situations

To be a bullfighter, you must learn to think like the bull.
– Spanish Folk Saying

We hold these truths to be self-evident, that all men are created equal;
that they are endowed by their creator with certain unalienable rights;
that among these are life, liberty and the pursuit of happiness.
– Thomas Jefferson

THE ARCHETYPICAL PHYSICIAN in the United States was, for a long time, a White, Anglo-Saxon male. But this has changed drastically over the last four decades.

There was a large influx of foreign-born, foreign-trained physicians during the perceived doctor shortage in the 1960s and 1970s. Advancements in the rights of women and minorities also were made during this time, and it gradually became easier for all qualified applicants to medical schools to equitably compete for entrance into the profession. This resulted in an increasing number of physicians who did not fit the classic male "WASP" mold. Soon after, these physicians began knocking at the doors of residency programs to get further training. Gradually, the once-barred doors of virtually all specialties opened. However, many groups still have particular problems gaining entrance into residencies.

Of note is that the federal Equal Employment Opportunity Commission (EEOC) has ruled that once you have obtained a residency position, you are an employee. This means that you are specifically protected under Title VII from discrimination in employment based on race, color, sex, religious beliefs, or national origin. You are also protected under the Equal Pay Act and the Age Discrimination in Employment Act.

Some excellent resources for medical students who don't fit the mold are the American Medical Student Association's (AMSA) groups and computer list serves for those students who are disabled; lesbian, gay, transgender, or bisexual; minorities; or women. AMSA also publishes information about these groups in *The New Physician*, often with contact phone numbers, e-mail addresses, and websites.

Women

The first woman to earn a U.S. medical school diploma, Dr. Elizabeth Blackwell, graduated from the Geneva Medical College in upstate New York in 1849. Despite many obstacles, she graduated first in her class. Yet, in 1921, more than 70 years later, only 8% of U.S.-hospital internships accepted women. Today, women account for about 26% of practicing physicians, 49% of medical students (and nearly 50% of first-year students), 41% of residents and fellows, but just 30% of medical school faculty members. On average, there is only one woman department head per medical school, and only 10% of medical school Deans are women.

It is no longer unusual for women to constitute the majority of a medical school class; they comprised more than half of the 2005 entering class at 51 U.S. M.D.-granting medical schools. In 1970, about one in 13 U.S. physicians (7.7%) was female; currently (2006), one in four physicians are women. It is estimated that by 2010, women will constitute one-third of all U.S. physicians.

This is a significant advance from the 1890s, when the new Johns Hopkins Medical School, because of its need for the funds that women were raising, and then only under duress, agreed to accept qualified women as medical students. In 1977, there were no female residents in more than a third of all specialties. In 2006, women were training in every accredited area except for a few minor subspecialties with few total trainees. Nineteen specialties had more than 1,000 female residents in training in 2006.

Nearly all women physicians say that they are satisfied with their careers. Those most satisfied have more children, have less stress at home, are strongly religious, and feel in control of their work life. Nevertheless, many would choose a different specialty or another career if given the chance.

About 55% of female physicians under 35 years of age are in Primary Care. About 65% of male physicians in this age group are in non-Primary Care specialties. This gender disparity is similar for physicians 35 to 54 years old. Forty-six percent of all women physicians specialize in General Internal Medicine, General Pediatrics, Family Medicine, or Obstetrics and Gynecology. In addition, only 67% of women physicians are Board-certified in their specialty, as opposed to 74% of men.

This does not mean that there is no longer discrimination against women trying to get residency positions. While the match rate for women is better than for men in Family Medicine, Internal Medicine, Anesthesiology, Emergency Medicine, and Diagnostic Radiology, the reverse is true in some other specialties. Obstetrics and Gynecology, Pediatrics, Psychiatry, Pathology, General Surgery, and Orthopedic Surgery all have consistently higher match rates for men than for women. In the first four of the latter specialties, it has been suggested that a form of reverse discrimination is occurring: Program directors may be attempting to reverse the preponderance of women in those specialties by giving preference to male applicants (Figure 13.1).

One of the biggest discrepancies is in General Surgery, which is practiced by almost 5% of male physicians, but only 2% of female physicians. While there has been a marked increase in the number of female surgical residents, a greater percentage of women who apply have failed to match than have men. A survey of both male and female physicians cited General Surgery, Orthopedic Surgery, and Urology as the specialties that most restrict opportunities for women, although the percentage of women residents in these specialties has risen in recent years.

Respondents in this same survey cited Family Medicine, Obstetrics and Gynecology, Pediatrics, and Internal Medicine as having an equal or higher rate of opportunity for female physicians. In Internal Medicine, a much higher percentage of women than men practice General Internal Medicine, despite any subspecialty training.

FIGURE 13.1

Women's Representation in Selected Specialties

Specialty	% of All Physicians in this Specialty	% of Physicians in the Specialty that are Women	% of Residents in the Specialty that are Women
Internal Medicine	17%	30%	40%
Pediatrics	9	51	67
Family Medicine	8	31	51
Psychiatry	5	31	51
General Surgery	5	13	25
Obstetrics/Gynecology	4	39	74
Anesthesiology	4	21	27
Radiology	3	14	26
Emergency Medicine	2	21	30
Orthopedic Surgery	1	4	9

Adapted from: American Medical Association. *Physician Characteristics and Distribution in the U.S.* Chicago, IL: AMA, 2005, various tables; and Association of American Medical Colleges. *AAMC Data Book.* Washington, DC: AAMC, 2005.

If a woman candidate presents herself as firm and assertive, she is often labeled "strident and aggressive." If she demonstrates a milder, more traditionally feminine image, she runs the risk of a "meek and wimpy" label. In essence, it is often a lose-lose situation.

Greater awareness of federal laws prohibiting discrimination against women in hiring and during employment, as well as a change in social attitudes toward professional women, have made discriminatory practices more complex and subtle. These practices are often based upon the irrational fears of potential employers, which are not only unfair but also arbitrary. These employers are frequently disturbed by the idea of working with women as equals. One possible result is the under-representation of women on residency faculties. The percentage of women faculty members varies greatly by specialty, and their academic ranks are lower than those of their male colleagues (Figures 13.2 and 13.3).

One example of widespread discrimination is seen in the discrepancy between the average male and female physicians' income. Female physicians in practice (and not working for the federal government) still receive an average of 40% less annual net income than their male counterparts. This is only partially explained by differences in specialty, practice setting, age, and productivity. The exact amount varies by specialty, but this trend pervades medical practice.

Sexual Harassment

Unfortunately, nearly half of women physicians report having been harassed on the basis of gender, and more than a third report having been sexually harassed by patients, peers, or attending physicians. The frequency of both is about the same during medical school and training. (It decreases somewhat when the physicians enter practice.)

FIGURE 13.2

Gender of Medical School Faculty, by Rank

| Academic Rank | Men | | Women | |
	Number	Percent of All Faculty*	Number	Percent of All Faculty*
Professor	23,373	21.2%	4,076	3.7%
Associate Professor	17,990	16.3	6,682	6.1
Assistant Professor	28,613	26.0	17,085	15.5
Instructor	6,335	5.8	6,110	5.5
Total	**76,311**	**69.3%**	**33,953**	**30.8%**

*Percentages may not total 100% due to rounding error.
Adapted from: AAMC Faculty Roster System, 2005.

FIGURE 13.3
Women M.D. Faculty in Various Specialties

Specialty	% of All M.D. Faculty within Each Specialty Who are Women	% of Women M.D. Faculty within Each Specialty Who are Full Professors	Ratio of Men to Women Faculty Who are Full Professors
Pediatrics	45%	11%	3.5
Public Health	44	7	3.2
OB/GYN	44	12	5.1
Physical Medicine	41	13	3.0
Family Medicine	41	7	3.5
Psychiatry	39	12	4.8
Dermatology	38	9	5.0
Pathology (All)	30	6	5.3
Anesthesiology	30	6	6.9
Neurology	30	10	7.4
Internal Medicine	29	11	7.1
Ophthalmology	26	9	7.5
Emergency Medicine	26	4	7.1
Radiology	25	8	6.4
Otolaryngology	22	10	10.2
Surgery	16	10	17.0
Orthopedic Surgery	12	6	34.0

From: AAMC Faculty Roster System, 2005.

The EEOC definition of sexual harassment is:

> Unwelcome sexual advances, requests for sexual favors, and other verbal or physical conduct of a sexual nature constitute sexual harassment when:
>
> 1. submission to such conduct is made either explicitly or implicitly a term or condition of an individual's employment;
> 2. submission to or rejection of such conduct by an individual is used as the basis for employment decisions affecting such individual; or
> 3. such conduct has the purpose or effect of unreasonably interfering with an individual's work performance or creating an intimidating, hostile, or offensive working environment.

Sexual harassment, including physical harassment, sexual slurs, and sexual advances, is common. It is experienced more frequently by women than men and, in residency, varies by specialty. Figure 13.4 lists those specialties with the highest and lowest reported incidence of sexual harassment. Married women and those with children suffered less harassment than single women. Most women say they do not report harassment because they fear a negative impact and because they do not believe action

---

FIGURE 13.4

Relative Incidence of Sexual Harassment*

1. Urology	11. Otolaryngology
2. Family Practice (renamed Family Medicine)	12. General Surgery
	13. Pediatrics
3. Psychiatry	14. Orthopedic Surgery
4. Emergency Medicine	15. Radiology
5. Obstetrics/Gynecology	16. Radiation Oncology
6. Internal Med–Pediatrics	17. Dermatology
7. Neurological surgery	18. Transitional Year
8. Neurology	19. Anesthesiology
9. Physical Med & Rehab	20. Ophthalmology
10. Internal Medicine	21. Pathology

*Ranked from highest (1) to lowest (21) incidence.

Adapted from: Baldwin DC, Daugherty SR: Distinguishing sexual harassment from discrimination: a factor-analytic study of residents' reports. *Acad Med.* 2001;76(10):S5-7.

---

would be taken, even though virtually all teaching hospitals have policies regarding the sexual harassment of residents. Individuals who sexually harass residents generally have a higher professional status. One study showed that while lesbian physicians suffer no more harassment than their heterosexual peers, they report these offenses four times as often.

During the residency selection process, women are also often asked sexist, blatantly illegal questions. See "Illegal Questions" in Chapter 20 for more information.

Even without discrimination, women in medicine have unique personal problems that have no easy solutions. The training period of medical school and residency cuts directly across the childbearing years. This results in women physicians having fewer children, and at a later age, than non-physician women. Only 60-70% of married women physicians have children, compared to 90% of their married male counterparts.

Additional information for and about women in medicine can be obtained from the American Medical Women's Association (AMWA), (703) 838-0500; www.amwa-doc.org. This organization provides student members with educational loans, scholarships, and awards; use of a bed-and-breakfast program; and a bimonthly journal. Another source of information is Women Physicians Congress, American Medical Association,

(312) 464-5622; www.ama-assn.org/go/wpc. This section of the AMA serves as an information resource on issues relating to women physicians. Many individual specialties also have separate societies for women physicians. You can locate them through the main specialty society, AMWA, or the AMA.

Marriage, Pregnancy, & Children

The problems associated with adjusting to marriage and having children during medical training were once thought to be solely a woman's concern. Not any longer. While women do have unique biological concerns regarding pregnancy, both men and women physicians now frequently base career decisions, including choosing a residency, on how they will affect their family. The major concerns include maintaining the family relationship, coping with pregnancy, and caring for children.

Marriage

Half of all medical students marry during medical school or residency training, and more than 60% of physicians divorce within ten years after completing residency. (At least one study showed that Psychiatrists have the highest divorce rate at 50%, followed by Surgeons with 33%.) Up to 70% of medical marriages are dysfunctional, in part, because physicians often hold a position of unquestioned authority at work and it can be difficult to relinquish this role at home. Residents' marriages are at particular risk for work-related difficulties, since they work longer hours, have more trouble "winding down" after work, are sleep deprived, and are often too tired to participate in social or leisure-time activities.

Does this mean that your partnership is doomed? No! All new professionals have the same stresses. One key to success is to lend your partner as much support for his or her career as you deserve for your own. Another is for both partners to recognize that, at least during residency, theirs will not be the idyllic marriage that balances a thriving career with a loving and active family life. Ultimately, residents with successful marriages cope better, remain more productive, and are happier than those whose marriages are foundering.

More than three-fourths of medical students' domestic partners play a significant role in deciding which residency programs they apply to, where they accept interviews, and how they rank the programs. Partners influence these decisions more than medical school faculty, residents, other family members, or classmates. Many partners travel to the interview sites and investigate job opportunities while there. Ultimately, while nearly 60%

of male and female medical students try to satisfy both their own and their partner's needs when selecting programs, nearly 33% of male and 20% of female medical students make their final selections based primarily on their own needs.

Dual-physician marriages have their own difficulties. In physician-physician marriages, both earn less money individually than other physicians, and each is less likely to feel that their career takes precedence over their spouse's. However, they feel as successful as other physicians in achieving their career and family goals, and benefit more from shared work interests. Nevertheless, the women in these partnerships, are more likely to make professional sacrifices for their spouses than are their cohorts who are married to non-physicians.

Balancing personal and professional goals, and the responsibilities accompanying each, can be a major challenge for both men and women—although women have more stressors. Significant social expectations on women physicians, apart from their medical careers, can create tension between their private and professional lives. This contributes to the fact that only 66% of female physicians marry, compared to 90% of both non-physician women and male physicians. In addition, since up to 70% of married women physicians are married to other physicians, the complications mount.

Compared with women physicians partnered with non-physicians (usually other professionals), the women in physician-physician relationships are more likely to bear the primary responsibility of caring for their children and home. Many do this by working fewer hours and subordinating their career to that of their partner. As many as half of all women physicians change their career plans because of marriage or family responsibilities.

In the end, however, marriage enhances well-being. Married men and women are generally happier and less stressed than single people. Men benefit more from marriage than do women. However, both show decreased stress, which can help to enhance physicians' lives—especially during residency.

Pregnancy & Family Leave

Among the most stressful personal situations that residents must deal with are pregnancy and child rearing. Increasing numbers of women are having children during their medical training. Before 1950, 24% of women physicians with children had them during medical training. Since then, more than half of all women physicians with children had their first child during residency. Approximately 7,500 current women residents will become pregnant at least once during their training. Many more residents will experience fatherhood.

Maternity/paternity leave (often now incorporated into "family leave") has lengthened over time, although women are still unhappy with the amount of time off they receive for pregnancy and childbirth. These policies have been problematic for at least two reasons. First, women residents who have been pregnant feel that the leave, if less than six weeks long, is inadequate. Second, since these policies only apply to a subset of residents (parents, usually mothers), extended leave can wreak havoc on schedules and on the baseline educational requirements that must be met for Board certification.

Leave policies are ultimately the responsibility of the sponsoring institution. The ACGME's *Essentials of Accredited Residencies in Graduate Medical Education: Institutional and Program Requirements* stipulates that residency applicants in all specialties must be informed, in writing, of parental leave policies and that this information must be included in resident's contracts. In addition, it states: "There must be a written institutional policy on leave (with or without pay) for residents that complies with applicable laws. The institution must provide residents with a written policy concerning the effect of leaves of absence, for any reason, on satisfying the criteria for completion of a residency program."

It should be noted, however, that most programs actually deal with pregnancies on an *ad hoc* basis. Therefore, how individual programs interpret the requirements varies. *FREIDA* indicates whether a program has written maternity, paternity, and/or family leave policies. It also frequently lists the maximum time allowed for each—although many list "NGO" ("negotiable"). As women become an even greater presence in medicine, longer pregnancy leave, greater flexibility in residency programs, and increased availability of childcare for medical students and residents will become mandatory.

The Federal Family and Medical Leave Act, which took effect in August 1993, applies to most residents. It requires employers having 50 or more workers to grant up to 12 weeks of unpaid leave each year to new fathers and mothers (including adoptive and foster parents) after they have worked at the job for one year. The same amount of leave time must be available for employees to seek medical care for themselves or to care for their spouse, child, or parent with a serious health condition. Sick leave, vacation, and personal leave time can be incorporated into this time period so that it may not all be unpaid. Approximately three-fourths of teaching hospitals have a written parental leave policy. At these hospitals, maternity leave averages 64 days (range: 21 to 180 days), and paternity leave averages 46 days (range: 1 to 120 days). At many institutions, much of this leave time is unpaid.

As evidenced by the relative paucity of adequate paternity leave policies (at least one hospital generously offers just one day off), male residents may have more difficulty than women getting time off to fulfill their parental responsibilities around the time of birth. More male residents will become parents than will women residents because there are more male residents, and most of them are married to non-physicians.

The 1978 Pregnancy Discrimination Amendments to the Civil Rights Act of 1964 state that women affected by pregnancy, childbirth, or related medical conditions are to be treated the same as disabled employees for all employment-related purposes, including being covered by fringe-benefit programs. A number of states also have laws governing the rights of pregnant employees.

Most women physicians who have been pregnant during their residency report inequitable treatment during their pregnancy, ranging from unconscious slights to actual harassment. To lessen stress, some women physicians suggest trying to plan pregnancies for the time between the second and third years or during the fourth year of medical school, during the senior year of residency (not a surgical residency), during a year off, or after residency. (Of course, pregnancies often cannot be "planned.") If you become pregnant, give your (hopefully supportive) colleagues adequate notice that you will be taking leave.

Pregnant residents usually have lifestyles that they would not recommend to their patients—long hours, rigorous physical activity, poor eating and sleeping habits, and exposure to disease. Fortunately, studies have shown that these stressors have had little effect on the success of their pregnancies, although there appears to be a higher-than-expected incidence of preeclampsia and preterm labor (but not preterm delivery). Additionally, female resident physicians have fewer induced abortions than do their non-physician counterparts (Figure 13.5).

According to an AMA review, pregnant residents should take breaks every few hours; take a longer "meal" break every four hours; maintain adequate hydration; regularly vary their work positions by sitting, standing, and walking; and minimize heavy lifting, especially if associated with bending.

Up to one-third of women who were pregnant during their residency training would counsel others to avoid the experience. They found that the farther along they were in their residency, the easier the pregnancy was to

FIGURE 13.5
Pregnancies and Complications

Complication	Non-Physicians	Physicians
Mean age at first delivery (yrs.)	25.2	27.0
Mean number of children	2.9	1.8
Stillbirths/1000 births	3.7	3.2
Spontaneous abortions (%)	12.5	12.7
Elective abortions (%)	13.1	11
Premature delivery (%)	7.6	12.4
Pregnancy-induced hypertension (%)	7	5.4
Diabetes (%)	1	1

Adapted from: Pinhas-Hamiel O, Rostein Z, Achiron A, et al.: Pregnancy during residency—an Israeli survey of women physicians. *Health Care for Women International.* 1999;20:63-70.

manage, since their work schedules were more flexible and coworkers were more supportive.

The most obvious issue for women is fatigue—both during and after pregnancy. Consider whether the pregnancy, unexpected circumstances related to the pregnancy, or caring for an infant might delay your progression through, or graduation from, medical school or residency. In part, this will depend on your support system, especially at home. Also, consider the financial aspects of pregnancy. How much will *you* have to pay for your (and the baby's) medical care and for the delivery? You will probably have to buy furniture, clothing, and other baby supplies (toys, car seat, stroller, diapers, etc.).

If you are considering pregnancy during your training, you may want to look for large training programs that might have more flexibility to modify schedules for pregnancy leave, or investigate training programs that clearly state their maternity leave policy in their application material. (It is becoming more common for these policies to be titled "Parental," "Family," or "Maternity/Paternity/Adoption" leave, rather than "Maternity" leave.) *FREIDA* includes a question about maternity and paternity leave for each program.

Children

Childcare can be an enormous burden for residents, especially if both parents work. Women carry most of the child-rearing burdens in our society, and cannot be both residents and parents without some help. Childcare facilities, although relatively common in the business world, have yet to appear in the medical field on a regular basis. Even where hospitals offer childcare, it is often not available to residents' children. See the discussion of childcare in Chapter 10.

It is very difficult to find routine childcare services that can accommodate a resident's extremely long (and sometimes unexpectedly longer) hours. Start searching for childcare during pregnancy. Consider a nanny service, live-in childcare, a regular baby-sitter, or a day care center. Make sure that you have a back-up plan in case something unexpected happens at the hospital. Some resources containing helpful tips for men and women are listed under "Parenting" in the *Annotated Bibliography*.

Couples Matching

Resistance to matching couples at the same institution seems to have faded with the reality of nearly 4,000 new physician-physician couples each year. However, matching couples in the same training program, which occurs much less often, may still pose a problem. This may be due to the faculty's concerns about the effect upon both the individual residents and the esprit de corps of the entire program if there is any strife between the couple or a breakup. This concern is not at all assuaged by the marginal commitment to each other shown by some interviewing couples.

Using the NRMP Couples Match often reduces the strain in two-physician (medical student) marriages/relationships. Rather than being more difficult than individual matches as might be expected, couples that match through the NRMP PGY-1 Couples Match actually have about the same match rate as do individuals going through the regular NRMP Match. Part-time, also described as "Shared-Schedule," positions are available in some programs (see below).

In most cases, problems revolve around the process of successfully matching as a couple. It is particularly troublesome when both partners do not use the NRMP Match, are from different medical schools, or are in different years of training. The latter is the only problem that will be addressed here. The others will be discussed in Chapter 22.

If you and your partner are in different years of medical school training, there are three viable options for you.

1. The senior partner goes through the Match for his or her specialty. The junior partner can then concentrate his or her efforts on the geographic area compatible with their partner's Match results. However, this could mean separation for one or more years, which may be unacceptable.

2. The senior partner goes through the Match and then the junior partner transfers to a medical school in the same geographic area to complete his or her medical school training. Some schools, especially private schools that rely on income from tuition, make

transferring out very difficult. For information about transferring schools, search "Transfer Policies for Applicants to Medical Schools" at www.aamc.org/students/medstudents. On that site, you can search either by the type of transfer policy or by the school.

3. The senior partner limits selections on his or her rank order list to the geographic area of the junior partner's medical school and matches into a less desirable spot if necessary. When the junior partner graduates, both partners can enter the Match again, with the senior partner seeking an advanced position. In the past, this was accomplished by the senior partner first matching into a "Preliminary" or "Transitional" year—both of which are becoming less common as residency funding tightens.

There is no question that the whole Match process causes a great deal of stress among physician couples. And, if programs are not chosen with care, the stress does not end there. Couples must find out how flexible the programs will be in scheduling both on-call and vacation time. Ask for details about how to request time-off and schedule changes. With both partners in training, flexible scheduling may be needed if you are to see each other at all. Absence may make the heart grow fonder, but in excess it can devastate a relationship. Check for scheduling flexibility before you rank a program.

Part-Time (Shared-Schedule) Positions

A shared-schedule position is one in which two residents, who usually pair up before interviewing and applying to programs, agree to each spend less than full-time in a single residency slot. In essence, they share one position.

This can be done either by having each participant spend less time per day at work or, more commonly, by alternating the weeks or months worked. This requires a great deal of forbearance on the part of a lot of people. First, the partners must be willing to work together and be flexible. Second, the program must be willing to work within the agreed-upon format. At present, very few residency applicants apply for part-time positions; in some years, none apply.

In many ways, physicians seeking part-time residency training face similar problems to those encountered by couples trying to match— although *they are completely different arrangements*. Part-time positions came into their own in the late 1970s, when changes in attitudes resulted in a federal law (now lapsed) that required most programs to offer positions to physicians who were only willing to commit limited time to residency training. (That law specified that each resident work no more than two-thirds time for no less than half-time pay. You can try to figure that one out for yourself.)

No two shared-schedule positions are ever structured in exactly the same way. *The key is to obtain the arrangement with the program, whatever it is, in writing. Be sure to get it in writing before you rank programs for the Match.* If you require scheduling in a specific manner, then get this agreed to and spelled out in advance with both your partner and the program. Chapter 22 contains the special rules for entering the NRMP Match for shared/part-time positions.

Part-time programs appear to have worked well for those involved in them; however, fewer than 9% of programs (701 programs in 2006) offer "shared-schedule/part-time" positions (Figure 13.6). Most are in Family Medicine, General Internal Medicine, Pediatrics, and Psychiatry. The national societies and Boards in other specialties may be unfamiliar with this type of program, even if some of their residencies offer it.

The number of part-time positions varies by geographic region. Less than 1% of residency programs in the Mountain States (AZ, CO, ID, MT, NM, NV, UT, WY) offer part-time positions, while in the East-North Central region (IL, IN, MI, OH, WI), 18% of programs offer these positions. Less than 1% of military and Puerto Rican programs offer part-time positions.

A trainee's need for a part-time residency position often results from other pressing needs, including family considerations, the simultaneous pursuit of another profession or training program, and significant involvement in outside activities. Individuals in this type of program spend less time in any single year working, but, by the time they finish, they will spend as much or more total time in training than do full-time residents.

Usually, two physicians, both entering the same year of training, agree to split one residency position. The individual method by which a split position is achieved varies greatly from program to program. There are several keys to success:

1. You must find a flexible partner to pair with you, preferably *before* you begin to look for programs. This will often be a spouse, significant other, or good friend from school.

2. You must find a program willing to work with you in arranging a part-time position. Both *FREIDA* and the AMA's *GMED Companion* list programs that have said they will accept shared positions. The percentage of programs with shared-schedule/part-time positions varies widely among major specialties. While no General Surgery programs offer part-time positions, they are offered by 40% of Preventive Medicine programs and 22% of Pediatrics programs.

FIGURE 13.6

Shared-Schedule/Part-Time Positions Offered by Specialties

Specialty	Number of Programs with Shared/ Part-Time Positions	Percent of Programs with Shared/ Part-Time Positions
Allergy & Immunology	7	10%
Anesthesiology	9	7
Colon and Rectal Surgery	2	5
Dermatology	3	3
Emergency Medicine	3	2
Family Medicine	54	12
Family Medicine–Psychiatry	4	40
Internal Medicine	46	12
Internal Med–Neurology	3	43
Internal Med–Pediatrics	18	18
Internal Med–Physical Med & Rehab	1	11
Internal Med–Preventive Med	1	14
Internal Med–Psychiatry	4	24
Medical Genetics	5	10
Neurological Surgery	4	4
Neurology	10	8
Neurology–Psychiatry	3	30
Nuclear Medicine	3	5
Obstetrics & Gynecology	2	<1
Ophthalmology	7	6
Orthopedic Surgery	1	<1
Otolaryngology	1	1
Pathology, Anatomical & Clinical	7	5
Pediatrics	44	22
Peds/Medical Genetics	1	9
Peds/Physical Med & Rehab	3	60
Peds/Psychiatry–Child Psych	4	40
Physical Medicine & Rehabilitation	3	4
Plastic Surgery	1	1
Preventive Medicine (all areas)	27	40
Psychiatry	60	33
Radiology, Diagnostic	8	4
Thoracic Surgery	4	4
Transitional	4	3
Urology	3	3

Data derived from: American Medical Association. *GMED Companion: An Insider's Guide to Selecting a Residency Program 2005–2006*. Chicago, IL: AMA, 2005; and *FREIDA*.

3. During the application process, you and your partner will have to work together closely and interview together. This will emphasize to the program that you are applying as a team.

4. Get an agreement *in writing* from each program about how their part-time position will work *before* you list it in the Match. Otherwise, both you and the program will be going blindly into a nebulous arrangement from which it is unlikely that any party will emerge happy.

Shared-schedule residencies do work, but the amount of preparation that is necessary to make them work successfully is enormous. Getting a good partner, choosing the right program, and making certain that all parties understand and agree to the details from the beginning are the keys to success.

Gay, Lesbian, Bisexual, & Transgender Applicants

Gay, lesbian, bisexual, and transgender (GLBT) medical students and physicians are a largely invisible minority, although they are becoming more visible within the medical profession as our society becomes more accepting of diversity. Maturing societal attitudes now recognize diverse sexual orientations and many individuals feel more comfortable identifying themselves as gay, lesbian, or bisexual. Medical organizations of gay, lesbian, and bisexual physicians have thousands of dues-paying members, and membership is growing. These groups' unique health concerns, including AIDS, have forcefully gained the profession's attention: The AMA now recognizes the Gay and Lesbian Medical Association as one of their specialty committees.

As mentioned in other sections, however, medical practitioners generally have conservative attitudes toward their life and work, as exemplified by the difficulty that many national physician organizations have approving resolutions banning discrimination on the basis of sexual orientation. Two national surveys found that 40% of General Internists and 50% of Internal Medicine residents had witnessed homophobic comments in their workplace. A 1996 study showed that about 10% of physicians would oppose openly gay and lesbian physicians seeking residency training in Obstetrics and Gynecology, Urology, and Pediatrics, and that about 10% would not refer patients to them no matter what their specialty. Another study of Psychiatry residents and faculty and Family Medicine residents found that one-third were homophobic.

GLBT residency applicants may encounter fears that they are among the estimated 5,000 HIV-infected physicians. This fear represents more than mere homophobia; it denotes concerns about employing physicians who have a disability that may require prolonged absences, as well as other problems with which residency directors would rather not have to deal.

Therefore, GLBT residency applicants face difficult and, ultimately, very personal decisions regarding their sexual orientation or gender identity. Is this an aspect of your life you want to be open about during the interviewing process? Should you include some of your gay-identified activities and affiliations on your application or CV? What happens if those activities become part of your interview? Many applicants will simply choose to avoid the topic and its possible negative impact on their getting a residency spot.

As one medical student, Lydia Vaias, wrote in *JAMA*, "Interviews are uncomfortable, scary processes for everyone. They are particularly terrifying for lesbian and gay people, because we must grapple with telling who we are, without revealing an integral aspect of ourselves." Moreover, a medical school's respect for diversity may stop short of transgendered applicants. For support around these issues, consider joining a GLBT medical student list serve.

There is an additional problem for gays and lesbians. Even if you are in a committed relationship, your partner will not qualify for "spousal" benefits, except in a few states or hospitals. Since these benefits are worth a substantial percentage of your income, this may be a significant loss.

Two national groups lend assistance and support to gays, lesbians, and bisexuals in medicine: Gay and Lesbian Medical Association, (415) 255-4547; www.glma.org; and the Lesbian, Gay, Bisexual & Transgender People in Medicine (LGBTPM), which is an advocacy group within the American Medical Student Association, (800) 767-2266; www.amsa.org/advocacy/lgbtpm/. There are also a number of local groups in larger cities, and specific groups within some medical specialties.

Psychiatric Illness

Some medical students require psychiatric interventions, due either to pre-existing illnesses or to new conditions that appear during medical school. Why should this distinguish them from others needing medical treatments?

Some medical boards ask for complete psychiatric records of all physicians who have had psychiatric treatment when they apply for or renew their medical license. In those states that require residents to have a medical license, this includes individuals accepted to residency positions.

Residency director Norman Fost, M.D. (also a bioethicist), deals with such requests by leaving this space blank when completing forms. Instead, he attaches a note stating, "All of our residents and faculty have emotional problems. Some are sensible enough to seek professional help. If I believed Dr. X's problems interfered with his/her ability to perform duties of the position he/she is applying for, I would tell you."

Perhaps your Dean of Students can treat these requests the same way.

Underrepresented Minorities

The term "underrepresented minority" is based on government definitions of those groups that have fewer physicians than would be expected from the groups' population. The Association of American Medical Colleges (AAMC) defines those "underrepresented in medicine" as "those racial and ethnic populations that are underrepresented in the medical profession relative to their numbers in the general population." Generally, this term refers to Blacks (African-Americans), Native Americans/Alaskan Natives (including Native Hawaiians), and individuals of Hispanic Origin (Cuban/Mexican-American/Puerto Rican/Other Hispanic). Though there certainly are other minority groups facing many of the same problems, these are the groups with the largest number of U.S. medical school graduates that appear to be underrepresented in residency programs—especially in the subspecialties. In recent years, they have comprised about 21% of practicing U.S. physicians and 12.5% of all physicians in U.S. residency programs (Black, 5.3%; Hispanic Origin, 6.3%; Native Hawaiian/Pacific Islander, 0.6%; Native American/Native Alaskan, 0.3%).

Underrepresented minority physicians are more likely to enter a generalist specialty (Family Medicine, Internal Medicine, and Pediatrics) than are physicians from other racial or ethnic groups. Among those entering generalist specialties, they are four times more likely to practice in socioeconomically deprived areas as are other physicians.

Although there has been an increase in the number of minority physicians in all specialties, relatively few of these specialists are on the faculties of medical schools (Figure 13.7). Approximately 10% of full-time medical school clinical faculty are minority physicians: Many of these are at the three predominantly Black schools and the three Puerto Rican schools. The faculty at these six minority schools comprises less than 2% of the total medical school faculty in the country.

Minority faculty representation is important because these individuals provide role models for minority medical students. Their absence creates an enormous void that is hard for other faculty to fill. Because this absence is especially acute in many of the non-primary care specialties, some minority medical students feel considerable social pressure to enter

FIGURE 13.7

***Minority Representation on Medical School
Faculties in Various Clinical Specialties***

Department	Native Amer	Black	Mexican Amer	Puerto Rican	Other Hispanic	% of Specialty's Faculty*
Anesthesiology	<0.1%	4.0%	0.5%	0.8%	2.8%	8.2%
Dermatology	0.0	2.1	0.5	0.8	1.1	4.5
Emergency Med	<0.1	4.7	1.0	0.9	1.8	8.5
Family Medicine	0.2	5.9	1.6	1.5	2.0	11.2
Internal Medicine	<0.1	3.2	0.6	0.8	2.6	7.3
Neurology	<0.1	1.2	0.5	0.2	2.3	4.3
Obstetrics/Gynecology	<0.1	7.0	0.7	1.3	2.6	11.7
Ophthalmology	<0.1	1.8	0.4	0.4	2.6	5.3
Orthopedic Surgery	<0.1	2.2	0.4	0.6	1.0	4.3
Otolaryngology	<0.1	2.3	0.2	0.1	1.9	4.6
Pathology**	<0.1	1.2	0.6	0.2	3.2	5.3
Pediatrics	<0.1	3.6	0.7	1.2	3.1	8.7
Physical Med/Rehab	0.0	4.1	0.4	2.0	2.0	8.5
Psychiatry	0.1	3.1	0.6	0.8	2.5	7.1
Public Health	0.3	4.7	0.0	0.5	1.7	7.2
Radiology	0.1	2.1	0.3	0.7	2.4	5.6
Surgery	0.1	3.2	0.5	0.8	2.3	6.9

*Totals may vary due to rounding errors.
**Includes Basic and Clinical Pathology.
Adapted from: *AAMC Data Book.* Washington, DC: *AAMC*, 2005.

primary care and "return to their communities." If they do enter a sub-specialty, they often are made to feel like traitors, since many subspecialists' services are not readily available to minority communities.

A higher percentage of minority medical students plan to enter Family Medicine, Internal Medicine, Pediatrics, Psychiatry, Obstetrics and Gynecology, and General Surgery compared to their classmates. They do not plan to go into the smaller specialty and subspecialty areas in comparable numbers. Because role models are not available to show them alternative routes for their careers, they may feel that their options are more limited than those of the majority of medical students.

As Dr. Freeman Favors, a Black Emergency Physician, said, "Many minority students think to themselves 'I don't see minorities in this specialty, so why try to get in?'" This becomes a self-fulfilling statement. It keeps many minority students from even applying to them, so many specialties accept only a handful of minority residents. Dr. Favors wasn't intimidated, and he has done very well in his chosen field. He exhorts minority students to be courageous when setting their professional goals. He also suggests that minority students who desire to enter hard-to-match-with specialties look for regions of the country where their minority is underrepresented. As he says, "They can be at a competitive advantage by being a 'rare gem' at such programs and institutions."

No matter what specialty minority medical students want to enter, it appears that they do consistently worse in obtaining residency positions compared to other students. Many reasons have been given for this. While racial and ethnic barriers have fallen in some specialties, there still appears to be an "invisible quota system," due to reluctance by some to rank too many minority candidates for the Match. This may be because some faculty members still feel uncomfortable having more than one or two minority residents in a program. Given the uncertainty of the Match, ranking a lot of minority candidates could result in several such students matching with their program. This is probably equally true in those programs using a non-NRMP matching process.

During the past decade, programs with the highest percentage of minority residents and fellows have been those in municipally owned hospitals, those in the western United States, those with major university affiliations, and those at hospitals with 700 or more beds. Programs with the smallest number of minority residents and fellows (as a percentage of total residents and fellows) have been in small hospitals (399 or fewer beds) that are university-owned, those run by the Veterans' Administration, and those in the southern United States.

Pressure is being put on medical schools to increase the number of both minority faculty and minority residents. Grants to encourage minority faculty's education and research provide strong incentives, as do the embarrassing statistics published by the AMA, the AAMC, and the federal government about minority representation in each school and specialty. State governments that fund health-related positions also look at these numbers: If you are a minority student, this could work to your advantage. To get a good position, however, you still have to be as good as, or better than, the competition—and be able to demonstrate that to interviewers and selection committees. This is one reason why you are reading this book: To learn how to do exactly that.

Of particular concern is one study that showed that 20% of Blacks and Hispanics (including Puerto Ricans) were not in a residency program three years after graduation from medical school. At present, the reasons for this are unclear, but these findings suggest that these physicians entered medical practice (probably in primary care areas) at a disadvantage when compared to their fully trained colleagues.

Harassment

About one-third of underrepresented minority residents felt that they had suffered ethnic discrimination during their first year of residency. In most cases, this is expressed as racial or ethnic slurs, favoritism toward other groups, poor evaluations, and denied opportunities.

Minority women physicians experience harassment based on their ethnicity at a rate six to nine times that of White women. Black women physicians have the highest rate; 35% of those less than 50 years old experienced harassment during training and 32% experienced it in their practice. Forty percent of Muslim women had experienced ethnic harassment.

Native American Applicants

Physicians identified as Native Americans make up considerably less than 0.5% of all U.S. physicians. One must be at least one-eighth Indian to be considered a Native American or an Alaskan Native. Most of these physicians practice in the West and the South. There are only about 55 Native American physicians per 100,000 Native Americans in the population. This is the lowest ratio of any ethnic group's physicians to their population in the United States. It is, therefore, unlikely that a Native American medical student will come across a role model either in his or her home environment or at medical school. Recent studies suggest that about half of all current Native American physicians are in primary care specialties. In 2005, only 0.3% of all residents were either Native American or Alaskan Natives.

It is not always apparent that one is a Native American. Listing membership in the Association of American Indian Physicians on your application is an unobtrusive way of mentioning that you are a minority candidate. All other things being equal, this might give you an edge.

For more information about and for Native Americans in medicine, contact: Association of American Indian Physicians, (405) 946-7072; www.aaip.com.

Black Applicants (African-Americans)

Today, there are approximately 90 Black physicians per 100,000 Blacks in the population. Of these physicians, about 25% graduated from one of the three predominantly Black medical schools: Meharry Medical College, Morehouse School of Medicine, and Howard University Medical School. As of 2005, only 5% of all physicians in residency programs were non-Hispanic Blacks.

Approximately 25% more Black physicians choose primary care specialties than does the general population of physicians. There are usually role models available for Black medical students, either at the medical school or in the community. Most medical schools have some Black faculty members, albeit not in all specialties.

Yet, discrimination does exist within the medical fraternity. One study showed that if a residency program uses USMLE Step 1 scores to screen applicants for interviews, Black applicants suffer disproportionately. As you expand your horizons to search for the ideal training program, be aware that you may have to do more to prove yourself than other candidates. And, unfortunately, this reality may persist throughout your training, as well as afterwards. For more information, contact: National Medical Association, (202) 204-1223; www.nmanet.org/; or the Student National Medical Association, (202) 882-2881; e-mail: snmamain@msn.com.

Hispanic Applicants

Hispanic applicants should know that many interviewers are unaware that the term "Hispanic" represents a diverse classification category. "Hispanic" includes persons of Cuban descent, Puerto Ricans, Mexican-Americans (Chicanos), and those of Latin American or Central American descent. Federal government guidelines do not consider all of them minorities; in medicine, some definitely are not minorities. Cuban-Americans, for example, are represented in medical schools to a greater extent, as a percentage of the population, than nearly any other subgroup in the United States.

However, even including all Hispanic physicians, there are only about 80 Hispanic physicians in practice per 100,000 Hispanic population compared to approximately 202 White physicians per 100,000 White population. But 61% of Puerto Rican physicians have graduated from the three medical schools in Puerto Rico. Partially due to language and cultural barriers, relatively few of these graduates apply to mainland training programs.

In recent years, only about 2% of new interns were Puerto Rican, 1.8% were Mexican-American, and 1.8% were "other Hispanics." As of 2005, only 6.3% of all physicians in residency programs classified themselves as Hispanic. As the U.S. Hispanic population grows, fluency in both Spanish and English will become a definite plus for any applicant. If you have this skill, promote it in your application materials. For more information, contact: National Hispanic Medical Association, (202) 628-5895; www.nhmamd.org.

Physically Impaired Applicants

The subgroup of physically impaired medical students is unique. The individuals in this group are singular both among medical students, for their tenacity and drive to overcome the obstacles to get where they are, and among the physically impaired, since they are able enough to complete medical school's clinical requirements.

There are currently about 3,000 practicing U.S. physicians with major physical disabilities. (Estimates of the number of physicians with disabilities range from 2.5% to 4%.) Of those medical students with known physical impairment (only about 0.25% of all medical students), approximately 25% have visual disabilities, 42% have neurological or musculoskeletal impairments, 8% have an auditory disability, and 14% have learning disabilities. By 1995, more than one-third of all teaching hospitals had made accommodations under the Americans with Disabilities Act for disabled residents. While some residency programs may hesitate to take a physically impaired individual, this attitude is normally due to ignorance.

Educate these educators! Explain to them that you have been able to do what was necessary, with only "reasonable accommodations," in each of the clinical settings to which you were exposed. You may have to not only tell them in detail, but also show them. For, while federal legislation protects an individual from discriminatory questioning (such as being asked about the extent of your disability), it is permissible for interviewers to inquire about, and even to test, your ability to perform the job for which you are applying. Don't worry about this. If you did it in medical school, you can do it anywhere. Show your stuff!

As an example, after being denied admission to more than two dozen medical schools in the early 1990s, James B. Post IV, a quadriplegic since age 14, graduated in 1997 from Albert Einstein College of Medicine in the top 15% of his class. He planned to enter an Internal Medicine subspecialty. Upon graduating from medical school, he had little trouble getting a residency position. A Physician Assistant, whom he pays for, helps him. Einstein had previously graduated a paraplegic who became a Pathologist. In the past decade, there have been up to ten quadriplegics in U.S. medical schools at any one time. In December 2004, a blind medical student graduated near the top of his class at the University of Wisconsin-Madison, where he was also completing a Ph.D.

In the past, a physician's disability usually influenced his or her specialty choice if it occurred before or during medical school. Severely handicapped individuals usually entered Physiatry, Psychiatry, Pathology, or Anesthesiology. Those with disabilities that occurred later tended to stay in their original specialties, if they could. Many severely handicapped medical students and physicians now employ sophisticated medical assistive technology that helps them use necessary equipment or interpret clinical results. Three of the most common devices are rising electronic chairs that enable paralyzed practitioners to stand over an OR table, voice-activated or "reading" computer programs, and the "Optacon" that converts EKG images into vibratory signals for the visually impaired.

Under the Americans with Disabilities Act of 1990, "disability" is defined as a physical or mental impairment that substantially limits one or more major life activities (e.g., caring for oneself, performing manual tasks, walking, seeing, hearing, speaking, breathing, learning, and working). Under the Act, persons are considered disabled if they have a record of such an impairment or they are regarded as having such an impairment. The Act requires potential employers to make "reasonable accommodations" for disabled job applicants and workers, as long as the accommodations do not impose "undue hardships" on their business operation. If you are a disabled residency applicant, that applies to you. In addition, if you are not currently disabled but become disabled once you are a resident, they must make reasonable accommodations for you.

While having a contagious disease (such as tuberculosis or HIV) is considered an impairment, current illegal- or excessive legal-drug use, alcoholism that interferes with performance, sex-related behavior and disorders, and certain behavioral disorders (including pyromania, kleptomania, and compulsive gambling) are *not* covered by the Act.

If you believe that your impairment will hinder you when taking the USMLE, be certain, well before the application deadline date, to contact the examining agency: National Board of Medical Examiners (NBME) or the Educational Commission for Foreign Medical Graduates (ECFMG) for Steps 1 and 2, and the state or territorial licensing authority for Step 3. They will advise you on the documentation to submit so that they can arrange the special accommodations necessary for you to take the test. Special accommodations that they can make include granting extra time for the test or extra rest breaks, providing a reader or recorder, and using visual aids or enlarged-print examinations. If you test under any special conditions, your score reports and transcripts will include a note to that effect.

One caveat for those who do not think that they have a physical impairment that could keep them out of a training program: At least one-third of the Ophthalmology programs, all Aerospace Medicine programs, and a smattering of other programs test applicants for color vision and stereognosis. (This is perfectly legal if all applicants are screened and they can show that the requirement is job related.) Some applicants, especially men, fail. You may want to find out whether you have this physical impairment prior to setting your heart on one of these specialties.

For more information about resources for physically impaired physicians, contact: the U.S. Equal Employment Opportunity Commission, (202) 669-4900; TTY: (202) 669-6820; e-mail: info@ask.eeoc.gov; www.eeoc.gov.

Osteopathic Physicians

As an Osteopathic physician, you have one of two problems in getting a residency position, depending upon how you intend to approach your training: The limited number of Osteopathic specialties to choose from, or the intransigence and constantly shifting rules of some Osteopathic licensing bodies.

The growth in the number of Osteopathic medical students now far outpaces that of students at M.D. medical schools. Between 1970 and 2006, the number of D.O.s doubled, the number of Osteopathic schools increased from 9 to 20, and the number of graduates nearly *tripled*. By 2006, there will be nearly 2,900 D.O. graduates each year. However, D.O.s can be certified by an Osteopathic specialty board only in the following specialties:

Addiction Medicine	Orthopedics
Allergy & Immunology	Pathology
Anesthesiology	Pediatrics
Dermatology	Proctology
Emergency Medicine	Radiology
Family Practice	Physical Medicine &
Internal Medicine	Rehabilitation
Neurology & Psychiatry	Rheumatology
Obstetrics/Gynecology	Sclerotherapeutic Pain
Occupational & Preventative	Management
Medicine	Sports Medicine
Ophthalmology &	Surgery
Otolaryngology	

These graduates could enter D.O. internships, if they wanted to: The 5,434 funded Osteopathic internships, as well as the funded residency and fellowship positions would be sufficient to meet their needs if they were in the specialties that these new physicians desired to enter; for the most part, they aren't (Figures 13.8 and 22.10). This means that many Osteopathic graduates must look to the M.D. side of the profession for their training. The American Osteopathic Association's (AOA) Intern/Resident Registration Program (the "Match") and the Military's matching program are the only ways to get an AOA-approved internship (see Chapter 22).

AOA-approved training provides three types of internships: Transitional/Rotating (also called "Traditional"), Specialty Emphasis, and Specialty Track. *Transitional/Rotating internships* are the traditional program, with physicians rotating through the core specialties during the year.

The *Specialty Emphasis internship* is intended for the student who has special interest in Anesthesiology, Emergency Medicine, Family Practice, General Surgery, Psychiatry, or Diagnostic Radiology. Similar to traditional rotating internships, it offers additional concentration within one specialty. However, completing a special emphasis internship is *not* credited toward the first year of a residency in the specialty.

Specialty Track internships, while providing exposure to core disciplines, have most of the rotations in one specialty. Program graduates gain credit for both the internship and the first year of residency training. They are available only in Internal Medicine, Internal Medicine/Pediatrics, Obstetrics/Gynecology, Otolaryngology/Facial Plastic Surgery, Pediatrics, and Urological Surgery at institutions which have AOA-approved Osteopathic residencies in those specialties.

Osteopathic graduates say they "jump ship" to M.D. programs because they believe these programs provide better training, pay higher salaries,

FIGURE 13.8
Osteopathic Internships

Specialty	Number of Programs	Approved Positions	Funded Positions
Anesthesiology	6	147	142
Diagnostic Radiology	6	249	215
Emergency Medicine	27	829	699
Family Practice	88	1,540	1,248
Internal Medicine	60	1,312	1,100
Internal Med/Pediatrics	1	22	18
Obstetrics/Gynecology	26	833	671
Otolaryngology/Facial Plastic Surg	16	461	402
Pediatrics	15	444	348
Psychiatry	3	144	98
Surgery, General	15	498	422
Urological Surgery	2	83	71
TOTAL	**265**	**6,562**	**5,434**

Information from: American Osteopathic Association, http://opportunities.aoa-net.org, July 2005.

and include specialty training that is unavailable in Osteopathic programs. That is not surprising since there are only 13 Osteopathic teaching hospitals with more than 300 beds in the United States. Osteopathic educators now see AOA-approved postgraduate programs becoming a haven for D.O.s interested in surgical or other non-Internal Medicine and non-Family Practice specialties. As one said, defending students who do M.D. residencies, "students do not see anything distinctive in what Osteopathic graduate medical education training programs have that would differentiate them from [M.D.] programs . . . these choices may be the result of enlightened decision making and not necessarily an indication of disloyalty." If you intend to pursue ACGME-approved (M.D.) training, as did nearly two-thirds of recent Osteopathic graduates (including government and other joint AOA-ACGME-approved programs), you will have to deal with both the American Osteopathic Association (AOA) and the programs themselves.

About 10% of all residency programs in the United States have both AOA and ACGME (D.O. and M.D.) accreditation. About 11% of Osteopathic medical students plan on entering one of these programs. Another 47% plan on doing an M.D. residency. Another 10% plan on entering a federal government-sponsored residency (that both M.D. and D.O. groups must recognize). Only about 32% plan on entering a residency approved by only the AOA.

In the past, the AOA has made it very hard to pursue training at ACGME-approved programs. As a D.O., you cannot get a medical license in five states (FL, MI, OK, PA, WV) if you have not completed an AOA-approved internship. Some states may also require completion of an AOA-approved residency. Yet, increasing numbers of Osteopathic graduates coupled with low numbers of funded internship positions in many specialties have forced the AOA to create policies that allow for approval of some ACGME training.

Generally, if you want to do an AOA-approved residency, you are required to complete an AOA-approved internship. Recognizing the need to keep Osteopathic physicians associated with the profession, the AOA enacted Resolution 42, which allows Osteopaths in ACGME internships or residencies to apply for AOA approval of their training. To be eligible, you still must show hardship due to "unusual or exceptional circumstances"; however, the AOA has broadened their definition of these circumstances: Only 4 out of 400 applicants have been denied approval since the resolution was enacted in 2000.

The "Catch 22" is that before the internship or residency program can be considered, you must have been accepted into the program. In addition, you must complete the six core rotations included in a traditional AOA Rotating internship and participate in at least one Osteopathic medical education activity, such as attending an annual meeting of the appropriate Osteopathic specialty College or giving an Osteopathic clinical presentation at your ACGME program.

Both current and past trainees can apply for approval using a streamlined, one-page form available on the AOA's website. Internship applicants must submit a letter verifying the list of rotations, a letter explaining their "exceptional circumstances" (and supporting documents), documentation of their Osteopathic educational activity, and a non-refundable fee based on the number of beds in the hospital (e.g., $1,300 for 300 or more beds). Residency applicants must show proof of completion of an AOA-approved internship, proof of acceptance into a residency program, verification of ACGME program approval, and a non-refundable application fee of $120 (in 2006). Surgery residents must also submit the program director's *curriculum vitae*, a description of patients and procedures generally seen in the program, and a description of the program. You can petition the AOA for approval within three months of the start of your training. Notify them upon completion of any requirements. You must also provide "adequate documentation that similar training is not available within the Osteopathic profession."

After you submit an application and the fee to the AOA for approval, it is forwarded to the appropriate Osteopathic specialty College or Academy. They review it and make a recommendation to the AOA, which can then require an on-site review. (*You* must pay the $1,700 [2006] fee for the site review.) If the AOA approves the program, you must submit annual reports to them.

In addition, even though you will generally be eligible to take the AMA's specialty board examination upon successful completion of an ACGME-approved training program, in the past, you could not take the AOA's specialty examination in the same field without an AOA-approved internship. (You may take COMLEX Level 3, but you must request the application directly from COMLEX.) Again, to keep Osteopaths within the profession, the AOA has created (at least temporarily) a "Reentry Pathway" to enable those Osteopaths with ACGME-approved internships to be eligible for board certification. Note that if you do not have AOA specialty board certification, you will not be eligible for staff privileges in your specialty at some Osteopathic hospitals. This may not be important to you now, but things do change.

Another way of circumventing AOA requirements is to train in an ACGME-approved program that has also been approved by the AOA. For internships, the AOA will approve (or has already approved) most of the Military's Transitional (or equivalent) programs and, as of 2001, ACGME Transitional programs in a pilot program.

Over the past 15 years, increasing numbers of ACGME-approved Internal Medicine and Family Medicine programs have also become accredited by the American Osteopathic Association, so that both M.D.s and D.O.s will be eligible for Board certification and licensure. This cooperation grew out of a need for more primary care residents, an increasing number of D.O. students without a corresponding increase in Osteopathic residency positions, and the M.D. programs' only alternatives—taking international medical graduates or having open positions. In recent years, 60 ACGME-accredited institutions had such dual-accredited programs, which opened an additional 705 positions for Osteopathic graduates.

Perhaps this is why many of the Osteopaths training at M.D. institutions are in federal programs. The military has many good training programs under the direction of either M.D.s or D.O.s, or both. They are usually at very busy hospitals with adequate amounts of both resident responsibility and teaching from the staff. The AOA's procedures for approving Federal/Military internship training can be found on their website: http://www.do-online.osteotech .org/index.cfm?PageID=sir_app formsmilitary. Be sure to include your orders and a copy of the rotation schedule signed by your director.

More Osteopathic graduates are entering ACGME-approved training programs each year. Between 1986 and 2006, the number of D.O.s entering PGY-1 positions in M.D. residency programs has grown 250%. However, you must recognize that, for whatever reason, ACGME-approved training in some specialties is almost completely off-limits to Osteopaths (Figure 13.9). Chief among these are General Surgery and various surgical specialties, such as Colon and Rectal Surgery, Neurological Surgery, Orthopedic Surgery, Otolaryngology, Pediatric Surgery, Thoracic Surgery, and Urology.

If you apply to ACGME-approved programs, make certain that you explain, in detail, exactly what your COMLEX scores mean (unless you took the USMLE—a smart move), what your curriculum consists of, and what the grading scale on your transcript signifies. Remember that these may be significantly different from the scores, curricula, and grading scales seen in applications from M.D. students.

Also, be careful about your Dean's letter. While most Deans of Osteopathic medical schools send out respectable letters that are comparable to those sent out by M.D. Deans, some send out almost cursory statements. One wonders if these are sent only to ACGME-approved programs, in an attempt to "keep you in the fold"?

FIGURE 13.9

Osteopathic Graduates in ACGME-Approved Programs

Specialty	Number in Training	% of all Available M.D. Positions
Allergy/Immunology	8	3%
Anesthesiology	472	10
Cardiovascular Disease	76	4
Child/Adolescent Psychiatry	38	6
Colon & Rectal Surgery	1	2
Critical Care Medicine (All)	60	6
Dermatology	19	2
Emergency Medicine	338	8
Endocrinology	16	3
Family Medicine	1,170	13
Gastroenterology (IM)	44	4
Geriatrics (IM & FP)	13	5
Hand Surgery (All)	1	17
Hematology/Oncology (IM)	46	5
Infectious Diseases (IM)	23	3
Internal Medicine	1,097	5
Internal Med–Pediatrics	64	4
Nephrology (IM)	38	5
Neurological Surgery	1	<1
Neurology	90	7
Nuclear Medicine	5	3
Obstetrics & Gynecology	310	7
Ophthalmology	17	1
Orthopedic Surgery	20	<1
Otolaryngology	10	1
Pathology	102	5
Pediatrics	442	6
Pediatric Surgery	0	0
Physical Med/Rehabilitation	190	17
Plastic Surgery	1	<1
Preventive Med/Pub Hlth (All)	24	8
Psychiatry	286	6
Pulmonary Diseases (IM)	2	2
Radiation Oncology	8	2
Radiology, Diagnostic	139	3
Rheumatology (IM)	31	9
Surgery, General	177	2
Thoracic Surgery	4	1
Transitional Year	52	4
Urology	10	1

Adapted from: Appendix II, Table 1. JAMA. 2005;294(9):1129-31.

While you will encounter problems when crossing over to enter ACGME-approved programs, if that is the training that will meet your future needs, by all means, go for it!

Common Questions

The following are some common questions Osteopathic medical students ask:

As an Osteopathic medical student or graduate, can I participate in the National Residency Matching Program (NRMP)? Yes, you participate as an "Independent Applicant." For additional information, see Chapter 22, *The NRMP & Other Matches*. To apply to most programs, you must now also participate in the Electronic Residency Application Service (ERAS) (see Chapter 12). As of July 15, 2005, you can apply for Osteopathic internships on ERAS.

Should I take the USMLE or the Osteopathic licensing exam (COMLEX)? As an Osteopathic student, generally, you will want to take *both* the USMLE and COMLEX, since comparative results show that the COMLEX is a little easier to pass than the USMLE (Figure 7.3) and some state D.O. licensing boards may not recognize the USMLE. The main reason to take the USMLE is that residency directors at M.D. programs can more easily judge your qualifications against other applicants. If you take only the COMLEX and apply for an M.D. residency, be sure to explain how the test is scored. If possible, send them copies of the official information sheet that came with your scores. Also, attach a small "cheat sheet" summarizing your performance.

What options do I have if I am in or have taken an Osteopathic internship? You have three options for residency training. First, you can directly contact Osteopathic or M.D. residency programs with openings and apply to them. (See "Not Using a Match," page 570.) Second, you can apply to an M.D. residency program through the NRMP Advanced Match, either as a senior student or during your intern year. Finally, you can simply enter the NRMP Match during your intern year to begin an M.D. residency at the PGY-1 level. The option you choose depends upon your personal situation and the competitiveness of the specialty you want to enter.

How much discrimination against D.O.s is there among M.D. residency directors? To deny that many M.D. residency programs discriminate against D.O.s would be foolish. Many residency directors do not understand that Osteopathic training parallels that of M.D. schools. This discrimination, however, varies by the area of the country and by the specialty. In areas where many D.O.s practice and Osteopathic medical schools have been established, there is minimal discrimination. Where there are few D.O.s, ignorance abounds. As to specialties, residency programs in General Surgery and its subspecialties remain the major areas that automatically reject many D.O. residency applicants.

Older Applicants

Many students now enter medicine either after they have raised a family or as a second career. In the last decade, the number of students over 28 years old entering medical school has doubled. This group now comprises about 34% of all graduating students, with 10% being at least 30 years old. Older students may have some unique problems in medical school, and they may face some obstacles when applying for residency positions.

First, because older students may have more debt and more financial responsibilities than younger students, they may be tempted to jump into the most lucrative practice they can in the shortest amount of time. Many may decide to bypass specialties in which they have a real interest but whose training takes longer. Bad move! If you have invested the time, lost income, and endured strife getting through medical school, aim for the goal you really want. Apply to the specialty that most interests you. The extra year or two of training will pay you back immeasurably in the satisfaction you (and your family) have in your work during your career.

The second difficulty older applicants face is the negative attitude of some residency faculty members. They may perceive the older applicant as possessing maturity, but not enough stamina and energy to complete a demanding residency. Spending time with the program faculty, either in a clinical setting on a formal rotation or in educational rounds, may overcome their hesitation. During your interviews, describe your high energy level within the context of other answers. One example might be, "I stayed by her bedside all night in the ICU, monitoring her status and adjusting her medications. It was exhilarating." Finally, many older applicants come to medicine after other life experiences to truly serve humanity. Many faculty will respond positively to a heartfelt description of why you made such a difficult life decision. Tell them.

Physicians who are making a mid-career switch—changing specialties—are a subgroup of older applicants. The most common reasons physicians give for changing specialties, either during residency or after they are in practice, are: (1) they become enlightened or (2) they become disillusioned with their prior specialty. While about 40% of those who change specialties are generalists, 60% are specialists. Of those who change specialties late in their career (40 to 69 years old), the most common profile is a woman international medical graduate with a hospital-based practice in an Internal Medicine subspecialty, Emergency Medicine (probably not residency-trained with this profile), a Pediatrics subspecialty, or Pathology.

Some physicians are forced to change specialties due to physical disabilities. Others need to change specialties, often to a primary care specialty, to find a job where they want to live. Residency directors may be reluctant to accept these applicants unless they can adequately demonstrate that they have come to terms with making the specialty change. Programs are not looking for applicants who do not really want to be in their residency.

The first question residency directors ask is "Are you seeking to enter our specialty or simply running away from the one you are in?" That is a darn good question—one you need to ask yourself before starting the process. Why do you really want to do this? At the least, it will cost you extra time, decrease your income, and alter your lifestyle or where you live.

If your extensive qualifications are used as a reason to not hire you as a resident, note that a New York Federal District Court ruled that an employer declining to offer a position on the grounds that the candidate is "overqualified" may be violating the Age Discrimination in Employment Act. According to the court, the term "overqualified" may simply be a code word for too old.

Physicians face multiple problems in making such a change. The most obvious problem for those going back to residency after being in practice is the resultant change in lifestyle. Going from a practicing physician's salary to a resident's salary can be a rude experience for both the physician and his or her family. Ego damage can also be a problem. The shift from the role of omnipotent attending to lowly resident can be quite a blow—especially when some of the residency faculty are younger than you (or sometimes, your children).

Occasionally, physicians who have left clinical practice for administration or research decide to reenter the clinical world. This may be a daunting step. As one returnee noted, "My greatest fear was my ignorance—the amalgam of what I had forgotten combined with what had been added to the realm of practice since I had last been there." The key is to choose a supportive program that will provide a curriculum tailored to your individual needs. This may be harder to find than you assume.

The specialties that most commonly receive trainees who previously were in other specialties are Anesthesiology (sometimes called "the Foreign Legion of Medicine" for all the escapees from other specialties in its ranks), Diagnostic Radiology, Emergency Medicine, Family Medicine, Internal Medicine, and Neurology. Practitioners most commonly leave Internal Medicine for other specialties.

The keys to successfully making a mid-career switch are to adequately prepare yourself and your family for the changes, to carefully investigate what you are getting into, and to make contact in advance with potential residency directors. If you plan to take training in the town where you practice, attend some teaching conferences and make arrangements to observe or participate clinically with some of the attendings. Knowledgeable residency directors will see an applicant who comes to residency training with prior clinical experience as a real bonus—if you can show them that you know what you are getting into and that you want to be there.

Military/Public Health Service

Two basic questions come up when discussing your involvement in military residencies. First, what is involved in a commitment to the Armed Forces medical system? Second, how is playing this game different from competing in the normal application and matching processes?

There are several factors to consider when looking at military residencies. The most obvious is financial. If you are in the School of Medicine of the Uniform Services University of the Health Sciences (USUHS), you are obligated to do a military residency. The military is obligated to find you a first-year training slot. You have saved a great deal of money, and will pay it back with the years you commit to the service at much lower pay than your civilian counterparts receive.

If you have enrolled in the three- or four-year Armed Forces Health Professions Scholarship Program (HPSP), the military will pay for your tuition, expenses, and required books. They will also give you a stipend for living expenses. In return, you owe them four active duty tours of 45 days during each year of medical school, four years of active duty as an Armed Forces doctor, and four years of inactive reserve duty. If your residency lasts more than four years, you will owe more time. You have, of course, avoided a large debt by obligating yourself to military service. In addition, if you train in a military residency, you can expect a higher rate of compensation than if you were in a civilian residency. But you don't get something for nothing. Your colleagues will normally make up the difference after they finish training and begin their medical practice, although most will also be saddled with a large educational debt.

Military residencies typically involve a greater time commitment than civilian residencies, as you can be pulled after the first internship year to fill General Medical Officer (GMO) openings, tours that can last two to three years. These GMO tours as a "sick call" doctor provide unique opportunities. After the tour, you will continue your specialty at the second-year level, and these years are subtracted from your time commitment. Also, be aware that as a member of the Independent Ready Reserves after completing your active duty obligation, you can be called up at any time while you are building a practice. Finally, since the September 11th attacks, the military reserves the right to keep you in the service in times of crisis. So, even if you have served your contracted time, you could be prevented from leaving until the crisis is resolved.

Military medicine is changing rapidly as the armed forces are downsized, more dependent medical care is being outsourced to the civilian sector, and military physicians are finding themselves deployed overseas more often and for longer periods of time. Simultaneously, battlefield medicine is going "high tech," with many cutting-edge developments to assist military physicians in the field.

As noted above, Osteopathic medical students might want to consider military residency training. The American Osteopathic Association is usually willing to recognize as valid any residency that is done in the military. This provides Osteopathic graduates a chance at what may be a more intense and varied residency experience than they could obtain in the civilian world. Additionally, successful completion of a military residency generally allows the Osteopathic physician to apply for both M.D. and Osteopathic specialty boards. Make sure, however, that the individual program has been approved by the AOA *before* you start your training.

Finally, if you have your heart set on entering the specialty of Aerospace Medicine, you will normally need to join the Air Force or the Navy to get a residency position. And you usually will not be able to enter the residency directly from school or even after your internship. These programs routinely require applicants to have some experience, as well as to have passed short courses in Aerospace Medicine offered through the military. However, there are two civilian residency programs in Aerospace Medicine: One at Wright State University School of Medicine in Dayton, Ohio, and the other at the University of Texas in Galveston. If you are interested in training for Hyperbaric and Undersea Medicine, you will normally have to join the Navy.

If you want to do a military residency, how do you obtain a position? All U.S. Army and most Navy residency programs (all specialties) use the Electronic Residency Application Service (ERAS), although each branch also has its own application. (Chapter 12 has information about ERAS.) According to former U.S. Army Surgeon General Ronald R. Blank, the Army, Navy, and Air Force fill their first-year residency positions with graduates of the Uniformed Services University of the Health Sciences, medical students with an individual military commitment (often through HPSP), and those in the Reserve Officers' Training Corps. Only individuals on active military duty can participate in Armed Forces residency programs.

The military's selection system for matching applicants with programs is similar to the NRMP Match in that both applicants and programs send in rank order lists. However, representatives of the military teaching hospitals meet, exchange information about the candidates, and make the selections, rather than having it done impartially by computer. Priority is given to those on active duty at the time of selection and to graduates of the F. Edward Hebert School of Medicine, Uniformed Services University of the Health Sciences (military medical school) in Bethesda, Maryland. The selections are then finalized. There are generally many more applicants for military residency positions than there are available slots.

The military match occurs early in the senior year. Therefore, competing in the military match means you have to make career decisions very early. Finding out about military training programs is often more difficult than getting information about civilian programs. Your best sources of information, aside from the "Green Book" and *FREIDA*, are military residents, military physicians, and your military branch's Medical Personnel Counselor. These latter individuals vary greatly in quality and interest. Be certain to cross-check any information they give you.

Early planning and preparation are very important. Military residencies are extremely competitive, and the number of open spots varies from year to year depending on the military's needs. The residencies and subspecialties offered are also based on projected military needs, so if there are sufficient personnel in a particular specialty, acquiring training in it may be extremely difficult. To verify what has been approved each year for the Air Force, check the "Specialties" Table on their HPSP website at http://ci.afit.edu/cimj/specialties_table.asp.

You should be able to get a good idea of the programs you wish to attend, since military specialties have only three to five residency programs each. To get into the specialty and the military residency program you desire, you are highly encouraged to do your "away" rotation (subinternship) in that specialty and at that site during or immediately after your third year of medical school. Arranging for this rotation can often take six months or more. Your activities during this subinternship are not much different than those described for a civilian subinternship. Be sure that both the residency director and the department chairman know who you are and are impressed with the job that you do. Try to set up your residency interview during your rotation. Also secure a letter of recommendation from a military doctor as one of your two letters of recommendation for the Match—not required, but certainly helpful.

You must submit applications to military residency programs the summer before your senior year. Interviews start shortly thereafter, and ROLs are due in mid-September, while civilian students are still interviewing. Be sure to wear a well-fitting, clean, and starched Class A uniform to your residency interviews. Military bearing is important, just as it is during your clerkships. Health Professions Scholarship Program (HPSP) students should also interview at some civilian programs and enter the NRMP PGY-1 Match. However, if there are spots open in a military training program, you will not receive a deferment to a civilian program unless (1) your service decides it needs more physicians in your chosen field than its own training programs can provide or (2) you are a highly competitive student. With fewer students applying for HPSP scholarships, it is highly likely that you will do a military residency, particularly in the Army, which has more openings and more specialties than the other services. Nevertheless, you will need to apply to civilian programs as a backup. If you do match with the military, you must drop out of the NRMP PGY-1 Match. But your money won't be refunded.

One important note: If you owe an obligation to serve in the military or PHS, but either did not match with a military program or there is no military program in your specialty (e.g., the Air Force does not have a Neurological Surgery program), you will need a civilian residency. No civilian program will want you as a resident, however, if they cannot be assured that you will be around for the duration of the program. The Navy, for example, has had a gloomy record of pulling their people out of training after the PGY-1 year to go on sea duty. Therefore, civilian programs will want to see a *written commitment* from the service allowing you to complete your training before going on active duty. There should be no difficulty in obtaining this before it is time for the civilian training programs to make up their rank lists for the Match.

The military services also sponsor some physicians during their civilian training programs. Residents in this program receive officer's pay, some benefits, and a salary bonus. The military obligation is equal to the time sponsored, with a minimum of two years.

Your active duty begins when you finish residency, unless you are given permission to go into a fellowship. Be aware that permission for fellowship subspecialization, an increasingly attractive option for many students, is often declined: You may serve your time, for example, as a general surgeon, instead of receiving more training in a Cardiothoracic Surgery fellowship. Military fellowships are highly competitive, and you may be given preference if you have seen active duty or plan on a military career, which makes the investment more worthwhile for the military.

Any moonlighting you do, either during your residency or while practicing medicine in the military, is subject to the approval of your commanding officer; most institutions have standard forms to request permission. While moonlighting, you are not allowed to care for (or at least charge) patients covered by the Military Health System, since you are already being paid to serve this community.

Students in the **National Health Service Corps' (NHSC) Scholarship Program** are required to enter (and complete) an approved primary care residency program; failure to do this will incur financial penalties. Acceptable programs include those in General Internal Medicine, Family Medicine, Internal Medicine–Pediatrics, Internal Medicine–Family Medicine, General Pediatrics, Obstetrics/Gynecology, and General Psychiatry. D.O.s must complete a Transitional/Rotating year before beginning one of the above residencies. The NHSC must approve your completed *Deferment Request Form* and your educational plan, although not the specific program, in advance. Note that military residencies are not acceptable.

In general, physicians who have completed military residencies strongly recommend not making a decision to go into military medicine based on financial need or on recruiters' glowing promises, but rather on a desire to participate in the Armed Forces. As one person put it, "The best advice I *never* heard while contemplating signing up for military medicine is that it is a good thing to do only if you if you think you would enjoy being in the military anyway. If you have concerns about deployment, spending several years living in undesirable places far from family, or the unique aspects of military medicine, do yourself a favor and do not sign up." Make certain that this option is for you and you understand the obligations involved before you sign on the dotted line.

An excellent guide for those considering the Armed Forces Health Professions Scholarship Program is available online at http://lukeballard .tripod.com/HPSP.html. The author wrote this unofficial guide, with lots of inside tips and good advice, while in the Air Force HSPS. For information on physicians in military and federal service, contact the Military Medical Student Association, www.militarymedicine.org/; or the Association of Military Surgeons of the United States, (800) 761-9320 or (301) 897-8800; www.amsus.org.

14

International Medical Graduates

If you really want to do something, you'll find a way;
if you don't, you'll find an excuse.

– Anonymous

INTERNATIONAL MEDICAL GRADUATES (IMGs), often referred to as foreign medical graduates (FMGs), include all those who have graduated from any of the approximately 1,400 medical schools outside the United States, its possessions, and Canada. IMGs functionally break down into three subgroups:

1. **U.S. IMGs (USIMGs).** Those individuals who are currently citizens or permanent residents of the United States, but who received their medical degree outside the United States, Puerto Rico, or Canada. About a third of IMG physicians who have obtained U.S. residency slots in recent years are in this category. (Permanent Residents or "Green Card" holders are treated as U.S. citizens during the residency application process.)

2. **Foreign National IMGs (FNIMGs).** Individuals who are not U.S. citizens and who received their medical degree from a medical school not approved by the LCME, usually located outside the United States, Puerto Rico, or Canada.

3. **Exchange Visitor IMGs (EVIMGs).** The largest subset of FNIMGs applying for residency slots, these individuals are in the United States only temporarily as Exchange Visitors (with J-1, or occasionally H-type visas) to study, teach, or do research. This group must have a firm offer of a residency position to apply for their visa. Many, if not most, of this group will have attended U.S. medical schools.

Each group has unique problems in terms of acquiring U.S. residency positions. But since EVIMGs and FNIMGs have such similar problems, they will be discussed together. (Note that foreign nationals who graduate from U.S., Canadian, or Puerto Rican medical schools are not considered IMGs.)

By 2005, more than 200,000 (about 25%) of the physicians practicing medicine in the United States were trained outside the United States, Puerto Rico, and Canada. Their practices tend to be medical, rather than surgical (Figure 14.1). In 2005, about 80% of IMGs worked in patient care, with 72% in office-based practices (nearly one-quarter of all office-based U.S. physicians). Most IMGs work in New York (16%), California (11%), Florida (8%), New Jersey (6%), or Illinois (6%).

While IMGs account for 26% of physicians in residency training, they comprise only 22% of PGY-1s. About 20% of non-U.S. citizen IMG residents come from India, and 10% come from the Philippines, with the balance relatively evenly divided among other nations. About 40% of IMGs train in New York or California, with almost half training in Internal Medicine or a Medicine specialty. Nearly 34% of all primary care residency positions are filled by IMGs. About 33% of IMGs pursue post-residency fellowships, while only about 27% of U.S. medical graduates do so. Women comprise less than 30% of all IMGs in U.S. residencies, with nearly half of them in primary care (compared to one-third of male IMGs).

The Negative Image

The prestigious *Academic Medicine* described some residency faculty members' perceptions of why IMGs experience problems in U.S. residency programs. These were:

- Difficulty with medical or non-medical English.
- Differences in medical education.
- Length of time since graduation from medical school and last clinical experiences.
- Older, with more family and financial obligations.
- Cultural differences in their approach to and beliefs about communication, authority, gender roles, interpersonal relationships, and the role or status of physicians.
- Traumatic experiences as persecuted minorities, refugees, or new immigrants.

Large numbers of IMGs continue to practice and train despite a lot of negative press. Over the past several years, IMGs have had much lower scores on USMLE Step 1, Step 2CK, and Step 2CS than U.S. medical

FIGURE 14.1

IMGs Practicing Medicine in Various Specialties

	Number of IMGs	% of All Physicians in Specialty that are IMGs	% of all IMGs
Internal Medicine	50,653	34%	23.3%
Nuclear Medicine	485	33	0.2
Pathology	6,031	33	2.7
Physical Med/Rehab.	2,239	32	1.0
Psychiatry	12,335	31	5.7
Pulmonary Diseases	2,962	31	1.4
Cardiovascular Disease	6,632	30	3.1
Neurology	3,924	30	1.8
Anesthesiology	11,007	29	5.1
Pediatrics	18,931	28	8.7
Child & Adolescent Psychiatry	1,897	28	0.9
Gastroenterology	3,086	26	1.4
Medical Genetics	118	26	0.1
Allergy & Immunology	1,007	24	0.5
General/Family Medicine	20,464	22	9.4
Colon & Rectal Surgery	261	21	0.1
Thoracic Surgery	1,087	21	0.5
Radiation Oncology	837	20%	0.4%
General Surgery	7,698	20	3.5
Obstetrics/Gynecology	7,489	18	3.4
Radiology (All)	1,592	18	0.7
Urological Surgery	1,699	16	0.8
Gen. Preventive Med	288	15	0.1
Neurological Surgery	724	14	0.3
Occupational Medicine	378	14	0.2
Plastic Surgery	849	13	0.4
Public Health	210	12	0.1
Otolaryngology	994	10	0.5
Emergency Medicine	2,468	9	0.1
Ophthalmology	1,488	8	0.7
Aerospace Medicine	36	7	<0.1
Orthopedic Surgery	1,671	7	0.8
Dermatology	660	6	0.3

Adapted from: American Medical Association. Physician Characteristics and Distribution in the U.S., 2005. Chicago, IL: AMA, 2005, Tables 1.5, 1.14.

students and graduates (Figure 7.3). These widely reported results do not improve the negative image of IMGs within the medical community.

Negative incidents over the past two decades, including "worthless" medical degrees granted by some Caribbean medical schools, led the ECFMG to establish web-based assistance, the Credential Verification Service (www.ecfmg.org/cvs/index.html), where residency directors, among others, can quickly verify ECFMG Certification. The incidents also led four jurisdictions (Pennsylvania, Puerto Rico, Texas, and Virginia) to ban international medical students from taking clinical clerkships in their hospitals in their state. (Texas grants an exception for rotations if the hospital has an accredited residency in the same specialty.) Fourteen other states (AR, AL, CA, CT, DE, DC, FL, GA, KY, MA, ME, NJ, NY, and OR) regulate IMGs in clinical clerkships. New York reportedly has the toughest regulations (and most expensive process) to certify non-U.S. medical schools to send their students for clerkships. In addition, AAMC rules preclude U.S. medical schools from "co-mingling" their own students with students from non-U.S. schools during required clerkships. (Some hospitals have gotten around this by using "separate-but-equal" ward teams.) These restrictions, however, attack the mechanism through which foreign-trained medical students demonstrate their clinical competence and subsequently get residency slots and become licensed. (Twenty licensing boards evaluate the quality of a clinical clerkship when deciding whether to grant a license to an IMG.)

Licensing, Funding, & Residency Positions

There are thousands of IMGs in the United States who have not been able to obtain a license to practice medicine. In many cases, this is because residency programs will not accept them for training: *all jurisdictions in the United States require at least one year of postgraduate training in the U.S. or Canada for licensure* (Figure 7.10). Fourteen jurisdictions require IMGs to have at least two years of training for licensure and 29 require three years. This exceeds what most jurisdictions require from U.S. graduates. In addition, 25 licensing boards (AL, AR, CA, CO, CT, DC, GA, GU, ID, IN, KY, LA, MN, MS, MO, MT, NM, ND, OK, OR, PR, RI, SD, TN, VT) maintain lists of state-approved foreign medical schools whose graduates are eligible for a medical license. However, 16 U.S. licensing boards allow IMGs to take USMLE Step 3 before obtaining graduate medical education in the U.S. or Canada. Thirty-nine states will endorse the Licentiate of the Medical Council of Canada (LMCC) for a U.S. license when held by an IMG.

Residency programs, especially those that train large numbers of international medical graduates, are also concerned about changes in Medicare laws that severely restrict the programs' and hospitals' reimbursement for training non-U.S.-medical school graduates. These residency programs often operate on a shoestring as it is; threatening to further restrict their funds has had the desired effect of closing down many training opportunities for international medical graduates.

There is little question that many, if not most, residency programs discriminate against IMGs. Yet, Section 102 of the 1992 Federal Health Professions Education Extension Amendments (PL 102-408) states:

> Graduates of Foreign Medical Schools.–The Secretary [of Health and Human Services] may make an award of a grant, cooperative agreement, or contract under this title to an entity [including a medical school] that provides graduate training in the health professions only if the entity agrees that, in considering applications for admissions to a program of such training, the entity will not refuse to consider an application solely on the basis that the application is submitted by a graduate of a foreign medical school.

How much sway this law holds over residency directors is unknown, since most probably are not aware of it. Studies show that some residency programs discriminate against IMGs as early as when they send out application materials. As residency positions decrease, however, enterprising IMGs will certainly begin making them aware of the law.

What does sway residency directors, however, is the past performance of IMGs in residency programs. For example, IMGs, especially those who contract with residencies outside a matching program, have a higher attrition rate than U.S. graduates. Also, IMGs pass some specialty board examinations, such as Internal Medicine's, only about two-thirds as often on their first try as do U.S. graduates. Since residency programs are judged, in part, on their graduates' pass rates, this is important to residency directors.

Despite all the unfavorable press and the tough requirements, the number of IMGs in U.S. residency positions increased from just over 12,000 in 1989 to nearly 27,000 in 2004. The number of IMGs in first-year residency positions increased over this same period from 2,689 to more than 6,100. USIMGs (U.S. natives and permanent residents) make up about 11% of first-year residents, but 40% of all first-year IMG residents. In the 2005 NRMP Match, IMGs made up a large proportion of those entering some specialties, such as Family Medicine and Internal Medicine (Figure 14.2).

The American Medical Association's International Medical Graduates Section tackles licensure, discrimination, and visa issues on behalf of IMGs. For information, go to the AMA's website at www.ama-assn.org/go/membergroups and select the Section by name. The website contains interesting, although not necessarily the most current, information.

FIGURE 14.2

Types of Applicants (Percentages) Filling PGY-1 and Advanced Positions in Specialties through NRMP Match[1]

Specialty	% Filled by U.S. Senior Students	% Filled by Osteopaths & U.S. Grad. Physicians	% Filled by IMGs, Fifth Pathway, & Can. Grads	% Total Positions Filled thru NRMP
Anesthesiology	70%	10%	16%	95%
Emergency Medicine	82	14	4	98
Family Medicine	49	7	38	82
Internal Medicine	57	6	36	97
Obstetrics/Gynecology	71	10	19	95
Orthopedic Surgery	93	5	2	99
Pathology[2]	68	14	18	91
Pediatrics	76	8	16	97
Psychiatry	66	10	23	96
Radiology, Diagnostic	86	10	4	93
Surgery, General[4]	81	8	11	99
Transitional	92	4	4	95
Osteopaths Unmatched[3]	—	31%	—	—
5th Pathway Unmatched[3]	—	—	40%	—
U.S. IMGs Unmatched[3]	—	—	45%	—
FNIMGs Unmatched[3]	—	—	44%	—
Total Unmatched[3]	**6%**	**40%**	**47%**	—

[1]Numbers in the columns for percent of graduates matching within a specialty may not add up to total percentage matched due to rounding.
[2]A significant number of entry-level positions (PGY-1 or above) are offered outside the Match.
[3]The percentage is of those going through the entire NRMP process. Between 4% (U.S. Seniors) and 40% (U.S.- and foreign-born IMGs) of the candidates either withdrew before the Match or did not submit a Rank Order List.
[4]Categorical positions.
Derived from: National Residency Matching Program. *Results and Data 2005*. Washington, DC: NRMP, 2005 (April).

ECFMG Certification

International medical school graduates must get ECFMG Certification to be eligible for: (1) acceptance into an ACGME-accredited residency or fellowship position in the United States; (2) a visa for entry into the United States as a medical trainee; (3) a medical license in most states; and (4) an application to take USMLE Step 3 (Figure 14.3). (Fifth Pathway students do not need an ECFMG Certificate, and Oklahoma does not require it for licensure.) The ECFMG issues about 6,000 new Certificates annually.

Note, however, that 16 states have requirements for appointment to a residency position in addition to an ECFMG Certificate for IMGs. These states are Alaska, Arizona, California, Connecticut, Iowa, Kansas, Kentucky, Louisiana, Michigan, Minnesota, Nevada, New Jersey, New Mexico, Pennsylvania, Texas, and Vermont.

FIGURE 14.3

**Requirements to Practice Medicine, Do Post-Graduate Training, or
Be a Clinical Research Fellow in the United States (Patient Contact)**

	USMLE	ECFMG Certification	Applicable Visas
American Citizen/Permanent U.S. Resident: Graduate of LCME-accredited U.S., Canadian, or Puerto Rican Medical School	✔		
Foreign National: Graduate of LCME-accredited U.S., Canadian, or Puerto Rican Medical School (EVIMG)	✔		✔
American Citizen/Permanent U.S. Resident: Graduate of Foreign Medical School (USIMG)*	✔	✔	
Foreign National: Graduate of Foreign Medical School (FNIMG)	✔	✔	✔

*An alternative for U.S. citizen/permanent resident IMGs is to enter the Fifth Pathway Program. In that case, they do not need to get an ECFMG Certificate.

To qualify for an ECFMG Certificate, you must be either a *student* attending a medical school listed in the current edition of the *International Medical Education Directory*, published by the Foundation for Advancement of International Medical Education and Research (FAIMER), or a *graduate* of a medical school that is listed in this directory (your graduation date must be within the "Graduation Years" listed for the school).

If you have graduated, you must document completion of the educational requirements to practice medicine in the country in which you received your medical education. This must include at least four years of medical study for which credit was received. Foreign nationals must also have an unrestricted license or certificate to practice medicine in their own country. The specific credentials accepted for each country are listed in the annual *ECFMG Information Booklet* (see below). Those licensed only in stomatology, in ayurvedic or homeopathic medicine, and those awarded only the diploma of Physician–Epidemiologist–Hygienist, Physician–Cyberneticist, Physician–Biophysicist, Licensed Medical Practitioner, or Assistant Medical Practitioner are not eligible for an ECFMG Certificate.

The ECFMG website (www.ecfmg.org) contains a wealth of information, including one of the most important resources for IMGs, the *ECFMG Information Booklet*. This publication describes the steps in the ECFMG certification process, lists the contact information and application requirements for the various items necessary to obtain an ECFMG Certificate, and lists the medical credentials that the ECFMG accepts for each country. The ECFMG website also lets you download the *USMLE Bulletin of Information*.

For those who already have or are about to get their ECFMG Certificate, the site also provides an entry into ERAS (acts as your Dean's office). The Credential Verification Service on the site allows program directors, hospitals, and other employers to verify that you do, indeed, have an ECFMG Certificate.

OASIS

Accessible via the ECFMG website, the Online Applicant Status and Information System (OASIS) is a very useful tool for ECFMG applicants and ECFMG-certified physicians. Individuals can use OASIS to check the status of their Certificate, including whether the ECFMG has received their medical education credentials, or to request permanent validation of their Certificate. Those eligible for ECFMG certification can get information on the status of their USMLE application, scheduling permits, score reports, and transcript requests. (While exam results are not available on OASIS, you can use the system to check whether the results have been mailed.) If you are sponsored by the ECFMG, you can also use OASIS to determine the current status of your J-1 visa sponsorship.

The system also allows you to verify that the ECFMG's information about you, including name-of-record, contact information, and the status of your ECFMG financial account, is correct. If the information is wrong, address and other contact information can be changed online, but name changes must be submitted on a separate form. If necessary, you can also make advance payments to your ECFMG financial account through OASIS. If you use ERAS, you will use OASIS to request and pay for the ERAS token.

OASIS is free of charge and can be accessed 24 hours a day, seven days a week, by individuals with a USMLE/ECFMG Identification Number and a special password. More information about OASIS, including how to obtain a password for this service, can be found at https://oasis2.ecfmg .org/. Technical difficulties should be reported to: oasis@ecfmg.org.

Application Process

You must submit an application and the required documentation to the ECFMG. Processing this application may take several months, since education credentials must be verified by your medical school. To speed up the processing on all paperwork, always use the same (formal) name that is on your medical school diploma. Once the ECFMG has assigned you a number, use that on any correspondence with the ECFMG, licensing bodies, and residency programs.

USMLE

IMGs can apply for Step 1, Step 2 Clinical Knowledge (CK), and Step 2 Clinical Skills (CS) of the USMLE through the ECFMG using the Interactive Web Application on the ECFMG website. You can complete the online application in one sitting, or save it and return to complete it later. Alternatively, you can print a paper application.

If you receive approval to take the exam, you will receive a receipt showing the date of the exam, the test center's address, and the cost. About four weeks before the exam, an official admission permit that includes the time and location of the test will be sent out. As of 2005, students must have completed at least two years of medical school before taking Step 2CK or Step 2CS. While eligible IMGs can take the USMLE Steps in any sequence, they must pass Step 1, Step 2CK, and Step 2CS to meet the medical science examination requirement for ECFMG Certification. The ECFMG recommends that IMGs complete their core clinical clerkships, including patient contact, before taking Steps 2CK and 2CS. Students who are unable to obtain an appropriate visa to enter the United States to take Step 2CS may request a full refund of the examination fee.

The ECFMG administers the USMLE to IMGs at about 300 centers in the United States and Canada, and at more than 100 other locations. The computerized tests are administered throughout most of the year. Each test takes one day. There is no limit to the number of times an applicant can take a Step or Step component, although some states impose their own limits—both on the number of times Steps can be taken and on the length of time taken to complete the entire (Steps 1 through 3) process. Note that IMGs desiring to enter the United States on an H-1B visa (work permit) must pass Step 3 before they can obtain the visa. (For more information about the USMLE, see Chapter 7.)

While there are rumors to the contrary, the USMLE Steps 1, 2CK, and 2CS are scored identically for all examinees. It usually costs more to take these exams outside the United States or Canada, however, since an "International Test Delivery Surcharge" is added. The current charges and cities with ProMetrics testing sites are listed on the ECFMG website.

To apply to take Step 3, an applicant must have obtained an M.D. degree or equivalent; passed Steps 1, 2CK, and 2CS; obtained an ECFMG Certificate or completed a Fifth Pathway program; and met any other specific requirements imposed by the state licensing board administering the test. Information about specific state requirements is available from the individual state board or The Federation of State Medical Boards of the U.S., P.O. Box 619850, Dallas, TX 75261-9850 USA; (817) 868-4000; www.fsmb.org.

If history is any guide, those IMGs with the best chance of passing the USMLE are younger than 30 years old, male, native English speakers, FNIMGs, and educated in countries with a low infant mortality rate and a high per capita income. Those with the least chance of passing the USMLE are those over 40 years old, female, non-native English speakers, those taking the test more than 10 years after medical school, USIMGs, and those educated in countries with a medium to high infant mortality rate and medium per capita income.

ECFMG English Language Examination
All IMGs must be fluent in spoken and written English.

Applicants for ECFMG certification are no longer required to take the Test of English as a Foreign Language™ (TOEFL®) or the ECFMG English Test. As of June 2004, the ECFMG accepts a passing score on USMLE Step 2 Clinical Skills (CS) as evidence that an individual's written and spoken English is sufficient to practice medicine in the United States. (This test has a separately scored subcomponent that assesses English language proficiency.) However, the ECFMG does recommend that IMGs take the Test of Spoken English™ (TSE®), offered by the Educational Testing Service®, for self-assessment before taking Step 2CS. (They suggest that you should receive a score of at least 45 on the TSE.)

If you have previously taken TOEFL or the ECFMG English Test, check with the ECFMG to see if the results are still accepted for the purposes of entering graduate medical education.

Even if your ability to read and write English is excellent, your chances of obtaining the residency you want (or any residency in the United States) may be improved if you take a *conversational* English course. (This is also true for those native English speakers who are not familiar with American idioms.) Unlike the standard English course, this type of course prepares people to speak American English. It is a skill you will need as a resident and later as a practicing physician.

Clinical Skills Assessment (CSA®)
The ECFMG Clinical Skills Assessment (CSA), a test of clinical and communication skills, has been supplanted by USMLE Step 2 Clinical Skills (CS). (See Chapter 7, "USMLE".)

Applicants who have already passed the CSA are not required to pass Step 2CS to meet the eligibility requirements for Step 3 and for ECFMG Certification. If students were certified by ECFMG and the CSA pass date on their certificate is June 14, 2001, or later, they may request a permanent validation sticker for their CSA date. A passing performance on the CSA before June 14, 2001, however, remains subject to expiration (three years from the exam date) for the purpose of starting a residency in the United States.

Applicants who have *both* passed the *former* ECFMG CSA *and* achieved a score acceptable to ECFMG on an English language proficiency test (such as TOEFL or the former ECFMG English Test) can use these passing performances to satisfy the clinical skills requirement for ECFMG certification.

Tips for All IMGs

Several hints have been passed on to me from IMGs who used previous editions of this book. Some of the most useful were from Bill Groves, M.D., who got his first choice of residency program. He wrote:

> If you are in an interview and cannot remember anything at all, and your English is deteriorating rapidly [even if you are native English speaker, as is Dr. Groves], remember how many babies you have delivered, how many times you did CPR, and how many times you were alone. Your education may at times have lacked quality, machinery, or medications, but it did not lack vitality.

> If the program apologizes for having IMGs and the resident apologizing is from Bangladesh, there is a double standard here, and no doubt friction between the residents and administration.

> If a program director calls you and says that all the competing programs are dropping out of the Match, that all of his slots will be filled by early February, and that you need to sign onto one of his remaining two slots immediately, don't do anything precipitously. Call the Match to check on his story—it is probably untrue. Yet you might want to take his interest as a compliment and consider the offer.

> It may seem unfair that American graduates can take clerkships right up until they begin residency, while you are barred from any contact [with patients, which may represent a year of decay of your clinical skills]. Do not doubt, however, that the law applies to you and will be enforced. Your temporary license may depend upon adhering to state requirements. If necessary, work temporarily in another state, and write the AMA for information and help.

What Dr. Groves did not mention is that there may be an even greater image problem for USIMGs than for FNIMGs. While foreign-born physicians have a reason for training outside the United States, it is often assumed that USIMGs could not measure up to U.S. standards and so had to leave the country. While this may be true for some, the fact remains that many qualified applicants are rejected by U.S. schools simply because there are not enough positions. USIMGs, at least, do not have to broach the language or cultural barriers faced by their foreign-born counterparts.

Non-U.S./Non-Canadian Citizens (FNIMGs)

International medical graduates who are not U.S. citizens generally encounter the biggest problems in obtaining residency training positions. Many programs just will not accept such applicants. Often, they will not state this plainly for fear of legal reprisal, although some programs have begun stating in their program information that they will accept only graduates of U.S. medical schools as applicants. However, Sec. 102 of the Health Professions Education Extension Amendments of 1992, quoted above, may help. While it is unclear how much effect this law has had, it certainly is ammunition.

While selection committees have some problems evaluating an IMG's credentials, the problem is not as grave as it was in the past. The USMLE has provided an even playing field to assess all medical school graduates' level of knowledge. Apples can now be compared directly with other apples (if you don't mind being an "apple").

Some U.S. residency programs actually prefer international graduates. Though this may seem paradoxical, they feel that way for a very good reason. The medical system views residencies with a high percentage of international medical graduates as inferior—even if their training is just as good as any other program. This message is clearly sent to U.S. graduates. Therefore, only the poorest U.S. students apply to such programs. This, according to the directors of some of these programs, is in direct contradistinction to the high quality of international medical graduates who are applying to their programs.

As an FNIMG, the best way to get a residency position is to apply to a program that has a relationship with your medical school. Some programs have drawn excellent graduates from one or two specific foreign medical schools over the years. They have developed good contacts within the schools and are not afraid, as are many other programs, of encountering forged documents, inflated grades, or poor quality instruction.

Some international graduates are forced to take residency slots that are unfunded. In some cases they are called externships; in others they actually count toward completion of a residency. It is not unusual to see offers of payment for a residency slot from either the applicants themselves or a third-party acting on their behalf. Proposals of $25,000 or more per year (plus any cost for salary, benefits, and allowances) have been offered for competitive positions. There is concern, however, that many of the individuals filling these positions are not treated as equals, do not get similar responsibilities, or do not end up with training equivalent to that of other residents in the same program.

A good method for evaluating whether you, as an IMG, have a reasonable chance of getting accepted into a program in a particular specialty is to check Figures 14.1 and 14.2 or the charts in *JAMA*'s annual "Medical Education Issue" to see how many foreign-trained residents are currently training in or entering that specialty. In addition, check with your school to see if there are any particular programs in the United States with which they have a working relationship.

Even if you get a residency position, you have to worry about your visa. About 45% of IMGs hold J-1 Exchange Visitor visas or H-1B visas. J-1 visas are limited to the time typically required to complete the advanced medical education program. This means the time required for board certification by the American Board of Medical Specialists for a specialty and subspecialty. The maximum time is seven years. This limitation mostly affects individuals who extend their program to include research or chief resident years and then want to do a fellowship. (The "residency/fellowship" time includes a practice year for those specialties which require a year of practice to qualify for the Board exam, such as Pathology and Occupational Medicine.)

Exchange-Visitor visas are typically given only to individuals in ACGME-accredited training programs. The ECFMG will still sponsor IMGs in non-ACGME-accredited programs for Exchange-Visitor visas if the subspecialty is recognized by the parent American Board of Medical Specialties (ABMS) board (e.g., Trauma fellowships and some subspecialty areas of Obstetrics/Gynecology and Ophthalmology). The Immigration and Naturalization Service (INS) has recently restated that to obtain a J-1 visa, individuals must first get a letter from their home country confirming the need for them to get U.S. medical training. In addition, the INS bans residents with J-1 visas from moonlighting.

The ECFMG usually sponsors physicians in training for their J-1 visas. Although you can leave the United States at any time with this visa, you must have proper documentation to reenter the United States (a valid J-1 visa stamp in the passport and either a duplicate copy of the IAP-66—the J-1 application form—or the pink copy of the current IAP-66 endorsed by the ECFMG). If you have questions about this, check with the ECFMG.

J-1 visas normally require the holder to return to their *home country* for a minimum of two years after training. This requirement also extends to relatives holding J-2 dependent visas. Occasionally, exceptions are made if the home country writes a "no objection" letter, the IMG qualifies for a hardship or asylum waiver, or a U.S. government agency requests a waiver because they have a need for the individual. Visas and the laws governing them, however, constantly change.

In December 2004, a law was signed exempting IMGs who have completed medical residencies in the United States from having to leave the country for two years once they have completed their studies, as required by their student visas. Instead, they may apply for a work visa if they agree to practice in a medically underserved area for at least three years. (It extends the J-1 waiver program for two more years.) The law also allows physicians to practice in primary care *or in a medical specialty* if a local shortage in the requested specialty can be demonstrated, exempts waiver recipients from caps on H1-B visas (the visas used by the majority of IMGs seeking to work in the United States), and allows for up to five physicians in each state to work in regions not specifically designated as underserved by the Department of Health and Human Services.

While it is easier to obtain a visa to be a "Research Scholar" or a "Professor," those entering the United States as an Exchange Visitor with these designations are not allowed to transfer into a residency program for at least 12 months after arriving.

For current information about visas for IMG residents, see the ECFMG's online *Exchange Visitor Sponsorship Program Reference Guide* (www.ecfmg.org/evsp) or contact the ECFMG/Exchange Visitor Program, P.O. Box 41673, Philadelphia, PA 19101-1673 USA; (215) 823-2121. The bottom line, though, is that the United States has increasingly been trying to prevent international medical graduates from obtaining advanced medical training in this country.

U.S. International Medical Graduates (USIMGs)

Most of the problems described above also exist for U.S. citizens/permanent residents who have taken their medical school training outside the United States.

What you have going for you is that you are a native English speaker, so you should have no trouble passing the English Language Proficiency component of USMLE Step 2CS. What you have going against you is that you did not have the experience of attending a U.S. medical school. In 2004, 49% of IMGs in U.S. residency training programs were U.S. citizens or permanent U.S. residents. (Only 14%, however, were native U.S. citizens.) This is an increase from 1988, when USIMGs made up only 41% of IMGs in U.S. residencies. Of the 2,091 USIMGs who completed the NRMP

PGY-1 Match in 2005, only 1,143 (55%) obtained a residency position. This is just slightly lower than the rate for foreign-born IMGs (56%).

USIMGs will feel the impact of restrictions now being imposed upon all international medical graduates. Getting into a residency will become harder and harder as time passes and the laws become more strict. In the future, it will take more than just excellent grades and good examination scores for you to get any position at all, let alone in the specialty that you desire.

Transferring to a U.S. School

The best advice for getting into a residency is to do everything possible to transfer into a U.S. medical school prior to graduation, although that is getting more difficult. To accomplish this, you will have to do very well in your studies in the first two or three years of medical school, in addition to performing well on Step 1 and both parts of Step 2 of the USMLE as administered through the ECFMG. Doing well on the USMLE will be an impressive accomplishment, since USIMGs have consistently done worse on licensing examinations than their foreign-born counterparts. Perhaps FNIMGs take the test more seriously—you should too. Study!

In recent years, most students who have transferred to U.S. schools had high GPAs after completing at least two years of medical school, did very well on the USMLE, and transferred to private schools or to schools in states where they were official residents. (Note that you cannot "transfer" once you have received your medical degree.)

No one keeps a master list of which schools will accept transfer students from non-U.S. medical schools, although Deans of Students at international schools with large numbers of U.S. citizens do keep lists of U.S. medical schools that have accepted their students. To locate a school that might accept you:

1. Check information in the "Transfer Policies for Applicants to Medical Schools" area at www.aamc.org/students/medstudents.
2. Contact U.S. medical schools directly to inquire about their willingness to take USIMGs. Do not be "picky" about their location.
3. Mail inquiry letters to the admissions offices of all U.S. medical schools. For any school where you have any kind of "tie" (such as birthplace, undergraduate school, long residence, parents' residence, etc.), specifically mention that connection.
4. If you have to limit the number of letters sent, concentrate on the non-Ivy League private schools. State schools will often accept only students who are considered residents.

5. Also write to Osteopathic medical schools. They often are more flexible than M.D. schools.

Fifth Pathway Program

If you cannot transfer to a school in the United States, you may be eligible to enter a *Fifth Pathway Program*. The Fifth Pathway route allows students in countries that require a year of internship or of social service before granting the M.D. degree (primarily Mexico) to qualify for their M.D. and medical license by taking a year of supervised clinical training at a U.S. medical school. Finishing this program is a route to medical licensure without getting an ECFMG Certificate and having to deal with its attendant requirements. More than 7,000 individuals have completed the Fifth Pathway Program since it was initiated in 1971. To qualify for this program, students *must be U.S. citizens/permanent residents or Canadian students with a Student Visa who are not U.S. citizens* and have:

1. Completed their undergraduate premedical studies at a U.S. college or university with grades and scores acceptable for entrance into a U.S. medical school.
2. Within two years of beginning the Fifth Pathway Program, completed all formal requirements except the internship and social service at a foreign medical school listed in the *World Directory of Medical Schools* published by the World Health Organization.
3. An academic record acceptable to New York Medical College.
4. Passed USMLE Step 1.
5. Completed at least three years of medical school.
6. *Not* completed their internship/social service requirement.
7. *Not* received their M.D. degree.
8. *Not* met the ECFMG's certification requirements.

Two U.S. medical schools accept Fifth Pathway students: New York Medical College (NYMC) in Valhalla, New York, and Poncé University in Puerto Rico.

The NYMC program charges a $100 application fee, with an additional non-refundable $500 reservation fee once the student is accepted. To receive an application, complete the short pre-application form on their website. If you qualify, they will send an application. For 2006, tuition and fees (including USMLE Step 2) were $28,500. Contact NYMC at (914) 594-4489 or (914) 594-3651; www.nymc.edu/depthome/fifth.asp.

Poncé School of Medicine also charges a $100 application fee and an additional non-refundable $500 reservation fee upon acceptance. Applicants must be bilingual in English and Spanish. Their 2006 tuition was $17,500; required fees were $3,500. Poncé School of Medicine can be reached at (787) 840-2575; www.psm.edu; e-mail: admission@psm.edu.

NYMC now has at least eight participating hospitals in New York, New Jersey, and Connecticut. Priority is given to students from Mexican medical schools, since New York State recognizes these schools. Students from Semmelweis Medical School in Hungary have also gone through NYMC's program, but they must be placed in hospitals outside New York. Also, NYMC now admits Canadian students who are not U.S. citizens but who have a Student Visa.

NYMC's Fifth Pathway program lasts 12 months, with starting dates in January and July. The clinical programs offered vary among the hospitals. From this springboard, USIMGs are usually able to leap into residency slots. During their Fifth Pathway year, students generally apply to residencies through the NRMP Match as Independent Candidates. The school gives students a Clinical Skills Standardization Patient Course to prepare them for USMLE Step 2CS, and allows students to take time off to go for residency interviews.

Although Fifth Pathway graduates who have passed USMLE Steps 1, 2CS, and 2CK are eligible for licensure in 52 U.S. jurisdictions (but not in Guam and the Virgin Islands), individual states may apply their own requirements and restrictions. Mississippi and South Carolina, for example, accept Fifth Pathway graduates only if the applicant is also certified by an ABMS Board (in other words, has completed both a residency and Board certification). Such restrictions can occasionally lead to horror stories, as one physician related:

> I had been accepted in an Orthopedic Surgery residency in my home state after finishing the Fifth Pathway program. I was ecstatic! However, the residency was notified that the state's Board of Medical Examiners had decided not to accept the Fifth Pathway route to licensure. Since residents were required to be licensed, I could not take the position and had to sit out a year until I could reapply somewhere else.

For more information about the Fifth Pathway program, contact: the Licensure and Certification Section, American Medical Association, 515 N. State St., Chicago, IL 60610.

Canadian Citizens

Canadian citizens are not IMGs, but the United States has a somewhat schizophrenic attitude toward Canadian medical school graduates. While the same association that accredits U.S. schools accredits Canadian medical schools and there is no question that their training is excellent, there is still ambivalence in many sectors about considering Canadian applicants for residency positions. In part, this stems from the dissimilarity of the entire Canadian educational system and the resultant difficulties in comparing Canadian applicants with those from U.S. schools. This can be at least partially remedied by including as much explanation as possible about your training, grades, honors, etc., with your application materials.

However, aside from the problem of comparing applicants, there also is concern about the lack of reimbursement in the future if Canadians are taken into residency training programs. Some state monies have already been withdrawn from programs that have Canadian trainees. Therefore, it is wise for any Canadian considering training at a U.S. program to first check to see if the program will seriously consider Canadian applicants.

Even if you want to eventually practice medicine in the United States, it may not be as important as it seems to do a U.S. residency. That is because 37 U.S. states and territories will issue a medical license by endorsement to graduates of accredited Canadian medical schools who hold a Licentiate of the Medical Council of Canada. Those that don't are Delaware, Florida, Georgia, Guam, Hawaii, Idaho, Louisiana, Michigan, Mississippi, Missouri, Montana, New Jersey, North Carolina, South Carolina, Utah, Vermont, and the Virgin Islands.

Nevertheless, increasing numbers of Canadian medical school graduates now seek residency training in the United States, although they still constitute less than 1% of physicians in U.S. residency programs. This increase may be due to several factors: Canada's medical education system forces specialty decisions earlier than in the past, they have reduced the number of residency positions, and Canadian provinces now make it very difficult for physicians to change specialties, or even to get licensed in their own specialty in another province.

The Canadian government forcefully discourages Canadian graduates from taking U.S. residencies. Canadians wishing to enter a U.S. residency program must get a J-1 visa, which requires a letter of support from their province's Ministry of Health. For the most part, Canadian officials are reluctant to provide these letters if they need more physicians in your particular specialty in the Province. For more information, contact your province's Ministry of Health.

Finally, to be seriously considered as an applicant, it will be necessary to get an immigration card approving your working in the United States before you apply. Otherwise, even if you match with a program, you may not be able to work there. Without an immigration card, no program will consider you.

15

Preparing For The Interview

Every new answer raises a new question.

– Folk Saying

NO MATTER HOW IRRATIONAL it may seem, the 10 to 30-minute interviews that you will have at the residency programs will count more, in most cases, toward getting you into the program than the total weight of your previous 3½ years of medical school. That's not just my personal belief. Several studies have shown this to be true. It is not only the most important part of the resident-selection process, but also the most costly and most time-consuming. So now that you are preparing to go for interviews, put your best effort toward doing a good job. This is where it all comes together!

The Mock Interview

How well will you do when you are actually sitting in the hot seat being interviewed for that residency slot you want above all others? Do not wait until you sit in the real chair to find out! When you think that you are prepared to go on the interview circuit, arrange for a mock interview. This practice instills confidence and stifles anxiety, makes you calmer and more organized, and helps you sound better during the real thing.

A mock interview is to an interview what near-drowning is to drowning. In both cases, you think that you are going to die, but in the former, you live through it. Your mock interview should closely imitate the actual interview. You must prepare for it in exactly the same way that you will prepare for your real interviews. Dress the same, carry identical materials with you, and go over your answers to the questions just as you will before interviews at the residency programs. If you don't feel anxiety, you're not doing it correctly. This interview must be as realistic as possible so that you will get the most accurate and useful feedback.

Who should conduct the mock interview? Ideally, your mentor and a specialty adviser, if you have one, since they are probably used to interviewing residency applicants. If not, the Dean of Students or another faculty member in the specialty with interviewing experience and your mentor should interview you. Tell them, if they do not know, that you want the mock interview to be as realistic as possible. You want them to ask you the "difficult" questions and treat you in the same manner they would treat any candidate—not as someone they already know. Then you want feedback on the way you presented yourself, the manner in which you were dressed, how you handled the questions, and an overall assessment of areas to improve before you hit the interview trail.

One useful technique for self-critique is to audio- or videotape the interview. Would you hire the person you hear or see? What seems wrong with the applicant (you)? How can you improve your interview performance next time? As with all other parts of the application process, this takes a little extra effort. Experience has shown that it pays off in a big way.

Besides the formal mock interview, it also helps to go over interview elements in your mind during those times when you are commuting, waiting for others, or holding retractors. Review potential questions and situations, as well as those from previous interviews. To remember the areas you want to review before the real interview, use the mnemonic "SHOWTIME."

- **Self**: What do you know about yourself? Have you adequately assessed your own knowledge, skills, and desires?

- **History**: How did you decide to enter this specialty and this program? Which aspects of your personal history can help you relate to an interviewer in this specialty, and this interviewer in particular?

- **Originality**: What makes you unique? What have you accomplished, experienced, or set as a personal goal that sets you apart from the crowd?

- **World View**: What do you believe in? Why are you striving for this particular goal? What will it mean in your life? How does this program fit into these goals?

- **Tell**: How are you presenting yourself? Remember that the impression you make begins at the moment you first interact with hospital and residency personnel and extends through every contact. For the interview itself, practice effective verbal commu-

nication, including looking alert and interested, appearing organized, and listening carefully.

- **Illustrate:** Practice non-verbal communication, including maintaining eye contact, sitting forward, gesturing effectively, and
smiling—when appropriate. This is vital, since more than half
the message may be delivered through non-verbal cues.

- **Manage:** Use well-placed questions and time-awareness to manage the interview. Be sure to get your key message across while
fully (but not endlessly) answering the interviewer's questions.

- **Engage:** Throughout the interview, try to discuss those areas
about which you are enthusiastic so that your conversation is
animated and stimulating for the interviewer. If you enjoyed the
interview, it is likely that the interviewer did also.

The "SHOW" part should not be recited as a litany, but rather used
when questions arise in any of the applicable areas. Two things you probably want to memorize, or at least get down pat enough so that they sound
smooth, are your opening introduction to the interviewer and a two- or
three-sentence summation of your message (your strengths and desire to
come to the program). The "TIME" elements are how you convey your
message. Practice both.

Give the right non-verbal signals. Use a strong handshake to communicate energy and drive. Maintain eye contact. For successful eye contact,
you must hold the interviewer's gaze for three to five seconds or until a
thought or sentence is complete. Don't glance around the room; this indicates that you are bored. Avoid nervous mannerisms such as doodling or
tapping your fingers. Smile often. Avoid slouching and other forms of bad
posture that make you seem to lack confidence. Send a positive message.
For example, lean forward in the chair to show interest and alertness.

Don't sweat over past interviews, just think about how they could have
gone better. This frequent review will keep you ready to face the next interview without needing too much last-minute preparation.

Timing

Students always have many questions about the timing of the actual interviews. Because there is very little information or guidance offered to
applicants, they must wallow through the morass of scheduling, traveling,
and interviewing on their own. The most common question is whether to
do an interview close to home or at the bottom-choice program first as a

trial interview, thereby getting an idea of the interview process. Neither of these is advisable.

As discussed above, you should learn how to go through the interview process by participating in a mock interview with your mentor and specialty adviser prior to embarking on your first trip. If you can avoid it, do not waste any real interviews on "practice." The programs that you consider weak based upon their written material may surprise you with their strengths when you visit them.

Ratings Inflate As the "Season" Goes On

A number of studies on interviewing show that programs' ratings of applicants become more favorable as the "season" progresses. Although one emergency medicine study showed no relationship between the date interviewed and the match list position, this may not hold true for all specialties—or even for all programs within a single specialty.

Just as the requirements to get an interview slot are reduced when the composition of the entire applicant pool is uncertain, interviewers' evaluations tend to be lower for the candidates interviewed early. This is, in part, because early interviewees are being compared to a hypothetical "best applicant" rather than the available applicant pool. As reality sinks in, interviewers tend to raise their ratings to more accurately reflect a candidate's true position in comparison with his or her cohorts. This suggests that it is better for you to interview in the second half, if not near the end, of the interview season.

Last Interviewed Are Remembered Best

Unless you are among the last applicants interviewed, the impression you make will tend to fade as faculty members interview other applicants. When they make their selection decisions, the faculty will best remember those individuals who are interviewed last.

The difference in the rate of selection between candidates interviewed in the second half of the season and those interviewed in the first half is only a few percentage points. But don't you want those points to work for you rather than against you? If so, plan to interview late. If you can manage it, schedule your interview on or near the last available date that each program offers. This can often be done easily if you get your materials to the program early. You will be offered an interview when there is still a wide choice of available dates. Scheduling your interviews at the end of multiple programs' interview schedules may not be as difficult as you might imagine, since various programs end their interviewing at different times.

After you schedule your interviews, send each program a letter or e-mail confirming your interview date, time, and location. Keep a hard copy for your records (in case your computer crashes) and take it with you as a reminder on your interview trip.

Not My Top Choice

What should you do when your "bottom" program offers you an invitation to interview and you have yet to hear from your "top" programs? As they say, "A bird in the hand . . .".

Schedule interviews at those programs that offer you an interview and where you would actually be willing to go as a resident. This should logically be all the programs to which you apply—unless you get additional information after you submit your application. Do this for three reasons:

1. You may find that one or more of these "bottom" programs actually perfectly meets your needs when you visit.

2. You may not hear from any other programs, so you need to make certain that you have an opportunity to train in the specialty that you have chosen.

3. Residency programs know that applicants will face this dilemma and, especially late in the interview season, expect a certain percentage of applicants to cancel their interviews.

Hopefully, you will eventually interview at some of your top choice programs, but you may not like them as well as the programs where you have already interviewed.

Time Off—Arranging the Senior Schedule

You must have the necessary time off to go to interviews. The average senior medical student spends 18 days away from school on the interview circuit. However, over one-fourth spend more than 21 days on the road. This requires a little advance planning.

When should you go for interviews? If you are applying to a specialty that has a second-year Match right out of medical school, such as Neurology, Urology, Neurological Surgery, Otolaryngology, or Ophthalmology, you will interview from September through December. If you are applying to programs through the standard NRMP PGY-1 Match (most of you will be in this group), interview season generally runs from November through early February. Some programs interview during only a portion, often the mid- to latter parts, of these time periods.

There are two ways to arrange for time off to interview; you can either take vacation or take an elective or research block that will allow you to obtain the time off you need. While attractive, this latter option must be investigated carefully. If you make a mistake, and cannot get the time off once you are on such a rotation, you may miss some important interviews. You cannot afford this. If possible, talk with the faculty member responsible for the rotation ahead of time. Find out if you will be able to have days off for interviews. If you know the specific dates or blocks of time, write them down, give the faculty member a copy and have him or her sign the copy that you keep. This way a faulty memory at the last minute will play no part in determining your future.

By the way, if you have followed the schema proposed in this book, you should have plenty of vacation time available. While the interview circuit is usually no holiday (though it can be, see the next section), taking vacation time at this point may ease some of the pressures that can exist if you are trying to sandwich interviews among other responsibilities.

Wait-Listed?

If you get a letter from a residency program saying that you are "wait-listed" for an interview, do not despair. Residency programs sometimes send such letters when they think that there is little chance that an applicant really is serious—such as someone from the other end of the country.

Write a short note thanking them and saying that you are still interested. One applicant who did this almost immediately got a letter back from the program that was her top choice offering her an interview. She later matched with that program.

Travel Arrangements

The extensive traveling that you undertake during the interview process may be the most that you have ever done. It may be your first real chance to see many other parts of the country. It will also be a rude introduction to the frequent delays, cancellations, and sardine-can-like accommodations of our nation's air travel system.

Simply traveling to many parts of the country, packing and unpacking in hotels, and finding your way around strange cities will be very tiring—not to mention costly. More than 60% of all senior medical students find the cost of interviewing burdensome—the average student spends more than $1,600 on travel. There are, however, some methods to decrease your fatigue and to make traveling the interview circuit more tolerable, if not actually pleasant.

Clustering Interviews

The first method to consider is the possibility of clustering your interviews. This can be done either chronologically (to use available blocks of time) or geographically.

It is not unusual for some applicants to fly back and forth across the country several times, as well as to make many side trips, for interviews. Clustering interviews geographically, however, saves both time and the considerable effort that is involved in traveling great distances. It also, of course, saves money. Clustering reduces your interviewing costs by lessening your time away from home (usually spent in hotels) and the amount of traveling you do. These costs, aside from the clothes you bought for the interview, can run anywhere from nothing to $5,000 or more. It will depend upon the geographical range in which you evaluate programs, the level of your accommodations, and your savvy in clustering interviews to use available transportation in the least expensive manner possible.

To cluster interviews, it is essential that you have both luck and flexibility. The harder you work on the problem, the luckier you will become. Flexibility results from getting your materials to programs early. This will allow you a maximum number of interview dates to choose from. Luck is involved with being offered interviews at the right programs in time for you to arrange clusters. Work with the residency secretaries to try to arrange these clusters of interviews. Most of the time they understand your situation and are willing to try to help you out.

Some obsessive-compulsive individuals will try to schedule multiple interviews day after day for a period of time. This is very dangerous. They will eventually become stressed out, and may have fewer options if they encounter transportation delays. Remember, bad weather shuts down many of the nation's major airports during the interview season. In addition, they will have too little time to digest the information obtained from one interview before getting involved in the next one.

One method some applicants have used to obtain additional insight into a program is to informally drop by the hospital the evening after the interview, or the next morning, to talk with residents. This provides an opportunity to get a better perspective on the information gained in the midst of hectic interviewing. While they are there, some applicants also take time to get a feel for the community in which the program is based. If you plan to do this, build in enough extra time, particularly if you are clustering your interviews.

Special Fares

Another way to save money is by using special fares available from airlines, railroads, and bus companies. Often these allow you unlimited travel during a specified period of time. With the deregulation of the travel industry and its resultant fierce competition, the rates, rules, and special offers change with dizzying frequency. Check with several travel websites or travel agents until you are satisfied that you are getting the best possible value for your money. Don't forget to tell travel agents that you are a medical student. "Medical" indicates that you may generate very good business in the future; "student" may entitle you to special rates on some carriers. Remember, the only people paying full fare for transportation, especially air travel, are those having someone else pay for their trip. And the savings can be astronomical. Frequent-flyer programs can also save you money by providing discount or free car rentals, airline tickets, and hotel accommodations.

While getting low airfares has become more complicated, there are some specific strategies you can use. Once you know which cities you will visit for interviews, determine the standard 21-day advance-purchase fare. Then, if you find a fare that is 45% to 50% less, book it immediately. Such discounts are usually available only for limited times and there may be only a few seats available at that rate. You can also save up to 70% off the price charged by major airlines by flying one of the no-frills, low-cost carriers.

The cheapest airfare may be to a lesser-used airport or to an adjacent city, from which you will have to rent a car or arrange other transportation. These ticket prices may be reduced 33% or more and, even with increased transportation costs, the total cost may be less. The best airline deals may be found on the Internet, where many airlines post their lowest fares. You may also want to bid for tickets at one of the online auctions or contact one of the discount agencies available through the AAMC, AMSA, and similar groups. These are often listed in *The New Physician*.

If you buy a full-discount, restricted ticket (as you probably want to do), always check the rules first. Most are non-refundable, charge a fee to change flights or dates, and cannot be changed to a lower fare, even if it is later advertised. Still, it may be worth it.

If you must rent a car, the average daily rate varies depending upon which basic plan you choose. Generally, the pricing packages are (1) a daily rate with a mileage charge; (2) a daily rate with a limited number of free miles per day; (3) a daily rate with unlimited mileage; and (4) a rate that has free mileage over an extended period. Rates also vary according to the size and the style of vehicle, and additional fees (such as drop-off fees) can increase the cost. Special promotional rates are often available, especially over weekends, but should be specifically requested in advance.

Check several rental companies. Local car rental agencies and those not located at the airport (but who will pick you up at the airport) often have much lower rates than the national companies. You can get their phone numbers from the phone books at your library or off their websites. If you do drive to your interview, check ahead to find out where to park. At many medical centers, visitor parking can be almost impossible to find.

Surviving Air Travel

Most residency applicants fly to lots of interviews. Traveling for business is a vastly different experience than flying for pleasure. As a business traveler, you must do everything possible to save time and fly comfortably. Figure 15.1 lists suggestions gleaned from thousands of business travelers on how to do this.

Cheap Housing

The American Medical Association Alliance runs the Physicians-In-Training Host Program (formerly the Community Welcoming Program) to help students reduce interviewing costs, get to know the community surrounding their potential residency program, and introduce them to local medical society and Alliance members. Using volunteer hosts, the program tries to find housing for AMA student members going on residency interviews. They will try to fulfill requests for housing for one- or two-night stays for up to three interview dates. Requests must be received at least two weeks prior to the expected stay.

For more information and the application for housing, go to www.ama-assn.org/go/alliance and click on "Membership Resources" on the right sidebar and then, at the bottom, click on "Spouses of residents and medical students." A link to "Housing for Resident Interviews" appears. (Why does the AMA make their site so user-unfriendly?) If you have trouble, call the Alliance at (312) 464-4470.

The American Medical Women's Association runs a "Bed and Breakfast Program" for its student members traveling to residency interviews (and also for physician members going to job interviews or conferences). When a member calls the AMWA office with her trip details, they supply a list of volunteer hosts in the requested city so that she can call to make appropriate arrangements. There is no fee. For further information, call AMWA at (703) 838-0500 or e-mail: info@amwa-doc.org.

FIGURE 15.1

Air Travel Made Easier

- Take early morning or late-night flights. In the late afternoon or evening, delays are common. (Late-night flights may also be less expensive.)

- Go a day before you must arrive—or at least not on the last flight of the day to your destination. Interview season occurs during the worst travel weather of the year, so your flight may be canceled or delayed.

- You may get "bumped" from your flight, meaning there is no room for you even though you have a confirmed reservation. The airline may ask for volunteers to give up their seat for a negotiated sum. But, if you arrive on time and are bumped without volunteering, the airline may owe you a required fee depending on how long you will be delayed and the price you paid for the ticket. If the airline can get you to your final destination within one hour of the original arrival time, there is no compensation. If they can get you there between one and two hours after your original arrival time, the airline must pay you the one-way cost of your ticket up to $200. If they cannot get you there within two hours of the scheduled time, the compensation is doubled, up to $400. In some cases, they also add free tickets—so getting bumped may be a good deal if you have time to spare.

- Keep your travel agent's phone number handy. (Many have toll-free numbers.) If your flight is canceled, call the agent to rebook you, rather than standing in line with the angry masses.

- Have a copy of that month's *Official Airline Guide* (or a copy of the relevant pages) to help reschedule flights if necessary. Your library or some of the more-traveled faculty may have a copy.

- If you arrive at the airport early, try to get on an earlier flight.

- Board the plane as soon as possible. It is easier to find storage space for your carryon bags.

- Sit in the front of the plane to be one of the first off the plane.

- Get an aisle seat. You can get to the bathroom easier and get off the plane faster. (You may, however, be disturbed by the "inside" passengers climbing over you to get out.)

- If you are right-handed, sit on the right side of the plane. That way, people passing you in the aisle won't jiggle your arm when you work or eat. If you plan to sleep on the plane, get a window seat so other passengers won't crawl over you to get out. Ask for a seat in the exit row to get more legroom. On some planes, though, those seat backs don't recline.

- Carry foam ear plugs or a small music player with earphones if you want to sleep on the plane or if you fly on a small (usually commuter) plane. Carry eyeshades if you want to sleep.

- Join the airlines' frequent flier clubs. You may be able to board earlier and get special perquisites. Use one airline and its affiliated hotel and car rental companies as much as possible to maximize benefits.

FIGURE 15.1 (continued)

- If you will fly a lot on one airline, consider joining their airport club. The relaxation between flights may be worth the cost of a one-year membership. Join hotel and car rental clubs if you will be using them frequently.

- Don't check luggage, if at all possible. Use a carryon bag with wheels and, if necessary, a garment bag that clips onto it.

- If your checked bags are damaged or lost, maximum reimbursement is only $1,250. Keep a list of what is in your bag, file a claim with the airline's baggage claim department on arrival, and keep your baggage claim receipts. They will normally get your bag to you (if you stay in the same city) by the next day.

- Dress comfortably. Unless you will go directly to your interview, carry your interview clothes and dress casually for the flight.

- Pack a snack and a small bottle of water. Many airlines no longer offer meals, and flight delays often prevent travelers from eating between flights. Order special meals, such as vegetarian, weight-watcher, or kosher, if meals are served on the flights. They are usually fresher than other meals.

- Do exercises on the airplane:
  - *Neck Stretches*: Flex and extend your neck 5 times anteriorly-posteriorly to and away from the chest and 5 times laterally toward the shoulders. Then rotate your head from side to side 5 times, holding it at full rotation for 3 to 5 seconds.
  - *Shoulder Stretch*: Link fingers and hold them in front of your chest. Lift them above your head, breathing in while stretching toward the ceiling, and hold your breath and position for 3 seconds. Bring your arms behind your head while breathing out. Hold your breath and position for 3 seconds.
  - *Arm Isometrics*: Push down on the armrest for the count of 5 and then pull up on the armrest for the count of 5. Repeat 5 times.
  - *Lower-Back Stretch*: Clasp your knee with both hands, pull it to your chest, and hold it there for the count of 5. Repeat with other leg.
  - *Leg/Foot Stretch*: With your shoes off, press firmly with your palms on both knees. Dorsiflex your foot so your heels are touching the floor and your toes are raised as high as possible. Then plantar flex so that your toes touch the floor and the heels are raised. Repeat quickly 8 times.

- Use the airplane restroom before landing. This may save up to 20 minutes on the ground if you are first to the taxis or car rental counters.

- Shuttle/taxi/train/rental car: Ask the residency program you are visiting for the best and the cheapest (they may be different) ways to get from the airport to the hospital. Trains will usually be the cheapest and fastest transportation method—but may not be the safest method at certain times of the day. Also, you may have to lug your baggage a distance to get to the train. A useful alternative is an airport shuttle. Remember to get the cheaper round-trip ticket. Taxis are for those who don't have to watch their budget and cars are for special situations or for additional sightseeing in the area.

- Use a skycap to avoid taxi lines. A small tip can save lots of time.

Another source for information about inexpensive housing is the residency program at which you are interviewing. If such information is not included in the material they send, call the residency's secretary and ask about good, inexpensive, and *safe* housing near the hospital. You will not be the first one to ask, and the program probably has a list of good places to stay. They may have a special deal with special rates for applicants at local hotels. Some programs even offer housing in a resident's or faculty member's home to applicants who request it. This is especially true if your host is an alumnus of your medical school.

If you decide to go it alone, make sure the location will allow you to make the interview on time. Check out their security in advance—especially if it is in a crime-prone area, as are many locations around large teaching hospitals. If the establishment offers free services, such as breakfast, take advantage of them.

Get enough sleep. Before turning in, make sure that the curtains are tightly closed—and bring along some clothespins to keep them closed. Use a sleep mask for added darkness and a pair of soft earplugs for quiet. Make sure to test the mask and earplugs at home to become used to them—and to be sure you can still hear your alarm clock. Check the alarm clock (bringing yours is even better) to make sure that it works. Then go to bed in time to get enough sleep and still get to the interview a little early (to reduce your stress).

During your personal time, take advantage of the local area, including the museums, sporting or cultural events, and shopping. To avoid the common feelings of isolation, stay in touch with friends and family via phone or e-mail. If you don't have a cell phone with lots of long-distance minutes, now is the time to get one. Also, exercise as you would at home. Check with your hosts or the hotel about nearby, safe exercise areas.

Simultaneous Vacationing

As mentioned, the interview circuit is no picnic. But in some situations, you can turn it into a real vacation. Try to chronologically cluster interviews but, if there is a break in your interview schedule, investigate vacation spots in the surrounding area. This can give you a relaxing break in the action—a needed rest period at a relatively low cost, since you are already nearby. If you have a spouse or significant other, he or she might want to meet you at this spot. A friendly face is sometimes a very welcome sight and helps to bolster the spirits. And having someone to talk to and to share your experiences with may add to the relief. Given the stresses of medical school and the anticipated heavy work schedule to come, you and your spouse or significant other (if you have one) probably need a vacation anyway!

Updating Information about the Programs

As the time for your interviews draws near, recontact the programs where you will be interviewing to request any new or updated information and recheck their websites. The material that you were initially sent was prepared the previous spring or earlier. Many things could have changed at the program. Some might even affect whether you still want to go to that institution for an interview. Other changes may affect your final program rankings.

The best time to ask about any changes in the program is when you arrange a date for your interview. If there is new written material, ask them to send you a copy. If it is not yet available, ask for as much information about the changes as possible.

Undoubtedly, you will be a more appealing candidate to the interviewers if you know up-to-date information about their program. If you don't, they will wonder why. So be sure to get the latest available information on the program before you leave for your interviews. Ask about changes once again when you are at the program—of the program director, the residency secretary, and the current residents.

Communicating with the Programs

Once you send your initial application packet, you will mostly communicate with programs by phone and e-mail.

The first time you should contact the programs is about a month after you have requested that your material be sent to them. Find out if it has all arrived. If not, what is missing?

How you communicate with a program is very important. It is amazing that the nicest, most sophisticated individuals often have a terrible phone "presence." Your voice over the phone and your attitude on it will make a big impression on a program. Don't think that you can behave any way you want to on the phone because you are *only* talking to the residency secretary! And don't express your extreme annoyance at being put on hold in rather crude terms.

As in many businesses, a secretary who interacts with applicants often has a major impact on who is selected—both for interviews and for final positions. Many residency directors ask their secretaries for input. And most take this input very seriously. Polish your phone technique. Polish up those residency secretaries. They can be either your allies or your enemies. Make them think of you as a nice person, the kind that they want as a resident in *their* program.

E-mail is the modern way to communicate, and this also goes for residency programs. Increasingly, programs notify applicants via e-mail when they are selected for interviews. They also request that specific questions be forwarded either to the residency directors or to their assistants via e-mail. As with other correspondence, be certain that your e-mail messages to the programs are coherent, spell-checked, and grammatically correct. One way of improving your e-mail messages is to write them on a word processor and then paste the messages into your correspondence. As noted previously, be certain that your e-mail address doesn't appear sophomoric, such as "hotstuff@xyz.com."

16

Looking The Part: Interview Attire

In your town, your reputation counts; in another, your clothes do.

– Talmud, Shabboth

I base most of my fashion sense on what doesn't itch.

– Gilda Radner

THE KEY HERE IS TO DO what others do—but better. Yes, there is a "uniform" to wear. It is conservative, tasteful, and neat. It looks like upper-middle-class success. And it works. Of course, you wore jeans and sweat-shirts during your first two years of medical school. Maybe you wore less as an undergraduate. You love to hang around the wards dressed in a wrinkled scrub suit, looking just like the residents. Don't imitate their sloppy dress; residents already have their training slots. Now is the time for you to shine—both literally and figuratively.

One interviewee, medical student Scott Fishman, described this uni-form as "remarkably drab . . . a ridiculous costume . . . a rite of passage." He went on to say that, "sitting there waiting for our turns outside the interviewer's office, we all look like we are going to a funeral." Perhaps. But better to wear the uniform and appear to go to a funeral than not wear it and attend your own.

No, you don't have to go out and spend lots of money that you don't have on clothes you can't afford. Just do what you can to get into the uni-form. Ideally, interviewers should not be aware of your clothes; you want them to remember you, not what you wore. The proper dress for residency interviews is essentially identical, no matter where in the country you are applying. Appropriate dress can help you a little. The wrong outfit will destroy you.

Remember that in the first seven seconds, interviewers make decisions based on your visual cues: your clothes, grooming, walk, stance, etc. After that, they begin evaluating you through your verbal skills.

Men

The Suit

A suit is the standard dress for an interview. It should be solid or pinstripe, navy or gray. "The men who run America," says John T. Molloy, author of *Dress for Success*, "run it blue, gray, and dull." Do not wear a suit with bright or avant-garde colors or designs. "If you try to spruce up the look," Mr. Molloy continues, "you're in trouble."

The suit doesn't have to be expensive or in the latest style, but it should be tailored and well-cut. If you don't have or cannot afford a suit, wear a navy-blue sport jacket with matching pants. If you don't have these either, it is time you visited a clothing store. Charge the bill to your future. Serious and solid is the image you are looking for in your outfit. And *before* you show up at your first interview, make sure that your clothes fit well. Few things distract an interviewer more than an applicant fidgeting with his tight collar.

The Shirt

Wear either a white or pale-blue solid-color shirt. Long sleeves are in order if you plan to remove your jacket. Avoid stripes, loud colors, or any weird designs. Shirttails should be long enough to keep the shirt tucked in, even when you raise your arms. With the top button fastened, your collar should fit snugly, but not so tightly that your eyes bulge.

The Tie

Wear a tie—even if you are a laid-back individual. An open-neck shirt and gold chain just won't cut it. Your tie should be solid, have repeating stripes (rep), small polka dots, or repeating small insignias (club). Avoid gaudy bright colors, large patterns, and black. The "power colors" are red and navy. Knot the tie so its tip meets the belt and put the back of the tie through the label, so the ends stay together. Do not wear a bow tie. It gives the impression that you're odd and out of touch with this decade.

The Shoes & Socks

Wear black or very dark brown conservatively designed shoes. Make sure that they are in good repair and shined. Dirty shoes are male applicants' most common clothing error. Also make sure that there are no holes in your soles; if there are, keep your feet flat on the floor. Wear calf-length plain socks that match your suit.

Accessories

The key here is sedate. Limit *jewelry* to a watch and wedding band (only if you are married). If you wear a watch, avoid anything unusual such as a dive watch or one with a picture of Spiderman on the front. No lapel pins, no ID bracelets, no tie clasps, and—definitely—*NO EARRINGS OR OTHER IMPLANTED JEWELRY!* No matter what the protestations, that little flash of gold will cost you big points. Save it for later. Inappropriate or too much jewelry will elicit very strong negative responses.

If you wear an *undershirt*, a crew neck looks best, since it doesn't show through a shirt. A plain, dark leather *belt* with a small square buckle works well. If you wear *suspenders*, be sure that they button to your pants. If you carry a *wallet*, it shouldn't bulge out of your pocket.

If you wear *glasses*, make sure that they are in standard frames. No initials on the lenses or unusual colors. It's best not to wear tinted or photo-gray lenses, since they tend to place a barrier between you and the interviewer. Also, keep the lenses clean.

The *pen* and *pencil* you carry should look classy. They do not have to be gold, but they should not look like you got them from hospital stores or the local drug rep. And don't stick them in a shirt-pocket protector. To look the part of a serious candidate and have a convenient place to make notes and store papers, carry a small, folding, zippered, leather-covered *note pad* with the materials you need. If you use a PDA to take notes, make sure that you can use it to make your notes quickly; otherwise, revert to a pen and paper.

Grooming

As for personal grooming, be neat, squeaky clean, and conservative. Your *hair* should be short and a natural color. If it's shorter than you like it, it's probably close to the right length. Ask your mentor (if he or she is over 35 years old), a parent, or close (older) friend to advise you on this. Definitely, no ponytails and no punk or otherwise unusual haircuts. Make sure all hair has been very recently trimmed and washed. Invest in a good haircut about one week before the interview; haircuts look best after one week. If you wear facial hair, avoid goatees and handlebar mustaches as these have strong negative connotations. Keep any tattoos covered. Trim and manicure your *nails*. Remember, you are about to be a physician, putting your hands on, and in, patients.

The *odor* the interviewer perceives should be minimal—and then only that of deodorant or nervousness. Avoid after-shave; you are not going on a date. If you are concerned about your breath, carry breath mints. And, above all, no alcohol within 24 hours of the interview. There are enough perceived and anticipated problems with drug abuse among housestaff. You do not have to show the interviewers that you could be part of the problem.

The bottom line is that you want to look as much like a successful upper-middle-class physician as possible. Wear the garments symbolizing the successful individual in our society. You certainly did it to get into medical school. It's time to do it again. There is no need to flaunt your lifestyle in your dress. Leave your personal preferences out of this. They can only harm you.

Women

The Suit

Although styles are changing in the workplace, the standard dress for a woman going to an interview is still the suit. In this case, it is a skirted suit. A good skirted suit suggests that you are an upper-middle-class professional—just the image you want to project. Don't be led down the path to destruction by following fads or fashion. The classic suit is the uniform of success. Find out what woman accountants or lawyers who work for large firms wear. This will be the "classic" style.

In purchasing a suit, choose wool, linen, or a synthetic that simulates either. The fabric should be solid, tweed, or plaid. For solid suits, the three best colors are gray (a couple of shades lighter than charcoal), medium-range blue, and dark maroon. Stay away from bold, flashy patterns. The skirt should extend to just below the knee (no miniskirts!) and the matching jacket should be a blazer cut with long sleeves.

Two alternatives to the suit are a tailored dress or a skirt worn with a jacket. Neither is as powerful as the suit, but if you do not feel comfortable in a suit, these are two reasonable substitutes.

The Blouse

The blouse should be simply cut, not too frilly or lacy, and the neckline must not be too low. If it's equivalent to a man's shirt with one button open, it will be acceptable. The blouse should be cotton, silk, or a look-alike synthetic. Usually it will be white, cream, or pastel—not red or fuchsia. In general, it should be in a solid color that complements the suit.

The Shoes

Shoes should be simple pumps, closed at the toe and heel, and not brand new. They should be in a dark or neutral color that is compatible with your suit. The heels should not be more than 1½ inches high. Do not wear boots. Most residency applicants will be doing a lot of walking around the hospital; be sure that you will survive in the shoes you wear.

Accessories

Although a *scarf* is not as essential as a man's tie, it can be eye-catching if used properly. Wear silk or a look-alike synthetic and tie it in an ascot, necktie, or scout style. If worn, a scarf must have simple lines and no frills to detract from the center of attention—your face. *Hosiery* should be skin-colored.

As with men, the less *jewelry* you wear the better. Aside from a simple watch and wedding ring (if married), be careful about what other ornaments you wear. While a brooch or a simple necklace is often very suitable, multiple rings, bracelets, or anything ornate or gaudy is not. Very simple earrings or gold studs should be limited to one per ear. The appropriate watch is plain gold or silver. Wear nose rings only for religious reasons.

If you need to wear an *overcoat*, make sure that it is long enough to cover the bottom of your skirt. Multiple coat styles are acceptable; furs are not. If you wear *gloves*, make them leather. They should match your coat in color.

Do not carry a purse. Carry a leather zippered case, attaché case, or leather-bound zippered notebook with any necessities, including a PDA if you use one. This connotes power and authority. Put everything that you need in it, but do not overstuff it or keep it sloppy—you may have to open it during an interview. Some students have written that using the zippered notebook is less awkward when carried to lunch, labs, or on ward tours. If using an attaché case, include a small leather-covered notepad. Avoid the drug company pens you use on the wards.

Grooming

As for the more personal items, such as hair, makeup, and perfume, just remember that you are going on a job interview, not on a date. If the interviewer is aware that you are wearing *perfume*, you are wearing too much. Similarly with *makeup*—it works best when it is not obvious. Be especially careful to avoid obvious eye shadow or eyeliner. *Nails* should be manicured. Your *hair* should be clean and conservative in appearance. If it is long, it is often a good idea to put it up to keep it from looking sloppy. Many consultants recommend that women should avoid hairstyles that cover either eye, and that their hair should be pulled away from the jaw line and ears so they will look more serious.

The bottom line is that you dress for the interview in a uniform. Although there is considerable variation allowed, for maximum success, applicants should adhere to the standard style. As one woman physician who did very well in her resident interviews said about the wardrobe, "sophistication and maturity are the keys to success."

Clothing as Camouflage

Clothes can hide real or perceived problems. For those "Doogie Howser" types who think they look too young to be taken seriously, dressing conservatively will age you a bit. Wearing glasses, even if you normally wear contacts, also helps.

Some people are self-conscious about their weight. Clothes can help disguise those extra pounds. Both men and women can wear slightly longer, or hip-length, suit jackets, and women can wear a loose jacket over a business dress or flared skirt. The key is to be certain that your clothes fit well. Even thin people look heavy if their buttons are popping out or their collar is too tight.

Wear the "Uniform" Stylishly

Now that you have acquired the uniform, make sure that you get the most out of it. Your clothes must appear neat, clean, and pressed. Do *not* travel in your clothes and show up five minutes before the interview looking like a Raggedy Anne doll that has gone through the washer. If possible, arrive at the interview city the night before, having traveled in your normal attire. You will get a good night's sleep and put on your freshly pressed uniform the next morning to go to the interview. Be sure to have the appropriate garments, such as overcoat, umbrella, etc., to protect your uniform in case of inclement weather. When you get to the interview site, slip into the restroom and give yourself a last-minute inspection.

Once you dress correctly for your interview, forget about your clothes. They should be a natural part of you. Think of these clothes like new hiking boots. You don't want to go 20 miles in a new pair without breaking them in first. If you aren't comfortable in these fancy duds, wear them a few times before you hit the interview trail.

Packing

When packing for interviews, the motto should be "less is more." That will often be the only way to get all the necessities into the allowable size and number of bags. Two simple techniques for doing this are either to limit the time you have to pack to 20 minutes per city you will visit, or to put out everything you want for your trip—and then put half of it away.

Sophisticated travelers decrease the amount they carry by making sure that all their clothes go with everything else, by packing clothes that can serve more than one function, and by avoiding the tendency to pack for each potential "what if?" that could happen on the trip. Wear the bulky items. You can always stow a heavy coat in the overhead bin.

Packing lists ease pre-trip anxieties. Once you make a decision about what to take with you on one trip, use the same packing list for subsequent trips. That way you won't forget anything. Keep the list with you to serve as a record of your belongings in case your bags are lost.

How to Pack a Suitcase

Whether you use a large suitcase or a smaller carryon, the goal is for your clothes to arrive intact and as pristine as possible. To accomplish this, place trousers, skirts, dresses, shirts, blouses, and jackets (all zipped or buttoned, and folded along their natural seams) in the suitcase, alternating side to side. Frequent travelers know that if suits, skirts, and dresses are neatly folded and placed in a plastic cleaner's bag, they will stay neat and pressed. You can even roll them up and they will remain pristine! (I know it seems bizarre, so try it out at home to prove to yourself that it works.)

Only after all items are partially in the suitcase should the remainder that are outside the suitcase be folded in, one garment over the other (Figure 16.1). Each item will then cushion the others and help prevent creases. Pack shoes, stuffed with toiletries, rolled-up socks, belts, etc., along the hinged side of the bag. Finally, stuff rolled T-shirts, under-garments, sleepwear, and sweaters in any available space to cushion the contents and keep them from shifting. When you unpack, the result should be neat and clean clothing.

On multi-day trips, where you won't unpack and stay at the same location, put the items you will wear together on the same layer, so you can simply reach in and pull them all out at the same time. Put smaller items for each day, such as underwear, in plastic bags. To reduce the stress of residency interview trips, take along a memento of home, such as a family picture, a favorite book, or even a pillow (if you are not traveling by air).

What to Do If Your Suitcase Doesn't Show Up

Use Carryon, If Possible

A danger when flying is that your checked baggage won't show up—at least not in time to do you any good. The fact that it appears back at your home the day after the interview is little consolation for being forced to dress in "low camp" style for the interview at your most desired program. The solution, especially if you are only going to be away from home for one or two days, is to use a carryon suit bag and an under-the-seat bag. This often provides enough packing capacity and alleviates any worry about your uniform not showing up. And, since you don't have to retrieve your bags, it also saves you time at the airport.

FIGURE 16.1
Packing a Suitcase

Before packing, every garment should be buttoned, zippered, belted, and folded along natural creases.

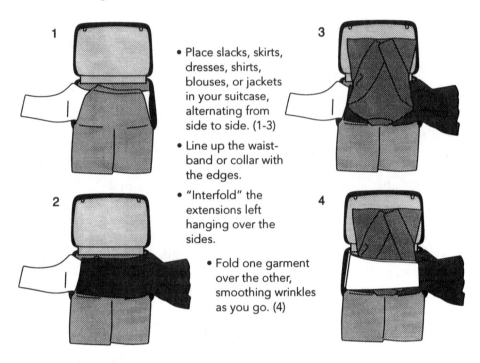

- Place slacks, skirts, dresses, shirts, blouses, or jackets in your suitcase, alternating from side to side. (1-3)

- Line up the waist-band or collar with the edges.

- "Interfold" the extensions left hanging over the sides.

  - Fold one garment over the other, smoothing wrinkles as you go. (4)

Each item will cushion the other, helping to prevent creases.

It is *essential to carry with you* the interview schedules, airline tickets and schedules, travelers checks, credit cards, drivers license or other ID, jewelry, hotel and automobile confirmations, medications, and the phone numbers and addresses for your travel agent and interview contacts. I have seen more than one distraught applicant whose checked bag containing his interview materials, not to mention his clothes, had been lost.

Be careful when choosing your carryon bags. Each airline, and even each model or configuration of seats on a particular plane, has different allowable space and different rules for carryons. These days, traveling with as little baggage as possible is the best bet. Most airlines now limit you to one carryon bag and a personal item such as a purse or a briefcase. It is wise to check with a travel agent or the airline to avoid bringing bags that won't fit in the overhead bin or under the seat. If possible, get a carryon with wheels so you can roll it—your back will thank you.

Honesty Works (The Sympathy & Uniqueness Votes)

Okay, so you weren't able to use the carryon method—and now your baggage is somewhere between here and Outer Mongolia. You have an interview in three hours and are wearing hand-me-downs from a backwoods orphanage. What should you do?

First, don't panic. Any faculty member who will be interviewing you has undoubtedly had a great deal of airline travel experience. And anyone with that amount of experience has also had his or her bags misplaced by the airlines—often more than once. However, you need to make some show of good faith. First, badger the airline representatives. If you present a good enough sob story, they might front you money for a decent shirt and tie (or blouse and scarf). You will need at least this much. Then, when you get to the interview, apologize to everyone you meet for your appearance. The "airline-lost-my-luggage" story never fails to both get the sympathy (or empathy) vote and keep that applicant in the interviewers' minds. A good story and a good attitude may actually win you some points.

Tax Tip

Since you may have just spent substantial sums on phone calls, travel, and transportation, you may be asking yourself whether these expenses are tax deductible. The answer is yes and no.

Most applicants are medical students who have no substantial income. Without income, they pay no taxes, so there are no deductions. In any event, students will be applying for their first job in medicine, so Uncle Sam would not allow the deductions anyway.

If, however, you are already working as a physician and are now applying for a residency or fellowship position, keep a careful record of your expenses (including postage, copying, phone calls, travel, and lodging). These may be deductible as job search expenses if you itemize your income tax return.

FEEDBACK FORM*

Much of the most valuable information in this book comes from students like yourself. Please share your experiences.

I would like to pass on the following information or experience for inclusion in the next edition of this book:

_____

_____

_____

_____

_____

_____

_____

_____

_____

_____

_____

Name (please print)

_____

Address

_____

_____

_____

E-mail (optional)

*Please return to:

Kenneth V. Iserson, M.D., Galen Press, Ltd.

P.O. Box 64400, Tucson, Arizona 85728-4400 USA

or e-mail: sales@galenpress.com

17

The Visit

*Hiring decisions are made in the first 30 seconds of the interview—
the balance of the time is used to justify the decision.*

– An axiom in the personnel field

Illusions are comforting; just don't rely on them.

– Folk Saying

OKAY, SO YOU HAVE YOUR INTERVIEWS set up and you are ready to go and "knock their socks off." Remember that it is not only your interview performance but also how you conduct yourself throughout your entire time at a program that will determine whether the faculty ranks you highly. So, here are some last minute tips to help you smooth out any remaining rough spots in the way you will present yourself.

Timeliness

To mangle an old saying, "Timeliness is next to Godliness." You will make a major impact on all interviewers, a significantly *negative* impact, if you are late for your appointments. Excuses are fine for your mother, your spouse, and, sometimes, your friends and teachers. But they work poorly on prospective employers. Faculty's time is valuable, and they have set some of it aside to interview you. Don't waste their time, or yours, by being late.

Of course, unavoidable delays do occur. Unexpected bad weather and transportation breakdowns are the two most common causes (especially during the interview season—with the worst weather of the year). If you run into difficulties that will cause you to be late, have the courtesy to call ahead. Even if you only think that you *might* be delayed due to these or other valid factors, let the program know early. They will then be able to reschedule people and, possibly, to work you in at a later time or on a later date. Do not leave them wondering what happened to you. Even if you do not care about that program, leaving them hanging is extremely discourteous and unprofessional, and it may cost you a position at another program. Remember that many academics know each other—and they do talk about applicants when they get together. *The key is to show up on time, ready for action!*

Confirm Your Interview

Although you are expected to be on time and at the correct location, either you or the program may have made a scheduling error. It is very embarrassing for an applicant to show up on the wrong day for a scheduled interview because of a communication error.

Occasionally there is a disaster at the residency program that mandates that interviews be postponed or rescheduled. Mistakes happen, especially when there are dozens or hundreds of individuals interviewing at the same program during a short time period. And since you may very well be on the road, there may be no way to contact you about such a situation. The professional way to avoid complications is to call to confirm your interview a day or two before traveling to the program. That way you stand little chance of making a wasted trip or being embarrassed by a scheduling mistake.

Know the Schedule

If you can get your interview schedule for each program before you arrive, so much the better. Have them fax or e-mail it to you. You will then know how to pace yourself throughout the visit. You will also be able to plan specific activities for any "free-time" blocks. These periods can be used to visit the library, the wards, the other teaching hospitals in the program if they are nearby, and the cafeteria. Since this could be the food you eat for the next several years—how bad is it?

If you cannot get your entire schedule, at least find out what time you begin. Recheck your information the afternoon before to make certain that it is correct. You cannot afford to be late. It usually helps if you are early. Even if you have never been early for anything in your life, this would be an excellent time to start.

Once you get started on your interviews, it is up to the interviewers themselves, and the residency secretary, to keep everyone on schedule. Many interviewers have a bad habit of running over their allotted time. Do not let this make you uncomfortable. However, when you get to the next appointment late, apologize immediately and explain that you just got out of your last interview with Dr. X. If it happens to you, it has happened to others—and faculty members will understand and not count it against you. They probably are already aware of their colleagues' foibles.

Leave Some Time Flexible

Now that you have gotten the interview and have worked hard to make a good impression, do not ruin it all by running out early. Would you leave a fancy dinner party before dessert? Of course not. Scheduling departing flights out of town without giving yourself enough flexibility to "eat dessert" is the same situation. If you book yourself too tightly, you will not have any leeway in case your interviews run overtime. When they do, it will usually be because one or more of the faculty has an extra interest in your candidacy. This is a golden opportunity; don't blow it.

Also, you may find you have a greater interest in a program than you initially thought you would. In that case, you may want to investigate that program's finer points while you are there. You will need some extra time to do this. Remain a little flexible.

Attitude

SMILE! It doesn't cost you anything. Of course you are prepared to be on your best behavior with interviewers. But astute program directors are just as interested in how you act outside the formal interview setting as in how you act in it. This tells them more about how you will act during day-to-day program activities, how you will interact with your peers, and whether you will be able to get along with the ancillary medical staff.

Be pleasant to everyone, and be pleasant at all times. This does not mean you must fawn over the residents and bow down to the secretaries. It does mean, at the least, that you should not ignore them. They are real people. Treat them as the friendly individuals they probably are. Be pleasant and try to interact with them warmly. This also holds true for other applicants. If the other applicants like you, this is often seen as a very positive point in your favor. When applicants are observed as a group, those who get along with others can be clearly identified. And working well with a team is a key ingredient in being a successful resident.

The bottom line is that input from sources other than the interviewers is often very important. You should consider yourself under observation the entire time you interact with the program. The show doesn't stop until you walk out the hospital door at the end of the day, and it continues with every phone and written contact you make with the program.

One point worthy of mention is that reviewing your own medical school file may help you prepare for these interactions. The narrative part of your file usually contains a wealth of information from faculty and residents concerning how others perceive you. Take time to read through it before your interviews. Insights that you gain could lead to more positive interactions with the interviewers, as well as improvements in all your personal relations.

Uniqueness

Interviewers, like all individuals, receive only a small portion of the information directed at them. There is a great deal of "noise" between the sender's encoded message and the receiver's decoding of that message (Figure 17.1). Receivers take this information and change it to fit their preconceived ideas. It is from this information that they make decisions. As a residency applicant, you battle three communication devils.

Selective Exposure

People are constantly exposed to a tremendous amount of stimuli. They really notice only exceptional deviations from normal patterns. These deviations can either be positive (beneficial to you) or negative (counterproductive to you). It is essential that you be noticed—and noticed positively.

FIGURE 17.1

Elements in the Communication Process

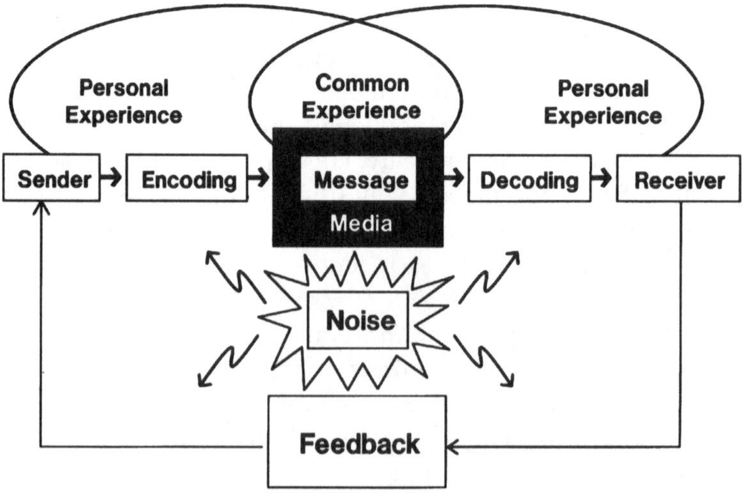

Selective Distortion

People tend to interpret data in ways that support, rather than challenge, their preconceptions. These preconceptions of you will, most likely, be based upon the written material that you have supplied to the program. It is your job to add to the positive feeling you have already worked so hard to create.

Selective Retention

People forget much of what they learn. And they forget it quickly. Your job is to make sure that they remember you.

Knowledge

About the Specialty

You have worked hard to get interviews for a position in your chosen specialty. Be certain you know a great deal about that specialty before you arrive at the programs. This does not mean medical knowledge; you will acquire that during your residency. It means that you should know about the specialty's culture.

- What do the practitioners in the field really do?
- What types of procedures do they perform?
- What level of reimbursement should they expect?
- How do other specialists perceive them?
- Do they have opportunities for subspecialty training?
- What are the requirements to take the specialty's board examination?
- What is the outlook for the specialty in the future?

These are the types of questions that you should have asked yourself while making an informed decision about which specialty you wanted to enter. Faculty members want to know that you have made the effort to learn about their specialty before committing your entire professional life to it.

If you do not have this information, you may not have fully thought out your decision, and could later be very unhappy. Unhappiness is bad for both the resident and the faculty. It leads to depression, anger, and poor performance. It can also cause a resident to drop out of a program before graduation. Therefore, demonstrate that you have seriously thought about your career choice. Know about the specialty. Read the specialty journals and newsletters concerning pending changes within the field. The latter, if you can get copies, are the most current. Read the editorials to know about the specialty's "hot topics." The more you know about a specialty, the more committed to it you will appear. And commitment is one of the most important qualities interviewers seek.

About the Program

Just as you must know the basic information about your chosen specialty, you also need to know about each program you visit.

You initially received a lot of information in the program's packet, from their website, and from *FREIDA*. If you were as careful as you should have been, you also have received additional updated written or oral information. Review this information before going into the interview. No matter whether this is your first interview or the twentieth, it is a major *faux pas* to confuse basics about the program where you are currently interviewing with information from another program. Be sure that you have the facts about the current program firmly in your mind before you set out in the morning. If you, like most people, have a little trouble keeping the details straight, write yourself some notes for reference.

Another way to get additional information about a program is to run a MEDLINE search on the faculty. Looking at articles written by the faculty will give you an idea of their medical interests. It may also provide some insight into questions they might ask you or subjects they might like to discuss. In any case, the more you know about a specific program before going into the interview setting, the better the chance that you will leave highly regarded and be well-remembered.

Many programs use more than one hospital for training. If possible, see them all, even if you are only scheduled for interviews at one or two of them. They may not want to show you the other institution(s) for a very good reason—you would not rank the program if you saw them!

Talk to Residents for the Real Story

If you haven't talked to the current residents, assume that you really do not know very much about the program. Be very wary of any program that either does not give you the opportunity or that does not insist that you talk to some of its residents. Residents often see things quite differently than the attending physicians. And their perspectives, while not necessarily the same as those you might have in the same situation, may be much closer to yours than those of the faculty. These talks are usually informal, and because of limitations on the residents' time, may occur in a group setting. Nevertheless, the residents' opinions, viewpoints, and insights about the program should strongly influence how you will rate it for each of the factors on your "Must/Want" Analysis.

If there is a senior medical student on rotation in the department while you are there, try to talk to him or her. You cannot afford to miss this valuable perspective. One other source of information might be a graduate from your medical school who is currently training at that institution. Even if not in the same program to which you are applying, he or she will have intimate knowledge of the institution, and may even know something about your prospective department. Graduates from your *alma mater* may also feel some loyalty to you—and give you otherwise "forgotten" information. You will probably be able to locate such graduates through either your Dean of Students or your school's Alumni Office.

Basic Rules

Once you actually get to the interview site there are some very basic things that you need to do, aside from answering any questions in a satisfactory manner. In fact, questions and answers may, in some cases, be merely window dressing for the actual interview process.

The "behavioral interview" is becoming more common as laws increasingly limit the questions that interviewers can ask. Behavioral interviewers are much more interested in whether you look and act like you would fit into a job rather than whether you can answer any specific questions. They look for communication skills, physical presence, motivation, truthfulness, and how suited each applicant is to be a resident in their program.

All good interviewers look for small, but important, details. Some of these are discussed below.

Show Enthusiasm for This Program

It is important to show your enthusiasm for the specialty. But being enthusiastic about entering the training program *at which you are currently interviewing* makes interviewers rate you even more highly. Base your eagerness on the strong points that you gleaned from the program's packet of information. Generally the areas of which the program is most proud are included in their packet. So basing your interest on these areas will get the best results.

An amazing number of applicants arrive at programs with the attitude that either: (1) they are browsing and will not reveal that they really *want* a position at the program; or (2) the attitude toward the program that they demonstrate while interviewing will not influence their selection as a potential resident. Both approaches are wrong. Show enthusiasm! If you cannot work up any enthusiasm for a program, perhaps you should not be interviewing there. Also, if you can't garner enthusiasm for the program and specialty now, you won't be able to do it during your third 30-hour on-call stint in a week.

Know How to Pronounce Your Interviewers' Names

How do you say Dr. Llnoyphthg? You don't know? How could that be when he will be interviewing you in five minutes? It may seem petty, especially with some of the difficult or unique pronunciations of names in the medical world, to expect you to know how to pronounce, on the first try, all the names of the people that you will meet. But it is expected. So you should know how. Remember that, above all else, a person's name is a unique part of him or her. Mispronouncing an interviewer's name can, even if subconsciously, leave a negative impression of an applicant.

At the start of the day, ask the residency secretary how to pronounce any difficult or unusual names among those listed on your interview schedule. As she tells you, write each down phonetically so you will be able to repeat it correctly when necessary. If this is not possible, listen carefully when the individual introduces him- or herself to you. If it is a difficult name, repeat it and ask if you said it right. Don't slip up on this simple point of etiquette.

Enter & Depart in a Polite, Assured Manner

Look confident! Walk into the interview with your head up, shoulders squared, looking poised. Pause briefly as you enter the room to assert your strong presence. If you slink into an interview like a scared rabbit, how are you going to look to an interviewer? Certainly not like one of the people likely to get a spot in their residency program. Remember that initial impressions are very important. In the first minute, interviewers determine whether applicants meet their expectations. Let your body send a message of confidence, calmness, and control.

Greet interviewers with a firm, but not bone-crushing, handshake. This goes for both men and women. The dainty dead-fish handshake used by many women, as well as some men in the past, connotes only meekness and a lack of authority. Avoid it like the plague. Extend your hand to the other person with the thumb up and out. Make sure that the web between your thumb and index finger meets the other person's web. Try to shake hands from the elbow, not the shoulder or wrist. It is also desirable to have reasonably dry hands. If your palms have a tendency to sweat when you get nervous, dry them off just before meeting each interviewer. One solution to sweaty palms is to sit, before interviews, with your palms exposed to the air rather than stuffed in a pocket or lying face down in your lap.

Also greet the interviewer with an enthusiastic voice and manner. When you begin speaking to an individual, the actual words you speak are much less important than the manner in which you say them. The first thing an interviewer notices is your tone of voice. You will also be judged by your enthusiasm, facial expressions, gestures, and posture. Therefore, try to act as if you are really pleased to have an opportunity to talk with the faculty and residents. Practice this with some critical observers at home. You must not sound forced or pretentious. If you do, you will do yourself more harm than good. Sincere enthusiasm will greatly enhance your entire visit.

During the interview, sit comfortably straight, leaning slightly forward in the chair. This demonstrates your interest through nonverbal cues. You can prove this to yourself. Have a friend (trying to keep a neutral expression in both instances) first face you, sitting forward in a chair. Then have the individual lean back in a relaxed posture. If you were the interviewer, which candidate would interest you more?

Other negative body-language traits include resting your head on your hand, tilting your head to one side (the coy look), and fiddling with your beard, hair, mustache, or earrings. Keep your head upright and your hands away from your head. Likewise, don't fiddle with your clothes, pen, or anything else.

Look your interviewer in the eyes. Applicants who look away when they answer questions suggest either that there is something less than honest about their answers or that they are afraid of the situation. Those who look away when the interviewer is talking (a true kiss of death) indicate that they do not care about what the interviewer is saying. Obviously, neither situation is favorable. Always try to look an interviewer in the eyes. Some experienced interviewers suggest looking at a person first in one eye, then the other. The recipient gets the feeling that the listener is listening intently; the listener avoids a glazed look some people get when they look at a person only in one eye (a common behavior). If you plan to try this, practice ahead of time; the first few times you do this you may be distracted and not hear what the speaker is saying.

Acknowledge what the interviewer is saying by nodding, and with brief verbal phrases such as "I see," "Of course," or "Yes." Try not to use expressions such as "wow," "awesome," or "rad," which connote something other than professionalism. It helps to vary the expression you use so you don't sound wooden or monotonous.

Your exit from the interview must also be graceful and enthusiastic. As speechwriters know, the last thing heard will be remembered best. Shake your interviewer's hand and say again how glad you are to have had a chance to talk with him or her. Offer to provide any other information he or she might desire about you. You will rarely, if ever, be taken up on this offer. State that you look forward to working with him or her. This should take less than 15 seconds and appear very smooth. It would not hurt to practice this one little segment so you don't appear awkward. As you can see from some television interviews, even the best speakers and the most intelligent individuals often look like dolts when terminating an interview. Don't let this be your downfall.

You Are Not Selling a Medical Student— You Are Selling a Promise

Forget that you are a medical student. In the interview scenario, you are the promise of a bright future. You will be the specialty's finest clinician, a noted researcher, a diligent healer of indigent patients, and a solid member of the medical community. You will achieve this because you are an extremely hard worker who is compulsive, intelligent, responsive to teaching, happy in your work, and no trouble to the faculty.

That is the promise you are selling. To get into your chosen program, you must project the ability to make this promise a reality. How can you make a contribution to this program? You are the salesman. You are the product. Go forth and sell.

Materials for the Interview

Although it may seem rather silly to detail what you need to take with you to interviews, it is surprising how many applicants seem to forget some of the necessary basic materials. In addition to the basics, two forms, the *Interview Notes*, Figure 17.2, and your *"Must/Want"* Analysis (see Figure 10.1 for a blank copy) are suggested as part of your standard interview equipment. These will aid you later when you evaluate each program and write your follow-up letters.

General Materials

The first two items that you need to bring with you are the *directions to the interview site and the phone numbers* to contact the program if you get lost or are delayed. Next, carry along whatever *information you have received from the program*. Not only should you review it immediately prior to setting out for the interview in the morning, but you may also want to consult it during the interview day to refresh your memory or recheck questionable points brought up in conversation. It helps to have a paper copy as a backup in case your PDA fails.

Of course, you should have a *list of questions* that you want to ask at each program (see Chapter 19), as well as a pad of *paper* and a *pen* to record the answers. Test your pens to make sure that they work. Bring a *photograph* of yourself to give to the residency secretary when you arrive. Also, if you have any additional credentials or paperwork that will be vital for the program to have, such as a written military deferment for training, be certain that you bring these with you.

Finally, bring *something to read*, be it a specialty journal, a news magazine, or a newspaper. At most programs, you will spend a lot of time waiting. If you have something to occupy your mind, it will make you more alert and less cranky. And don't forget to turn off your cell phone or pager!

Interview Notes

The Interview Notes form (Figure 17.2) is designed to give you an organized method for remembering key information obtained during interviews. It will also act as a reminder when you want to send follow-up notes or materials to individual interviewers. Write the phonetic spelling of the interviewers' names on this form. The *Companion Disk for Getting Into A Residency* will print out blank Interview Notes forms.

Some students have written that they took the elements from the "Must/Want" Analysis that were key to their decision making and abstracted the information onto a separate form. They used that form to take notes during the interview day. If this serves your needs, go for it.

Your "Must/Want" Analysis As an Interview Checklist

The "Must/Want" Analysis you previously completed (see Figure 10.1) can now act as an interview checklist (example, Figure 17.3). Its use both simplifies your evaluation of each program and helps you discriminate among them. The factors on your personal "Must/Want" Analysis and the weights you assigned to each one will remain constant for all the programs you visit.

Immediately following your visit to each program, score on a 1 to 10 scale (10 is perfect) how well the program does in each category. Even if you have previously given some items "Scores" based on written materials, those "Scores" should be considered tentative until confirmed during the site visit. Then multiply the "Weights" by the "Scores" for each factor to obtain the factor "Total." Adding the values in the "Total" column will give you your personal ranking for the program ("Program Evaluation Score").

FIGURE 17.2
Interview Notes

Program _____

Address _____

_____

Secretary _____

Telephone _____

E-mail _____

INTERVIEWER   NOTES

1._____   _____

_____   _____

_____

2._____   _____

_____   _____

_____

3._____   _____

_____   _____

_____

4._____   _____

_____   _____

_____

5._____   _____

_____   _____

_____

6._____   _____

_____   _____

_____

OTHER NOTES

_____

_____

_____

_____

FIGURE 17.3

"Must/Want" Analysis As an Interview Checklist—An Example

PROGRAM #2–Mako General Hospital   DATE INTERVIEWED: January 30

Clinical Experience	WEIGHT X	SCORE =	TOTAL
On-Call Schedule	5	6	30
Patient Population	2	5	10
Responsibility	14	8	112
Setting	7	8	56
Volume	10	8	80
Geographic Location			
Part of Country	1	2	2
Specific City	1	1	1
Reputation			
Program Age and Stability	2	5	10
Faculty			
Availability	5	4	20
Interest	7	7	49
Stability	3	3	9
Curriculum			
Number of Conferences	1	7	7
Special Training	6	9	54
Types of Conferences	2	5	10
Esprit de Corps	8	7	56
Research Opportunities/Training			
Knowledge	5	3	15
Materials	2	8	16
Time	7	8	56
Facilities			
Clinical Laboratory Support	1	2	2
Library/Media	2	6	12
Safety/Security	3	5	15
No Restrictive Covenant	MUST	Yes	OK
Benefits: Health			
Health Insurance	MUST	Yes	OK
Hospitalization	MUST	Yes	OK

FIGURE 17.3 (continued)

	WEIGHT	X SCORE	= TOTAL
Benefits: Non-Health			
Childcare	MUST	Yes	OK
Disability Insurance	MUST	Yes	OK
Educational Leave: Funding Available	1	8	8
Time Off	2	9	18
Liability Insurance	MUST	Yes	OK
Vacation	1	7	7
Moonlighting	2	2	4

TOTAL OF ALL WEIGHTS = _100_

PROGRAM EVALUATION SCORE = 659

This "Program Evaluation Score" can later be compared to those calculated after you visit other programs. In some cases, of course, your ratings may suffer from the same problem that interviewers face; early ratings will tend to be lower because they are compared to an ideal, whereas later ratings will tend to be higher since they are being scored in comparison to programs you have already visited. If this is taken into account, you should have no difficulty in correctly interpreting the scores.

The numbers in Figure 17.3 are based on the "Weights" given by our hypothetical applicant from Chapter 10. If you compare Figure 17.3 with Figure 10.9, you will note that some of the "Scores" (in boldface) and "Totals" for this program have been changed based on information obtained during the site visit and interviews. The applicant now has a more complete picture of this program; its "Program Evaluation Score" is now 659.

Behavior at Lunch

Applicants often go to lunch with the program's residents or faculty members. Several rules apply to this experience, as well as to any business lunch—for that is exactly what it is.

Stay away from alcohol! You need to be on your toes, not under the table. Even if you don't lose your wits after imbibing alcohol, your afternoon interviewers may be teetotalers, and thus discount you as a viable candidate if you have been drinking.

Do not eat too much. The postprandial tide is a very effective soporific. You don't want to sleep through the afternoon's activities, do you?

Use good table manners. If you have never learned them before, now would be an excellent opportunity. You will need to know how to eat in a reasonably civilized manner throughout your medical career. Start this behavior at the interview lunch. Common errors that cost people jobs include: holding your fork like a knife, talking with your mouth full, not putting the napkin in your lap, not breaking bread before you eat it, and pushing food onto the fork with your thumb. Even in the hospital cafeteria, some table manners are necessary. If you need help, ask a civilized friend.

Pitfalls abound during meals. For example, a tale is told of Admiral Rickover, the father of the U.S. nuclear submarine service, who personally interviewed every officer applying to be a sub captain. If a person salted his food without tasting it, he was eliminated as too rash a decision-maker. Be wary.

If you go to a restaurant, don't order the most expensive items. Also, order food that is easy to eat. Avoid any food that you cannot control. If you aren't skilled at twirling "strand" pasta, don't order it—it will be too messy. Shellfish that requires squeezing and digging, ribs, corn on the cob, and fried chicken are all too difficult to eat daintily. Also, avoid foods that can cause accidents and embarrassment. Soups, creamy dressings, desserts, and greasy hand-held foods, such as tacos, can easily end up on your brand-new clothes. Onions and garlic can make even the most stalwart interviewer want to avoid you.

Never eat all the bread in the basket. If it is in front of you, pass it around before you take any; same with the butter. Once you get it, tear your roll gently; don't saw it with a knife. And don't butter all your bread at once. You also don't want to blow on the soup; you may splatter it on others. Only cut and take one bite of food at a time—and always use your knife (not the fork) to cut your food. In a fancy restaurant with lots of cutlery, use the outer silverware first, reserving those above your plate for dessert.

Sit up straight in the chair without hovering over your plate or leaning backward on the chair's back legs. Keep your elbows off the table and, as your mother said, never talk with food in your mouth. If you are asked a question just as you are about to put something in your mouth, go ahead and eat it, and think about your answer while you chew. To acknowledge the question, look at the person and nod. If you feel a bit of food between your teeth, swish silently and unobtrusively. If you notice someone else with food in his or her teeth, mention it unobtrusively. Don't do as one interviewee did at a Chinese restaurant. She popped an entire fortune cookie into her mouth, then removed the fortune and read it to her dining companions!

Don't share another person's appetizer or dessert unless invited to do so—and then, ask the waiter to split it for you. As for the napkin, rest it in your lap; never use it as a bib. When you finish your meal, don't place your napkin in the center of a dirty plate—put it next to the plate.

During the conversation, generally avoid religion, politics, and sexual preferences. The best advice is to use lunch to ward off true hypoglycemia. Consider that meal as simply another part of your interview. Do your real eating after you have left the program for the day and can relax.

18

The Perfect Applicant

How do you make silk purses out of a sow's ear? Start with silk sows.

– Samuel P. Martin III, M.D.

Perfection is in the eye of the beholder.

– Proverb

Note: No updates were found in the medical literature for the figures in this chapter.

BY NOW, AS YOU PREPARE to go for your first interviews, you are probably wondering just what residency directors are looking for in an applicant. There is no absolute answer, but here are some program directors' thoughts on the subject.

The *fundamental rule is that there is no perfect applicant.* Although program directors constantly search for the beast known as the "perfect applicant," they know that this hunt is very similar to the quest for the Holy Grail, a fruitless endeavor. And yet, just as with the Holy Grail, the search continues.

As an applicant, you are probably paranoid enough to want to compare yourself against the perceived ideal of residency selection committees and program directors. While the ideal candidate varies from specialty to specialty and from program to program, there are some basics that seem to hold true for all.

A residency director in a competitive specialty once told me that his perfect applicant would be "a minority woman who graduated from Harvard Medical School at the top of her class, got honors in all her required third-year clinical rotations, had been elected to AOA, had a Ph.D. with a record of significant research and funding, scored in the 99th percentile on USMLE Steps 1 and 2, acquired superior reference letters from top colleagues in our specialty with whom she had worked closely and who said they wanted her in their program, had a dynamite personality, knew a lot about and loved the specialty, and had the energy of a 13-year-old."

"Why," I asked, "are you looking for these criteria?"

He explained that women and minorities are generally under-represented in medicine and, if possible, he wanted to help correct this. Election to AOA, top class ranking at a good medical school, and high U.S. Medical Licensing Exam (USMLE) scores were the only standard criteria across all medical schools he could use to measure candidates. "Of course the USMLE Step 1 has little to do with clinical medicine, but what else is there?" he asked, rather frustrated.

The answer is that excellent performance in third-year clinical clerkships is another, although less accurate, measure of performance. Since medical schools vary so much in their grading schemes (many do not have grading systems discriminating enough to obtain class ranks), it is often very difficult to know what a particular grade means. The courses also frequently vary in their levels of difficulty and intensity. The closest thing to uniformity among medical schools comes in the third-year required clinical clerkships. Excellent grades in these courses usually suggest at least a modicum of clinical knowledge and ability.

Letters from colleagues in the field, especially those who have worked with the applicant, who want the applicant in their own program and who are available to honestly answer questions over the phone are often the most significant part of an application package. Unlike the typical Dean's letter where every student appears to "walk on water," this is the closest thing to an honest appraisal one can get.

"But why include the other criteria?" I asked.

"No matter how good an applicant is," he continued, "he or she has to fit in with our program's residents and faculty. This is where our opportunity to talk with and interview the applicant comes in. And, because our program is so intensive, we need people with a great deal of energy and enthusiasm. The Ph.D. and research are there to be certain that I never get an applicant who meets all the criteria. If I did, I would probably be disappointed."

I asked him if he had ever met anyone, applicant or not, who met these criteria. Smiling, he replied that of course he hadn't, but he could still look for her.

What this residency director is seeking in applicants is little different from what the vast majority of program directors seek when deciding whom to interview. One survey showed that the most common traits that program directors look for include: grades in required and elective rotations in the specialty, grades in other clerkships, class rank, USMLE Step 2 scores, and AOA membership (Figure 18.1).

FIGURE 18.1

Relative Importance of Academic Criteria When Selecting Residents in Various Specialties

	Ortho-ped	Gen Surg	OB/Gyn	Ophth-amal	Peds	Fam Med	Int Med	Emer Med	Psych	PM&R	Path	Rad-Onc	DX Rad	Anesth
Grades in required clerkships	2	1	1	1	1	1	1	2	1	2	8	4	3	1
Number of honors grades	4	4	2	2	3	3	3	3	2	5	6	2	2	7
Sr. specialty elective grades	1	8	9	5	2	2	6	1	3	1	3	1	10	2
Class rank	5	2	5	3	4	6	5	4	7	10	2	5	1	2
AOA honorary membership	5	2	7	3	7	7	4	6	9	10	5	7	4	9
USMLE Step 2 score	7	7	4	6	8	4	2	7	8	5	9	8	8	6
Med. sch. academic awards	8	6	6	8	5	8	7	5	6	10	3	8	6	5
USMLE Step 1 score	3	5	3	7	9	9	8	9	11	5	10	10	5	4
Med. school's reputation	8	10	8	9	10	10	9	8	4	8	7	10	7	9
Other senior elective grades	10	12	11	10	5	5	10	9	10	3	11	5	11	7
Published med. sch. research	12	9	10	11	12	12	11	11	5	4	1	2	9	11
Grades in preclinical courses	11	11	12	12	11	11	12	12	12	9	12	12	11	12

*Criteria with identical numbers were considered by the residency directors to be equivalent.

Adapted from: Wagoner NE, Suriano JR: Program directors' responses to a survey on variables used to select residents in a time of change. Acad Med. 1999;74(1): 51-58.

The importance of various criteria may vary among specialties. Figure 18.2 shows the importance given to the same criteria by residency directors in Family Practice (now Family Medicine) and Obstetrics and Gynecology. Based on similar studies, the Family Medicine criteria seem to mirror those of Internal Medicine, Pediatrics, and Psychiatry, while the Obstetrics and Gynecology criteria reflect those of other surgical specialties.

Most program directors have a good idea of what they are looking for in a resident. If they really know what they're doing, they have written these criteria down (it is an ACGME rule to do this), discussed them with the rest of the department, and given a copy to all interviewers. As an applicant, you should be able to determine what programs are seeking based on what they highlight in their written materials, how their program is structured, and the institution(s) in which they reside. Make a list of the top three or four criteria you believe each program is seeking and stress, in the interviews, your qualities that match these criteria.

FIGURE 18.2

Importance of Information to Residency
When Selecting Interviewees and Ranking Applicants

Selecting Interviewees*

	FP	OB/GYN
Dean's letter	1	2
Well-written personal statement	2	6
Transcript	3	1
Application form	4	5
USMLE scores	5	3
Letter from known/respected colleague	6	4

Ranking Candidates *

	FP	OB/GYN
Interview	1	1
Dean's letter	2	3
Well-written personal statement	3	7
Transcript	4	2
Application form	5	6
Letter from known/respected colleague	6	5
USMLE scores	7	4

*1 is the most important factor and 7 is the least important factor among those listed.

Adapted from: Taylor CA, Weinstein L, Mayhew HE. The process of resident selection: a view from the residency director's desk. *Obstet Gynecol.* 1995;85:299-303.

What residency directors *really* want are residents who will perform well clinically in their program without causing the faculty too much agitation or grief. Among knowledgeable employers, the jargon for an applicant who will easily fit into the program, requires minimal coaching to do extremely well, and already has proven clinical skills and judgment is "plug and play."

No matter what criteria are used, the system is imperfect. The best that can be said about AOA election, high USMLE scores, clinical honors in medical school courses, high class rankings, and positive interviews by faculty is that individuals who meet these criteria usually do not perform dismally in training programs. Their performance is, in fact, usually above average. Similarly, those who performed near the bottom of their class in medical school continue to do the poorest in residency. Individuals who seem to fare the worst during residency are those who took leaves of absence or had academic difficulty during medical school, or those with below-average performance in their required clinical clerkships.

Residency directors have different levels of concerns about applicants, depending upon what they see and hear. Figure 18.3 shows how they feel about some common things they see in residency candidates' histories.

FIGURE 18.3
Items in Applicant's History That Worry Residency Directors

Very Concerned
- Received disciplinary action in medical school.
- Treated for alcoholism.
- Received failure in a required clerkship.
- Took extended time to graduate for academic reasons.
- Has learning disability.
- Failed USMLE Step 1 prior to passing.
- Passed USMLE with minimal scores.

Worrisome
- Graduated in lower third of class.
- Received a failure in a preclinical course.
- Had mediocre preclinical grades but strong clinical evaluations.

Concerned
- Has family responsibilities.
- Did not participate in extracurricular activities in medical school.

Adapted from: Wagoner NE, Suriano JR: Program directors' response to a survey on variables used to select residents in a time of change. *Acad Med.* 1999;74(1):51-58.

Applicants and residency directors seem to place different values on applicant qualities. Some studies have shown that directors most admire personal characteristics, while students believe that their knowledge and skills are more important attributes in getting a residency position.

Regardless of studies or personal opinions, however, program directors will give up neither their search for the ideal resident nor their use of measurement criteria for applicants. Their job is still to weed through the morass of applications to cull out a group of potential residents. And since precious little else is available to help them make this decision, these are the criteria they will use and by which you will be measured.

19

The Interview

A job interview is like being on trial for your life.

– Russian Proverb

He who asks is a fool for a minute; he who doesn't is a fool forever.

– Chinese Proverb

BEFORE BEGINNING THE INTERVIEW, keep in mind some research-based information about the process. First, interviewers develop a stereotype of a good applicant and then try to match the candidates to it. By reading the program information carefully, you may get a hint of what they think the "perfect" applicant is. Also, see Chapter 18, The Perfect Applicant.

The typical residency faculty member is unskilled at employment interviews and makes many errors when evaluating applicants. A typical rating error is the "halo effect," when they are overly influenced by a single favorable or unfavorable trait. Unfortunately, unfavorable information carries more weight than favorable information, so the halo effect is more likely to work against you than for you.

Related to this, if several outstanding candidates have been interviewed in succession, an average candidate who follows them will look worse than he or she is because of the comparison. The reverse is also true: an average candidate will look better when following several poor ones. You can't do much about these factors, but they are worth remembering as you head into the lion's den.

Know Your Questions

It is important to know not only what questions you want to ask, but also what you are searching for in the replies. You will be looking for specific answers, e.g., the percentage of residency graduates that have passed the specialty's board examination on the first try, as well as observing the interviewers' attitudes toward the subjects you raise. Also notice their attitudes toward you as a person and toward residents in general. Are they friendly and open? Or haughty and cold? This could make a big difference in how you rank the program.

Know when to ask your questions. You will rarely run out of questions before you run out of opportunities to ask them. Most programs try to allow applicants the opportunity to have their questions answered fully. They gain as much, or more, information about you from your questions as they do from your answers to their questions. But wait for the proper time. Let the interviewers ask their questions first. Wait for them to ask if you have any questions of your own (Figure 19.1).

When you ask your own questions, do so in a courteous, diplomatic manner. More than one applicant has "gone down the tubes" by trying to cross-examine interviewers. Doing so is crass and demonstrates immaturity. Ask your questions in a way that expresses enthusiasm for a positive answer. Rather than the question, "What problems have you had with accreditation?" you might inquire, "There haven't been any accreditation problems, have there?" The first is accusatory, the second merely inquisitive. Get your information. But be nice about it.

Ask simple, straightforward, open-ended (requiring more than a "yes" or "no" answer) questions. Do not ask questions with multiple parts or that are too long to easily follow. If you ask these types of questions, you may not get the information you want, but you will probably make a negative impression on the interviewer.

FIGURE 19.1

Typical Interview from the Interviewer's Viewpoint

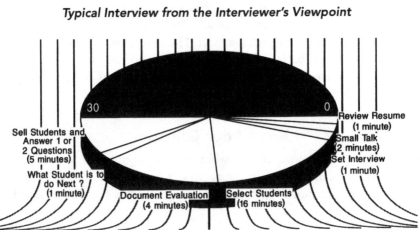

Finally, ask the right people the right questions. At the start of your interview day, ask the residency secretary which individuals you will meet with and what their positions are within the program. Ask the residency or department director about changes in the program or the current status of prior residents. Do not ask them about the call schedule or resident esprit de corps. These are questions to ask residents.

Print a list of your questions in advance so that you can easily refer to it (and read it) during your interviews. (It's probably easier during interviews to have a printed list than to be fiddling constantly with your PDA.) What are some of the questions you should ask, and what should you look for in the answers? The list below is divided into questions you should ask the faculty and those that you will want to ask residents. Some you may want to ask of both groups, especially Question 23, "Could you give me (show me) an example?"

The List—To Ask Faculty

1. What is the program's educational philosophy?
Before you begin your interviews, review your notes about the program. Reread the statements from their website and written material about their educational goals and objectives. Some programs emphasize preparation for an academic career; most try to produce strong clinicians who will work in the community. Ask the residency director to clarify any vague points so that you can determine if their goals are consistent with yours.

This leads naturally to your next question: What do you look for in a candidate to meet those goals? You then have a golden opportunity to briefly list your qualities that match their needs.

2. How have your graduates done on the specialty's board exam?
Although the primary goal of residency training is to prepare you to practice in your chosen field, an important milepost during your career will be passing the specialty's board examination. In many cases, passing "the Boards" determines the type and level of position you can fill. How have this program's residents done when they took their specialty board exams? If they have all passed, was this on the first try? This can be asked tactfully, as in "Did any of them have to take their Boards more than once?" Did they fare as well on the oral exams (you should already know if they have these in your chosen specialty) as they did on the written exams?

Residency directors should know this type of information. Although information on specific graduates is, of course, confidential, the cumulative data should be available to all residency applicants. If it isn't, then there may be a problem.

You also want to know how residents have done on the specialty's in-training examinations. These tests, usually given annually, mirror subsequent performance on specialty board exams. In addition, does the program have any conferences or special programs to help their residents prepare for the specialty's boards?

The information you glean from these questions indicates, in part, the amount of didactic teaching, reading time, and interaction with the faculty that you will receive at this program. As might be expected, graduates of high-volume, high-workload programs often have worse records on board examinations than do those from lower volume programs. However, this is not always true, so it is important to get the specifics from each program you visit.

3. Is there much faculty turnover?

Tread gently in this area—it may be very sensitive. But do tread. You need to know about faculty stability. It gives a strong indication about the staff's and, by extension, the entire program's esprit de corps. If there is a large or rapid turnover in faculty positions, it may indicate that all is not well, even if there is a pretty façade.

There are several ways to get this information. If the program sent you a list of instructors with its material, simply ask how many of these individuals will still be there in July. Otherwise, you can ask if any faculty members have recently been added—"As replacements?" you ask not so naively—or if any of the current staff will be leaving in the near future. This last is the least favorable way to ask the question. If you hear from the residents, however, that either the residency director or the department director is planning to leave, ask about it. These are two changes that can markedly affect the program's tenor.

You might feel that faculty turnover is their business, not yours. Wrong! Would you make reservations at an expensive French restaurant for your birthday celebration if you thought that the chef/owner was going on vacation—and being replaced by the short-order cook from the greasy spoon next door? Don't go hungry. Ask before you commit to a reservation.

4. How would you characterize faculty–resident relationships?

This might provide an interesting insight into how the program really functions. Listen for overly positive answers, as well as those that are negative or dismissive of the relationship or of their residents. If you ask several faculty members this question, you may discern a pattern. Most important, you want to compare the answers from the faculty with those from the residents on the same topic. (See Questions 25 and 27.)

5. Are there non-clinical responsibilities?

Of course you will be doing clinical work, and you need to talk to the residents about this. But what other requirements are there? If you arrive at a program expecting nothing but clinical work and there are additional requirements, you may be upset. Find out about all your obligations ahead of time.

There are usually four categories of extra activities:

1. *Research.* Either the development and implementation of a research project or participation in ongoing research may be required.
2. *Projects.* Development of or participation in projects, such as those designed around medical student education, or in specialty society activities may be strongly encouraged.
3. *Writing.* Written case reports, abstracts, and book reviews may be mandatory.
4. *Administration.* Either a specialty board or the program may require spending time as chief resident. This usually includes a number of administrative duties.

These extra activities may demand a considerable amount of your time during your residency training. They may also contribute greatly to your education. But to make a rational decision about which program to choose, you need to know what extra activities each program requires.

6. Is this program particularly strong or well known in any special areas?

If you have learned of any special training the residency offers from their brochure, website, residents, or other interviewees, you may want to ask for more details. You also want to know about other special courses, some of which may be too new to list in the brochures or which have not yet started. These will be extra perquisites of attending this program, and the interviewers will generally be thrilled that you asked. This allows them to show off their program to its best advantage.

When evaluating the interviewers' answers, remember that programs in which you do not plan to participate, such as an international elective that won't fit in with caring for your three young children, are of no benefit to you. They may, however, demonstrate the program's educational direction, which is very useful to know.

7. How is the training divided?

This question is primarily for individuals who are applying to a combined residency program, such as Emergency Medicine–Pediatrics and Internal Medicine–Pediatrics. Each combined program operates a bit differently, so you will need to inquire about the details for each. Specifically, you want to find out how long you will work as a de facto intern in each specialty and when you will begin to assume significant patient care responsibility. Ask the faculty and the residents from all parts of the program.

You also want to know how well your predecessors have been made to feel a part of both programs academically and socially. Were they seen as "outsiders" in one or both of the programs, or have they been welcomed and easily integrated into both?

8. What types of clinical sites are used?

Residency programs generally use a variety of clinical settings, including private, public, and Veterans Administration hospitals; private-practice preceptors; and distant rotations for specialized training. Which types does this program offer—or require? Are there a wide variety of both outpatient and inpatient facilities appropriate for your education in this specialty? Or have the sites been chosen for reasons other than optimal resident education (for example, because they provide some resident funding)? Do the types of clinical facilities mimic the medical practice you envision yourself having?

Logistical questions associated with this are: Are any of these rotations out of town? Is housing (and, if distant, transportation) supplied? If the primary residency is in an urban center with good mass transit, you may want to ask whether you will need a car for some rotations.

Since residents spend virtually all their time in clinical settings, this information is very important. Be aware that many older, poorer, and badly funded residency-associated hospitals and clinics don't have enough staff (you do the "scut" work), up-to-date working equipment (you make do using available materials), or the necessary variety of clinicians (you must refer interesting patients to other facilities) to provide you with the quality experience you need.

9. What patient population will I encounter?

The patients you see during residency determine, in large part, the types of learning experiences you have. The obvious groups to ask about include the mix of adults and children, the ratio of men to women (especially important in Veterans' Hospital-based programs), and the percentages of acute (including trauma) and chronic problems. Less obvious factors are the patients' social mix, including private versus public patients (often with differing expectations and stress levels); the different cultures of and languages spoken by patients; and the racial mix (this may suggest emphasis on certain diseases).

10. Is training offered in medical Spanish or other languages?

Spanish is becoming the second language in medicine throughout the United States. Learning the basics is a skill that will help you throughout your career.

Some programs assist their residents in learning at least basic medical Spanish so that they can communicate with their patients. In some areas of the country, another language may be needed to speak with patients. Does the program offer opportunities to learn these languages? More important, do they pay for them? Are they part of the residency curriculum or an elective? And, if such classes are offered, does the department make it easy for residents to attend?

11. Are there elective opportunities?

Each of us has a unique view of what our professional life will be like. Some may envision a life in private or group practice, while others believe their career will involve research, teaching, or foreign travel. Since most residency programs are structured to fit the generic physician entering the specialty, you may need specific educational opportunities to learn something about particular specialty areas—either to gain expertise or to find out if that is the direction you want to follow. Does this program allow sufficient time and flexibility to sample these different environments?

The easiest way to determine this is to ask both how much elective time is built into the program and how it has been used. The answers describe the program's standard pattern.

Next, you want to know the official policy, so it is best to ask the program director. Find out the specific scope of elective experiences that are permitted. Are there geographical restrictions on where you can go? Can you sample only certain clinical or non-clinical areas? Is there any funding for electives? Also ask about faculty contacts that will make it easier to arrange such electives, especially off-site.

Note that even if you are currently not interested in areas outside the specialty's mainstream practice, you will grow as a clinician during your residency. Having the option to explore different tracks may become important to you.

12. Are there research opportunities?

Some applicants may envision careers in academia or research. If you are one of them, you will certainly want to enter a residency that can provide you with the resources and guidance to do research.

Start with the question "What research projects are the department's faculty and residents working on now?" That will give you a range of interests and the level of activity. Then, if one of the projects interests you, focus on that. Will you have a mentor? Is that person funded for his or her research? Is that individual amenable to working with residents? How fairly have residents been treated when working with faculty members on research projects in the past? (Have the residents done the work and been given secondary credit?)

Also find out about available facilities, funding, time, and support staff, such as statisticians, to do research. Does the department or institution provide these? Is research required, tolerated, or actively encouraged? In addition, if you do research and it is accepted for presentation at a national meeting, will the department pay your way there? Will they give you the necessary time off? Ask now to avoid disappointment later.

Finally, you should attend one or more of your specialty's national meetings while you are in residency. National meetings are excellent places to make job contacts, meet residents from other programs, and gain additional insight into the specialty, so going to them can be very important. Does the program allow residents time off to attend them? Do they provide any funding for these trips? If so, is the funding available only if you are presenting at the meeting, or is it available to all residents?

13. Are administrative, bioethics, and legal training available?

Although academicians have been slow to recognize it, medicine is also a business—sometimes a dangerous business. How much training in the administrative and legal aspects of medical practice will you get at this program? Will you have hands-on training dealing with insurance, billing, contracts, hiring, and similar problems? Or are you expected to learn it all at the "school of hard knocks" after you begin your own practice?

Will you receive in-depth training about the legal pitfalls now so common in medicine, or will this come only after your first malpractice suit? How about the ethical issues involved in your specialty?

Does the program offer a formal course of bioethics instruction? As medicine advances, practitioners must more frequently ask, "Just because I can do it, should I?" Bioethics helps answer this and other difficult clinical (and research) questions. Although the requirements for residency training now include the areas of law, ethics, and socioeconomics related to medicine, most training programs do not offer instruction in these areas. If you find one that does, it indicates that they have a dynamic and forward-looking residency director.

14. Is there a mentor/adviser system? How does it work?

Everyone expects to do well in his or her residency program. Problems can develop, however. The first hurdle may be simply learning the rules and the culture of a new institution. Having an experienced person to guide you through this maze can work wonders. This may be a senior resident "buddied" with a new trainee, a faculty member at the program, or both. Is there a formal system of assigning "mentors" for new residents? If so, how are these assigned: randomly, by mutual interests, by sex, or by race? If a mentor/adviser system exists, it suggests that the program is at least trying to ease your transition from medical student to resident. Later you may want to ask residents how well this mentoring system works.

Another recent innovation at some residencies is financial counseling. It's an excellent idea, since many residents carry an enormous debt burden and the repayment rules keep changing. Does this residency have such a program?

15. What types of resident evaluations are used? How often?

Interns struggle through their first year in one of two modes (sometimes alternating between them): they believe they are doing a dynamite job or, more frequently, they believe they are learning little and their performance is marginal. Neither extreme is usually the case. But in the strange world of neophyte medicine, it is hard to know where you stand without some feedback.

How often does the program supply this feedback? What mechanisms are used? In the past, many residents went through one or more years of training blissfully unaware that the faculty thought their performance was less than adequate, only to be suddenly dropped from the program. This was especially common in Surgical training programs. Residency programs must now demonstrate to reviewers their mechanisms for evaluation.

Many Internal Medicine programs use not only periodic formal evaluations, but also "Early Warning Notes" and "Praise Cards," developed by the American Board of Internal Medicine, to deliver feedback between formal evaluations. Unfortunately, most faculty members are not used to giving individual residents constructive feedback while they are working with them, so formal evaluations become very important in gauging how well you are doing.

Another evaluation method is the in-service examination given by many Boards. These measure "book knowledge," and are used to compare residents at the same level of training across the United States. Ask if such exams are available at the program. Will you be allowed time off to take the exams (including the night before so you won't fall asleep during the test)? How are the results used—to help the resident assess his or her strengths and weaknesses, or to eliminate "weak" residents? Does the program offer standardized evaluation examinations or other methods of self-assessment in addition to the national in-service tests? It is nice to know how you are doing compared not only to your peers locally, but also to all other residents with whom you will take your specialty board examination when you finish the program. These tests are one way of finding out.

16. How has health care reform affected this program and institution?

This is far from an idle question. The 1990s saw the most devastating and grievous insult to medical education in this century. Medicare rules and punitive actions (fining medical schools and residency faculties millions of dollars) have forced most teaching hospitals to seriously restrict many residents' clinical independence.

Medicare also has a demonstration project to pay 49 New York hospitals $400 million to decrease the number of residency positions by 20% to 25%. Their idea was that if this could be implemented nationwide, it would decrease the total number of U.S. physicians. By 1999, at least 16 of these hospitals had dropped out of the project (less than two years after it began), which is an indication of how much work residents do in hospitals.

In addition, the encroachment of managed care organizations has siphoned off many patients from hospitals' teaching services and clinics. Even when the patient census has remained stable, declining reimbursement has often decreased the number of ancillary staff, available services, and any amenities residents once had. What actions have this residency program and teaching institution taken to assure that trainees continue to get a quality clinical education? Are they financially stable? Have these changes adversely affected residents' and faculty's esprit de corps?

17. Do you anticipate changes in the program's curriculum?

This is another of those questions that you should ask the residency director. It is a safe inquiry and can be asked directly.

Are changes in the curriculum expected in the near future—if so, why? "Near future" is defined as your time in the program. Residency programs may anticipate changes based upon modifications of board requirements, alterations in the patient base, or new directions being taken by the specialty as a whole or the faculty in particular. These changes may make a difference in your evaluation of the program—either favorably or unfavorably.

In some cases, only general ideas about anticipated changes can be set forth. Usually the faculty is not dissembling, but rather demonstrating both their hopes for the program and the complexity involved in altering many training curricula. In any case, know that no matter what you are told, some changes most likely will take place during your training. No program's curriculum is chiseled in stone.

You can elicit this information from the faculty and residents by asking "What has changed since you came to this program?" This is an easy and non-threatening way to get a sense of the frequency and types of curriculum changes at the program.

18. What is the program's accreditation status?

This is another sensitive question. Does that specialty's Residency Review Committee accredit the program? (Actually, it is the Accreditation Council for Graduate Medical Education that accredits the programs, but let's not quibble.) This indicates that the program is certified to prepare residents for the specialty's board examination. There are four possible answers to this question.

The first answer is "No, the program is not accredited." If you go through such a program, which is not in the NRMP Match since it is not accredited, *you will not be eligible to take the specialty's board exam.* A negative answer to this question should, in virtually all cases, eliminate this program from your consideration.

The other possibilities all come under the "Yes" category. The simplest is "Yes, full accreditation." This means that the program has been accredited without restrictions for a number of years. This is as good as it gets.

Two other possibilities are "Yes, provisionally" and "Yes, on probation." The former indicates that the program either has not been in existence long enough to get a full accreditation or has had enough recent changes to warrant being considered a "new" program. The problems here, common to all new programs, revolve around the question of stability.

The response, "Yes, on probation," indicates that the program is having major problems and is in danger of losing its accreditation. If that happens, any resident in the program may be left in the lurch, struggling to find another program to enter in mid-training. That is neither a pleasant possibility nor an easy thing to do.

Although you can indirectly look for information about accreditation in *FREIDA* (since non-accredited programs will not be listed) and some programs may mention their accreditation status in the material that they send to applicants, it is worthwhile confirming this at the interview; things do change. You should ask this question of the residency director. The most diplomatic way to do this might be, "You do have full accreditation?" This allows a complete answer. If the program does have full accreditation, there will be a simple answer. If not, the residency director will have an answer already prepared for you. Sit back and take it all in. It may "get a little deep" at this point and you may have to lift your feet off the floor part of the time.

19. *Is this a pyramidal program?*
Most often found in Surgery and Surgical specialties, a pyramidal training program is structured so that only a percentage, usually about half, of those starting in the PGY-1 year will be allowed to finish the entire program. This is usually because the program needs "bodies" to accomplish much of the clinical work, but only has enough significant procedures, such as major operations, to accommodate a few chief residents. If you plan to go into such a program, e.g., "Categorical" General Surgery, be prepared for intense competition with your peers. However, if you are applying only for a one- or two-year "Preliminary" position prior to entering a subspecialty such as Orthopedic Surgery, it might work in your favor. If you are accepted into the program, it will mean that fewer of the Categorical residents will have to be dropped from the pyramid. Make certain that you ask this question—the information, although very important to you, often will not be offered spontaneously.

Programs may no longer be pyramidal according to the ACGME's rules. Many residents, however, report that de facto pyramidal programs still exist.

20. *Have any housestaff left the program before graduating? Why?*
Residents leave training programs for many reasons. Most residencies have had residents leave, usually because of illness, family circumstances, or simply changing their minds about which specialty to enter. This information is not what you are after. You want to know whether any residents have left because they were unhappy with the program, the faculty, or the training they were receiving.

A way to ferret out these individuals may be to ask, "Have any of the residents who have left this program gone into another program in the same specialty?" These are usually the folks who were dissatisfied with the program. Simply ask why they left. Although you may not get specifics, the tenor of the answer may be enough to let you know if there is a potential problem for you.

21. Where are your graduates?

This question is actually a two-parter. The first part asks, "Where are your graduates geographically?" Are they practicing in the vicinity of the program or spread throughout the United States? Are they primarily concentrated in major cities or in rural communities? This gives you a realistic perspective about the program's orientation. Training programs reflect the needs of the populations they serve. The places where residency graduates feel comfortable working reflect the training that they have received.

The second part of the question asks, "What types of jobs do your graduates have?" Are they working primarily in academic centers, in private communities, in group practices, in research, in administration, or in other specific areas? Or are they in many diverse areas of practice? Again, this is highly reflective of the scope and quality of the training the residents in a program receive.

Ask this question in a general manner. If either part is not answered, follow up with a more specific question designed to get the missing information. You might ask to see the map on which residencies often post the location of their graduates. If you locate a residency graduate in your home area, you can gain valuable insight into the program by talking with this individual.

What percent of the program's graduates enter fellowships? The answer to this is relatively straightforward. It leads, however, to an opportunity to ask about how much help the faculty provides in obtaining fellowships—and shows that you have an interest in them. That may be good, unless you are speaking with a general Internist or Pediatrician, who may not be as enamored with applicants who desire to do something other than primary care.

22. Do you help your graduates find jobs?

This may be a new question to many residency faculty. In the past, there was little problem finding work once a resident finished training. Today, with a "doctor glut" in some specialties, there are fewer choice jobs to go around. So, you might need some help to find them, especially if you are interested in entering a difficult market, such as southern California. Ask if the program will help you.

If they say you are on your own, it indicates that they: (1) have little regard for your future welfare, and (2) have little understanding of what their job as teachers really entails. In either case, you are now forewarned.

If they do offer help to residents in finding employment after training, what have they done for recent graduates and current residents? Are there individual counseling sessions? Are faculty contacts used to get positions? Will the faculty review job offers with the residents?

These are but a few of the possible ways in which the program can assist residents in getting their first jobs. You are having a hard enough time getting into a residency. Ask this question now to avoid as many problems as you can when you finish your training.

23. *Could you give me (show me) an example?*

This is one of the most important questions you can ask during interviews. Ask it to supplement questions you ask of faculty and residents.

In the process of trying to ascertain whether you would fit into a program, you need to have some firm information, not unsubstantiated statements. "Our resident on-call schedule is very benign," says the chief resident. "Could you show me the current month's schedule?" you ask. After you see the schedule, you will know if it really is as easy as they claim it is. If it is just the resident's interpretation of what "benign" means, you will know that too.

Many answers to questions lend themselves to confirmation or explanation. This is a safe, pleasant, and enlightening way to get further information about important points. You can never ask this question too often.

The List—To Ask Residents

24. *Would you choose this program again? Why or why not?*

This is the key question to ask residents. It will most likely produce the answers that will best help you to determine your fit with the program. As always, ask this question in a non-confrontational, low-key manner. No doubt this is not the first time the resident has been asked—or contemplated—this question. There is usually a great variation in the answers among the residents. You are looking for general consensus (good or bad), rather than the opinions of "outliers" who love or detest the program for unique reasons.

Faculty members at weak or dysfunctional programs hope that you will not ask this question of their residents. Beware! Some may actually limit your access to residents so that you don't get this feedback.

Two natural follow-up questions are: Which parts of the program do you like the most? Which do you like the least? And, while free time may not be a large part of your residency existence, you do want to know whether the resident (and their significant other) like the city and the area. Listen closely. You may have to "sell" the city to your family before they agree to consider moving there.

25. What contact will I have with the clinical faculty?

The material that the program sent to you listed 42 faculty members. Did they mention how often you will have contact with all of them? With *any* of them? The faculty only helps you if you have direct contact with them. If faculty members hide in their offices or labs rather than attend in the clinics, wards, emergency department, or operating rooms, they might as well not be there.

So, the questions that you should ask the residents are: "How often are the faculty members present?" and "How often do you want faculty input but find that it is not available?" You might want to also ask "How available are they on nights and weekends?" As a resident, you certainly want to be able to exercise some independent thought and judgment. But you need adequate guidance from knowledgeable faculty during residency training. Does this program really offer it?

Also, do the faculty and residents interact informally, such as at holiday parties or on basketball or volleyball teams? This often provides a way to make closer contacts with faculty members who may then wish to help you develop your career.

26. What has changed since you came to the program?

How quickly and significantly does this program's curriculum change? By asking senior residents what has changed since they arrived, you can easily find out this information in a non-threatening way. This is a question to also ask the faculty.

Their answers will provide a picture of the frequency and types of curriculum changes at the program. For example, have there been changes (major or minor) in the program's curriculum, rotations, or electives? How about the program's overall structure? Have there been major faculty changes? Most important, have there been changes in the patient mix or resident responsibilities? Do they think that these changes have been good for the program and for their education?

27. Do residents regularly have an opportunity to formally evaluate faculty and the program? What changes have been made recently as a result of this feedback?

This question really asks, "How important is the educational mission?" Feedback on the faculty's performance is an essential part of all education.

If the residency is serious about education, it will have a good evaluation system. Virtually all residencies, however, will say that they have an evaluation system, since the residency review boards generally require it. What is really telling is if they can recite substantive changes that have been made based on these evaluations. That means that they not only have the system, but also value their residents' opinions.

When asking this question, you may also get information on the institution's or residency's grievance policy, such as that used for harassment. Listen closely. Is the resident telling you about problems they have had, or how they have used the system to avoid problems?

28. How much didactic time is there? Does it have priority?

If it is not in the material that you have already received, find out how much time is spent in lectures, seminars, journal clubs, and other didactic activities. If a current monthly schedule is available, ask for a copy to peruse at your leisure.

The more important question, which you need to ask of one or more residents (not the faculty), is "Which has a higher priority, attending conferences or performing clinical duties?" In most training programs, residents must, at least occasionally, attend to clinical duties while conferences are in progress. But if this is the norm rather than the exception, kiss any meaningful answers about the number of didactic sessions good-bye. If you cannot attend the teaching sessions, they don't exist. Remember that didactic sessions may have a significant impact on your learning, and on passing your in-service training exams and specialty board examinations.

29. What type of clinical experiences will I have?

Residencies are supposed to teach physicians to be excellent clinicians. For that, they must provide adequate clinical experience. How many clinical experiences will you have and how diverse will they be?

In surgical or procedural specialties, will you be performing procedures, or mostly watching? Is there a struggle between services or among residents on the same service for some procedures? At what level do residents graduate to more advanced procedures? In General Surgery, for example, if third- and fourth-year residents are still doing appendectomies, there is a definite problem. Similarly, if senior Pediatric, Family Medicine, or Internal Medicine residents "hog" every tube and line placement, it suggests that they have not had enough experience doing these procedures. Have previous graduates felt comfortable performing all necessary procedures by the time they graduated? If not, you should question whether such a marginal program is right for you.

A special situation exists in Obstetrics and Gynecology. Few programs now teach their residents how to perform elective abortions. If you plan (or think you might want) to do these procedures in your practice, ask specifically whether this training will be available to you.

Aside from the easily recognized procedures, how much responsibility do residents at each level have for managing patients; that is, for making the crucial decisions? (It is usually more difficult to decide *when* it is appropriate to do a procedure than to actually do it. That's what being a doctor is really about.) Will you have increasing responsibility for patient care, progressively making more decisions as you show that you have the requisite knowledge and ability? Or will you be "thrown into the middle of the pool" the first day without adequate supervision? Or, perhaps worse, will you be kept in the "wading pool" for most of your residency?

Some programs offer unique learning opportunities, for example, new diagnostic or therapeutic techniques (such as neurohyperthermic therapy), older but rarely available methodologies (such as hyperbaric chambers), or special training in areas of faculty expertise. As a resident, will these opportunities be available to you?

30. What is the relationship between this program and other specialties?

While you may expect to learn medicine from your own faculty and co-residents, the truth is that you will often learn as much or more from attendings and residents on other services. How well do the various specialties get along at the program's teaching institutions? Is there cooperation, strife, or open warfare among them?

This is an important issue. For example, how will you be treated when you rotate on other services? What type of interactions will you have when calling for or doing consultations, or when treating patients in cooperation with other services? Good inter-service relationships can make residency much less stressful and a more educational experience.

31. Tell me about the on-call rooms, meal plan, cafeteria, library, computer access, and parking.

You've already experienced a variety of call rooms during your clinical years. That was only a taste. When you use the call rooms night after night, their ambiance (or lack thereof) can greatly affect your outlook on life and work. Not only should you be told about the call rooms, but if possible, go see those at the institutions you visit during your interview trip. That way you can evaluate and compare them.

No resident has ever died from hospital food (at least I don't think so). But when you get a chance to eat, it's a lot better if the food is tasty, looks good, has some variety, is served in a setting with at least some semblance of quiet and a pleasant décor, and is inexpensive (or free). There is a huge monetary benefit, not to mention morale boost, if food is provided. Some programs even provide meals when residents are not on duty. More hospitals are finding that jazzing up their cafeterias improves their image with hospital staff, trainees, and patients' families. How do the cafeterias at the locations you will work measure up? Can you tolerate this food, setting, and cost for the duration of your residency?

The library is the bellwether of an institution's educational commitment. Is it stocked with useful and up-to-date materials, staffed with knowledgeable and helpful people, and open long (or all) hours? Does the library have audiovisual and computer materials to supplement printed material? How about access to online databases? When you need to access material for tomorrow morning's grand rounds, are the library's facilities adequate?

Our world is computerized, and the medical field, although currently lagging behind other segments of society, is no exception. Practitioners need to be computer literate, using the Web and local networks as readily as their stethoscopes. Does the residency provide access to computers and use them for teaching? Is Internet access available in the clinical areas? Are computer labs or specialists available to residents? How about special computer courses? It's no longer enough to know how to take a medical history and do a physical examination. You also need to know how to access computerized medical records, lab results, bedside nurses' notes, clinic schedules, library materials, databases, and, eventually, billing records.

Finally, how about parking at the hospital and clinics? Is it difficult to find or expensive? If you drive to your residency interview, you may get a taste of what the parking is like. Is this the norm for residents, or just for visitors?

32. Will I have time to read?

Your educational reading reflects a personal decision about what is important to you. However, if residents consistently answer that they are too tired to read, it suggests a deficiency in the program rather than in any individual. Education in any specialty depends on supplementing clinical experiences with reading. You cannot learn all you need to know on the wards, in the clinics, or in the OR. Reading will be important to you. Ask whether you will have time to do it from those who know—the residents.

The answer to this question will also help to identify those departments that have residency programs primarily to fulfill their service commitments, rather than to educate.

Ask senior-level (PGY-2 and above) residents this question; nearly all interns will tell you that they are too tired to read. That is certainly understandable given their schedules.

33. What support staff is available? Are they helpful?

Residents commonly feel overworked because there are too few people to perform what are typically non-physician tasks. You owe it to yourself to find out how much "scut" work the residents at a program typically perform.

Who starts routine IV lines, draws blood, and does clerical work? Who pushes patients to x-ray or to radiation oncology for treatments?

Does the institution provide an adequate level of nursing and ancillary support? Is this staff supportive, or merely an obstacle to good patient care? Are there backup teams you can call when you are swamped with admissions?

Even if institutions have sufficient numbers of support staff, their quality and interest in helping you may vary based on personnel policy and tradition. What is it like at the institutions through which residents in this program rotate?

While faculty may be able to tell you about some of the available clinical support, ask the residents for the real answers. Don't complain after the fact. Find out in advance.

34. What is the call schedule?

There are two main things that directly affect your life during residency—and they both relate to the call schedule. The first is the amount of time you will actually work. The second is who arranges the schedule.

Ask the residents how much time they actually work at each level of training. Some states, such as New York, and all specialties have officially limited the number of hours their residents can work. As of July 2003, the rules are that all residents must work no more than 80 "duty hours" per week, averaged over a four-week period. "Duty hours" includes all clinical, academic, and administrative activities related to the residency program or patient care. This includes in-house on-call time. Every seven days (averaged over a four-week period), residents must also have at least one continuous 24-hour period free of all educational, clinical, and administrative responsibilities. Residents must also have at least 10 hours for rest and personal activities between all daily duty periods and after in-house call.

In-house call must be no more often than every third night. Taking call from home is not limited, although any time a resident spends in the hospital is counted toward their 80-hour maximum, as is any "in-house" moonlighting (e.g., moonlighting within the residency program, the sponsoring institutions, or the non-hospital sponsor's primary clinical sites).

Although data from 2004–2005 suggest there is high compliance with the duty-hour standards, not everyone plays by the rules. Faced with ever-tighter budgets, many residency directors skirt the rules so the institution can avoid the cost of adding residents. Some of the worst offenders, at least in New York, have been the private hospitals. Surgical specialties and Obstetrics and Gynecology, due to the nature of their practices, continue to have the longest hours. Programs in surgical specialties, in particular, applied for an increase to an 88-hour-a-week limit.

Not many years ago, an applicant got a Surgical internship after having, he thought, asked all the appropriate questions. He expected to work long hours, but was astonished when he found that in addition to taking call in-house on alternate nights, he had to take call from home when he was off duty! Ask in advance so you don't get any nasty surprises.

At many programs, the residency director, the secretary, a chief resident, or some unnamed individual in a back office makes the schedule, leaving residents feeling helpless. Indeed, the lack of control over one's life is one of the biggest stressors among residents. Some programs allow the residents themselves to generate the call schedule (as well as conference, vacation, and off-service schedules). If a program offers this, your mental health will be better for it.

Also, find out if days off are built into the schedule. Although all residents are supposed to be allotted days off (a minimum number is usually four/month), many programs do not explicitly build them into the schedule, and then apply pressure on residents to work even on "free" days. This leads to rapid burnout, frustration, and disgust with practicing medicine and the specialty. Avoid this by asking whether days off are scheduled, and how many there are per month.

35. Do you have a plan for sick days?

A natural part of the on-call resident schedule is an arrangement for coverage in case of illness, injury, or personal crises within the resident staff. It will happen, if not to you, then to some of your colleagues—and you will be affected. If there is a plan, and there probably is, what are the "payback" arrangements and who arranges the backup? The less onerous these arrangements are, the better.

36. Do I need a medical license? A DEA number?

All U.S. medical licensing authorities require residents to have educational licenses, permits, certificates, or registrations. Generally, the institution pays for this, and supplies the licensing board(s) with a list of resident names. Some licensing agencies may require you to pay the fee, which ranges from free to $225 (Washington State). Fourteen states require that residents have passed USMLE Step 1; Mississippi and Montana each require passing Steps 1, 2C, and 2S.

37. What are your moonlighting rules?

Moonlighting—working outside the residency program for income and experience—has long been common. If you have dependents or large expenses, this extra income may be vital. Depending upon the nature of the moonlighting, the experience can be invaluable. At the least, it may be the first time that you feel like a physician, fully responsible for your patient's care. By itself, that is a worthwhile, enlightening, and often scary experience.

Questions to ask about moonlighting include: Does the program allow, tolerate, or encourage moonlighting? Are opportunities available nearby? How are they arranged? Is there a specific individual (often a senior resident) that coordinates them? Is moonlighting permitted both within and outside of the training facilities? Do current residents moonlight? If so, at what PGY level do they begin and what pay do they receive?

38. What is the patient population I will see?

Patients (their numbers and age distribution, the nature of their diseases, and who cares for them in what settings) are the basic element of all medical training programs. If the program lacks an adequate number of patient encounters, it doesn't matter what else it offers.

It is necessary to first ascertain how many patients the residents care for. But aside from this, you also need to know how much time is spent and how much autonomy residents have when caring for private patients. While some programs have many patients coming through their offices or hospital beds, private practitioners often take care of the majority of them.

Find out about the patient population served and the distribution of disease processes. Some teaching hospitals have an overabundance of a few types of disease processes, such as penetrating trauma, tertiary oncology, or AIDS. A skewed distribution does not provide adequate training for clinicians who will eventually serve a more diverse population with more common diseases. Today, as more medical care is being delivered in outpatient settings, residents should see patients in the clinics and outpatient surgeries.

Finally, ask if there are medical students on the service. If there are, ask if you will be responsible for teaching them. Whether this is a plus or minus for you, find out in advance what to expect.

39. Do the residents socialize as a group?

This is one element, or at least demonstrates one element, of esprit de corps. Are the social events program-wide or institution-wide? This may or may not be important to you. If it is, you may also want to ask about the ratio of married to single residents (in the program or institution), how many have children, and how often social events occur.

Does there seem to be any particular activity that is of special interest to the residents, or do their interests vary? Is socializing related to educational activities, such as journal clubs? Or are they separate events, such as volleyball games or picnics? Note that if the socialization is resident-organized, it may vary considerably from year to year.

Confirm Questionable Points

A number of the questions that you raise may be critical. Which questions these are will depend upon your own "Must/Want" Analysis. However, you may not get straight answers to some of them. This may be because no one knows the answer at the moment. For example, in October no one may really know how many of the faculty will still be on-site next July. But you may be getting the runaround for other, more nefarious, reasons. If you ask the residency director about how much faculty interaction there is with residents and the hemming and hawing begins, then you will need to get the real story. This is where the technique of cross-checking facts becomes useful.

Whenever you have some doubt about the answer to an important question, repeat the question to another interviewer. Or better yet, if it is appropriate, ask a resident in the program. In fact, if the issue is extremely important to you, ask everyone you talk to the same question. But be sure not to do so within earshot of others you have already asked (or will ask) that same question—it will be taken as a sign that you doubt their honesty, which, of course, you do. Remember that the program is trying to sell its product to you at the same time that you are selling yourself to it. Not all salesmen are honest. *Caveat emptor!*

Things Not to Ask

There are specific questions that must not be asked during an interview, even though they are important to you. These questions basically involve four areas: salary, benefits, vacation, and competition. Let's discuss each one individually, so you will know what information to get from the *appropriate* sources.

Salary

The *salary* you will receive as a resident will, in large part, depend upon three factors.

1. The mean salaries of housestaff around the country in the previous year.
2. The type of institution in which the residency is located.
3. The region of the country in which the institution is situated.

Most institutions base their resident salaries upon a variation from the mean salary that residents are receiving nationally. The variations in many cases are based upon the cost of living in the region of the country where the institution is located. In addition, those programs that have a relatively difficult time attracting residents, such as community and non-university hospitals, will tend to have higher salaries. Those with very large numbers of applicants will generally offer lower salaries. But, of course, you would be more than happy to do the residency for free, wouldn't you? Probably not. However, this is the attitude to take during the interview process. Salary will keep you alive and pay your bills—but do not try to find out what it will be during the interview. What are you, money-hungry?

The only exception to this rule is if you have any hint that the position is unfunded. Despite rules to the contrary, these positions still exist. They are most commonly found in highly competitive fellowships (post-residency) and at some institutions whose residents are mostly international medical graduates. If this is the case, and you are still interested in the position, at least ask about the non-salary benefits offered.

Benefits

Benefit packages are very important to you as a resident—as they will be for the rest of your career. Virtually all such packages include malpractice insurance and some type of medical insurance. Other benefits may be food or housing allowances, uniforms, cleaning expenses, disability insurance, moving expenses, parking, tuition fee waivers for the affiliated school, and childcare, to name some common ones (Figures 10.4 and 10.5).

Remember, if you can use the benefit, it counts as additional salary. However, if the program offers benefits that you cannot use, such as Obstetric care when you are not planning any children for now, the value of this benefit is lost to you. Do make certain that the medical insurance is comprehensive enough to cover serious illness or injury. You probably already are in debt up to your eyeballs and cannot afford steep medical bills.

Asking a faculty member about the benefit package, however, is generally like talking to your pet rock. He or she will normally have no idea what his or her own benefit package is, let alone yours. Don't make your interviewer look stupid. Avoid this topic during the interview.

Vacation

If you don't think that *vacation* is important, wait until you have been up most of every night for a week. At that point, dreaming about an upcoming vacation may be all that keeps you going. Most interns have three weeks or less of vacation, while most residents in their second or higher years have at least three weeks of vacation each year. In some programs, the vacation can all be taken at one time; in others, it must be taken as one-week blocks. The latter obviously doesn't allow much time for travel.

Asking an interviewer about vacation is akin to inquiring whether you would actually have to do any work during the residency. While everyone understands that vacation—even a resident's vacation—is important, interviewers assume that during the interview you will concentrate on the great educational experience that they offer, rather than your time off.

Competition

Who is your *competition*? It doesn't matter! Asking about other applicants will serve no good purpose and only directs an interviewer's attention away from you. The key, as has been stressed throughout this book, is to put your own best efforts before the residency faculty and let them select you based upon what they see. Forget the others. Concentrate on selling yourself.

Okay, so where do you find out about salary, benefits, and vacation? First, look at the packet that the residency sent to you. Normally, you will discover most of the information there. If not, then three other excellent sources are *FREIDA* (which you have already accessed), the residency secretary, and the people in the institution's Graduate Education office. In fact, the latter site is the place where you can get the most up-to-date information. It is also the spot where you can obtain the data and still remain relatively anonymous. If all else fails, put your questions in writing when you get home and address them to the director of the institution's Housestaff or Graduate Education office. Even by mail, try to avoid querying the program directly about these non-educational areas.

Things Not to Do

Just as there are certain questions that you should avoid, there are certain things that you should not do during the interview. The following are attitudes or actions that will evoke a negative response from an interviewer.

Show Discouragement

Be upbeat! This is your time to shine. One poor interview should not influence the rest of your visit. Remember that the interviewer may not have thought it was a poor interview at all. Looking "down in the dumps" will destroy any positive effect that your interview could possibly have made.

Stand up straight. *SMILE*—it won't break your face. If you cannot find the courage to smile through some adversity now, you are really going to be in trouble when you get into your residency.

Disparage Other Programs, Faculty, or Applicants

You might very well be asked about the other programs that you have visited. The question could be phrased as, "Tell me about the poorest programs that you have visited." Although this may be tempting—you may have interviewed at some really horrendous places—back up a minute to redirect the question. Say that you are not in a position to determine which programs are poor, but there may be some that do not seem to meet your needs. Then you can describe specific aspects of programs that you feel did not fully meet your expectations. But go easy. If you really berate a program that you have visited, the interviewer might wonder what you will say about his or her program when you go elsewhere.

Do not say anything derogatory about faculty at another institution. It should go without saying that you will not berate faculty at the institution at which you are interviewing. No matter what you think, academic medicine, especially within the confines of any one specialty, is rather close-knit. There is a good chance that the person you are describing is well-known to the interviewer.

Falsify Background

Although it may appear that you could say almost anything about your background during the interview and get away with it, you do so only at great risk. The first danger is that you will immediately be discovered.

Not many years ago, a residency applicant was eloquently describing his activities in the Emergency Medical System. He stated that he responded to calls frequently even while in medical school. It was quite an impressive achievement. Yet, as he went on with his story, it became obvious to the interviewer that he was being less than honest. For, while he was describing activities in the opposite end of the country, it just so happened that the interviewer was also from that area and picked up on major factual errors in the story. These were confirmed by a call to his medical school.

The second danger is even worse. If information that you provide when you apply for any job, including a residency position, is later found to be false, it is grounds for immediate dismissal. Thus, giving fraudulent information puts you in jeopardy throughout your residency. Stick to the truth. Make it appear as favorable as possible, but stick to the truth.

Inappropriate Humor

There is a place for humor in interviews. A good laugh can be enjoyed, but, unfortunately, rarely is during residency interviews. However, humor should not be offensive. Even if laughter ensues after you tell an off-color, sexist, or racist joke, you almost certainly will have lowered yourself in the eyes of the interviewer.

In fact, off-color or inappropriate humor is considered by a large number of administrators to be the major breach of etiquette in the workplace. If you have an uncontrollable urge to tell these types of jokes, at least keep them out of the interview.

Drink Coffee, Smoke, Chew Gum, or Bite Nails

Four activities that you must not do during an interview are drink coffee, smoke, chew gum, and bite your nails. You may very well be offered coffee by each interviewer. They mean well. But do they also offer you a bathroom break in the middle of the interview? No! And if you are concentrating on a full bladder instead of the interviewer's questions, you could end up in deep trouble. Avoid diuretics.

There are three problems with smoking. The first is that it is unlikely that your interviewer smokes, since the habit is now relatively rare among physicians. The second is that smoking looks bad during an interview. So, even if you are addicted, hold out until the interview is over—or you have left the program for the day. The smell that lingers on your clothes and breath, if you smoke, will not endear you to non-smoking interviewers. Third, interviewers may be biased against hiring smokers. As of yet, no programs have gone public with an explicit ban on hiring smokers, but it is likely that it would be legal. There is no protection under current civil rights legislation for smokers. This makes it legal for an interviewer to inquire whether or not you are a smoker. Note, of course, that if they inquire, it can only be a (un-Lucky?) strike against you. About 25% of personnel directors admit that if offered two equivalent applicants, they would hire the non-smoker.

Chewing gum is absolutely out. It evokes a fatuous, sophomoric image that will destroy everything that you have worked so hard to achieve. If blowing bubbles is your "thing," hold out until you leave the hospital. No one is physiologically addicted to chewing gum (except, perhaps, nicotine gums—use patches during interviews). One stick of gum at the wrong time can cancel your chance for a residency slot that you really want.

Finally, even though you are nervous and your common response is to bite your nails, restrain yourself when at residency programs. It signals your neuroses to interviewers. For clinicians, it also demonstrates potentially dangerous, infection-producing behavior.

Stressful Interviews

Stress interviews were very common at one time. Interviewers asked questions to purposely make applicants confused, fearful, and hostile. Employers believed they could weed out applicants who couldn't handle stress. The applicants they actually eliminated were individuals with enough self-esteem to determine that they didn't want to work for people who treated potential employees like dirt. While the business world long ago learned not to use this method, some residency programs still use the technique. Others treat applicants shabbily because that is how they treat their residents.

Panel Interviews

The most common type of interview is the one-on-one serial interview, in which you go from interviewer to interviewer, with each asking his or her own questions. Occasionally, though, you will be faced with a rather unusual interview scenario—the panel or group interview, in which from two to 20 individuals will all be interviewing you at the same time. There is a reason business people call this the "gang bang." It is generally considered a rather poor interview technique, both from an employer's and from an applicant's perspective. However, it is still in use, primarily because it is thought to save the interviewers' time. Some people also believe this technique is useful for jobs that require sophisticated communication skills— such as that of a physician.

These interviews will generally be conducted using either a question or a scenario format. In the question format, each panel member asks his or her own questions. In the scenario format, you discuss one or more cases with the entire panel.

The best approach is to look at the individual who asked the question when you answer. In the case of the scenario, since it is a question from the entire group, look at all the members while answering. If an individual member asks you a follow-up question, look at that person when answering. Do not try to determine the most influential people on the panel and direct most of your attention to them. The others will feel slighted. When the panel members meet together later to discuss the candidates, your implied insult will damage your chance of getting a residency position.

A particularly nasty variation used at some residency programs is to sit the applicant between the wings of a V-shaped table facing the interviewers seated on both outside wings. They then pepper interviewees with questions, alternating sides to make candidates swivel their heads back and forth to answer each question. One applicant quickly adjusted by simply slowing down and completely turning to face each questioner when she answered. Her solution was to avoid getting flustered. You could also get up and move your chair back so the angle to view the interviewers is not so acute.

Even worse is another technique that is employed (thankfully) by only a few Gestapo-like programs. At the end of an interview day, they bring two students at a time into a roomful of faculty. They then rapidly ask the students the same questions at the same time. This is really an abuse of power; my suggestion, if this happens to you, is to stand up, thank them for their time, and leave without participating.

If you are faced with any type of panel interview, remember that it will be as unnerving an experience for everyone else as it is for you. So, keep cool and knock their socks off!

Non-Interview Visits

There is one type of program visit, still very rare, to which you may be invited. This is the non-interview visit, which is essentially the same as a traditional interview visit, but without the interviews. While it has the same implications as any other invitation to visit a residency, the programs handle it somewhat differently.

At present, only a few of the most highly selective programs use this type of visit. You are not rated on the basis of your performance during the visit (unless you act really obnoxious). Rather, the residency faculty screens applicants based on their performance in undergraduate or medical school, on the USMLE, and by using other written materials they feel are important. They then assume that all of those they invite for a visit to their program would make acceptable residents.

Residencies use the non-interview visit primarily to show an applicant the program. During the visit, applicants normally have multiple opportunities to see the physical plant, didactic program, and social milieu of the residency. They are usually given many opportunities to interact with faculty and residents, and to have all their questions answered. Generally, they are given a better picture of the program than would be possible during a more traditional visit. Applicants invited for these visits get the maximum possible information; this ensures that those ranking the program highly are doing so with a sound knowledge of what they are getting into.

There are several principles upon which this system is based. The first is that the interview system, especially when using physician-interviewers who are untrained in personnel selection, is as likely to give erroneous information as valid facts. A second is that creating a program with happy residents is best assured by giving applicants as much information as possible about it ahead of time. The last assumption is that if you have qualified applicants, those that are happy to come to a particular program for training make the best residents and, therefore, the best program.

This system is, at best, considered avant-garde. You probably will not be exposed to it. But if you are, do not be put off by it. You should still handle yourself in the same manner described elsewhere in this book.

Silence

The most stressful time during any interview can be a period of silence. This is an invitation to reveal all of your twitches, nervousness, and insecurity. It is also an opportunity to show self-assurance. Be strong!

Silence occurs for several reasons. Rarely are physician-interviewers disciplined enough, or nasty enough, to impose a period of silence simply to test an applicant. Rather, they may remain quiet while they contemplate a question or your answer. They also may suddenly have remembered that they didn't turn off their headlights when they parked their car that morning. Don't feel that a period of silence is negatively directed at you.

Some people respond to silence during an interview by fidgeting. They brush their hair back, move around in their chair, straighten their clothes, or mutter to themselves. Others try to break the silence by repeating (or worse, contradicting) what they just said. Don't do it; sit still, be calm, and be quiet—it too will end. One way experienced individuals combat periods of silence in interview-like situations is to simply begin counting the time to see how long the period lasts. It will seem like days, but it rarely lasts more than 15 seconds.

You, too, can occasionally use silence to demonstrate your contemplative side. If an interviewer asks a particularly deep or thoughtful question, you don't have to jump in immediately with an answer, even if you are prepared for it. Wait a few seconds as you "think" it through. Rather than appearing impulsive, you now seem to be a deep thinker.

Control the Interview—Gently

As you will see in the next chapter, it is often possible to steer the interview in a direction that is beneficial to you. You can mold your answers to interviewers' questions in such a way as to bring out some of your most favorable points. However, this must be done subtly. Some interviewers may see your pushing an interview in a specific direction as being impudent. This, of course, would be counterproductive. So, if you can, steer the interview in a beneficial direction—but do it so gently that the interviewer does not notice.

Reasons Why Interviews Fail

Inadequate Preparation

The first reason that interviews fail is due to inadequate preparation on the applicant's part. This book helps you to prepare for the residency interview. In the end, however, it is up to you to know about the specialty, the program, the faculty, your own ambitions and desires, and the questions that you will probably be asked during interviews. It takes hard work on your part to get ready for interviews, but in the end it is worth it.

Not Listening to Questions

The second reason is because the applicant does not listen to the interviewer's questions. This results in discommunication, distorting the messages coming in and going out. This is what happens when you let your mind wander during an interview—and it spells disaster. Remember that an interview is a battle of wits. If your thoughts stray during this war game, you lose!

Even fast talkers listen faster than they talk. We usually speak only 100 to 150 words per minute, but we process about 600 spoken words a minute. This provides a lot of time for our minds to wander—usually spent thinking about what we are going to say next rather than about what is being said. Since we can only listen or think, we may miss what the other person is saying. When we think and our eyes wander (even momentarily), the speaker knows that we are not listening. The epitome of ignoring the interviewer and the interview is the apocryphal candidate whose cell phone rings during the interview, excuses herself, and proceeds to answer the phone.

Use "active listening." This involves briefly summarizing what you think the speaker has just said. It shows that you are carefully listening, allows the speaker to correct any misimpressions you may have gotten, and helps the conversation move forward. Don't wait until the end of the interview to do this, but rather intersperse it several times during the interview. For example, after the interviewer has described some attributes of their program, say "As I understand it, this residency's strengths are . . .." You might then continue with "How about . . .?".

Since many residency interviews are conducted in busy offices, clinical settings, or even hallways, you may have to concentrate very hard on the interview to avoid the ever-present distractions, sometimes justifiably called "interview blockers" (Figure 17.1). This can be difficult, but your experiences working in noisy patient-care areas should help you to concentrate on the task at hand. And don't just listen to the question, listen to *how the question is asked.* Many times an interviewer will give the astute listener clues to the answer that he or she is looking for. Figure 19.2, "Guidelines for Effective Listening," should help you out.

When speaking, use your normal voice rather than the higher pitch that people often use when they are nervous. Avoid using "fillers" to pad a pause in the conversation, such as "um," "er," "ah," or "you know." Rather, simply pause or use "and," "or," or "but" to join your thoughts together.

Also, never mechanically "give your presentation," downloading your spiel in a rote manner. Rather, keep in mind an outline of your "message" and interject it at appropriate points in the conversation.

Occasionally your mind may go blank during an interview. It's okay. Just apologize to the interviewer and simply ask for a moment to think about the question or, second best, ask the interviewer to repeat the question. As Sam Donaldson, the television newsman, said, "Even the pros get tongue-tied."

One caveat. If you have carefully read the questions and answers in Chapter 20, you may be planning how to answer what you think will be the next question. Or, you may be analyzing how you might interact

---

FIGURE 19.2

Guidelines for Effective Listening

1. Demonstrate attentiveness.
2. Listen for "what" and "why" questions.
3. Listen for key issues.
4. Mirror back the interviewer's message.
5. Don't interrupt the interviewer.
6. Ask clarifying questions.
7. Identify feelings and attitudes in the interviewer.
8. Don't waste time evaluating the interviewer.

during your residency with the faculty and residents you have met. Stop! Turn off that mental audiotape and listen to the interviewer. By now you should be able to answer questions without rehearsing, and there will be plenty of time later to analyze your visit. Concentrate on what the interviewer is saying.

If you really listen, and you still can't understand what an interviewer is looking for, ask for clarification. This might also work (once) if you miss a question completely—but it would be unwise to count on using it repeatedly. Remember that the most ego-gratifying thing you can do for interviewers is to listen to them.

If you are asked a question you just don't know how to answer, be honest and say so. Perhaps you can say, "I'll have to think about that. Can we come back to that later?" Normally, the interviewer will oblige. It is then your responsibility to return to the question before the end of the interview. At that point, if you still cannot come up with an answer, say that you will continue to think about it and get back to the interviewer by letter. Then, in your thank-you letter, give that interviewer an answer to his or her question. In these cases, honesty (and thoughtfulness in later responding by letter), rather than bluffing your way through an answer, may be your key to success.

Answering Questions Not Asked

A third reason for interview failures is that interviewers may get annoyed by having questions answered that were not asked. Many students, while attempting to highlight their strengths, routinely give answers that have no relation at all to the questions that were asked (much like politicians).

Here, you are treading the fine line between guiding the interview and destroying it. Answering a question about your spare-time activities with a description of your medical school awards makes no sense. Rather, talk about the rock band you organized or the Internet bulletin board you established. These both answer the question and highlight your initiative and talents.

Similar applicant behavior that interviewers detest includes answering questions with questions, telling jokes to change the subject, and answering with gibberish. Like reporters, good interviewers simply repeat their original question until they get a straight answer. Also, because interviewers are human, answers that might work one day may not work on another. Many factors can influence an interviewer's behavior (Figure 19.3).

FIGURE 19.3
Factors Influencing an Interviewer's Behavior

- Age and Stage in Life Cycle
- Cultural Background
- Interests
- Prior Experiences

- Goals/Aspirations
- Successes/Failures
- Mood
- Personality

Rambling

A fourth way to wreck your interview is to ramble, thus providing superfluous information. Interviewers are easily bored—not surprising given the number of applicants they must often see in one day.

If you have a lot of information to impart in answer to a specific question, tell the interviewer the main points, and then ask if he or she would like you to continue. For example, if you are asked to describe your medical school rotation in your chosen specialty, give the highlights in several sentences and then ask if the interviewer would like to know more. Since you are watching the interviewer while you answer, you may note nonverbal cues indicating that you have said enough. In general, keep your answers brief, to the point, and interesting.

Giving Warning Signals

The fifth reason that interviews fail is that the applicant inadvertently gives warning signals to the interviewer that there may be an unstable personality lurking behind a deceptive smile. Trained interviewers seek specific warning signs (Figure 19.4).

Very few faculty interviewers are sophisticated enough in the techniques of employment interviewing to consciously recognize these signs. Being good clinicians, though, they unconsciously assimilate clues and will give the applicant a poor rating. It would be a good idea to review the warning signs and make certain that you do not demonstrate any unintentionally.

Interview Disasters

Life is often stranger than fiction, and so are some interviews. One national employment agency described some of the more unusual occurrences during interviews for professional positions:

FIGURE 19.4
Warning Signs for Interviewers

- Inconsistent answers during the interview.
- Inconsistencies between what is said in the interview and past performance.
- Abrasiveness or any other personality quirk that makes the interviewer uncomfortable.
- Evasiveness.
- A pattern of unhappiness in former jobs.
- Blaming others for all the applicant's problems.
- Dullness when responding to questions.
- A pattern of taking advantage of, or of deceiving, other people.

Adapted from: Perham JC. Spotting bad apples: the warning signals. *Dun's Business Month*. October 1986, pp. 54-56.

- At the outset of the interview, the applicant sat down in the interviewer's chair and insisted that the interviewer sit elsewhere.
- When an applicant was asked about loyalty, he showed the interviewer a tattoo of his girlfriend's name.
- An applicant pulled out a tape recorder, saying that he taped all interviews.
- Another left the dry cleaning tag on his jacket, saying that he wanted to demonstrate just how neat and clean he was.
- When told to take his time answering questions, an applicant began writing out the answers before speaking.
- During the interview, an applicant received three cell phone calls.
- Another brought his five children and the family cat to the interview.
- At the end of the interview, the applicant asked if she could use the fax machine to send out some personal letters.

Hopefully, you won't make these types of errors. Just think, if this is how other applicants behave, you don't have much to worry about. Of course, most medical students are smart enough to avoid such crass behavior.

Sell Yourself

The bottom line during an interview is that you must sell yourself. At the same time, you also need to elicit information. To have the best chance of being ranked highly by the programs, you must do a good job of showing your own wares. Interviewers are looking for specific attributes in applicants (Figure 19.5). When talking with the individuals at each program, remember that interviewers rate these elements in the applicants they interview. Although every program has a different rating form for interviewers to complete, the essential items will always be the same (Figure 19.6).

It is your job to point out how closely you resemble the interviewer's ideal candidate by exhibiting the sought-after traits. Remember, if you don't sell yourself, no one else will do it for you!

FIGURE 19.5
Personality Traits Interviewers Seek

Personal	Professional
• Enthusiasm	• Reliability
• Motivation/Initiative	• Honesty/Integrity
• Communication skills	• Pride
• Chemistry	• Dedication
• Energy	• Analytical skills
• Determination	• Listening skills
• Confidence	• Ability to get things done
• Humility	• Initiative
• Emotional control	• Good work habits/work ethic
• Common sense	• Good judgment
• Good interpersonal skills	• Motivation to achieve
• Adaptability	• Problem-solving skills
• Intelligence	

FIGURE 19.6
Interviewer's Rating Form

Applicant Name _____ Date _____

Scale: 1 = *Very Weak*   10 = *Very Strong*

General

_____ Physical appearance (dress, grooming)
_____ Character (reliability, honesty, integrity)
_____ Timeliness
_____ Knowledge about specialty
_____ Knowledge about program
_____ Computer literacy
_____ Energy

Intellect

_____ Mental ability   _____ Judgment
_____ Flexibility   _____ Communication ability

Emotions

_____ Work ethic   _____ Personality (fits program)
_____ Motivation   _____ Teachable
_____ Attitude   _____ Sense of humor
_____ Stability   _____ Outside interests
_____ Self-confidence

Record

_____ USMLE/COMLEX score   _____
_____ Class rank   _____
_____ Medical school   _____
_____ Quality of reference letters _____
_____ Clinical performance (general) _____
_____ Clinical performance (specialty) _____
_____ Honors/Awards   _____
_____ Research   _____

_____ **Total**   _____ **Number of Scored Items**

_____ **Average of Scored Items**

20

The Questions—
The Answers

Silence is the only good substitute for intelligence.

– Folk Saying

Judge a person not by his answers, but by his questions.

– Voltaire

WHAT MUST YOU REMEMBER in the process of preparing for the interview? And what must you remember during the interview? Only two things: *prepare in advance* and *sell yourself by showing your best qualities.*

Interviews generally start with some simple pleasantries and then move on to the skills/attitude evaluation (Figure 19.1). In this part of the interview, no matter what the format or the type of questions asked, most program directors look for three qualities in applicants: *intellectual strength, energy,* and *personal compatibility* with faculty, staff, and current residents.

Interviewers don't really want "the truth." They want "correct" answers. If you believe there is no such thing as the correct answer to a typical interview question, you are sadly mistaken. Good interviewers know exactly what they are looking for in a resident. They know how to extract the needed information in a way that is disarmingly benign. Their questions are simply tools with which to hammer out an impression of the applicant.

Intellectual Strength

Program directors already know a great deal about your performance in this arena. Reference letters, USMLE/COMLEX scores, transcripts, and narratives of clinical performance have preceded you. That is what got you in the door for the interview. Now it is time to see if you can think on your feet. Can you apply what you know to new situations? Are you really interested in learning, or just in getting through a program so you can go into practice? Do you know about anything other than medicine? Was it your quick smile rather than a solid intellect that got you your good grades? Do you believe that you have very little left to learn? Basically, the interviewer is trying to determine what you know, how well you are able to use what you have learned, and if you really want to learn any more.

Energy

Residents spend the majority of their time attending to patient care duties. No matter where a program is located or what the specialty is, fatigue, stress, and depression are pervasive. This is especially true during the PGY-1 year. The less this manifests itself in a program's residents, the fewer the problems with which the faculty must deal and, consequently, the happier they are. Make them happy. Demonstrate that you have the good humor, self-confidence, and stamina to go the distance. But don't just say the words—show them by your actions during the entire interview process.

Personal Compatibility

Remember that you are being hired to join an established group of practicing physicians, albeit at a very junior level. You will be responsible for the care of the faculty's patients. You will be their representative to the medical and non-medical communities. They will have to live their professional lives with you for the duration of your training.

A "personality" already exists for the group, the residency, the department, and the institution. Will you fit in? Will they be comfortable with you? A little thought and a lot of care are necessary here. A hyper-aggressive image may work in some locales, but fail in others. Modify the image you project to meet the situation. But don't fool yourself. If you will not fit in with a group, it is better to find that out during the interview, rather than after you arrive for a several-year stint as a resident.

Presenting Yourself

Show Your Best Qualities

As you answer the interviewers' questions, remember to highlight your best qualities to *sell yourself!*

And do not sell yourself short! Know what your strengths are. Know what the residency is looking for. If you don't have an obvious opportunity to let the interviewers know how well you meet their needs, make an opportunity. This may come through answering questions—all questions—with different strength areas you want to demonstrate. Or it may come in the form of a "question" at the termination of the interview, e.g., "Is it true that many Orthopedic Surgeons have woodworking as a hobby? I have a workshop at home and have made prize-winning furniture." Remember, if you don't sell yourself, no one will do it for you.

Prepare

When getting ready for the interview, it is absolutely essential to *prepare, prepare, prepare!* How many hours have you spent studying and preparing for exams? A thousand? Five thousand? The interview is, perhaps, the toughest exam of your life. Make sure that you spend enough time studying for it. The steps to preparing for an interview are very straightforward: learn to talk about yourself easily, and learn the types of questions interviewers ask and what they hope to learn from your answers. Then combine these and formulate your answers in advance.

Talking About Yourself

Talking about yourself can be very difficult. Most people are loath to extol their own virtues. You must be ready to tell the interviewers your positive qualities so that they hear them loud and clear.

First, put yourself in the position of the residency faculty where you will be interviewing. What job skills and personal characteristics would you want in an individual applying to *your* program? You should be able to get a good idea from the material you have collected from the specialty societies and the program, and from talks with residents and specialists in the field. Write these characteristics down. Then write out questions that you would ask an applicant to your program.

Second, list your strengths that match these characteristics. This step requires a good bit of objectivity. You may need some help from your adviser or a close friend. The following exercise will help you to get in the habit of thinking and talking positively about yourself.

Exercise

List *three accomplishments* of which you are proud and what each accomplishment indicates about you:

1. _____

_____

2. _____

_____

3. _____

_____

Next, list *three abilities* you have that will make you valuable as a resident in the specialty for which you are applying:

1. _____

   _____

2. _____

   _____

3. _____

   _____

Now, can you use these accomplishments and abilities in a short narrative that describes you? If you can, you have made a good start toward a successful interview.

Finally, write some great answers to the questions you developed. Be sure to incorporate your accomplishments and abilities into your answers. But do not memorize them word for word—they will sound forced. Guests on television talk shows prepare by making a list of the ten questions they *don't* want to be asked—and then developing answers for each of them. Note that this process may change a bit as you gain interview experience. But the process gets easier each time you do it. And it is worth the effort.

It's said that the famous lawyer, F. Lee Bailey, doesn't believe that he has won so many difficult cases because he is any smarter than his opponents—it is just that he is more obsessive-compulsive. Preparation is his key to success. Your preparation will be your key to getting a residency position.

Types of Questions

Typical interviewers use only five types of interview questions, although they can be phrased in many different ways. Recognizing the type of question the interviewer asks helps you determine what information he or she is seeking.

Closed Question

These questions ask for specific information and a simple, definitive answer. "How many years were you an undergraduate?" for example, deserves merely a simple answer, such as "four years." Nothing deep here. Interviewers use closed questions to elicit information seemingly absent from the application materials.

Open-Ended, Informal Question

These questions also ask for specific information, but require more in-depth answers. Such a question might be "What clinical experiences have you had in this specialty?" While the question requires specific information, it allows the applicant a chance to speak and become relaxed.

Open-Ended, Attitudinal Question

These questions determine how well an applicant organizes his or her thoughts before speaking. An example is "What do you think of physician advertising?" Most interviewers want to see if the answer is concise and to the point.

Probing Question

Interviewers ask probing questions as follow-ups to open-ended questions. They become especially useful after the applicant has given an answer expressing an opinion. An example of this type of question is "Why do you feel that way?" This forces applicants to defend and further explain their previous answer. It also allows an interviewer to control the direction of the interview.

Sometimes an interviewer will go back to an earlier answer, quote the applicant, and ask a question, such as "You said you felt this area of the country was more progressive medically than your medical school's area. Why is that?"

Leading Question

Interviewers use leading questions to direct applicants' answers or to see if they have the gumption to express their own opinions. Unfortunately, it is not always easy to tell what is expected. Such a question might begin, "Residents in our specialty should go back to an every-other-night call schedule," and be followed by, "Don't you agree?" The interviewer may be serious or merely prodding the interviewee into an untenable position. If the intent is unclear, a way to find out before answering is simply to ask, "What makes you think that?"

Interview Techniques

Interviewers have numerous methods to trap the unwary applicant. They may, for example, ask three questions together at the start of the interview. Are you cool enough to remember them without being prompted? One way to help remember them is to repeat them back "for clarification" after they are asked.

The interviewer may also give conflicting opinions about the same topic to see if the applicant will simply agree with both. Wrong move! Don't be a wimp! Suggest to the interviewer that the opinions "seem to conflict, if I understand you correctly."

Some interviewers treat the interview more like a psychological test by asking interviewees to complete sentences. Examples might be:

"If I were 10% more assertive, I would . . ."

"I sometimes act inappropriately when . . ."

"If I could say anything I wanted right now, I would say . . ."

As for psychological tests, about half of all U.S. companies use them, and about a fourth give formal personality tests to job applicants as part of the interview process. This has not yet caught on among residency programs. Prospective employers use these tests to measure "The Big Five"—emotional stability, extroversion, openness to new experiences, agreeableness, and conscientiousness. These test results (which can be faked by knowledgeable test takers) can then be validated in the interview. Residency faculty think that they can get the same information without using these tests.

Some savvy residency directors interview applicants twice—although one time may be during lunch or in a more informal setting. They may ask some of the same questions again. The second time they are interviewed, applicants are generally more relaxed and may give more complete information or even respond differently to the same questions.

Now, what are some of the specific questions you are likely to be asked?

Questions & Answers

The following questions are those that residency applicants have been asked over the past several years. Following the prototypical question and a discussion of possible answers, I have listed similar questions that applicants have been asked. Some are much more thoughtful or original than the classic questions—such as "Why do you want to be a (fill in the specialty)?"—which nearly all applicants get tired of answering. Perhaps some interviewers will read this list and buff up their interviewing "act." It is impossible to prepare for or to predict every possible question. However, if you prepare for the questions listed below, you will have the self-confidence to answer anything an interviewer asks.

These questions are often used in strange ways by interviewers. One residency applicant reported that she had been asked the main questions from this list *in the order in which they appear*! Don't count on this happening to you.

1. *How are you today?*

What a pleasant way for an interviewer to begin. A simple ice-breaker, you think. Wrong! Sophisticated interviewers use this and similar questions as rapid and effective screening tools. "Gee, it's raining outside and I got soaked coming here," said one applicant. "I'm really frustrated that my plane was late and that I had trouble getting a cab," whined another.

"Great!" "Wonderful!" or "Really happy to be here!" is always your reply to this question. Interviewers look for individuals who stay upbeat even under adversity. The travails on the interview circuit are insignificant compared to those during residency. Simple opening questions delivered in an off-hand manner often expose an applicant's true personality far better than the well-rehearsed "deep" questions that most applicants have come to expect.

Most people find the first three minutes of an interview to be the most difficult. Breaking the ice has tripped up many excellent candidates. You can ease this awkward moment—and make many interviewers grateful— by asking a question about a photograph, book, or other object in the office you are sitting in. The interviewer then has the ball and must answer (giving you a little breathing space), and the interview starts on a warm, friendly note.

The point is there are no innocent questions!

• Did you have any trouble finding us or getting here?

• You're looking a little flustered. What's wrong?

2. *Do you have any questions?*

This is the "behavioral" interviewer's classic opening. The interviewee is expected to take the initiative right from the start. Many applicants ask standard questions and, therefore, waste this opportunity. When the "any questions" opportunity begins an interview, ask questions that highlight your strengths and knowledge of the specialty. Get this information from reading recent "throwaway" journals or news magazines for this specialty, such as *Internal Medicine News*.

Use this question to demonstrate the special expertise you can bring to their program, and that you are achievement-oriented. An example might be, "I recently read in *Family Medicine News* that Family Medicine expects to be more involved in sports medicine. I have a real interest in this area based on my work as a football trainer in college, and I have taught new trainers. Do other people at this program also have an interest in sports medicine?"

Faculty members most commonly ask this question because they are poor employment interviewers. They often do not know what other questions to ask. Since many applicants report this is the most common question they are asked, make a long list of your own questions to use as answers. Never answer "No," since, no matter what the situation, a negative answer indicates that you have a less-than-serious interest in that program.

- Do you know much about our program?
- If you were in my (the interviewer's) seat, what would you ask? Okay, now answer those questions.

3. Tell me about yourself.

This is the granddaddy of open-ended questions (although, of course, it isn't really a question). You have the opportunity to say almost anything you want. You can put your best foot forward or stick it right in your mouth. This question gives you, by design, no hint of how to answer it. You can go off on almost any tangent. And if the interviewer is any good, you will be able to talk for as long as you want. The longer you talk, however, the less chance there is that you will score high on the interviewer's list of candidates.

To answer this question, and similar open-ended questions as well, first respond briefly and succinctly to the single question, "What motivates you?" For example, you might cite your most applicable qualities by stating, "I am a hard worker with a real interest in ENT. I like both the diagnostic and therapeutic aspects of the specialty and seem to be good at the technical procedures that I have been allowed to do."

Then stop. Ask the interviewer if you should continue. This demonstrates that you understand the interactive nature of interviews and that you have consideration for the other person's role. When you ask whether you should continue, many interviewers will direct you to other areas to discuss further. This will help both you and the interviewer a great deal by allowing you to answer the questions that the interviewer really wanted to ask.

- Which three adjectives best describe you?
- Tell me a story about yourself that best describes you.
- If you were going to die in five minutes, what would you tell someone about yourself?
- If you died right now, what would you want on your tombstone?

- Of which accomplishments are you most proud?
- Do you have any hidden achievements or qualities of which you are secretly proud? What are they?
- What are your team-player/leadership qualities?
- What might give me a better picture of you than I can get from your résumé?
- Tell me about your adolescence.
- How have you changed since high school?
- What was the most important event in your life?
- What shaped you and got you to where you are today?
- What was the most difficult thing you have ever done?
- If you could be on the cover of any magazine next month, which one would it be? What would the caption say?
- What do you like to cook?
- How would your best-friend/roommates/relatives describe you? What negative things would they say?
- Why did you write . . . in your personal statement/essay?
- What do you recall about your day before you go to sleep at night?
- What one thing do you want conveyed to the residency committee?

4. What are your strengths and weaknesses?

This question represents the "Tell me about yourself" question phrased negatively. It asks, "Tell me what's wrong with you."

Would you want to answer that question? Of course not. And it is extremely unlikely that you will ever come up against it. But an inquiry about your strengths and weaknesses, essentially the same question, is very common. Basically, the interviewer asks you to jump off a cliff of your own design. All you need to do is to redesign the cliff so you can climb rather than jump.

First, answer the question about your strengths concisely. The only danger is talking too much. Then work on the other half of the question, the dangerous part.

Everyone has weaknesses. "Each and every one of you has something that makes you a jerk," said a Lieutenant Colonel briefing a group of officers about to be promoted to General. "Get in touch with your 'inner jerk' and work on losing that ugly part of your personality." Okay, so a little bit of you is a "jerk." How do you respond?

At this point, you must turn your "weaknesses" into more strengths. What character flaws would the faculty in this specialty approve of? Is your weakness that you are obsessive about completing your work in an exacting manner? Or is it intolerance for those clinicians who do not perform their patient-related tasks with a professional attitude? Maybe it is an inability to go home at night unless all your work is completed. These are, undoubtedly, the types of "failings" that the faculty will be interested in encouraging rather than disparaging. But in relating these faults, show at least a little remorse about having them. Don't be glib.

- Tell me about your "secret identity," the part of your personality that you don't share with strangers.
- Are there any skeletons in your closet that you want to tell me about?
- How well do you take criticism?
- What is your pet peeve?
- If you could change one thing about your personality, what would it be?
- What are your three strongest qualities?
- What are your two worst qualities?
- Have you demonstrated leadership in any extracurricular activities?

5. If you could be any cell in the human body, which would you choose to be, and why?

This is not much different from the directive to "Tell me about yourself." It is, however, a bit more inventive and has been used by many interviewers, especially in Internal Medicine, ever since it found its way into *The New England Journal of Medicine* (1990;323:838). Unfortunately, you may have a hard time not being reminded of *Saturday Night Live's* Baba WaWa's similar question, "If you could be any kind of twee . . . ?"

The neuron was overwhelmingly favored by applicants for Internal Medicine internships, and by those for Gastroenterology and Geriatric fellowships. Most applicants said they wanted to be neurons "to be in control, to be stimulated and stimulating, and to be the center of all things." Since you are now prepared in advance for this question, try to be original. Don't be surprised if this question pops up along the interview route.

- Do you see yourself as more relaxed/casual/informal or as more serious/dedicated/committed?

- Which is more important, the ability to organize, structure, and prioritize, or the ability to be flexible, modify, and make do as needed?
- Which is more important, knowledge or imagination?
- If you could be any kitchen object, what would you be?
- If you could sing any one song beautifully, which one would you choose?
- What is the strangest Halloween costume you ever wore?

6. If your house was burning, what three objects would you save?

Some residency interviewers really believe Freudian analysis will help them choose the best residents. While this may seem to be essentially the same type of question as the one above, think again. This question narrows the scope to a very concrete and personal level by asking, "What do you value in your own life?" How important are material objects to you? Are you "sensitive" enough to reach for your beloved's picture, or are you "sensible" enough to grab the car keys and credit cards?

There is no one correct answer to this question. The best answer depends upon the nature of the person asking the question. Sometimes the questioner actually wants to know whether you have planned ahead or can think quickly, since a fire is a real possibility in our lives—unlike turning into a tree or a cell. Note that in real life, many people die trying to get objects out of a burning home. Current recommendations are to save only people. You might want to throw that into the mix.

An alternate form of this question is "If you had to repack your belongings, what wouldn't you have brought with you?" This question is even more concrete, at least for the majority of students traveling to interviews. The follow-up questions will certainly be "Why leave that behind?" and "Why did you bring it?" Pack carefully.

- If you had unlimited money and two free hours (one day, one week, one month) what would you do?
- If you had three wishes, what would they be? (Shades of *Aladdin!*)
- What in your life is most important to you?
- If you could bring any three things with you for a six-month stay on a deserted tropical island that has a basic vegetable supply and potable water, what would they be? This is different than the house fire question, since you have time to plan and the outcomes are survival and pleasure.

7. What kinds of people are your friends?

"Know my friends, know me," goes an old expression. People attract similar folks as friends. An applicant's description of his friends often gives interviewers deep insights into his personality. This type of question essentially asks you to talk about yourself in the third person.

Answer this question as if you were describing yourself. Interviewers often respond favorably when married applicants state that their spouse is their best friend. Describing a spouse's glowing personal attributes only serves to enhance the applicant, as long as these attributes are not used as a contrast to the candidate's own qualities.

- Describe your best friend/roommate/spouse and their life.
- How are you similar and dissimilar to your best friend?
- How would your friends or coworkers describe you?
- Has someone ever come to you for help with a major personal crisis? What have you done to alleviate their emotional pain?

8. Who are your heroes?

Related to the question "Tell me about yourself," this is a deep probe into your psyche. It evaluates your self-image, direction, and goals. How the interviewer interprets your answer may, to some degree, reflect his or her own personality, age, and background.

This is perhaps the most difficult interview question to answer. In an age without obvious heroes, your choice will, by necessity, be very personal. There are several possible responses to this question.

One answer you may have already thought of is that you have no heroes. You have, however, just completed many years of schooling, during which you had many new experiences and met countless interesting people as teachers, friends, and patients. Viewed from that perspective, it would be an unusual, and perhaps very narrow-minded, individual who could not find someone to look up to as a role model.

Another possible answer is to cite a family member, friend, or personal acquaintance. The follow-up question, of course, will be "Why?" There should be some identifiable attribute this person demonstrates that justifies your distinguishing him or her as your hero. A parent, sibling, or spouse is usually a very good choice. It shows respect for your family and a firm commitment to your roots. If you choose a physician as your hero, be prepared to explain how you are trying, or will try, to emulate that person's attributes in your professional life.

Historic or public figures are perfectly acceptable answers. These heroes can be drawn from science, education, or many other fields. But tread lightly if your hero is a contemporary religious or political figure. An interviewer's bias may affect your evaluation if your choice of a hero exemplifies major philosophical differences between the two of you.

The worst answer is to name a contemporary star of television, the movies, or popular music. In that case, both you and your answer will probably be seen as very superficial.

- What is your favorite movie? Why?
- What is the last book you read?
- What do "success" and "failure" mean to you?
- If you could accomplish only one thing the rest of your life, what would that be?
- What do you believe?
- Do you have any Black, Hispanic, etc. role models in medicine? (Usually addressed only to minority applicants by minority faculty.)
- What physician characteristics do you admire most? Least?
- If you could dine with anyone from the past, present, or future, who would it be?
- Among the people at your school, whose work or life do you admire? Why?
- Tell me about your father/mother.

9. What do you do in your spare time?

The primary danger here is in giving too long an answer. Everyone likes to talk about him- or herself and this is an invitation to do just that. But keep it brief. If you collect rocks, for example, you might say, "I am an avid rock collector and have been for about ten years. I have had the opportunity to travel across the United States and Canada pursuing my hobby." Then stop. If the interviewer wants to know any more, he or she will ask.

Your answer should show that you are not a couch potato (although a computer aficionado is okay). Do not describe activities that may cause injuries resulting in prolonged sick leave. Also, pick a non-controversial topic; avoid discussing hunting, guns, or religion unless you are certain that you will not raise the interviewer's hackles. In general, speak about community-oriented and people-centered activities. The focus of the rock collector's description might be the people she meets at collector's conventions.

The questioner usually wants to learn three things from this query.

First, does the applicant have any interests outside medicine? An interviewee with no outside interests sends a serious danger signal. Residents who have no outlet for the anxieties, stresses, and frustrations of residency training may decompensate—and become a problem for the residency faculty. If you have no overriding outside interest, simply mention what you do in your spare time. Yes, spending lots of time with your spouse and children is certainly an outside interest.

Second, is the applicant more enthusiastic about his or her avocation than about the prospect of training for and practicing in this medical specialty? The key here is to show equal enthusiasm for both.

Third, the interviewer is screening out those applicants who are so wrapped up in themselves that they will not be able to pay any attention to their patients, peers, and faculty. How do they spot these individuals? They are the ones who go on and on and on about their other activities with no prompting—even after the interviewer gives negative cues, such as turning away from the applicant, coughing, or even standing up. Answer questions about your outside activities, as you have answered the other questions—fully, briefly, and with enthusiasm.

- What are your favorite games and sports? Why?
- Have you done any volunteer work?
- Why did you choose these activities?
- If you had a completely free day, what would you do?
- What is the most bizarre thing you have ever done (or did in high school or in college)?
- What was the most unusual occurrence in your life in the past month?
- Do you think you can remain intensely focused on learning this specialty for the length of the program? For the rest of your professional career?
- Would you work if you didn't have to? Why?
- Besides your future medical accomplishments, what do you wish to be known for by your peers, friends, and family?
- Where have you traveled? Why?
- What non-medical magazines do you regularly read?
- What have you contributed to groups and activities in which you participated?
- What have you learned from your volunteer work?

10. *It says on your résumé that . . .*
You wrote that you have a particular skill or learning experience. That may have been one reason you got this interview. Okay, show us how you would apply it.

This request is not made in the abstract. Rather, the interviewer gives you a specific situation, usually associated with medical practice, and possibly with the residency, and asks you to show your stuff. You wrote that you had experience working in a medical clinic for indigent patients. They ask you how you would obtain necessary medications for a child whose parents did not have the money to pay for them. Or you wrote that you served as the student on your hospital's bioethics committee. What elements do you look for when doing a bioethics consultation, asks the interviewer.

In some cases, the request can be even simpler. The interviewer starts speaking to you in Spanish or Russian. Well, you said you could speak it.

Anything you put in your résumé is fair game for the interviewer, including your extracurricular activities, publications or research, ability in a foreign language, travel, etc. Don't embellish! You are certain to run across at least one interviewer who will want to speak to you in Serbo-Croatian if you said you speak it fluently. If you said you participated in a study of histamine in rats, an interviewer is sure to ask you to explain how you could study the chemical's role in headaches or toxic presentations during your residency.

Since you may be asked about them, bring any written materials, such as articles, book chapters, etc., listed in your résumé to the interview, Even if they haven't been published, bring a draft copy so you can show it to interviewers if asked.

This is called the "predictive interview technique." It is very effective when the interviewer can make a specific connection with something in the applicant's history. For interviewees, this can be either a wonderful or a devastating experience. Be careful what you put in your application materials.

- What did you like about Kuala Lumpur (to an applicant who said he had worked in a medical clinic there)?
- How would you design a study to test whether drug Z works in congestive heart failure (to an applicant who says she has done several drug-related studies)?

11. *In what situations are you most efficient and effective?*

Medicine, and especially residency, is best practiced by those who are time-efficient. Residency directors know that those who can manage their time well will often make excellent residents. Part of managing time, however, is knowing what makes you efficient. Have you thought about how you optimize your use of time? Do you know the strategies that help you accomplish tasks faster, more successfully, and in a timely manner?

A particular interest in some specialties is whether you can multi-task. That is, can you walk and chew gum at the same time? Or, more to the point, can you successfully handle multiple patient-related tasks for multiple patients at once? This is essential to function well in emergency departments, busy clinics, and on hectic ward services.

- When are you least efficient and effective?
- How do you handle interruptions when you are busy?
- When are you most creative?
- What makes you procrastinate?
- Do you see time as your ally or your enemy?

12. To which organizations do you belong?

People join organizations that further their own agendas, be they recreational, spiritual, political, or professional. The organizations you belong to reflect your goals, background, and interests. The question here is: How much do you want to reveal?

The groups you join often loudly signal your religion, political or sexual orientation, and cultural heritage. Since prejudice exists in many guises, it may be best to simply discuss the professional medical organizations to which you belong. These should include the student arm of the specialty's national organization, and might also include the AMA, AOA, or AMSA.

Most interviewers now understand that pressing you for information about other organizations might violate state and federal hiring rules. Note, however, that anything you included in your application materials is fair game during interviews. If you list an organization on your résumé, the interviewer may ask you about it.

- Your name sounds Hispanic (Arabic, Italian, Vietnamese, etc.). Is it?
- How did you learn to speak (non-English language)?
- When was the last time you went back to (country of origin)?
- Why do you think you are a minority?
- Would you have any trouble working in this predominantly Catholic (LDS, Jewish, etc.) hospital?

13. What are your plans for a family?

You probably will be asked a variety of questions that are not only uncomfortable, but also patently illegal under state or federal statutes. These questions also provide ammunition for discrimination-in-hiring lawsuits. (These suits are rarely brought, however, because discrimination is hard to prove in court.)

The litmus test to see whether a question is illegal is to ask yourself, "Is it important to my job as a resident?" If it is relevant, then the question is probably legitimate. (The law, however, can be convoluted. See Figure 20.2.)

Questions about family, childcare, and birth control are most often directed at women applicants. Other candidates may hear inquiries about race, nationality, physical infirmities, religion, and other subjects that are illegal for employers to raise. (See also Chapter 13, "Marriage, Pregnancy, & Children" and "Illegal Questions" later in this chapter.)

How should you respond to such questions? This can be very tricky. There are several possible approaches. The most common one is to just answer the question in the most favorable manner possible. It is the most politic thing to do and will not eliminate you from the pool of potential candidates. For questions about family planning, you could simply state that you have no plans to interrupt your training to have a family at the present time. If you already have children, you might directly address the interviewer's concerns by stating that your past performance demonstrates that your family responsibilities will not detract from your work or affect your ability to show up on time. Directly answering such questions may be preferable to saying "I prefer not to answer." Just as when invoking your Fifth Amendment rights, the listener will often infer the most negative response.

You may not, however, want to answer such questions, either because of the answer that you would have to give or because your principles just will not allow it. You then have three choices.

The first choice, which will still permit you to remain a viable candidate, is to laughingly ask whether the answer to the question, or the question itself, is relevant to being a resident. If you do this lightly, the interviewer will be able to back off from the question without losing face.

If you derisively ask whether the question is relevant, or simply state that the question is illegal (your second choice), you will be on the interviewer's black list. Don't plan on getting into that residency program. But, if you do not get in and you still want to, you have the option of taking legal action against the program for violating your civil rights (your third choice). This has been done successfully in the business world many times. It is only a matter of (a short) time until these suits become frequent in the medical community. In fact, they may become commonplace enough that there will be much firmer control over the entire interview process in order to avoid legal entanglements.

Still, you should approach these illegal and uncomfortable questions in a relaxed manner. This will yield the best results.

A legal way to ask such questions might be "Is there anything about your personal life that may affect your performance in this demanding residency?" Your answer is "No."

- How important is your family to you?
- How do you plan to juggle marriage (relationship) and medical practice?
- What do your parents do for a living?

14. If you could no longer be a physician, what career would you choose?

Once again, let's see who is really hiding beneath the polished veneer. How deeply are you committed to medicine? Is it an interesting part of your life or is it the core of your existence? How easily can you come up with an answer that you find acceptable? How upset do you seem by such a prospect?

Very few people can fake a response to something this important. Interviewers, especially those who live and breathe medicine, use this question to find people who have the same level of commitment. Older interviewers may ask this more frequently, since many distrust the resolve of younger generations.

One other reason for asking this question is that some studies suggest that there is a high correlation between alternate career choices and certain specialties. Those going into Anesthesiology or Radiology, for example, usually select highly technical professional fields, such as engineering, research, the "hard" sciences, law, architecture, or finance-related business. Those entering Pediatrics tend to select teaching, other health-related professions, the humanities, the arts, or non-professional careers.

Variations of this question may also be used to test an applicant's grasp of reality. The interviewer may ask, "What do you think you will do when you stop practicing medicine (at the end of a career)?" Others will probe even a strong answer to see whether applicants have considered any alternatives if they suddenly cannot practice medicine, at least in their specialty.

- Why did you choose to be a physician?
- If your brain was the only part of your body that worked, what would you do with your life?
- What will happen if you develop a debilitating disease while in residency?

15. You seem really interested in research. How will you incorporate that interest into your residency and career?

Are you sure you want to go to *this* residency? If you are interviewing at a program within a research institution, the interviewer may simply be assessing the strength of your interest in research and, perhaps, how strong a clinician-researcher you might be. However, if the interview is at a program that is primarily or solely clinical, the question may be asking how well you investigated the program before applying, whether your goals are consistent with those of the program, or if you will be happy going through this residency. This is a very legitimate faculty concern. If you have research as a possible career goal, be sure to apply to programs that share this interest.

- What are the most important traits for a clinician/researcher?
- How will your research alter scientific thought? Help mankind?
- Let's discuss the details of the research you have done.
- How did the idea come to you for any research you initiated?
- How might acupuncture work? Do we know enough about physiology and biophysics to determine that?

16. In what subspecialty would you like to practice?

It is perfectly reasonable to say that you plan on practicing the primary specialty. But you may already have your heart set on becoming, for example, a cardiologist or neonatologist. Residency faculty know that a great many applicants, especially in the "primary care specialties" (General Internal Medicine, General Pediatrics, Family Medicine, Obstetrics/Gynecology), plan to take subspecialty fellowships. Feel free to tell them that you are *considering* that course. Realize, though, that many residents change their minds about which specialty to enter once they get more clinical experience, so couch your answer with the reality that your future is not certain and you will make your decision at the appropriate time during your residency training.

If you do specify a subspecialty in which you are interested, be prepared for questions about that medical area. Also, you may be asked what you know about how well that subspecialty is represented at that residency's training institutions and program. Do you know who the subspecialists are? Do you know how much time you will spend with them during your residency? Given your interests, if that subspecialty is not well represented at their institutions, why did you choose to interview at their program?

- In light of the bleak future for subspecialists, why would anyone go into Cardiology or Gastroenterology today?

17. *How do you make important decisions?*

As you discuss some very important life decisions you have made, the interviewer may wonder how you came to these decisions. Individuals vary in how they make important decisions. This reflects their personality and thought processes. Are they thoughtful, deliberate, and slow, or are they inattentive, impulsive, and quick? Or, does their decision-making method vary appropriately with the situation?

Be prepared to discuss your own decision-making strategies with interviewers. Think carefully before responding to this question, however. They may respond by asking if the method you describe matches the method you used to make your decisions to enter medicine and to apply for the specialty. Or they may inquire about how this process affects your ability to perform in specific clinical situations or to make other obvious life decisions, such as those revealed by your résumé.

If you use the Must/Want Analysis to help decide on the qualities you want in a residency, take a copy (without the program's ratings) to your interview and show it to any interviewer who asks you this question. They will probably be impressed with your logical and deliberate decision-making process.

- Are you a "risk-taker" or "safety-minded"?
- What made you choose your undergraduate major/minor?
- How did you select your undergraduate/medical school?
- What was the biggest obstacle in your life? How did you overcome it?
- What was the most difficult stand or position you ever defended? Why was it difficult?
- What was the most difficult decision you have had to make in your life? How did you make it?

18. *What were the major deficiencies in your medical school training?*

This is your opportunity to demonstrate some realistic insight into the past three-and-a-half years of your life. How well did your basic science courses prepare you for your clinical rotations? What were the strongest elements in your training? Where were the holes that you need to fill? No one believes that any medical school is perfect; residency faculty know this as well as anyone. However, avoid taking major swipes at your school. You will be an alumnus of the residency program at which you train no less than you will be an alumnus of your medical school. While a rah-rah response is not appropriate, neither is downgrading the training that you have received. Remember, your medical school training has gotten you as far as this interview.

While mentioning any deficiencies in your training you have the perfect opportunity to talk about your plans to remedy the deficit. These may include taking extra work or courses during the balance of your senior year and electives you plan to take while in residency.

- Why did you choose your medical school? How satisfied are you with your decision?
- What preclinical (clinical) medical school courses interested you the most?
- Did you enjoy your medical school classes? Why?

19. How do you explain your . . . (low grades? leaves of absence? poor clinical narratives?)

Not everyone who reads this book has an unblemished, stellar record. In fact, very few medical students do. Most have some areas of their records that require an explanation. Perhaps you failed a basic science course or a USMLE Step, and had to repeat it. Or maybe you had to take a leave of absence at some point in your training. You should expect to be asked about these deficiencies if the faculty members interviewing you are at all on the ball.

You already know what these issues are, and you need to be prepared to explain them. If there is a good justification for a questionable action, such as having to take time off due to a death in the family or a personal illness, explain. But if the poor grade or poor clinical performance on a rotation was, as is usual, due to your failure to put forth your best effort, just say so. Do not give excuses; they will sound lame to almost everyone except you. Your answer should be a variation of the terse military response, "No excuse, sir." Say that you did not give the course, rotation, etc. your best effort. If you think you can get away with it, blame it on immaturity, ignorance, or youth. This works best if the problem occurred during your first year in school, especially if you can demonstrate that you have expended more effort in subsequent years. If you have any questionable areas hanging over your application, be prepared in advance to answer for your aberrant behavior.

- If you could begin your schooling again, what would you change?
- Have you ever dropped a class? Why?
- Have you ever quit or been fired from a job? Why?
- With these grade(s) in (medical school subject[s]), how did you even get an interview here?
- Do you use drugs?

- Do you like to study? How do you study best? What motivates you to keep studying?
- What did you do during this (specified) period of time?

20. Have you always done the best work of which you are capable?

If you imagine that you can just answer yes or no to this question, you haven't gotten the drift of the interviewing business yet. The correct response to this question must not only show that you have put in a tremendous effort, but also demonstrate humility—by acknowledging that you could often have done a better job.

How to do this? Simply say that you have always striven to do the best possible job that you could, but the results did not always match your effort. This again stresses that you are a hard worker, you are humble, and you understand your limitations—all positive attributes. And this is all nicely wrapped up in that one-sentence answer. Very elegant.

- What have been your biggest failures in life?
- What have you done to ensure that these failures won't happen again?

21. With which types of people do you have trouble working?

This question asks, "Why won't you fit into the clinical team that exists at this residency?" In essence, what personality problems do you have? Will Rogers said, "I never met a man I didn't like." Maybe so, but most people have some difficulties with arbitrary, obnoxious, and loud individuals. This is not, however, what you want to say. The correct answer, if you cannot honestly state that you usually get along with everyone, is that you generally have problems with those individuals who do not pull their own weight.

This is also the answer to the parallel question, "What qualities drive you crazy in colleagues?" Again, this emphasizes your interest in, and ability to do, hard work. At the same time, it will normally hit a responsive chord in the interviewer, who also probably dislikes picking up the workload for slack colleagues. No one, of course, ever recognizes this problem in him- or herself.

Some interviewers will attempt to get the names of negative references by asking, "Who didn't you get along with in medical school or in past jobs?" Luckily, this is an unusual request, if only because programs are besieged with too many applicants to follow up on the information. If you are asked for such references, your willingness to provide them and your ability to explain why you didn't get along with certain individuals will say a lot about your self-confidence, honesty, and insight.

- Describe the best/worst attending or resident with whom you ever worked.
- Do you prefer to work under supervision or on your own?

22. With which patients do you have trouble dealing?

The interviewer in this case is trying to determine whether you will generate multiple patient complaints—a situation that faculty and administrators abhor.

No one expects you to be thrilled when you have to deal with whining, abusive, demanding, alcoholic, or drug-seeking patients. Most physicians do not like to treat such patients. You should state that while there are certain personalities that irritate you, you attempt to recognize these patients and then try even more than usual to act in a professional manner during interactions with them. This demonstrates professional maturity, survival skills, and common sense.

If you really dislike dealing with certain racial, ethnic, or age groups, or with people in general, you should probably reconsider your decision to pursue a medical career.

- What are patients most afraid of when they visit a doctor?
- If I called the last patient you took care of, what do you think they would say to me?
- What would you find most difficult to deal with if (when) you were a patient?

23. How do you normally handle conflict?

Hopefully, you can answer that your interactions with people rarely lead to conflict but, when there is conflict, you try to work the problem through to a reasonable and amicable settlement.

You may want to prepare an example of just such a situation that you faced and how it was resolved. Optimally, this example will demonstrate that the conflict was handled in a thoughtful and good-natured manner, with good will restored at the end. Your attitude, facial expressions, and body language when telling such a story will reveal much about your personality and your real ability to harmoniously work with others.

- How do you respond when you are having problems with a nurse, patient, another medical student, resident, or attending physician?
- What do you do if your senior resident or attending tells you to do something you know is absolutely wrong (medically or morally)?

- Have you ever challenged a teacher in class or a supervisor, resident, or attending physician at work? What were the circumstances?
- How do you handle disagreements with more senior colleagues, peers, nurses, and ancillary medical staff?
- How do you handle criticism, whether it's fair or unfair, from a superior, a subordinate, a peer, or a family member?
- What was the most useful criticism you ever received? Why?
- What was your most difficult/stressful life experience? How did you handle it?
- What frustrates you the most?

24. With what subject or rotation did you have the most difficulty?
Similar to the question concerning your strengths and weaknesses, this one asks you to incriminate yourself. You cannot plead the Fifth Amendment, so you need to know how to work through it. If you obviously had problems with a course, as evidenced by a poor grade or dismal narrative evaluations, you will have to address this. Do so in a direct manner. Otherwise, use the same strategy you used for the strength and weakness question. Pick "difficulties" that will exhibit some of the strengths that you want the interviewer to see.

For example, by stating that your Internal Medicine rotation was difficult because of the vast amount of information you needed to assimilate through extensive reading and clinical time, you will impress the interviewer with both your insight and your hard work. Discussing the time it took you to master suturing techniques on your Surgery rotation suggests to the interviewer that you have gained a clinical skill that is a prerequisite to training in the specialty. In general, you should emphasize that any trouble that you have had was the result of the long hours you spent (explanation, not a complaint) in the learning process. However, if you really did poorly in a course or on a clinical rotation, you are probably being asked to explain why you did so poorly (Question 19).

Commonly, the interviewer will have already spotted your problem area and will also ask, "How will that affect your performance as a physician?" Of course, your answer is that it won't affect your performance, since you already have (or plan to) overcome any problems in this area through hard work or extra training.

- Tell me about your first day in anatomy. How did it change you?
- What has been your greatest challenge?

25. Why do you want to go into this specialty?

This is probably the question most often asked of residency applicants. The question poses two dangers. The first lies in not having a good answer. If you have gone through the steps in this book, you will have no trouble answering the question. You initially found out what aspects of medical practice you enjoyed and then matched them to the specialty that encompassed most of them. Then, you talked with multiple specialists working in the field, read as much as you could about the field, and tested your choice by spending volunteer time working in the specialty. With this background to support your answer, you should have little trouble convincing the interviewer that you have firm and valid reasons for entering the specialty.

The second danger is that interviewers will ask you this question so often—sometimes two or three times at each program—that you will become bored with your own answer. This will be obvious in your response and will reflect poorly upon your candidacy. Since each interviewer tends to ask applicants similar questions, your response will be compared with the answers from the other candidates they have seen. Be enthusiastic when replying to this question—every time. Try to take a new tack when answering the question with different interviewers. This way you will avoid repeating the same phrases, which will sound stale and trite not only to you but also to the interviewers. You have an excellent answer to this question; make certain that your delivery is just as good.

- What would you be willing to sacrifice to become a (specialist)?
- What is the greatest sacrifice you have already made to get where you are?
- If (this specialty) did not exist, what would you do?
- How much did lifestyle considerations fit into your choice of a specialty?

26. Why did you apply to this program?

No specialty has only one training program. So this question comes up quite often in interviews. Having based your program selections on your personal "Must/Want" Analysis, you have some excellent answers to this question. Maybe the program is particularly strong in research, which is an area you value highly. Or perhaps the faculty is outstanding. Your answer to this question should include whatever attracted you to the program. In addition, it never hurts to say that the program also got a strong recommendation from your specialty adviser.

Review all material you have about the program, as well as your personal evaluation of it, before beginning the day's interviews. If you remember to individualize your answer for each program, you should have no problem. Your knowledge about the program should include:

- Residency size
- Academic mission
- Key faculty names & specialties
- Research opportunities
- Number of key procedures performed
- Patient volume
- Clinical training sites
- Elective opportunities
- Patient population mix
- Percent women, minorities, or IMGs admitted

If you don't have some of this information, that's okay. Make sure you ask for it at your first opportunity.

A more personal way of asking this question is, "Why are you willing to leave the West (or Northeast, Midwest, etc.) to come here to train?" Rather than obviously directing the question toward the program's educational elements, the question appears to be asking a more personal question. Without thinking, you may answer, "Well, I don't really want to live anywhere but the Boston area, but I heard this was a good program and I thought I'd take a look." Bad move! You have fallen into the interviewer's trap. It is not even worth considering you as an applicant now, since you said you would be unhappy away from Boston. The better answer is to say (hopefully with some truth) that you are willing to move anywhere there is a fine training program in this specialty. Then tell the interviewer what you consider to be the program's fine qualities.

- What qualities are you looking for in a program/residency?
- What interests you most about this program/residency?
- What have you heard about our program that you don't like?
- Are you applying here because it is a familiar environment?
- What do you think you will contribute to our specialty or to your community?
- How can you be sure that (specialty) is the right career for you?
- You said (a statement) in your application essay. What did you mean?
- What would you want your patients to say about you?
- What can be done to ensure that physicians are in (specialty) for the "right" reasons?
- Why do you want to leave (city or state where you live)?
- What do you think will be the most difficult aspect of living in this city, coming as you do from . . . ?
- Do you know what you are getting into? Have you talked with physicians about what a career in our specialty is really like?

27. What will be the toughest aspect of this specialty for you?

This is another way of asking you about your strengths and weaknesses. Only the most skilled interviewers usually ask this form of the question.

Every specialty has complex areas to master; each specialty has its onerous aspects. What do you foresee as difficult areas for you? Your answer may deal with your learning to master certain skills or with the vexing areas of the specialty's practice.

It would be unrealistic for you not to recognize some difficult areas of the specialty, and failure to cite some might indicate that you know little about the specialty, yourself, or both. A good way to answer this question is to note one or more small or commonly recognized difficult areas, such as physics training in Radiology, and describe how you intend to overcome any problems you might have. The fact that you envision only small problems will either placate the interviewer or lead to other questions to be certain that you haven't missed the big picture.

If the question is asked in the form of the "most enjoyable" part of the specialty for you, answer in the most specific terms you can. Cite examples of experiences you had while working in the specialty that excited you, stimulated you to read further, or suggested interesting research opportunities. The more specific you can be, the better your answer will be received, and the better the interviewer will remember you.

- How will you handle the least interesting or least pleasant parts of this specialty's practice?
- What qualities are most important in this specialty?
- What would you be willing to sacrifice to become a (specialist)?
- What is the greatest sacrifice you have already made to get where you are?
- Are you willing to work graveyard shifts and all weekends for a month or more at a time?
- How long have you stood on your feet at one time?
- Have you ever noticed negative aspects of (specialty) physicians with whom you have come in contact?
- What negative aspects do you see to pursuing a (specialty) career?

28. Why should we take you in preference to the other candidates?

Danger! This is one of those questions designed to quickly lead you down the garden path to disaster. What is your first response? Most of you would attempt to defend yourself against attack, probably by trying to compare yourself favorably with other candidates whom you either know or imagine. Wrong move.

Start by acknowledging that you will not make the decision about who gets into the residency. State that you are not qualified to make that type of decision. In addition, acknowledge that there undoubtedly are many good candidates applying to the program. Then, state that you can really only describe your own qualities and ask the interviewer if he or she would like you to do just that. If the answer is yes, you have an excellent opportunity to tout your best qualities and finest achievements.

Obviously, to answer the interviewer's initial question, you will want to stress those qualities that distinguish you from other candidates. You should concentrate on some of the areas mentioned previously—*energy level*, the *desire to do and to learn*, and the *ability to get along with others* under all circumstances. Never disparage other candidates. Only stress your own excellence.

- What can you add to our program/residency class?
- What computer experience do you have?
- What are some of the qualities a good physician should possess? Do you possess them?
- How will your background in . . . be of any use in this specialty?
- If you were on our residency committee, what would you look for in an applicant?
- Why should I tell the residency committee to pick you?
- If we had one spot left in the residency class, what one of your attributes qualifies you more than any other candidate?
- What makes you unique?
- Give me your sales pitch.

29. I don't think you'd be right for this program/specialty.

Medicine has some pretty crass folks populating its ranks, but very few would actually invite you for an interview and really mean it when they tell you that you would not be right for their program, much less the specialty.

If you are told this, recognize it for the ploy that it is. It is meant to fluster and confuse an applicant. A rather nasty maneuver, used only by cruel interviewers, it can easily be sidestepped if you see it coming. This is a statement that can only be answered successfully with a question. That question is "Why do you say that?"

If you come out swinging to defend yourself, you lose. Put the interviewer on the defensive by asking the question in your nicest, most polite manner. This will throw him or her off guard, and you might even receive an apology.

- Describe your ideal residency program in this specialty.
- Montana . . . Hmm . . . Isn't that where the Unabomber lived?
- I see that neither of your parents graduated from high school. What does that say about your genetic background?
- How would you contribute to this residency's reputation?

30. What is your energy level like?

Although this may be an interviewer's standard question, watch out. Some only ask this of applicants who demonstrate less-than-adequate energy levels during their interviews. If you feel yourself fading, pump out a little more adrenaline and beef up your act. Now is the time to show your energy level. If you can't do it now, what will it be like at 3 A.M. while you are on call?

A question about your energy level must be answered with an enthusiastic "Very high." A very brief anecdote of just how high it is would be appropriate. An example might be, "I was able to make rounds on all my Medicine patients and write notes each morning before the residents even arrived." Try to make your anecdote appropriate to the specialty for which you are interviewing.

- When do you work harder than you ordinarily do?
- How many hours of sleep do you require each night?
- How well do you function without adequate sleep?

31. How well do you function under pressure?

Every physician, at one time or another, has been under pressure while practicing medicine. Some specialties have frequent stressors, and the physicians in them seem to thrive under this stress. Asking you about your performance under stress is, therefore, a natural question. The interviewer wants to know two things. First, have you thought about the pressures inherent in residency training, as well as those peculiar to this specialty? And second, are you up to them?

Assuming that you have gone through all the right steps to select this specialty, your answer should indicate that you operate at peak performance under the type of stressful conditions encountered in the specialty. Cite specific examples of your past performance under stress. Be sure that the examples, however, do not show that the stress resulted from your negligence, procrastination, or obstinacy. Assure the interviewer that you are up to the challenges this specialty has to offer.

A potential curve ball here may be a secondary question dealing with the administrative stressors brought on by government and third-party payer interference with medical practice. This question may be raised because it is constantly, and annoyingly, on many practitioners' minds. If this topic is raised, either state that you are certain that you will learn to handle these problems during residency, or respond by simply asking the interviewer "What are the biggest problems you are facing in this area?" In all likelihood, the interviewer will be pleased to speak about the subject at length. Be a good listener.

- How do you handle stress?
- Can you handle stress without the resources you are accustomed to relying on?
- When was the last time you cried?
- Have you ever faced death? How did you handle it?

32. *Tell me about the patient from whom you learned the most.*
This is a favorite question of elderly professors, as well as smarter young interviewers. It examines your medical knowledge, your insight into the patient's condition, your ability to think quickly, your attitude toward medicine and learning, and your compassion. If an interviewer asks this question, the balance of the interview remains on the same topic. How, then, should you approach it?

To be able to answer this question satisfactorily, you must prepare at least two patient cases in advance. Try to choose examples at least somewhat relevant to your chosen specialty. Select patients in whose care you were intimately involved. These should be people you helped treat for a prolonged period of time—either during many concentrated hours or periodically over time. If they had a specific disease or injury, read about it in depth. If they had a multisystem disease, be able to describe its effect on the various organs grossly and microscopically, as well as clinically.

What was it that you learned from these patients? Was it just the nature of the disease? Normally, this will not be enough. Did you learn something about your own limitations as a physician, the patient's fears and perceptions of the medical system, or the workings of the health care system itself? If you did, be prepared to say so. Also, know the follow-up information on the patients. If they were discharged, review their medical records to find out how they are doing now. If they died, did you attend the autopsy? (Attending your patients' autopsies is a good idea throughout your training—it reveals to you both what you missed and what you were powerless to change.) If you did not attend, obtain a copy of the autopsy report and read it. Following up on interesting patients demonstrates both your concern for them and your excitement in learning.

If you have prepared for this question and have begun to answer it appropriately, the interviewer may interrupt with a "war story." Sit back, listen, and enjoy. You did just fine.

Over the years, applicants throughout the country have consistently said that being prepared for this question was the best advance planning they did for their interviews.

- What were your most memorable experiences in medical school/college?
- If you had to choose the single most valuable thing you have ever learned, what would it be?
- What was the (non-medical) situation in your life when you had the greatest responsibility?
- Tell me about the non-physician health care provider who most influenced you.

33. What error have you made in patient care?

This is very similar to the question above, concerning the patient from whom you learned the most. In fact, the case illustrating your biggest error may be the same as the one from which you learned the most. If it is, say so. This question is used to test your humility, to ascertain whether you were allowed to do enough on your own as a medical student so mistakes were possible, and to determine whether you can learn from your mistakes. Obviously, these are all significant issues. Make sure you have prepared your reply before you visit any programs.

- What is your greatest fear about practicing medicine?
- What is your greatest fear about entering this specialty?
- What was the worst thing that ever happened to you? Why?

34. Where do you see yourself in five (ten) years?

Some realism, as well as the ability to read what the program and the specialty desire, is required to accurately answer this question. The questioner is attempting to find out if you have some life goals—and if these are consistent with the training that the program has to offer.

Have you looked beyond your existence as a trainee? Are you realistic? Do you expect to be the Surgeon General of the United States within the decade following the completion of your residency? Or perhaps you propose to be a full professor and head of a department at a major medical school. Both expectations are, of course, not practical in the near future. On the other hand, applying to a high-powered academic residency program as preparation for working part-time at a small neighborhood clinic also may not demonstrate much realism.

The problem of incongruent goals stems from your evaluation either of your own abilities or of the program's goals for its residents. Residency faculties usually have at least a general vision of what they would like most of their graduates to do with their careers. They want your goals to be consistent with those of the program. This is beneficial to both you and them. For example, if a training program has been designed primarily to produce academic physicians, residents who hope to become community doctors will be very unhappy in it, and the faculty may be very dissatisfied with those residents as well.

To answer this question, you should have previously analyzed the program's written materials. Do they promote goals consistent with your personal goals? If the two widely diverge, perhaps you should consider looking elsewhere. Do not, however, be too certain about your final career direction. Many, if not most, residents significantly change their career orientation during or shortly after training. This should not upset you; it is a normal part of learning and maturation.

So, answer this question by giving a general response while listening to the interviewer. Try to understand the diversity of learning experiences that exist within the training program. Leave enough latitude in your reply, however, to allow for other possibilities in your future. Also, always phrase your answer in terms of a probability that may change with training, experience, and age.

- In ten years, in what specialty and under what circumstances will you be practicing? Who will be paying for your services?
- What are your life goals? What have you done to accomplish them?
- How would you describe "success"?
- Draw a picture of yourself in ten years.

35. *How do you see the delivery of health care evolving in the twenty-first century?*

This can be a very tricky question. It tests your knowledge of current events and politics, as well as your humility in recognizing that you do not have the ultimate answer. The interviewer, though, may think that he or she does. Only people who already have definite opinions about the trends in health care will ask this question. They actually may want to use it as a jumping-off point from which to expostulate on their pet theory. Since people like to hear themselves talk, give the interviewer a chance to say what is on his or her mind while appearing interested and you will do just fine.

Respond by giving a broad answer to the initial question, such as "I expect that there will be numerous changes, not only in the way medicine is practiced, but also in the way it is paid for." You can go on to add that you do not have any definitive answers. This will give the interviewer a chance to jump in and give you either the lecture that was lying in wait, or at least some definite hints as to what he or she is thinking. You do not want to stick your neck out without some guidance.

This question is probably the closest that you will get to a direct inquiry about your political views, which is illegal in pre-employment questioning. Listen closely, nod your head a lot, and do not go out on a limb without some support. If you want some solid background, read the Institute of Medicine's *The Nation's Physician Workforce: Options for Balancing Supply and Requirements* (Washington, DC: National Academy Press, 1996).

- Would you be willing to work under a single-payer (government-run) health care system?
- How little would your annual take-home pay have to be for you to leave medicine for another field?
- What are your thoughts about homeopaths, naturopaths, and herbal medicine?
- How do you think a socialized medical system will affect medical progress?
- If you were made King of the United States, what one thing would you change about health care delivery? Why?
- What is managed care? HMOs? PPOs? Capitation?
- What is the biggest challenge facing health care delivery?
- What does "a cross-cultural approach to healing" mean?
- What will you do as a physician to curb the rising costs of medicine?
- What is the nurse's role and how much responsibility should a nurse be given for patient care?
- Where does the money go in a prepaid medical system?
- What recent newsworthy medical event or announcement would you like to discuss?
- What is your least healthy personal habit?
- What is the solution to the health care crisis?

36. What problems will our specialty face over the next five (ten) years?

This question is an important variation on the question about health care in general. It provides an opportunity for you to take the broad concepts related to changes in health care and direct them toward the specific specialty to which you are applying. Have you given the specialty's future any thought? Have you given your own future enough thought? The information you obtained to answer the general question (above) about health care in the next century should give you plenty of ammunition to carry on a conversation about changes that might occur in this specialty. Of course, your wealth of knowledge about the specialty will also come in handy here.

As mentioned in the question relating to general changes in health care, give the interviewer an opportunity to sound off if it seems like that is what he or she wants to do. Listen actively. Be ready to jump in gently with an idea or two of your own, but don't argue. Some interviewers may bait you to see if they can make you angry or upset. No matter what they say, keep your cool. Remember that at least one of you has to remain professional.

- What do you think is the number one issue facing our specialty today?
- What would have to happen for you to leave (specialty) for another type of medical practice?
- Will new technological developments change our specialty? For better or for worse?

37. If a patient just stabbed your best friend . . . ?

A favorite question of many interviewers is the ethics scenario. In virtually all cases, it involves a situation in which there is no "correct" answer. However, as with all ethics questions, there are wrong answers.

The key to answering this question (the question itself is usually, "What would you do?") is to tell the interviewer that you need a moment to think about it. Then think through at least one answer that does not violate your personal values. Relate this to the interviewer. It is best if you do not give responses based upon your religion. Generalities, such as protecting patient autonomy or avoiding paternalism, work best.

Do not appear dogmatic; state that you are sure that there are other possible options. The interviewer may want to discuss the problem. If so, listen to the options presented and discuss them. Do not argue! Try to see the interviewer's point of view, but do not escalate the discussion into a religious debate or a shouting match. There's an old saying which suggests that one should never discuss religion or politics with friends, or you are bound to lose them. That applies just as well to residency interviewers.

- What would you do if the housestaff had a "job action" (strike)?
- What would you do if you saw another resident or physician snorting cocaine at a nightclub? On the job?
- What do you think about using animals in medical research and teaching?
- Should physicians be involved in assisted suicide or active euthanasia?
- What ethical questions will the health care delivery system face in the future?
- Should applicants who say they don't want to treat patients with (AIDS, hepatitis B, life-threatening plague, etc.) be admitted to our specialty?
- What would you do if you knew Dr. X was cheating on the in-service exam?
- Is health care rationing ethical?
- Would you treat a colleague and a patient, each coming to you with an unwanted pregnancy, differently?
- How would you respond if a resident or a colleague wanted to keep a therapeutic error a secret from a patient and the patient's family?
- What do you think of hospitals that refuse admission to patients without insurance?

38. What do you think of what is happening in the (economy, Middle East, Congress)?

The interviewer is trying to find out if you have pulled your head out of your medical books in the past four years. It's wise to prepare for this question by reading weekly news magazines for a month or two prior to the interview season. It is also prudent to read the newspaper and, if possible, watch the morning news on the day of your interview.

As for the question itself, hope that it is on a relatively innocuous subject. If not, don't antagonize the interviewer by giving a polarized viewpoint. Try to take a balanced view—looking at both sides of the issue, e.g., "on the one hand . . ., but on the other hand . . .." This shows that you do not have your head in the sand and that you are a diplomat—both desirable qualities.

- What is the last non-medical book you read?
- Are physicians doing enough to improve public health policies?

- Are physicians doing enough for women's issues?
- What do you think is the largest problem facing American society on a statewide or a national basis?

39. Teach me something non-medical in five minutes.

This is now the question I use most often. It shows me a great deal about applicants, including how well many of them think on their feet. It is also more fun to start off an interview this way than with many of the routine questions most interviewers ask.

With this directive, applicants have a marvelous opportunity to discuss something in which they are an expert—and the interviewer has guaranteed that he or she will pay rapt attention. Pick a topic that you know really well and that you can explain a small piece of to a novice in five minutes.

But which topic is best? Is it something about your hobby, something unique you learned in childhood, something from a previous job, or something truly different, such as a lesson you learned through a difficult experience? The keys here are to pick a topic that will interest listeners, that fascinates you, and that can be successfully taught in the allotted time. Among the topics applicants have discussed are how to tie fishing lures, how to write a simple computer program, and how to select a melon. Not that I always understood them, but they were always interesting. Often this directive leads naturally to further questions about the topic.

Many applicants and interviewers find this the best, and most productive, interview question.

- Without using your hands, tell me how to tie a shoelace.
- How are art and medicine similar?
- What is "beauty"?
- Why are manhole covers round?
- Why is it called "the practice" of medicine?
- If you were the residency director for the next five minutes, how would you evaluate your performance halfway through your first year of residency.
- Give an example of a problem you solved and describe how you went about solving it.

40. Does the reverse side have a reverse side?

The comedian Steven Wright has made a career of asking unanswerable questions. Many of the questions attributed to him are actually from anonymous sources. This type of question can rattle, provoke, or amuse residency interviewees, depending on the intensity of the situation, their ability to understand spoken English, and the interviewer's attitude.

If you recognize that you are being asked this type of question—and most interviewees immediately will—laugh. Giving any other response is ridiculous.

- When the light goes out, where does it go?
- Why are there five syllables in the word "monosyllabic"?
- How come Superman could stop bullets with his chest, but always ducked when someone threw a gun at him?
- When I erase a word with a pencil, where does it go?
- Why do we wait until a pig is dead to "cure" it?
- Why do we put suits in a garment bag and garments in a suitcase?
- How many ping pong balls fit in an airplane?

41. Why are beer cans tapered at the top and bottom?

This is a "brainteaser" question. Such questions actually have real answers, and often there are several possible answers. Unless you have a clear answer, take a few seconds to think through the problem and then verbally reason out what you can. Don't expect to come up with a definitive answer; they are generally too obscure. The interviewer just wants to see your reasoning process.

For the beer can question, the answer is simply to save aluminum. The can top needs to be thicker (more aluminum) to allow the flip top to work without ripping the can. Tapering reduces the amount of metal needed. And the bottom taper is to allow the cans to be stacked. Tapering also makes the cans stronger, but it wasn't why this design was originally used.

- Why are manhole covers round? (Unlike square ones, they cannot accidentally fall through the hole. Also, they can be rolled, don't need to be rotated to fit, and round holes are easier to dig than square ones.)
- How would you weigh a jet plane without using a scale and not cutting it into pieces? (One possibility: Put plane on a barge. Draw line at the water level. Remove plane and add objects of known weight until line is again at water level.)
- If you could remove any one of the 50 states, which would it be? (You don't have enough information to answer the question. What does "remove" mean? From the U.S.? Only the land? Or the people and the land? Also, why would you want to remove a state?)

42. Tell me a joke!

Several residency applicants say that they have been asked to tell the interviewer a joke—and that it was their greatest interview challenge. Don't improvise. It may be prudent to have one or two hilarious jokes that are clean, non-sexist, non-racist, non-religious, etc. As a source for this type of material, you might want to check out *Reader's Digest*.

- Name as many words that start with the letter "F" as you can in 10 seconds. (Careful now!)

43. Where else have you interviewed?

This is many residency directors' favorite question. Don't become paranoid when you hear it. In most cases, they are not trying to test your interview choices. They are doing two things.

The first is determining whether you have selected programs in a reasonably sufficient quantity and of a quality to assure that you match with a program.

The second reason they ask is usually to find out current information about other training programs. Often, you are the best source of information that is available to them about other residency programs. Interviewers will be interested in pumping you for facts. Give them what they want. Tell them about what is going on in the places you visited. You may have to review all of your notes before each interview. If you just do not remember some of the specifics, be honest enough to say so. The interviewer will appreciate this. Be enthusiastic. But, as mentioned before, under no circumstances should you say anything derogatory about other programs or other faculty. If you say negative things about other programs to this interviewer, what will you say about this program when you go elsewhere? Negative comments are a sign of immaturity. Avoid them.

44. What if you don't match?

Okay. Now let's see you sweat a little. This question is most often asked during interviews for residency positions in the most-difficult-to-match-with specialties and programs. If you are not prepared for this question, you may internalize it and consider that it is a backhanded way of suggesting that you had better make other plans, since you won't be getting into a residency in this specialty. Keep cool. That is not why applicants are usually asked this question.

The interviewer is trying to determine whether you have had the foresight to plan for contingencies. Planning ahead says something about your personality. Not making alternative plans if you are applying to an Orthopedic Surgery or Emergency Medicine program is just plain foolish. And people who do foolish things with their lives are not the people these programs look for as residents. They also do not want applicants who are so uncommitted to the specialty that they say, unconcernedly, that they will simply train in another specialty if they do not match in this one. Interviewers would like you to mention alternative plans that include methods for getting into one of the specialty's training programs.

One such plan may be that you have also applied to some one-year programs, such as Preliminary Medicine or Surgery or some Transitional programs, so you will have a training slot for the coming year if you do not match in the specialty. However, you will still be in a position to re-apply to the specialty in the following year.

45. Can you think of anything else you would like to add?

The answer to this question should always be "Yes." If the interviewer has neglected any critical area that further explains your qualifications for a residency position, mention it now. Even if nothing was omitted, use this opportunity to give an abbreviated summary of your sales pitch.

This is an alternate form of the frequent query, "Do you have any (other) questions?" that can be positioned at either the beginning or the end of the interview. This question can be a disaster at the end of a long interview day when you are tired, hungry, and sleepy—just like an intern. The wimpy response, "No, I think all of my questions have been answered," is not likely to score very many points with an interviewer.

Even if prior interviewers have already answered all your questions, ask one of them again. A very useful question, of course, is to ask for information that you wish to verify. Here you will have an opportunity to confirm or clarify the information. Another type of question to ask is one that will demonstrate your knowledge of the specialty's clinical or political activities. An example would be "What is your feeling about the new ultrasound treatment for cerebral tumors reported last month?" In any event, do not leave the interviewer in the lurch when you are given an opportunity to ask a final question.

• Is there anything else I should know about you?

46. If we offered you a position today, would you accept?

You are just finishing the last interview. Sitting with the residency director or department chief, you are suddenly faced with this question. Your first thought is "They can't ask me this. It's against Match rules."

Unfortunately, some programs disregard all rules, especially if they are desperate for good candidates. This question really puts you in a bind. If the program is clearly your top choice, you have no problem. If it isn't, or if you have not seen enough programs to know yet, what do you say? A perfectly reasonable response is, "I would love to accept a position in this program. I feel obligated, however, to keep the (six) other interview appointments I have made. I will be finished with these interviews in two weeks and could let you know then." Usually programs will accept this answer. Take care, though, to make sure you *really* do have a position guaranteed if you take them up on their offer (see Chapter 22, "Don't Believe Anything You Are Promised").

Illegal Questions

Interviewers continue to ask many applicants, especially women, blatantly illegal questions (Figures 20.1 and 20.2). A 2002 survey found that 86% of residency applicants had been asked illegal questions. The most common of these are about marriage and family plans. Indeed, asking women about childbearing and childcare is the most common gaffe interviewers make. Besides implicitly asking whether a woman has children, this assumes that she must be the sole person responsible for making childcare arrangements. (Wrong!) Also, if a female applicant inquires about the provisions for maternity leave, she is often written off as not being a serious candidate.

FIGURE 20.1

Illegal Questions—Sex Discrimination

1. What was your maiden name? (They can ask "What name is on your transcripts, diplomas, licenses, etc.?")

2. Do you wish to be addressed as Miss, Mrs., or Ms.?

3. Are you married? Single? Divorced? Separated? A single parent?

4. I notice that you are wearing an engagement ring. When are you going to be married?

5. What is your spouse's name? What does (s)he do for a living?

6. How does your spouse feel about your having a career?

7. Do you believe residents should use birth control?

8. Are you planning to have children? Anytime soon? (They can ask "Do you foresee any long-term absences during your residency?")

9. How will you take care of your children while at work? (They can ask "Is there any reason why you cannot be at work at 6 A.M. or stay in the hospital for in-house night call?")

FIGURE 20.2
Other Questions—Legal and Illegal Forms

Legal Form	Illegal Form
• How well can you handle stress?	• Does stress ever affect your ability to be productive?
• Are you currently using illegal drugs?	• What medications do you currently use?
• Do you drink alcohol?	• How much alcohol do you drink per week?
• Do you have 20/20 corrected vision?	• What is your corrected vision?
• Can you perform as a resident with or without reasonable accommodations?	• Would you need reasonable accommodations to perform your job as a resident?
• How many days were you absent from school last year?	• How many days were you sick last year?
• To what *professional* organizations, clubs, societies, and lodges do you belong?	• To what organizations, clubs, societies, and lodges do you belong?
• What languages do you speak, read, or write fluently?	• What is your nationality? How did you learn to speak, read, or write a foreign language?
• If you are not a U.S. citizen, do you have the legal right to remain permanently in the U.S.? If "no": What is your visa status? and Can you provide proof of eligibility for employment if hired?	• Are you a U.S. citizen?

Another set of illegal questions relates to disabilities. Under the Americans With Disabilities Act, if an individual has a visible disability (for example, uses a wheelchair or guide dog) or discloses voluntarily that he or she has a disability, the interviewer may not ask about its nature, its severity, the condition causing the disability, the prognosis, or treatments. They may ask about the applicant's ability to satisfy essential functions or requirements of the position, as long as all applicants are asked the same questions.

Since illegal questions are still being asked of all applicants (why this is allowed to continue is uncertain), it is important for you to be prepared for these questions.

How Should You React to Illegal Questions?

If you are asked these questions, there are three possible ways to respond:

Refuse to answer the query, perhaps stating that it is illegal to ask such questions or that it is none of the interviewer's business. Such an answer, however, while it is perfectly correct and legitimate, is likely to ensure that you will not get a residency position at that site.

Finesse the question. One way to do this is to ask the interviewer whether such information is really pertinent to obtaining a residency position. This gives the interviewer, who probably has been poorly prepared to do this type of interviewing, a chance to back off and save face at the same time. However, finessing a question must be handled with skill. Smile and be very pleasant while you parry these pointed questions. If you handle it correctly, you will still be a viable candidate for the program.

Answer the question. Most applicants take this tack, both in the medical field and in other employment situations. You can use either direct or indirect answers. For example, if asked about plans for a family and children, the direct answer might be "I plan to have children near the end of my residency." Since you might find this option distasteful, you could use an indirect answer, such as "My training comes first." These answers usually will not jeopardize your chance of obtaining a residency training position. Also, the interviewer probably does not even realize that he (or she) is being sexist and is violating both federal and state civil rights codes.

21

Post-Visit Follow-Up

We despise no source that can pay us a pleasing attention.

– Mark Twain

JUST BECAUSE THE INTERVIEW is over does not mean you have finished your visit. You still have some work to do to maximize the effort you have already expended. This includes writing a thank-you letter, providing additional requested materials, and adjusting and completing your "Must/ Want" Analysis for the program.

Thank-You Letter

The key to using post-interview thank-you letters effectively is to remember "out-of-sight is out-of-mind." Your letter reinforces the positive impression you left with the interviewers. Remember, you were not the only candidate interviewed that day. And, by the time the faculty gets your letter, they most likely have met more applicants.

Return yourself to the front of the interviewers' minds by sending them thank-you letters (see Figure 21.1). As with all aspects of the residency acquisition process, there are some rules to follow.

Send typed letters. Most of you would not want prospective employers to see your handwriting—even if you thought that they could read it. If your penmanship is particularly elegant, save it for a brief handwritten note at the bottom of a typed letter. That way you will achieve the maximum effect for each stamp you lick.

What should you include in the letter? First, direct the letter to the main interviewer—generally the residency director. In addition, mention all the interviewers. (Make sure that you save the list of names, with the correct spellings, of the people with whom you interview and tour the facilities.) Mention specific topics of mutual interest that were raised

531

FIGURE 21.1
Follow-up Letter Format
Use your personalized or laser-generated stationery, if possible.

Your Name
Your Current Address   Date

Interviewer's Name
Interviewer's Position
Interviewer's Department
Interviewer's Address

Dear Dr. [Interviewer's Last Name]:

Paragraph 1: Thank the interviewer for the courtesy and consideration shown to you during your recent residency interview. Mention the date you interviewed.

Paragraph 2: Reaffirm your interest in the program. Mention anything you may not have mentioned in the interview that enhances yourself as a candidate for their program and for the specialty. (Make it brief.)

Paragraph 3: Provide any information you said you would send to this interviewer, including additional documentation or answers to questions deferred during the interview. If you write this immediately following the interviews and do not have this information with you, say that you will be sending the additional information subsequently. Also, always offer to provide any additional information the program or interviewer might need.

Paragraph 4: A simple, positive closing sentence, such as "I look forward to working with you in the future."

> Sincerely yours,
>
> [Sign your name]
>
> Type your name

P.S. Don't forget a handwritten note!

---

during your interview, e.g., "the exciting new neonatal transport program" or "the unique border-medicine experience." Include enough personal information to ensure that the reader will remember your interview. Match the letter's formality to the tone of the interview you had. Don't go for wit or length; concentrate on making yourself memorable.

Don't forget the other interviewers. Many applicants who send thank-you letters ignore these folks, even though they often have a major say in deciding whether their program ranks a candidate. Send each of them a copy of the letter you send to the residency director, but hand write (print if your penmanship is terrible) a personalized note to each of them. Again, you want them to remember you. Your note should mention a subject that you discussed with them during your interview. Try to make it something that only you, and not other applicants, may have discussed.

One tactic to enhance these letters is to quickly peruse each interviewer's office and bookshelves during your interview to try to ascertain his or her personal interests. Look for something unusual or unique you can mention during the interview. This will provide you with a subject to use as a good memory jogger later on. Of course, you will need to make notations on your Interview Notes form (Figure 17.2) to remind you of what to write to whom.

Also, with the capability of computers and laser printers to produce quality photographs, it might be useful to have your picture on each of these letters, to better remind the interviewers who you are. Most local printing shops can quickly do this for you if you bring along a photograph.

Send the letters within 24 hours of the interview. You might not even be back home yet, and I know that trying to stop and produce these letters will be a major inconvenience. But it's worth the effort. Take materials with you on the road and get your thank-you letters out expeditiously. Some applicants now carry very small computers with them and stop by a local print-copy shop to print out their letters before they even leave the city where they interviewed.

Telephone Follow-Up

Although many job applicants follow up their interviews with phone calls, calling a residency director is usually counter-productive. Physicians are busy and do not like having their time wasted by sales pitches (from anyone). Unless you need to provide or obtain urgent information, or unless an interviewer specifically asked you to call, confine your follow-up messages to letters.

Specific Information

Occasionally, you will receive requests for additional information, either during the interviews or from the residency secretary. This information can include anything from additional reference letters to a copy of an article that you quoted during the interview. State in your thank-you letter that you will send the requested material as soon as possible. And then send it. It will, again, reinforce the interviewer's positive image of you.

If you have signed up for a military scholarship program (HPSP), be sure that the programs to which you are applying have a written deferment on file, even if it was not requested. If a program does ask for this document, they will not seriously consider you unless you can supply it to them.

Analyze Your Visit

There are two tasks to complete when analyzing your visit to each program. The first is to determine how well you performed. The second is to determine how well the program meets your needs. Let's discuss the personal analysis first.

The following questions will help you determine how well you did at the program, particularly in the interview setting. They are adapted from *The Robert Half Way to Get Hired in Today's Job Market* (Rawson, Wade Publishers: New York, 1981). Your analysis will also highlight problem areas to modify prior to visiting the next residency program on your schedule.

1. Did I look as good as I am capable of looking?
2. Was I as informed about the program and the specialty as I should have been?
3. Was I relaxed and in control of myself?
4. Did I answer the questions in a way that stressed my ability, enthusiasm, and suitability for that program?
5. Did I listen closely to the interviewers?
6. Did I unobtrusively steer questions toward points I wanted to stress?
7. Did I tailor my answers to fit the type of interviewer I was with at the time?
8. Did I present an accurate and favorable picture of myself to everyone that I met?

The second task is to analyze how well the program did. Use your previously prepared "Must/Want" Analysis form (Figure 10.1) for the program. Fill it out immediately. Rate the program's strength for each factor you listed. Use the 1-to-10 rating scale, with "10" being perfect.

Once you have completed the score for each factor (for example, Faculty Availability), multiply its "Weight" by its "Score" to get a "Total" for that factor. Then add up the factor "Totals" to give the final Total ("Program Evaluation Score") for the program. You may now put this sheet away until you have completed a similar form for each program that you visit.

Ranking the Programs for Success

Using the "Must/Want" Analysis

Once you have finished your interviews, you should have a file of completed "Must/Want" Analysis forms (Figure 10.1)—one for each program with which you have interviewed. Now you will see their true benefit. Rather than relying on a *gestalt* or gut feeling of your impressions, you can use your completed "Must/Want" Analysis forms to give you an accurate picture of how well each program meets your needs.

Rank the programs that you have visited in order, based upon your own needs and wants, by using the "Program Evaluation Score" that you assigned to each program. Simply arrange the evaluation forms with the Program Evaluation Scores in numerical order to find out what your rank-order list for the Match should look like. Rank the program that received the highest Program Evaluation Score first and the one with the lowest score last, if at all.

One key point, however. You may be somewhat depressed after first ascertaining what you want in a program and then interviewing. You probably found that no program meets every one of your expectations. Hey, that is what life is all about. *There is no utopia.* In looking for a residency, as with any job search, some compromises are necessary. You should choose the program that best fits your own needs. The "Must/Want" analyses help you do this.

A conceptual way of how to look at your evaluation of residency programs is provided in Figure 21.2.

List Enough Programs to Be Sure You Match

One of the keys to success in the Match is to rank enough programs. (It should go without saying that you must have interviewed at the programs that you list.) Several factors coincide to determine how many programs are "enough."

First, of course, is the specialty that you are trying to enter: The percentage of students who go unmatched in different specialties varies widely. There are tables that list the number of unmatched applicants in the

FIGURE 21.2

How Applicants Evaluate Residency Programs

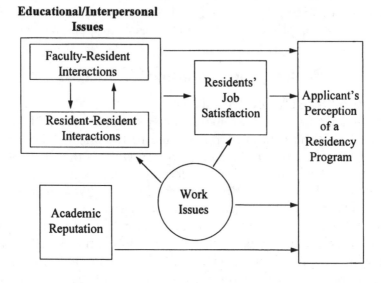

NRMP Data Book, available from either your Dean of Students or your medical library. Note, however, that the numbers are incomplete, since many positions in Urology, Neurological Surgery, Neurology, Child Neurology, Ophthalmology, and Diagnostic Radiology are filled outside the NRMP Match.

Nevertheless, by now you should know whether the specialty you have chosen is a "tough" or an "easy" match. If you still need some guidance, see the asterisk (*) ratings in Chapter 3. The tougher the specialty is to match in, the more programs you will have to interview with and rank. The number of applications graduates send to programs in their first choice of specialty is listed in Figure 11.2.

Geography also plays a part in the decision about how many programs to list. Some parts of the country are less desirable to medical school graduates than others. In some cases, this may have to do with the quality of programs located there. But it also is related to the ambiance of the surroundings. The deep South, the Midwest, and large industrial or inner cities are locations that often have very good programs but have fewer applicants than elsewhere. It might be to your advantage to rank programs in one of these locales if you are not the strongest of candidates.

Program match rates also depend upon the type of institution in which they are located. If you are looking mainly at university and major-medical-center programs, be prepared for stiff competition. While not necessarily the best, these programs are where most students apply. Of course, you want to meet your own needs, not those of your peers. Therefore, consider carefully the type of program you want. If you want a program at a big center, be prepared to do a little more interviewing and make a longer rank-order list.

Your assessment of your competitiveness really determines how many programs you rank. The greatest danger is that you will overrate yourself, interview at and rank too few programs, and then be left without a position. If in doubt, do a little extra. It will pay off with a greater chance of success and provide more peace of mind until you receive those Match results.

Hedge Your Bets As Necessary

Even if you have listed more programs than you think you will need to successfully match in the specialty of your choice, do not discard programs that you consider "sure bets" (weaker programs than those you have already ranked). Until you have a piece of paper in your hand stating that you have a residency position, nothing is certain.

Your best strategy (especially in the difficult-to-match-with specialties) is to list some "sure bets" at the bottom of your rank-order list, even if each of these is a slightly weaker program than others you have seen. Of course, if you think that the program is too weak, you may prefer not to match there. So, what should you do? Ask yourself, "Would I rather match at that program in the specialty of my choice, or not match in the specialty and take a chance on Unmatch Day?" If you can answer that question, you will know how to fill out the bottom of your rank-order list.

Plan ahead for all contingencies. That means interviewing at one or two less-competitive programs and, possibly, for a Transitional or Preliminary Surgery or Medicine slot. This will give you the "stoppers" on your list to be sure that you match. But it is your choice. If you are willing to "guts it out" and risk the Unmatch Day phone scramble to find an open slot, then the best of luck to you.

Go for the Gold

The preceding comments should not deter you from trying to secure the best residency position you can obtain.

As has already been mentioned, many of you will underestimate your own abilities and competitiveness. (Though a few of you will overestimate your chances.) Extend your sights and apply to the programs that you think will be the best for you. And, after you have applied and interviewed, make certain that you *rank your top choices first.*

Do not fill out your rank-order list in the order in which you think you will be selected by the programs. This will only decrease your chance of getting into the program you really desire. Put your prime program choices at the top of the list. Then rank the others in descending order of preference. That way, when Match Day rolls around, you can be confident that you have matched with the best program possible.

22

The NRMP & Other Matches

It is good to hope, but bad to depend on it.

— Folk Saying

THE "MATCH" IS OFFICIALLY KNOWN as the National Residency Matching Program (NRMP). It is how most medical students get their first-year (PGY-1, intern) training positions. Most of these positions are filled with the expectation on both the graduate's and the program's part that the entire training program will be completed.

About 21,400 first-year positions were offered in the 2006 NRMP PGY-1 Match. This number must be compared with the total number of students and graduates from U.S. and Canadian medical schools enrolled in the Match (about 17,600), plus the total number of international medical graduates (IMGs) in the Match (nearly 7,500). This works out to about 0.86 positions offered per participant. There are 1.5 positions for each U.S. senior M.D. and D.O. student in the Match.

In 2005, 67% of the available NRMP first-year positions were filled by graduates of medical schools approved by the Liaison Committee on Medical Education (U.S., Puerto Rican, and Canadian medical schools), another 20% were filled by IMGs, 4% were filled by Osteopathic graduates, and 9% were unfilled through the Match. Usually, but not always, these unfilled positions were in the least desirable programs.

In the 2005 Match, 94% of participating senior M.D. students and 69% of participating senior D.O. students from U.S. schools matched. About 53% of participating IMGs matched; U.S.-citizen IMGs matched more often (55%) than non-U.S. citizens (52%).

Separate Matches exist for Neurology, Child Neurology, Ophthalmology, Neurological Surgery, Plastic Surgery, and Urology. See each specialty's listing in Chapter 3 for details about their matching program. There is negligible involvement in the NRMP Match by Nuclear Medicine, Medical Genetics,

Preventive Medicine, Trauma Surgery, and many Internal Medicine sub-specialties.

Osteopathic medical students match with American Osteopathic Association (AOA)-approved internships and residencies (other than those in the military) through the *Intern/Resident Registration Program*. This matching program is run under the AOA's auspices by National Matching Services (see description on page 575).

The NRMP Match

In any competition, it is vital to know the rules *before* you play. This avoids having to learn through a process of trial and error. In as major an event in your life as the Match, learning as you go could be a disaster, so it behooves you to spend a few moments to become familiar with the way the system works. When you need more information or application materials, you can get them from your Dean of Students or the NRMP, 2450 N Street NW, Washington, DC 20037-1127; (202) 828-0566 or toll-free at (866) 617-5838 (8:30 A.M. to 5:30 P.M. Eastern time); e-mail: NRMP@aamc.org; www.nrmp.org. Contact information is the same for Fellowship matches, except that the phone numbers are: (202) 828-6077 or toll-free at (866) 617-5834.

History of the Match

Prior to 1951, the matching of medical students to internship positions was a rather sordid affair. Appalling abuses of the system occurred, such as weak programs pressuring students to take less-than-optimal positions early rather than waiting for an offer from their top choice. And, while there was a purported uniform announcement date for several years, it proved to be unworkable.

As evidence of just how badly a new matching system was needed, in 1951, more than 98% of hospitals and 97% of students participated in the first Match. Organized by the National Student Internship Committee, the program was a huge success and led to the establishment of the National Intern Matching Program.

This organization's name and its sponsors have changed several times over the years. Currently, it is organized as the National Resident Matching Program (NRMP). Its board of directors consists of representatives from the Association of American Medical Colleges, American Hospital Association, American Medical Association, American Board of Medical Specialties, American Medical Student Association, AAMC Organization of Student Representatives, Council of Medical Specialty Societies, AMA Medical Student Section, and the Consortium of Medical Student Organizations.

The original matching program used a card-sorting system, which was state-of-the-art in the early 1950s. This method, though it became antiquated, was not changed until 1970, when electronic data-processing techniques were introduced. But it was not until 1974 that the entire system was fully computerized. Currently, the entire computer program for the Match takes about six minutes to run. While the Match process has many flaws, as Winston Churchill said of democracy, it is "the worst [system] except all those other forms that have been tried from time to time."

Currently, a lawsuit is pending against the NRMP, its sponsoring medical organizations, and the hospitals that hire residents. Designed to destroy the NRMP, the suit contends that the current system restricts competition, depresses salaries, and deprives residents of the ability to negotiate their salaries and work hours. This case is being closely monitored: If the NRMP system is diluted or destroyed, most applicants will be adversely affected.

According to the AMA, one of the NRMP's sponsoring organizations,

> Experience before the institution of the "match" program suggests that its elimination might well result in lower compensation or worse working conditions. In any event, given Medicare funding limitations, if compensation increases dramatically, it is quite possible that there would be a reduction in the number of residency slots. The only certain result would be chaos in the process by which students select their residency programs and by which residency programs find the best students. Anxiety, pressure of deadlines and reduced information as the basis for making decisions would likely result. For the most highly competitive residency programs, there might even be a downward pressure on compensation. . . . residents might be asked to contribute to the cost of their "on the job" training through tuition possibly resulting in increased levels of indebtedness to pay for such tuition—to be offset by the higher compensation.

(The AMA was dismissed from the litigation in 2004.)

At present, have no fear about your colleagues destroying the system. Despite the suit, the NRMP Match will continue to operate.

The key element in the Match is the "algorithm" (see "NRMP Algorithm," page 549). The algorithm favors applicants, although how many residency programs this adversely affects is debatable. All categories of applicant (i.e., U.S. M.D. students, D.O. students, physicians, IMGs) are treated equally. As a result of complaints, the NRMP changed their matching algorithm in 1998 from one that favored programs (program-optimal) to one that favors applicants (student-optimal). (Another match, the San Francisco Matching Program, changed their algorithm in 1997 so that applicant preferences would always prevail.)

No matter what the truth is, of those students participating in the NRMP in 2005, nearly 63% matched with their first choice, 15% with their second choice, 9% with their third choice, 5% with their fourth choice, and the rest either got their fifth or lower choice of program or did not find a position in the Match.

The matching process has developed to the point where it can now accommodate all programs in all specialties that offer positions to senior medical students, regardless of the postgraduate level at which the program begins. However, many programs still do not participate in the NRMP Match.

"First-Choice" Residency Positions—A Warning

Medical students often boast about getting their "first-choice" of residency positions and medical schools proudly cite the number of their students who achieve this goal. These are misleading numbers, and ones to be very wary of in your own career planning.

Medical students are conservative by nature. But they also consistently underestimate their own worth. Hard to believe, but true! As a result, many settle for "safe" choices rather than aiming for their "dream" residency position. I speak with medical students from many medical schools, and the story is always the same: Even if they are AOA (medical school honorary), each student has what he or she feels is a valid reason why they are not as competitive as other students who are applying to what they consider the "best" residencies. So, they settle for something less than what they think will be optimal and don't even apply to these "best" residencies.

Over the years, some medical schools have strongly encouraged their students to apply both to "sure bet" positions and to positions within their own hospital system. The cynic in me suggests that this is done to boost the rate of "first-choice" residency matches and to make sure that their residency programs are filled.

The best course is to not fall into these traps. Always strive to get the best residency position that you can.

Participating Specialties

Most PGY-1 positions are offered through the NRMP Match. (Most programs in the NRMP Match require that you apply through ERAS.) The majority of those not offered are military internships. However, PGY-2 positions in many specialties either are not offered through any Match (you have to negotiate directly with programs) or are offered through the specialty's own Matching program. The number of specialties and programs participating in the NRMP Match changes from year to year, as does the number of positions offered in each of these specialties. The best sources for current information about each specialty are listed in the "Specialty Descriptions" in Chapter 3.

Intern Positions

Some PGY-1 positions for medical students are classified as "*Categorical (C).*" These are in the broad specialties and do not require preliminary graduate training. They are designed for individuals who want to remain in the same program throughout their residency. Categorical positions are found in Family Medicine, Internal Medicine, Pediatrics, Emergency Medicine, Obstetrics and Gynecology, General Surgery, and Pathology. In addition, other specialties whose Boards require a preliminary broad clinical experience can also offer Categorical positions if the individual program has made arrangements for this experience.

"*Preliminary (P)*" programs are designed for students seeking one or two years of broad prerequisite clinical experience prior to entering another specialty. They are available in Internal Medicine, General Surgery, and Transitional programs. They are not designed to act as entry points for a full residency in either Internal Medicine or General Surgery; occasionally, however, they can be used as just such a pathway.

Advanced Positions

There are also positions available through the NRMP's Matches beyond the PGY-1 year. These are "*Advanced*" residency positions (designated by an "A" in the *NRMP Directory*) and "*Fellowships.*" (Also see "Matching in Advance [PGY-2 and Above]," below.) Advanced residency positions are those positions above the PGY-1 level that are available for senior students. The presumption is that students will complete preliminary training before entering these programs. Fellowships are for individuals who have completed, or are about to complete, a residency in a primary specialty and desire more specialized training.

Advanced ("A")

Advanced ("A") programs offer positions *beginning at the PGY-2 or higher level* to senior medical students. The problem is that many programs offering such positions do not go through the NRMP PGY-1 Match. Applicants to these programs need to apply for the Advanced Position and also to the NRMP PGY-1 Match to fulfill their initial training requirement. This is especially true in Ophthalmology and Neurological Surgery. The internships accepted as prerequisites for further training in other specialties are listed in Figure 22.1. The numbers and types of training programs and of positions available, as of 2006, are listed in Figures 22.2 and 22.9.

FIGURE 22.1

PGY-1 Training Accepted by Various M.D. Specialties*

Specialty	Training							
	Internal Medicine	Pediatrics	Surgery	Family Medicine	OB/Gyn	Transitional	Neurology	Emergency Medicine
Anesthesiology	X	X	X+	X	X	**	X	X
Dermatology***	X	X	X	X	X	X	—	X
Neurology	X	—	—	—	—	**	—	—
Ophthalmology	X	X	X	X	—	X	X	X
Physical Med & Rehab	X	X	X	X	X	X	—	—
Psychiatry (3-yr prog.)	X	X	**	X	**	X	**	—
Diagnostic Radiology	X	X	X+	X	X	X	X	X
Radiation Oncology	X	X	X+	X	X	X	—	—

*The traditional PGY-1 (intern) year for Osteopathic (D.O.) physicians is acceptable to all AOA-approved specialties; few M.D. programs give credit for that year.

**Must be approved by program director.

***Broad-based clinical training year.

+Surgical subspecialty training also acceptable.

FIGURE 22.2

Medical Specialties, Programs, and Entry-Level Positions Offered

Column 1 is the total number of residency/fellowship programs. *Column 2* is the number of positions offered to medical students via a matching program. *Column 3* is the total number of entry-level positions.

The ACGME or AOA have not approved all the listed specialties.

Specialty	1#	2*	3+
Abdominal Radiology	34	0	123
Addiction Psychiatry	46	0	102
Adolescent Medicine	25	0	31
Adult Reconstructive Orthopedics	14	0	27
Aerospace Medicine	4	0	45
Allergy & Immunology	72	0	150
Anesthesiology	132	1,283	1,283
Blood Banking/Transfusion Med	48	0	74
Cardiology	170	0	778
Cardiothoracic Radiology	2	0	3
Chemical Pathology	3	0	4
Child and Adolescent Psychiatry	115	0	438
Child Neurology	119	164	164
Clinical Cardiac Electrophysiology	82	0	183
Clinical & Laboratory Immunology	1	0	2
Clinical Neurophysiology	90	0	263
Colon & Rectal Surgery	39	0	72
Cornea/External Disease++	64	0	73
Craniofacial Surgery++	19	0	19
Critical Care (Anesthesia)	49	0	48
Critical Care (IM)	32	0	91
Critical Care (Surg)	85	0	170
Cytopathology	85	0	152
Dermatology	111	316	404
Dermatopathology	47	0	85
Developmental/Behavioral Peds	22	0	21
Emergency Medicine	133	1,332	1,477
Emergency Med-Internal Med	11	23	23
Endocrinology (IM)	119	0	266
Endovascular Surg Neuroradiology	3	0	5
Facial Plastic Surgery++	37	0	38
Family Medicine	469	2,761	3,442
Family Med-Internal Med	3	5	6
Family Med-Psychiatry	10	16	21
Female Pelvic Med & Reproductive Surg*	24	0	24

FIGURE 22.2 (continued)

Specialty	1[#]	2[*]	3[+]
	5	0	10
Forensic Pathology	39	0	82
Forensic Psychiatry	43	0	101
Gastroenterology	156	0	421
Geriatric Medicine (FM)	31	0	71
Geriatric Medicine (IM)	100	0	471
Geriatric Psychiatry	60	0	162
Glaucoma[++]	54	0	62
Gynecologic Oncology	33	0	39
Hand Surgery (All)	67	0	145
Hematology (All)	90	0	167
Hematology & Oncology (IM)	123	0	428
Infectious Disease	139	0	322
Internal Medicine, Categorical	364	4,768	4,768
Internal Medicine, Preliminary	291	1,987	1,987
Internal Med-Dermatology	4	4	4
Internal Med-Emerg Med-Critical Care	1	0	1
Internal Med-Medical Genetics	1	0	2
Internal Med-Neurology	7	1	12
Internal Med-Nuclear Med	2	0	0
Internal Med-Pediatrics	101	390	465
Internal Med-Physical Med/Rehab	2	0	2
Internal Med-Preventive Med	7	3	5
Internal Medicine, Primary	56	290	290
Internal Med-Psychiatry	17	23	39
Interventional Cardiology	123	0	283
Maternal-Fetal Medicine[*]	59	0	73
Medical Genetics	48	2	96
Medical Microbiology	12	0	17
Medical Toxicology (EM)	20	0	34
Medical Toxicology (GPM)	4	0	6
Mohs Micrographic Surgery[++]	50	0	51
Musculoskeletal Oncology	9	0	27
Musculoskeletal Radiology	28	0	54
Neonatology	97	0	209
Nephrology	106	0	306
Neurodevelopmental Disabilities	8	0	10
Neurological Surgery[++]	95	156	158
Neurology[++]	128	524	524
Neurology-Diag Radiology-Neuroradiology	2	0	2
Neuropathology	36	0	36
Neuroradiology	87	0	259

FIGURE 22.2 (continued)

Specialty	1#	2*	3+
Neurotology (OTO)	12	0	10
Nuclear Medicine	62	0	107
Nuclear Radiology	21	0	38
Obstetrics & Gynecology	253	1,144	1,238
Occupational Medicine	33	0	108
Oncology	20)	0	76
Ophthalmology++	117	450	460
Ophthalmic Plastic/Reconstructive Surg	14	0	14
Orthopedic Sports Med	60	0	149
Orthopedic Surgery	152	610	661
Orthopedic Surgery of the Spine	12	0	27
Orthopedic Trauma	6	0	12
Otolaryngology	102	269	269
Pain Medicine (All)	117	0	217
Pathology (Anatomic & Clinical)	151	526	633
Pediatric Anesthesiology	43	0	137
Pediatric Cardiology	48	0	100
Pediatric Critical Care Med	59	0	119
Pediatrics-Dermatology	1	1	1
Pediatric Emergency Med (EM)†	11	0	21
Pediatric Emergency Med (PED)†	44	0	84
Pediatric Endocrinology	66	0	85
Pediatric Gastroenterology	51	0	69
Pediatric Hematology/Oncology	60	0	123
Pediatric Infectious Diseases	62	0	74
Pediatric Nephrology	37	0	39
Pediatric Neurosurgery++	16	0	20
Pediatric Ophthalmology++	40	0	48
Pediatric Orthopedics	23	0	36
Pediatric Otolaryngology++	20	0	26
Pediatric Pathology	28	0	41
Pediatric Pulmonology	46	0	57
Pediatric Radiology	44	0	87
Pediatric Rehabilitation Med	3	0	2
Pediatric Rheumatology	25	0	28
Pediatric Sports Medicine	8	0	0
Pediatric Surgery	31	0	31
Pediatric Urology	18	0	19
Pediatrics	204	2,269	2,868
Pediatrics/Dermatology	3	1	1
Pediatrics/Emergency Med	3	6	6
Pediatrics-Medical Genetics	12	1	7

FIGURE 22.2 (continued)

Specialty	1#	2*	3+
Pediatrics-Phys Med & Rehab	5	4	4
Pediatrics-Psychiatry-Child Psych	10	20	22
Physical Med & Rehabilitation	79	78	408
Plastic Surgery (All)++	90	80	587
Preventive Medicine, General	23	4	234
Procedural Dermatology	27	0	25
Psychiatry	181	1,026	1,389
Psychiatry-Family Med	10	16	21
Psychiatry-Neurology	10	0	10
Psychosomatic Med	14	0	21
Public Health	17	0	64
Pulmonary Diseases (IM)	30	0	117
Pulmonary Diseases & Critical Care Med (IM)	122	0	400
Radiation Oncology	79	137	137
Radiology, Diagnostic	191	1,018	1,106
Reproductive Endocrinology	29	0	32
Retina-Vitreous++	87	0	96
Rheumatology	108	0	198
Selective Pathology	22	0	88
Spinal Cord Injury Med	21	0	31
Sports Medicine (EM)	3	0	5
Sports Medicine (FM)	68	0	111
Sports Medicine (IM)	2	0	3
Surgery, General (Categorical)	245	1,051	1,051
Surgery, General (Preliminary)	292	1,331	1,331
Surgical Critical Care	84	0	170
Thoracic Surgery	97	0	158
Transitional Year	130	1,107	1,423
Trauma Surgery**	26	0	42
Undersea & Hyperbaric Med (EM)	1	0	2
Undersea & Hyperbaric Med (GPM)	1	0	2
Urology++	120	251	251
Vascular Neurology	22	0	44
Vascular Surgery	94	0	117
Vascular/Interventional Radiology	101	0	251

#Number of institutions participating. Some separate applicants into two or more "programs" based on whether they are applying as Categorical, Preliminary, Advanced, or Physician candidates.

*Positions at either the PGY-1 or the PGY-2 (Advanced) level available for medical student matching. Positions open only to physicians, labeled "R" on the NRMP's program list, are not included.

**Programs that meet guidelines of the American Association for the Surgery of Trauma; this subspecialty is not recognized by the ACGME.

+All entry-level positions available (at various years of training) in accredited programs. Some must be matched with during internship or residency; others are only in the Military match.

†Fellowship programs that follow residency. "Pediatrics/Emergency Med" is the combined residency program.

++Uses San Francisco or American Urological Assn. matches. Plastic Surgery uses NRMP only for PGY-1 year. Numbers derived from: *FREIDA*; the NRMP; Doug Perry, the San Francisco Match; and other sources.

All graduates of Osteopathic medical schools must complete an AOA-approved rotating internship before beginning Osteopathic specialty training (Figure 3.2), although Specialty Track internships in Internal Medicine, Obstetrics and Gynecology, Otolaryngology/Facial Plastic Surgery, Pediatrics, and Urological Surgery essentially eliminate the requirement for these specialties.

Fellowships

Some specialty programs have fellowship positions available through the NRMP, the San Francisco Matching Program, and the American Urological Association (Figure 22.9). Participation in these Matches is limited to individuals who have completed or are about to complete programs in the prerequisite specialties.

Nearly all fellowships require completion of the basic residency before beginning the program. See also the Fellowship descriptions in Chapter 3, listed either under the parent specialty or separately (designated by an "F" following their names).

NRMP Match Rules—General

NRMP Algorithm

The NRMP Match algorithm is complex; this is a brief summary:

1. The Match handles each applicant in sequence.
2. An attempt is first made to place an applicant into his or her most-preferred program.
3. If this is unsuccessful, an attempt is then made to place the applicant into the second, third, etc., choices on his or her rank-order list.
4. This process continues until there is a (tentative) match or until the applicant's listed programs have been exhausted.
5. When subsequent applicants go through the process, an attempt is first made to place them into their most-preferred program.
6. If a program they ranked highly has ranked them higher than applicants already tentatively matched, the new applicant gets the spot and the previously matched applicant goes back through the algorithm.
7. When an applicant is "bumped" from a spot and goes back through the Match, the process begins again with their first-choice program.
8. The Match is complete when all applicants have been matched with one of their choices or all the programs listed by applicants have filled their positions.

One element of this algorithm generally remains unstated: The NRMP allows several hundred hospitals each year to designate positions in one program that, if unfilled in the Match, can be transferred to positions in another program that can be filled.

Rank-Order Lists

The order in which you list the programs is called your Rank-Order List (ROL). The programs complete a similar list of candidates. After you complete the worksheets from the NRMP (found on their website), you can enter your ROL into the NRMP's computer system from any terminal with Microsoft Internet Explorer 4.5 or higher, Netscape 4.7 or higher, or another compatible program or browser. Java script must be enabled. (As of early 2006, Netscape 6.0 was not supported. Also, using Netscape from a Mac computer could cause problems.) If you have a problem, check with the NRMP website (search "Browsers") to find the latest system requirements.

The ROL can be entered in one or more sessions and can be modified as often as necessary until the posted deadline, usually in mid-February. *To complete the process, you must certify your list; otherwise, the NRMP does not recognize it as having been sent to them.* It is best to finish using the R3 System (Registration, Ranking, and Results) a few days before the deadline, since the system becomes very slow (due to heavy use by procrastinators) during the last 24 hours before the deadline. Applicants are responsible for the correctness of their individual rank-order lists. You can print a copy of your personal ROL at any time by clicking on the "Display/Print" button and then using your Web browser's print button. The NRMP accepts ROLs only via computer. Do not mail or fax them your list.

System security is guaranteed by granting access only to individuals with both an NRMP Code (which is also your AAMC ID) that is assigned when applicants register and a Password that applicants select at the same time. Participants can later change their password, if they wish to do so. Your password should be kept confidential (never share it with anyone else) and in a safe place.

Upon completing your ROL, "certify" the list by clicking on the "Certify" button and reenter your password. If you reenter your ROL after this, you will invalidate the certification and must recertify the list in order for the NRMP to accept it.

IMGs can participate in the NRMP Match, even without an ECFMG Certificate, *if the ECFMG notifies the NRMP that all requirements for certification have been met* before the Match is run.

In 2006, the basic NRMP Match registration fee for students in LCME-approved schools was $60. It was $90 for independent applicants. This fee allows the applicant, without additional charge, to rank up to 15 different programs on the ROL, as well as a total of 15 different PGY-1 programs on one or more Supplemental ROLs. In the Couples Match, each partner pays the individual fee and there is an extra $15 fee for submitting as a couple. This allows them to rank 20 different programs (including "unmatched") on their primary ROL and up to 20 different programs on all Supplemental ROLs. Each additional program pair listed costs $15. Each additional listed program on the primary or supplemental ROL for individuals or for couples costs $30.

Before entering your final ROL, complete the worksheets on the NRMP website. You will use them to check the accuracy of your submitted ROL, which lists only the "NRMP Program Code." On the worksheet, list the program's "Rank Order" (number 1 through as many as you choose to list); "Hospital Name/City, State"; "Program Description" (specialty and type of program, e.g., Surgery-Categorical); and "NRMP Program Code" (from the current *NRMP Online Directory*). The worksheet you use depends upon whether you are applying as an individual (including those applying for shared-schedule positions) or as a couple.

The Supplemental ROLs are used by students applying to one or more Advanced Programs for Students (listed as "A" in the *NRMP Online Directory*). The Advanced programs are listed on the Primary ROL. For each Advanced program or group of programs listed, you should enter acceptable associated PGY-1 programs on the Supplemental ROLs. Each Supplemental ROL will be designated by a letter (e.g., A through D). The same Supplemental ROL can be linked to more than one Advanced Program.

If, for example, you list six Advanced Programs, four of which are in widely dispersed locations and two of which are in the same city, then you will probably want to use one Supplemental ROL containing the PGY-1 programs for the two Advanced Programs in the same location. If you don't mind moving your residence between your first and second years, you can use the same Supplemental ROL for all the Advanced Programs to which you apply, no matter what their geographic location. The basic NRMP fee allows applicants to rank up to 15 Advanced programs and a total of 15 PGY-1 programs on their Supplemental ROLs. Each additional program listed costs $30.

Although there is no limit to the number of specialties (or programs) you can include on your ROL, it has been demonstrated that the individuals with the greatest success in the Match are those who rank only one specialty. However, if you are attempting to get into a highly competitive specialty, such as Emergency Medicine, this does not preclude you from listing some Transitional or Preliminary (Medicine, Surgery) programs at the bottom of your list.

Optimizing Your Rank-Order List

What techniques can you use to achieve the best possible outcome in the Match? There are two things to remember: *list your first-choice program first* and carefully *consider how many programs you should list.*

Applicants consistently do best if they list their top choice first. After listing the top choice, applicants might theoretically get better results if they listed programs based on knowing how all the other applicants rated programs—information which is unavailable. Therefore, *rank programs in the order of their acceptability to you*—not in the order in which you think you are acceptable to the programs. This will give you the best chance of matching with a program you think is optimal for you.

How long should your ROL be? If you apply to a highly competitive specialty (see ratings in Chapter 3) or to programs in an area of the country where matching is difficult, it's probably better to have a long ROL. If you apply to programs that are easier to match with, you may want to have a relatively short list.

The key to success is to consider, for each program you list, whether you would rather go to that program or whether you would prefer to be unmatched and take your chances in the scramble of unmatched candidates for positions. The higher the number of programs that an applicant lists on the ROL, the better the chance of matching (Figure 22.3). *For all applicants, the most common reason for not matching is that they do not list enough programs.* The same holds true for residency programs: Those that fill list approximately 9.4 candidates for each position. Programs that don't fill list only about 4.9 candidates per open position.

No matter how competitive (or non-competitive) the specialty, list all the programs with which you would like to match. If this isn't a long list, or if you are applying to a specialty that generally has many positions open after the Match, a reasonable strategy may be to list fewer programs (only those with which you *really* want to match). See Figure 22.4 for a decision tree to help you decide whether to rank a program.

Confidentiality

Match rules do not allow programs or applicants to ask each other how they will be ranked. The ROLs from both parties are considered confidential. Either party can, if they so desire, release this information to the other.

FIGURE 22.3

Average Number of Programs on Applicants' ROLs

Year	Number of Programs Applied to	
	Matched Applicants	Unmatched Applicants
1996	6.4	5.4
1997	6.9	5.2
1998	7.3	5.0
1999	7.4	5.1
2000	7.3	4.8
2001	7.4	4.7
2005	7.7	4.5

Adapted from NRMP information, November 2005.

What is said, however, is not binding. Many students have been grossly misled by a program's faculty member who told them that they would be "ranked high enough to match." Of course, many did not match with those programs although the students listed them first.

Programs are not supposed to offer contracts for appointment to applicants prior to the general announcement of NRMP Match results. To enforce this, applicants are expected to report any such offers to the NRMP, who will presumably take punitive action. In recent years, eight percent of students have reported that they were asked to make a commitment before a Match result, either the NRMP Match or a specialty match, was announced. So much for the ethics of academic physicians.

Match Results

Match results are released stepwise over the course of "Match Week" (Figure 22.5). All information is available to applicants through postings on the NRMP website; access requires an applicant's NRMP code and password.

Match Day is now in mid-March. Applicants can discover *whether* they matched at noon Eastern Standard Time (EST) three days prior to Match Day. The locations of filled and unfilled positions are posted at noon (EST) two days before Match Day. Unmatched applicants are then free to contact programs to try to acquire unfilled residency positions. This is commonly referred to as "The Scramble."

Matched applicants can discover to which programs they will be going at 1:00 P.M. on Match Day. Under the NRMP rules, both applicants and programs are bound by the Match results just as if they had already signed the official appointment documents.

FIGURE 22.4
NRMP Rank-Order List Decision Tree

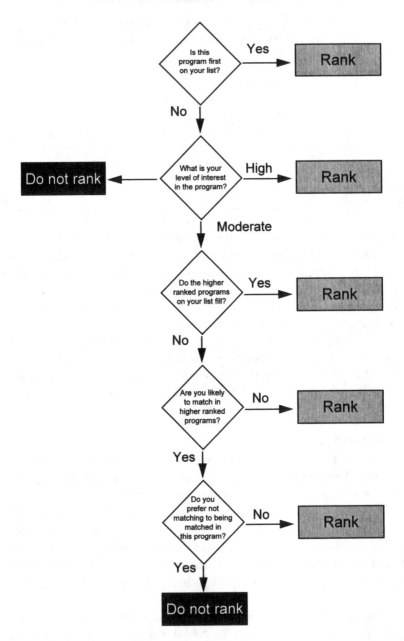

Adapted from a similar algorithm produced by Christopher Leadem, Ph.D., Dean of Students, University of Arizona College of Medicine, Tucson.

Employment Requirements

Even after you match with a program, you may need to successfully complete specific pre-employment requirements, such as drug testing, to get the position. If applicants must fulfill such requirements, they should be informed of this, preferably in the material provided by the institution, before they submit their rank-order list.

Non-U.S. citizens must have a current visa allowing them to enter a residency program, otherwise they cannot begin their residency, even if they have an ECFMG Certificate and have matched with a program.

Illegal Behavior

The NRMP considers two actions illegal for an applicant or a program. The first is supplying forged credentials or letters of recommendation to programs. This is not only illegal in terms of the Match, but also may be either a misdemeanor or a felony in some states. It certainly could prevent you from ever getting a license to practice medicine.

The second is for a program to refuse to accept an applicant who has matched into that program (program illegality) or for an applicant who has matched to refuse to accept the position (applicant illegality). While in the past the NRMP took action if it received "credible evidence" that such activities had occurred, the NRMP now expects that the individuals and programs will settle any disagreements themselves.

Schedule of Events

In 1987, a uniform national date for *releasing the Dean's letters was set at November 1*. (Dean's letters are now officially called "Medical Student Performance Evaluations," a name that no one other than medical bureaucrats actually uses.) Although not all Deans play strictly by the rules (some offer to essentially read the letter to program directors over the telephone), most Dean's letters go out on that date.

The dates for both the NRMP and the "early" (Ophthalmology, Neurology, Urology, Neurological Surgery, Plastic Surgery) Specialty Matches were also pushed back. This generally gives students an additional six weeks to complete the decision and application processes. For the NRMP PGY-1 Match, the rank-order lists are due in mid-February and Match results are released in mid-March. Although it varies by specialty, "early" Matches require their rank-order lists to be turned in by early to mid-January, with Match results released in mid- to late January.

The exact dates for the events in the Matching program change from year to year. Figure 22.5 gives a list of the *approximate dates* for each milepost in the process. For the exact dates each year, check the NRMP website.

Institution

All programs at teaching institutions that participate in the NRMP Main Match may accept senior U.S. students from M.D.-granting medical schools into their residency programs at the PGY-1 level only through the NRMP or another national matching program. Unfortunately, the same does not hold true for institutions' Advanced (PGY-2 and above) positions. Therefore, some Advanced positions may be offered through the Match, while others are matched in other ways. This practice leads to a considerable amount of confusion.

Name & Address Changes

The NRMP collects applicants' names, addresses, and e-mail addresses when they register. It is vital to keep at least your e-mail address current, since the NRMP and programs will first contact applicants using e-mail. Unfortunately, many e-mails sent to applicants are returned to the NRMP and the programs as "undeliverable."

You do not want to miss a message from the NRMP or a program; it can seriously affect your career. Get a stable e-mail provider and make sure that they continue to host your address. Also, use an e-mail "handle" that conveys a professional image: "ImTooSexy@aol.com" just doesn't do it, and might cost you an interview. If you need to change your e-mail address, you can do it instantaneously on the NRMP's website.

Withdrawal from the NRMP Matching Program

By signing the NRMP's contract to participate in their Match, you agree to withdraw from the Match only if you:

1. Accept an appointment from the military.
2. Decide not to pursue a PGY-1 training position in that year.
3. Otherwise obtain a residency position that begins in the current year.

In this last case, the program director must send a letter to the NRMP. (Matching through the Canadian Resident Matching Service [CaRMS] is not considered a withdrawal.) To withdraw from the Match, U.S. senior M.D. students need permission from their Dean. Independent applicants can withdraw themselves from the Match on the NRMP website.

Some students think that they can easily withdraw from the Match either by not turning in their ROL or by turning in a blank ROL. This is not true, because a list of all NRMP Match participants who have not turned in ROLs, or who have turned in blank lists, is sent to their medical school Dean.

FIGURE 22.5

Important Dates in the NRMP Application Process

March-November: Students request residency information materials from individual programs or get it from the programs' websites.

Early July: Applicants can register with ERAS (separate from the NRMP) and begin working on their ERAS application materials.

Mid-July: *NRMP Directory of Programs* is posted on the NRMP website (www.nrmp.aamc.org) and is updated weekly thereafter. Since programs actually start registering on September 1, most programs don't get their listings online until November or December. Until then, rely on *FREIDA* for information about which programs plan to participate in the NRMP.

Mid-August: Applicants can begin registering for the NRMP's Main Match (for PGY-1 and Advanced positions).

December 1: This is the initial NRMP registration deadline. After this date, there is an additional $50 charge. Applicants can technically register until the deadline for submitting their ROL. Don't do that! Register early so the programs will have your NRMP number when they want to rank you.

Mid-January to Mid-February: Applicants and programs enter their *Rank-Order Lists* using the *Registration, Ranking, and Results (R3) System* on the NRMP website.

January 31: Programs must submit their final program information on the number of available positions.

Mid-February: The *R3 System* closes. NRMP must have received both applicants' and programs' *Rank-Order Lists* by this time.

Mid-March:

Three Days Prior to Match Day – Applicants can find out if they matched at 12:00 noon (EST) via the NRMP website. The Dean of Students finds out at 11:30 A.M. (EST).

Two Days Prior to Match Day – At 11:30 A.M. (EST), program directors learn if their programs are filled, or how many unfilled positions they have. Unfilled positions are posted by specialty and program on the NRMP's website at noon (EST). At this time, unmatched students and programs can begin scrambling to fill the open positions.

One Day Prior to Match Day – Confidential list of applicants matched with each residency program posted to the NRMP website at 2:00 P.M. (EST).

Match Day – Match results posted on the NRMP website at 1:00 P.M. (EST).

Mid-March to Mid-April: Programs/applicants mail and receive letters of appointment.

The NRMP automatically withdraws candidates who cannot verify their medical school attendance or graduation, candidates who do not pay the required fees, IMGs who have not completed the ECFMG requirements, and Fifth Pathway students or graduates who have not completed USMLE Steps 1, 2CS, and 2CK.

Student Candidates

Schools
Although the majority of participants in the NRMP Match are students at U.S. schools granting M.D. degrees, you can participate even if you do not fall into this category. However, the rules change slightly depending upon the category into which you do fall.

LCME-Accredited Schools
Students from schools accredited by the Liaison Committee on Medical Education (LCME), which includes virtually all M.D.-granting institutions in the United States, Puerto Rico, and Canada, enter the Match by permission of their Dean. For students in U.S. schools, the medical school's Dean decides upon each student's eligibility to participate. The question the Dean must answer is, "Will the student graduate this year?".

Canadian Resident Matching Service (CaRMS)
Canada has its own electronic application service (AWS) and resident matching program (CaRMS). Both can be accessed through the CaRMS website (www.carms.ca). The CaRMS Match takes place in two rounds, or "Iterations," held one month apart. The first round matches only graduates of a Canadian medical school who do not have any prior post-M.D. clinical training. Some provinces (Newfoundland/Labrador, Quebec, Ontario, Alberta, and British Columbia) will consider students who are in their final year at an LCME-accredited U.S. medical school for the First Iteration, provided that they are Canadian citizens or have "Landed Immigrant" status.

All participants must have passed at least Part 1 of the Medical Council of Canada Qualifying Exam. Additional restrictions apply to non-U.S. international medical graduates and students (one is passing the Test of English as a Foreign Language, or TOEFL) and to graduates of Osteopathic medical schools.

Individuals may enter both the NRMP and CaRMS. However, since the CaRMS completes the First Iteration of its match before the NRMP is run, candidates who enter both programs essentially rank all Canadian programs on their list higher than the U.S. programs.

Applicants must inform CaRMS, in writing, if they have applied to both the CaRMS and the NRMP. If an individual matches through CaRMS, the NRMP automatically removes that applicant's name from the NRMP lists *unless they are notified not to do so*. If an applicant is in the NRMP Match to obtain an Advanced position beginning at the PGY-2 level, that applicant *must tell the NRMP not to withdraw* their rank list if they are matched through CaRMS.

The second round of the CaRMS Match is for unmatched candidates from the first round plus independent candidates, including IMGs and physician candidates. Any applicant matched to a position in the United States through the NRMP Match will be withdrawn from the Second Iteration of the CaRMS Match.

In most provinces, participants must be a Landed Immigrant or a Canadian citizen to obtain postgraduate training in the funded residency programs. The requirements for each province are available from the Canadian Resident Matching Service, 2283 St. Laurent Blvd., Suite 110, Ottawa, ON K1G 5A2, Canada; (613) 237-0075; (877) CARMS-42; e-mail: help@carms.ca; www.carms.ca.

AOA-Approved Schools

Students from medical schools approved by the American Osteopathic Association may also participate in the NRMP Match. However, PGY-1 programs available through the NRMP Match do not fulfill the Osteopathic licensing requirements in some states (FL, MI, OK, PA, WV). It is important that you check with the state *before* you decide to enter the Match.

If you want to participate in the Match, you do so as an Independent Applicant by logging onto the NRMP website. Your medical school will send the NRMP the required proof of your enrollment or graduation.

Non-LCME-Approved Schools

Students at or graduates of medical schools not approved by the LCME, which includes virtually all medical schools outside the United States, Puerto Rico, and Canada and a very few within these jurisdictions (you already know if you are in this group), can apply to the NRMP Match only as Independent Applicants. This includes international medical graduates (FNIMGs and EVIMGs), U.S. citizens graduating from non-LCME approved schools (USIMGs), and Fifth Pathway students.

To participate in the Match, each applicant must furnish proof that he or she has either completed all the requirements for Examination Council for Foreign Medical Graduates (ECFMG) certification, or obtained a full and unrestricted license to practice medicine in the United States. While you can sign up for the NRMP Match and submit an ROL without being certified by the ECFMG, you must have completed all necessary requirements for this certification by the time the ROL is due (mid-February). The NRMP will check with the ECFMG at that time. If you do not meet the requirements, you will not be allowed to proceed in the Match.

Couples Match

With the understanding that physician–physician couples were becoming more common, the NRMP instituted a Couples Match to assist couples in matching in the same geographic location. In recent years, couples' match rates have been comparable to those of students matching as individuals (Figure 22.6). The Couples Match is *not* only for those who are married or engaged. Any applicant pair can use this Match, including those who are dating, gay/lesbians, or even close friends. Independent applicants (e.g., Osteopathic students, graduate physicians, and IMGs) can also use the Couples Match.

There are significant differences between going through the Match alone and going through as a couple. The initial step in entering the Couples Match is simply for each member of the couple to enroll in the Match and indicate in the R3 System that they want to be in the Match as part of a couple.

Unlike those in a shared-schedule position (described in the next section), couples apply to and interview at programs separately. They should, of course, try to select programs in corresponding geographic areas. For example, if one partner applies only in Washington, DC and the other only in San Francisco, there would certainly be no way to find

FIGURE 22.6
NRMP Couples Match Results, 1987–2005

Year	Number of Couples	Number with Both Matched	Number with one Matched	Number with Neither Matched	Match Rate %
1987	347	316	14	17	93.1
1991	377	349	17	11	94.8
1995	499	433	33	33	90.1
1999	536	496	27	13	95.1
2001	561	518	25	18	94.6
2003	570	529	22	19	94.7
2005	606	552	39	15	94.3

Adapted from NRMP Data, 1987-2005, Table 14, at www.NRMP.org. Accessed January 2006.

programs where they could live together while they complete their residencies. However, if they both apply to programs in each city, there should be some compatible matches (see Figures 22.7 and 22.8).

The special worksheet and instructions for the Couples Match can be found on the NRMP's website (www.nrmp.org/res_match/special_part/ us_seniors/couples.html). After the partners apply to and interview at programs, each needs to evaluate the programs just as if he or she were matching as an individual. They then must work together to develop the combinations of programs to put on their Couples Rank-Order List Worksheet. Figure 22.8 is an example of one couple's list. Up to 400 pairs of programs can be listed without an extra charge. The programs are matched by rank order, and any combination of specialties and locations can be used. Note that PGY-1 choices on a Supplemental ROL are not paired in the Match. Therefore, any PGY-1 spots listed to accompany Advanced Programs should be geographically compatible with the partner's paired choices.

In many cases, programs will be listed more than once. This may be especially true for the higher-ranked programs. It is also possible for one partner to elect to be unmatched against the other partner's selection. This option is normally reserved for the bottom of the rank-order list, where it is used as a "stopper" to attempt to prevent both partners from going unmatched.

When entering the ROLs on the R3 System, each partner enters his or her choices independently. Be careful that the numbers of the choices for both partners' lists match. One safeguard is that the partners are required to have the same number of listings, even though some of those listings may be "unmatched" (NRMP Program Code = 999999999). Both appli-

---

FIGURE 22.7

Example of a Couple's Worksheet

Partner 1	Partner 2
Washington, DC–Prog A	San Francisco–Prog 1
Washington, DC–Prog B	Washington, DC–Prog 1
San Francisco–Prog A	San Francisco–Prog 2
	Washington, DC–Prog 2

This is the way each partner independently ranked the programs at which they interviewed. They now need to work together to form combinations of these selections within each geographic area for their Couples ROL. (This is shown in Figure 22.8.)

FIGURE 22.8

Example of a Couple's Rank-Order List

Partner 1	Partner 2
Washington, DC–Prog A	Washington, DC–Prog 1
San Francisco–Prog A	San Francisco–Prog 1
Washington, DC–Prog B	Washington, DC–Prog 1
Washington, DC–Prog A	Washington, DC–Prog 2
San Francisco–Prog A	San Francisco–Prog 2
Washington, DC–Prog B	Washington, DC–Prog 2
Unmatched	Any Program Listed Above

(Based on the individual preferences in Figure 22.7.)

cants need to know their partner's NRMP Applicant Code, not their R3 password, to enter an ROL in the Couples Match.

Four important things to note: First, if one partner withdraws from the Match, the other partner will be ranked as a single candidate using the ROL he or she submitted. Second, couples are treated only as a single unit, meaning that if they do not obtain a match using any of their pairs of programs, the NRMP will not run their lists independently to find a match. Third, the NRMP is not your mother. It does not inquire as to how or why a couple is trying to match together. However, your Dean of Students will know that you are using the Couples Match. If you wish this information to be kept confidential, you may want to make a special appointment to talk to your Dean. Finally, if both partners match to Advanced programs, their Supplemental rank-order lists are not treated as a unit in the Match. The couple function works only for the couple's primary ROLs. The NRMP considers any supplemental list individually and does not pair it with the partner's corresponding supplemental list.

Even more complicated for some couples are the problems that occur when both partners are not going through the NRMP PGY-1 Match. For example, if one partner is interested in Urology and the other in Internal Medicine, major problems can develop. Since Urology is one of the specialties that sponsors its own Match, there is no way that the NRMP's Couples Match will work for them. In this case, the best solution would be for the pair to make a tentative list similar in nature to that used by those going through the Couples Match. Then each partner should explain the situation to the program and department directors during their interviews. If you find yourself in this situation, ask them to make a commitment to you. If one residency position can be secured in advance, the partner can then attempt to match only with geographically compatible programs.

It is perfectly legal for program directors to make a commitment to you in advance. But programs participating in the NRMP PGY-1 Match are not allowed to offer you a contract. You, of course, have to place a great deal of trust in the program unless you are offered a contract to sign. Program directors cannot bind you to a commitment if they participate in the NRMP Match, and so they also need to trust you. Remember, if you do not deal honestly with the programs, the next couple coming through will have a much more difficult time.

Shared-Schedule/Part-Time Positions

A shared-schedule position, unlike the Couples Match, is one residency position held by two individuals. As explained in Chapter 13, the individuals involved want to do their training on a part-time basis, over a longer period of time than is normal. The NRMP provides a short description of their method for dealing with these positions at www.nrmp.org/res_match/ special_part/us_seniors/shared_residency.html.

Programs that say they offer part-time (shared-schedule) positions are most frequently found in Family Medicine, Pediatrics, Preventive Medicine, Internal Medicine, and Psychiatry. There is a separate listing of all programs offering shared-schedule positions in the AMA's *GMED Companion: An Insider's Guide to Selecting a Residency Program*, published annually and available at most medical school libraries. This information is also available in the program descriptions on *FREIDA*. The NRMP website has a much shorter list of programs that have made the commitment to offer shared-schedule positions (click "My Reports" in the menu after you register).

To participate in the NRMP Match for a shared-schedule position, notify the NRMP directly at (202) 828-0566 or toll free at (866) 617-5838. In reality, very few applicants choose to enter into this type of arrangement; most of those who contact the NRMP about part-time positions actually want to enter the Couples Match.

The NRMP issues shared-schedule applicant pairs a single NRMP Applicant Code to be used in the Match. In addition, a single combined name is used on the candidate list sent to the residency programs. For example, applicants Robert Smith and Mary Jones would be the candidate "Smith/Jones" for purposes of the Match. They would submit only one ROL, and could only be matched as a pair. If one of the pair drops out of the Match, the other must tell the NRMP whether he or she still wishes to participate as an individual. If so, the NRMP may assign them a new Applicant Code.

Physician Candidates

Physicians already in training or who have completed a training program can apply to enter the NRMP Match as Independent Candidates. Graduates of medical schools not approved by the LCME or AOA must furnish proof either that they have ECFMG Certification or that they have a full and unrestricted license to practice medicine in the United States. There are about 40 positions in fewer than 20 programs (labeled "R" on the program list at the NRMP website) that are open only to physician candidates.

Military Appointments

Military medical training programs usually will accept only those individuals already obligated to do military service because they attend the Medical School of the Uniform Services University of the Health Sciences, participate in the Health Professions Scholarship Program, or have another type of prior commitment. There are usually too few military positions available to accommodate the number of individuals who apply.

In order to have the best chance of obtaining a position, you will have to participate in both the Military and the NRMP PGY-1 Matches. The military selects their residents before the NRMP PGY-1 Match (except for the Army and Navy PGY-1 slots that are in the NRMP Match), so those individuals who do not get military positions will still be able to get a residency position through the NRMP Match. The NRMP and the American Osteopathic Association are automatically notified when individuals match into a military position. For more information on the Military Match, see "Military/Public Health Service" in Chapter 13.

Don't Believe Anything You Are Promised

Several years ago, an applicant, whom our program had ranked highly, called to say that she had not matched. That was rather surprising, since she was a very competitive applicant. Looking for a position, somewhat desperate, she admitted that she had listed only one program on her rank-order list. Why had she done this? Not for any of the common reasons related to family or other personal commitments. Instead, she had relied upon a promise from the residency director of a particular program, which was her first choice, that she would be ranked high enough to guarantee her a position. But that did not happen and she was left out in the cold. I have seen similar scenarios play out numerous times—often involving excellent students who have reason to believe that they will match with a particular program, only to find that they are either unmatched with any program or psychologically unprepared to go to their second-choice program.

The moral of such stories is that you should be extremely wary of any faculty member's promise to match you at a program. This holds true up until the point that either you get your Match results or you actually get a *firm and specific offer, in writing, from an individual authorized to make it.* (One student wrote saying he got just such a verbal offer and showed them this section of the book to demonstrate that he really did need a legitimate written offer. He got it.) If you fall for a specious promise, your dream of matching with the ideal residency may prove to be ephemeral.

According to surveys, residency programs contacted about two-thirds of applicants to inform them that they were being ranked highly. About one-third felt that programs lied to them, and one-quarter felt that programs made at least informal commitments to them. This doesn't portray medical educators as excellent role models.

As mentioned previously, couples with one or both partners applying to specialties outside the NRMP PGY-1 Match must take a calculated risk by asking for just such a commitment. In these cases, obtain the commitment from both the residency director and the department chairman, if possible. And make it clear that you are willing to sign a contract if it is offered.

Be aware, however, that *even a written contract for a position offered in the NRMP Match may not be valid.* The NRMP Match rules say that any contract for a position offered in the NRMP Match that is signed before the Match results are released is superseded by the results of the Match. Some specialties and programs, however, do not offer positions through the Match. If one of these programs offers you a position, they should simultaneously offer you a contract.

The AOA's Intern/Resident Registration Program states that programs can tell applicants that they are "very likely," "likely," or "unlikely" to be ranked in a top position for that program. Surprisingly, the only thing you can rely on is if they tell you that it is "unlikely." At least then you know not to buy real estate in that city.

What to Do If You Don't Match

If, for some reason, you do not match, you will be notified during "The Unmatch" or "The Scramble," the two days before Match Day. This does *not* mean that you have failed; *matching is not the final measure of your worth.* If you are currently enrolled in an LCME-approved medical school, there will be, in all probability, a formal mechanism in place to help you find a residency position. You will certainly not be the first individual in the school's history who did not match. And you will probably find some of your classmates in the same situation. By going through the steps in this book, you are less likely to find yourself unmatched than some of your classmates. In addition, the preparation you have already done will not be wasted. It will give you an edge, even if you do end up without a position. The first rule is: DON'T PANIC!

You may first want to consider whether the specialty you chose is still what you want. Many students have second thoughts after making their initial commitment. You now have a chance to reconsider—but you must reconsider quickly. As soon as you hear that you haven't matched, you must be on the telephone with residency programs. If you aren't sure about a specialty, one option is to pick one of the many Preliminary Surgery or Medicine slots that go unmatched. These may act as stepping-stones to PGY-2 openings in the new specialty of your choice.

If you decide that you still want to go into the specialty you initially selected, you will need to be geographically flexible. Training in the urban ghetto or the rural hinterlands (sites with many unmatched positions) may not be so bad after all; you will get a chance to expand your horizons, and you may even grow to like it. If you are flexible, you are almost sure to get a reasonable position in most specialties. (A few specialties, like Orthopedic Surgery, rarely have spots open after the Match.)

Telephone Match

If you find yourself unmatched, listen to the advice from your Dean of Students and proceed in an orderly manner to find a position. This search, unlike the deliberate steps you took to locate a residency slot before the Match, will be more like the harried and frenetic activity of a commodities broker with telephones to both ears at once.

If you are not currently a student at an LCME school, the process is the same. The only difference is that you will not have as much moral support.

Three days before Match Day, if you learn that you have not matched, contact both your adviser and the Dean of Students to find out what procedures and resources they have to help you. Two days before Match Day, the first day of "The Scramble," unmatched applicants and unfilled programs are free to search each other out and to contract for positions. Beginning at noon (EST), the NRMP posts lists of available residency positions on their website. Print out the relevant lists. When printing your lists, remember that some programs and specialties that would not initially consider you may be happy to seriously consider you now. After all, they need to fill their slots. Make a list of their telephone numbers, e-mail addresses, and websites before you begin by looking them up in *FREIDA*. If you want more information about a program than *FREIDA* supplies, look at the program's website.

List the programs in the order they interest you and call them in that order. If their line is busy, send the residency director an e-mail expressing your interest and detailing how best to contact you. Carry a beeper or cell phone so that you can be reached immediately

Have a copy of your Dean's letter, transcript, personal statement, NBME transcript, and reference letters available. Many programs that are interested in you will download your ERAS application after you contact them. Some will ask you to fax them these documents, so have a copy of your ERAS packet available. If possible, ask your specialty adviser to make personal calls to the programs to verify that you are an excellent candidate.

If the folks on the other end of the line appear somewhat curt, understand that they also feel oppressed by having to scramble to fill their residency position with the best available person. In addition, unlike you, their program is listed on the "Unmatched" website. This announces to the world that their program did not fill. They are not having a good day either, so be tolerant.

The best estimate is that 90% of the unfilled positions are filled by 5 P.M. local time on the first Scramble day. Therefore, be wary of programs that request that you go for an interview before being considered. At this stage of the game, *you need to conclude negotiations for a position by telephone and e-mail.* If you take the time to interview for a position and do not get it, your chances of getting any reasonable PGY-1 slot are almost nonexistent. At this point, both applicants and programs should be willing to interview and make decisions over the telephone and via e-mail. If they are not, they may not really be making a serious offer. You need a position, they need a resident—and you both need them *now.*

Another source of information about unfilled positions, both during the "Scramble" and at other times during the year, is the AAMC's Find-AResident website (www.aamc.org/findaresident). This subscription service is available to ERAS users for a nominal charge. Programs can post information about available positions for applicants to review. In addition, applicants can use their existing ERAS application to create an electronic résumé that can be easily downloaded and evaluated by the program directors.

Finally, remember that many "scramblers" enter excellent residencies, some get into difficult-to-enter specialties, and, despite this very temporary setback, most go on to become excellent clinicians.

Other Training Opportunities

If you haven't matched, there is another avenue to consider. That is postponing your training at the PGY-1 level to pursue parallel training. You may have an interest in pursuing a graduate degree (for example, an M.P.H. or M.S.) or in doing research. This is a perfect opportunity. It gives you a chance to regroup and rethink both your decision about a specialty and your method of pursuing it. In addition, success in this year, if it is used to advantage, may even bolster your chance of getting the position you want. The bottom line is, don't waste this year, even if you decide not to do an internship immediately.

Matching in Advance (PGY-2 & Above)

One of the most confusing and frustrating aspects of the Match is that not all specialties participate. And even in some of those that do, not all programs participate. Although listed in the *NRMP Online Directory*, Neurology, Child Neurology, Neurological Surgery, Ophthalmology, Plastic Surgery (PGY-4 positions), and Urology essentially do not participate in the NRMP Match.

Most of these specialties use separate Matches, sponsored by one of their academic societies, to fill their PGY-2 positions. (See Figures 22.2 and 22.9.) The positions are predominantly filled one or two years ahead of time by senior medical students who will enter these programs after finishing preliminary training. These specialty Matches require that rank-order lists be submitted by early January and they release their Match results in mid- to late January. Registration for Neurology, Child Neurology, Neurological Surgery, and Ophthalmology is $100, which includes the set-up fee for the San Francisco Matching Program's Centralized Application Service (CAS). Plastic Surgery (PGY-4) and the other fellowship matches require a $50 registration fee (costs are for the 2006 Match).

Information and applications for Neurology, Child Neurology, Neurological Surgery, Ophthalmology, and Plastic Surgery can be obtained by writing (designate which specialty) Matching Program, P.O. Box 45161, San Francisco, CA 94145-0161; www.sfmatch.org. The address for *overnight delivery only* is: SF Match, c/o Union Bank of California, Lockbox Dept-lockbox 45161, 460 Hegenberger Road, Oakland, CA 94621. The website also offers information about positions that have become available between the matches (click on "Vacancies").

FIGURE 22.9

Selected Specialties' Programs and Positions Available through Other (Non-NRMP-PGY-1) Matches

Specialty Match	Total Programs (Programs in Match)	Total Positions (Positions in Match)[+]
Abdominal Radiology*	34 (30)	97 (91)
Abdominal Transplant Surgery*	45 (45)	60 (60)
Breast Imaging/Women's Imaging*	23 (20)	38 (35)
Cardiovascular Disease*	170 (165)	778 (660)
Child and Adolescent Psychiatry*	115 (86)	438 (275)
Colon & Rectal Surgery*	39 (38)	72 (69)
Craniofacial Surgery#	19 (19)	19 (19)
Critical Care (Surgery)*	85 (68)	170 (117)
Gastroenterology*	156 (New)	421 (New)
Hand Surgery (All)*	67 (55)	145 (122)
Infectious Disease*	139 (115)	332 (271)
Interventional Radiology*	103 (81)	267 (189)
Maternal-Fetal Medicine*	59 (55)	73 (69)
Minimally Invasive Gastrointestinal Surgery*	96 (91)	137 (131)
Musculoskeletal Radiology*	28 (27)	54 (51)
MRI (Radiology)*	14 (14)	29 (29)
Neurological Surgery[#]	95 (91)	158 (156)
Neurological Surgery Fellowships[#]	20 (20)	21 (21)
Neuroradiology*	87 (71)	259 (174)
Ophthalmology Fellowships (Other)[#]	275 (230)	402 (308)
Otology-Neurotology[#]	8 (8)	9(9)
Pediatric Cardiology*	48 (45)	100 (45)
Pediatric Critical Care*	59 (47)	119 (93)
Pediatric Emergency Medicine*	55 (49)	105 (92)
Pediatric Hematology/Oncology*	60 (54)	123 (121)
Pediatric Radiology*	44 (17)	87 (34)
Pediatric Rheumatology*	25 (15)	28 (17)
Pediatric Surgery*	31 (29)	31 (29)
Plastic Surgery (PGY-4)[#,++]	68 (52)	137 (101)
Pulmonary Diseases (IM)*	30 (11)	117 (21)
Pulmonary Diseases & Critical Care (IM)*	122 (114)	400 (346)
Reproductive Endocrinology*	29 (26)	32 (29)

FIGURE 22.9 (continued)

Specialty Match	Total Programs (Programs in Match)	Total Positions (Positions in Match)[+]
Rheumatology (IM)*	108 (88)	198 (148)
Special/Combined Program in Radiology*	45 (41)	97 (91)
Thoracic Radiology*	12 (12)	16 (16)
Thoracic Surgery*	97 (95)	158 (139)
Ultrasound (Radiology)*	1 (1)	1 (1)
Urology**	120 (108)	251 (232)

[+] Many of the positions not in the Matches are offered through the U.S. Military.
* Match run by NRMP (Information from NRMP, December 2005).
# Match run by the San Francisco Match (Information from Douglas Perry, July 2005).
** Match run by the American Urological Association.
NEW: New program or specialty in 2006.
++ Plastic Surgery also offers an "integrated" program beginning at the PGY-1 level.

These programs use the Centralized Application Service (CAS) rather than ERAS. Much of the information you need to provide is the same as that for ERAS, and includes your personal data, achievements, employment history, activities, personal statement, references, and supporting documents. In addition, both online and paper applications for the individual specialties are available on the CAS website.

Information about the Urology Match can be obtained online from the American Urological Association's Matching Program at www.auanet.org/residents/resmatch.cfm. The Urology Match cost $75 in 2006.

Anesthesiology, Dermatology, Emergency Medicine, Physical Medicine & Rehabilitation, Psychiatry, and Diagnostic Radiology offer both PGY-1 and PGY-2 (Advanced "A") positions through the NRMP PGY-1 Match. Nearly all programs in these specialties participate in the NRMP Match.

The NRMP also runs many fellowship matches (Figure 22.9). Generally, rank-order lists must be submitted by early June. Most Match results are announced in late June, although it varies by specialty. Specific information is available by clicking "Fellowship Matches" at www.nrmp.org/.

Not Using a Match

Some residents get their positions without going through the NRMP or any specialty Matches. In recent years, nearly one-fifth of the residents in training programs had not gone through the NRMP Match to obtain their positions. Just how many of these individuals went through the specialty

Matches, and exactly which positions (and their quality) were obtained, is unknown. There are opportunities outside the Match, though. And it is important to know about these options.

Early Graduation

The NRMP PGY-1 Match is only for residency positions beginning in July. While not generally advertised, many programs (681 in 2006) have or can make positions available at other times. These are open for several reasons. For example, the program may not have been fully matched in previous years, it could be expanding, or a resident may have left voluntarily or been dropped from the program. Some programs have actually designed one or more positions to begin at midyear. Residency positions beginning in January, February, and March are not normally listed by the NRMP. However, there are not many of these positions (see "Programs offering multiple start dates" in each specialty's listing in Chapter 3).

One way to find positions that begin at times other than July is to use the AAMC's FindAResident system (described below). Another is to write to the programs and inquire. A list of programs that offer multiple start dates can be found both on *FREIDA* (use the "optional criteria" button to select "Start Dates other than June-July") and in the AMA's *GMED Companion: An Insider's Guide to Selecting a Residency Program* for the current year. Your inquiry to the program should be specific. Tell them when you want to start and whether you will have officially graduated. If your diploma will not be granted early, indicate whether you will have a letter from your school certifying that you have completed all the requirements for graduation.

If you go outside the Match, there are some additional rules to follow. These revolve around actually obtaining the position. Unlike using the Match, you will need to decipher when you are actually being offered a position and how firm the offer is. Most programs do not have as rigid a structure for interviewing or selecting applicants for midyear positions as they have for those that are available in July. The selection process, in fact, may be a little sloppy.

Aside from the other rules listed for optimal interviewing, you must also nail down exactly when and how you will be notified of the program's decision. It is perfectly reasonable to let the interviewers know that you are applying to more than one program for a midyear slot and, though you would *really* like to go to their program, you will, of necessity, have to accept the first available position. This, of course, is not completely true. If your second-choice program offers you a position, get at least a 24-hour delay to consider the offer. Virtually all programs will give you that long.

Then contact your first choice and press them for a decision. But don't bluff. While this may get you a position at your first-choice program, it might also leave you out in the cold if you force an early decision without having been offered a slot at another program.

Specifically, ask the residency director when you can expect to hear back from the program. Emphasize that an early decision is crucial. They will, undoubtedly, understand this. If you are a competitive candidate for the position, you will be seen as being even stronger at midyear. The program is not likely to wait for someone just a little bit better—that individual might not show up. So, be assertive. The day after you were supposed to hear a decision, assuming that you haven't, call the residency director's office and find out what is going on. In many cases, the program just will not have "gotten it together" enough to decide yet. Your demonstration of enthusiasm will be very effective. *For midyear matching, being assertive is the key to success.*

FindAResident™

FindAResident (www.aamc.org/findaresident) is available year-round to assist applicants seeking positions after the NRMP Match, those looking for advanced positions, and those wanting to transfer to a different program or specialty in mid-year. Some of the available slots are listed because they were unfilled in the Match and Scramble or because residents left the program.

FindAResident is a subscription service that, in addition to listing programs and their specific vacancies for applicants to review, allows applicants to create an electronic résumé for programs to view and evaluate. ERAS users may build their FindAResident résumé by downloading information from their existing ERAS application. Their Dean's and recommendation letters, however, cannot be posted. FindAResident services are available to ERAS users for $30 and to all other users for $75.

Applicants link their materials to one or more specialties so the programs in that specialty may access them. (If an applicant lists more than one specialty, the list is confidential; it is not available to the programs.) Students who register with the service can also search for posted positions by specialty.

Programs participating in the Match who have vacancies cannot post PGY-1 positions until *after* NRMP Match results have been released. Otherwise, they can update their listing at any time, so the database contains the most current and accurate information. Once a position has been filled, programs remove the position from the FindAResident database.

New Programs

New programs, specifically those that have just recently been approved to offer training but are not yet in the NRMP Match, are potential gold mines for those with initiative. Not only will there be less competition for slots, but you also have the potential of matching early, thus avoiding the hassle of sweating it out until March.

In addition, these programs offer you the unique opportunity to help shape a training program. The first residents through any program, though they encounter a lot of rough spots and often have no senior residents to act as role models, inevitably have closer contacts with the faculty than subsequent classes. They are frequently given more responsibility and obtain more intense training.

But how do you find out about these programs? There are a number of sources. Your mentor and the Dean of Students are the sources closest to home. Prominent individuals, especially other program directors and notable teachers in that specialty, often receive advance notification about new programs that have been approved to begin training residents.

Specialty societies are another source of information. Call and ask to talk to their Director of Educational Programs. New programs will often place advertisements in their specialty journals. Advertisements can also be found in general readership journals such as the *New England Journal of Medicine* and the *Journal of the American Medical Association*. Finally, search the Internet, especially FindAResident. Many new programs list themselves so potential applicants can find out about them before they are listed either on *FREIDA* or in the "Green Book."

Once again, the student who puts forth a little extra effort will reap gold from these opportunities. Also remember that new programs have fewer applicants. This is true not only for their first year, but also in the next few years. If you are not the most stellar of candidates, this source of training opportunities may be one of your best bets.

A warning, however. Every year, new graduates (often times, D.O.s) begin internships with the promise that the residency program is "about to be accredited." It often isn't, and the intern is faced with the daunting task of finding a residency position during the most stressful year of their life. A newly accredited program often works out amazingly well; a "soon-to-be accredited" program is a recipe for disaster.

Following Other Training

Some people suggest that you might have better luck getting into a highly competitive specialty, such as Neurological Surgery, Dermatology, or

Orthopedic Surgery, if you first complete specialty training in another area, such as Internal Medicine. The theory is that with the greater emphasis on patient care in teaching centers, any trainee who is already competent in basic patient care will be prized. In some cases, this might be true, but experience suggests otherwise.

Program directors ask the following questions: Why is someone who could go out and practice medicine applying for another training program? Are they unsure of themselves or their goals? Are they planning to become perpetual students? Are they even educable at this stage of their training? In addition, some recent federal rules restrict a program's reimbursement to training residents for their first completed specialty. So they ask, Do I want this applicant badly enough to reduce the Medicare payments we get for residents? Obviously, this is a risky road to follow—not to mention a long one. Think hard before you take this path.

Specialties without Matching Programs

Preventive Medicine (General, Occupational, and Public Health), Medical Genetics, Nuclear Medicine, Trauma Surgery, many Internal Medicine sub-specialties, and many smaller specialties and subspecialties do not have matching programs and do not, for all intents and purposes, participate in the NRMP Match. If you are interested in these specialties, you must apply to the individual programs and make individual contracts.

Non-Approved Programs

Of all the non-Match methods for getting a residency training position, this definitely has the most risk. "Non-approved" means that the Residency Review Committee for that specialty has not certified a program. These committees send out surveyors to assess training programs using preset criteria. A program that does not gain approval was probably deficient in more than one area that was felt to be essential for an adequate training program. *Training at a non-approved program may leave you unqualified to take the specialty's board examination.*

You should be aware of some other terms used to describe the accreditation of programs. Some programs have "provisional" approval. This only means that a program is relatively new or has undergone significant changes. However, if the program is on "probation," assess it carefully. It is in danger of falling into the "non-approved" category. And, while provisions are usually made to accredit the training of the most senior residents in such programs, those in subsequent classes may be in trouble.

Osteopathic Matching Program

Osteopathic medical students match with American Osteopathic Association (AOA)-approved internships and, as of 2006, residency programs (other than those in the Military) through the *Intern/Resident Registration Program*. These OGME-2 (second-year Osteopathic residency) positions are offered as combined internship/residency programs and will be available starting in the 2006 Registration program. Note that only the internship positions begin in that year; the residency positions are for the year following internship and are a continuation of the training program into which participants match. The Intern/Resident Registration Program is run under the AOA's auspices through National Matching Services (NMS), P.O. Box 1208, Lewiston, NY 14092-8208 USA; or 20 Holly Street, Suite 301, Toronto, Ontario, Canada M4S 3B1; (716) 282-4013 (U.S.) or (416) 977-3431; Fax: (716) 282-0611 (U.S.) or (416) 977-5020; e-mail: aoairp@ natmatch.com; www.natmatch.com/aoairp/.

As with the NRMP and other matching programs, applicants must still *apply* to the individual programs, usually through ERAS. Information about using ERAS to apply to Osteopathic programs is available at www .do-online.org (select "Students & Residents"). Matches between the programs and applicants are based on the rank-order list that each submits. The algorithm they use for the Match is applicant-optimal, i.e., it gives applicants' choices of programs a slight edge over programs' choices of applicants.

Students can match into three types of programs: Traditional Rotating Internships, Special Emphasis Internships, and Specialty Track Internships. *Traditional Rotating Internships* are offered only for one year. *Special Emphasis Internships* are in a specialty but do not decrease the length of training (offered in Anesthesiology, Emergency Medicine, Family Practice, General Surgery, Psychiatry, and Diagnostic Radiology). *Specialty Track Internships* are in a specialty and reduce the total years of training (offered in Internal Medicine, Internal Medicine/Pediatrics, Obstetrics/Gynecology, Otolaryngology/Facial Plastic Surgery, Pediatrics, and Urological Surgery). Special Emphasis and Specialty Track Internships can be offered as a one-year position or, more commonly, be combined with matching in the entire residency program. (See Figure 13.8.)

When selecting programs for your ROL, be certain to use the correct program identification number, found in the AOA's listing just before the abbreviated program description. The abbreviation "INT," as in "INT: TRADITIONAL ROTATING," means that applicants will match only for an OGME-1 (internship) year. A program listed as "CMB," such as "CMB: T/ANESTHESIOLOGY," indicates that it is an internship (in this case,

"Traditional") combined with a residency program and applicants will be matched for both the OGME-1 year and the subsequent years of specialty training (in this case, in "Anesthesiology").

Usually, but not always, combined programs will be in the same institution. A list of available internships and residency positions can be found at www.do-online.org (it is updated periodically). The list is sorted alphabetically by state, city, and institution, so you will need to go through the entire list to find any residencies in your chosen specialty.

In the past, many training programs or positions in training programs that seemed to exist in Osteopathic hospitals really didn't—because they were not funded. Including residency slots in the NMS Registration Program (essentially a match) should put an end to this practice, since the programs are required to offer contracts to all applicants that match with them. Figure 22.10 lists the number of recognized programs and positions in each specialty, as well as the number of positions that are actually funded. Check the AOA's website at http://opportunities.aoa-net.org for updated information on funded positions.

To be eligible to participate in the Registration Program (NMS Match), each student must register directly with the NMS by completing an Applicant Agreement form. To do this, go to the NMS site at www.natmatch.com/aoairp/aoareg.htm, and download, print out, and sign the Applicant Agreement. Then send it with $65 (U.S. funds, 2006) paid by check, by a money order drawn on a U.S. or Canadian bank, or by an *international* postal money order. You must put your AOA ID Number, which you get from your Dean's office or from the AOA Division of Postdoctoral Training at (312) 202-8276, on the form. The AOA recommends registering for their Match before mid-October of your senior year. Once your Applicant Agreement is processed, the NMS sends (by e-mail or snail mail) your confirmation that includes a "Code Number" for the Registration Program. You must give that number to each program to which you apply, so that they can list you on their ROL. To ensure that you don't miss vital messages from the NMS, be certain that any spam filter on your e-mail system accepts messages from "aoairp@natmatch.com," "matchinfo@natmatch.com," or any other address with "@match.com."

For those who have registered, the NMS sends a personalized packet of information by the end of November that includes instructions on preparing and submitting ROLs (including special instructions for those participating in the Couples Match or the Military Match) and the procedure for obtaining Registration Program results. Contact the NMS if you don't receive this packet in a timely manner. (See Figure 22.11 for a Registration Program timeline.)

For those wishing to match as couples, each partner must register individually. They indicate that they are part of a couple when they submit their ROLs. As with the NRMP, couples submit "pairs" of program rankings.

Students with military commitments generally participate in the Military Match, which is completed prior to both the AOA and the NRMP Matches. Osteopathic medical students must notify the NMS if they match through the military, so that they will be removed from the AOA Match. If students match through the AOA, the NRMP is notified and they are removed from the NRMP Match for those types of positions. For example, applicants that match through the AOA for an internship-only position (OGME-1) may not participate in the NRMP Main Match for a similar position that year. If they match to an Osteopathic combined internship/residency program (OGME-1 and OGME-2), they will be removed from the NRMP Match for both PGY-1 and PGY-2 positions.

If an applicant fails to match in the AOA Registration Program, they are provided with a list of unmatched programs, and should follow the procedures as discussed under "What if you don't match?" (page 565).

The Registration Program results are posted in mid-February at www.natmatch.com/aoairp/matres.htm. The results are binding. If an institution does not send a contract to a matched applicant within 10 working days of the Match, the applicant may be released from their obligations. If a matched participant does not sign a contract with that program within 30 days, he is banned from entering any other AOA-approved training program for one year. The only exception is if both the program and the applicant agree, in writing, to release each other from this obligation by signing the appropriate part of the intern contract.

Fewer than three-fourths of all Osteopathic graduates take Osteopathic internships. The number of new graduates choosing ACGME-approved (M.D.) programs ranges from 3% at some Osteopathic schools to 47% at others. In addition, nearly two-thirds of the Osteopaths taking specialty residencies do so in ACGME-approved programs. Of course, as the AOA notes: "*Students who do not participate in the Match, and choose to take allopathic (non-AOA-approved) first year graduate training instead of an Osteopathic internship, are not assured of receiving AOA approval for this training. Only interns who have received AOA approval for their training may receive credit for the internship year.*"

FIGURE 22.10

Osteopathic Specialties' Programs and Number of Positions

Specialty	Number of Programs	Number of Approved Positions*	Number of Funded Positions#
Anesthesiology	11	70	63
Cardiology	15	161	65
Child Psychiatry	1	2	1
Critical Care Medicine	3	8	5
Critical Care Surgery	1	2	1
Dermatology	18	98	65
Diagnostic Radiology	14	127	102
Emergency Medicine	36	631	518
Emerg Med–Fam Prac	5	28	17
Emerg Med–Internal Med	13	118	89
Endocrinology	1	2	1
Family Practice	144	1,606	1.271
Fam Prac–OMM	3	12	5
Fam Prac–OMM+1	1	3	3
Fam Prac–OMT	3	17	12
Gastroenterology	7	24	19
Geriatric Med–Family Practice	5	21	9
Geriatric Med–Internal Med	1	2	1
Gynecological Oncology	1	2	1
Hematology/Oncology	1	2	2
Infectious Diseases	2	8	4
Internal Medicine##	60	786	614
Internal Med–Pediatrics##	2	10	4
Interventional Cardiology	5	9	4
Maternal–Fetal Medicine	1	3	3
Nephrology	6	18	11
Neurological Surgery	9	57	50
Neurology	6	39	29
Neuromuscular Med+1	8	27	16
Neuromuscular Med–OMT	7	39	24
Obstetrics/Gynecology##	31	322	272
Oncology	1	3	1
Ophthalmology	9	42	37
Orthopedic Surgery	30	339	280
Otolaryngology/Facial Plastics##	18	93	81
Otolaryngic Allergy	1	3	0

FIGURE 22.10 (continued)

Specialty	Number of Programs	Number of Approved Positions *	Number of Funded Positions[#]
Pain Management	1	2	1
Pediatrics[##]	15	162	125
Pediatric Emergency Med	1	4	0
Pediatric Radiology	1	3	1
Physical Med/Rehabilitation	3	28	17
Plastic & Reconstructive Surg	2	9	5
Preventive Med–Public Health	1	3	3
Preventive Med–Occupational Med–Environmental Med	1	3	0
Proctology	1	2	2
Psychiatry	4	42	28
Pulmonary Medicine	2	5	0
Pulmonary Med–Critical Care	4	15	10
Rheumatology	3	6	3
Sports Medicine	10	33	20
Sports Med–Family Practice	3	14	7
Surgery (General)	37	337	288
Thoracic–Cardiovascular Surg	2	11	9
Urological Surgery[##]	5	37	32
Vascular/Interventional Radiology	1	1	1
Vascular Surgery (General)	8	19	11

* Number of residency positions, in all years of training, that the AOA has officially approved.

[#] Many programs list positions for which they do not have funding. This column lists only funded (real) positions available for Osteopathic physicians or students.

[##] A *specialty track* internship is available that can shorten the total residency length by one year.

Information from: American Osteopathic Association, http://opportunities.aoa-net.org, January 2006.

FIGURE 22.11

Osteopathic Intern/Resident Registration Program Schedule

June: Students can download the "Agreement" for the Registration Program from the National Matching Service (NMS) website, or use a form from the website to request that it be mailed to them (www.natmatch .com/aoairp/).

July–January: Students gather program information, apply to training programs (directly or through ERAS), and interview. (Deadlines for submitting applications and interviewing differ among programs.)

Mid-October: Students return completed Applicant Agreement Form and payment to NMS.

Early November: A list of programs participating in the Match is available on the website.

Late November: NMS sends the instructions for preparing and submitting the Rank-Order List (with special instructions for those in the Couples or Military Matches) to registered applicants.

Mid-January: Rank-Order List and Confirmation (ROLIC) system opens for students to input data.

Late January: NMS must receive Rank-Order List or Statement of Military Obligation.

Mid-February: Registration results released. Unmatched students receive a list of unfilled positions. Failure to receive a result on this date, for any reason, *does not* release students from the Registration Program.

Late February: Hospitals send contracts to matched applicants. Students must sign and return their contract to the institution within 30 days of its receipt.

July 1: Internship or residency begins.

23

You've Matched— Now What?

Eureka! Eureka!

– Archimedes

CONGRATULATIONS! You have gotten a residency position. You have matched! But you are still not through. As they say in tennis, it's the follow-through that makes winners. (I can't even hit the ball, but I know the rules.)

You will be firmly attached to this residency training program for the next several years. What you do in the next few hours and days will make a lasting impression on your new employers.

Telephone Follow-Up to Program

As soon as you find out where you have matched and can calm down to a reasonable level of intelligibility, make a phone call to your new residency director. The call should be brief and enthusiastic, even if the program was not your first choice. Tell him or her how glad you are to have matched with the program and how much you are looking forward to starting your residency training.

This also is a good time to ask if the program needs any additional information from you, their new resident. During this *short* phone call, keep in mind that you want to establish a positive image of yourself in the residency director's mind. Now that you have an employer-employee relationship, doesn't that seem wise?

Letter Follow-Up

Now that you have matched, you also have some letters to write.

The first is to the program with which you have matched. Repeat your enthusiastic response to matching with them and starting your residency training. Ask again if they need any additional information. Also, of prime importance, *give them sufficient addresses and phone numbers for the next several months* so they can send you any materials you might need. Every year some new interns fail to get their first few paychecks on time because they could not be reached in advance to fill out the necessary paperwork.

Your second letter should be to your adviser or mentor. This is the individual who has probably done the most to help get you the position that you wanted. Of course, it is most appropriate to tell your adviser about your Match results in person, as soon as possible. But also send a note of thanks, saying how much you appreciate all his or her efforts on your behalf. It is also proper, if you so desire, to give a small gift as a token of your thanks. This, however, is purely optional and will depend upon the relationship you have developed.

The final letters you should send are to those individuals who wrote your reference letters. Thank them for writing the letters and tell them where you will be going for training. They will appreciate your thoughtfulness and this will, hopefully, help you to continue these valuable professional ties that you have established.

Post-Purchase Dissonance

Have you ever thought long and hard before buying a car, a home, or a stereo—only to finally buy it and be fraught with uncertainty over whether you made the correct decision? Of course you have. It is normal human behavior. This behavior is called post-purchase dissonance.

You have just spent the past six months, and probably much longer, investigating specialties and residency programs before you "bought." You might now feel similarly uncertain about that choice. You may, from some source, receive additional information about your program (no matter whether it is correct or not) or about your specialty (significant or not), and suddenly you are unsure about the life decision that you have made. Don't worry! This happens to almost everyone. If you have gone through the steps outlined in this book, you will be just fine. Now is the time to relax and enjoy yourself—you've earned it.

You might also wonder if the program's faculty does not also feel some post-purchase dissonance. They often do. But if you have contacted them as outlined above, their dissonance, if they have any, will not be directed toward you.

Contracting with the Program

After matching, you should soon receive a contract to sign from the program. The contract and accompanying information a program sends you should specify:

- the length of the residency program
- the duration of your appointment
- the conditions for your reappointment
- your responsibilities in the program
- the amount of your salary
- the amount of other stipends (meals, uniforms, laundry)
- liability, health, and disability insurance coverage
- other benefits
- vacation and leave policies (including sick and professional leave)
- disciplinary and grievance procedures
- policies on sexual harassment
- policies on moonlighting

While no residency contract is perfect, programs should supply as much information as possible, in writing, before you start the residency. This will eliminate confusion later on.

Occasionally, the information in a residency contract will vary from that provided when you were interviewing. It is not unusual for programs to slightly alter the benefit programs as the sponsoring institution changes its benefits. If, however, there are important differences between this material and what you were initially told, immediately contact the program director to clarify the situation.

You might also want to look carefully for any pre-employment screening requirements, such as drug tests or infectious disease screens. The NRMP now takes the position that matching with the program is only part of the agreement, and that a prospective resident must pass any required screening before being hired. This is information that you should (ideally) know before you rank any program. Be certain that you look for it now, in case the program has a requirement you cannot pass.

Debt Management

As you embark on your new career, you may not want to think about the medical school debt that hangs heavy over most graduates' heads; but now is the time to do it. Before you leave your school, it may be wise to have a final meeting with the financial aid officer. He or she may be able to give you some advice about how to best handle your debt burden. Do it now. State medical boards are increasingly withdrawing medical licenses and imposing other penalties for those who don't repay their student debts.

Several other valuable tools exist to help residents manage their debts. The Association of American Medical Colleges (AAMC) runs a list serve called MONEYMATTERS for debt-ridden residents. They also have the *Layman's Guide to Educational Debt Management*, an excellent, detailed online publication. It discusses eight strategies for residents to use to manage their debt:

1. Know what you borrowed, from whom you borrowed it, and who services the loans.
2. Know the "relative cost" of your loans.
3. Know your grace periods and deferment and forbearance options.
4. Know your "decision points" and keep a calendar.
5. "Run the numbers" before choosing any repayment plan or consolidation option.
6. Keep good records.
7. Keep a budget and know when you need outside professional help.
8. Know and use your support systems.

These and several other invaluable resources can be accessed through the AAMC website (www.aamc.org). Be sure to check out their comprehensive online manual, *Monetary Decisions for Medical Doctors* (MD^2). Click on "For Students" and then on "Financing Your Medical Education." The forum can be accessed using a password that you get via the e-mail address at the site. Additionally, the AAMC periodically runs "Debt Management Workshops" for residents and posts information from recent workshops on their site. Check their website for dates and locations.

Helpful websites that offer information about consolidating loans include the U.S. Department of Education (www.ed.gov/index.jhtml). Click on "Financial Aid" in the "Information Links" box. This will lead you to information on obtaining and paying loans, and on loan consolidation. Information is also available from the Federal Direct Consolidation Loan Information Center (http://www.loanconsolidation.ed.gov/), and Sallie Mae (www.salliemae.com).

Your New Home

A number of websites exist to help you reduce the hassles of finding a new home. Some that seem to be good are listed below.

- www.homepath.com
- www.bestplaces.net (cost of living, crime rates, climate, etc.)
- www.homefair.com (links to realtors and mortgage payment calculators)
- http://realestate.yahoo.com (Under Tools, click on "Free School Reports" to find the best schools)

More sites are popping up all the time. Use your search engine to find them and you can eliminate a lot of aggravation.

Moving

If you have gotten a position far from where you now live, or you have just decided it is time to live in nicer quarters now that you will be getting paid (a little) for what you do, you need to move. Since this may be a new experience for you, and because many students have told me that they got "burned" when using movers, here are some helpful tips for hiring professional movers.

Call your local Better Business Bureau before contacting any mover, to find out if they have had any complaints lodged against them.

Contact and get estimates from at least three movers.

Get a written estimate. Estimates come in three forms: *Binding*, where the price remains fixed once the estimate is signed by both parties; *Non-binding*, where you can be charged almost any price; and *Not-to-exceed $X*, which sets an upper limit on cost.

Get details about charges not covered by the estimate. These may include packing, unpacking, surcharges for long distances from the house or apartment to the truck or for stairs (on either end of the trip), packing materials, and insurance.

Carry irreplaceable items with you. Do not entrust diplomas, other legal documents, heirlooms, family photographs, jewelry, safe-deposit-box contents, or other highly valued or easily breakable items to the movers. Take them with you.

Get adequate insurance for the possessions you will move. Check to see if your homeowners' insurance policy covers your possessions while the mover has them. *Basic (interstate) moving insurance* only pays you about 50 cents for each pound of material lost. The other options are *full-replacement-value insurance*, which costs about 85 cents per $100 of declared value of your goods; *depreciated-value-of-goods insurance* (what the goods are worth today), which costs about 25 cents per $100 of declared value of your goods; or a *full-replacement-less-a-deductible insurance* policy. This latter is relatively inexpensive, but you must pay the deductible before the insurance company pays anything.

Make a detailed list of all goods moved, including a list of everything in each box. The mover will make his own list of items and note whether furniture is "scratched," "dented," etc. Go over this list with the mover and be certain each item's condition is correctly stated on his list. Number the boxes so you will quickly know if any are missing. (While it may be a pain, be sure to account for each box or item at the end of the move—before the movers leave.)

Take photographs of any large or expensive items you must entrust to the movers, such as electronic equipment. Carry these photographs with you.

Carry contact numbers for your mover's dispatcher so you can locate your truck when it is delayed. (The frequent-mover's law: Never expect the truck to arrive when scheduled.)

Conclusion

Now you are ready to begin residency training. Let me welcome you to what will undoubtedly be one of the most stimulating and exciting periods of your professional life. You have planned well and have used your own wants and needs to guide your selection of both a specialty and a training program.

Good luck in all your future endeavors. You deserve it!

A New Beginning

To an intern, personal time is always reckoned in minuses. It is the time remaining when work-ups, conferences, dictations, and clinic sessions are taken away or it equals the time left over after work, sleep and errand running are subtracted from a day. Figured by whatever means, personal time often seems like a sum that is unaccounted for, the small amount that balances the ledger of hours. And in the tallying of hourly expenditures that every intern makes, it always lies on the debit side. Personal time is time still owed . . .

Having spent the last two years of medical school rotating disaffectedly from one clinical service to another—with hardly any involvement in patient care and hardly any sense of continuity—I gladly forfeited any claim to private time in order to have greater responsibility for patients and a more permanent station in life.

Hoffmann SA: *Under the Ether Dome: A Physician's Apprenticeship at Massachusetts General Hospital.* New York: Scribner, 1986, p. 209.

Glossary

AAMC—*see* Association of American Medical Colleges.

ABMS—*see* American Board of Medical Specialties.

Advanced Positions—Residency positions obtained through a matching program at least eighteen months before the slot opens and training begins.

Adviser—One of a number of faculty members who give you information about medical school, rotations, courses, specialties, and residency programs. This individual may also be your mentor.

AHA—*see* American Hospital Association.

Allopathic Physicians—*Not* M.D.s, but rather a therapeutic tradition believing that diseases are treated by producing a second condition that is incompatible with or antagonistic to the first.

AMA—*see* American Medical Association.

AMA-Fellowship and Residency Electronic Interactive Database Access—This AMA-produced computer program, popularly known as *FREIDA*, has in-depth information about nearly all residencies and many fellowship programs.

American Board of Medical Specialties—The group that authorizes "official" medical (M.D.) specialties and subspecialties.

American Hospital Association—A professional organization of U.S. hospitals. It lobbies for and monitors hospitals, and has a large say (through the JCAHO) in the setting and enforcement of hospital standards.

American Medical Association—An association of physician members which establishes standards of care, monitors legal issues, and lobbies members of the U.S. Congress on issues important to physicians and their patients. It has special sections for IMGs, residents, students, and young physicians. The AMA publishes the *Journal of the American Medical Association* (*JAMA*) and other specialty journals, as well as reliable resources on many health-related issues.

American Medical Women's Association—An independent organization which represents the interests of women physicians and medical students.

American Osteopathic Association—An association of Osteopathic physicians which establishes standards of care, monitors legal issues, and lobbies members of the U.S. Congress on issues important to physicians and their patients. It also sponsors its own Intern/Resident Registration Program. All Osteopathic medical students must be AOA members.

AMWA—*see* American Medical Women's Association.

AOA—*see* American Osteopathic Association.

AOA (award)—Alpha Omega Alpha, the best-known and most prestigious medical student honorary society.

Association of American Medical Colleges—An association of U.S. and Canadian medical schools which accredits schools in the United States, Canada, and Puerto Rico. The AAMC also conducts an annual meeting, provides consultation, and publishes useful directories and educational materials.

Audition Electives—Senior clerkships taken to demonstrate your abilities to the faculty at residencies you wish to attend.

Canadian Resident Matching Service—The Canadian equivalent of the NRMP Match. Formerly called the Canadian Intern Matching Service (CIMS).

CaRMS—*see* **Canadian Resident Matching Service.**

CAS—*see* **Centralized Application Service.**

Categorical Internship—A first-year residency position in Internal Medicine or General Surgery designed for those who plan to complete a residency in that field.

Centralized Application Service—A method for residency applicants to submit their applications through their Dean's office via the Internet. Specialties participating in the San Francisco Matching Programs use this system.

Clerkship—Structured clinical education provided to medical students.

Clinical Research Fellow—Designates either a U.S. physician or an IMG engaged primarily in research associated with patient care. Physicians in this category need full medical licensure if significant patient contact is involved, but no license if there is minimal patient contact under the supervision of a licensed physician.

Clinical Skills Assessment—A test formerly given by the Educational Commission for Foreign Medical Graduates to test clinical and communication skills. It has been supplanted by USMLE Step 2CS.

Clinical Years—The period of medical school when students "rotate" through the various clinical services. In a traditional four-year school, these are the third (junior) and fourth (senior) years.

COMLEX—*see* **Comprehensive Osteopathic Medical Licensing Examination.**

Comprehensive Osteopathic Medical Licensing Examination—A method of licensure available only to Osteopathic Physicians. It is a three-part written exam.

COTH—The Council of Teaching Hospitals, which publishes several references useful to residency applicants.

Couples Match—A method by which couples can rank their residency choices in program pairs for the NRMP Match so that they can stay in geographic proximity to one another.

CSA—*see* **Clinical Skills Assessment.**

Curriculum Vitae (C.V.)—A résumé.

Dean of Students—The key individual to ask for information about, and for assistance during, specialty selection and the matching process.

ECFMG—*see* **Educational Commission for Foreign Medical Graduates.**

Educational Commission for Foreign Medical Graduates—A nonprofit foundation sponsored by standard-setting associations and agencies to monitor the competency of graduates of foreign medical schools.

Electronic Residency Application Service—A method for residency applicants to submit applications through their Dean's office via the Internet. Most M.D. specialties and, as of 2006, Osteopathic internships use the system.

ERAS—*see* **Electronic Residency Application Service.**

EVIMG—*see* **Exchange-Visitor International Medical Graduate.**

Exchange-Visitor International Medical Graduate—A subset of FNIMGs applying for residency slots. These individuals are in the United States only temporarily as Exchange Visitors (with J-1 visas) to study, teach, or do research.

Externship—A clinical rotation taken at a location away from your primary teaching institutions.

Federation Licensing Examination—A medical licensing exam which is no longer given. However, a passing score may still be used for licensure.

Federation of State Medical Boards of the United States—This organization maintains contact information for individual medical licensing authorities and responds to inquiries regarding medical licensure.

Fellow—An academic term used to designate one engaged in postgraduate training after completing a residency program. Also used for experienced scholars engaged in research, writing, or teaching.

FLEX—*see* Federation Licensing Examination.

FMG—A term used by some organizations to indicate foreign-national physicians who are international medical graduates.

FMGEMS—*see* Foreign Medical Graduate Examination.

FNIMG—*see* Foreign-National International Medical Graduate.

Foreign Medical Graduate Examination—An examination once used to obtain an ECFMG Certificate, but not a medical license. It is no longer given.

Foreign-National International Medical Graduate—A non-U.S. citizen whose basic medical degree or qualification was conferred by a medical school not approved by the LCME, usually located outside the United States, Canada, and Puerto Rico.

FREIDA—*see* AMA-Fellowship and Residency Electronic Interactive Database Access.

FSMB—*see* Federation of State Medical Boards of the United States.

Green Book—The AMA-produced *Graduate Medical Education Directory*. This book lists most residency and fellowship programs. It also contains listings of the standards residency programs must meet and the requirements to take the specialty board examinations.

Health Maintenance Organization—A managed care plan under which medical treatment is prepaid through monthly premiums. HMO physicians are paid set salaries rather than collecting patient fees. Patients have a limited choice of physicians and, except in emergencies, must be admitted to HMO-designated hospitals.

Health Professions Scholarship Program—Military-sponsored scholarships for medical students.

HMO—*see* Health Maintenance Organization.

HPSP—*see* Health Professions Scholarship Program.

IAP-66—Visa document issued to a J-1 visa holder.

IMG—*see* International Medical Graduate.

Independent Applicants—Anyone in the NRMP Match who is neither a current student at nor a Sponsored Graduate of an LCME-approved medical school.

Individual Provider Association—The group contracting with independent physicians to provide services to an HMO's patients.

Intern—The historical term for individuals in their first year of training after medical school. While not officially used except to designate specific positions (Transitional, Preliminary, and Categorical internships), clinicians still commonly use the term.

Intern/Resident Registration Program—A matching program for obtaining AOA-approved internships and some Osteopathic residency positions.

International Medical Graduate—A foreign national educated at a U.S., Canadian, or an accredited Puerto Rican medical school (EVIMG); a foreign national who trains outside the U.S., Canada, and an accredited Puerto Rican medical school (FNIMG); or a U.S. or Canadian citizen who trains in a foreign medical school and then returns to the United States or Puerto Rico (USIMG).

IPA—*see* Individual Provider Association.

LCME—*see* Liaison Committee on Medical Education.

Liaison Committee on Medical Education—This organization accredits U.S., Canadian, and some Puerto Rican medical schools. Foreign-national graduates of these schools do *not* have to obtain an ECFMG Certificate to continue training in the United States.

License—A state's permission to practice medicine. Each state has its own licensure requirements.

Managed Care—Any type of health insurance that uses only specified physicians to see their patients. Examples include HMOs, IPAs, and PPOs.

Match Day—The day on which residency applicants participating in the NRMP or AOA Matches find out with which program they have matched.

Matching Programs—One of the various methods by which students or physicians obtain a position in a residency or fellowship training program.

Medical Student Performance Evaluations—A Dean's letter.

Mentor—The faculty member who helps guide you through medical school and the residency-application process.

Moonlighting—Extra clinical work done for pay, usually away from the institution where one is a resident.

MSPE—*see* **Medical Student Performance Evaluations.**

Must/Want Analysis—The best method to determine what you want in a residency program and which programs meet those needs.

National Board of Medical Examiners—The organization that produces national physician licensing examinations, including the USMLE.

National Board of Osteopathic Medical Examiners—An organization which gives the COMLEX, a licensing examination for Osteopathic physicians.

National Residency Matching Program—A national program to match applicants with accredited U.S. residency programs.

NBME—*see* **National Board of Medical Examiners.**

NBOME—*see* **National Board of Osteopathic Medical Examiners.**

NRMP—*see* **National Residency Matching Program.**

Objective Structured Clinical Examination—A patient-simulation examination used to test medical students.

OSCE—*see* **Objective Structured Clinical Examination.**

Participating Institution—One part of a multi-institutional graduate education program.

Part-Time Position—*see* **Shared-Schedule Position.**

PGY-1—Postgraduate Year-1. The internship year, otherwise known as the first year of residency.

PPO—*see* **Preferred Provider Organization.**

Preclinical Years—The period of medical school preceding clinical rotations, usually the first two years.

Preferred Provider Organization—A group of hospitals or physicians that contracts to provide comprehensive health coverage at a competitive rate. These networks combine aspects of a traditional health care system and an HMO.

Preliminary Internship—First-year positions in Internal Medicine or General Surgery designed for those who do not necessarily plan to complete a residency in that specialty. Many students who take these positions either are undecided about their career plans or intend to go into another field that requires prior clinical training.

Program—The designation for both a place and a curriculum to train residents.

R3 System—Stands for registration, ranking, and results. This is the name of the system used by applicants to register, enter their rank-order lists, and obtain results for the NMRP Match.

Rank-Order List—The program rankings each applicant submits and the applicant rankings each residency program submits to matching programs.

Research Scholar—Term used to designate an individual holding a Ph.D., M.D., or equivalent degree who is in a research training program. The term implies that the training involves no patient contact.

Résumé—Also called a curriculum vitae or C.V., it briefly summarizes a person's accomplishments.

ROL—*see* **Rank-Order List.**

San Francisco Matching Program—The organization which runs many of the "early" matches for specialties such as Neurology, Neurological Surgery, Plastic Surgery, and Ophthalmology.

Scramble—*see* **Unmatch Days.**

SFMP—*see* **San Francisco Matching Program.**

Shared-Schedule Position—One residency position shared by two individuals.

Special Purpose Examination—A one-day examination to test the knowledge base of physicians who seek licensure in a new state or relicensure in the same state at least five years after graduation from medical school.

Special Emphasis Internship—First-year training programs for Osteopathic physicians in Anesthesiology, Emergency Medicine, Family Practice, General Surgery, Psychiatry, and Diagnostic Radiology. Although these internships follow the curriculum of the specialty, they *do not* reduce the number of subsequent training years.

Specialty Track Internship—First-year training programs for Osteopathic physicians in Internal Medicine, Internal Med/Pediatrics, Obstetrics/Gynecology, Otolaryngology/ Facial Plastic Surgery, Pediatrics, and Urological Surgery. These internships usually shorten specialty training by one year.

SPEX—*see* **Special Purpose Examination.**

Sponsoring Institution—The main hospital or clinic responsible for a residency training program. Often it is also the primary training site.

Subinternship—A clinical rotation that gives a senior medical student added responsibility.

TOEFL—An examination called *Toward English as a Foreign Language.* Once used as the ECFMG English examination, it has been supplanted by USMLE Step 2CS.

Transitional Internship—Also called a "rotating internship," it allows interns to rotate through a variety of clinical services, usually in most of the same specialties they went through during their third-year clerkships.

Unmatch Days—The two days before Match Day when those who fail to match with a residency program begin to "scramble" for a residency position.

USIMG—A U.S. citizen whose basic medical degree or qualification was conferred by a medical school not approved by the LCME, usually located outside the United States, Canada, and Puerto Rico.

United States Medical Licensing Examination—The primary examination required to practice medicine in the United States. Implemented in 1994 as the only licensing exam for physicians (M.D.s or equivalent) without regard to their nationality or medical school.

USMLE—*see* **United States Medical Licensing Examination.**

Annotated Bibliography*

Knowledge is power.

– Hobbes, *Leviathan*

Medicine—The Big Picture

Bureau of Health Professions, Health Resources and Services Administration: *Changing Demographics: Implications for Physicians, Nurses and Other Health Workers*. Washington, DC: U.S. Dept. of Health and Human Services. Spring 2003. (http://bhpr.hrsa.gov/healthworkforce/reports/changedemo/Content.htm) This U.S. government report estimates the need for physicians in the larger specialties under several scenarios over the next 15 years. Definitely worth a look if you are interested in how your career plans might fit into the big picture.

Drayer J: *The Cost-effective Use of Leeches and Other Musings of a Medical School Survivor*. Tucson, AZ: Galen Press, Ltd., 1998. Hilarious stories, cartoons, and poems (based on Dr. Seuss) describing one medical student's trials and tribulations during medical school. A must read—if you don't take yourself too seriously.★

Iserson KV: *Demon Doctors: Physicians as Serial Killers*. Tucson, AZ: Galen Press, Ltd., 2002. Okay, so it is the dark side of medical history. But it's my book, and it's a great read. Not one case of euthanasia among them, these are real (and really fiendish) physicians who intentionally killed—for power, money, sex, or nationalism.★

Lewis S: *Arrowsmith*. New York: Harcourt Brace & Co., 1925. An inspiring classic that led many people to medicine as a career. It shows what physicians can do, as well as their limitations, in medical practice and in the laboratory. Although written in the pre-antibiotic era, the story remains as relevant today as it was then.★

London O: *Kill as Few Patients as Possible: and Fifty-six Other Essays on How to be the World's Best Doctor*. Berkeley, CA: Ten Speed Press, 1987. Funny, short essays illustrate this practicing physician's rules about how to be a successful (and compassionate) physician. While the essays are tongue-in-cheek, much of the underlying advice really will make you an excellent physician.★

Reynolds R, Stone J: *On Doctoring: Stories, Poems, Essays*. 2nd ed. New York: Simon & Schuster, 1995. Classic and pithy descriptions of physicians, medical practice, diseases, and patients. Contributors include physicians (Sir Arthur Conan Doyle, William Carlos Williams, Richard Selzer, and others) and noted writers (Anton Chekhov, Ernest Hemingway, Kurt Vonnegut, and Alice Walker). A book to be repeatedly read through an entire medical career.★

Schiedermayer DL: *House Calls, Rounds, and Healings: A Poetry Casebook*. Tucson, AZ: Galen Press, Ltd., 1996. Revealing the human vulnerabilities in doctor-patient relationships, this small book of verses provides powerful insight into how first-rate clinicians bond with the great variety of patients they encounter. Written by a practicing Internist with diverse experiences. It brings the humanity back into medical practice—something we all occasionally miss.★

---

*Code:
    ** See Chapter 9 for a more detailed description.
    ★ References marked with a star can be obtained through the *Galen Press Catalog*, P.O. Box 64400, Tucson, AZ 85728-4400; (800) 442-5369 or (520) 577-8363; fax (520) 529-6459; www.galenpress.com.

The Specialties

American Academy of Pediatrics: *Pediatrics 101: Facts, Figures and Other Intangibles.* This is an online (www.aap.org/profed/peds101.htm) positive overview of the specialty written by the specialty's leadership.

American Association for the Surgery of Trauma: *Trauma-Related Fellowships.* This online document (www.aast.org/fellowships/fellow.html) lists fellowships available for clinical work and for research. It also notes whether they comply with AAST guidelines. Well worth a look for those interested in pursuing this specialty.

American Board of Medical Specialties: *Which Medical Specialist for You.* A frequently updated online manual (www.abms.org) providing short descriptions of all recognized medical specialties and subspecialties. But note that such common subspecialties as Trauma Surgery and Hospitalist are not included, since they have not been officially blessed.

American College of Preventive Medicine's website (www.acpm.org) has a number of interesting links to information about the specialty and its activities. It is also the access point for the Association of Preventive Medicine Residents.

Carlson DW, Fentzke KM, Dawson JG: Pediatric hospitalists fill varied roles in the care of newborns. *Pediatric Annals.* 2003;32(12):802-10. The use of hospitalists to care for newborns is increasing. How will this affect patient care, education, and Pediatricians' practice in the future?

Colen BD: *O.R.: The True Story of 24 Hours in a Hospital Operating Room.* New York: Signet (Penguin), 1994. A Pulitzer Prize-winning author's gripping minute-by-minute account of the operating room, as seen from several perspectives. Surgeries range from extraordinary surgical feats to the mundane. After reading this, you will either be a confirmed surgeon or know why you don't want to enter this world.

Committee on Strengthening the Geriatric Content of Medical Training: Strengthening training in geriatrics for physicians. *J Am Geriat Soc.* 1994;42(5):559-65. A good description of the specialty, including the use of non-physician practitioners. It details what Geriatricians do in practice. An old article, but still worth reading.

DeLisa JA, Jain SS, Campagnolo DI: Factors used by physical medicine and rehabilitation residency training directors to select their residents. *Am J Phys Med Rehab.* 1994;73(3): 52-6. The title says it all. What does it take to get into a PM&R program? Despite being old, it contains valuable information.

Harkin KE, Cushman JT, Wei HG, eds.: *Emergency Medicine: The Medical Student Survival Guide.* 2001. Published by the Emergency Medicine Residents Association, this is sent free to all EMRA medical student members. Everything you wanted to know about Emergency Medicine, albeit with a very personal and sometimes biased slant. Topics include preparing for, applying to, and being successful in an Emergency Medicine residency and career. Also available to non-EMRA members from the ACEP bookstore at www.acep.org.

Narang AS, Ey J: The emerging role of pediatric hospitalists. *Clin Pediatrics.* 2003;42(4):295-7. As the use of Hospitalists increases, it makes sense that some will specialize in caring for children. This article explores the implications of this for both Hospitalists and Pediatricians.

Pawluch D: *The New Pediatrics: A Profession In Transition.* Hawthorne, NY: Aldine de Gruyter, 1996. Written by a sociologist, this book highlights the negative aspects of Pediatric practice, especially the "dissatisfied Pediatrician syndrome." Since it is always best to know the negatives about a specialty as well as the positives, it is definitely worth a look for those contemplating Pediatrics.

Richardson JD: Workforce and lifestyle issues in general surgery training and practice. *Arch Surg.* 2002;137(5):515-20. An experienced surgical educator speaks frankly about the problems with current surgical education—and about possible solutions. Read this to learn the frustrations you will face.

Sataloff RT: Education in laryngology: rising to old challenges. [Review] [35 refs] *Ann Otol Rhinol Laryngol.* 1999;108(11 Pt. 1):1046-52. A history of the specialty and the basic components of a good residency program.

Senf JH, Campos-Outcalt D, Watkins AJ, Bastacky S, Killian C: A systematic analysis of how medical school characteristics relate to graduates' choices of primary care specialties. *Acad Med.* 1997;72(6):524-33. What makes you think you want to enter a primary care specialty? Is it one of the factors described in this excellent study?

Silberstein EB: Trends in American nuclear medicine training: past, present, and future. *Seminars in Nuclear Medicine.* 2000;30(3):209-13. This is how Nuclear Medicine envisions its future.

Zussman R: *Intensive Care: Medical Ethics and the Medical Profession.* Chicago, IL: Univ. of Chicago Press, 1992. An excellent book for anyone considering a specialty in which they may spend time in the ICU. This well-written book gives the real scoop on what happens and what practitioners do there, rather than what they want you to think they do.★

Selecting a Specialty

Anderson MR, Jewett EA, Cull WL, Jardine DS, Outwater KM, Mulvey HJ: Practice of pediatric critical care medicine: results of the Future of Pediatric Education II survey of sections project. *Pediatr Crit Care Med.* 2003;4(4):412-7. The study summarizes the demographics and practice patterns of current Pediatric Critical Care physicians, and identifies issues that may affect future practice. Bottom line: PCCM physicians were increasingly women and working for more than 65 hr./week. Of note, 34% of respondents planned on leaving the field of critical care before retiring from medicine completely.

Azizzadeh A, et al.: Factors influencing career choice among medical students interested in surgery. *Curr Surg.* 2003;60(2):210-3. They concluded that prestige and career opportunities are more important to students seeking surgical residencies. Lifestyle and work hours during residency and perceived quality of patient/physician relationships were deterrents.

Burack JH, Irby DM, Carline JD, et al.: A study of medical students' specialty-choice pathways: trying on possible selves. *Acad Med.* 1997;72(6):534-41. Are you thinking about a primary care specialty? This paper describes factors that previous students considered important when either entering or rejecting a primary care career. No doubt you will recognize yourself in some of these vignettes.

Cochran A, Melby S, Neumayer LA: An Internet-based survey of factors influencing medical student selection of a general surgery career. *Am J Surg.* 2005;189(6):742-6. Interestingly, they concluded that medical students who choose surgical careers are not deterred by a negative perception of the lifestyle and workload, but are, instead, influenced by "personality fit" and mentors.

Cull WL, Yudowsky BK, Shipman SA, Pan RJ, American Academy of Pediatrics: Pediatric training and job market trends: results from the AAP's third-year resident survey, 1997-2002. *Pediatrics.* 2003;112(4):787-92. Comparison of annual surveys of graduating pediatrics residents demonstrating that there has been an increase in the number of female and U.S. underrepresented minority Pediatricians, and a decline in IMGs entering the field. Residents' educational debt has increased substantially, while starting salaries for Pediatricians have decreased.

Dorsey ER, Jarjoura D, Rutecki GW. Influence of controllable lifestyle on recent trends in specialty choice by U.S. medical students. *JAMA.* 2003;290(9):1173-8. Concludes that lifestyle plays a more important role in specialty selection than in the past. Today's medical students want to be in control of their time.

Ducatman BS: Be careful what you wish for. *JAMA*. 1997;278(14):1130. An insightful and beautifully written one-page piece on a student's experience with the consummate rural Family Practitioner—and reasons to rethink what seem to be idyllic career choices.

Hoff TH, Whitcomb WF, Williams K, Nelson JR, Cheesman RA: Characteristics and work experiences of hospitalists in the United States. *Arch Intern Med*. 2001;161:851-8. Who are Hospitalists and what are they actually doing? Do they enjoy their work and how "burnt out" do they feel? This survey of Hospitalists answers those questions.

Huddle TS, Centor R, Heudebert GR: American internal medicine in the 21st century: can an Oslerian generalism survive? *J Gen Int Med*. 2003;18(9):764-7. American Internal Medicine suffers an identity crisis, as managed care threatens what remains of the Oslerian ideal. Internists will have to adapt to continue to practice using the consultant-generalist model.

Kassebaum DG, Szenas PL: Medical students' career indecision and specialty rejection: roads not taken. *Acad Med*. 1995;70(10):937-43. So you think you know what specialty you want to enter? Think again—as many of your cohorts did. This article reviews the alternative decisions students made about their career choices as they proceeded through medical school.

Ko CY, Escarce JJ, Baker l, Klein D, Guarino C: Predictors for medical students entering a general surgery residency: national survey results. *Surgery*. 2004;136(3):567-72. This national survey of fourth-year medical students identifies factors related to the basic surgery clerkship that are associated with the decision to enter a General Surgery residency.

Leigh JP, Kravitz RL, Schembri M, Samuels SJ, Mobley S: Physician career satisfaction across specialties. *Arch Intern Med*. 2002;162(14):1577-84. The authors surveyed 12,474 physicians in 33 specialties. As might be expected, there were many variables, including age, geographic location, and income. However, they found no differences between men and women.

McAlearney AS: Hospitalists and family physicians: understanding opportunities and risks. *J Fam Pract*. 2004:53(6):473-81. As Hospitalists take on more in-patient care, what impact will this have on family practitioners' careers?

Newton DA, Grayson MS, Thompson LF: The variable influence of lifestyle and income on medical students' career specialty choices: data from two U.S. medical schools, 1998-2004. *Acad Med*. 2005:80(9):809-14. Lifestyle and income have become more important to medical students in their career choice, and the relative importance of these factors varies considerably between specialties. This study suggests that previous efforts to classify careers as those with controllable and uncontrollable lifestyles may mask important complexities.

Pathway Evaluation Program for Medical Professionals. 2003. As of early 2006, this tool is administered by Duke University School of Medicine in partnership with GlaxoSmith Kline. Once an on-site course offered at most medical schools, the *Pathway* program is now available online at http://medweb.usc.edu/pathways/intro.htm. This program contains some of the most complete descriptions of the major medical specialties and major subspecialties. It includes a background of each specialty, profiles of individual practitioners, and anecdotes about why individuals entered the field. It then details and rates, on a linear scale, how important 17 different aspects of practice are to the physicians in that specialty. These factors include continuity of care, schedule, diversity, autonomy, manual activities, security, and income. It also contains an exercise by which you can rate your interests against the typical profile in each specialty.

Tamaskar P, McGinnis RA: Declining student interest in psychiatry. *JAMA*. 2002;287(14): 1859. So you want to be a Psychiatrist? This very short piece does a good job of describing why students are avoiding the field, and discusses the many misconceptions that lead students to make this decision.

Taylor AD: *How to Choose a Medical Specialty.* 4th ed. Philadelphia, PA: W.B. Saunders, 2003. A correlate to the Pathway Evaluation Program and Chapter 4 in this book, Taylor's book provides an additional way to see if you are heading toward the right specialty.

Wachter RM: The hospitalist movement 5 years later. *JAMA.* 2002;287(4):487-94. An overview of studies on Hospitalists' efficiency, effectiveness, and how their care affects patients. Overall, a good "report card."

Weaver SP, Mills TL, Passmore C: Job satisfaction of family practice residents. *Fam Med.* 2001;33(9):678-82. This survey of Family Practice residents demonstrates that they had relatively high job satisfaction, which increased each year. Those in community-based programs were more satisfied than those in university-based programs.

Wetterneck TB, Linzer M, McMrray JE, et al.: Worklife and satisfaction of general internists. *Arch Intern Med.* 2002;162:649-56. A large survey sample showed that General Internists' role of managing patients with complex medical problems is associated with lower levels of job satisfaction than for Internal Medicine subspecialists and Family Practitioners.

The USMLE, Other Exams, and Licensure

American Medical Association: *State Medical Licensure Requirements and Statistics.* Chicago, IL: AMA, published annually. This is where to find the nitty gritty details about state licensure, both for U.S. (M.D., D.O.) and international medical graduates. It contains all the basic information about licensure requirements in every state and territory of the United States, including the requirements for taking the USMLE and COMLEX and additional requirements and fees. All the permutations and combinations of licensing are included in easy-to-read charts. It has contact information for individual state boards for additional information and updates, as well as hard-to-get information on IMG licensure requirements. It also lists the special licensing requirements for residents and requirements for clinical clerkships by IMGs.

Federation of State Medical Boards of the U.S., Inc: *Exchange–Section 1: USMLE and M.D. Licensing Requirements.* Dallas, TX: FSMB, published biannually. Contains the USMLE Step 3 eligibility requirements and administrative rules. Also has the requirements for initial licensure, licensure by endorsement, reregistration of one's license, licenses for postgraduate education, and special licenses.

—*Exchange–Section 2: USMLE and D.O. Licensing Requirements.* Dallas, TX: FSMB, published biannually. Contains the USMLE Step 3 eligibility requirements and administrative rules. Also lists the requirements for initial licensure, for licensure by endorsement, for reregistration of one's license, for licenses for postgraduate education, and for special licenses.

—*Exchange–Section 3: Licensing Boards, Structure and Disciplinary Functions.* Dallas, TX: FSMB, published biannually. Contains the basic structure and operation of each state medical board, their review and disciplinary functions, and contacts for both of these functions.

Flauta V: *USMLE Step 2CS for the IMG.* Infinity, 2005. This book contains several mock exams, and useful tips, including lists of questions to ask by body system and flashcard study materials. It also has a chart of the 35 most commonly seen cases, and a list of IMG-friendly hospitals to check out.

Modi RG, Shah NA: *COMLEX Review: Clinical Anatomy and Osteopathic Manipulative Medicine.* New York: Blackwell, 2005. This exam review was written by two fourth-year students at New York College of Osteopathic Medicine. It correlates anatomy with OMM and helps explain the more difficult concepts. A chart specifies which chapter to read for each exam.

National Board of Medical Examiners and The Federation of State Medical Boards of the U.S., Inc: *USMLE Step 1* (or *2CK, 2CS, 3*) *Bulletin of Information.* Published annually. These invaluable booklets list the current dates and eligibility requirements for the exams, as well as certification and registration procedures. Most important, there are subject/content outlines for each Step of the exam. The booklets, as well as other useful information, can be downloaded from www.usmle.org.

National Board of Osteopathic Medical Examiners: *[Annual] Bulletin of Information.* Contains all the necessary instructions to apply for, take, and interpret the COMLEX. Download from www.nbome.org.

Reteguiz J: *Mastering the USMLE Step 2 CS.* 3rd ed. New York: McGraw-Hill Medical, 2004. This interactive workbook prepares medical students for the Clinical Skills exam by simulating patient cases likely to be tested. In addition, it helps them to develop a checklist to better interact with SPs. It may also improve their performance on the OSCE.

Savarese RG, Fuoco GS, Bersen DG, Kaprow M: *OMT Review.* 3rd ed. Ft. Lauderdale, FL: Robert F. Savarese, 2003. The standard text for reviewing OMT material for both Levels 1 and 2 of the COMLEX. Available from the American Academy of Osteopathy at www.academyofosteopathy.org/.

The Paperwork

Hunt DD, MacLaren C, Scott C, et al.: A follow-up study of the characteristics of dean's letters. *Acad Med.* 2001;76(7):727-33. An excellent review of what is contained in Dean's letters. It should give you a good idea of what information might be included in a Dean's letter but that is not in yours, or what information you may want to suggest not be included in your own letter.

Taylor CA, Weinstein L, Mayhew HE: The process of resident selection: a view from the residency director's desk. *Obstet Gynecol.* 1995;85(2):299-303. This article contains the results of a survey of Family Practice and Obstetrics & Gynecology residency directors. The results seem to reflect the decision-making processes used by residency directors in Internal Medicine, Pediatrics, Psychiatry, and the surgical specialties.

Tysinger JW: *Résumés and Personal Statements for Health Professionals.* 2nd ed. Tucson, AZ: Galen Press, Ltd., 1998. A classic, this book guides you through the arduous process of describing your accomplishments in the best possible way to develop unique résumés and personal statements that reflect who you really are. Describes how to develop a personal inventory, and then how to use the inventory items to write a professional-looking document that will impress residency directors. Written by an educator with years of experience, it includes lots of examples to help you. Also discusses cover and thank-you letters. A must for all applicants.★

Venolia J: *Write Right! A Desktop Digest of Punctuation, Grammar, and Style.* 4th ed. Berkeley, CA: Ten Speed Press, 2001. A powerful and easy-to-understand pocket guide on how to avoid making mistakes on résumés, personal statements, and other important documents.★

Selecting a Residency Program

American Academy of Family Physicians: *Directory of Family Practice Residency Programs.* Kansas City, MO: AAFP, updated annually. (www.aafp.org/residencies). This substantial online directory (also available in printed form) lists all the currently approved Family Practice residencies. Information includes: How many positions exist at each level of training and what type of graduate (U.S. or IMG) is filling them; salary; benefits; whether moonlighting is permitted; night-call frequency; number of hospitals and Family Practice centers in the program; faculty to resident ratio; number and type (M.D., Ph.D., etc.) of full-time-equivalent faculty/staff; time spent working in a Family Practice center; number of Family Practice conferences; level of resident responsibility by postgraduate year; and resident research opportunities.

American College of Physicians/American Society of Internal Medicine. (www.acponline .org/residency). Updated annually, this is an online listing of programs by state, the track and combination residencies offered, and hospital type. Each program's individual pass rates on the Board examinations are also accessed through this site.

American College of Preventive Medicine: *Resident Directory At-a-Glance.* (www.acpm.org/ ataglance.htm). A detailed listing of the programs in all of the subspecialties. It often has information that *FREIDA* does not provide.

American Medical Association: *Fellowship and Residency Electronic Interactive Database Access (known simply as "FREIDA").* For most residency applicants, this system has replaced the "Green Book." Hundreds of items of information are available online about training programs and their parent institutions. However, the information that the programs provide is not validated by any outside source; always verify that the information is correct. Applicants can access the system at www.ama-assn.org/go/freida.**

——*Graduate Medical Education Directory.* Chicago, IL: AMA, published annually. Known as the "Green Book," the Directory includes information on nearly all ACGME-accredited and combined specialty programs. Also included are institutional and program requirements for all approved M.D. specialties/subspecialties and the requirements for medical specialty board certification. It is also available on CD-ROM. The *FREIDA* system has mostly replaced this book.**

——*GMED Companion: An Insider's Guide to Selecting a Residency Program.* Chicago, IL: AMA, published annually. Contains a list of those residency programs that have negotiable start dates, that offer part-time/shared-schedule residency positions, and that have on-site childcare, as well as other valuable information. Much of this information is also available on *FREIDA.*

American Medical Student Association: *AMSA's Student Guide to the Appraisal and Selection of House Staff Training Programs.* Reston, VA: AMSA, 1997. This short text describes many aspects of the residency selection process. It has a few questions you may want to ask during the residency interview.

American Osteopathic Association: *Yearbook and Directory.* (www.DO-online.org/Publications/ yearbooktoc.htm). Everything that an Osteopathic medical student, resident, or practitioner needs to know about the field is on this site. Under the section "Postdoctoral Education," it has a current listing of all AOA-approved internships and residency programs, the policies and procedures for entering the Intern/Resident Registration Program (Match), and the requirements for getting the AOA to approve non-AOA training.

American Urological Association: *Accredited Urology Training Programs.* This online directory (www.auanet.org/residents/) of the accredited Urology residencies can be searched by state or printed intact. While the listings duplicate much of the information in *FREIDA*, they do state how many applicants each program interviews, whether the two-year "pre-Urology" training must be at the same institution as the residency, and how much time is devoted solely to research. It also includes each program's unique AUA Match Number.

Association for Hospital Medical Education: *Transitional Year Program Directory* (formerly called the "Purple Book"). This site (www.ahme.org/publications/transitional.html) lists most of the available transitional programs, including contact information, months of required and elective rotations, presence of other training programs, type of individuals who match with the program, difficulty of getting a slot, night call frequency, and opportunities for a PGY-2 year at the same institution. Despite *FREIDA*, the site remains an excellent source of hard-to-come-by information.**

Association of Academic Physiatrists: *Directory of PM&R Residency Training Programs.* (www.physiatry.org/education/index.html). This online directory allows applicants to search for programs by state and by how many slots are open. It also notes whether there are available positions at any level of the residency. It does not, however, provide more information than is available on *FREIDA.*

Council of Teaching Hospitals and Health Systems Membership Directory. Available on the AAMC's website (www.aamc.org/teachinghospitals.htm), this is a listing of all teaching hospitals—alphabetically and by geographic location. Some hospitals have links from here to their websites. Even if they don't contain a lot of solid information, these sites can give you a sense of the hospital's milieu.

Raff MJ, Schwartz IS: An applicant's evaluation of a medical house-officership. *NEJM.* 1974; 291(12):601-5. A very extensive list of questions that can be used to supplement the "Must/Want" Analysis list. Although the paper is more than 30 years old, virtually all the questions are still pertinent.

Society of Academic Emergency Medicine: *Catalog of Emergency Medicine Residencies.* Continually updated information that is available only online (http://saem.org/rescat/contents.htm). More detailed than the *FREIDA* listings, it categorizes programs by state, by length, if M.D. or D.O., and whether they are a PGY 1-4, PGY 2-4, or PGY 1-3 program.

Society of Critical Care Medicine: *Fellowship Programs.* A list of available Critical Care fellowships in Internal Medicine, Pediatrics, Anesthesiology, and Surgery, including the address, the phone/fax numbers, and the fellowship director. See the website (www.sccm.org/professional_resources/fellowship-programs/index.asp) for other resources.

Society of General Internal Medicine: *SGIM Directory of Primary Care Internal Medicine Residency Programs.* (www.sgim.org/residencydir.cfm). A list of Internal Medicine residency programs with primary care orientation. The *Directory of General Internal Medicine Fellowship Programs* can also be accessed from this page. They can both be searched by geographic region and contain information similar to that found in *FREIDA.*

Yorke RF: Informed evaluation of pathology residency programs—a guide for pathology resident candidates. *Arch Pathol Lab Med.* 2000;124(6):853-8. What those seeking a Pathology residency should be looking for in a program, and what they should expect from their training.

Yudkowsky R, Elliott R, Schwartz A: Two perspectives on the indicators of quality in psychiatry residencies: program directors' and residents'. *Acad Med.* 2002;77(1):57-64. What makes a "good" Psychiatry residency? Program directors and residents have different views, and both are included in this paper.

International Medical Graduates

Educational Commission for Foreign Medical Graduates' website (www.ecfmg.org) provides all the necessary information about taking the USMLE; getting ECFMG-sponsored visas; submitting applications through ERAS using the ECFMG as your "Dean's office"; and getting credentials verified. It also provides a link to the FAIMER *International Medical Education Directory* (your school must be listed in this directory for you to obtain an ECFMG Certificate).

Foundation for Advancement of International Medical Education and Research (FAIMER): *International Medical Education Directory.* A searchable online (www.ecfmg.org/faimer/) list of international medical schools approved by the ECFMG. Graduates of the listed schools are allowed to obtain ECFMG Certification. If your school is not listed, you cannot attempt to practice in the United States.

Riley JD, Hannis M, Rice KG: Are international medical graduates a factor in residency program selection? A survey of fourth-year medical students. *Acad Med.* 1996;71(4):381-6. Does the presence of IMGs dissuade U.S. graduates from applying to certain residency programs? This study suggests that it does.

Vora AA: *The Successful IMG: Obtaining a US Residency.* Malden, Mass.: Blackwell, 2005. Information on preparing for the exams and getting a visa.

Women in Medicine

Association of American Medical Colleges: *Women in Medicine*. A website (www.aamc.org/members/wim/start.htm) with a bibliography; lists of meetings; a way to sign onto WIMSERV, an online discussion group; and contact information for the Association's specialists on women in medicine.

Beagan B: Micro inequities and everyday inequalities: "Race," gender, sexuality and class in medical school. *Can J Sociol*. 2001;26(4):583-610. It's more than just the overt discrimination that medical students and residents encounter, but also the "everyday practices of inclusion and exclusion that cumulatively convey messages about who does and who does not belong." Worth reading.

Brogan DJ, Frank E, Elon L, Sivanesan SP, O'Hanlan KA: Harassment of lesbians as medical students and physicians. *JAMA*. 1999;282(13):1290, 1292. The Women Physicians' Health Study of non-resident women physicians showed that lesbians are more likely than their heterosexual counterparts to experience sexual-orientation-based harassment during residency and practice.

Conley FK: *Walking Out on the Boys*. New York: Farrar, Strauss & Giroux, 1998. A very interesting book written by a female tenured neurosurgery professor at Stanford University School of Medicine who resigned her position to protest sexual harassment and gender-based discrimination. She has since regained her position and continues to be active in the movement against gender-based discrimination.

Frank E, McMurray JE, Linzer M, Elon L: Career satisfaction of U.S. women physicians. *Arch Intern Med*. 1999;159(13):1417-26. Are women who entered medicine pleased with their decisions? What do they like about medicine and what do they want changed?

Gautam M: Women in medicine: stresses and solutions. *West J Med*. 2001;174(1):37-41. Contains a list of specific practical steps that women physicians can use to decrease the stress in their professional and personal lives.

Langelan MJ: *Back Off! How to Confront and Stop Sexual Harassment and Harassers*. New York: Simon & Schuster, 1993. The title pretty much describes it, and the book delivers this message.*

McFarland FK, Smith AJ, West CA, Rhoades DR: African-American female physicians in South Carolina: role models and career satisfaction. *Southern Med J*. 2000;93(10):982-5. Why do women go into medicine? For the same altruism and role modeling that influences most other medical students. Their frustrations stem from the same sources as those of their colleagues.

McMurray JE, Linzer M, Konrad TR, Douglas J, Shugerman R, Nelson K: The work lives of women physicians—results from the physician work life study. The SGIM Career Satisfaction Study Group. *J Gen Intern Med*. 2000;15(6):372-80. This is what is really happening in the lives of women physicians.

Oancia T, Bohm C, Carry T, Cujec B, Johnson D: The influence of gender and specialty on reporting of abusive and discriminatory behavior by medical students, residents and physician teachers. *Med Educ*. 2000;34(4):250-6. Not surprisingly, this study found that female surgical residents adopt the prevailing culture during training, but after residency revert to behavior and attitudes more akin to their non-surgical peers. Good insights into how women "go along to get along" in surgical residencies.

Reed V, Buddeberg-Fischer B: Career obstacles for women in medicine: an overview. *Med Educ*. 2001;35(2):139-47. An international review of women in medicine. A good look at women's access to medical school, specialties they enter, promotion rates, frequency of part-time work, and salary inequities. It also reviews the obstacles women physicians face and what can be or is being done about them.

Sobecks NW, Justice AC, Hinze S, et al.: When doctors marry doctors: a survey exploring the professional and family lives of young physicians. *Ann Intern Med.* 1999;130(4)Pt.1:312-9. A useful survey of physician-physician marriages and their effect on the participants' professional and personal lives.

Wiebe C: From here to maternity. *New Phys.* 1995;44:40-4. A good description of some problems pregnant women physicians faced during medical school and residency. They also have some helpful suggestions.

Parenting

American Academy of Pediatrics: *Children's Health/Child Care.* An excellent web-based guide to childcare services, it gives detailed instructions on the different types of childcare services, what to look for, what questions to ask, and the different childcare needs of children as they grow and when they are ill. Available on the Medem website at www.medem.com/MedLB/bufferpage_aap.cfm. Click on "Child Care" or any of the other interesting topics about children and parenting.

Cujec B, Oancia T, Bohm C, et al.: Career and parenting satisfaction among medical students, residents and physician teachers at a Canadian medical school. *Can Med Assoc J.* 2000;162(5):637-40. Should you have children? While the more common question is "when?" this study suggests that medical students and residents are much more displeased with the time they have to spend parenting than are their colleagues in practice.

National Network for Child Care. The Learn section of their website (www.nncc.org) provides many articles dealing with childcare. Click on Childcare Evaluation and Assessment, then Parental Assessment to access a checklist of things to consider when selecting childcare. There is also a listing of childcare information (including regulations and licensing) by state at Tools/Resources. Even though the articles are on the Web, most of their authors are well known or the articles are on reputable academic sites.

Potee RA, Gerber AJ, Ickovics JR: Medicine and motherhood: shifting trends among female physicians from 1922 to 1999. *Acad Med.* 1999;74(8):911-19. How have things changed over the years? Is it better, or only different?

Disabled Students

Center for Disability Issues and the Health Professions. The website (www.westernu.edu/cdihp/home.xml) at the Western University of the Health Sciences has excellent links to up-to-date information for disabled medical students and residents.

Essex-Sorlie D: The Americans with Disabilities Act: I. History, summary, and key components. *Acad Med.* 1994;69(7):519-24. An excellent overview of the Americans with Disabilities Act and how it relates to medical schools. While it does not address questions of residency application directly, it gives enough information from which to extrapolate. Clear, concise, and not filled with legal mumbo-jumbo.

Helms LB, Helms CM: Medical education and disability discrimination: the law and future implications. *Acad Med.* 1994;69(7):535-43. A bit more about the legal background, relevant court findings, and possible directions of Americans with Disabilities Act implementation.

Takakuwa KM, Ernst AA, Weiss SJ: Residents with disabilities: a national survey of directors of emergency medicine residency programs. *Southern Med J.* 2002;95(4):436-40. The most recent study of the prevalence of known and suspected disabilities among physicians in residency, and the willingness of residency directors to provide resources to assist these residents.

Special Situations

Baldwin DC Jr, Daugherty SR, Rowley BD: Racial and ethnic discrimination during residency: results of a national survey. *Acad Med.* 1994;69(10Supp):S19-21. How commonly does racial and ethnic discrimination appear during residency training? Although 12 years old, this is one of the few papers that helps to assess the problem.

Burke BP, White JC: Wellbeing of gay, lesbian and bisexual doctors. *West J Med.* 2001;174(1): 59-62. Reviews the problems faced by these physician groups and discusses the questions they need to ask themselves about how their lifestyle may affect their choice of career and the discrimination they may face. Worth a read before "coming out."

Carling PC, Hayward K, Coakley EH, Wolf AMD: Part-time residency training in internal medicine: analysis of a ten-year experience. *Acad Med.* 1999;74(3):282-4. If you are considering doing a part-time/shared-schedule residency, see what others have experienced.

Lesko S: Women in medicine: challenges in part-time residencies. *Am Fam Physician.* 2002; 65(1):31. This very personal letter discusses the difficulties of actually finding a part-time residency position and advocates for them to be made available.

Mullan F: The journey back: a physician retrains. *JAMA.* 1997;278(4):281-3. An excellent description of an experienced (older) physician-administrator retraining to enter clinical practice.

Osteopathic Medicine

American Osteopathic Association: *Yearbook and Directory of Members.* This online (www.DO-online.org) compendium contains virtually everything anyone needs to know about Osteopathic medicine, including current information on Osteopathic residency programs, medical schools, and state-by-state and international licensure requirements.

—Division of Postdoctoral Training: Osteopathic graduate medical education. *J Amer Osteopath Assoc.* (Usually the November issue.) This annual article gives an overview of the number of available AOA-approved and funded residency positions, the number of graduates, how many D.O.s are taking ACGME-approved training, and new rules for specialty certification.

Cummings M, Lemon M: Combined allopathic and osteopathic GME programs: a good thing, but will they continue? *Acad Med.* 1999;74(9):948-50. Some residency programs are combined. Will they last? One perspective on this ever more common arrangement.

Gevitz N: *The D.O.'s—Osteopathic Medicine in America.* Baltimore, MD: Johns Hopkins Univ. Press, 2004. An entertaining and enlightening look at the development of Osteopathic medicine in the United States. It is required reading for all D.O.s and anyone else interested in Osteopathy.★

Lesho EP: An overview of osteopathic medicine. *Arch Fam Med.* 1999;8(6):477-84. As this article demonstrates, Osteopathic medicine is thriving. It reviews the history of the profession, its successes and problems, and its phenomenal growth. It also presents a large survey of patients. The biggest problem is that the public, and maybe your mother, still asks the question, "What is an Osteopath?"

Rogers FJ, D'Alonzo GE Jr, Glover JC, et al.: Proposed tenets of osteopathic medicine and principles for patient care. *J Amer Osteopath Assoc.* 2002;102(2):63-5. This is the updated philosophy of Osteopathic medicine.

Selecting Candidates and Interviewing

Biegeleisen JI: *Make Your Job Interview a Success.* 4th ed. New York: Prentice-Hall, 1994. The chapter, "63 Guaranteed Ways to Muff a Job Interview," is enlightening reading. It is also funny. Well worth the time, it may prevent you from making a serious *faux pas.*★

Edmond MB, Deschenes JL, Eckler M, Wenzel RP: Racial bias in using USMLE Step 1 scores to grant internal medicine residency interviews. *Acad Med.* 2001;76(12):1253-6. This study shows that when USMLE Step 1 scores are used as a criterion for residency interviews, Black students will suffer disproportionately.

Edmond M, Roberson M, Hasan N: The dishonest dean's letter: an analysis of 532 dean's letters from 99 U.S. medical schools. *Acad Med.* 1999;74(9):1033-5. You may be paranoid about how your Dean's letter will be written, but this study shows that many of these missives just seem to gloss over adverse information such as failing grades, repeating school years, and very low USMLE scores.

Gilbart MK, Cusimano MD, Regehr G: Evaluating surgical resident selection procedures. *Am J Surg.* 2001;181(3):221-5. This research paper gives some inside information on what Orthopedic Surgery residencies seek in candidates: work ethic, interpersonal qualities, orthopedic experience, and enthusiasm.

Girzadas DV, Harwood RC, Delis SN, et al.: Emergency medicine standardized letter of recommendation: predictors of guaranteed match. *Acad Emerg Med.* 2001;8(6):648-53. This study confirms the factors that go into a strong recommendation letter. You may want to forward a copy of the article to your letter writers.

Keim SM, Rein JA, Chisholm C, et al.: A standardized letter of recommendation for residency application. *Acad Emerg Med.* 1999;6(11):1141-6. Describes the standardized recommendation letter used by emergency medicine programs. This letter probably will show up, in some form, in other specialties.

Molidor JB, Campe JL: It's show time: mastering the art of being interviewed. *The Advisor.* 1997;18:21-6. An excellent mnemonic to use when faced with a stressful interview.

Molidor JB, Duff JL: Whatcha gonna do when they come for you? Preparing your responses for your interview. *The Advisor.* 1998;18:45-9. Another in this author's series on how to approach the high-stakes interview.

Wagoner NE, Suriano JR: Program directors' response to a survey on variables used to select residents in a time of change. *Acad Med.* 1999;74(1):51-8. What are program directors in various specialties actually searching for in residency applicants? This article gives some clues.

The Match

Association of American Medical Colleges: *Academic Medicine.* This journal is available at all medical school libraries or through your Dean's office. The June or July issue each year contains the results of the prior year's NRMP Match.

Englander R, Carraccio C, Zalneraitis E, Sarkin R, Morgenstern B: Guiding medical students through the match: perspectives from recent graduates. *Pediatrics.* 2003;112(3 Pt 1):502-5. A survey of PGY-1 Pediatrics residents asking about their satisfaction with their pre-match counseling and match results. Residents were very satisfied with where they matched, and less satisfied with the advice received. The top three resources were *FREIDA*, their adviser, and resident-to-student counseling. Only the *Green Book* was rated unhelpful.

National Resident Matching Program: *Results and Data [Annual] Match.* Washington, DC: NRMP. Known as the "Results Book," this details the outcome of the annual NRMP Match by specialty and institution. You can see a copy by asking your Dean of Students. Much of this information used to be in the *NRMP Directory*, and was of enormous interest to applicants. Unfortunately, it is now a little more difficult to come by, but it is worth seeking out.

Medical Practice

American Hospital Association: *AHA Guide.* Chicago: AHA, published annually. Contains a detailed listing and description of over 7000 teaching hospitals in the United States.

American Medical Association: *Physician Characteristics and Distribution in the United States.* Chicago: AMA, published annually. This book contains an extensive breakdown of the characteristics of physicians practicing in each specialty in the United States. It goes into the specifics of who, what, and where the physicians are. The descriptions are broken down both by specialty and by county.

—*Leaving the Bedside–The Search for a Nonclinical Medical Career.* Chicago, IL: AMA, 1996. It's no secret that many physicians, after some time in practice, find that they prefer not to be at the bedside, but rather in the lab, boardroom, lecture hall, or some other venue. This book explores some of the more common nonclinical options open to physicians (there are many more) and suggests ways to pursue them.

—*State Medical Licensure Requirements and Statistics.* Chicago, IL: AMA, published annually. This book presents in-depth information and statistics, by state, on medical licensure requirements. This is a particularly helpful book for international medical graduates and those seeking licenses in more than one state.

Association of American Medical Colleges: *AAMC Data Book.* Washington, DC: AAMC, published annually. It contains statistical information related to medical schools and teaching hospitals. (Available at all medical school libraries.)

Council on Graduate Medical Education: *Financing Graduate Medical Education in a Changing Health Care Environment.* Washington, DC: Health Resources & Services Administration, U.S. Dept. of Health & Human Services, 2000. This comprehensive document reviews the changing health care environment. It also specifically analyzes what needs to be done to improve funding for graduate medical education. Available on their website (www.cogme.gov/rpt15.htm).

Resident and Staff Physician: "Board Review Issue." (Annually in May.) Details the current utilization and rules for the various licensing examinations, as well as the licensing requirements (M.D. and D.O.) for each state. It also usually includes information on specialty societies and the current Board requirements in most specialties.

Villanueva AM, Kaye D, Abdelhak SS, Morahan PS: Comparing selection criteria of residency directors and physicians' employers. *Acad Med.* 1995;70(4):261-71. This article lays out what residency directors in Pediatrics, Surgery, Family Practice, and Internal Medicine seek in residency candidates' applications. It then compares the personal qualities they desire in residents with the qualities that academic medical centers, private practices, managed care organizations, hospitals, and other health care systems look for when hiring new physicians.

Zuger, A: Dissatisfaction with medicine. *NEJM.* 2004;350(1):69-75. This report examines the reasons for, and possible solutions to, the perception that physicians are unhappy with the practice of medicine. Good news: Most physicians still take satisfaction in their work. As the practice of medicine continues to evolve, the key may be to encourage students to have more accurate expectations of what a medical career entails.

General Information

American Medical Student Association: *The New Physician.* Published monthly and free with membership in AMSA. Has frequent articles about medical specialties, interviewing, the Match, international medical graduates, medical practice, and other topics of vital interest to medical students.

Medical Organizations' Contact Information & Websites

American Academy of Family Physicians (AAFP), P.O. Box 1120, Shawnee Mission, KS 662207-1210; (800) 274-2237 or (913) 906-6000; www.aafp.org.

American Hospital Association (AHA), 1 N. Franklin, Chicago, IL 60606-3421; (312) 422-3000; fax: (312) 422-4796; www.aha.org.

American Medical Association (AMA), 515 N. State Street, Chicago, IL 60610; (312) 464-5000 or 800-621-8335; fax: (312) 464-4184; www.ama-assn.org.

• AMA Medical Student Section, www.ama-assn.org/ama/pub/category/14.html.

• *FREIDA*, www.ama-assn.org/ama/pub/category/2997.html.

American Medical Student Association (AMSA), 1902 Association Drive, Reston, VA 20191; 800-767-2266 or (703) 620-6600; fax: (703) 620-5873; e-mail: amsa@amsa.org; www.amsa.org.

American Medical Women's Association (AMWA), 801 N. Fairfax Street, Suite 400, Alexandria, VA 22314; (703) 838-0500; fax: (703) 549-3864; e-mail: info@amwa-doc.org; www.amwa-doc.org.

American Osteopathic Association (AOA), 142 E. Ontario Street, Chicago, IL 60611; 800-621-1773 or (312) 202-8000; http://DO-online.org.

• Opportunities, http://opportunities.aoa-net.org/index.htm

American Urological Association Residency Matching Program, 1000 Corporate Blvd., Linthicum, MD 21090; (866) 746-4282, ext. 3919; fax: (410) 689-3939; e-mail: resmatch@auanet.org; www.auanet.org/residents/resmatch.cfm.

Association of American Medical Colleges (AAMC), 2450 N Street NW, Washington, DC 20037-1127; (202) 828- 0400; fax: (202) 828-1125; e-mail: amcas@aamc.org; www.aamc.org.

• Careers in Medicine, www.aamc.org/students/cim/

• Electronic Residency Application Services (ERAS), www.aamc.org/audienceeras.htm.

    – Send ERAS questions for ECFMG applicants to eras-support@ecfmg.org.

    – Send technical questions to the MyERAS Help Section at myeras@aamc.org.

• FindAResident, www.aamc.org/students/findaresident/start.htm.

Canadian Resident Matching Service (CaRMS), 2283 St. Laurent Blvd., Suite 110, Ottawa, Ontario K1G-5A2, Canada; (613) 237-0075; fax: (613) 563-2860; www.carms.ca.

Council of Medical Specialty Societies (CMSS), 51 Sherwood Terrace, Suite M, Lake Bluff, IL 60044-2232; (847) 295-3456; fax: (847) 295-3759; e-mail: mailbox@cmss.org; www.cmss.org.

Council of Teaching Hospitals (COTH), Association of American Medical Colleges, 2450 N Street NW, Washington, DC 20037-1127; (202) 828-0541; fax: (202) 828-1125; www.aamc.org/members/coth/.
- Most recent survey of housestaff stipends and benefits, www.aamc.org/data/housestaff/.

Educational Commission for Foreign Medical Graduates (ECFMG) www.ecfmg.org.
- ERAS/ECFMG, 3624 Market Street, Philadelphia, PA 19104-2685 USA; (215) 386-5900; fax: (215) 222-5641; eras-support@ecfmg.org; www.ecfmg.org/eras.
  - For completed documents by mail: ECFMG-ERAS Program, P.O. Box 11746, Philadelphia, PA 19101-0746 USA.
  - For completed documents by courier delivery: ERAS, ECFMG, 3624 Market Street, Philadelphia, PA 19104-2685 USA.
- ECFMG/USMLE Information, 3624 Market Street, Philadelphia, PA 19104-2685; (215) 386-5900; fax: (215) 387-9963; www.ecfmg.org.

Federation of State Medical Boards of the U.S., Inc. (FSMB), P.O. Box 619850, Dallas, TX 75261-9850; (817) 868-4000; fax: (817) 868-4099; www.fsmb.org.
- For USMLE Step 3 questions, e-mail: usmle@fsmb.org.
- For questions regarding test accommodations for USMLE examinees with disabilities, e-mail: exam@fsmb.org.
- For the Federation Physician Data Center (Board Action Data Bank and public access), e-mail: fpdc@fsmb.org.
- For the Federation Credentials Verification Service, e-mail: fcvs@fsmb.org.

Foundation for Advancement of International Medical Education and Research (FAIMER), 3624 Market Street, 4th floor, Philadelphia, PA 19104, USA; fax: (215) 386-9767; e-mail: imed@ecfmg.org; http://imed.ecfmg.org.

Gay and Lesbian Medical Association (GLMA), 459 Fulton Street, Suite 107, San Francisco, CA 94102; (415) 255-4547; fax: 415-255-4784; e-mail: info@glma.org; www.glma.org/home.html.

National Board of Medical Examiners (NBME), 3750 Market Street, Philadelphia, PA 19104-3102; (215) 590-9700; e-mail: webmail@nbme.org; www.nbme.org.

National Board of Osteopathic Medical Examiners (NBOME), 8765 W. Higgins Road, Suite 200, Chicago, IL 60631-4101; (773) 714-0622; fax: (773) 714-0631; e-mail: admin@nbome.org; www.nbome.org.

National Health Service Corps (NHSC), Health Resources & Service Administration, Bureau of Primary Healthcare, U.S. Dept. of Health and Human Services, Parklawn Bldg., 5600 Fishers Lane, Rockville, MD 20857; (301) 443-2086; http://nhsc.bphr.hrsa.gov.

National Medical Association (NMA), 1012 10th Street NW, Washington, DC 20001; (202) 347-1895; fax: (202) 898-2510; www.nmanet.org.

National Resident Matching Program (NRMP), 2450 N Street NW, Washington, DC 20037-1127; (866) 617-5838 or (202) 828-0566 (8:30 A.M. to 5:30 P.M. Eastern time); fax: (202) 828-4797; e-mail: NRMP@aamc.org; www.nrmp.org.

San Francisco Matching Programs (SFMP), (Specialty) Matching Program, P.O. Box 45161, San Francisco, CA 94145-0161; (415) 447-0350 [including Vacancy Line]; fax: (415) 561-8535; Overnight Mail address: SF Match, C/O Union Bank of California, Lockbox Dept-45161, 460 Hegenberger Road, Oakland, CA 94621; e-mail: help@sfmatch.org; www.sfmatch.org.

Additional URLs

Organization Name	Website
Aerospace Medical Assoc. (ASMA)	www.asma.org
Alpha Omega Alpha Student Research Fellowships	www.alphaomegaalpha.org/AwardsPrograms/StudentResearchPrize.htm
Amer. Acad. of Allergy, Asthma & Immunology (AAAAI)	www.aaaai.org
Amer. Acad. of Child & Adolescent Psychiatry (AACAP)	www.aacap.org
Amer. Acad. of Clinical Psychiatrists (AACP)	www.aacp.com/
Amer. Acad. of Dermatology (AAD)	www.aad.org
Amer. Acad. of Emergency Medicine (AAEM)	www.aaem.org
Amer. Acad. of Facial Plastic & Reconstructive Surgery (AAFPRS)	www.aafprs.org
Amer. Acad. of Neurology (AAN)	www.aan.com
Amer. Acad. of Ophthalmology (AAO)	www.aao.org
Amer. Acad. of Orthopedic Surgeons (AAOS)	www.aaos.org
Amer. Acad. of Osteopathy	www.academyofosteopathy.org
Amer. Acad. of Otolaryngology (AAO-HNS)	www.entnet.org
Amer. Acad. of Pain Medicine (AAPM)	www.painmed.org
Amer. Acad. of Pediatrics (AAP)	www.aap.org
Amer. Acad. of Physical Medicine & Rehabilitation (AAPMR)	www.aapmr.org
Amer. Assoc. for Geriatric Psychiatry (AAGP)	www.aagpgpa.org
Amer. Assoc. for Hand Surgery	www.handsurgery.org
Amer. Assoc. for the Surgery of Trauma (AAST)	www.aast.org/
Amer. Assoc. for Thoracic Surgery (AATS)	www.aats.org/
Amer. Assoc. of Clinical Urologists, Inc. (AACU)	www.aacuweb.org
Amer. Assoc. of Immunologists (AAI)	www.aai.org/
Amer. Assoc. of Neurological Surgeons (AANS)	www.aans.org
Amer. Assoc. of Neuromuscular & Electrodiagnostic Medicine (AANEM)	www.aanem.org/
Amer. Assoc. of Public Health Physicians (AAPHP)	www.aaphp.org
Amer. Board of Medical Specialties (ABMS)	www.abms.org
Amer. Coll. of Allergy, Asthma & Immunology (ACAAI)	www.acaai.org/

Organization Name	Website
Amer. Coll. of Cardiology (ACC)	www.acc.org
Amer. Coll. of Chest Physicians	www.chestnet.org
Amer. Coll. of Emergency Physicians (ACEP)	www.acep.org
Amer. Coll. of Gastroenterology (ACG)	www.acg.gi.org
Amer. Coll. of Managed Care Medicine (ACMCM)	www.acmcm.org
Amer. Coll. of Medical Genetics (ACMG)	www.acmg.net/
Amer. Coll. of Nuclear Medicine	www.acnucmed.org
Amer. Coll. of Obstetricians & Gynecologists (ACOG)	www.acog.org
Amer. Coll. of Occupational & Environmental Medicine (ACOEM)	www.acoem.org
Amer. Coll. of Osteopathic Emergency Physicians (ACOEP)	www.acoep.org
Amer. Coll. of Osteopathic Family Physicians (ACOFP)	www.acofp.org
Amer. Coll. of Osteopathic Internists (ACOI)	www.acoi.org
Amer. Coll. of Osteopathic Obstetricians & Gynecologists (ACOOG)	www.acoog.org/
Amer. Coll. of Osteopathic Pediatricians	www.acopeds.org
Amer. Coll. of Osteopathic Sclerotherapeutic Pain Management, Inc. (ACOPMS)	www.acopms.com
Amer. Coll. of Physician Executives (ACPE)	www.acpe.org
Amer. Coll. of Physicians (ACP)	www.acponline.org
Amer. Coll. of Preventive Medicine (ACPM)	www.acpm.org
Amer. Coll. of Radiology (ACR)	www.acr.org
Amer. Coll. of Rheumatology	www.rheumatology.org
Amer. Coll. of Sports Medicine (ACSM)	www.acsm.org
Amer. Coll. of Surgeons (ACS)	www.facs.org
Amer. Congress of Rehabilitation (ACRM)	www.acrm.org
Amer. Federation for Aging Research (AFAR)	www.afar.org
Amer. Foundation for Urologic Disease, Inc. (AFUD)	www.afud.org/
Amer. Gastroenterological Assoc.	www.gastro.org
Amer. Geriatrics Society	www.americangeriatrics.org
Amer. Medical Directors Assoc. (AMDA)	www.amda.com
Amer. Neurological Assoc. (ANA)	www.aneuroa.org
Amer. Nuclear Society (ANS)	www.ans.org/
Amer. Occupational Therapy Assoc., Inc. (AOTA)	www.aota.org
Amer. Orthopedic Soc. for Sports Medicine	www.sportsmed.org
Amer. Osteopathic Acad. of Orthopedics (AOAO)	www.aoao.org
Amer. Osteopathic Acad. of Sports Medicine (AOASM)	www.aoasm.org
Amer. Osteopathic Coll. of Dermatology (AOCD)	www.aocd.org
Amer. Osteopathic Coll. of Occupational & Preventive Medicine (AOCOPM)	www.aocopm.org
Amer. Osteopathic Coll. of Physical Medicine & Rehabilitation (AOCPMR)	www.aocpmr.org
Amer. Osteopathic Coll. of Radiology	www.aocr.org

Organization Name	Website
Amer. Osteopathic Coll. of Ophthalmology & Otolaryngology (AOCOOHNS)	www.aocoohns.org
Amer. Pain Society	www.ampainsoc.org/
Amer. Pediatric Soc. : Soc. for Pediatric Research (APS-SPR)	www.aps-spr.org
Amer. Pediatric Surgical Assoc. (APSA)	www.eapsa.org
Amer. Physical Therapy Assoc. (APTA)	www.apta.org
Amer. Psychiatric Assoc. (APA)	www.psych.org/
Amer. Roentgen Ray Soc. (ARRS)	www.arrs.org
Amer. Soc. for Clinical Pathology (ASCP)	www.ascp.org
Amer. Soc. for Dermatologic Surgery (ASDS)	www.asds-net.org/
Amer. Soc. for Investigative Pathology (ASIP)	www.asip.org
Amer. Soc. for Reproductive Medicine (ASRM)	www.asrm.org
Amer. Soc. for Surgery of the Hand	www.hand-surg.org
Amer. Soc. for Therapeutic Radiology & Oncology (ASTRO)	www.astro.org
Amer. Soc. of Anesthesiologists (ASA)	www.asahq.org
Amer. Soc. of Clinical Oncology (ASCO)	www.asco.org
Amer. Soc. of Colon & Rectal Surgeons (ASCRS)	www.fascrs.org
Amer. Soc. of Dermatology (ASD)	www.asd.org/
Amer. Soc. of General Surgeons (ASGS)	www.theasgs.org
Amer. Soc. of Hematology (ASH)	www.hematology.org
Amer. Soc. of Nephrology (ASN)	www.asn-online.org
Amer. Soc. of Plastic Surgeons	www.plasticsurgery.org
Assoc. for Hospital Medical Education–*Transitional Year Program Directory* (*The Purple Book*)	www.ahme.org/ publications/ transitional.html
Assoc. for Research in Otolaryngology (ARO)	www.aro.org
Assoc. of Academic Physiatrists	www.physiatry.org
Assoc. of American Indian Physicians (AAIP)	www.aaip.com
Assoc. of Military Surgeons of the U.S. (AMSUS)	www.amsus.org
Assoc. of Teachers of Preventive Medicine (ATPM)	www.atpm.org
Cardiothoracic Surgery Network	www.vascsurg.org
Child Neurology Society	www.childneurology society.org
Coll. of Amer. Pathologists (CAP)	www.cap.org
Congress of Neurological Surgeons	www.neurosurgeon.org/
Emergency Medical Residents' Assoc. (EMRA)	www.emra.org
Federal Direct Consolidation Loan Information Center	www.loanconsolidation .ed.gov/
Federal Student Aid (FSA)	http://studentaid.ed.gov/ PORTALSWebApp/ students/english/repaying .jsp?tab=repaying

Organization Name	Website
Foundation for Digestive Health & Nutrition	www.fdhn.org/html/awards/awards.html
Foundation for Reconstructive Plastic Surgery	www.frps.org
Genetics Societies websites	www.faseb.org/genetics
Genetics Society of America	www.genetics-gsa.org/
Infectious Diseases Soc. of Amer. (IDSA)	www.idsociety.org
International Medical Education Directory (IMED)	http://imed.ecfmg.org
Lesbian, Gay, Bisexual, & Transgender People in Medicine (LGBTPM)	www.amsa.org/advocacy/lgbtpm/
Marshall Univ. Medical H.E.L.P. Program	www.marshall.edu/medicalhelp/
Military Medical Student Assoc. (MMSA)	www.militarymedicine.org/
National Hispanic Medical Assoc. (NHMA)	www.nhmamd.org/
National Institutes of Health Clin. Rsch. Training Prog.	www.training.nih.gov/crtp
National Matching Services (NMS)	www.natmatch.com
New York Medical College-Fifth Pathway	www.nymc.edu/depthome/fifth.asp
Pathway Evaluation Prog. for Medical Professionals	http://medweb.usc.edu/pathways/intro.htm
Radiological Soc. of North America, Inc. (RSNA)	www.rsna.org
Renal Physicians Assoc.	www.renalmd.org
Sarnoff Endowment	www.sarnoffendowment.org
Soc. for Academic Emergency Medicine (SAEM)	www.saem.org
Soc. of Critical Care Medicine (SCCM)	www.sccm.org
Soc. of General Internal Medicine (SGIM)	www.sgim.org
Soc. of Hospital Medicine (SHM)	www.hospitalmedicine.org
Soc. of Nuclear Medicine (SNM)	www.snm.org
Soc. of Thoracic Surgeons (STS)	www.sts.org
Soc. of Toxicology	www.toxicology.org
Student Doctor Network	www.medstudents.net
The Amer. Orthopedic Assoc. (AOA)	www.aoassn.org
The Endocrine Society	www.endo-society.org
Thomson Prometric Testing	www.prometric.com
U.S. Equal Employment Opportunity Comm. (EEOC)	www.eeoc.gov
U.S. Medical Licensing Exam (USMLE)	www.usmle.org
Univ. of Kansas School of Med.	www.kumc.edu/som/medsos/opp.html
Univ. Missouri-Kansas City, Institute for Professional Preparation	http://web1.umkc.edu/ipp/
Women Physicians Congress (WPC)	www.ama-assn.org/ama/pub/category/18.html
Women's Health.gov	www.4women.gov/index.htm

Index

– A –

AAMC. *See* Association of American Medical Colleges
Abdominal Radiology, 96
    match, 569
    programs and positions, 545
Abdominal Transplant Surgery, 101, 569
Addiction Medicine. *See* Addiction Psychiatry
Addiction Psychiatry, 22, 91, 545
Administrative duties, required in residency?, 457
Adolescent Medicine, 20-21, 85, 545
Adoption. *See* Family leave
ADTS. *See* Applicant Data Tracking System
Adult Reconstructive Orthopedics, 78, 545
Advanced (A) residency positions, 543
    matches, 568-70
Adviser
    choosing an, 145
    mock interview and, 408
    specialty, 149-50
    See also Mentor
Aerospace Medicine, 22
    IMGs in practice, 391
    military residency, 385
    programs and positions, 545
African-Americans, 371-2. *See also* Minorities
Age discrimination, 382-3
Air travel, tips, 416-7
Alaskan Natives. *See* Minorities
Allergy & Immunology, 20, 30-31, 110
    D.O.s in M.D. training, 380
    IMGs in practice, 391
    number of practitioners, 26
    part-time positions, 365
    Pediatric, 85
    programs and positions, 545
Alpha Omega Alpha, 220
Alternative health plans, 19
Alumni, information from, 437
American Medical Association
    Graduate Medical Education Library, 236
    Green Book, 234
    Women Physicians Congress, 356
American Medical Assoc. Alliance
    interview accommodations and, 415
American Medical Student Assoc., 211, 351, 367, 414

American Medical Women's Assoc.
    awards, 220
    interview accommodations and, 415
American Osteopathic Association, 385, 540, 559, 575
    M.D. training and, 377-9
American Urological Assoc. Match, 104
Americans with Disabilities Act, 374
Analysis, personal traits, 117-21
Anatomic Pathology, 21, 82. *See also* Pathology
Anesthesiology, 20, 32-33, 111
    acceptable PGY-1 training for, 544
    Advanced (A) positions, 570
    Critical Care, 40
    D.O.s in M.D. training, 380
    IMGs in practice, 391
    managed care and, 19
    minority faculty, 369
    number of practitioners, 26
    Osteopathic programs & positions, 32, 376, 578
    part-time positions, 365
    PGY-1 positions, 115, 143
    programs and positions, 545
    subspecialties, 20
    who matches?, 394
    women faculty, 355
    work hours, 140
AOA. *See* Alpha Omega Alpha; American Osteopathic Association
Applicant Data Tracking System, 307, 314, 316
Applicants
    changing specialties, 382-4
    older, 382-4
    married, 357-62
    minority, 368-72
    perfect, 447-52
    physically impaired, 373-5
Applications, 299-349
    completing, 302
    directly to programs, 143-4, 574
    ERAS, 305-17
    IMGs and, 308
    neatness, 299
    number to submit, 295-8
    organizing, 300-3
    program requirements, 303

requesting, 300
submitting, 5, 347
timing, 3, 300
to multiple specialties, 232
Universal, 304
See also Centralized Application
Service; ERAS
Aptitudes, personal assessment, 113-32
Association of American Medical Colleges
Careers in Medicine, 116
FindAResident, 572
MONEYMATTERS, 584
Audition electives. *See* Electives, away
Awards, 219-21

— B —

Benefits
at residencies, 238-9
don't ask, 475
health, 277-9
non-health, 279-85
Bisexual students, 366-7
Black applicants, 371-2. *See also* Minorities
Blood Banking/Transfusion Med, 21, 82,
545. *See also* Pathology
Breast Imaging/Women's Imaging, 96, 569

— C —

CAF. *See* Common Application Form
Canadians, 405-6
Canadian Resident Matching Service,
558-9
NRMP Match and, 394, 558-9
Careers in Medicine, 115, 116
Cardiac Surgery, 20, 102.
See also Thoracic Surgery
Cardiology, 20, 33-35, 110
D.O.s in M.D. training, 380
IMGs in practice, 391
match, 569
number of practitioners, 26
Osteopathic programs & positions, 578
Pediatric, 85
PGY-1 positions, 115
programs and positions, 545
work hours, 140
Cardiothoracic Radiology, 96, 545
Cardiovascular Diseases. *See* Cardiology
Career, changing, 231
CaRMS. *See* Canadians
CAS. *See* Centralized Application Service
Categorical (C) positions, 543
Internal Medicine, 546
Surgery, 101
CCS. *See* Computer-based Case Simulation

Centralized Application Service, 76, 570
Changing specialties, 229-31, 382-4
Chemical Pathology, 21, 82, 545
Child and Adolescent Psychiatry, 22,
35-36, 91, 110
D.O.s in M.D. training, 380
IMGs in practice, 391
match, 569
Osteopathic programs & positions, 91,
578
programs and positions, 545
See also Psychiatry
Child Neurology, 22, 36-37, 71, 85,
10, 545
Child Psychiatry. *See* Child &
Adolescent Psychiatry
Child Psychiatry/Peds/Psych, 35, 91. *See
also* Child & Adolescent Psychiatry
Childcare, 361-2
as selection factor, 282-4
at residencies, 238
Children, 357-62
Clerkships, 164
exams and, 165
specialty, 161
third year, 113, 160-1
Clinical & Laboratory Dermatologic
Immunology, 20
Clinical & Laboratory Immunology, 20, 21,
545
Clinical Biochemical Genetics, 20
Clinical Cardiac Electrophysiology, 545.
See also Cardiology
Clinical clerkships. *See* Clerkships
Clinical Cytogenetics, 20
Clinical experience
as selection factor, 255-60
clinical years, 154
pre-clinical years, 152-3
pre-med students, 151-2
volunteer time, 150-4
Clinical Genetics, 20
Clinical laboratories, as selection factor,
273
Clinical Molecular Genetics, 20
Clinical Neurophysiology, 22, 71, 545
Clinical Pathology, 21, 82. *See also*
Pathology
Clinical setting, as selection factor, 258-9
Clinical Skills Assessment, 398-9
Clothes, for interview, 421
men, 422-4
packing, 426-8
women, 424-5

Colon & Rectal Surgery, 20, 37-38, 111
  D.O.s in M.D. training, 380
  IMGs in practice, 391
  match, 569
  number of practitioners, 26
  part-time positions, 365
  programs and positions, 545
COMLEX, 188-96
  cost, 191
  fairness of, 206
  importance to applicants, 199
  irregular behavior, 196
  Level 1, 191, 194
  Level 2CE, 191, 194
  Level 2PE, 192, 195
  Level 3, 191, 196
  licensure and, 196
  preparation for, 193, 200
  resident selection criteria, 199
  retaking, 190-1
  scores, 192-3
  special testing accommodations, 190
  test day, 191-2
  tips, 202-5
Common Application Form, 309. *See also*
  ERAS
Communication process, 434
Competition, don't ask, 476
Complementary & Alternative Medicine,
  38-39
Comprehensive Osteopathic Medical
  Licensing Examination. *See* COMLEX
Computer-based Case Simulation, 184-5
Conferences, as selection factor, 268-9
Contracts for positions
  outside the Match, 565
  residency program, 583
Cornea/External Disease, 76, 545. *See also*
  Ophthalmology
Couples
  matching, 241, 362-3
  NRMP Match and, 560-3, 565
    not using, 562
    partner's influence, 357
  Osteopathic Match and, 577
Craniofacial Surgery, 545, 569
Critical Care Medicine, 20, 21, 40-42, 111
  D.O.s in M.D. training, 380
  entry via
    Anesthesia, 32, 545
    Emergency Medicine, 44
    General Surgery, 101, 545, 578
    Internal Medicine, 40, 545
    Pediatrics, 40

  match, 569
  Osteopathic programs & positions, 578
  Pediatric, 85
  programs and positions, 545
  Pulmonary Disease and, 93
  Trauma Surgery and, 103
Critical Care/Pulmonary Disease, 41, 93
CSA. *See* Clinical Skills Assessment
Cuban-Americans, 372
Curriculum, as selection factor, 267-99
Curriculum vitae. *See* Résumé
Cytopathology, 21, 82, 545

— D —

D.O.s. *See* Osteopathic physicians
Dean of Students
  aptitude/interest tests &, 114
  choosing adviser, 145
  contact book, 245
  Dean's letter and, 336
  ERAS and, 306-7
  help on Unmatch Day, 566
  information on subinternships, 213
  mock interview and, 408
  NRMP *Results & Data* and, 241
  requirements for AOA honorary, 220
  residency information and, 245
  school-specific awards and, 220
  specialty information and, 245
  summer job and, 208
  Universal Application for Residency
    and, 304
Dean's letter, 331, 336-8
  check carefully, 336
  IMGs, ERAS and, 312
  information in, 331
  late, 337-8
  late awards and, 221
  national template for, 332-5
  OSCE and, 207
  Osteopathic, 379
  residency program requirement, 337
  uniform date for, 337
Debt
  career choice and, 137-8
  educational, 134, 137-8
  management of, 583-4
Dental insurance, as selection factor, 279
Dermatology, 20, 42-43, 110
  acceptable PGY-1 training, 544
  Advanced (A) positions, 570
  D.O.s in M.D. training, 380
  fellowships, 42
  IMGs in practice, 391

managed care and, 19
minority faculty, 369
number of practitioners, 26
Osteopathic programs & positions,
376, 578
part-time positions, 365
PGY-1 positions, 143
programs and positions, 545
subspecialties, 20
women faculty, 355
work hours, 140
Dermatopathology, 20, 21, 42, 43, 82, 545.
See also Dermatology; Pathology
Developmental–Behavioral Pediatrics, 21,
85, 545
Diagnostic Radiology, 22, 95-97, 110
acceptable PGY-1 training for, 544
Advanced (A) positions, 570
D.O.s in M.D. training, 380
fellowships, 96
Nuclear Radiology and, 96
Osteopathic programs & positions,
376, 578
programs and positions, 548
part-time positions, 365
who matches?, 394
See also Radiology
Disability insurance, as selection factor,
280-1
Disabled students, 373-5. *See also* Learning
Disabilities
Discommunication, 482
Drug testing, 555

— E —

Early graduation, and Match, 571-2
ECFMG
Clinical Skills Assessment, 398-9
certification, 394-9
English language exam, 398
ERAS and, 307
transcripts, 312
ineligible practitioners, 395
Information Booklet, 395
OASIS, 396
USMLE and, 397-8
Educational conferences, 238
Education benefits, as selection factor, 284
Education leave, as selection factor, 281
Electives
advantages/disadvantages, 214-6
applying for, 218
away, 162, 218
home or away?, 218

preparation for, 216-7
senior year, 212, 214-9
specialty, 161
specialty choice and, 214, 216-7
subinternship, 213-4
timing of, 218-9
Electronic Residency Application Service.
See ERAS
Emergency Medicine, 20, 43-46, 110
Advanced (A) positions, 570
D.O.s in M.D. training, 380
Emergency Medical Service
Administration, 44
IMGs in practice, 391
managed care and, 19
number of practitioners, 26
Osteopathic programs & positions,
376, 578
part-time positions, 365
PGY-1 positions, 115, 143
practitioners' characteristics, 122
programs and positions, 545
subspecialties, 20
who matches?, 394
women faculty, 355
work hours, 140
Emergency Med–Family Practice, 44, 46,
578
Emergency Med–Internal Med, 45
Osteopathic programs & positions,
376, 578
programs and positions, 545
Emergency Med–Pediatrics, 45
Endocrinology, Diabetes & Metabolism, 20,
46-47, 85, 110
D.O.s in M.D. training, 380
Osteopathic programs & positions, 578
Pediatric, 85
Endocrinology (IM), 545
Endovascular Surgical Neuroradiology, 96,
545
ENT. *See* Otolaryngology
Equal Employment Opportunity
Commission, 351
ERAS, 176, 305-8
ADTS, 307, 314
assign documents, 313-4
Canadians, 307
Common Application Form, 309
completing forms, 309
components, 306
computers and, 314
cost, 315-6
Dean and, 316

Dean's letter and, 312
Dean's Office Contact, 306
documents, 309
ECFMG and, 316-7
Fifth Pathway, 310, 311
IMGs and, 307-8, 312, 315-6
letters of recommendation, 311
military applicants, 307
MyERAS, 307
Osteopathic applicants, 306-7
personal statement and, 309-10
photograph and, 312
PostOffice, 307
program selection, 312-3
registration, 307
résumé and, 310-1
specialties using, 305
support, 314
transcripts and, 312
Esprit de corps, as selection factor, 269-70
EVIMGs, 389. *See also* IMGs
Exams, 5
clinical grades and, 165
COMLEX. *See* COMLEX
OSCE, 206-7
Shelf, 205
Special Purpose, 198
TOEFL, 398
USMLE. *See* USMLE
Exchange Visitor IMGs. *See* EVIMGS;
IMGs

— F —

Facial Plastic & Reconstructive Surgery, 80
match, 568
programs and positions, 545
Faculty
as selection factor, 265-6
number of, 238
residency information and, 244
Family leave, 358-61
as selection factor, 284
specialty policies on, 359
Family Medicine, 20, 47-50, 110
applicant selection criteria, 450
D.O.s in M.D. training, 380
Geriatrics, 52
IMGs in practice, 391
managed care and, 19
minority faculty, 369
number of practitioners, 26
part-time positions, 365
PGY-1 positions, 115
practitioners' characteristics, 122
Preventive Medicine and, 90

programs and positions, 545
subspecialties, 20
who matches?, 394
women faculty, 355
work hours, 140
See also Family Practice
Family Medicine–Internal Med, 49, 545
Family Medicine–Psychiatry, 49
part-time positions, 365
programs and positions, 545
Family needs, as selection factor, 261
Family Practice, 48
Osteopathic programs & positions, 376,
578
See also Family Medicine
Family Practice–Emergency Med, 46
Family Practice–OMM, 48, 49, 578
Family Practice–OMT, 48, 49, 578
Feedback form, 430
*Fellowship and Residency Electronic
Interactive Database Online.* See *FREIDA*
Fellowships, 549
Burn Surgery, 88
Cardiology, 34
Colon & Rectal Surgery, 37, 111
Craniofacial Surgery, 88
Critical Care, 40, 111
Dermatopathology, 42
Diagnostic Radiology, 96
Emergency Medicine, 44
Endocrinology, Diabetes & Metabolism,
46, 110
Gastroenterology, 50, 111
Geriatrics, 51
Hematology–Oncology, 54, 111
Hospitalist, 58
Infectious Diseases, 58, 110
matches, 549, 569-70
Microsurgery, 88
Mohs Micrographic Surgery, 42
Neurological Surgery, 69-70
Ophthalmology, 569
Orthopedic Surgery, 78
Otolaryngology, 80
Pediatrics, 85
Pediatric Surgery, 84
Physical Med & Rehabilitation, 86
Plastic Surgery, 88
Procedural Dermatology, 42
Psychiatry, 91
Rheumatology, 97
Sports Medicine, 99
Surgery, 101
Trauma Surgery, 103
Women's Health, 106, 107

Female Pelvic Med & Reproductive
Surgery, 74, 545
Fifth Pathway, 397, 404-5
ERAS, 310, 311
letters of recommendation, 311
licensure, 405
NRMP Match, 394
See also USIMGs
FindAResident, 567, 571-2
FMGs. *See* IMGs
FNIMGs, 389, 400-402. *See also* IMGs
Foot and Ankle Orthopedics, 78, 546
Foreign Medical Graduates. *See* IMGs
Foreign National IMGs. *See* FNIMGs
Forensic Pathology, 21, 82, 546
Forensic Psychiatry, 22, 91, 546
FREIDA, 236, 237-40, 571
Unmatch Day and, 567
Future, of medicine, 12-19
Future, of specialties, 140-3

— G —

Gastroenterology, 20, 50-51, 111
D.O.s in M.D. training, 380
IMGs in practice, 391
match, 569
number of practitioners, 26
Osteopathic programs & positions,
50, 578
Pediatric, 85
programs and positions, 546
Gays, 366-7
General Internal Medicine, 59
managed care and, 19
PGY-1 positions, 115
See also Internal Medicine
General Practice, 26, 47. *See also* Family
Medicine
General Preventive Medicine, 111. *See also*
Preventive Medicine, General
General Psychiatry. *See* Psychiatry
General Surgery, 22, 100, 110
IMGs in practice, 391
PGY-1 positions, 115, 143
See also Surgery; Surgery, General
Genetics. *See* Medical Genetics
Geography, as factor when
ranking programs, 536
selecting programs, 12-13, 260, 262-3
Geriatric Medicine, 20, 51-53, 110, 546.
See also Geriatrics
Geriatric Psychiatry, 22, 52, 91, 110, 546
Geriatric–Family Practice, 48, 578
Geriatric–Internal Med, 578

Geriatrics, 51
D.O.s in M.D. training, 380
via Family Medicine, 48, 52, 578
via Psychiatry, 52
Glaucoma, 76, 546. *See also*
Ophthalmology
*GMED Companion: An Insider's Guide to
Selecting a Residency Program*, 236
Grades
as resident selection criteria, 159-65
basic sciences, 162
clinical, 163-5
senior electives, 162
specialty clerkships, 161
third-year clerkships, 160
See also Transcript
Graduate Education Office, 476
Graduate Medical Education Directory.
See *Green Book*
Graduate Medical Education Library, 234,
236
Green Book, 234
special requirements, 234
using with *FREIDA*, 240
Gynecologic Oncology, 21, 74
Osteopathic programs & positions, 578
programs and positions, 546
Gynecology. *See* Obstetrics & Gynecology

— H —

Hand Surgery, 21, 22, 53-54, 111
entry via
General Surgery, 101
Orthopedic Surgery, 78, 110
Plastic Surgery, 88
match, 569
programs and positions, 546
Handicapped students. *See* Physically
impaired students
Head & Neck Cancer Surgery, 80
Health Benefits
as selection factor, 277-9
insurance, 278
Health Professions Scholarship Program,
384, 387
Hematology, 20, 21, 82, 546. *See also*
Pathology
Hematology–Oncology, 54-56, 111
D.O.s in M.D. training, 380
Osteopathic programs & positions, 55,
578
Pediatric, 55, 85
programs and positions, 546
Hispanics, 372. *See also* Minorities
HMO participation, 19

Holistic Medicine. *See* Complementary &
Alternative Medicine
Hospital
facilities, as selection factor, 273-5
size, at residencies, 239
Hospitalist, 57-58
Housing
as selection factor, 281
finding, 584-5
How to Choose a Medical Specialty, 114
HPSP. *See* Health Professions Scholarship
Program
Hyperbaric Medicine. *See* Undersea &
Hyperbaric Medicine

— I —

ICU Medicine. *See* Critical Care
Ideal applicant, 447-52
Illegal questions, 304, 504-6, 528-30
IMGs, 389-406
AMA and, 393
applications and, 308
California letter, 311
Canadians, 405-6
clerkships and, 392
CSA and, 399
ECFMG Certification, 168-9, 394
English-language exam, 398
ERAS and, 307-8, 314, 315
Fifth Pathway, 404
general tips, 399
GMED Companion and, 236
ineligible practitioners, 395
letters of recommendation, 311
licensure requirements,196, 197, 392
non-practicing physicians, 392
NRMP Match and, 559-60
practicing in various specialties, 391
requirements for U.S. training, 6, 395
specialties and, 394
transcripts and, 312
USMLE and, 397, 398
visas, 393, 399, 401-2, 555
See also Canadians; FNIMGs; USIMGs
Income
potential and debt, 137
specialty, 134, 136
Industrial Medicine. *See* Occupational
Medicine
Infectious Diseases, 20, 58-59, 110
D.O.s in M.D. training, 380
match, 569
Osteopathic programs & positions,
58, 578

Pediatric, 85
programs and positions, 546
Information, on residencies, 233
Integrative Medicine. *See* Complementary
& Alternative Medicine
Intensive Care. *See* Critical Care
Interests, self-testing, 114
Intern/Resident Registration Program, 540,
575-80
algorithm, 575
military match and, 577
rank-order list, 576
results, 577
schedule, 580
See also National Matching Services
Internal Med–Dermatology, 546
Internal Med–Emerg Med–Crit Care, 545
Internal Medicine, 20, 59-63, 111
Allergy & Immunology, 30
Categorical, 546
Critical Care, 40
D.O.s in M.D. training, 380
Geriatrics, 52
IMGs in practice, 391
Infectious Diseases, 58, 110
minority faculty, 369
number of practitioners, 26
Osteopathic programs & positions,
376, 578
part-time positions, 365
PGY-1 positions, 115, 143
Practitioners' characteristics, 123
Preliminary, 546
subspecialties, 20, 61, 115, 546
who matches?, 394
work hours, 140
Internal Med–Emergency Med. *See*
Emergency Med–Internal Med
Internal Med–Med Genetics, 546
Internal Med–Neurology, 62
part-time positions, 365
programs and positions, 546
Internal Med–Nuclear Med, 546
Internal Med–Oncology, 110
Internal Med–Pediatrics, 63-65, 110
D.O.s in M.D. training, 380
Osteopathic programs & positions,
376, 578
part-time positions, 365
programs and positions, 546
Internal Med–Physical Med & Rehab, 62
part-time positions, 365
programs and positions, 546

Internal Med–Preventive Med, 63
   part-time positions, 365
   programs and positions, 546
Internal Medicine, Primary, 61, 63
   PGY-1 positions, 143
   programs and positions, 546
   training, 60
Internal Med–Psychiatry, 63, 365, 546
Internal Medicine–Women's Health, 107
International Medical Education Directory,
   395
International Medical Graduates. *See* IMGs
International Medicine, 44
Internet, program information from, 243
Internships, 228, 543
   Categorical, 543
   Osteopathic, 375-7, 381-2
   Preliminary, 228, 543
   residency application during, 228
Interventional Cardiology, 20
   Osteopathic Fellowship, 578
   programs and positions, 546
Interventional Radiology Match, 569
Interview, 453-88
   analyzing, 534-5
   answering unasked questions, 484
   applicant selection criteria, 450
   appropriate attire, 421-6
   ask the right people, 455
   body language, 439
   confirm questionable points, 474
   entering and leaving, 438-40
   evaluations, 410
   failures, 482, 485-6
   inadequate preparation, 482
   interviewer's perspective, 454
   listening skills, 482-4
   making an impression, 410
   materials, 440-4
   mock, 407-9
   never-ending answer, 485
   panel, 479-80
   post-visit follow-up, 531-6
   preparation for, 407-9, 431-2, 435-6,
      491-2
   questions and answers, 489-528
   questions to ask, 453-74
   rating form, 488
   scheduling, 212, 409-11
   selling yourself, 440, 487, 490
   SHOWTIME mnemonic, 408-9
   stressful, 479-81
   travel arrangements, 412-9
   types of questions, 492-3
   vacationing and, 418
   wait list, 412

Interview questions
   do not ask, 474
      benefits, 475
      competition, 476
      salary, 475
      vacation, 476
   to ask faculty, 455-66
      accreditation?, 463-4
      administrative opportunities?, 460-1
      changes in the program?, 462-3
      combined residency training?, 458
      elective opportunities?, 459
      faculty turnover?, 456
      give me an example?, 466
      graduates and specialty boards?,
         455-6
      have housestaff left program?, 464
      help getting jobs?, 465-6
      interaction with residents?, 456
      language training?, 459
      medicare punitive audits?, 462
      mentor available?, 461
      non-clinical responsibilities?, 457
      patient population?, 458
      program's educational goals?, 455
      pyramidal program?, 464
      research opportunities?, 460
      resident evaluations?, 461-2
      special programs?, 457
      types of clinical settings?, 458
      where are your graduates?, 465
   to ask residents, 466-74
      call schedule?, 471-2
      clinical experiences?, 468-9
      computer facilities?, 470
      dea number?, 473
      didactics versus clinical?, 468
      do residents socialize?, 474
      facilities adequate?, 469-70
      faculty presence?, 467
      give me an example?, 466
      library adequate?, 470
      medical license?, 473
      moonlighting rules?, 473
      patient population?, 473-4
      program changes?, 467
      relationship with other
         programs/specialties?, 469
      sick days?, 472
      still choose this program?, 466
      student evaluation of faculty?, 467-8
      support staff?, 471
      time to read?, 470
   when to ask, 454
Interview rules, 437-40

Interview trip
  lost suitcase and, 427
  packing, 426-8
  tax tip, 429
  things not to do, 477-9
  See also Residency program visit
Interviewers
  behavioral factors, 485
  know names, 438
  perspective, 454
  rating form, 488
  techniques, 493-4
  traits they seek, 487, 489-90
  warning signs to, 485-6

— J —

Jobs after training, as selection factor,
  12-13, 272
Journals, specialty information and, 244
Junior internship. *See* Subinternship

— L —

Lab coats, as selection factor, 282
Learning disabilities, USMLE and, 202.
  See also Special testing accommodations
Length of training, specialty choice and,
  138-9
Lesbians, 366-7
Letters of recommendation. *See* Reference
  letters
Liability insurance. *See* Malpractice
  insurance
Library, as selection factor, 274
Licensing examinations, applicant selection
  factor, 165. *See also* USMLE; COMLEX
Licensure, 196
  graduate education requirements, 197
  Osteopathic, 378-9
  IMGs, 392
  suggested changes, 198
  pathways to, 196
Life insurance
  as selection factor, 280
  at residencies, 239
Lifestyle, specialty choice and, 139-40
Listening skills, 482-3
Loans, educational, 134, 137-8
LORs. *See* Reference letters

— M —

Magnetic Resonance Imaging, 96
Malpractice insurance, 136
  as selection factor, 282
  at residencies, 239

Managed care, 17-19
Marriage, 357-8
Maslow's Hierarchy of Needs, 157
Master of Public Health, 75
Match
  Abdominal Radiology, 569
  Abdominal Transplant Surgery, 569
  Advanced (A) positions, 569-70
  after other training, 573
  algorithm, 541
  behavior after you match, 581-6
  Breast Imaging/Women's Imaging, 569
  Cardiovascular Disease, 569
  Child & Adolescent Psych, 569
  Colon & Rectal Surgery, 569
  Cornea/External Disease, 76
  couples and, 362-3, 560-3
  Craniofacial Surgery, 569
  Critical Care, 569
  early graduation and, 571-2
  Gastroenterology, 569
  Glaucoma, 76
  Hand Surgery, 569
  Infectious Disease, 569
  Interventional Radiology, 569
  Maternal–Fetal Medicine, 569
  military, 386-7
  MRI Radiology, 569
  Musculoskeletal Radiology, 569
  Neurological Surgery, 569
  Neuro–Ophthalmology, 76
  Neuroradiology, 569
  new programs and, 573
  non-approved programs, 574
  non-NRMP PGY-1, 569-70
  not matching, 565-8
  not using a, 570-4
  NRMP, 540-64
  Oculoplastics, 76
  Ophthalmology, 76, 569
  Otology–Neurotology, 569
  Pediatric Cardiology, 569
  Pediatric Critical Care, 569
  Pediatric Emergency Medicine, 569
  Pediatric Hematology/Oncology, 569
  Pediatric Ophthalmology, 76
  Pediatric Radiology, 569
  Pediatric Rheumatology, 569
  Pediatric Surgery, 569
  Plastic Surgery, 569
  programs not in a, 574
  Pulmonary Diseases, 569
  ranking programs, 535-8, 552
    decision tree, 554

Reproductive Endocrinology, 569
Retina, 76
Rheumatology, 570
Thoracic Radiology, 570
Thoracic Surgery, 102, 570
Ultrasound (Radiology), 570
Urology, 104, 570
Thoracic Surgery, 102
Vascular Surgery, 105
Match Day, 553, 557
Matching programs, 6
CaRMS, 558
Child Neurology, 539
Fellowships
Child & Adolescent Psychiatry, 35
Colon & Rectal Surgery, 37
Obstetrics & Gynecology, 74
Pediatrics, 85
Radiology, 96
San Francisco Matching Program
Craniofacial Surgery, 89
Facial Plastic Surgery, 89
Neurological Surgery, 69, 70, 539
Ophthalmology, 76, 739
Otology/Neurotology, 80
Neurology, 539
Osteopathic Intern/Resident
Registration Program, 540, 575-80
Plastic Surgery, 539
Thoracic Surgery, 102
Urology, 539, 570
Maternal and Fetal Medicine, 21, 74
match, 569
programs and positions, 546
Osteopathic programs & positions, 578
See also Obstetrics & Gynecology
Maternity leave, 359. *See also* Family leave
Meals, as selection factor, 281
Medical Administration. *See* Medical
Management
Medical benefits, at residencies, 238-9,
277-9
Medical Genetics, 20, 65, 111
IMGs in practice, 391
number of practitioners, 26
part-time positions, 365
programs and positions, 546
subspecialties, 20
Medical licensure. *See* Licensure
Medical Management, 66, 115
Medical Microbiology, 21, 82, 546
Medical Oncology, 20. *See also*
Hematology–Oncology
Medical Student Performance Evaluations.
See Dean's letters

Medical Toxicology, 20, 21, 22, 44, 66-7,
90, 546
Medicare
punitive audits, 462
residents' salaries and, 230, 392
specialist participation in, 19
Medicine, future of, 12-19, 140-3. *See also*
Internal Medicine
Men, faculty in specialties, 354
Mentor
choosing a, 145-50
clinician as, 147
interacting with, 148
mock interview and, 408
residency information and, 244
role, 145
summer job and, 208
supplement with specialty adviser, 149
teacher as, 147
wrong choices, 148
Mexican-Americans. *See* Minorities,
Hispanics
Military, 384-8
Aerospace Medicine, 30, 385
after internship, 223
ERAS and, 307, 385
why do it, 388
Military Match, 386-7
NRMP Match and, 564
Military residencies
applications, 385
information sources, 386
Osteopaths and, 379, 385, 577
payback obligation, 384, 387
subinternship and, 386
Minimally Invasive & Gastrointestinal
Surgery, 101, 569
Minorities, 368-72
harassment, 371
Hispanics, 372
medical school faculty, 369
women, 371
Mock interview, 407-9
Mohs Micrographic Surgery, 546
Molecular Genetic Pathology, 20, 21
Moonlighting, as selection factor, 285-6
Moving, 585-6
MRI Radiology Match, 569
MSPE. *See* Dean's letter
Musculoskeletal Oncology, 78, 79, 546
Musculoskeletal Radiology, 96, 546, 569
Must/Want Analysis, 248-54, 287-93
as interview checklist, 441, 443-4
examples, 253-4, 288-93
form, 251-2

instructions, 250
post-visit completion, 444, 534
rank programs using, 535-8

— N —

National Health Service Corps, 388
National Matching Services, 575
National Medical Association, 372
National Residency Matching Program.
  See NRMP
*National Residency Matching Program
  Online Directory*. See NRMP *Online
  Directory*
Native Americans, 371. *See also* Minorities
Native Hawaiians. *See* Minorities
Neonatal–Perinatal Medicine, 21, 67-68,
  85, 110, 546
Neonatology. *See* Neonatal–Perinatal
  Medicine
Nephrology, 20, 68-69, 110
  D.O.s in M.D. training, 380
  Osteopathic programs & positions,
    68, 578
  programs and positions, 546
Neurodevelopmental Disabilities, 21, 22,
  546
Neurological Surgery, 20, 69-70, 110
  D.O.s in M.D. training, 380
  fellowship match, 569
  IMGs in practice, 391
  match, 69-70, 569
  number of practitioners, 26
  Osteopathic programs & positions, 578
  part-time positions, 365
  programs and positions, 546
Neurology, 22, 70-72, 110
  acceptable PGY-1 training for, 544
  Child. *See* Child Neurology
  D.O.s in M.D. training, 380
  IMGs in practice, 391
  match, 71
  minority faculty, 369
  number of practitioners, 26
  Osteopathic programs & positions,
    71, 578
  part-time positions, 365
  programs and positions, 546
  women faculty, 355
Neurology–Diag Rad–Neuroradiology, 546
Neurology–Psychiatry, 365, 546
Neuromuscular Med+1, 578
Neuromuscular Med–OMT, 578
Neuro–Ophthalmology 76, 546
Neuropathology, 21, 82, 546

Neuroradiology, 22, 96, 546, 569
Neurosurgery. *See* Neurological Surgery
Neurotology (OTO), 21, 80, 547
NHSC. *See* National Health Service Corps
NMS. *See* Intern/Resident Registration
  Program; National Matching Services
Non-health benefits, as selection factor,
  279-85
Non-interview visits, 480-1
Non-NRMP PGY-1 Matches, 568-70
NRMP Match, 540-64
  algorithm, 541, 549
  Canadian Resident Matching Service
    and, 559
  Canadians and, 394
  confidentiality, 552
  cost, 551
  couples match, 362-3, 560-3
  fellowships, 543
  Fifth Pathway and, 394
  first-choice, 542
  history of, 540-1
  illegal behavior, 555
  IMGs and, 394, 559-60
  Match Day, 553, 557
  military match and, 564
  not matching, 565-8. *See also* Scramble
  Osteopathic students and, 394, 559
  part-time positions, 563-4
  physician candidates, 564
  positions available in, 539
  programs' promises and, 564-5
  ranking programs, 535-8
    couples and, 561-2
    decision tree, 554
  Rank-order list, 550-2
  results, 553
  rules, 549-52
  schedule, 555-8
  students and, 558-64
  U.S. students and, 394
  UnMatch Day, 553, 557, 565-6
  withdrawal from, 556-8
NRMP Online Directory, 241
*NRMP Program Results & Data: [Year]
  Match* (online), 241, 536
NRMP Results & Data: [Year] Match (book),
  143, 241, 536
Nuclear Cardiology, 34
Nuclear Medicine, 20, 72-73, 111
  D.O.s in M.D. training, 380
  IMGs in practice, 391
  number of practitioners, 26
  Osteopathic training, 72

part-time positions, 365
programs and positions, 547
Nuclear Radiology, 22
Diagnostic Radiology and, 96
programs and positions, 547
Nutrition. *See* Endocrinology, Diabetes &
Metabolism

— O —

Objective Structured Clinical Examination.
See OSCE
Obstetrics and Gynecology, 21, 73-75,
110-1
applicant selection criteria, 450
D.O.s in M.D. training, 380
fellowship match, 74
IMGs in practice, 391
managed care and, 19
minority faculty, 369
number of practitioners, 26
Osteopathic programs & positions,
376, 578
part-time positions, 365
practitioners' characteristics, 123
programs and positions, 547
PGY-1 positions, 115, 143
subspecialties, 21, 74
who matches?, 394
women faculty, 355
work hours, 140
Occupational Medicine, 22, 75-76, 110,
376
Oculoplastics, 76
On-call rooms, as selection factor, 275
On-call schedule, as selection factor, 255-6
Oncology, 110
programs and positions, 547
Osteopathic fellowships, 578
See also Hematology–Oncology;
Musculoskeletal Oncology
Ophthalmic Plastic & Reconstructive
Surgery, 547. *See also* Oculoplastics
Ophthalmology, 21, 76-77, 110
acceptable PGY-1 training for, 544
D.O.s in M.D. training, 380
IMGs in practice, 391
match, 76, 569
minority faculty, 369
number of practitioners, 26
Osteopathic programs & positions, 578
part-time positions, 365
PGY-1 positions, 115
programs and positions, 547
women faculty, 355
Organized housestaff, 285

Orthopedic Sports Medicine, 21, 78, 99,
547
Orthopedic Surgery, 21, 77-79, 110
D.O.s in M.D. training, 380
IMGs in practice, 391
matches, 78
minority faculty, 369
number of practitioners, 26
Osteopathic programs & positions,
78, 578
part-time positions, 365
PGY-1 positions, 115, 143
programs and positions, 547
subspecialties, 21, 78
who matches?, 394
women faculty, 355
work hours, 140
Orthopedic Surgery of the Spine, 78, 547
Orthopedic Trauma, 78, 547
OSCE, 206-7
Dean's letter and, 336
Osteopathic Emergency Med–Fam Practice,
46. *See also* Emergency Med–Family
Practice
Osteopathic Fam Practice–Emergency Med,
46. *See also* Family Practice–Emergency
Med
Osteopathic Manipulative Medicine, 26
Osteopathic physicians, 375-82
approval for M.D. training, 377-8, 379
COMLEX and, 381
Comprehensive Medical Licensing
Exam. *See* COMLEX
Dean's letter, 379
discrimination and, 381-2
ERAS and, 306-7
Intern/Resident Registration Program,
575-80
rank-order lists, 576
schedule, 580
internships, 375-7, 381, 575
licensure, 196, 378-9
GME requirements and, 197
M.D. programs and, 377-80
military match and, 577
military training, 379
NRMP Match and, 381, 394, 559
number in practice, 26
programs & positions, 578-9
residencies, 109, 576
specialty training, 23-25. *See also*
individual specialties
Osteopathic residencies. *See under*
individual specialties
Osteopaths. *See* Osteopathic physicians

Other specialties' presence, as selection
    factor, 267
Otolaryngic Allergy, 80, 578
Otolaryngology, 21, 79-81, 110
    D.O.s in M.D. training, 380
    IMGs in practice, 391
    match, 80
    minority faculty, 369
    number of practitioners, 26
    Osteopathic training, 80
    part-time positions, 365
    PGY-1 positions, 115
    programs and positions, 547
    subspecialties, 21, 80
    women faculty, 355
Otolaryngology/Facial Plastic Surgery, 376,
    578
Otology. *See* Neurotology
Otology–Neurotology Match, 569
Otorhinolaryngology. *See* Otolaryngology
Outpatient visits, 239

— P —

Packing, for interview, 426-8
Pain Management. *See* Pain Medicine
Pain Medicine, 20, 22, 81-82, 86, 91, 111
    Osteopathic fellowships, 579
    programs and positions, 547
Parental leave. *See* Family leave
Parenting, 361
Parking, as selection factor, 274
Part-time positions, 363-6
    as selection factor, 286
Pathology, 21, 82-83, 110
    D.O.s in M.D. training, 380
    IMGs in practice, 391
    managed care and, 19
    minority faculty, 369
    number of practitioners, 26
    part-time positions, 365
    PGY-1 positions, 115
    programs and positions, 547
    subspecialties, 21, 82
    who matches?, 394
    women faculty, 355
    work hours, 140
*Pathway Evaluation Program for Medical
    Professionals*, 115, 116, 155
Patient population, as selection factor, 256
Patient volume, as selection factor, 259-60
Pediatric
    Allergy–Immunology, 30, 85
    Anesthesiology, 547

Cardiology, 21, 34, 85, 110, 569
Critical Care, 21, 40-41, 85
Dermatology, 20
Endocrinology, 21, 47, 85
Gastroenterology, 21, 51, 85, 111
Hematology–Oncology, 21, 55, 85, 111
Infectious Diseases, 21, 58, 85
Nephrology, 21, 85
Neurology, 85
Neurosurgery, 20
Ophthalmology, 76
Orthopedics, 78, 79
Otolaryngology, 21, 80
Pathology, 21
Pulmonology, 21, 85, 111
Rheumatology, 21, 85, 98, 569
Sleep Medicine, 21
Sports Medicine, 21, 85
subspecialty matches, 569
subspecialty programs & positions, 547
Transplant Hepatology, 21
See also individual subspecialties
Pediatric Emergency Med., 20, 21, 45, 85,
    569
    Osteopathic programs & positions, 579
Pediatric Radiology, 22, 96, 97, 569
    Osteopathic fellowships, 578-9
Pediatric Surgery, 22, 83-84, 101, 110
    D.O.s in M.D. training, 380
    match, 84, 569
    programs and positions, 547
Pediatrics, 21, 84-86, 110
    D.O.s in M.D. training, 380
    fellowships, 85
    IMGs in practice, 391
    managed care and, 19
    minority faculty, 369
    number of practitioners, 26
    Osteopathic programs & positions,
        376, 579
    part-time positions, 365
    PGY-1 positions, 115, 143
    practitioners' characteristics, 124
    programs and positions, 547
    subspecialties, 21, 85
    who matches?, 394
    women faculty, 355
    work hours, 140
Pediatrics–Internal Medicine. *See* Internal
    Med–Pediatrics
Pediatrics–Physical Med & Rehab, 22, 86
    part-time positions, 365
    programs and positions, 548
Pediatrics–Primary, 143

Pediatrics/Psych/Child Psych, 35, 85, 91
    part-time positions, 365
    programs and positions, 548
Perfect applicant, 447-52
Perinatology. *See* Neonatal–Perinatal
    Medicine
Personal needs, as selection factor, 262
Personal statement, 327-9
    ERAS and, 309-10
    example, 330
Personal trait
    analysis, 117-9
    synthesis, 121, 128-32
        examples, 120, 126-8, 132
        specialty characteristics and, 131-2
PGY-1 positions, 115
    accepted by specialties, 544
    arranging for, 144
    Categorical (C), 543
    filled through NRMP, 143
    Preliminary (P), 543
PGY-2 Advanced (A) positions, 543
    matches, 568-70
    See also San Francisco Matching
        Program
Photograph, and ERAS, 312
Physiatry. *See* Physical Medicine &
    Rehabilitation
Physical Medicine & Rehabilitation, 22,
    86-87, 110
    acceptable PGY-1 training for, 544
    Advanced (A) positions, 570
    D.O.s in M.D. training, 380
    IMGs in practice, 391
    minority faculty, 369
    number of practitioners, 26
    Osteopathic programs & positions, 579
    part-time positions, 365
    programs and positions, 548
    subspecialties, 22
    women faculty, 355
Physically impaired students, 373-5
Physicians
    changing specialties, 382-4
    future need, 140-3
    number in practice, 26
    managed care and, 19
    work hours, 140
Physicians-In-Training Host Program, 415
Plastic & Reconstructive Surgery, 579
Plastic Surgery, 22, 88-89, 110
    D.O.s in M.D. training, 380
    fellowships, 88
    IMGs in practice, 391

    match, 89, 569
    number of practitioners, 26
    part-time positions, 365
    programs and positions, 548
    subspecialties, 22
Plastic Surgery in Head & Neck, 21-22
Postgraduate training, length of
    M.D., 108
    Osteopathic physicians, 109
Post-purchase dissonance, 582
Post-visit follow-up, 531-5
Pre-clinical years, 152-3
Pregnancy, 357-61
    during residency, 358-61
    women physicians' complications, 361
Preliminary (P) positions, 543
    Internal Medicine, 61
    Surgery, 101
Preparing for the interview, 407-20
Preventive Medicine, 22
    Aerospace Medicine, 29
    Family Medicine and, 90
    Occupational Medicine, 75
    part-time positions, 365
    subspecialties, 22
    See also Public Health
Preventive Medicine, General, 89-90
    IMGs in practice, 391
    programs and positions, 548
    subspecialties, 90
    training, 90
Preventive Med/Occupational
    Med/Environmental Med, 75, 579
Preventive Med–Public Health
    D.O.s in M.D. training, 380
    Osteopathic programs & positions, 579
Primary Care Internal Medicine. *See*
    Internal Medicine
Primary Care specialties, 13
Problem-based learning, 165
Procedural Dermatology, 548
Proctology, 37, 579. *See also* Colon &
    Rectal Surgery
Program stability, as selection factor, 264
Programs, residency. *See* Residency
    programs
Psychiatric benefits, as selection factor, 279
Psychiatric illness, 367-8
Psychiatry, 22, 90-92, 111
    acceptable PGY-1 training for, 544
    Addiction, 91
    Child & Adolescent, 35, 91
    D.O.s in M.D. training, 380
    Forensic, 91

Geriatric, 52, 91
IMGs in practice, 391
managed care and, 19
minority faculty, 369
number of practitioners, 26
Osteopathic programs & positions, 376, 579
Pain Medicine, 91
part-time positions, 365
PGY-1 positions, 115, 143
practitioners' characteristics, 124
programs and positions, 548
subspecialties, 22, 91
who matches?, 394
women faculty, 355
work hours, 140
Psychiatry–Peds–Child Psych. *See* Child & Adolescent Psychiatry
Psychiatry–Family Med, 548
Psychiatry–Neurology, 548
Psychosomatic Medicine, 22, 91, 548
Public Health, 92-93
Gen Prev Med &, 22
IMGs in practice, 391
minority faculty, 369
programs and positions, 548
women faculty, 355
Public Health Service, 384-8
after internship, 223
Puerto Ricans. *See* Minorities
Pulmonary Diseases, 20, 93-94, 111
Critical Care and, 93
D.O.s in M.D. training, 380
IMGs in practice, 391
match, 569
number of practitioners, 26
Osteopathic programs & positions, 94, 579
programs and positions, 548
Pulmonary Medicine, 579
Pulmonary Med–Critical Care, 579
Pulmonology. *See* Pulmonary Diseases
Purple Book Online, 229, 241

— Q —

Questions
clerkship expectations and, 164
illegal, 304, 504-6, 528-30
types of, 492-3
Questions and answers, 494-528
able to work under pressure?, 517-8
always do your best work?, 510
any questions?, 495-6
any subjects/rotations very difficult?, 512

anything else to add?, 527
current world events?, 523-4
deficiencies in your medical training?, 508-9
family/significant other?, 504-6
health care in the future?, 520-1
how are you?, 495
how do you explain. . . ?, 509-10
how do you handle conflict?, 511-2
if a patient stabbed your friend?, 522-3
if we offer you a position?, 527-8
if you don't match?, 526-7
interest in research?, 507
interest in subspecialty?, 507
made any medical errors?, 519
other interviews?, 526
patient who taught you the most?, 518-9
problems the specialty faces?, 522
spare time activities?, 501-2
specialty's toughest aspect?, 515
teach me something non-medical., 524
tell me a joke!, 526
tell me about yourself., 496-7
time management skills?, 503-4
unanswerable questions, 524-5
what cell would you be?, 498-9
what memberships?, 504
what would you save?, 499
where will you be in 5/10 years?, 519-20
which alternate career?, 506
why should we take you?, 515-6
why this program?, 513-4
why this specialty?, 513
with which patients can't you work?, 511
with whom can't you work?, 510-1
your decision-making process?, 508
your energy level?, 517
your friends?, 500
your heroes?, 500-501
your resume says. . .?, 502-3
your strengths/weaknesses?, 497-8
you're not right for us., 516-7
Questions to ask, 453-74

— R —

Radiation Oncology, 22, 95, 111
acceptable PGY-1 training for, 544
D.O.s in M.D. training, 380
IMGs in practice, 391
programs and positions, 548
Radiological Physics, 22

Radiology, 22, 95-97
  fellowship match, 96
  IMGs in practice, 391
  managed care and, 19
  minority faculty, 369
  number of practitioners, 26
  Osteopathic training, 96, 579
  Pediatric, 96, 97
  programs and positions, 547-8
  PGY-1 positions, 115
  subspecialties, 22
  ultrasound and, 96
  women faculty, 355
  work hours, 140
  See also Diagnostic Radiology;
    individual subspecialties
Rank-order list
  couples and, 561-2
  decision tree, 554
  hedge your bets, 537
  NRMP Match, 550-2
  optimizing, 552
Recommendation letters. *See* Reference
  letters
Recruitment incentive, as selection factor,
  284
Reference letters, 329, 338-44
  ERAS and, 311
  elements of, 342
  format, 343
  senior electives and, 219
Renal Medicine. *See* Nephrology
Reproductive Endocrinology, 21, 74
  match, 569
  programs and positions, 548
Reputation, as selection factor, 263-5
Research
  Aerospace Medicine, 29
  Allergy & Immunology, 30
  Anesthesia, 32
  as selection factor, 270-2
  designing projects, 209
  required in residency?, 457
  student projects, 208-12
Residencies. *See* Residency programs
Residency fairs, 245
Residency interview. *See* Interview.
Residency program visit, 431-46
  confirm schedule, 432
  flexibility during, 433
  interview rules, 437-40
  know about program, 436
  know about specialty, 435
  lunch behavior, 444-6
  make an impression, 433, 434-5, 437

  non-interview visit, 480-1
  post-visit follow-up, 531-5
  punctuality, 431
  questions to ask, 453-74
  talk to residents, 436
  things not to do, 477-9
  See also Interview; Interview trip;
    Questions and Answers
Residency programs
  applicant evaluation of, 536
  communicating with, 419-20
  criteria for selecting residents, 159-221,
    449
  exams, 165, 199-200
  awards, 219-21
  grades, 159-65
  factors in selecting, 254-87
  information about, 233, 236-45
  interview. *See* Interview
  length of, 108-9, 138-9
  multiple start dates and, 571
  new, 573
  non-approved, 574
  number of, 545-8
  number of applications to, 295-8
  Osteopathic, 578-9
  program codes, 240
  promises from, 564-5
  ranking in Match, 535-8
  requirements, 234
  selecting, 247-93
    using Must/Want Analysis, 248, 287
    examples, 288-93
  specialty directories, 243
  visiting. *See* Residency program visit
  with no match, 574
Residents
  information from, 436
  work schedule, 238
Responsibility level, as selection factor,
  257-8
Restrictive Covenants, as selection factor,
  275-6
Results & Data Book, NRMP, 241
Résumé, 317-27
  action words, 320
  checklist, 321
  commercial preparation, 326
  disasters, 319, 322
  ERAS and, 310-1
  examples, 323-4
  graphics, 326-7
  layout, 318-9, 325
  printing, 327
  writing a, 319-20

Retina Match, 76
Retina–Vitreous, 548
Rheumatology, 20, 97-98, 110
  D.O.s in M.D. training, 380
  match, 570
  Osteopathic fellowships, 98, 579
  Pediatric, 85, 98
  programs and positions, 548

— S —

Safety/security, as selection factor, 275
Salary, 239
  as selection factor, 263, 276-7
  average for specialties, 135
  don't ask, 475
  specialty choice and, 134-8
  unfunded positions and, 475
San Francisco Matching Program, 568, 570
  algorithm, 541
Schedule
  senior, 212-9
  third (clinical) year, 160-1
Scramble, 553, 557, 565-8
Selective Pathology, 82, 548
Selling yourself, 440
Senior electives, 216
Senior schedule
  arranging, 212-9
  interviewing and, 411
Sexual harassment, 354-6
SFMP. *See* San Francisco Matching Program
Shared-schedule positions, 363-6
  as selection factor, 286
Shelf exams, 205
SHOWTIME interview mnemonic, 408-9
Sick leave, as selection factor, 279
Sleep Medicine, 20, 22
Space Medicine. *See* Aerospace Medicine
Special Purpose Examination, 198
Special testing accommodations
  COMLEX, 190
  USMLE, 169, 177
Special training, as selection factor, 269
Specialty
  approved, M.D., 20-22
  approved, Osteopathic, 23-25
  choosing a, 113-44
  clerkships, 161
  competitiveness, 295
  descriptions, 27-107
  faculty, 354
  future need, 13-17, 140-3
  IMGs and, 394
  knowledge about, 245, 435

lifestyle, 139-40
  Osteopathic residents, 380
  physicians in practice, 26
  practitioners' characteristics, 122-5
  Primary Care, 13-17
  programs and positions, 545-8
  program requirements, 234
  switching, 229-31
  with no match, 574
  women in, 353, 355
  work hours, 139, 140
Specialty adviser, mock interview and, 408
Specialty certification, American
  Osteopathic Assoc. and, 377
Specialty choice, 7-26
  AMA's resources, 155
  AAMC's Careers in Medicine, 116, 155
  debt and, 9, 137-8
  decision too fast, 229
  Directory of Graduate Education, 155
  important factors, 11, 133-44
  indecision, 223-32
  length of training and, 138-9
  lifestyle and, 139-40
  making a decision, 225
  not deciding, 232
  *Pathway Evaluation Program for Medical
    Professionals*, 115, 116, 155
  process, 10
  reading, 154-5
  salary and, 134
  talk with specialists, 155
  testing, 150-4
  timing, 227
  work hours and, 139-40
  your interests and. *See* Personal trait
  your needs and, 156. *See also*
    Must/Want analysis
Specialty descriptions, 27-107
Specialty information, 233, 244
  Dean of Students and, 245
Specialty Matches, 568-70
  CAS and, 570
  Osteopathic programs & positions,
    578-9
  programs and positions, 545-8, 569-70
SPEX. *See* Special Purpose Examination
Spinal Cord Injury Medicine, 22, 86, 548
Sports Med–Family Practice, 99, 579
Sports Medicine, 20, 44, 98-100
  match, 99
  Orthopedic, 78, 99
  Osteopathic programs & positions, 579
  Primary Care, 99

programs and positions, 548
via Family Medicine, 48
Subinternship, 213
military and, 386
Subject exams, 205
Summer job, clinical, 207-8
Surgery, 22, 100-101
Categorical PGY-1 positions, 101, 548
Critical Care, 40
General, 22
minority faculty, 369
Osteopathic programs & positions, 101, 579
patient volume and, 259
PGY-1 positions, 115
practitioners' characteristics, 125
Preliminary PGY-l positions, 101, 548
programs and positions, 548
subspecialties, 22, 101
women faculty, 355
See also individual subspecialties
Surgery of the Hand. *See* Hand Surgery
Surgery of the Spine, 79
Surgery, General
D.O.s in M.D. training, 380
managed care and, 19
number of practitioners, 26
Osteopathic internships, 376
programs and positions, 548
who matches?, 394
work hours, 140
Surgical Critical Care, 22, 41, 548

— T —

Test of Spoken English, 398
Therapeutic Radiology. *See* Radiation Oncology
Thoracic Radiology, 96, 570
Thoracic Surgery, 22, 102-3, 110
D.O.s in M.D. training, 380
IMGs in practice, 391
match, 570
number of practitioners, 26
Osteopathic programs & positions, 102, 579
part-time positions, 365
programs and positions, 548
Thoracic–Cardiovascular Surgery. *See* Thoracic Surgery
Time off, interviewing and, 411
Timing, interviews, 409-12
TOEFL, 398
Transcripts, 345-7
ERAS and, 312

interpreting, 346-7
Transgender students, 366-7
Transitional Internship
advantages/disadvantages, 227-9
D.O.s in M.D. training, 380
no credit for, 228
part-time positions, 365
programs and positions, 548
who matches?, 394
Transitional Year Program Directory, 229
Transplant Hepatology, 20
Trauma Surgery, 101, 103, 548
Travel, 412-9
accommodations, 415-8
clustered interviews, 413
packing, 426-9
special fares, 414
surviving air travel, 415-7

— U —

Ultrasound, Radiology and, 96, 570
Under the Ether Dome, 586
Undersea & Hyperbaric Med, 20, 22, 90, 385, 548
Unfunded positions, 475
Unions, housestaff, 285
United States Medical Licensing Examination. *See* USMLE
Universal Application for Residency, 304-5
Unmatch Day, 553, 557, 565-6. *See also* Scramble
Unmatched, what to do?, 565-8
Urogynecology/Reconstructive Pelvic Surgery, 74
Urological Surgery, 22, 104-5, 110
D.O.s in M.D. training, 380
IMGs in practice, 391
match, 104, 570
number of practitioners, 26
part-time positions, 365
Osteopathic programs & positions, 376, 579
PGY-1 positions, 115
programs and positions, 548
Urology, 22. *See also* Urological Surgery
USIMGs, 389, 402. *See also* IMGs
Fifth Pathway, 404
transferring schools and, 403
USMLE, 166-88
application for, 168
cost, 171-2
ECFMG and, 397-8
fairness of, 206
IMGs and, 397

importance to applicants, 199-200
irregular behavior, 177
licensure and, 196
not taking, 205-6
Osteopaths and, 381
pass rates, 175
preparation for, 172, 200-202
resident selection criteria, 199
retaking, 176, 201-2
sample questions, 185-7
scheduling, 169-71
scores, 174-6
special testing accommodations, 169, 202
Step 1, 167, 178-9, 201
Step 2, 167, 179-83
Step 3, 167, 169, 183-5
test day, 172-4
tips, 202-5
transcript, 176-7

— V —

Vacation/leave policy, 239
as selection factor, 281
don't ask, 476
interviewing and, 418
Vascular Neurology, 22, 71, 548

Vascular Radiology, 110
Vascular Surgery, 22, 101, 105-6, 111
match, 105
Osteopathic programs & positions, 579
programs and positions, 548
Vascular/Interventional Radiology, 22, 96
Osteopathic Fellowships, 579
programs and positions, 548
Visas, 393, 399, 401-2, 555
Volunteer time
testing specialty choice, 150-4

— W —

Win-lose decision model, 226
Win-win decisions, 225
decision model, 227
Women in medicine, 352-7
minorities, 371
pregnancy during residency, 360
resources, 356
Women Physicians Congress, 356
Women's Health Medicine, 106-7
Work hours, and specialty decision, 139-40
World Directory of Medical Schools, 404
Writing required in residency?, 457

About the Author

Kenneth V. Iserson, M.D., M.B.A., FACEP, FAAEM, is a noted medical teacher, clinician, researcher, and bioethicist. A past president of the Society of Teachers of Emergency Medicine and a Professor of Emergency Medicine, he directed the residency program in Emergency Medicine at The University of Arizona College of Medicine in Tucson for a decade.

In addition, he now runs the *Recursos Educacionales en Español para Medicina de Emergencia* (www.reeme.arizona.edu) Project. Using online distance learning technology, the project distributes (at no cost to users) Emergency Medicine-oriented Spanish-language teaching programs throughout the world.

Dr. Iserson frequently speaks to medical students, advisers, and residency directors on the complex process of selecting a medical specialty; choosing a residency program; and applying to, interviewing for, and obtaining a position at a desired residency program.

Dr. Iserson is also the author of the following books, all published by Galen Press, LTD., Tucson, AZ (www.galenpress.com):

- *Death to Dust: What Happens to Dead Bodies?, 2nd ed.*
- *Ethics in Emergency Medicine, 2nd ed.*
- *Get Into Medical School! A Guide for the Perplexed, 2nd ed.*
- *Grave Words: Notifying Survivors about Sudden, Unexpected Deaths*
- *Pocket Protocols: Notifying Survivors about Sudden, Unexpected Deaths*
- *Demon Doctors: Physicians as Serial Killers*
- *Dying to Know: A Compendium of the Morbid, Mortal, & Macabre (December 2006)*

Galen

Galen of Pergamum (A.D. 130–201), the Greek physician whose writings guided medicine for more than a millennium after his death, inspired the name, Galen Press. As the father of modern anatomy and physiology, Galen wrote more than 100 treatises while attempting to change medicine from an art form into a science. As a practicing physician, Galen first ministered to gladiators and then to Roman Emperor Marcus Aurelius. Far more than Hippocrates, Galen's work influenced Western physicians, and was the "truth" until the late Middle Ages when physicians and scientists challenged his teachings.

Galen Press, LTD., which publishes non-clinical, health-related books, follows Galen's advice that "the chief merit of language is clearness . . . nothing detracts so much from this as unfamiliar terms."

Also by Galen Press, LTD.

After-Death Planning Guide
Kenneth V. Iserson, M.D.

Civil War Medicine: Challenges and Triumphs
Alfred Jay Bollet, M.D.

*The Cost-Effective Use of Leeches
and Other Musings of a Medical School Survivor*
Jeffrey A. Drayer, M.D.

Death Investigation: The Basics
Brad Randall, M.D.

Death to Dust: What Happens to Dead Bodies?, 2nd ed.
Kenneth V. Iserson, M.D.

Dying to Know: A Compendium of the Morbid, Mortal, and Macabre
Kenneth V. Iserson, M.D.

Ethics in Emergency Medicine, 2nd ed.
Edited by Kenneth V. Iserson, M.D.; Arthur B. Sanders, M.D.;
and Deborah Mathieu, Ph.D.

Get Into Medical School! A Guide for the Perplexed, 2nd ed.
Kenneth V. Iserson, M.D.

Grave Words: Notifying Survivors about Sudden, Unexpected Deaths
Kenneth V. Iserson, M.D.

House Calls, Rounds, and Healings: A Poetry Casebook
David Schiedermayer, M.D.

Résumés and Personal Statements for Health Professionals, 2nd ed.
James W. Tysinger, Ph.D.

Demon Doctors: Physicians as Serial Killers
Kenneth V. Iserson, M.D.

*Pocket Protocols: Notifying Survivors about Sudden,
Unexpected Deaths*
Kenneth V. Iserson, M.D.

For more information, please contact:

Customer Service, Galen Press, LTD.
P.O. Box 64400, Tucson, AZ 85728-4400 USA
Tel: (520) 577-8363   Fax: (520) 529-6459
www.galenpress.com

Pocket Protocols
Notifying Survivors about Sudden, Unexpected Deaths
Pocket-sized booklet containing the protocols from *Grave Words*
ISBN: 1-883620-05-8 $ 6.95 (bulk discounts available)

Slides for *Grave Words*

- Slide sets of the protocols and other tables from *Grave Words*
- Build your own Death Notification or Death & Dying Course using the specialized slide sets

Slide Set	Number of Slides
A. Main Protocol for Death Notification 66	
B. General Set: Sudden Death/Nurse Interactions/ Grief/Communication/Survivors' Questions 49	
C. Chaplains/Religions 41	
D. Emergency Medicine/Trauma 35	
E. Phrases: Helping and Hurtful 23	
F. Telephone Notification Protocol 20	
G. Students' Deaths 17	
H. Emergency Medical Services 16	
I. Telling Friends 16	
J. Children: Telling & Grieving 13	
K. Obstetrics 14	
L. Disaster Survivors' Protocol 10	
M. Organ Donation 10	

Prices: **Item 1:** Complete set of 330 slides $ 395.00
     Item 2: Main Protocol + Any three other sets $ 345.00
     Item 3: Main Protocol + Any two other sets $ 295.00
     Item 4: Main Protocol + Any one other set $ 250.00
     Item 5: Individual set $3.00/slide

Items 1-4: Includes one copy each of **Grave Words** and **Pocket Protocols**. Shipping $15.
Item 5: Add shipping of $10 for first set and $2 for each additional set.

To order, and for more information, please contact Galen Press, LTD., at:
P.O. Box 64400, Tucson, AZ 85728-4400 USA
Tel: (520) 577-8363   Fax: (520) 529-6459
www.galenpress.com

Previews: We keep our prices low by not offering previews. See our 30-Day Guarantee.

30-Day Money Back Guarantee: You may return your purchase *within 30 days* for a refund of the purchase price. (Shipping costs not refundable.)

Order Form

Yes! . . . Please send me:

_____ copies of **Iserson's Getting Into A Residency: A Guide for Medical Students, 7th ed.** @ $38.95 each $ _____

_____ copies of **The Companion Disk** @ $12.00

_____ copies of **Grave Words: Notifying Survivors about Sudden, Unexpected Deaths** @ $38.95 each $ _____

_____ copies of **Demon Doctors: Physicians as Serial Killers** @ $28.95 each $ _____

_____ copies of **Death to Dust: What Happens to Dead Bodies?, 2nd ed.** @ $48.95 each $ _____

_____ copies of **Ethics In Emergency Medicine, 2nd ed.** @ $39.95 each $ _____

_____ copies of **Résumés and Personal Statements for Health Professionals, 2nd ed.** @ $18.95 each $ _____

_____ copies of **Death Investigation: The Basics** @ $24.95 each $ _____

_____ copies of **Civil War Medicine: Challenges and Triumphs** @ $44.95 each $ _____

_____ copies of **Get Into Medical School! A Guide for the Perplexed, 2nd ed.** @ $36.95 each $ _____

_____ copies of **House Calls, Rounds, and Healings: A Poetry Casebook** @ $12.95 each $ _____

_____ copies of **The Cost-Effective Use of Leeches and Other Musings of a Medical School Survivor** @ $14.95 each $ _____

AZ Residents – Add 7.65% sales tax $ _____

Shipping: $3.95 for 1st Book, $1.50 / each additional $ _____

Priority Mail: **ADD** $3.00 for 1st Book, $2.00 / each additional $ _____

TOTAL ENCLOSED (U.S. funds only) $ _____

❏ Check   ❏ VISA   ❏ MasterCard   ❏ Institutional Purchase Order

SHIP TO: Name _____

    Address _____

_____

    City/State/Zip _____

    Phone **(required)** _____

CREDIT CARD Number: _____

Expiration date: _____ Signature: _____

Send completed form and payment to:

Galen Press, Ltd.	Tel (520) 577-8363
PO Box 64400-R6	Fax (520) 529-6459
Tucson, AZ 85728-4400 USA	Orders: 1-800-442-5369 (US/Canada)

www.galenpress.com

Also available through your local bookstore.

Bulk Discounts Available

Pocket Protocols
Notifying Survivors about Sudden, Unexpected Deaths
Pocket-sized booklet containing the protocols from *Grave Words*

ISBN: 1-883620-05-8 $ 6.95 (bulk discounts available)

Slides for *Grave Words*

- Slide sets of the protocols and other tables from *Grave Words*
- Build your own Death Notification or Death & Dying Course using the specialized slide sets

Slide Set	Number of Slides
A. Main Protocol for Death Notification	66
B. General Set: Sudden Death/Nurse Interactions/ Grief/Communication/Survivors' Questions	49
C. Chaplains/Religions	41
D. Emergency Medicine/Trauma	35
E. Phrases: Helping and Hurtful	23
F. Telephone Notification Protocol	20
G. Students' Deaths	17
H. Emergency Medical Services	16
I. Telling Friends	16
J. Children: Telling & Grieving	13
K. Obstetrics	14
L. Disaster Survivors' Protocol	10
M. Organ Donation	10

Prices:
Item 1: Complete set of 330 slides	$ 395.00
Item 2: Main Protocol + Any three other sets	$ 345.00
Item 3: Main Protocol + Any two other sets	$ 295.00
Item 4: Main Protocol + Any one other set	$ 250.00
Item 5: Individual set	$3.00/slide

Items 1-4: Includes one copy each of **Grave Words** and **Pocket Protocols**. Shipping $15.
Item 5: Add shipping of $10 for first set and $2 for each additional set.

To order, and for more information, please contact Galen Press, LTD., at:

P.O. Box 64400, Tucson, AZ 85728-4400 USA

Tel: (520) 577-8363   Fax: (520) 529-6459

www.galenpress.com

Previews: We keep our prices low by not offering previews. See our 30-Day Guarantee.

30-Day Money Back Guarantee: You may return your purchase *within 30 day* for a refund of the purchase price. (Shipping costs not refundable.)

Order Form

Yes! . . . Please send me:

_____ copies of ***Iserson's Getting Into A Residency: A Guide for Medical Students, 6th ed.*** @ $38.95 each $ _____

_____ copies of ***The Companion Disk*** @ $12.00

_____ copies of ***Grave Words: Notifying Survivors about Sudden, Unexpected Deaths*** @ $38.95 each $ _____

_____ copies of ***Demon Doctors: Physicians as Serial Killers*** @ $28.95 each $ _____

_____ copies of ***Death to Dust: What Happens to Dead Bodies?, 2nd ed.*** @ $48.95 each $ _____

_____ copies of ***Ethics In Emergency Medicine, 2nd ed.*** @ $39.95 each $ _____

_____ copies of ***Résumés and Personal Statements for Health Professionals, 2nd ed.*** @ $18.95 each $ _____

_____ copies of ***Death Investigation: The Basics*** @ $24.95 each $ _____

_____ copies of ***Civil War Medicine: Challenges and Triumphs*** @ $44.95 each $ _____

_____ copies of ***Get Into Medical School! A Guide for the Perplexed, 2nd ed.*** @ $36.95 each $ _____

_____ copies of ***House Calls, Rounds, and Healings: A Poetry Casebook*** @ $12.95 each $ _____

_____ copies of ***The Cost-Effective Use of Leeches and Other Musings of a Medical School Survivor*** @ $14.95 each $ _____

AZ Residents – Add 7.65% sales tax $ _____

Shipping: $3.95 for 1st Book, $1.50 / each additional $ _____

Priority Mail: **ADD** $3.00 for 1st Book, $2.00 / each additional $ _____

TOTAL ENCLOSED (U.S. funds only) $ _____

❏ Check   ❏ VISA   ❏ MasterCard   ❏ Institutional Purchase Order

SHIP TO: Name _____

 Address _____

_____

 City/State/Zip _____

 Phone **(required)** _____

CREDIT CARD Number: _____

Expiration date: _____   Signature: _____

Send completed form and payment to:

Galen Press, Ltd.   Tel (520) 577-8363
44400-R6   Fax (520) 529-6459
728-4400 USA   Orders: 1-800-442-5369 (US/Canada)

www.galenpress.com

Also available through your local bookstore.

Bulk Discounts Available